D1219445

18. 33

Attitude Measurement

Attitude Measurement

Edited by
GENE F. SUMMERS
University of Illinois

RAND McNALLY & COMPANY / Chicago

Rand McNally Sociology Series

EDGAR F. BORGATTA
Advisory Editor

BF
323
.C5
S85

Copyright © 1970 by Rand McNally & Company
All rights reserved
Printed in U.S.A. by Rand McNally & Company
Library of Congress Catalogue Card Number 70:98447

To Mom, Dad and Phyllis

ALMA COLLEGE
MONTEITH LIBRARY
ALMA, MICHIGAN

PREFACE

Attitudes have been studied almost exclusively by using self-reported beliefs, feelings and action tendencies. Treating self-reports as virtually the only window onto the psychological world of the individual is most unfortunate. To be sure, the self-report is a legitimate source of information. One way to know how another person feels about an issue or event is to ask him. But it is only one way. When a person responds to a direct question regarding his beliefs or feelings he may or may not report them accurately. This is not an indictment of those persons who respond to our questions. There are, after all, compelling reasons, conscious and unconscious, why persons may not give completely accurate self-reports.

There can be an indictment made of researchers who recognize the fallibility of self-report data and then continue to use such data exclusively, with little or no effort to estimate the amount of distortion created. There is always some discrepancy between the "true" value of that which a scientist wants to measure and the readings given by his instrument. The indictment therefore, is not brought because researchers use a fallible source of information, for all sources of information are fallible. It is, rather, the failure to sufficiently cross-check the procedures that produce the readings which is cause for apprehension. The problem is not peculiar to one group of attitude researchers or even one social science discipline. Research on attitudes is done by people from all the social sciences and the fixation on the self-report seems to plague researchers indiscriminately.

This single-minded concentration upon self-report data is a barrier to a clearer understanding of attitudes and their relation to behavior. The seriousness of the problem has prompted me to request several of my colleagues to prepare statements on related issues. The primary objective in assembling this collection of essays and previously published works is to encourage the emergence of a strategy of attitude research that builds upon a multiple data base. In the Introduction I shall attempt to develop a framework within which such a manifold base can be used without doing injustice or violence to existing theory and measurement techniques. The essays and reprinted materials are organized into six sections, which reflect the main dimensions of this framework.

A number of considerations guided the selection of materials. First, selection and organization of articles and essays was made to support the primary objective of encouraging a multiple data base approach in attitude research.

Second, an effort was made to provide the reader with examples of each major approach with preference given to those which have been highly evaluated by other professionals. Other things being equal, or nearly so, preference was given to the most recent work.

Third, an effort was made to expose the limitations of each approach since it must be recognized that every approach to attitude measurement has limitations. To accomplish this, it was generally necessary to request new essays since none were to be found in the recent literature. Although the authors of original essays often went beyond discussing the limitations of an approach, this was one of their objectives. The essays that are particularly critical reviews are those by Seiler and Hough (Chapter 8), Dotson and Summers (Chapter 11), Heise (Chapter 14), Ross (Chapter 17), Webb and Salancik (Chapter 19), Kidder and Campbell (Chapter 20), Woodmansee (Chapter 35), and Mueller (Chapter 36).

To guard against a potential failure of the reader to recognize the fundamentals of all measurement, regardless of the approach, four chapters on basic considerations were included. These are fairly lengthy but comprehensive and complementary. Cook and Selltiz (Chapter 1) develop the strategy of multiple indicators in attitude research, a thesis which is amplified by this book. Garner and Creelman (Chapter 2) deal with methods and problems of scaling. Bohrnstedt (Chapter 3) discusses reliability and validity in an unusually cogent and clear exposition, and Campbell and Fiske (Chapter 4) treat in greater detail the logic of validity assessment.

As is every editor, I am deeply indebted to many people and organizations. Without the cooperation of the authors and original publishers, the reproduction of the several articles would have been impossible. I am most obliged to my colleagues who graciously accepted the responsibility of preparing manuscripts. A short biographical sketch of each contributor appears on pp. xiii–xviii. I especially appreciate the encouragement and many helpful suggestions of Edgar F. Borgatta and Louis E. Dotson. Without their continuing support it is doubtful that the volume would have been completed. To my colleague, Edward J. Janeski of the Instructional Materials Division, University of Illinois, who applied his professional art skills to the task of preparing the necessary figures and graphs, I wish to convey my deep appreciation. I wish also to thank Patricia Neef, Suzanne Saltiel and Dorothy Behunin for their expertise in handling the many details of preparing and typing the manuscript. Finally, and most importantly, I must say thank you to my wife and children for their patience and understanding and for sharing with me the joys of cutting and pasting.

GENE F. SUMMERS

Urbana, Illinois
October, 1969

CONTENTS

THE AUTHORS

GEORGE W. BOHRNSTEDT is Associate Professor of Sociology at the University of Minnesota. He is, with Edgar F. Borgatta, Associate Editor of *Sociological Methodology, 1970*. His publications have been important contributions to research methods and statistical analysis in sociology.

DONALD T. CAMPBELL is Professor of Psychology at Northwestern University. He is co-author of *Experimental and Quasi-experimental Designs for Research, Unobtrusive Measures*, and *The Influence of Culture on Perception*. His numerous articles have established him as one of the nation's leading authorities on research design and attitude measurement.

ERNEST JOHN CHAVE was Professor, College of Divinity, University of Chicago. In addition to co-authoring the monograph with L. L. Thurstone, from which Chapter 6 is taken, he wrote *Personality Development in Children* as well as numerous articles in religious education.

STUART W. COOK is Professor of Psychology and Program Director, Institute of Behavioral Science, University of Colorado. He is co-author of *Human Relations In Interracial Housing* and *Attitudes and Social Relations of Foreign Students*. He is also co-editor of *Research Methods in Social Relations* and has written numerous articles on attitudes and attitude measurement. In recent years he has been directing a program of research to assess the validity of a multiple-indicator approach to attitude measurement.

C. DOUGLAS CREELMAN is Associate Professor of Psychology, University of Toronto. His published experimental and theoretical works have appeared in the *Journal of the Acoustical Society of America*, the *Journal of Experimental Psychology* and *Perceptual and Motor Skills*.

MELVIN L. DEFLEUR is Chairman of the Department of Sociology, Washington State University. He is the author of *The Flow of Information* and *Theories of Mass Communication* as well as numerous articles in professional journals.

LOUIS E. DOTSON is Associate Professor of Sociology, University of Tennessee. His research has focused upon attitude measurement with special emphasis upon testing the Guttman model of attitude components. His publications have appeared in the *Public Opinion Quarterly* and the *Sociological Quarterly*.

ALLEN L. EDWARDS is Professor of Psychology at the University of Washington. His research and writing are well known in the fields of research design, statistics and attitude measurement, appearing in books such as *Techniques of Attitude Scale Construction, Statistical Methods, Experimental Design In Psychological Research, Statistical Analysis* and in numerous professional journals.

DONALD W. FISKE is Professor of Psychology at the University of Chicago. His major publications include *Assessment of Men, Prediction of Performance in Clinical Psychology, Functions of Varied Experience* and *Psychosomatic Specificity*.

N. L. GAGE is Professor of Education and Psychology at the School of Education, Stanford University. He is editor of the *Handbook of Research on Teaching,* co-editor of *Readings in the Social Psychology of Education* and co-author of *Educational Measurement and Evaluation.* In addition he has contributed numerous articles to professional journals on interpersonal perception, interpersonal behavior, and the theory of teaching.

WENDELL R. GARNER is Professor of Psychology at Johns Hopkins University. His research activities have dealt primarily with problems in perception, cognitions and psychometrics. He has contributed to many of the professional journals in psychology including the *American Psychologist, Perception and Psychophysics* and the *Quarterly Journal of Experimental Psychology.*

LOUIS GUTTMAN is Professor of Social and Psychological Measurement at The Hebrew University, Jerusalem, and Scientific Director, The Israel Institute of Applied Social Research. While his graduate training was in Sociology at the University of Minnesota, he has been a major contributor to research on quantification in many fields. His first significant work was Scalogram Analysis and his most recent work has been the development of facet analysis.

KENNETH R. HAMMOND is Professor of Psychology and Program Director of Research on Cognitive Processes, Institute of Behavioral Science, at the University of Colorado. He is co-author of *Teaching Comprehensive Medical Care, Introduction to Statistical Method,* and editor of *Psychology of Egon Brunswik.* He is also the author and co-author of many journal articles on cognition, conflict resolution, and methodology.

DAVID R. HEISE is Associate Professor of Sociology, Queens College, City University of New York. His works in Sociolinguistics and research methodology have appeared in such publications as *Psychological Monographs, Genetic Psychology Monographs, American Sociological Review* and *Sociological Methodology, 1969.*

RICHARD J. HILL is Professor of Sociology and Director of the Institute for the Study of Social Change, Purdue University. While his research activities have been unusually outstanding for their scope, social psychology, particularly measurement problems, is central. This is evident in his books *Public Leadership, Management Training Effectiveness, Sociological Measurement* and his numerous journal articles.

RICHARD L. HOUGH is Assistant Professor of Sociology, The College of Wooster. He has contributed articles to several professional journals in the field of sociology of religion. For the past three years he has been working with Professor Summers, analyzing the consequences of rural industrialization.

ESIN KAYA is Chairman of the Department of Educational Psychology, Hofstra University. His major research activities have been in evaluating educational practices. Reports of these activities have appeared in numerous professional journals such as *Journal of Educational Sociology* and *Exceptional Children.*

FRED KERLINGER is Professor of Educational Psychology and Head, Division of Behavioral Sciences, New York University. His research and writings have been focused primarily upon test construction and statistical problems. His most recent book, *Foundations of Behavioral Research,* is recognized as a leading text in the field.

LOUISE H. KIDDER is a doctoral candidate and Research Assistant in Psychology, Northwestern University. For the past two years she has been working closely with Professor Campbell on social attitude research.

FRANKLIN KILPATRICK is Dean of the College of Graduate Studies, University of Delaware. His career as a psychologist includes authorship of research publications and theoretical expositions in many journals and several books such as *Human Behavior from the Transactional Point of View, Explorations in Transactional Psychology* and *The Image of the Federal Service.*

FRANK KREVANICK is Staff Psychologist, Southeast Louisiana Hospital, Mandeville, Louisiana. While performing his duties there he is completing requirements for the doctoral degree in Psychology at Louisiana State University.

WILLIAM KRUSKAL is Professor and Chairman of the Department of Statistics, University of Chicago. Internationally known for his work in statistics, he is Associate Editor of the *International Encyclopedia of the Social Sciences* and has been a frequent contributor to the major journals of statistics and mathematics.

JAMES L. KUETHE is Professor of Educational Psychology, State University of New York at Albany. His work on the "social schemata" is an intriguing and promising approach to a variety of measurement problems including attitudes.

BERNARD KUTNER is Associate Professor and Director, Center for Social Research in Rehabilitation Medicine, Albert Einstein College of Medicine, Yeshiva University. While carrying on research in medical sociology he has maintained an active research interest in social attitudes and continues to contribute to the leading journals of social psychology. His most recent work has been on cognitive functioning and prejudice.

RENSIS LIKERT is Professor of Psychology and Sociology and Director, Institute for Social Research, University of Michigan. His early work with Professor Gardner Murphy led to his development of the summated rating technique of attitude measurement which is one of the standard tools of all attitude researchers. During the 1930s and 1940s he was a prominent figure in the development of the field of public opinion research, publishing *Public Opinion and the Individual* in 1938. In recent years he has turned his attention to industrial psychology and organization analysis as is indicated in his two most recent books, *New Patterns of Management* and *The Human Organization.*

JAMES C. LINGOES is Professor of Psychology at the University of California, Berkeley. While trained as a clinical psychologist at Michigan State University, his research has concentrated upon multivariate analysis of qualitative data and computer applications in behavioral science. He has been a frequent collaborator with Professor Louis Guttman in the development of nonmetric analytical techniques.

LAWRENCE S. LINN is Research Sociologist, Center for Advanced Study in Organization Science, University of Wisconsin, Milwaukee. In addition to his research on social attitudes he is engaged in medical sociology with special reference to mental health. These interests are often joined profitably as is evident in his publications in leading journals of mental health and social psychology.

ALBERT J. LOTT is Professor of Psychology and Behavioral Science at the University of Kentucky. For several years he has been a consistent and frequent contributor to the literature on interpersonal attitudes. Much of his research has been devoted to studying the relation of learning theory to interpersonal attitudes: His most recent book is *Negro and White Youth* with the collaboration of Bernice Lott.

DANIEL J. MUELLER is Assistant Professor in Educational Psychology, University of Indiana. His current research deals with isolating factors which differentiate university honors students.

CHARLES E. OSGOOD, Professor of Psychology and Communications at the University of Illinois, is perhaps best known to the field of attitude research as the originator of the Semantic Differential Scale. He is equally eminent as an experimental methodologist. His works include *The Measurement of Meaning, Method and Theory in Experimental Psychology,* and *An Alternative to War or Surrender.* The latter book is indicative of his prominence in the field of international relations.

GARY W. PORIER is Assistant Chief Psychologist, Department of Mental Health, Frankfort, Kentucky and is a doctoral candidate in Clinical Psychology, University of Kentucky. His doctoral research is a study of the effects of parental pressure among schizophrenics and normals.

HAROLD M. PROSHANSKY is Professor of Psychology at The City University of New York. His contributions to research on attitudes and intergroup relations are extensive and include co-authorship of a chapter in the *Handbook of Social Psychology,* and editorship of a special issue of the *Journal of Social Issues.* He is also co-editor of *Basic Studies in Social Psychology.*

ROBERT E. RANKIN is Professor of Psychology, Central Michigan University. His research activities have focused upon social attitudes and public opinion both in the laboratory and in the field. His most recent monograph, *Air Pollution and the Community Image,* indicates his current research efforts.

JOHN ROSS is Reader in Psychology, The University of Western Australia. He is co-editor of *Measurement in Personality and Cognition.* In addition he has authored numerous articles on experimental psychology, personality measurement, and psychometrics.

JERRY R. SALANCIK is a doctoral candidate in Social Psychology at Yale University. In addition to the chapter in this volume he is co-author of *The Interview.* Prior to his study in social psychology he received the Master of Science degree in Journalism from Northwestern University.

LAUREN H. SEILER is a doctoral candidate in Sociology and NIMH Fellow, University of Illinois. His doctoral research is concerned with the relation of significant others to mental health. For the past three years he has worked closely with Professor Summers on a study of the consequences of rural industrialization.

CLAIRE SELLTIZ is Associate Professor of Psychology, City College of the City University of New York. Her work has been primarily concerned with attitudes and research methodology, and she has authored and co-authored several books and numerous articles. Her books include *How To Conduct a Community Self-Survey of Civil Rights, Research Methods in Social Relations,* and *Attitudes and Social Relations of Foreign Students in the United States.*

CAROLYN WOOD SHERIF is Associate Professor of Psychology, Pennsylvania State University. Her research and writing have covered several areas of psychology and sociology, but social attitudes and group behavior continue to be the dominant theme. She is co-author of several books, including *Reference Groups, Attitude and Attitude Change,* and *Social Psychology* and author and co-author of numerous journal articles.

MUZAFER SHERIF is Professor of Social Psychology in the Department of Sociology and Director, Psychosocial Studies Program, Pennsylvania State University. Beginning with his work on the autokinetic effect Professor Sherif has for over three decades been one of the true pioneers of social psychology. His books include *The Psychology of Social Norms, Social Judgment, In Common Predicament: Social Psychology of Intergroup Conflict and Cooperation, Social Interaction: Process and Products* and *Social Psychology.*

BENJAMIN SHIMBERG is Director, Vocational Technical Educational Projects, Educational Testing Service. As his position suggests, i 1 recent years his research has been in areas other than attitudes. His writing includes *Meeting The Test* as well as contributions to professional journals.

GEORGE J. SUCI is Associate Professor of Child Development, Cornell University. He is co-author of *Measurement of Meaning* with Charles Osgood and Percy Tannenbaum. He has also contributed much to professional publications in psychology and child development.

GENE F. SUMMERS is Assistant Professor of Sociology at the University of Illinois. Attitude measurement, youth aspirations, and community change have been central concerns in his research and writing. He is co-author of *Before Industrialization: A Social System Base Study of a Rural Area,* and has written a number of articles in sociology and education journals such as *Social Forces, Sociological Quarterly, Contemporary Education,* and *Educational and Psychological Measurement.*

PERCY H. TANNENBAUM is Professor of Communications and Psychology, Director of Research and Chairman of the Ph.D. Group in Communications, University of Pennsylvania. In addition to co-authoring *Measurement of Meaning,* he is Co-Editor of *Cognitive Consistency Theories* and has published nearly one hundred articles in a variety of journals.

DONALD THISTLETHWAITE is Professor of Psychology at Vanderbilt University. His research and writing have concentrated on attitude scaling methods, attitude change through communication, and theories of learning. His articles have appeared in numerous professional journals such as the *Psychological Bulletin* and the *Journal of Abnormal and Social Psychology.*

Louis L. Thurstone was Professor of Psychology at the University of Chicago. He was one of the leading figures in psychology during the first half of the twentieth century. His many books and articles were influential in the formative stages of several areas of psychology—social psychology, educational psychology, theory of personality, and tests and measurement. The seminal quality of his work is evident in the fact that his monograph on attitude measurement is still a basic reference in the field of social psychology.

Charles R. Tittle is Assistant Professor of Sociology, Indiana University. In addition to his contributions to the study of attitudes he is conducting research on formal organizations and has published several articles in that field. He is currently directing a study of inmate organization in an institutional setting.

Robert N. Vidulich is Chairman of the Department of Psychology, Memphis State University. His research efforts are directed primarily to problems of language behavior, conformity, and prejudice. He has contributed frequently to leading professional journals in psychology.

William Wallace is Assistant Professor of Psychology, University of Nevada. Most of his work has been in learning and experimental psychology and has appeared in such publications as *Psychological Bulletin* and *Psychological Review*.

Eugene J. Webb is Professor of Organizational Behavior, Graduate School of Business, Stanford University. Much of his research and writing has been devoted to the problems of data collection procedures where human behavior is the object of analysis. As a result of these efforts he has co-authored two books, *The Interview* and *Unobtrusive Measures: Nonreactive Research in the Social Sciences*. His current activities include a sequel to *Unobtrusive Measures*.

Frank R. Westie is Professor of Sociology, Indiana University. His research covers several areas of social psychology and includes attitude measurement, intergroup relations and social anthropology. His major works have been on attitude theory and measurement and have appeared in leading journals in both sociology and psychology.

Carol Wilkins [Giniger], now affiliated with The K. S. Giniger Company, Inc. Publishers, was an undergraduate student at Sarah Lawrence College at the time she co-authored Chapter 26.

John J. Woodmansee is Assistant Professor of Psychology, Wake Forest University. His research on pupillography as a measure of attitudes has been extremely important in providing further knowledge about this novel and initially promising approach to attitude measurement. His research reports have appeared in a number of professional journals.

Penny R. Yarrow is not currently affiliated with an academic institution. She has been pursuing a career of wife and mother since graduation from Sarah Lawrence College where she co-authored Chapter 26.

Attitude Measurement

INTRODUCTION

Gene F. Summers

Measurement is the assignment of numbers to observations according to some set of rules. This is true whatever the phenomenon being observed. When that phenomenon is attitude, the process of measurement becomes complicated, since attitude cannot be observed directly but must always be inferred from behavior. There are, of course, many other variables familiar to the social scientist that may be inaccessible to direct observation—intelligence, personality traits, values, and motives are only a few which have this same quality.

When measuring phenomena that are inaccessible to direct observation, it is helpful to conceptualize the measurement process as consisting of three subprocesses: (1) identification of behavioral specimens that are acceptable as a basis for making inferences about the underlying concept, (2) collection of the behavioral specimens, and (3) treatment of the behavioral specimens so as to convert them into a quantitative variable. While it is instructive to separate these subprocesses of measurement analytically, it must be remembered that in execution they are inextricably interwoven. Therefore, decisions as to what is acceptable as a basis for

The author is grateful to George Bohrnstedt, Edgar F. Borgatta, Donald T. Campbell, Dorothy Darroch, Russell Darroch, Bill Gunter, André D. Hammonds, David R. Heise, Richard Hough, Leon S. Robertson, and Lauren Seiler for critical comment on earlier drafts.

inference may preclude some methods of specimen collection as well as restrict the manner in which the specimens can be treated. Thus a decision concerning one aspect of the problem will automatically affect the degrees of freedom for the other two.

ACCEPTABLE BEHAVIORAL SPECIMENS

What is acceptable as a basis for inference inevitably turns upon what is meant by attitude. Over the years many definitions of attitude have been proposed. Those offered by our contributing authors serve to illustrate this variety. Cook and Selltiz (1964) prefer "to think of attitude as an underlying disposition which enters, along with other influences, into the determination of a variety of behaviors toward an object or class of objects, including statements of beliefs and feelings about the object and approach-avoidance actions with respect to it." Kidder and Campbell (Chapter 20) contend that "a host of seemingly unrelated terms such as acquired drive, belief, conditioned reflex, fixation, judgment, stereotype, valence, to mention only a few, are functionally synonymous with the concept of attitude. All describe the residues of past experience which are the stuff of which attitudes are made. They are the underlying processes, or the behavioral manifestations of underlying processes, which are

1

products of learning." With some expressed ambivalence Ross defines attitudes as "those mental structures which organize and evaluate information." In a statement which was originally published in 1928, Thurstone declares, "The concept 'attitude' will be used here to denote the sum total of a man's inclinations and feelings, prejudice or bias, preconceived notions, ideas, fears, threats, and convictions about any specific topic." Although these examples should not be considered a representative sample of attitude definitions, they do indicate the diversity a truly representative sample would present.

Despite the wide variety of interpretations of the meaning of attitude there are areas of substantial agreement. First, there is general consensus that an *attitude is a predisposition to respond* to an object rather than the actual behavior toward such object. The readiness to behave is one of the qualities which is characteristic of attitude.

A second area of substantial agreement is that *attitude is persistent over time*. This is not to say that it is immutable. The rather large body of literature on attitude clearly indicates that while it is amenable to change, the alteration of attitude, especially that which is strongly held, requires substantial pressure. Consequently, the persistence of attitude contributes greatly to the consistency of behavior which introduces a third area of agreement.

Attitude produces consistency in behavioral outcroppings. Attitude as a latent variable gives rise to consistency among its various manifestations whether they be in the form of verbalizations about the object, expressions of feeling about the object, or approach or avoidance of the object. This aspect of attitude was stated cogently by Campbell when he wrote: "An individual's social attitude is a syndrome of response consistency with regard to social objects." (1963, p. 96)

Fourth and finally, *attitude has a directional quality*. Not only does it imply a routinization of behavior in the form of consistency in outcroppings, it has a motivational quality. There is general agreement

that attitude connotes preference regarding outcomes involving the object, evaluations of the object, or positive-neutral-negative affectations for the object. This facet of attitude as a concept has been noted from the very earliest discussions, and it has been argued that the concept of attitude should be limited or restricted to this dimension. Whether one argues for constriction of the concept to only the affective dimension or for a more multifaceted conception of attitude, it is clear that affect is an important dimension of attitude.

Perhaps currently the most popular conception of attitude is that formulated by Katz and Stotland (1959) and by Krech *et al.* (1962). According to this view an attitude consists of three components: (1) cognitive, (2) emotional, and (3) action tendency. Under the cognitive component are subsumed the beliefs one has about an object. The number of elements in this component varies from person to person. An individual may believe a great many things to be true about one object, such as his mother (or father), and know very little, if anything, about another object, such as his sociology professor. Obviously, there are objects about which we know nothing. It should be noted also that some objects are more complex than others and therefore are capable of generating more bits of information to be known. While all beliefs one has about an object are subsumed under the cognitive component, it is the evaluative beliefs that are the most critical to attitude as a dispositional concept. They include beliefs about the desirable or undesirable, acceptable or unacceptable, and good or bad qualities of the object. According to Krech *et al.* (1962), beliefs about how one should or should not treat the object are also aspects of the cognitive component. There is, therefore, a very deep penetration of the normative order of society into the cognitive component of attitude.

The emotional component is sometimes known as the feeling component and refers to the emotions or feelings attached to an attitude object. Bipolar adjectives commonly used in discussing elements of this component are love-hate, like-dislike, admire-detest, and others connoting feelings of a favorable or unfavorable order. It is noteworthy that when an individual is able to verbalize these feelings they are more than mere feelings or emotions. They are also cognitions. But they are cognitions that are significantly different from those of the cognitive component. Cognitions of feelings and emotions refer not to the object but to the one who cognizes, the individual who is responding to the object. This is worthy of note because in much research dealing with attitude the individual is asked to indicate in some manner his beliefs about an object and also his feelings toward the object. That is, he is requested to reveal his cognitions of the object and himself. Verbalizations from these two categories of cognitions are then correlated to determine patterns of consistency. One might call these cognition-to-cognition correlations. Correlations of this type are particularly vulnerable to irrelevancies such as the individual's need to be consistent, his introjection of the perceived normative order, or his desire to help or hinder the researcher. Recognition of the intrusion of such irrelevancies is important to establishing acceptable bases for inferences as well as selecting approaches to the collection of behavioral specimens.

From the standpoint of measurement it would be better if behavioral specimens other than verbalizations of feelings and emotions could be identified and used. The relation of feelings and emotions to physiological processes offers one possible avenue to a more acceptable behavioral specimen upon which to base inferences about the emotional component of attitude. Some of the efforts in this direction are included in Section 6 of this volume.

The action tendency component incorporates the behavioral readiness of the individual to respond to the object. It is generally accepted that there is a linkage between cognitive components—particularly evaluative beliefs—and the readiness to respond to the object. Furthermore, there is the general notion that evaluative beliefs and the direction of the response readiness will tend to be consistent. Thus, if an individual believes the Democratic (or Republican) party is a good party and stands for good goals and practices, he will probably be in a state of readiness to respond to it in a helpful, supportive way.

In addition to the linkage between the cognitive and action tendency components there is a linkage between the emotional and action tendency components. This second linkage is presumably mediated by the physiological relation of emotional states of the organism and readiness to respond. It can perhaps be illustrated best by reference to research on stress behavior. Funkenstein (1957) found that subjects who reacted to stress with outwardly aggressive behavior also had an above normal amount of norepinephrine in the blood. Norepinephrine, an enzyme secreted by the adrenal gland, is directly related to such emotions as anger and fright. This sequential relation of object-emotional state-bodily reaction was discussed earlier by Simmons and Wolff (1954). While it is generally recognized as a plausible explanation of the linkage between emotion and readiness to respond, the intricacies need further clarification.

The conceptualization of attitude outlined by Katz and Stotland does appear to incorporate the major areas of agreement among the wide variety of attitude definitions. One of the unfortunate aspects of the development of attitude theory and attitude measurement is that each has developed more or less without reference to the other. The conceptualization of attitude presented above does allow for a closer interplay between theory of attitude and measurement.

What is called for as a basis of inference regarding attitude are specimens of behavior that reveal the individual's beliefs, feelings, and action tendencies with respect to the object in question. Postulating three major components of attitude and making consistency among them a basic proposition of the theory directs attention to types of behavior that may serve as legitimate bases of inference. Doing so also suggests a strategy which has been grossly neglected in attitude research. Any behavioral outcropping that reflects or manifests the individual's cognitions, particularly his evaluative beliefs, about an object may serve as a basis for inference. Similarly, any outcropping that manifests an emotion, in either verbalized or physiological form, may be important as a basis of inference. Behavioral manifestations that reveal an individual's readiness to act toward an object, whether positively or negatively, may be used as a tentative basis for inference with regard to attitude. A systematic typology of bases of inference founded directly upon the Katz and Stotland conceptualization of attitude has not been developed.

In the absence of such a systematic typology the work of Cook and Selltiz (Chapter 1) is a useful schema for ordering the acceptable bases of inference. While it is not dependent upon the Katz and Stotland statement of theory, their classification is derived from a definition of attitude that is wholly consistent with it. As was indicated above, Cook and Selltiz regard attitude as an underlying disposition that enters into the determination of one's beliefs, feelings, and approach-avoidance actions with respect to an object.

From that conceptualization of attitude they identify five bases of inference: (1) self-reports of beliefs, feelings, and behaviors; (2) observation of overt behavior; (3) reaction to or interpretation of partially structured stimuli which involve the attitudinal object; (4) performance of "objective" tasks which involve the attitudinal object; and (5) physiological reactions to the attitudinal object or representations of it. There is a double-edged advantage inherent in their identification of bases of inference. On the one hand, they draw attention to the conceptualization of attitude. On the other, they provide a means whereby the multitude of methods for collecting behavioral specimens and techniques for treating the specimens can be organized. The ordering of specimen collection and treatment procedures leads to

another major advantage. It calls attention to weaknesses in the existing procedures and suggests a reformulation of research strategy that, if followed, could lead to important gains in our understanding of attitude.

Historically, attitude measurement has relied very heavily, almost exclusively, upon the use of self-reports of individuals' beliefs, feelings, and behaviors toward an attitudinal object. This methodological single-mindedness is inconsistent with the conceptualization of attitude. It ignores the variegated nature of outcroppings of an individual's attitudes in his behavior. Moreover, to pursue attitude measurement from only one basis of inference sacrifices the opportunity to examine the theoretical postulate of consistency among the various behavioral outcroppings of attitude as an underlying concept or latent variable. Cook and Selltiz were perhaps the first to argue in detail the need for a research strategy which makes use of several bases of inference.

There is yet another, more purely methodological, case to be made for a "multiple-indicator" approach to attitude measurement. Every method or instrument of measurement runs the risk of containing method-specific irrelevancies. Ideally one would like to have an instrument or method that measures the variable in question and is unaffected by the presence of any other variables—a perfectly valid instrument. However, it is clear that the "readings" taken from any instrument or by any method are fallible. A part of the reading obtained is due to the instrument's sensitivity to irrelevancies, to variables other than the one being measured. Some of the sensitivity to irrelevancies may be peculiar to the instrument being used. Any other instrument we use may also have its idiosyncratic sensitivities. But by using more than one instrument, each with its own peculiarities, it is possible to get a convergence of readings, which we can assume to be due to the variable we are trying to measure. This is what Campbell and Fiske in Chapter 4 refer to as convergent validation, a confirmation by different measurement procedures.

The logic of this argument can be extended beyond the problem of instruments of measurement and measurement methods to bases of inference in attitude research which requires an approach that allows for the confirmation of inferences about attitudes from different types of behavioral specimens. Self-reports are but one such type of behavioral specimen. The others noted above need to be used in conjunction with the self-reports, thus enabling researchers to examine the convergent validation of inferences. This point is developed more fully by Webb and Salancik (Chapter 19) who argue: "Our knowledge of attitudes is anchored in information collected from a single method in restricted settings—verbal self-reports in the laboratory. Methodologically, this is regrettable." By joining a theory of attitude such as that of Katz and Stotland with the bases of inference outlined by Cook and Selltiz and taking the methodological approach to validation suggested by Campbell and Fiske we have an emergent research strategy for a more fruitful approach to attitude measurement.

SPECIMEN COLLECTION

The collection process is intricately related to the specimen. While some collection processes are usable for more than one specimen (or type of specimen), other processes are applicable to only one type of specimen. It has been suggested that the Cook and Selltiz typology of bases of inference is useful in ordering procedures for collecting specimens. Therefore, we shall discuss the procedures for specimen collection within that framework in an effort to illustrate its utility.

Self-Report

The procedure for collecting self-report specimens of behavior is rather obviously indicated by the label itself: the researcher confronts the person directly and asks him how he feels about a particular person, thing, or event, or what he thinks about it or is pre-

pared to do about it. However, the matter is not quite as simple as that, since there are a number of possible ways in which the researcher can approach the respondent.

The primary dimensions separating the various procedures for obtaining self-report specimens are two: (1) method of administration (group versus individual) and (2) method of enumeration; (respondent versus researcher) (Summers and Hammonds, 1969). By taking all possible permutations of these two dimensions, four procedures for specimen collection are recognizable:

(1) group administered, respondent enumerated;
(2) group administered, researcher enumerated;
(3) individually administered, respondent enumerated;
(4) individually administered, researcher enumerated.

The group administered, respondent enumerated procedure is perhaps the most popular, and for obvious reasons. The researcher who can assemble a fairly large aggregation of willing or captive respondents and distribute a questionnaire that they complete privately saves considerable time and effort. This procedure is reasonable and useful when proper attention is given to its limitations.

In general it is not an easy matter to assemble a group of respondents who represent a probability sample from a population to which the researcher wishes to generalize his findings. A proper sample of bankers throughout the United States would be difficult to assemble, for example. There are, of course, several "captive" respondent pools readily available to researchers, especially researchers with academic appointments. College and university classrooms house rather obvious respondent pools, as do secondary schools. The sampling bias is clear in such aggregations unless, of course, the purpose of the research is to study student attitudes.

In addition to the problem of assembling a representative group, there are limitations stemming from the respondent's enumeration of the questionnaire. If he misinterprets a question, inadvertently omits a question, or otherwise distorts his response, the researcher probably will not detect the mistake or omission until he begins his analysis of the specimens. By then it may be too late to make the correction simply and easily, and often it will be impossible. Despite such limitations, the group administered, respondent enumerated questionnaire is widely used as a procedure for collecting self-report specimens.

While the group administered, researcher enumerated questionnaire is a logical possibility, it is virtually impossible on practical grounds. Quite obviously an effort to question several people simultaneously and record their answers individually would be an exercise in chaotic futility. Yet this procedure might be employed when the respondents' answers need not be recorded as individual responses. Conceivably a researcher might be concerned with the collective beliefs, feelings, or action tendencies of a series of small groups of individuals such as school boards, city councils, families, and the like. In such cases the behavioral specimen would be a group datum rather than an individual datum. Most attitude research, however, deals with the attitudes of individuals rather than of groups; for that reason the group administered, researcher enumerated procedure is rarely used.

The individually administered, researcher enumerated procedure, however, is rather widely used. The standard interview in survey research, wherein the researcher (or his representative) meets face-to-face with the respondent, asks him questions, and records his answers, is a very common adaptation of this procedure. The telephone interview, which is like the standard interview except that the respondent and researcher do not see each other, is another frequently used adaptation of the procedure. Both standard and telephone interviews are useful when behavioral specimens are to be collected from a widely scattered sample of respondents. Obviously, both techniques are time consum-

ing, require a rather large staff of research assistants, and, therefore, are generally expensive. It is difficult, also, to assure standardization of the questioning process, since several different interviewers are involved who are not likely to have the same phonetic qualities in their interrogation process. Furthermore, the respondents are more likely to ask questions of their own, thus making standardization of the interviews even more difficult. It is also known that characteristics of the interviewers, such as sex, age, race, or mode of dress, may affect the self-reported beliefs, feelings, and action tendencies of the respondent (Summers and Hammonds, 1966). Regardless of the limitations of the individually administered, researcher enumerated procedures, when self-report specimens are required from respondents who are not easily assembled the researcher may find he has little choice but to use them.

There is one additional self-report procedure, which is sometimes used when respondents are very widely scattered geographically and/or when budgetary considerations limit the use of interviewers. This procedure is the mailed questionnaire, which is individually administered and respondent enumerated. Its limitations are enormous and virtually impossible to overcome. For example, large proportions of the mailed questionnaires typically are never returned, thus adversely affecting the representativeness of the sample from which behavioral specimens are collected. Also, once the questionnaire is in the hands of the respondent, the researcher can never be sure behavioral specimens collected are actually those of the intended or supposed respondent: the respondent's spouse, other members of the family, or friends may "help" in framing the respondent's self-report. Finally, the researcher's assistance in interpreting a question to the respondent is an impossibility. While the use of mail questionnaires in attitude research seems to be on the decline, they once were widely used and are still used in certain types of research such as those dealing with business practices, personnel procedures, associational membership trends, or curriculum trends in higher education where consultation with organizational records is required before questions can be answered.

As has already been noted, the use of self-reports as behavioral specimens is clearly the dominant approach to the study of attitudes. Not only is the heavy emphasis upon self-report specimens unfortunate on theoretical grounds, it is likewise a mistake in view of the fallibility of the procedures used for collecting them. While the procedures for collecting other types of specimens are also fallible, their use in conjunction with self-reports may lead to a firmer understanding of the attitude that presumably underlies all types of behavioral specimens.

Observation of Overt Behavior

Making direct observations of respondents' overt responses to the attitudinal object might appear, at first glance, to be the most desirable approach to gathering behavioral specimens. After all, the ultimate aim of attitude research is better understanding and prediction of overt behavior. The degree of correspondence between attitude and behavior on the theoretical level, or between self-reported attitudes and overt behavior on the measurement level, has been an important issue in the history of attitude research. Important studies dealing with the issue are those of LaPiere (1934), Saenger and Gilbert (1950), Kutner, Wilkins, and Yarrow (1952), DeFleur and Westie (1958), Linn (1965), and Tittle and Hill (1967). Their overall conclusion is that verbally expressed or self-reported attitudes do not correspond perfectly with overt behavior toward the attitudinal object. In fact, in some studies such as LaPiere's, the correspondence is slight. The conclusion in order is that direct observation of overt behavior toward the attitude object is no more free of irrelevancies than are other approaches to the collection of behavioral samples. There are several sources of such irrelevancies. First, the physical presence of the stimulus object may result in a suppression of privately held beliefs, feelings, and action tendencies (Summers and Hammonds, 1966). For example, employees who intensely dislike their supervisor probably will not say so in his presence. Furthermore, in a behavioral situation there are more objects than the one on which the attitude research is focused. One's overt behavior in any given situation is a consequence of the total field of forces impinging upon him; it is not limited to the influences stemming from the attitude under study. The value of direct observation, then, comes from its contribution to the convergent validation process, not from its intrinsic superiority as a process for collecting behavioral specimens.

There are a number of ways direct observations can be collected. They vary with the nature of the situation being observed and the timing of the observation. It is sometimes possible to observe the reactions of people to the attitudinal object in real-life situations without their being aware that their behavior is being watched and recorded. When this situation exists, the observation is nonreactive. The observation per se does not become an influence upon the behavior of the individual being observed. The studies in Section 5 by Kutner, Wilkins, and Yarrow; Campbell, Kruskal, and Wallace; and Gage and Shimberg all have this quality. Webb et al. (1966) have described a very large number of ingenious and imaginative efforts to develop nonreactive measures for attitudes as well as other phenomena. Many, if not most, of the nonreactive measurement efforts have involved unobtrusively observing the behavior of individuals in real-life situations. But it would be a mistake to conclude that all efforts to observe overt behavior directly in an unobtrusive and nonreactive fashion have centered on real-life situations. Direct observations also can be made in contrived situations. However, in collecting behavioral specimens from contrived situations it is essential that the persons being observed believe that their actions will have real consequences. Linn's study (Chapter 27) is a good example of an effort to contrive a situation in which respondents' behaviors can be observed directly. The aspect of the Kutner, Wilkins, and Yarrow study involving telephoning for reservations and mailing inquiries about reservations is an equally good example of a contrived situation which appeared to have been accepted as "real" by the respondents. Whether the observational situation is contrived by the researcher or merely exploited by him, the critical element is that the respondents accept as a fact that they must live with the consequences of their actions.

Direct observations of overt behavior need not be concurrent with the behavior. Sometimes behavior leaves a trace of residue which can be examined later. Personal documents such as diaries, letters to intimates or biographies can be important and valuable residues of past overt behavior. Thomas and Znaniecki (1918–1920), who were among the first persons to seriously attempt to measure attitudes, relied very heavily upon such personal documents to assess the attitudes and values of Polish peasant immigrants in the United States. The study by Gage and Shimberg measuring senatorial progressivism demonstrates that public documents as a residue of overt behavior can be used to draw inferences. The researcher must remember that in observation of traces and residues of overt behavior, as in all direct observation, there is the possibility that the behavior may possibly have been affected by influences other than the attitude in question. There is also the further potential limitation that important aspects of the overt behavior were not recorded, and that ignorance of the omission may lead the researcher to erroneous inferences. Furthermore, when using traces and residues, the researcher has little freedom to control which elements of the overt behavior will be selected as behavioral specimens. There is the final limitation that most overt behavior simply does not leave traces or residues at all.

Overt behavioral responses to the attitude object are highly desirable behavioral specimens in attitude research, even though there are limitations to the use of direct observation. While some researchers have appeared to assume that direct observation is a more reliable and valid indication of the respondent's attitude, that interpretation is of dubious value. It is perhaps more worthwhile to view direct observation as a collection procedure which can contribute to the convergent validation of attitude measurement. It does have the attractiveness of being less susceptible to reactive arrangements. Therefore, the need for more ways to collect behavioral specimens by direct observation is important in attitude research and significantly challenges the imagination and creative abilities of the researcher.

Reaction to Partially Structured Stimuli

The causes of any given specimen of behavior are to be found in the psychological makeup of the person, in his environment, or in both. Ordinarily the person's behavior is a function of both his environment and his own psychological composition. In attitude research we are concerned with the contribution of attitude (a quality of the person) to his behavior. One strategy for clarifying that contribution is to limit, insofar as possible, the contribution of other influences. This can be done by minimizing the structure of the environment and thereby minimizing its utility for the person as a system of cues for behavior. When this is accomplished it is reasonable to assume that the manifest behavior is the product of the person's psychological attributes. This is the logical basis of the many projective techniques used in psychological research and in clinical psychology. The extension of this logic to attitude measurement is simple and obvious. If the object is included in an otherwise highly unstructured stimulus field, the person's response to the object must be largely, if not wholly, determined by what the person contributes to the situation.

Typically, the techniques for collecting behavioral specimens that are reactions to partially structured stimuli involving the attitude object or its symbolic representation are quite similar to the self-report techniques.

But there are important differences. The first and most important characteristic is disguised intent. This is what Kidder and Campbell refer to as the indirection of a test. The respondent has categories and dimensions in mind while answering which are different from those used by the researcher in interpreting the respondent's behavior. For example, respondents in Kuethe's research (Chapter 22) were allowed to place objects cut from felt onto another felt background in any way they pleased. Their placements of the objects were recorded and interpreted in terms of the kinds of social schemas which they revealed. The content of the set of objects used was noted to determine its effect on the social schema used by the respondent. One of the most widely cited indirect techniques for measuring attitudes among adults is one developed by Proshansky (Chapter 21). He selected a number of ambiguous photographs of labor situations from magazines and newspapers and interspersed them in a standard set of Murray's Thematic Apperception Test cards. The scenes were then shown to respondents who were given a few minutes in which to write a brief description of what was happening in each scene. Proshansky found that labor-management attitudes measured in this manner correlated substantially (.77 and .67) with self-report measurements of the same attitude.

A second characteristic of techniques in this approach is that the respondent is led to believe that there are no correct or incorrect answers. Any answer is acceptable. In fact, the respondent is usually encouraged to be as idiosyncratic and self-descriptive as he likes. In the typology of techniques developed by Kidder and Campbell, those having this feature are said to be voluntary. "In the voluntary test the respondent is given to understand that any answer is acceptable, and that there is no external criterion of correctness against which his answers will be evaluated."

A third characteristic that generally sets this approach to specimen collection apart from the self-report techniques is the open-ended or free-response format for responding to the partially structured stimuli. The respondent must construct his response to the stimulus situation presented without assistance from the researcher. This is true in the Kuethe and Proshansky techniques noted above. By using the free-response format the researcher does not limit or artificially expand the respondent's range of possible behaviors. Also, the free-response format does not run the risk of the researcher's imposing his own set of categories and concepts upon the respondent. The respondent is not forced to view the world through the eyes of the researcher but is encouraged to report it as he sees it.

As a final word about specimen collections using partially structured stimuli it should be noted that the researcher's instructions to the respondent are also an integral part of the stimulus situation to which the respondent reacts. It is a serious risk to overlook that fact. Highly unstructured pictures, inkblots, wordless cartoons, and the like can take on a great deal of structure in the view of the respondent if the researcher is not careful in presenting the task. Therefore, whether a particular technique belongs in this category of behavioral specimen collection procedures or in the self-report category depends greatly upon the researcher's ability to maintain indirection. The techniques employed to collect specimens of reaction to partially structured stimuli are generally characterized by indirection, partially structured stimuli, and voluntary responses in a free-response format. The Kuethe and Proshansky contributions to Section 4 are clear examples of this type of approach to specimen collection. Kidder and Campbell provide a detailed review of techniques related to this basis of inference.

Objective Tasks

The techniques used for collecting specimens by observing performance of objective tasks also have a close resemblance to the self-report techniques. Both involve the confrontation of the respondent by the researcher or his assistant. The respondent is aware that he is being tested. What distinguishes the techniques in this approach from those of the self-report approach is their indirection. The respondent is led to believe he is being tested in the usual sense of the term, as in an achievement or information test. However, the researcher has in mind a set of categories into which the respondent's reactions will be fitted that are different from those the respondent has in mind as he performs the task. The success of the technique depends heavily upon this deception.

The presence of indirection suggests that the techniques of this approach are also similar to those used for collecting reactions to partially structured stimuli. True, they both are characterized by indirection. However, unlike the partially structured stimuli techniques, the objective task techniques are not voluntary. "In contrast, in an objective test the person is told, either explicitly or implicitly, that there is a correct answer external to himself, for which he should search in selecting his answer" (Kidder and Campbell). In the respondent's own thinking he is describing the world as it is, and in doing so he is unintentionally and unknowingly reflecting his own interpretation of that world. It is the inevitability of this phenomenological introjection into the objective task that is the primary assumption underlying the use of performance of objective tasks as a basis for inference. "The assumption common to [techniques in this approach] is that performance may be influenced by attitude, and that a systematic bias in performance reflects the influence of attitude" (Cook and Selltiz). The contributions of Hammond, Thistlethwaite, and Selltiz and Cook to Section 4 are illustrative of the efforts to apply this logic to the collection of behavioral specimens.

Physiological Reactions

"At the opposite extreme from measures relying on a subject's verbal report of his beliefs, feelings, etc., are those relying on physiological responses not subject to conscious control" (Cook and Selltiz). Physiological responses to the presence of an attitudinal object or its representation may be either conditioned or unconditioned. In the case of the unconditioned response it is assumed that the magnitude of the physiological responses is directly related to the arousal and/or intensity of the feeling component of attitude and that the relationship should hold, within limits, for all persons. As Cook and Selltiz point out, there are problems of inference involved because most physiological reaction measures indicate only the extent of arousal and not the direction of the feeling. This limitation is also dealt with by Mueller (Chapter 36). There was an early belief that the pupillary dilation and constriction could indicate the direction of feeling or affect. However, the work of Woodmansee (Chapter 35) dampens that enthusiasm and early optimism. It is perhaps more likely that use of behavioral specimens of this type will depend heavily upon conditioned physiological responses as a basis for inference.

The inferential process involved in the use of conditioned physiological responses rests upon learning theory. Most physiological responses are susceptible to conditioning. When a physiological response has been conditioned to an evaluative concept such as good, bad, desirable, or nice, the presentation of an object that is perceived as having that quality will elicit the physiological response. As an example, Volkova (1953) conditioned subjects to salivate in response to the word GOOD. With the response firmly conditioned, presentation of such statements as "The Young Pioneer helps his comrade" brought maximum salivation, while such statements as "The Fascists destroyed many cities" produced minimum salivation. The logic of the inferential process used when dealing with conditioned physiological responses is to run this learning process in reverse. Thus, if it is noted that the presentation of an attitude object is associated with an increase in the acidity of the saliva, it is necessary to know to what attitudinally relevant concept the acidity of saliva has been conditioned before inference can be made as to direction of the attitudinal response. Robertson and Dotson (1965) have reported using acidity of saliva as a conditioned response to stress. Stress is generally regarded as undesirable and hence it is a reasonable hypothesis that increased acidity of saliva is related to unfavorableness toward the attitude object (stress). However, low acidity could not be taken to mean favorableness toward an object. Acidity of saliva, as are most physiological responses, is sensitive to influences other than those with which the researcher is concerned. Thus, it is as difficult to collect specimens of physiological responses without introducing irrelevancies as it is to collect other types of specimens.

TREATMENT OF BEHAVIORAL SPECIMENS

The collection of specimens is meaningful only when the things observed have some relevance to the variable or concept about which we wish to gain further knowledge. When the specimens do reflect the variable, we are in a position to further our understanding of the phenomenon.

However, a collection of specimens is little more than a stack of questionnaires, several cartons of interview schedules, reels of used recording tape, polygraph record sheets, etc., until it is treated in some manner that allows one to grasp the dimensions of the aggregate.

The Scale of Number

Mathematics and statistics provide us with extensive knowledge of the scale of number and the multitude of meaningful manipulations that can be performed with the scale. It is, of course, much more efficient and parsimonious to manipulate numbers than the actual objects they represent. But in order to gain the efficiency of numerical manipulation as a shorthand for object manipulation, certain specific relations between the variable being studied (attitude), the specimens (self-reports, direct observations, etc.), and the scale of number must obtain. The scale of number has many properties, and they are integral to the manipulations that can be performed on the scale—addition, subtraction, multiplication, and division. Which manipulations of the number scale are appropriate are determined by those properties of the scale that are applicable to the concept being studied and to the specimens collected. The most important properties of the scale of number are presented below.

Each number is an entity, distinguishable from any other number. This is the *nominal* property of the scale of number. The scale also has an *ordinal* property. We consider 1 to be larger than 0, 2 to be greater than 1, 3 than 2, and so forth. Numbers are not only ordinal in scale, they are equidistant. The distance between 1 and 2 is the same as that between 2 and 3, 3 and 4, or any other two adjacent numbers. This is the *interval* property of the scale of number. There is finally the property of *equality of ratios*. The number 4 is twice 2; 8 is twice 4; 64 is twice 32. The frequency with which 2 can be subtracted from 4, 4 from 8, and 32 from 64 is a constant 2. Therefore, the ratio is 2. It is this property of equality of ratios that makes possible the manipulations of multiplication and division. It must be remembered that the scale of number possesses *all* these properties. In order for the researcher to take full advantage of them in his manipulations of specimens he must assign the numerals to his specimens so that the integrity of the scale of number is maintained. Therefore, the researcher must determine whether or not the variable he is studying (attitude) *and* his specimens have all the properties of the scale of number. If so, and that is seldom the case, the researcher is free to use all manipulations that are possible with the scale of number and to interpret the resulting "score" accordingly. If it is not possible to assume total isomorphism between the properties of the concept, the specimens, and the scale of number, it may be possible to assume an isomorphism between them on at least some properties of the scale. Notice that in the four properties of the scale of number mentioned, the equality of ratios assumes the other three; the interval property assumes the ordinal and nominal properties. And the ordinal property assumes the nominal. The question then becomes one of determining which properties may be legitimately assumed for the concept being studied (attitude) and the behavior specimens collected. The properties that may be legitimately claimed determine the rules by which numerals may be assigned to the specimens and the manipulations that may be employed.

Attitude as a concept is generally assumed to have all properties of the scale of number. First, since attitude is conceptualized as a continuous variable, points along its continuum are identifiable and are nominally different. If the continuum is seen as extending from extreme "positive" to extreme "negative" with respect to the attitudinal object, any two nominally discrete points along it will differ in amount of positiveness (or negativeness). Attitude, therefore, has an ordinal property. Next, it is possible to locate points along the attitude continuum that will be equidistant in psychological meaning (positiveness or negativeness); thus, attitude has an interval property. Finally, attitude theorists generally assume that it is possible to locate points that will legitimately maintain equality of ratios. This is the equivalent of saying that point A on the attitude dimension is twice as positive as point B. Given an isomorphism between the properties of the concept and those of the scale of number, any limitation on the application of the scale of number in attitude research must rest with the properties of the specimen.

Unlike the concept of attitude, specimens cannot be said to have the properties of the scale of number a priori. Whether or not properties of the scale of number are appropriate to a given set of specimens depends upon the conditions under which they were collected. However, two generalizations are in order.

First, all specimens have the nominal property and most have the ordinal property.

Second, few known specimens have the equality of ratios property. Hence, to answer which properties of the scale of number are appropriate for a given set of specimens usually requires deciding between ordinal and interval properties. Whatever the decision regarding the extent of isomorphism of the specimens and the scale of number, procedures (or rules) for assigning numbers to the specimens must not presuppose greater isomorphism than exists. For example, one must not assign numerals to specimens and manipulate those numerals as if they had an equality of ratios property when the specimens are no more than ordinal. To do so would lead to misinterpretation of the numerical scores. The converse is equally important. The researcher should take advantage of all the properties of the scale of number that the specimens possess in order to use his information maximally.

Scales and Data Sources

Attitude scaling is a special application of the general process of psychological scaling which is concerned with developing scales of measurement for abstracted properties of human experience. Every scaling effort involves three sets of variables. As Garner and Creelman state in Chapter 2, "The three variables are *stimuli,* a set of objects which we have chosen to use, *subjects,* to whom the objects are presented, and *responses* which are required by the experimental situation." The attribute to be scaled is a property of the subjects. For some attributes there is a corresponding physical dimension of the stimuli as when the attribute is sensory experience of size, brightness, loudness, and the like. For other attributes, such as attitudes, there is no physical counterpart in the stimuli. This difference complicates the processes of attitude scaling somewhat, but the complications are not insurmountable. One of the major contributions of Thurstone to attitude measurement was the demonstration that the assumptions and techniques of psychophysical scaling could be applied to attitude measurement (Chapter 6). Since Thurstone's work of the 1920s and 1930s, considerable advance has been made in the development of techniques of attitude scaling. Most of these advances have been based upon self-reported behavioral specimens. It is for this reason that the selections dealing with psychological scaling techniques (see Sections 2 and 3) have been presented as illustrative of the quantification of self-report specimens.

The association of attitude-scaling techniques with self-report behavioral specimens is not complete, however. The application of some attitude-scaling techniques to non-self-report specimens is possible. For example, Guttman's scalogram analysis can be used with several other types of specimens, as is demonstrated by Gage and Shimberg. The chief reason for the wider applicability of scalogram analysis is its unique feature which permits the scaling of subjects and stimuli simultaneously. (See pp. 54–55 for a brief explanation of this feature.)

A number of the scaling techniques, however, including those of Thurstone and Likert, are not easily adapted for use with non-self-report specimens. They require that the researcher experimentally control the stimuli and the modes of response. Situations presented to subjects, who respond to them, must contain predetermined combinations of the stimuli and possible responses to them. These are generally presented as a series of statements describing a variety of potential responses to the stimuli, and the subject indicates his agreement or disagreement with each descriptive statement. Conceivably, similar pairing of potential responses to the stimuli could be presented to the subjects by means other than written statements. For example, a subject could be observed in a small group discussion where all the other members of the group were confederates of the researcher. During the course of the discussion the subject's reaction (his agreement or disagreement with statements made by the confederates which combine the stimuli

and potential responses) could be recorded. These specimens would then be amenable to standard Thurstone or Likert scaling procedures.

Yet it is clear that attitude scaling has been developed largely in conjunction with self-report specimens. The measurement procedures typically employed with specimens other than self-reports are much less sophisticated and less powerful. There are, no doubt, many reasons for this developmental trend in attitude measurement. Webb and Salancik cite the popularity of operationalism as a major influence. Related to that is the historical fact that attitude scaling was initiated by researchers with training in the tradition of psychophysical measurement, which depends heavily on self-reports. The norms and values of that research tradition have been promulgated over the past forty years with only minor shifts in orientation. And it has been fruitful for the field of attitude measurement even though there are inherent limitations with exclusive reliance upon this tradition.

Other types of specimens have been used but with less frequency than self-reports. The clinical tradition in psychology has relied heavily upon subjects' reactions to partially structured stimuli. Specimens of this type generally have no more than the ordinal property and are often only nominal. This means, of course, that treatment of such specimens must be relatively weak when viewed in relation to the full range of properties of the scale of number. Responses to objective tasks represent an effort to merge the psychophysical and clinical traditions. And the potential contribution of this merger has scarcely been tapped. The works of Hammond and Thistlethwaite indicate the promise of this approach.

Direct observation as a source of behavioral specimens is associated with the tradition of participant observation in anthropology and sociology. Here again the properties of the scale of number which can be assumed are generally quite limiting. It is hardly an exaggeration to say that most direct observation specimens have only the nominal property, a few possess the ordinal property, and virtually none achieve the interval level.

It is fairly obvious that scaling of observations with only nominal or ordinal properties is extremely limiting if attention is properly given to the restrictions that are imposed because of limited isomorphism between the observations and the scale of number. The scales that are possible are of the nominal and ordinal levels. At best, all one can hope to do is order subjects by saying that A is more positive than B, who is more positive than C.

It is easy to understand why researchers from a tradition in which ordinal scale properties are taken for granted may fail to develop an enthusiasm for using behavioral specimens that generally do not allow one to rise above the ordinal level of scaling. It is an understandable response, but not a wise one. First, the self-report specimens, while sometimes permitting one to reach the interval level of scaling, are fallible. Scales for measuring attitudes that are based on self-report specimens may be just as invalid and unreliable as those based upon any other specimen type. Second, since the fallibility of scales based on self-report specimens may be correlated with the specimen, it is essential that scales using other behavioral specimens be developed and applied in conjunction with self-report scales. This point is central to the strategy for validity assessment presented by Campbell and Fiske.

The scaling of physiological reaction specimens represents a tradition based in physiology. Here the level of measurement may be generally higher than for other types of specimens. Interval level scales are common and ratio level scales are not rare. Why, then, have researchers not turned to this type of specimen as a favored window into the attitude domain? The chapters by Woodmansee and Mueller provide a rather clear answer. In short, the physiological reaction specimens are often of dubious relevance to attitude. That there is an emotional or feeling component to attitude is commonly ac-

knowledged theory, and physiological specimens of emotional response are possible. The difficulty occurs because most physiological specimens reflect only the arousal level of the emotion and are incapable of reflecting the direction of the emotion, which is what the attitude researcher is concerned with. Therefore, the validity of physiological reaction measures is somewhat suspect.

In this introduction attention has been directed to the importance of the isomorphism between the behavioral specimens and the scale of numbers. In doing so, attention has been limited to the manifest properties of the specimens. The reader must be made aware that behavioral specimens have latent as well as manifest properties. As Garner and Creelman state, "The manifest properties of the data are, as the term suggests, the evident, easily seen, and interpreted properties. The latent properties are those which must be extracted from the data, which are inherent, but are not readily perceivable." This distinction between manifest and latent properties will not be elaborated here because it is central to the discussion of Garner and Creelman. Nevertheless, the problems dealt with in Section I are equally relevant to both properties. Generally, the latent properties more fully approximate the properties of the scale of number than do the manifest properties.

Reliability and Validity

Attitude measurements are meaningful only when they accurately reflect the attitude. Inaccuracy of, or discrepancy between, the observed attitude score and the "true" score is known as measurement error. That is, the observed attitude score, X_o, is the true attitude score, X_t, plus the error in measurement, X_e. Formally,

$$X_o = X_t + X_e. \tag{1}$$

From (1) it follows simply that

$$X_e = X_o - X_t. \tag{2}$$

Ideally one would like to have $X_t = X_o$ and thereby eliminate measurement error.

This is seldom, if ever, achieved in practice, however. Therefore, one must always be concerned with the consequences of measurement error. And, since in practice one never knows the true score, X_t, estimating the magnitude of error in measurement is always problematic.

The consequences of measurement error center primarily upon whether or not the error is randomly distributed about the true score. When X_e is randomly distributed the alegebraic sum of the errors will be zero, and therefore the mean of the observed scores, $E(X_o)$, will be unaffected by the errors. $E(X_o)$ remains an unbiased estimate of $E(X_t)$ in spite of the measurement error. However, because the errors are random, it follows that repeated measurement of the same individuals will result in departures between the two sets of scores. Thus, the correlation of one set with the other will result in a correlation of less than unity. The *reliability* of a measuring instrument (or procedure) is defined as its ability to produce identical scores on repeated application to the same subjects in the absence of change in their true scores. It is clear, therefore, that the presence of random errors of measurement adversely affects the reliability of the measurement procedure.

When measurement error is not random it adversely affects the *validity* of the measurement procedure. That is, the observed score is influenced systematically by another variable to which the measurement procedure was not intended to be sensitive. In this case we may rewrite (1) as

$$X_o = X_t + X_r + X_s, \qquad (3)$$

where X_r is random error and X_s is systematic error. To be completely accurate, (1) should be written as (3), because in every situation $X_e = X_r + X_s$. However, in classical reliability theory X_s is assumed to be zero, $X_s = 0$, and the term is merely dropped from the formal equation. By reinserting X_s in (1), the relationship of true scores, observed scores, random error, and systematic error is more readily recognizable.

Both X_r and X_s may be zero, in which case $X_o = X_t$; the measurement procedure would be valid *and* reliable. X_s may be zero while $X_r > 0$, in which event the measure would be valid but unreliable. The converse is possible. X_r may be zero while $X_s > 0$. Here the measurement is perfectly reliable but invalid, and does not reflect the true score of attitude it purports to represent. The more likely condition in practice is one in which $X_r > 0$ and $X_s > 0$.

There is no way of knowing, a priori, the magnitude of X_r and X_s. They must be estimated from the observed scores, X_o. The problems and techniques of estimating validity and reliability are beyond the purpose of this introduction, but a number of them that are central to attitude measurement are discussed by Bohrnstedt in Chapter 3. For a more extensive introduction to these matters the reader will find the following most helpful: Gulliksen (1950), Horst (1966), and Lord and Novick (1968).

CONCLUSION

There are numerous potential sources of invalidity and unreliability in attitude measurement as in any measurement effort. They range from improper conceptualization of attitude, to inappropriate choice of behavioral specimens, to errors in the collection of specimens, to misapplication of numerical treatment. The thesis of this introduction is that attitude measurement needs to devote more attention to the collection and treatment of specimens other than self-reports. The thesis was generated by a concern for improving the validity and reliability of attitude-measurement procedures—especially validity.

According to Campbell and Fiske, "Validation is typically *convergent,* a confirmation by independent measurement procedures.... For the justification of novel trait measures, for the validation of test interpretation, or for the establishment of construct validity, *discriminant* validation as well as convergent validation is required. . . . Each test or task employed for measurement purposes is a *trait-method unit,* a union of a particular trait content with measurement procedures not specific to that content. . . . In order to examine discriminant validity, and in order to estimate the relative contributions of trait and method variance, *more than one trait* as well as *more than one method* must be employed in the validation process."

The application of this logic to attitude measurement is straightforward, simple, and compelling. Yet evidence of its use is extremely scarce. The work of Tittle and Hill (Chapter 30) goes part of the way by examining the convergent validity of several independent measures of a single attitude. But what is needed is the application of the complete multitrait-multimethod strategy. And with its application *types of behavioral specimens* (direct observation, self-report, etc.), as well as techniques for treating specimens, need to be interpreted as methods. Apparently the only systematic efforts along this line are those currently being carried out by Cook and his associates (1968). Even here there are no reports available indicating that the maximum application of the multitrait-multimethod strategy has been pursued.

In counterpoint to the need for using types of behavioral specimens as methods is the need to interpret attitude *components* (beliefs, feelings, action tendencies) as traits. Attitude theory claims that the components are distinct but that they tend to be consistent. The validity of this theoretical assertion can be meaningfully examined as a convergent-discriminant validation problem.

The selection of materials for the chapters that follow was largely determined by a firm belief that the limitations presently associated with specimens other than those collected by self-report procedures can be reduced, if not eliminated; that the long-standing reliance upon self-reported specimens is inconsistent with the canons of science; and that the multitrait-multimethod paradigm offers a research strategy that permits an evaluation of the extent to which attitude and its components, procedures for collecting specimens, and techniques for

treatment of the specimens are achieving convergent and discriminant validity. It is hoped that the selections argue well for these biases.

REFERENCES

Campbell, Donald T.
  1950 "The indirect assessment of social attitudes." Psychological Bulletin 47:15–38.
  1963 "Social attitudes and other acquired behavioral dispositions," in Sigmund Koch (ed.), Psychology: A Study of a Science. Volume 6. New York: McGraw-Hill.
Campbell, Donald T., and Donald W. Fiske.
  1959 "Convergent and discriminant validation by the multitrait-multimethod matrix." Psychological Bulletin 56:81–105.
Campbell, Donald T., William H. Kruskal, and William P. Wallace.
  1966 "Seating aggregation as an index of attitude." Sociometry 29:1–15.
Cook, Stuart W., and Claire Selltiz.
  1964 "A multiple-indicator approach to attitude measurement." Psychological Bulletin 62:36–55.
Cook, Stuart W.
  1968 Studies Of Attitude and Attitude Measurement: Final Technical Report. Boulder: Institute of Behavioral Science, University of Colorado. (AF Grant No. 436–66. Mimeographed.)
DeFleur, Melvin, and Frank Westie.
  1958 "Verbal attitudes and overt acts: an experiment on the salience of attitudes." American Sociological Review 23:667–673.
Funkenstein, D. H., *et al.*
  1957 Mastery of Stress. Cambridge: Harvard University Press.
Gage, N. L., and Ben Shimberg.
  1949 "Measuring senatorial 'progressivism'," Journal of Abnormal and Social Psychology 44:112–117.
Garner, W. R., and C. D. Creelman.
  1967 "Problems and methods of psychological scaling," in Harry Helson and William Bevan (eds.), Contemporary Approaches to Psychology. Princeton: Van Nostrand Co.

Gullicksen, H.
1950 Theory of Mental Tests. New York: Wiley.

Hammond, Kenneth R.
1948 "Measuring attitudes by error-choice: an indirect method." Journal of Abnormal and Social Psychology 43:38–48.

Horst, Paul.
1966 Psychological Measurement and Prediction. Belmont, Mass.: Wadsworth.

Katz, D., and E. Stotland.
1959 "A preliminary statement to a theory of attitude structure and change," in Sigmund Koch (ed.), Psychology: A Study of a Science. Volume 3. New York: McGraw-Hill.

Krech, David, Richard S. Crutchfield, and Egerton L. Ballachey.
1962 Individual In Society. New York: McGraw-Hill.

Kuethe, James L.
1964 "Prejudice and aggression: a study of specific social schemata." Perceptual and Motor Skills 18:107–115.

Kutner, Bernard, Carol Wilkins, and Penny Rechtman Yarrow.
1952 "Verbal attitudes and overt behavior involving racial prejudice." Journal of Abnormal and Social Psychology 47:649–652.

LaPiere, R. T.
1934 "Attitudes vs. actions." Social Forces 13:230–237.

Linn, Lawrence S.
1965 "Verbal attitudes and overt behavior: a study of racial discrimination." Social Forces 43:353–364.

Lord, Frederick M., and M. R. Novick.
1968 Statistical Theories of Mental Test Scores. Reading, Mass.: Addison-Wesley.

Proshansky, Harold.
1943 "A projective method for the study of attitudes." Journal of Abnormal and Social Psychology 38:393–395.

Rankin, Robert E., and Donald T. Campbell.
1959 "Galvanic skin response to Negro and white experimenters." Journal of Abnormal and Social Psychology 51:30–33.

Robertson, Leon, and Louis E. Dotson.
1965 "Instrumental and expressive parental roles and reaction to frustration." Paper presented to the American Sociological Association, Chicago (August).

Saenger, Gerhart, and Emily Gilbert.
1950 "Customer reactions to the integration of Negro sales personnel." International Journal of Opinion and Attitude Research 4:57–76.

Simmons, L. W., and H. G. Wolf.
1954 Social Science in Medicine. New York: Russell Sage Foundation.

Summers, Gene F., and André D. Hammonds.
1966 "Effect of racial characteristics of investigator on self-enumerated responses to a Negro prejudice scale." Social Forces 44:515–518.
1969 "Toward a paradigm for respondent bias in survey research." Sociological Quarterly, 10:113–121.

Thistlethwaite, Donald.
1950 "Attitude and structure as factors in the distortion of reasoning." Journal of Abnormal and Social Psychology 45:442–458.

Thomas, William I., and Florian Znaniecki.
1918– The Polish Peasant in Europe and
1920 America. 5 Volumes. Boston: Richard Badger.

Thurstone, L. L.
1928 "Attitudes can be measured." American Journal of Sociology 33:529–554.

Tittle, Charles R., and Richard J. Hill.
1967 "Attitude measurement and prediction of behavior: an evaluation of conditions and measurement techniques." Sociometry 30:199–213.

Volkova, B. D.
1953 "Some characteristics of conditioned reflex formation to verbal stimuli in children." Sechenov Physiological Journal 39:540–548. U.S.S.R.

Webb, Eugene J., D. T. Campbell, R. D. Schwartz, and L. Sechrest.
1966 Unobtrusive Measures: Nonreactive Research in the Social Sciences. Chicago: Rand McNally.

SECTION **I** **Basic Considerations**

Overview

Attitudes are not open to direct observation. Their existence and their strength must be inferred from what is observable. One must therefore choose behaviors which are acceptable as bases of inference. Traditionally, self-reported beliefs, feelings and/or intentions to act with respect to an object have been used as the primary basis of inference. The emphasis upon self-reported specimens of behavior is both unnecessary and unfortunate. Cook and Selltiz present several reasons why this is true and argue for a multiple-indicator approach to attitude measurement. The classification of methods which they suggest rests upon the type of behavioral specimen that is used as a basis of inference.

To understand human behavior it is necessary to sort the mass of things people do and say; to arrange them in clusters which are behaviorally and theoretically meaningful, such as academic performance, conformity to the demands of others, or aggression. In attempting to explain why people do (or do not) manifest these behaviors, intervening constructs are often introduced. For example, postulate that academic performance is enhanced by intelligence; low self-esteem leads to conformity; and aggressive behavior is an outcome of frustration. Testing the correctness of such propositions obviously requires measurement of the behaviors and the intervening variables.

Attitude is a very popular intervening variable among social psychologists. Consequently, much attention has been given to the problems of attitude measurement. Indeed, the peculiar features of attitude measurement have been so greatly stressed that it is well to remember that many of the problems of measuring attitudes are common to the measurement of other psychological variables. The chapter by Garner and Creelman makes quite clear the value of recognizing common bonds of problems and methods between psychological scaling and attitude scaling.

All measurement must be accurate to be useful—accurate in several ways. An instrument of measurement must provide "readings" which represent that which the user of the instrument purports to measure. When we plan to measure attitudes we want an instrument which is insensitive to intelligence, social class, tendencies of the respondent to give socially desirable answers, or anything else except attitudes. The instrument must be valid. How this is achieved and the degree to which it is achieved are extremely important.

An instrument must be consistent in the readings it provides when applied to an object which is unchanged; it must be reliable. There are several ways in which reliability may be conceived. For example, one may think of reliability as consistency over time, or one may see it as the degree of consistency among the items constituting the instrument. As with validity, the problems of increasing the reliability and assessing the reliability of instruments is critical in attitude measurement.

Validity and reliability are intimately related. For example, an instrument with low reliability cannot provide valid measures of anything to which it might be applied. But the interrelation of these two qualities of instruments goes beyond this simple level of functional contingency as Bohrnstedt points out in Chapter 3. He also provides an explanation of how validity and reliability of instruments may be assessed and offers insights into ways of increasing both.

In order for a measure to be accepted as valid several criteria must be met. Perhaps the two most basic are: 1) it must provide scores which agree with other measures of the same object, and 2) it must not show convergence with measures from which it is supposed to differ. These two processes of validation are defined by Campbell and Fiske in Chapter 4 as convergent and discriminant validation, and a lucid and cogent discussion of the manner in which the multitrait-multimethod correlation matrix makes possible the assessment of the convergent and discriminant aspects of the validation process is then presented. The basic feature of the strategy is to combine several traits and more than one method into a single correlational analysis. The multitrait-multimethod design is a powerful and parsimonious tool even though its execution may not be feasible in all field studies of attitude.

CHAPTER 1

A Multiple-Indicator Approach to Attitude Measurement[1]

STUART W. COOK AND CLAIRE SELLTIZ

At least since LaPiere's report (1934) of the discrepancy between the actual reception accorded him and a Chinese couple and the answers to a questionnaire about accepting Chinese as guests, investigators have been concerned with the fact that different procedures designed to assess the same attitudes have often led to quite different placements of the same individuals, and that observed behavior toward a social object (person, group, etc.) is frequently not what would have been predicted from a given instrument intended to measure attitude toward that ob-

From Stuart W. Cook and Claire Selltiz, "A multiple-indicator approach to attitude measurement." *Psychological Bulletin*, 1964, *62*, 36–55. Copyright 1964 by the American Psychological Association, and reproduced by permission of the authors and publisher.

[1] This paper was prepared as part of a program of research on the measurement of social attitudes supported by grants from the National Science Foundation and the Air Force Office of Scientific Research. Many of our colleagues have contributed to our thinking about the problems discussed here. In particular, we have gained insights and clarified our ideas through discussions with Donald T. Campbell, Isidor Chein, Barbara S. Dohrenwend, John S. Harding, Marie Jahoda, Irwin Katz, and M. Brewster Smith. It is perhaps unnecessary to add that there is no implication that any of these colleagues completely share the point of view expressed here.

ject. There have been several types of reaction to such observed discrepancies. One has been to assume that there is a "true" attitude toward the object, which one or both measures have failed to gauge correctly. A second has been to assume that there are different "classes" of attitudes toward a given object —for example, "verbal attitudes" and "action attitudes"—which should not necessarily be expected to correspond. Another has been to equate attitude with behavior, using "attitude" simply as a descriptive term summarizing observed consistencies in behavior. Still another reaction has been to think of attitude as an underlying disposition which enters, along with other influences, into the determination of a variety of behaviors toward an object or class of objects, including statements of beliefs and feelings about the object and approach-avoidance actions with respect to it.

We prefer the latter position; first, because for us, as for others (e.g., Allport, 1954) the observation of regularities in social behavior seems to point to the operation of relatively stable underlying dispositions toward classes of objects. Further, we believe that apparent inconsistencies in social behavior may often best be understood in terms of the operation of such stable underlying dispositions in shifting relation to other influences on behavior. Finally, if validly distinguished, a dispositional concept has, by its very nature, a wider range of situational relevance—including projectability into relatively novel situations—than a simple descriptive concept of equating attitude with behavior in specified situations.

We assume that two classes of variables, in addition to an individual's attitudinal disposition toward a given object or class of objects, influence his behavior in situations involving the object or symbols of the object (including the behavior constituting his responses to instruments designed to measure attitude toward the object): (*a*) *other characteristics of the individual,* including his dispositions toward other objects represented in the situation, values he holds that are engaged by the situation, his motivational state, his expressive style, and so on; (*b*) *other characteristics of the situation,* including its prescriptions as to appropriate behavior, the expectations of others in the situation with respect to the individual's behavior, the possible or probable consequences of various acts on his part, and so on.

In this view, an attitude cannot be measured directly, but must always be inferred from behavior—whether the behavior be language in which the individual reports his feelings about the attitude-object, performance of a task involving material related to the object (e.g., recall of statements which take a position with respect to the object), or actions toward a representative of the object-class (e.g., avoidance of such an individual). Lazarsfeld (1959) takes a similar position in his discussion of latent structure analysis. He points out that there is a probability relation between an indicator and the underlying trait of which it is taken as an indication; that is, a given trait does not invariably produce a given behavior. He stresses that, in consequence, some inconsistency will always be found between different measures of a hypothesized trait, and that the task of the investigator is to combine them into an "in-dex" or "measurement" which represents the best inference that can be made from the manifold of empirical operations to the underlying characteristic they are assumed to reflect.

This orientation leads to emphasis on the need for a number of different measurement approaches to provide a basis for estimating the common underlying disposition, and to the expectation that data from these approaches will not be perfectly correlated. However, it seems to us that it should be possible to increase the correspondence among the indicators by careful analysis of other factors that are likely to affect response to a given measuring instrument and by efforts to reduce or control the influence of those factors. Ideally, the goal would be to develop one or more measures from which the effects of all probable response determinants other than attitude toward the relevant object would be removed. This goal, however, seems unlikely of achievement; therefore it seems to us important to work with a number of different measures, in each of which an effort is made to eliminate or control in some systematic way some identifiable influence on response other than the attitude in question. Since different influences will be controlled in different measures—and thus, conversely, different influences in addition to attitude will affect responses on the different measures—there will remain a lack of full correspondence among scores on the different measures.

Social scientists have long recognized that factors other than an individual's attitude toward an object may influence both his response to instruments designed to measure the attitude and his behavior toward the object in everyday life. Much recent work in the field of both personality and attitude measurement has been concerned with identifying the effects of such "extraneous" variables as the tendency to agree (or to disagree) with statements regardless of their content (e.g., Bass, 1955; Cronbach, 1946, 1950) or the wish to give a socially acceptable picture of oneself (e.g., Edwards, 1953, 1957; Taylor, 1961). Another interest has been in the development of indirect methods of attitude assessment (for a review of such methods, see Campbell, 1950). But attempts to develop indirect measures have, for the most part, been sporadic, and there has been little effort to examine systematically the relation of different indirect measures to each other or their relative susceptibility to such influences as agreeing response set or social norms.

Despite the general awareness of measurement problems, examination of reports of experimental research on attitudes shows the following picture: First, even investigators who hold very sophisticated theoretical positions about the nature and functions of attitudes and the conditions for attitude change commonly use only a single attitude measure —typically quite crude—in testing hypotheses derived from those theoretical positions. Second, most investigators are aware of the possibility that responses to these instruments may be influenced by factors other than the attitudes they are intended to measure. Third, efforts are made to guard against the intrusion of such factors or to rule out interpretations based on the possibility that they have been operative. These safeguards usually take one or more of the following forms: sampling (e.g., selection of groups of subjects believed to differ in susceptibility to the extraneous influences most likely to be operative in the measurement situation), experimental design (e.g., the introduction of control groups), internal analysis of the data (e.g., considering how the responses of subgroups of subjects might be expected to differ if one determinant rather than another were operative).

We do not mean to minimize the importance of such procedures. In any given study they may quite convincingly rule out the possibility that responses have been influenced by factors other than subjects' attitudes toward the object in question. Nevertheless, it seems to us that effort directed toward improving measuring instruments might be at least equally useful.

AN EXAMINATION OF DIFFERENT TYPES OF MEASURING INSTRUMENTS IN TERMS OF THE KINDS OF EVIDENCE THEY PROVIDE AS A BASIS FOR INFERENCES ABOUT ATTITUDE

In most current research on attitudes, efforts directed specifically toward improving measuring techniques are limited to such matters as assuring anonymity, attempting to separate the measurement from the experimental sessions, varying the order of presentation of items or the context in which they are embedded. If we are to go beyond such limited steps, a more systematic analysis of the characteristics of measuring instruments is needed than is yet available. This paper is a first step toward such an analysis. Our purpose is not to present a detailed review of the different kinds of instruments that have been used to measure attitudes; this has been well done by others (Campbell, 1950; Deri, Dinnerstein, Harding, and Pepitone, 1948; Weschler and Bernberg, 1950). Rather, we propose to examine broad classes of measurement techniques from the point of view of the kinds of evidence they provide and thus the nature of the inferences involved in estimating attitude. By "the nature of the inferences involved" we mean the grounds for believing that attitude toward the presumed object is a determinant of responses to the measuring instrument, and the bases for inferring the nature of the attitude from the characteristics of the responses (i.e., for considering a given response as indicative of a positive or a negative disposition toward the object).

We have found it useful to think in terms of five major groupings: (*a*) measures in which the material from which inferences are drawn consists of self-reports of beliefs, feelings, behavior, etc., toward an object or class of objects; (*b*) measures in which inferences are drawn from observed overt behavior toward the object; (c) measures in which inferences are drawn from the individual's reactions to, or interpretations of, partially structured material relevant to the object; (d) measures in which inferences are drawn from performance on objective tasks where functioning may be influenced by disposition toward the object; and (e) measures in which inferences are drawn from physiological reactions to the object. Not all of the measures discussed have been used as attitude tests in the formal sense, but for each of them there is reason to believe that attitude may be an important determinant of response and thus that the technique could serve as a basis for inferences about attitude.

In assessing the adequacy of an instrument as an indicator of attitude, consideration of its susceptibility to other influences is as important as consideration of the grounds for believing that underlying disposition toward the object is a determinant of response. In examining measuring instruments from the point of view of the possible influence of factors other than attitude, we shall consider two major aspects: (a) the probability that overt responses may deviate from "private" responses—that is, the ease with which an individual can alter his responses to present a certain picture of himself; (b) the probability that private responses may be influenced by determinants other than attitude, in the absence of any attempt to distort responses.

Possibilities of influence of private response by factors other than attitude are, of course, almost limitless; we shall discuss only those that seem most probable with respect to each type of instrument. Susceptibility of overt response to distortion—that is, the possibility of discrepancy between private and overt response—would seem to be a function of three characteristics of the instrument: the extent to which its purpose is apparent, the extent to which the implications of specific responses are clear, and the extent to which responses are subject to conscious control.

In discussing the susceptibility of measures to distortion of responses and techniques developed to lessen the probability of distortion, we assume that with respect to many attitudes the settings in which tests are usually administered tend to exert pressures in a constant direction. It seems reasonable to suppose that most respondents, presented with tests in an academic setting or under the auspices of some other "respectable" organization, will assume that the responses which will place them in the most favorable light are those which represent them as well adjusted, unprejudiced, rational, openminded, and democratic. Moreover, since these are ideal norms at least in much of the American middle class, the pressures specific to the test situation are likely to coincide with inner pressures toward maintaining an image acceptable to the self as well as to others. By "controversial social attitudes" we mean attitudes with respect to which such norms are operative. Some of our discussion, and especially some of our examples, concern techniques for making it easier for the individual to reveal himself as not well adjusted, not unprejudiced, etc., or for making it harder for him to portray himself, falsely, as well adjusted, unprejudiced, etc. While some assumption as to the probable direction of pressures operating in the situation is necessary for the concrete details of certain techniques, the principles involved do not hinge on the specific direction of pressures; given testing situations in which there is reason to believe that the pressures are predominantly in a different direction, the techniques can be modified accordingly. And many of the techniques require no assumption about the probable direction of pressures, being designed to reduce the effects of extraneous influences in any direction.

Measures in Which Inferences Are Drawn from Self-Reports of Beliefs, Feelings, Behaviors, etc.

By far the most frequently used method of securing material from which to make inferences about an attitude is to ask an individual to reveal—either in his own words or through acceptance or rejection of standardized items—his beliefs about the attitudinal object, how he feels toward it, how he behaves or would behave toward it, how he believes it should be treated.

The basis for inference is clear: it is axiomatic in all definitions that an individual's attitude toward an object is indicated by his beliefs, feelings, and action orientation toward it. The nature of the inference is also clear: it is assumed that the relationship between attitude and expression is a direct one and that the attitude corresponds to the manifest, common-sense implications of the stated belief or feeling. For example, a stated belief that the object has characteristics usually considered desirable is taken as reflecting a favorable disposition toward it, and a stated belief that it has characteristics usually considered undesirable is taken as reflecting an unfavorable disposition. Similarly, a report that the person avoids contact with the object is taken as indicating an unfavorable disposition toward it, while a report that he does or would willingly enter into contact with it is taken as indicating a favorable disposition.

In some definitions, attitude is considered identical with, or simply a summary of, beliefs, feelings, behavior, etc., toward the object; thus no problem of inference arises. However, in such definitions some criteria must be adopted for choosing which behavior constitutes the population of "attitudinal responses" to be sampled. The choice of such criteria would, we believe, depend upon an analysis essentially similar to our consideration of "extraneous influences" in the remainder of this paper.

Self-report measures have a number of characteristics that make them susceptible to distortion of overt responses. The purpose of the instrument is obvious to the respondent; the implications of his answers are apparent to him; he can consciously control his responses. Thus a person who wishes to give a certain picture of himself—whether in order to impress the tester favorably, to preserve his own self-image, or for some other reason—

can rather easily do so. This difficulty has long been recognized, and in recent years it has been extensively investigated under the rubric of "social desirability." A number of techniques have been devised to make the purpose of the instrument or the implications of the responses less apparent; to make it easier to give answers that may be considered undesirable; and to make it harder to give, falsely, answers that may be considered desirable. Some of these techniques are focused primarily on reducing the likelihood that responses will be distorted in an attempt to meet the investigator's expectations or to please him; others are addressed to reducing the influence on responses of a desire to maintain a certain self-image as well as that of a desire to please or impress the investigator.

One of the simplest approaches to making the purpose of the instrument less apparent is the inclusion of items not relevant to the attitudinal object in which the investigator is interested. A variation of this approach is to include in each of the items a number of aspects in addition to that in which the investigator is interested; for example, if the investigator is interested in attitudes toward one or more racial groups, each item may refer to a hypothetical person characterized not only in terms of race but of age, sex, religion, occupation, etc. Approaches of either sort serve only to make the purpose of the test less obvious. They do not completely conceal or disguise it, nor can they do so within the format of self-report measures, which by definition call for the individual's own account of his reactions to the attitudinal object.

Among the simplest, and most frequently used, approaches to making it easier to give answers that may be considered undesirable are assurances of anonymity, statements to the effect that "there are no right or wrong answers" or that "people differ in their views on these things," emphasis on the importance of honest answers in order to contribute to scientific knowledge or some other presumably desirable outcome, efforts to build up rapport between questioner and respondent and to create the impression that the questioner will not disapprove of whatever views may be expressed.

Other approaches are built into the instrument itself: including items to which an unfavorable reply is likely to be considered acceptable (e.g., "Would you be willing to have a ditch digger as U.S. Congressman from your district?"—Westie, 1952, 1953), in order to break down a possible set to give uniformly favorable replies; including in the statement of a view that may be considered undesirable a qualification or a justification of it (e.g., "It is best that Jews should have their own fraternities and sororities, since they have their own particular interests and activities which they can best engage in together, just as Christians get along best in all-Christian fraternities."—Adorno, Frenkel-Brunswik, Levinson, and Sanford, 1950); wording questions in such a way that they assume the respondent holds certain views or has engaged in certain kinds of behavior (e.g., "When did you first . . . ?"—Kinsey, Pomeroy, and Martin, 1948).

Other approaches are designed to make it difficult to give, falsely, what may be considered a desirable answer. In the measurement of personality, a major effort in this direction has been the use of forced-choice tests, where the respondent is asked to indicate which of two statements, matched in terms of social desirability but differing in their implications with respect to traits or needs, is closer to his own views or more descriptive of his own behavior. This approach has not been extensively used in the measurement of attitudes.

In addition to their susceptibility to conscious distortion in order to give the picture the individual wishes to present of himself, responses to self-report measures may be influenced by another set of characteristics presumably unrelated to attitude toward the object in question—characteristics frequently labeled "response set" or "expressive style." It has long been noted that some individuals have a consistent tendency to agree (or to disagree) with items presented to them, regardless of their content; or to select, with more than chance frequency, the alternative which appears in a given position; or to give extreme (or moderate) answers.

A number of techniques have been devised to reduce the effects of such tendencies on scores that are to be taken as indicative of attitudes. Perhaps the simplest and the most common approach to the problem of influence by a tendency to agree (or to disagree) is to vary the wording of items in such a way that for approximately half of them agreement represents a favorable response to the attitudinal object, and for half an unfavorable response. Other approaches to this problem involve setting up the instrument in such a way that responses do not take the form of expressing agreement or disagreement with one statement at a time. The instrument may consist of pairs of statements representing roughly opposed points of view on a given issue, both statements being worded positively or both worded negatively; the subject is asked to indicate which is nearer his own position, or to indicate his position on a scale running between the two statements. The following pair of items from an unpublished scale of attitudes toward freedom of speech, developed by students of Donald T. Campbell at Northwestern University, illustrate this approach:

A. Fascists and Communists are entitled to preach their beliefs in this country.
B. Only those who are in agreement with this country's philosophy of government are entitled to preach their beliefs.

In other instruments, the problem, at least in its obvious form, is avoided by using items that call for free response—open-ended questions, sentence stubs to be completed with the individual's own responses, etc.

An approach to correcting for the effects of a tendency to give extreme answers, or moderate answers, consists in providing matched pairs of items, one referring to the attitudinal object, the other referring to some control object, and scoring in terms of the discrepancy between the two responses. For example, if respondents are asked only, "Would you be willing to have a Negro bookkeeper live in the same apartment building you live in?" and are provided with a 5-point response scale, it is impossible to determine whether respondents who answer "very willing" differ from those who answer simply "willing" in attitude, in response style, or in both. Providing a parallel item with respect to a white bookkeeper and scoring on the basis of discrepancy between an individual's responses to the Negro and the white removes the effects of response style from the score (Westie, 1953).

Susceptibility of self-report measures to the two kinds of influences discussed so far—desire to present a certain picture of oneself, and response sets unrelated to the content of items—clearly leads to the possibility of distortion of responses in the obvious sense of lack of correspondence between the overt responses and the individual's private beliefs, feelings, policy views, etc. Still other factors, however, may influence his private beliefs and feelings as well as his overt responses. While private beliefs, feelings, and action orientations with respect to an object are by definition at least partially determined by the individual's attitude toward the object, they may be influenced by other factors as well—for example, by the availability of information, or by other values the individual holds. Thus, a person who has an essentially devaluing attitude toward Negroes may nevertheless have learned, and state as his belief, that there is no difference in the chemical composition of the blood of Negroes and whites; on the other hand, a person whose disposition toward Negroes is not devaluing may know and state as his belief that the average scholastic achievement of Negroes in the United States is lower than that of whites. A person with a devaluing attitude toward Negroes may nevertheless believe that they should not be deprived of the right to vote, because he sees this right as an essential ingredient of democracy; a person whose attitude toward Negroes is not devaluing may be opposed to laws forbidding discrimination in the sale and rental of housing because he places great store on the right of an owner to do with his property as he sees fit.

To the extent that such other influences affect different items differently, or affect only certain items, this problem has been attacked by examining responses for consistency, eliminating items which show low agreement with total scores, or eliminating those to which responses do not fall on a unidimensional scale.

A given technique may help to reduce or correct for extraneous influence from more than one source. For example, scoring in terms of discrepancy between responses to items concerning the attitudinal object and comparable items about a control object may provide a correction for the effects of other values or meanings engaged by the items as well as for response sets. Asking the respondent to choose which of two statements is closer to his views may help to eliminate the influence both of response set and of concern with the acceptability of responses, if the alternatives provided are equivalent in both respects.

Not only may a given technique serve more than one function; a given instrument may embody a number of techniques designed to reduce the influence of extraneous factors. For example, in Westie's (1953) Summated Differences Test, the subject is presented with hypothetical persons of specified race (Negro or white) and occupation (eight occupations, ranging from ditch digger to banker, plus "the average man"), and asked to indicate, on 5-point scales, his willingness to accept each of these 18 hypothetical persons in each of 24 relationships—a total of 432 items. Some of the items are such that a negative answer is likely to be considered acceptable by most people (e.g., unwillingness to vote for a machine operator, whether white or Negro, as President of the United States is not likely to be seen as an expression of "prejudice"), thus presumably breaking down a possible tendency to give uniformly favorable answers whether through an acquiescent response set or through a desire to give a picture of oneself as unprejudiced. The large number of items, and the format of the questionnaire, make it extremely unlikely that the subject can remember or check his response to a given item with respect to one racial group when he is answering the comparable item concerning the other group. Scoring on the basis of discrepancy between parallel items referring to whites and Negroes takes account both of possible response sets and of the influence of the specified occupation and the specified situation. Thus, this instrument adds to the basic social distance questionnaire a number of techniques designed to make the focus of the investigator's interest less apparent, to make it easier to give answers that might be considered undesirable, to correct for possible response sets, and to some extent to take account of other values or meanings that may affect responses.

Measures in Which Inferences Are Drawn from Observation of Overt Behavior

Many investigators have pointed out the desirability of using measures in which overt behavior toward members of a class of objects would serve as a basis for inferences about attitude toward the object-class. As with self-report measures, the basis for inference is clear; all definitions of attitude specify that behavior can be taken as an indicator of attitude. And, as in the case of self-report measures, the usual assumption is that there is a simple correspondence between the nature of the behavior and the nature of the underlying attitude; for example, that friendly behavior toward a member of a given class of objects indicates a favorable attitude toward the object-class.

There has been much less extensive development of measures of this sort than of self-report measures. Situations capable of eliciting behavior toward an attitudinal object are more difficult to devise and to standardize, and more time-consuming and costly to administer, than self-report measures. Although some measures of this type have been devised,

they have not been widely enough used to provide much evidence as to their specific strengths and weaknesses nor to stimulate efforts to correct for shortcomings. However, analysis of their characteristics can provide estimates as to their probable susceptibility to influences other than attitude and possibilities of reducing such susceptibility.

Attempts to develop behavioral measures have followed three general lines. One consists in presenting subjects with standardized situations that they are led to believe are unstaged, in which they believe that their behavior will have consequences, and in which the attitudinal object is represented in some way other than by the actual presence of a member of the object-class. For example, subjects may be asked to sign a petition on behalf of an instructor about to be discharged for membership in the Communist party, to contribute money for the improvement of conditions for migratory workers, to indicate whether they would be willing to have a Negro roommate. DeFleur and Westie (1958) have attempted to develop a measure of this sort which is appropriate for use in many different testing situations. In their procedure, as part of a larger program of research, white subjects viewed a number of colored photographic slides showing a young Negro man and a young white woman, or a young white man and a young Negro woman, in a social setting; subjects described the pictures and answered specific questions about them. At the close of an interview following this session the measurement procedure being discussed here was introduced. DeFleur and Westie describe the procedure as follows: The subject was told that another set of such slides was needed for further research, was asked if he (or she) would be willing to be photographed with a Negro of the opposite sex, and then was given "a standard photograph release agreement," containing a variety of uses to which such a photograph would be put, ranging from laboratory experiments where it would be seen only by professional sociologists, to a nationwide publicity campaign advocating racial integration. The subject was asked to sign his name to each use of the photograph which he would permit. These investigators report that subjects "uniformly perceived the behavioral situation posed for them as a highly realistic request."

Such devices differ from self-report measures with similar content in that, in the behavioral measures, the subject either actually carries out the behavior (signs a petition, makes a contribution, etc.) or is led to believe that his agreement to do so will lead to real-life consequences (being asked to pose for a photograph to be put to specified uses, being assigned a Negro roommate, etc.).

Another approach is to present the subject with an admittedly staged situation and ask him to play a role—perhaps to behave as he would in such a situation in real life, perhaps to take the part of someone else or to act in some specified way. Stanton and Litwak (1955) presented actual and potential foster parents with situations of interpersonal stress in which they were instructed to behave in a given way (defined as not manifesting specified undesirable or neurotic kinds of behavior); for example, in one scene the subject was instructed that he was to play the role of a married man, having dinner with his parents; the investigator, playing the role of the man's father, treated his son like a child, criticized his wife, and put him in the wrong. These investigators found that ratings based on a half-hour's role playing were better predictors of subjects' behavior as foster parents (as rated by case workers who had sustained contact with them) than were ratings based on 12 hours of intensive interviewing by a trained social worker. Stanton, Back, and Litwak (1956) reported that a role-playing approach was successful in discovering the limits of positive and negative feelings about public housing projects on the part of slum dwellers in Puerto Rico. These investigators have stressed the importance of designing the scene specifically to elicit responses relevant to the particular behavior or attitude in which the investigator is interested.

A third behavioral approach, used in the study of attitudes toward social groups, has been to ask for sociometric choices among individuals some of whom are members of the object group, preferably under circumstances that lead the participants to believe that such choices will have consequences in the form of subsequent assignment in some situation. Early applications of this technique to the study of intergroup attitudes were made in studies by Moreno (1943) and by Criswell (1937, 1939), in which patterns of choices by school children were analyzed in terms of the development of cleavage along racial lines. Subsequently, sociometric techniques have been used in research evaluating the effects of certain experiences on attitudes (e.g., Mann, 1959a; Mussen, 1950a, 1950b) and of the relations among different aspects of attitudes (e.g., Mann, 1959b).

There are differences among these three kinds of behavioral measures—situations appearing to the subject to be unstaged, role playing, and sociometric choice—in characteristics that affect the probability that overt responses will correspond to responses that would be shown if the individual were not concerned with presenting (to others or to himself) a certain picture of himself. Let us consider first the extent to which their purpose is apparent to the respondent. To the extent that the purportedly unstaged situations are accepted as genuine, the respondent will not see them as designed to get information about his attitudes; thus one possible source of pressure to give responses that are likely to be considered desirable is eliminated. Nevertheless, the implications of his behavior as revealing certain characteristics may be apparent to him; even if he accepts a question about his willingness to pose with a Negro or to have a Negro roommate as genuine, he may be aware that a positive answer will have the effect of presenting him as unprejudiced, a negative answer as prejudiced. Thus, even in the absence of awareness that he is being tested, an individual may be motivated to give a response that differs from his spontaneous private one, in order to present himself to the questioner as unprejudiced or to maintain his own image of himself as one who behaves in an unprejudiced way. The sociometric choice method would appear to be similar in these respects, though it may perhaps be assumed that, in the absence of special influences calling attention to racial or ethnic group membership, the implications of the choices are less likely to be apparent. In the case of role playing, the extent to which the purpose of the situation and the implications of responses are clear presumably depends on the convincingness with which the situation can be presented as a measure of some other characteristic, such as acting ability.

All of these behavioral approaches have characteristics that may operate to make it easier to respond in ways that may be considered undesirable. In many situations it is possible to justify a negative response on neutral or acceptable grounds: one does not believe in signing petitions, or he does not like to have his picture taken, or he prefers Persons A and B to X and Y because they share his interest in music. Or, in the role-playing situation, his behavior is shaped not by his own reactions toward the attitudinal object but by interest in the dramatic requirements of the situation. (To the extent that these alternative explanations are real possibilities, however, they introduce other problems about interpretation of the behavior as an indicator of the attitude in which the investigator is interested.)

Some characteristics of the behavioral approaches may reduce the probability that the individual will modify his behavior in order to present an acceptable picture of himself. When responses are expected to have real-life consequences, the anticipation of such consequences may counterbalance the wish to make a good impression. In a social distance questionnaire, if one wishes to present himself (to the tester, or to himself, or both) as unprejudiced, there is little effective pressure against saying that one would be willing to work with a Negro, or to have a Negro roommate; but if the question is posed in a context where a positive reply is seen as lead-

ing to assignment of a Negro as a co-worker or a roommate, one must weigh his willingness to accept that consequence against his wish to appear unprejudiced. In role playing, the pressure for quick response to unanticipated stimulus situations probably operates to lessen conscious control of behavior in order to produce a desired impression. Faced with the necessity of doing or saying something to keep the situation going, the individual may not have time to consider the impression he is making; to the extent that this is so, this approach may be thought of as reducing the individual's conscious selection of his response.

Thus behavioral measures seem to be less susceptible than simple self-report measures to distortion of response in the interest of presenting a certain picture of the self. But they are at least as susceptible as self-report measures to the effects of other extraneous influences. It has sometimes been suggested that the model of behavioral measures would be apparently unstaged situations in which a member of the object-class is present. But it is clear that behavior in everyday life situations (which this model seeks to approximate) is not determined exclusively by attitude toward the presumed attitudinal object. In the case of behavior toward minority groups, for example, social custom is a major determinant; in communities with segregated transportation systems, almost all white people—regardless of their attitudes toward Negroes or toward segregation—sit in the white section, whereas in communities with unsegregated transportation systems, very few white people—regardless of their attitudes—refuse to sit next to Negroes. Other values may override attitudes toward the presumed object; an individual who feels physical revulsion at the experience of eating with Negroes may nevertheless do so because he has come to believe that the ideals of democracy, or religious principles of brotherhood, or the position of the United States in the eyes of the world, require that all men be treated as equals. Finally, other characteristics of the object individuals may predominate over their ethnic identification in determining response to them. Thus, LaPiere (1934) concluded that the factors which most influenced the behavior of hotel and restaurant personnel to the Chinese couple with whom he was traveling "had nothing to do with race"; rather, it was the quality and condition of their clothing, the appearance of their baggage, their cleanliness and neatness, and above all, their self-confident and pleasant manner, that determined reactions. Observations such as this suggest that, to the extent that one is interested in tapping generalized dispositions toward a given group rather than in predicting behavior in specific situations, behavioral measures that call for response to a symbolic representation of the group may be less subject to influence by extraneous factors than measures that call for response to members of the group who are physically present.

Campbell (1961) has suggested an approach to the use of behavior measures which is based on the premise that different situations have different thresholds for the manifestation of hostile, avoidant, or discriminatory behavior. He suggests that, in order to secure evidence about an individual's attitude, it is necessary to place him in a number of situations with differing thresholds— ranging, for example, from eating with a Negro at a business men's luncheon club (assumed to be a situation with a low threshold for nondiscriminatory behavior—in other words, one in which it is easy to behave in an unprejudiced way) to renting one's house to a Negro (assumed to have a high threshold for nondiscriminatory behavior). The lowest-threshold situation in which an individual exhibits discriminatory behavior would indicate his position on a scale of attitude with respect to the group in question. Such a procedure would be effective in taking account of pressures that are constant for all, or most, individuals; it would not, it seems to us, rule out the effects of differences in the strength for different individuals of such influences as concern with social approval, other values seen as relevant to the situation, etc.

Measures in Which Inferences Are Drawn from the Individual's Reaction to, or Interpretation of, Partially Structured Stimuli

The characteristic common to techniques in this category is that, while there may be no attempt to disguise the reference to the attitudinal object, the subject is not asked to state his own reactions directly; he is ostensibly describing a scene, a character, or the behavior of a third person. He may be presented with a photograph of a member of the object-class (usually a person of a given social group) and asked to describe his characteristics; or he may be presented with a scene in which members of the object-class are present and asked to describe it, to tell a story about it, to predict the behavior of one of the characters, etc. The stimulus material may be verbal rather than pictorial; for example, the subject may be asked to complete sentence stubs referring to a hypothetical third person.

The bases for inferences about attitudes are those common to all projective tests: assumptions that perception of stimuli that are not clearly structured is influenced by the perceiver's own needs and dispositions; that, asked to provide an explanation or interpretation for which the stimulus presented gives no clear clue, the subject must draw on his own experience or his own dispositions or his own definitions of what would be probable or appropriate; that, asked to attribute behavior to others, especially under speed conditions, the most readily accessible source of hypotheses is the individual's own response disposition. As in self-report and behavioral tests, the usual assumption is that the expressed response corresponds directly to the individual's attitude; for example, that attribution of desirable characteristics to a member of a given group represents a favorable attitude toward that group, that interpretation of a scene as one in which there is hostility toward a member of a given group represents a hostile attitude toward the group, that attribution of a positive (or a negative) response to a hypothetical third person with respect to a given object reflects a positive (or a negative) disposition toward the object in question.

A major reason for the development of such techniques is the assumption that, by disguising the purpose of the instrument and the implications of responses, they lessen the probability of distortion of responses in the interest of presenting a certain picture of the self. They are presented to the respondent not as measures of attitudes but as tests of imagination, verbal fluency, ability to judge character, social sensitivity, or some such characteristic. To the extent that the respondent accepts these explanations, he presumably is unaware not only of the purpose of the test but of the implications of his responses as revealing his own attitudes. Even if the subject does realize that he is expressing his own attitude, it is assumed that it may be easier to express views that may be considered undesirable if one does not explicitly acknowledge them as his own. In some instances the questions asked are nonevaluative, so that the implications of one or another response are quite unlikely to be apparent to the respondent; for example, "What is the [nonexistent] colored man in the corner doing? [Horowitz & Horowitz, 1938]."

Questions have been raised, however, about the validity of the assumption that responses, even though spontaneous and undistorted, reflect the individual's own attitude toward the object. While it seems clearly established that an individual's response may reflect his own disposition, it is not certain that it necessarily does so. Given a scene in which the roles of Negro and white are ambiguous, an individual who describes the Negro as being in a menial position may be reflecting his own devaluing disposition toward Negroes; on the other hand, he may simply be reporting the arrangement most commonly observed in our culture. Similarly, the responses he attributes to a hypothetical third person may be based either on his own response disposition or on his estimate of how most people would react in such a situation. Attempts to secure evidence as to whether responses to instruments of this type do in fact reflect the individual's own attitudes have followed two lines: examination of the correspondence between estimates of attitude based on these measures and estimates based on other measures (usually of the self-report type); and examination of data secured from instruments of this sort in the light of predictions about patterns of results.

Several studies have found significant correspondence between results of measures of this type and scores on self-report measures. Proshansky (1943) found high correlations between scores based on a standard self-report scale for measuring attitude toward organized labor and scores based on descriptions of briefly-exposed ambiguous pictures of relevant social situations. Riddleberger and Motz (1957) found that subjects who scored high and those who scored low on a self-report measure of attitude toward Negroes differed in their explanations of how the people in a pictured interracial group had met. Sommer (1954), using a modified form of Brown's (1947) adaptation of the Rosenzweig Picture-Frustration Test, was able to identify with considerable success not only individuals who scored high and those who scored low on a self-report scale of attitude toward Negroes but a subgroup who had been instructed to respond to the Picture-Frustration Test as if they were unprejudiced, even though their self-report scores were unfavorable.

However, in view of the assumption that an important characteristic of tests of this type is their relative lack of susceptibility, as compared with self-report measures, to efforts to present a certain picture of the self, correspondence with scores based on self-report measures is a dubious criterion. Getzels (1951), recognizing this fact, approached the problem by predicting conditions under which speeded completions of third-person sentence stubs would differ from completions, by the same respondents, of the same sentence stubs presented in the first person. He made two predictions: (a) that first- and third-person responses would differ on items subject to strong social norms not fully internalized by all members of the group and would not differ on items not subject to such norms; and (b) that in the case of the former items, more socially acceptable answers would be given on the first-person form than on the third-person form. Both predictions were strongly supported. Getzels recognized the possibility that responses to the third-person form might be based on estimates of how most people would respond rather than on the subjects' own response dispositions. Accordingly, he asked the subjects to estimate how most people would respond to the items about Negroes, and found no difference between the average estimates made by those whose third-person responses had been favorable and those whose third-person responses had been unfavorable.

A number of techniques involving perception—in a more literal sense—of ambiguous or unstructured material may be considered in this category. For example, a number of psychologists have been investigating the possible relation of attitudes to perception of stimuli presented under stereoscopic conditions of binocular rivalry. Bagby (1957), presenting pairs of cards differing in cultural content (e.g., a bullfighter and a baseball player) to subjects from Mexico and the United States, found that Mexicans tended to see the card with Mexican content, U.S. Americans those with content familiar in the United States. Pettigrew, Allport, and Barnett, (1958), presenting to residents of South Africa pairs of pictures of individuals from different racial groups, found that Afrikaners deviated most consistently from other groups in their responses, overusing the "European" and "African" categories, underusing "Colored" or "Indian."

A study by Bray (1950) made use of unstructured visual material in a different way. Taking off from Sherif's (1935) finding that estimates of movement in the autokinetic phenomenon are markedly influenced by the estimates given by others, Bray investigated the effects of estimates by confederates who were identified as members of minority groups. He had the hypothesis that the extent and direction of such effects would be influenced by the subject's attitude toward the minority group. Here the unstructured perceptual material did not refer to the attitudinal object, but simply provided an opportunity for expressing indirectly a response to the attitudinal object—the physically present, minority-group member.

Again, there are problems about the nature of the inferences that can be drawn. Bray, for example, did not find the direct relationship he had predicted between attitude toward the minority group (as measured by self-report scales) and responses to the minority-group members' estimates. In the case of binocular rivalry, in what way, if at all, does attitude influence perception? Does one see the picture with the most familiar content? Does one see the member of the racial group toward which he is most favorable, or the one toward which he is most hostile, or of which he is most afraid?

Questions such as these point both to the need for further research on the usefulness of these techniques as measures of attitude and to potentially fruitful lines of investigation of the relation between attitudes and response to various kinds of materials under various conditions.

Measures in Which Inferences Are Drawn from Performance of "Objective" Tasks

Approaches in this category present the respondent with specific tasks to be performed; they are presented as tests of information or ability, or simply as jobs that need to be done. The assumption common to all of them is that performance may be influenced by attitude, and that a systematic bias in performance reflects the influence of attitude.

For example, the subject may be asked to memorize material, some of which is favorable to the attitudinal object, some unfavorable, perhaps some neutral or irrelevant. The assumption is that material congenial with the subject's own position will be learned more quickly and remembered longer. Some empirical support is available for this assumption; for example, in a study by Levine and Murphy (1943), using material about the Soviet Union, and one by Jones and Kohler (1958) using statements about segregation. Or the subject is given a test of "information," in which at least some of the items referring to the attitudinal object either have no correct answers or are so unfamiliar that it can be assumed that few if any respondents will know the correct answers; alternative responses believed (by the investigator) to indicate relatively favorable or relatively unfavorable dispositions toward the object are provided. The assumption here is that, when forced to make a guess on ostensibly factual questions where he has no objective basis for an answer, the subject is likely to choose the alternative most consistent with his own attitudinal disposition. This assumption, too, is supported by some empirical evidence; for example, studies by Hammond (1948) and Weschler (1950) of attitudes toward labor and toward Russia, and by Rankin and Campbell (1955) of attitude toward Negroes. Or the task may be a test of "reasoning," in which syllogisms or other logical forms are presented, and the subject is asked to indicate which of a number of conclusions can appropriately be drawn. Items referring to the attitudinal object are paralleled by similar items with neutral or abstract content; scoring is on the basis of the number and direction of errors on the attitudinally relevant items as compared with the control items. The assumption is that reasoning may be swayed by attitudinal disposition, and thus that errors on the attitudinally relevant items reflect the individual's own position, if the parallel neutral items have been answered correctly. Watson (1925), Morgan (1945), and Thistlethwaite (1950), among others, have developed instruments of this type. Thistlewaite found a significant difference between Northern and Southern college students in frequency of errors on items dealing with Negroes (as compared with errors on the neutral items), and no corresponding difference on items dealing with Jews, women, or patriotism.

Other measures place the emphasis on the material being judged or on the outcome to be achieved rather than on the ability involved in achieving it. For example, the subject is asked to sort items about the attitudinal object in terms of their position on a scale of favorableness-unfavorableness, ostensibly in order to help in the construction of a Thurstone-type scale. The assumption here is that the rater's own attitude toward the object—especially if it is extreme—influences his judgments of the favorableness of statements about the object. Despite the earlier belief that ratings of items for Thurstone scales are not affected by the raters' own attitudes, a number of recent studies (e.g., Hovland and Sherif, 1952) have found such effects.

It seems reasonable to suppose that most subjects accept these tasks at face value; presumably only someone with rather sophisticated knowledge of research techniques in the social sciences would be aware of their attitudinal implications. Thus it seems reasonable to suppose that they may be relatively impervious to distortion in the interest of presenting a desired picture of the self.

Again, however, there are questions about the nature of the inferences to be drawn. If a subject shows marked and consistent bias, it seems reasonable to infer that he has an attitude toward the object strong enough to affect his performance. If he does not show consistent bias, however, are we to infer that his attitude is not strong, or not consistent? In other words, how sensitive are such measures? Is it possible that individuals with equivalent attitudes differ in the extent to which their performance on such tasks is influenced by those attitudes?

Another problem has to do with the direction in which attitude influences the response, and, conversely, with the nature of the inference to be drawn from a given response. Responses may reflect either wishes or fears; a member of the Communist party may overestimate the number of Communists in the United States, but so may a member of the

John Birch Society. A person who underestimates the number of Negro doctors in the United States may do so on the basis of his feeling that Negroes do not have the ability to become doctors, or he may do so on the basis of his belief that opportunities for Negroes to obtain medical training are limited.

Judgments of the favorableness or unfavorableness of statements are subject to a similar problem of interpretation. Hovland and Sherif (1952), working with items about Negroes, found that ratings by Negro subjects and by white subjects who actively supported desegregation differed from ratings by "average" and by anti-Negro white subjects. However, other investigators (e.g., Manis, 1960; Weiss, 1959), working with statements about different attitudinal objects, found that subjects with extreme attitudes—whether favorable or unfavorable—showed similar patterns of ratings, which differed from those made by subjects with moderate attitudes.

As with the preceding category, these problems of interpretation point to the need for caution in inferring the attitude of a given individual from a single test of this sort, but they seem to point also to the probable usefulness of further empirical investigation of the relation of scores based on such measures to those based on tests providing other grounds for inference.

Another group of measures presented as objective tasks or tests of ability focus on the extent to which the attitudinal object figures prominently in the subject's organization of his environment, that is, its salience for him. The kinds of data appropriate for inference about the salience of an attitudinal object differ in some respects from the kinds appropriate for inference about the nature or direction of the attitude. Measures of salience have been developed primarily with respect to attitudes toward social groups. They are of two types: techniques for assessing the tendency to classify individuals in terms of group membership, and techniques for assessing the tendency to subordinate individual differences to group identification.

One technique for assessing the tendency

to classify individuals in terms of group membership, originated by Horowitz and Horowitz (1938), may be presented as a test of concept formation. It consists in presenting to a subject sets of photographs of individuals differing in race, sex, age, and socioeconomic status and asking him to select those which "belong together." For example, one set may contain photographs of three white boys, one white girl, and one Negro boy. If the subject replies that the white girl does not belong, this is taken to mean that for him sex is a more important basis for classification than race; if he replies that the Negro boy does not belong, the inference is that race is a more important category for him than sex.

Another technique for assessing the tendency to classify individuals in terms of group membership, presented as a test of memory, involves the clustering, in recall, of verbal symbols for which alternative classificatory principles are available. This technique rests on the finding from studies of verbal behavior that when words drawn from various categories are presented in random order, subjects tend to recall them in clusters, with several words representing a given category being recalled together even though they were not next to each other in the list presented. In studying the salience of race as a basis for classification, a subject would be presented, in random order, with names of people from several different occupational categories—for example, baseball players, musicians, political figures, actors, one name in each category being that of a Negro. The extent to which names of Negroes are grouped together in recall would provide the basis for inference as to the salience of race as a basis for classifying individuals.

A measure of the tendency to subordinate individual differences to group identification, originated by Horowitz and Horowitz (1938), consists in showing the subject a number of photographs of individuals of different ethnic groups and then asking him to identify, from a large number of photographs, those he has already seen. The task is presented as one involving perception and/ or memory. Scoring is in terms of the proportion of correct responses to individuals of a given social group as compared with the proportion of correct responses with respect to individuals of other groups. The inference here is that accuracy in identifying whether or not pictures of specific individuals of a given social group have previously been seen is decreased by the tendency to subordinate individual differences to group identification.

Seeleman (1940–41), using pictures of whites and Negroes, found a high correlation between scores on this measure and scores on a self-report questionnaire designed to measure attitude toward Negroes, with the less-favorable subjects less accurate in identifying whether the Negro pictures had previously been exposed. The question whether there is, in general, a correlation between salience of an attitudinal object and favorableness of disposition toward it is an interesting problem for empirical investigation.

Measures in Which Inferences Are Drawn from Physiological Reactions to the Attitudinal Object or Representations of It

At the opposite extreme from measures relying on a subject's verbal report of his beliefs, feelings, etc., are those relying on physiological responses not subject to conscious control. These may be measures of a subject's reaction—for example, galvanic skin response (GSR), vascular constriction—to the presence of a member of the object group or to pictorial representations of situations involving members of the object group. For example, Rankin and Campbell (1955) compared GSRs obtained when the experimenter was a Negro with those obtained when the experimenter was white; Westie and DeFleur (1959) recorded GSR, vascular constriction of finger, amplitude and duration of heartbeat, and duration of heart cycle, while the subjects were viewing pictures of whites and Negroes in social situations. Hess and Polt (1960) have photographed pupillary constriction in response to unpleasant stimuli and

pupillary dilation in response to pleasant stimuli.

Or the measures may involve responses, such as salivation, blinking, vascular constriction, that have been conditioned to a verbal stimulus, and, by a process of semantic generalization, appear in response to words or concepts that are similar in meaning to the original stimulus. For example, Volkova (1953) has reported a series of experiments in Russia in which subjects were conditioned to salivate in response to the word GOOD; subsequently, such statements as "The Young Pioneer helps his comrade" brought maximum salivation, while such statements as "The Fascists destroyed many cities" brought minimum salivation.

In the case of unconditioned physiological responses to the presence or the representation of the attitudinal object, the basis for inference comes directly from the concept of attitude. Just as all definitions of attitude include beliefs, feelings, and overt behavior as indicators of attitude, so do all definitions, explicitly or implicitly, include physiological responses. It is assumed that the magnitude of the physiological reaction is directly and positively related to the extent of arousal or the intensity of feeling; thus, the greater the physiological response, the stronger and/or more extreme the attitude is presumed to be. Here again, however, there are problems in inferring the nature of the attitude being reflected. Most measures of physiological reaction give direct indications only of the extent of arousal; they do not reveal whether the corresponding emotion is pleasurable or unpleasurable. In general, in attempts to assess attitudes toward social groups via measurement of physiological responses, it has been assumed that the range of affect is not from strongly favorable to strongly unfavorable but rather from accepting, or neutral, to strongly unfavorable; thus the inference has been drawn that the greater the physiological response, the more unfavorable the attitude. If Hess' technique of photographing pupillary constriction-dilation can be adapted to the study of attitudes, it would provide a much firmer basis for inferences about the direction of attitude, since the reaction being measured shows a differential response to pleasant and unpleasant stimuli.

In the case of the conditioned physiological responses, the basis for inference is somewhat different, stemming from learning theory. A response that has been conditioned to a given stimulus tends to generalize to stimuli that are similar. Thus, if a response that has been conditioned to the concept "good" appears when the attitudinal object is presented, the inference is that the subject considers the object good—that is, that his attitude toward it is favorable; if the response does not appear when the attitudinal object is presented, the inference is that the subject does not consider it good—that is, that his attitude toward it is not favorable.

The purpose of the physiological measures may or may not be apparent to the subject. In the Westie and DeFleur (1959) study, for example, subjects presumably realized that the physiological measures were being used as indicators of their reactions to the interracial pictures. In the Rankin and Campbell (1955) experiment, on the other hand, subjects were led to believe that they were taking part in a word-association study and that it was their GSRs to the stimulus words (rather than to the Negro and white experimenters) that were being investigated. Whether or not the purpose is clear to the subject, the fact that the responses measured are not subject to conscious control would seem to eliminate the possibility of modification of responses in order to present a certain picture of the self.

However, physiological responses may be quite sensitive to influences other than those in which the investigator is interested—both to other aspects of the stimulus material and to other environmental influences. It is difficult to control the experimental situation so completely that other factors are ruled out as possible determinants of the response.

Again, questions such as these point to the need for extreme caution in drawing inferences about the attitude of a given individual from a measure of this type. But, again, they point to encouraging possibilities for empirical research and to the opportunity to greatly increase our understanding of attitudes and their relation to various kinds of response, by the use of instruments yielding different types of evidence.

REFERENCES

Adorno, T. W., Else Frenkel-Brunswik, D. J. Levinson,, and R. N. Sanford.
  1950   The Authoritarian Personality. New York: Harper.
Allport, G. W.
  1954   "The historical background of modern social psychology." In pp. 3–56 of G. Lindzey (ed.) Handbook of Social Psychology. Vol. 1. Theory and Method. Cambridge, Mass.: Addison-Wesley.
Bagby, J. W.
  1957   "A cross-cultural study of perceptual predominance in binocular rivalry." Journal of Abnormal Social Psychology 54:331–334.
Bass, B. M.
  1955   "Authoritarianism or acquiescence?" Journal of Abnormal Social Psychology 51:616–623.
Bray, D.
  1950   "The prediction of behavior from two attitude scales." Journal of Abnormal Social Psychology 45:64–84.
Brown, J. F.
  1947   "A modification of the Rosenzweig Picture-Frustration Test to study hostile interracial attitudes." Journal of Psychology 24:247–272.
Campbell, D. T.
  1950   "The indirect assessment of social attitudes." Psychological Bulletin 47:15–38.
  1961   "Social attitudes and other acquired behavioral dispositions." In S. Koch (ed.) Psychology: A Study of a Science. Vol. 6. Investigations of Man as Socius: Their Place in Psychology and the Social Sciences. New York: McGraw-Hill.
Criswell, Joan H.
  1937   "Racial cleavages in Negro-white groups." Sociometry 1:87–89.

1939 "Social structure revealed in a socio-metric retest." Sociometry 2:69–75.

Cronbach, L. J.
1946 "Response sets and test validity." Educational and Psychological Measurement 6:475–494.
1950 "Further evidence on response sets and test design." Educational and Psychological Measurement 10:3–31.

DeFleur, M. L., and F. R. Westie.
1958 "Verbal attitudes and overt acts: An experiment on the salience of attitudes." American Sociological Review 23:667–673.

Deri, Susan, Dorothy Dinnerstein, J. Harding, and A. D. Pepitone.
1948 "Techniques for the diagnosis and measurement of intergroup attitudes and behavior." Psychological Bulletin 45:248–271.

Edwards, A. L.
1953 "The relationship between the judged desirability of a trait and the probability that the trait will be endorsed." Journal of Applied Psychology 37:90–93.
1957 The Social Desirability Variable in Personality Assessment and Research. New York: Dryden Press.

Getzels, J. W.
1951 "The assessment of personality and prejudice by the method of paired direct and projective questions." Unpublished doctoral dissertation. Harvard University.

Hammond, K. R.
1948 "Measuring attitudes by error-choice: An indirect method." Journal of Abnormal and Social Psychology 43:38–48.

Hess, E. H., and J. M. Polt.
1960 "Pupil size as related to interest value of visual stimuli." Science 132:349–350.

Horowitz, E. L., and Ruth E. Horowitz.
1938 "Development of social attitudes in children." Sociometry 1:301–338.

Hovland, C. I., and M. Sherif.
1952 "Judgmental phenomena and scales of attitude measurement: Item displacement in Thurstone scales." Journal of Abnormal and Social Psychology 47: 822–832.

Jones, E. E., and Rika Kohler.
1958 "The effects of plausibility on the learning of controversial statements." Journal of Abnormal and Social Psychology 57:315–320.

Kinsey, A. C., W. B. Pomeroy, and C. E. Martin.
1948 Sexual Behavior in the Human Male. Philadelphia, Pa.: Saunders.

LaPiere, R. T.
1934 "Attitudes vs. actions." Social Forces 14:230–237.

Lazarsfeld, P. F.
1959 "Latent structure analysis." In S. Koch (ed.) Psychology: A Study of a Science. Volume 3. Formulations of the Person and the Social Context. New York: McGraw-Hill.

Levine, J. M., and G. Murphy.
1943 "The learning and forgetting of controversial material." Journal of Abnormal and Social Psychology 38:507–517.

Manis, M.
1960 "The interpretation of opinion statements as a function of recipient attitude." Journal of Abnormal and Social Psychology 60:340–344.

Mann, J. H.
1959 "The effect of inter-racial contact on sociometric choices and perceptions." Journal of Social Psychology 50:143–152. (a)
1959 "The relationship between cognitive, affective and behavioral aspects of racial prejudice." Journal of Social Psychology 49:223–228. (b)

Moreno, J. L.
1943 Who Shall Survive? (Orig. publ. 1934) (Rev. ed.) Beacon, N.Y.: Beacon House.

Morgan, J. J. B.
1945 "Attitudes of students toward the Japanese." Journal of Social Psychology 21: 219–227.

Mussen, P. H.
1950 "The reliability and validity of the Horowitz Faces Test." Journal of Abnormal and Social Psychology 45:504–506. (a)
1950 "Some personality and social factors related to changes in children's attitudes toward Negroes." Journal of

Abnormal and Social Psychology 45: 423–441. (b)

Pettigrew, T. F., G. W. Allport, and E. O. Barnett.
1958 "Binocular resolution and perception of race in South Africa." British Journal of Psychology 49:265–278.

Proshansky, H. M.
1943 "A projective method for the study of attitudes." Journal of Abnormal and Social Psychology 38:393–395.

Rankin, R. E., and D. T. Campbell.
1955 "Galvanic skin response to Negro and white experimenters." Journal of Abnormal and Social Psychology 51:30–33.

Riddleberger, Alice B., and Annabelle B. Motz.
1957 "Prejudice and perception." American Journal of Sociology 62:498–503.

Seeleman, Virginia.
1940– "The influence of attitude upon the
1941 remembering of pictorial material." Archives of Psychology, New York 36 (No. 258).

Sherif, M.
1935 "A study of some social factors in perception." Archives of Psychology, New York No. 187.

Sommer, R.
1954 "On the Brown adaptation of the Rosenzweig P-F for assessing social attitudes." Journal of Abnormal and Social Psychology 49:125–128.

Stanton, H., K. W. Back, and E. Litwak.
1956 "Role-playing in survey research." American Journal of Sociology 62:172–176.

Stanton, H. R., and E. Litwak.
1955 "Toward the development of a short form test of interpersonal competence." American Sociological Review 20:668–674.

Taylor, J. B.
1961 "What do attitude scales measure: The problem of social desirability." Journal of Abnormal and Social Psychology 62: 386–390.

Thistlethwaite, D.
1950 "Attitude and structure as factors in the distortion of reasoning." Journal of Abnormal and Social Psychology 45:442–458.

Volkova, B. D.
1953 "Some characteristics of conditioned reflex formation to verbal stimuli in children." Sechenov Psychological Journal, USSR 39:540–548.

Watson, G. B.
1925 "The measurement of fairmindedness." Teachers College, Columbia University Contributions to Education No. 176.

Weiss, W.
1959 "The effects on opinions of a change in scale judgments." Journal of Abnormal and Social Psychology 58:329–334.

Weschler, I. R.
1950 "An investigation of attitudes toward labor and management by means of the error-choice method." Journal of Social Psychology 32:51–67.

Weschler, I. R., and R. E. Bernberg.
1950 "Indirect methods of attitude measurement." International Journal of Opinion and Attitude Research 4:209–228.

Westie, F. R.
1952 "Negro-white status differentials and social distance." American Sociological Review 17:550–558.
1953 "A technique for the measurement of race attitudes." American Sociological Review 18:73–78.

Westie, F. R., and M. L. DeFleur.
1959 "Autonomic responses and their relationship to race attitudes." Journal of Abnormal and Social Psychology 58: 340–347.

CHAPTER 2 Problems and Methods of Psychological Scaling[1]

W. R. GARNER AND C. D. CREELMAN

Quantification, measurement, scaling—these are all words which connote the use of numbers to describe phenomena. Whatever the term used, quantitative methodology has been the hallmark of a maturing science, and so it is with psychology. Quantitative methodology and measurement play very broad roles in psychology, as they do in any science.

One of the first uses of quantitative method is to specify the conditions of an experiment exactly, so that these conditions can be accurately reproduced on another occasion, and perhaps by another experimenter. For instance, we specify the physical intensity of a light, or of a tone stimulus, in exact terms, so that there can be no ambiguity to other psychological scientists about the conditions of our experiment.

From W. R. Garner and C. D. Creelman. "Problems and Methods of Psychological Scaling," Pp. 1–33 in Harry Helson and William Bevan, (Eds.), *Contemporary Approaches to Psychology*. Princeton: D. Van Nostrand, 1967. Copyright 1967 by D. Van Nostrand, and reproduced by permission.

[1] The preparation of this chapter was supported in part by Contract Nonr-24(55) between the Office of Naval Research and The Johns Hopkins University. This is Report No. 23 under this contract. Reproduction in whole or in part is permitted for any purpose of the United States Government. Creelman was supported by a National Institute of Mental Health Post-doctoral Fellowship No. 12,140.

In addition to precise statement of the conditions of the experiment, quantitative method should also include treatment of the data obtained. We need to be able to state the results of the experiment in a form which can be checked exactly by another experimenter. We use statistical techniques to describe the results of an experiment, and often also to estimate the likelihood that the same results, within a stated margin of error, would occur if the experiment were done again.

We can also use more abstract mathematics to show relations between dependent and independent variables, and the effect of the independent variable on some aspect of behavior. A mathematical equation can summarize and show most relationships between variables far more efficiently, and perhaps with greater meaning, than can the simple listing of experimental conditions and results. In recent years psychology has seen considerable use of such abstract mathematics to describe phenomena.

These uses of quantitative method are not unique to the science of psychology, nor are they the primary topic of this chapter. Rather, we shall be concerned with the measurement of psychological attributes, the problem area which has come to be called psychological scaling.

THE NATURE OF ATTRIBUTES

An attribute is an abstracted property of human experience. There are two critical aspects of this definition, each of which poses some special problems in the measurement of attributes, and at times this fact has led to some confusion about the nature of psychological scaling. The first aspect is that an attribute is an *abstracted* property of something, it is not the thing itself. Interestingly enough, while this fact makes for many of the difficulties of measurement, it is not unique to psychological measurement. When we talk about measuring something in an everyday situation, we are not really talking about measuring an object, or an event, but some abstracted property of it. When we measure length, or weight, for example, we are not measuring the object which has the length or the weight, but we are measuring some abstracted property, or dimension, of the object.

The second aspect of our definition is that an attribute relates to psychological experience—and it is this aspect which both makes it uniquely psychological and creates difficulties. Perhaps we can clarify this problem somewhat by contrasting an attribute (of experience) with a physical dimension which may be closely related to the experience. A sound can have a physical intensity, and we can measure its intensity with standard techniques of physical measurement. And we can experience loudness, but the loudness is not the same as the physical intensity. The loudness is something we experience; the intensity is something which is an aspect of the stimulus itself.

We speak, casually, of the loudness of a sound, rather than the loudness of our experience. Ordinarily there is little confusion created by our doing so. But when we become concerned about the measurement of loudness, the distinction becomes important, since we are required to investigate the properties of the attribute of loudness, even though we cannot in a direct physical sense get at the thing we are trying to measure.

This distinction between the attribute and the dimension of the physical object or event is fairly easy to see in those cases where there is an obvious physical counterpart of the attribute in which we are interested. In other cases, the distinction is more subtle. For example, when people are the stimuli we are interested in, and we want to measure something like leadership ability, or attitudes, it is often difficult to realize that the measurement we are concerned with is still not of the external stimulus, but of the underlying experienced attribute. If anything, the distinction becomes even more important in such cases.

THE NATURE OF MEASUREMENT

Psychological scaling is concerned with devising scales of measurement for psychological attributes. Before we present specific techniques for such measurement, it might be well to discuss the nature of measurement in more general terms, and then some of the special problems involved in the measurement of psychological attributes.

Measurement, in its broadest sense, is the assignment of numerals to objects, according to some specified rule. But this definition is much too simple, and even misleading, unless we consider the special problems of the use of numerals. Numerals are just symbols —the "1," "2," "53," etc., which we write or print. Thus if the problem of measurement were simply the problem of assigning numerals to objects by using some rule, we could use any rule we wish, as long as we use it consistently.

The Scale of Number

The numerals, however, represent a particular kind of scale—the scale of number. The numeral "1" stands for a single object, the numeral "2" stands for two distinct objects, and each numeral we use has a direct meaning in that it represents a number of objects or events. The scale of number is a scale of counting, and it is the simplest and most fundamental scale of measurement we have.

In a strict sense, the numerals can have any properties—mathematical or otherwise—we wish to assign them. But since the numerals represent the fundamental scale of number, they are often assumed to have the properties of the scale of number. For example, suppose we have 12 objects. We can carry out several operations with these objects, and we can also carry out the equivalent operations with the numerals themselves. We can add 3 objects to our 12, and then if we count again, we will have 15 objects. But we can add the numeral "3" to the numeral "12" and get the same result somewhat faster. Or we can subtract objects, or their equivalent numbers, and either way we get the same result. We can even divide the 12 objects into two equal groups, and if we count each group we will find there are 6 objects in each group—a fact we can just as easily ascertain by doing the division on paper.

There are many properties of the scale of number, but when we assign numerals to attributes or dimensions other than number, we need to be careful to determine which properties of the scale of number are applicable. This problem has nothing to do with determining the properties of the scale of number; rather we must determine the properties of the attribute itself, and then be sure that the numerals are assigned so that the numerals properly reflect the properties of the attribute.

Some Properties of Scales

We have briefly alluded to some properties of the scale of number, but the more important properties need further explanation. These properties are often used to describe the nature of a psychological scale, since they limit the interpretation of scale values.

Nominal scales—The simplest and most fundamental property of the scale of number is that of naming or identifying items or ob-

jects. As a simple example, we can ask each of several people what sex they are, and then assign to each the code number "1" if they say they are male, and the code number "2" if they say they are female. Such a use of numerals is measurement in a very primitive sense; it is the assignment of numbers according to a rule. But note that the only property of the scale of number which is applicable is the *identity* relation, namely, that all objects given the same number have the same sex. Here we can use no other property of the scale of number. For example, we cannot say that females are "more" than males, or that they are twice as much as males, even though the numerals represent these properties of the number scale.

Note, however, that we are free to change the assignment of numerals as long as we change all females together and all males together. We could have called females "1" and males "2." The reason we could do this is that the quality being "measured" does not have any measurable property other than identity or equivalence. The general point of our illustration is simply this: *The permissible rules for the assignment of numerals to objects depend on the properties of the attribute being measured,* and not on the properties of the scale of number. Thus we cannot determine what the permissible rules are without knowing something about the properties of the attribute itself.

Ordinal scales—A second property of the scale of number is that of *order:* the number "10" is larger than the number "6," and in fact is larger than all numbers less than 10. Note that this property assumes the nominal property, since the same numeral would still be used for all objects which are identical.

The simplest use of ordinal scales in psychology is when we rank order a set of objects with regard to some attribute, and each object is assigned a single numeral to reflect its ordinal position. But we can also use a rank scale and have several different objects assigned the same rank number. The school grading scale of "A," "B," "C," "D," and "F" is such a scale, even though letters are used rather than numerals, since all "A" grades are better than all "B" grades, etc.

With the nominal scale we say that we could translate the numerals in any fashion which retained the identity relation. With an ordinal scale we can translate with any rule which preserves the original ordering of the numbers assigned to the objects. In other words, once a set of numerals is assigned, we are free to change them by writing any new set of numbers as long as the new numbers are a monotonic positive function of the original numbers.

Once again, whether we use the ordinal property of the scale of number for the assignment of numerals to objects depends on whether the attribute itself has the ordinal property. If it has, then we can use this more restrictive rule.

Interval scales—A third, and even more restrictive, property of the scale of number is that of *equality of intervals*. If we add 6 objects to 24 objects to get 30 objects, the 6 objects are the same as if we add them to 40 objects to get 46 objects. Thus the numerical difference between 30 and 24 represents the same amount of number as does the difference between 46 and 40. The numerically equal intervals represent equal differences in number, and if an attribute has this same property, then the rule for assigning numerals should ensure that this property is properly reflected. Note that with the particular numerical example just used, we could change all the numbers by adding a constant, and it would not change the numerical value of the difference. Thus the intervals would still be equal.

If we are talking about actual number, of course, then we could not change the 6 and have it mean the same thing any longer, since 6 additional objects are just that, no more and no less. But if we are representing an attribute which does not have all the properties of the scale of number but does have the equal interval property, then we could multiply all of our numerals by a constant, and the two differences would still be equal. In other words, with interval scales we can translate

our scale by any linear positive function—which is a more restrictive translation than the monotonic positive function permissible with the ordinal scale. In mathematical form, we are allowed to assign any new set of numerals, as long as the condition that

$$y' = a + by$$

is satisfied, where y is the original numeral and y' is the transformed numeral. The important condition, the equality of differences, will still hold with the new numbers.

There are innumerable examples in psychology where the ordinal property of the scale of number can be assumed for a psychological attribute; but with interval properties we are on less sure ground, and frequently the interval property is assumed but cannot be proven to hold.

The IQ scale is a good example of an assumed interval scale, since the difference between an IQ of 120 and one of 130 is assumed to be the same as the difference between IQ's of 90 and 100. Note that the entire scale could be moved up to center around 200, rather than 100, and it would not change any of the properties of the scale. So also could we double all the numbers and it would not change the equal interval property. So the actual numerals assigned are quite arbitrary, with the restriction that the assumed equal interval property must be reflected in the numerals.

Ratio scales—An even more restrictive property of the scale of number is *equality of ratios*. The numeral "10" is twice the numeral "5," and so is the numeral "90" twice the numeral "45." Thus these two ratios are equal, and so are their counterparts in the scale of number, since in each case if the larger number is divided into groups each containing the respective smaller number, there will be exactly two groups. This property means that the numerical operations of multiplication and division are applicable to the attribute being measured—and in the case of a scale of number, they are.

Notice that in this case we are not free to transform the original numbers by adding or subtracting a number, because if we did, the ratios would no longer be equal. If we are dealing with any attribute which has the ratio property, then we can multiply all of the numerals by a constant and still retain the ratio property. What we may not do is add or subtract a constant. Thus if we have a scale with ratio properties, we can translate our numerals such that

$$y' = by$$

where y' is the numeral transformed from the original y.

In psychological research there are few examples of attributes which we can be sure have the ratio property. The difficulty has to do with the problem of an absolute zero. Notice that any permissible transformation of a ratio scale does not change the zero point on the scale, although the permissible transformations of an interval scale do. In fact, the basic requirement for a scale with ratio properties is that there exists an absolute zero—which means literally that no amount of the attribute exists. It is not sufficient to have a zero point on a scale, unless we can also be sure that the zero represents an absolute lack of the attribute.

The problem in psychology is twofold. First, there are not many attributes which can reasonably be assumed to have an absolute zero. For example, what would an absolute zero of intelligence be? Or what is the absolute zero of attitude toward the Republican Party? There can be neutrality of feeling, and the neutral position is often used as the zero point on a scale, but it does not represent an absolute lack of the attribute. The zero is simply a position between positive and negative attitudes. Or as still another example, what would the absolute zero of pitch be? It is difficult to picture what we mean by "no amount of pitch," since pitch exists as a difference, but not strictly as a magnitude.

The other aspect of the problem has to do with our ability to determine the true, or absolute zero even if it might logically exist. Consider the psychological attribute of brightness, for example. We can produce a condition of no amount of light, but such a physical situation does not guarantee an absolute lack of brightness, since it is possible to have a blacker black than we have ever experienced. In neurological terms, we know that complete absence of light does not produce complete absence of nerve activity (Kuffler, FitzHugh, and Barlow, 1957), so it seems quite reasonable that absolute psychological black might never be experienced. So also with things like loudness; there may be a meaningful zero, but we probably can never experience it directly.

The scale of temperature gives a physical example of this problem. It has been known for some time that there is an absolute zero of temperature (which does not, of course, correspond to the zero of either the Fahrenheit or Centigrade scales), but physically producing such a condition is quite a different problem. The existence of an absolute zero could be deduced from the behavior of measurable temperatures, and its value relative to the Centigrade scale was finally determined. But historically the task of getting a ratio scale was made difficult by the inability to work directly with absolute zero.

This example points out another way of characterizing a ratio scale; it is one on which no negative numbers can be assigned. We can see that this is the case with counting objects, as in the scale of number, and with the Kelvin scale of temperature. In each case it is meaningless to speak of less than zero number of objects, or of a temperature less than absolute zero.

Other scale properties—The four kinds of scales we have discussed are certainly four of the more important scale types currently in use, but by no means are they the only ones possible. There are many other combinations of the properties of the scale of number which could also be properties of a psychological attribute. For example, it is possible that we can know that one interval on a scale is larger than another, but not be able to specify exactly how much larger it is. In such a situation, we could have not only an ordering of objects, but also an ordering of the intervals between objects. Coombs (1950) has in fact proposed such a scale, which we shall discuss in a later section. It is also possible to have a true ratio scale for intervals between objects, but only an interval scale for the objects themselves. Such a situation would occur if we could identify and measure a zero difference between objects, and at the same time be sure of the ratio properties of the differences.

Power Versus Restriction in Scaling

Frequently one hears of the power of a scale, and by power is usually meant the kinds of mathematical properties we have been discussing. A ratio scale is more powerful than an interval scale because it not only tells us about the numerical intervals of the measured attribute, but it also tells us about the ratios. And an interval scale is in turn more powerful than an ordinal scale because it tells us everything the ordinal scale does, but tells us about intervals as well. Psychological scalers usually try to devise scales with at least interval properties, even if some assumptions must be made in order to obtain the greater power. There are real advantages to the greater specification of an attribute which the more powerful scales provide.

There is, however, another side to this problem from the point of view of the scaler. He is more restricted in his use of numbers with the more powerful scales. As we have seen, with a scale as weak as the nominal scale, the only restriction on the scaler is that he use the same number for identical objects or amounts of an attribute. But with an ordinal scale, he must assign the numbers so as to reflect the ordinal relations inherent in the measured attribute; and with more powerful scales, he is even more restricted. With the scale of number itself, the most powerful scale, he of course has no choice at all, but must assign numbers to attributes in an exactly specified manner—the number "10," for example, can be used for ten objects only, not more or less.

The more powerful scale has greater utility once it has been established, but the scaler has much less freedom in establishing the scale values of the more powerful scale in the first place. In effect, the scaler is always in a certain amount of conflict. He wants to establish as powerful a scale as possible, but he is much less sure that he has done so correctly than if he had attempted to establish a weaker scale. Often the scale produced is a compromise between a scale with maximum power and a scale with minimum restriction on the scaler.

THE BASIC SCALING PROBLEM

Any scaling experiment will be concerned with three sets of variables, and it will be well at the outset to understand the different role each of the three plays. In the most simple case this is easy to visualize. The three variables are *stimuli*, a set of objects which we have chosen to use, *subjects*, to whom the objects are presented, and *responses* which are required by the experimental situation. The role that each of these variables can play in the scaling process can vary, but it is always the case that an analogous set of three variables must be chosen. Each is important, and each must be carefully considered.

It might be well to recall that the problem of psychological scaling is the problem of assigning numerals to an attribute—which is an abstracted property and not to be confused with the object itself. Nevertheless, often the only way we can specify how much of the attribute corresponds to a stated numeral is to point to a particular object as an illustration. Thus, as a practical matter, we do end up assigning numerals to objects—but our purpose is not to say that the object is the numeral. Rather, it is to say that this object can call out the attribute in this amount.

Likewise, while we are interested in the effect of the stimulus objects on the persons to whom they are presented, it is true that all we have to go on are the responses that we obtain from our subjects. Then a double inferential chain is necessary (in the scaling process). First the stimuli are chosen to represent the world of possible stimuli in some representative fashion, and then the responses are taken to represent the experience of the subject in some meaningful sense. The response must also reflect the aspect of the experiment that we are interested in. This is not always as easy as it might seem. For instance . . . the response from a subject to the effect that he "sees" a very weak light can not always be taken at face value, but it is determined by many aspects of the situation beyond the intensity of the light itself.

We have been talking about objects as the sources of the attribute, although some of our illustrations have used people as the objects. In reality, if we think of the objects as stimuli, we can scale any one of three variables—the stimuli, the subjects, or even the responses. For example, there need be no simple relation between the responses used by the subject in the experiment and the underlying metric of the attribute. Certainly if the responses are verbal rather than numerical, we need to scale the responses before we can scale the stimuli; in fact, one can hardly be done without the other. If we manage to assign numerals correctly to the stimuli, then we must also find a numerical scale for the responses, since we are looking for a functional relation between the stimuli and the responses.

It is also quite possible that we could determine the amount of an attribute corresponding to the subject himself. This is commonly the case when we measure attitudes. The function of the objects now is to provide a way for the subject to express an amount of an attribute in himself, the subject, rather than the object. For example, if the objects have a predetermined amount of the attribute, then we can determine the subject's perception of himself by finding which objects he will accept as representative of himself, or desirable to him.

Abelson (1960) has expressed these interrelations in another form. He distinguishes between *agents, objects,* and *modes* as the three variables required in a psychological scaling problem. While his distinctions leave

some ambiguity, in principle they are sound. To illustrate with a reasonably simple case, suppose we want to scale the loudness of several traffic sounds. Our scaling problem then becomes one of assigning numerals to various sounds, which are the objects, in such a way that the underlying attribute is properly reflected.

But we must have some agent which defines the attribute, so we use one or more subjects to judge the loudness of the stimuli. The subjects, then, are the agents through which we determine the scale values to assign to the stimuli.

The agent expresses his judgment through a mode, which is the actual set of responses which he is allowed to use.

This is a useful way to visualize the scaling problem, and yet we shall see that it is an oversimplification (as are most ways of describing the problems of psychological scaling). There are some scaling techniques in which both the stimuli and the subjects are scaled from the same set of data, so that the objects and the agents play interchanging roles in the same scaling problem. And there are other cases where the stimuli and responses are scaled from the same set of data, and in a real sense play interchanging roles as objects and modes.

What should be kept clear, however, is that we are interested in scaling an attribute, an abstraction about the perception of either stimuli, people, or even of responses. Since our interest is in the abstracted attribute, we can scale it with reference to one or more of these three basic variables, sometimes simultaneously, or at least from the same set of data.

The problem of generality—There is another reason why our original three-variable framework used the term *subjects* rather than *agents,* and that is to illustrate a pervading problem in all psychological research. To a greater extent than other sciences, psychology must always face, and attempt to answer, the question of the generality of an experimental result—and generality usually, but not always, means with respect to some specified population of people. We could use just one subject as our agent to scale the loudness of stimuli, with a single response mode, but we don't do so because we want some assurance that the scale obtained is not unique for our one subject. Thus we use several subjects and pool or average data across them in order to have the greater generality which average data give us. Or, alternatively, we can look for differences between subjects to determine how generally applicable the scale is.

If our intent is to establish differences between subjects, then frequently the objects become the means of establishing generality. We might want to know, for example, whether sounds seem louder to one person than to another. But we would ordinarily be unwilling to draw such a conclusion on the basis of judgments about a single stimulus. Rather, we would want to know whether subject A always rates auditory stimuli as louder than does subject B. Thus either subjects or objects can be used to establish generality. In still other cases, we would want to establish generality across responses, since the scale we obtain should not be unique to a particular set of possible responses. If subjects are, for example, asked to judge the brightness of a light, the scale we obtain should be the same whether he uses responses between zero and ten, or between zero and one hundred.

Latent Versus Manifest Scaling

The data obtained to construct a psychological scale may be used in many ways. But there are differences in how the scale can be constructed other than those we have discussed, and one of the major differences is whether the latent or the manifest properties of the data are used to construct the scale.

The manifest properties of the data are, as the term suggests, the evident, easily seen, and interpreted properties. The latent properties are those which must be extracted from the data, which are inherent, but are not readily perceivable. The latent properties are just as important as the manifest properties, perhaps even more so. Psychological scaling techniques have tended more and more to the use of latent properties, for a variety of reasons.

When we distinguish between scales based on manifest or on latent properties of data, we are not concerned with whether the data themselves have manifest properties: All data do. Rather, our concern has to do with the measurement properties of the scale we construct in relation to the measurement properties of the manifest data. Ordinarily, scales based on latent properties will have measurement properties different from, and usually more powerful than, the measurement properties of the responses (the manifest data). Indeed, the object of most latent scaling techniques is to arrive at such stronger measurement properties. There are three major points in the construction of a psychological scale which are relevant to the question of whether we have a scale based on manifest or on latent properties.

The nature of the subject's response—The first, and frequently most important consideration, is the nature of the response required of the subject. We can require him to use nominal, ordinal, interval, or even ratio scale types of responses, and if we intend to use the manifest properties of the data, then we can construct a scale with no more powerful measurement assumptions than the subject was asked to use. For example, if we ask subjects simply to order several stimuli for aesthetic preference, then we cannot construct an interval or a ratio scale based on manifest properties of these data.

The assumed property of the response—It is not necessary, of course, that the experimenter assume the responses have the measurement properties the subject was told to use. If the subject was instructed to make ratio judgments of the brightness of lights, we need not assume that he was able to do so. We might assume that he was only capable of making interval, or perhaps just ordinal, judgments. Logically, it is possible to assume more powerful properties of the response continuum than the subject used, even though it is rarely done. For instance, we could instruct the subject to rank order a set of stimuli, and then assume that in reality the ranks represent an interval scale. If we do so, then we would be tapping a latent property of the data, since the interval property was not evident.

The assumed property of the scale—The scale finally constructed will not necessarily have the same measurement property as the responses used by the subject, or even the same as that assumed by the experimenter. One can, as we shall see, assume only that the subject made ordinal responses, but from these an interval scale can be constructed, if some further assumptions are made in treating the data.

When the nature of the response, the assumed properties of the response, and the assumed property of the scale are congruent, then we have a scale based on manifest properties of the data. If they are not congruent, then the scale is to some extent based on latent properties. It should be clear that the distinction between latent scales and manifest scales is not a sharp dichotomy. Rather, there are all degrees of variation from scales based entirely and simply on manifest data, to scales based partially on latent properties of the data, to scales which bear little relation to any evident or manifest properties of the data.

Why Latent Property Scales?

The construction of a scale based on manifest data is basically so simple and straightforward that we can wonder why latent property techniques are used at all. If we can directly ask a subject how loud a tone is, or how beautiful a tree is, why not do so and be done with it? The answer lies in the very nature of the psychological scaling problem itself.

In psychological scaling we try to assign numerals so as to reflect the properties of an attribute—the abstraction which cannot be directly observed. Therefore, when we have used manifest data we have begged what may be the most important question of all, whether there is, in fact, such an attribute, and if so, what its properties are. To use manifest properties of the response requires a very powerful pair of assumptions. We must assume that the attribute exists and has the measurement properties which we assign to it; and we must also assume that these properties can be directly reflected by the subject in his manifest response.

It is not sufficient to say that we have a scale for an attribute because we can show a functional relation between a set of objects and a set of scale values. We must first determine what the properties of the attribute itself are (Does it have an absolute zero, for example?), and then what numerals to assign the objects having the property. In other words, we must establish a relation between the attribute itself and some aspects of the scale of number.

Scales based on latent properties of data are much like hypothetical constructs or intervening variables (Green, 1954); they are mathematically constructed to explain relations between other variables. Rarely do such scales have properties more powerful than an interval scale, but they usually are assured of this property in a meaningful way. A scale based on manifest data where the responses have ratio properties may frequently appear to have such properties; but the greater power of the ratio scale comes at considerable cost. There is seldom any clear evidence for the meaningfulness of the presumed attribute in the first place.

Most latent scale techniques have experimental or mathematical converging operations (Garner, Hake, and Eriksen, 1956) built into them. Converging operations serve as separate checks on the legitimacy of the concept. For, after all, an attribute (by definition not directly observable) is just that—a concept, and a concept is quite meaningless unless it is both abstracted and general. To identify a concept from a single experimental or mathematical operation is to establish meaningfulness by fiat, a procedure which is hardly in good scientific taste. The latent techniques thus generally provide greater generality, even though at a possible cost in measurement power.

SOME SCALING TECHNIQUES

Each scaling problem poses different requirements of technique, so there have been many different scaling techniques developed. Many differences in technique are due to differences in the attributes or the objects to be scaled. These differences make it difficult to organize the various techniques in a meaningful fashion. Some means of organizing the techniques must be found if we are to present a clear picture. We could organize them according to the nature of the attribute, according to the nature of the objects to be scaled, or even according to the nature of the responses used. But these methods do not recognize the most important related aspects of a psychological scale, namely, what its measurement properties are and how the scale is related to the underlying attribute.

We have, therefore, chosen to organize the techniques according to these two major criteria: First, the measurement properties of the scale; and, second, whether the scale is based primarily on latent or on manifest properties of the data. In describing the kinds of scales, we shall use terms like "manifest-interval," which means that the scale obtained has interval properties, and that these properties were inherent in the manifest response.

Internal consistency of scales—Before describing the specific techniques, one other comment is worth making about the experimental problems of psychological scaling. Good experimental technique requires some check on the internal consistency of the data. The concept of internal consistency is an important one, and we shall frequently refer to it. Basically it is concerned with the validity of a particular scaling procedure, or with the validity of the assumption that a particular attribute can be scaled with the specified scale properties.

The essence of the concept is this: If a scale has the assumed properties, and if the particular scaling technique is valid for determining these properties, then the experimental results should show certain internal relations which are consistent with the assumed properties. To illustrate, let us suppose that we are trying to establish an ordinal scale for three objects, A, B, and C. If a large number of subjects all agree that A is greater than B, and that B is greater than C, then they should also agree that A is greater than C in order for these data to be internally consistent. If instead they all agree that C is greater than A, then we have a reliable result (reliable because of intersubject agreement), but we would question the legitimacy of the scale because of the lack of internal consistency. As another example, suppose that we have found experimentally that A is twice as much of something as B, and that B is twice as much as C. Then our experimental procedure should also show that A is four times as much as C. If it does not, then we reject the assumption that proper ratio scaling has been accomplished.

If a set of data are not internally consistent, we are not always sure why. It may be that the assumption of the existence of a scale with the specified properties is in error. Or it may simply be that our experimental technique is inadequate for determining the scale. If data are not internally consistent, then we often try another technique to determine whether it is the original technique which is at fault rather than the assumption about the properties of the attribute itself.

Many scaling procedures have checks or internal consistency as an integral part of the technique itself. In particular, the latent techniques frequently contain and even emphasize such checks because of the importance of the assumption of scalability with these techniques. With the manifest techniques, such checks can (and should) be made, but ordinarily they involve carrying out more than a single experiment.

Manifest-Ordinal Techniques

The ordinal property of psychological scales is so commonly accepted that essentially all scales with only ordinal properties are based on manifest data. In other words, latent techniques are not usually used to obtain ordinal scales because most experimenters are willing to accept the ability of the average subject to make ordinal judgments.

Rank ordering—Probably the simplest of all scaling techniques is simple rank ordering. A subject is shown a set of stimuli to judge, say, for his aesthetic preference; or a supervisor is asked to rank the employees under his supervision; or a subject is asked to judge the brightness of several gray stimuli. In each case, if there are relatively few objects to rank, the subject is simply required to place the objects in rank order, or to assign a rank number to each object. These rank numbers are then taken to be the scale values.

In order to provide some generality to the scale and thus to provide some check on the validity of the assumption that there is an attribute to be scaled, several subjects or raters may be required to rank the same objects. The data of Table 1 show ranks from an hypothetical example where four raters each rated five workers. The rank numbers can then be summed to give a composite rank

TABLE 1

RELATIVE RANKING OF WORKERS IN A SHOP BY DIFFERENT RATERS. THE OVER-ALL RANKING IS FROM THE SUMS OF THE RANKS GIVEN EACH WORKER

Raters	Workers				
	Joe	Bill	Andy	Jack	Sam
Foreman	2	1	3	4	5
Superintendent	3	2	1	5	4
Shop steward	2	1	4	3	5
Psychologist	3	2	4	1	5
Sum of ranks	10	6	12	13	19
Average rank	2.5	1.5	3	3.25	4.75
Over-all rank	2	1	3	4	5

scale, or we can take averages for each worker to obtain an average rank. It should be clear, however, that these average ranks, with their unequal numerical spacings between stimuli, do not give scale properties beyond those of ordinal scales. To avoid any misinterpretation of the meaning of such average ranks, it is better to reassign whole rank numbers to the objects, as has been done in Table 1.

Pair comparisons—If we have a relatively small number of objects to be ranked, a slightly more sophisticated technique can be used, one which provides a greater check on the internal consistency of the ordinal assumptions. With this technique, the objects, say ten of them, are formed into all possible pairs. (With ten objects, there are 45 such pairs.) Now these pairs are presented one at a time, and the subject is required to state which stimulus has the greater amount of the relevant attribute, or which person, say, is more skilled as a machinist. Thus with this technique, instead of each subject ranking all ten objects at one time, he ranks two objects in each of 45 pairs.

The advantage of this technique is that it provides a check on the ability of subjects to rank the stimuli in the first place, because if the objects really have a consistent ordering for the subject, then many of the pair judgments are predictable from others. To illustrate, suppose that one subject chooses A as greater than B, and then chooses B as greater than C. It is now clear that he should also choose A as greater than C, and if he fails to do so more often than would be predicted on a chance or error basis, we have cause for rejecting the assumption that the objects can be ordered with respect to the specified attribute.

Table 2 shows a set of hypothetical data from a pair comparisons experiment, displayed in the usual form. In this table the stimuli are listed both across the top and down the side, and each cell represents a single pair which has been judged. The entry in a cell of the table shows the proportion of choices (out of all subjects making the

TABLE 2

PAIR-COMPARISON METHOD OF RANKING*

		Paintings							
		A	*B*	*C*	*D*	*E*	*F*	*G*	*H*
Paintings	A	(.50)	.30	.14	.06	.06	.02	00	00
	B	.70	(.50)	.38	.22	.12	.08	.08	00
	C	.86	.62	(.50)	.32	.30	.14	.10	.06
	D	.94	.78	.68	(.50)	.32	.36	.18	.08
	E	.94	.88	.70	.68	(.50)	.38	.16	.10
	F	.98	.92	.86	.64	.62	(.50)	.36	.10
	G	1.00	.92	.90	.82	.84	.64	(.50)	.22
	H	1.00	1.00	.94	.92	.90	.90	.78	(.50)
Sum of proportions		6.92	5.92	5.10	4.16	3.66	3.02	2.16	1.06
Rank		1	2	3	4	5	6	7	8

* Entries in the table are the proportion of 50 subjects who rated each painting across the top as better than the painting listed at the side. Final ranking of the paintings is done from the sums of the proportions, which reflect the number of occasions each painting is preferred to all others.

choices) on which the stimulus listed at the top was chosen over the stimulus listed at the side. In the illustration, 50 subjects were required to choose between pairs of paintings, on the basis of aesthetic preference. For instance, painting "A" was preferred to painting "B" by 35 of the 50 subjects, for a proportion of .70. Likewise all subjects preferred painting "A" to painting "H."

In this type of experiment, like simple ranking, data from just one subject could give us the rank values for the objects—if his pair choices were internally consistent. However, we can obtain greater generality by pooling responses across subjects, as we have done in our illustration. If we now simply sum the total number (or proportion) of times that each object is chosen when it is paired with each of the others, we have an average rank scale. And again as with rank ordering, the stimuli should be assigned whole rank numbers, since the differences in numbers of choices do not necessarily reflect differences in the intervals between objects. Thus we still have just an ordinal scale, one based on manifest ordinal properties of the judgments.

Category ranks—Both the ranking and pair comparisons techniques are feasible only when we have a reasonably small number of objects to be scaled. With as many as 20 objects, ranking becomes very difficult, and pair comparisons (with 190 pairs of objects) becomes prohibitively difficult. We then must resort to a somewhat modified ranking or ordering technique.

With the category ranks technique, fewer rank categories are used than there are objects to be judged. For example, we might have 60 different stimulus patterns to be judged for goodness of pattern, but we ask the raters to use just five different response categories, and to use these categories as ranks only. In our illustration in Table 3, there are just five rank categories, in which rank "1" means the best patterns, and rank "5" means the poorest patterns.

With this technique, of course, each rank category will be used for many different stimuli, but the different subjects or raters will not all assign the ranks to the stimulus objects in exactly the same way. So for each stimulus we will have a distribution of rank categories. From this distribution we could compute a mean rank, as has been done in Table 3, but this procedure is open to question because the rank categories do not have interval properties. A better procedure, also shown in Table 3, is to compute the median rank assigned to each stimulus by interpolating from the cumulative frequency distribution for each stimulus, and these median ranks are shown in the table. Again, reassigning whole rank numbers to the stimuli is appropriate, since the differences in median rank do not indicate interval properties of the attribute in question.

Guttman's scalogram analysis—There are two scaling techniques which lead to ordinal scales that depend to some extent on latent properties of the data. One of these is Guttman's Scalogram technique (1950), which produces a scale on which both stimulus objects (usually test items) and subjects can be placed. The essence of the technique is the determination of the validity of the ordinal assumption for an attribute. Unless it can be shown that both objects and subjects can be ordered with regard to a single attribute, then Guttman argues that we have no grounds for attempting to produce an ordinal scale at all. This technique is most appropriate with attributes such as abilities, where both stimuli and subjects can be presumed to elicit the attribute.

While the Guttman technique has been developed to a considerable degree of sophistication, we will describe it only sufficiently to show the basic principles which are operating.

The kinds of stimulus items used for a Guttman scale are usually those which can be answered dichotomously—accept or reject, right or wrong, etc. The requirement of the technique is that only those items can be used which can consistently be ordered with regard to preference or ability, and that sub-

TABLE 3

THE METHOD OF CATEGORY RANKS*

Rank	Stimulus Patterns					
	1	2	3	4	19	20
1	.50	.40	.45	.30	.10	00
	.50	.40	.45	.30	.10	00
2	.30	.35	.15	.25	00	.10
	.80	.75	.60	.55	.10	.10
3	.05	.15	.15	.20	.15	.10
	.85	.90	.75	.75	.25	.20
4	.10	00	.15	.10	.40	.40
	.95	.90	.90	.85	.65	.60
5	.05	.10	.10	.15	.35	.40
	1.00	1.00	1.00	1.00	1.00	1.00
Median	1.50	1.79	1.83	2.30	4.13	4.25
Mean	1.90	2.05	2.30	2.55	3.90	4.10
Rank	1	2	3	4	19	20

* The upright numbers are the proportion of the raters placing each of the patterns listed across the top into each of the categories of "goodness of pattern" listed down the side. The slanted numbers are the proportion of raters giving the listed rank or better, obtained by adding down each column. The median is obtained from an interpolation to find the rank number which 50 per cent of the raters exceed for each pattern. The mean category values for each pattern are listed as well.

jects can also be consistently ordered with respect to the items. The example we have chosen is shown in Table 4, with five arithmetic questions. These items are chosen to correspond to an increasing level of difficulty, such that the simple addition problem is easier than the double-digit addition problem, and so on. If these items do in fact represent a single attribute continuum, then subjects should be right on all problems easier than the most difficult one they solved, and they should be wrong on all problems more difficult than the easiest one they failed. Thus the subject who correctly answered the last item should have correctly answered all other items; and the subject who failed the first item should have failed all other items, because they are more difficult.

This requirement, of perfect ordering of the stimulus objects, means that there are only six possible scores, and each possible score represents a single subject scale type. The six possible scores, of course, are the numbers from "0" through "5," and each number is uniquely associated with a particular pattern of right and wrong answers. Thus a "3" means that these subjects were right on the third item and all items less difficult, but were wrong on the last two items.

There are, naturally, many difficulties involved in establishing such a scale with more realistic types of items, and with items which are not answered dichotomously, and these problems are discussed in Stouffer, et al. (1950). But the basic concept of this technique is not difficult, and it is of interest because of its central emphasis on the internal consistency check as the primary requirement which must be satisfied. We have noted that most scaling techniques do have some degree or form of internal consistency check inherent in them, but none of the other techniques so thoroughly establishes the validity of the fundamental assumption involved in all psychological scaling, namely, that an attribute actually exists with the assumed or stated properties of measurement. Far too often this assumption remains just that, an assumption, with little clear proof of its validity.

Coombs' unfolding technique—Coombs (1950) has described a scaling technique which also locates both stimulus objects and subjects on the same attribute. His technique makes direct use of ranking by subjects, and it is in this respect based on manifest properties of the data. But his technique also, with sufficient data, makes possible the determination of an ordering of the intervals—leading to what Coombs calls an ordered metric type of scale, a scale which is intermediate between those with ordinal and those with interval properties.

The best way to explain the unfolding

TABLE 4

AN ARITHMETIC TEST WHICH ESTABLISHES A GUTTMAN SCALE

Test Items	Subjects					
	A	B	C	D	E	F
1. 2 + 2 = 4	−	+	+	+	+	+
2. 11 + 23 = 34	−	−	+	+	+	+
3. 6 × 12 = 72	−	−	−	+	+	+
4. 48 ÷ 4 = 12	−	−	−	−	+	+
5. 78 ÷ 13 = 6	−	−	−	−	−	+
Number correct	0	1	2	3	4	5

* The items are arranged in order of difficulty, and the subjects are arranged in order of ability. A "plus" means that the subject listed at the top got the item correct, and a "minus" means that he failed the item. All possible sets of scores are listed.

technique is to start with the end product desired and see what kinds of data could occur if this scale were so. We have, following Coombs' terminology, a J scale of some attribute, which is a scale on which stimuli can be located, and on which the desired or preference position of the subject can also be located. To illustrate, let us suppose that we have five different levels of sugar concentration in a soft drink, and we know the scale values of the attribute of sweetness, but also the preference position of each subject with regard to the attribute of sweetness.

Figure 1 shows two possible J scales. On the J_1 scale, we have located all five stimuli

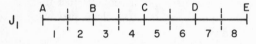

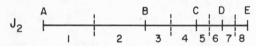

Figure 1. Two different J scales on which five stimuli (A through E) are located as points. The numbers indicate possible ranges of positions where subjects could also be located. Each subject position will lead to a different order of preference. Courtesy of D. Van Nostrand Company, Inc.

equidistant—thus we are temporarily assuming these five stimuli to constitute a known equal interval scale. Now each subject will have some preferred sweetness, so each subject can also be located along the scale. The arabic numerals indicate ranges within which subject preferences can lie, and each range will have a different effect on the responses given by the subject.

In the actual experiment, we ask each subject to rank order his preference for the five sweetnesses, and we assume that he will rank order according to the nearness of the actual sweetness to his preferred sweetness. With this assumption, we can predict exactly what the rank orders of the five stimuli will be for each range of possible preference positions.

The rank orders for each preference position are:

1	ABCDE	5	CDBEA
2	BACDE	6	DCEBA
3	BCADE	7	DECBA
4	CBDAE	8	EDCBA

For this particular J scale, no other rankings can possibly occur, and if in an experiment we obtain only these rankings out of all the possible rankings of five things (5!, or 120), then we have learned two things: First, we know that the stimuli can in fact be ordered; and, second, we can determine the ordering by unfolding the various rankings of preferences to give us the original scale of stimuli themselves. The term "unfolding" is used because in effect the subject, in making his preference rankings, folds the scale of sweetness over, using as a hinge his own position on the scale, and in reconstructing the scale, we, in effect, unfold the rankings.

But now let us see what would happen if the intervals between the stimuli on the J scale were not equal. The J_2 scale of Figure 1 shows such an hypothetical scale, and once again we can ask what rankings could be produced by subjects if their preference positions were in the intervals indicated by the arabic numerals. In this case, the following preference rankings could occur:

1	ABCDE	5	CDEBA
2	BACDE, or BCADE, or BCDAE	6	DCEBA
3	BCDEA, or BCDAE	7	DECBA
4	CBDEA, or CDBEA	8	EDCBA

Where there is more than one possible preference ranking for a given range of positions, the exact ranking depends more precisely on the position of the subject's preference. Altogether, with this set of scale values for the sweetness attribute, 11 different rankings can occur, and once again, we can reconstruct the ordering of the stimuli by unfolding the preference ranks.

While we shall not go into more detail on the unfolding technique, it should be clear by now that for any particular scale of sweetness, a limited number of possible preference rankings can occur, and if we have enough different subjects rank the stimuli to obtain a large number of different preference positions, then we can not only learn the ordering of the stimuli, but we can also order the sizes of intervals between the stimuli. Thus we can obtain an ordered metric scale.

Notice that with both the Coombs and the Guttman techniques, internal consistency is a critical part of the procedure. Furthermore, in both techniques the same basic principle is used to determine internal consistency: to limit the number of possible results which can occur and which are acceptable as satisfying the measurement requirements for the scale. In the Guttman technique, with dichotomous items, it is possible for 2^n patterns of results to occur with n different items, but only $(n + 1)$ results are accepted as satisfying the ordinal requirements. In the Coombs technique, there are $n!$ ways of ordering n items, but for any scale spacing, only $[\frac{1}{2}n(n - 1) + 1]$ possible orderings will occur. In our example of five stimuli, there are 120 ways of ordering the stimuli, but only 11 ways for any one actual spacing.

Manifest-Interval Techniques

The principal aspect of the manifest-interval scale techniques is that some direct response is required, and either because of instruction to the subject, or assumption on the part of the experimenter, the data are treated as though they have interval properties. The major differences in technique have to do with the kinds of stimulus objects used, and the limitations these put on the experimental procedure.

Equisection—Suppose that we want to determine psychological scale values for stimuli which are on a true physical continuum—one which can be manipulated easily to produce continuous variation. There are not many physical continua of this sort which are of interest to the psychological scaler, but there are some. Both frequency and intensity of sounds can be so manipulated; so also can

physical brightness, and even hue or saturation, with a sufficiently complicated apparatus; electric shock, vibration, and the intensity of odors are others.

For our example, we shall use intensity of sounds, with loudness being the psychological attribute whose scale we wish to determine. The procedure is fundamentally very simple: We provide two tones of fixed intensity, and then require that the subject adjust the intensity of other tones until he has them arranged to provide a series of equal loudness intervals.

Each of the tones thus produced, plus the two tones which defined the original range of loudness, is assigned a numerical value with equal interval spacings to correspond to the assumption that the tones produced by the subject provide an interval scale of loudness. In order to provide generality to the resultant scale, we would ordinarily have each subject make the adjustments several times, and we would use several different subjects. Some measure of central tendency (usually the mean) of the intensities is then used to define the average value of the points on the intensity continuum which provide an interval scale of loudness.

The number of stimuli which are to be adjusted by the subject is a matter of choice on the part of the experimenter. In the limiting case, where two end stimuli are provided, and the subject then adjusts a single stimulus to a value midway between the two, the method is called "bisection," because the subject is required to bisect an interval.

In order to provide a check on internal consistency, it is a good procedure to use at least two different sets of values for the fixed end stimuli, and have the ranges overlap. Then we would want to use enough stimuli in each range to give a substantial overlap in the number of stimuli common to both sets. In the illustrative data shown in Figure 2, seven stimuli (two end stimuli plus five adjustable stimuli) were used with two ranges of intensity (50 to 90 db sound pressure level, and 70 to 110 db). The same subjects were required to adjust five stimuli within each range, and the data shown in Figure 2 are averages of the adjusted intensities. For each

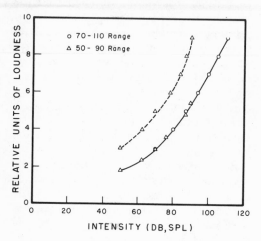

Figure 2. The equisection technique, using seven stimuli over two different ranges of audio power. The solid line shows the final scale, and the data for the 70 to 110 db range. The dotted line shows the untransformed data for the 50 to 90 db range. These were transformed to yield the final scale by the formula $y' = .58y - .025$. (After Garner, 1954a). Courtesy of D. Van Nostrand Company, Inc.

range, the numerical values 3 through 9 were assigned to the seven stimuli. This is shown by the dots for the higher range, and the triangles connected by dotted lines for the lower range.

To construct the final scale, shown by the solid line, the interval size of 1 unit was contracted for the data from the lower range, and the whole curve was moved downward by subtracting a constant. It should be remembered that with an interval scale we are free to use any linear transformation of the scale values, which is to say that we can adjust both the intercept and the slope to provide the best fit of the two overlapping sets of equisection data. In other words, we use two degrees of freedom from the lower values to establish our scale unit for the upper values, and it should now be clear why it is best to use several intermediate stimuli in equisec-

tion. If we had only two overlapping points, then with two degrees of freedom to determine the scale values, we can assure that the two sections of the curve will fit together in the overlapping range. It would still be possible for the two sections to provide an apparently discontinuous function, but an oddly shaped or broken curve would be our only check on the validity of the interval assumption.

On the other hand, if three or more stimulus values overlap, then the curvature, or the shape of the function, can be seen to be the same or different for the same range of intensities. Clearly if our assumption that an interval scale can be formed is valid, then we should obtain the same scale for the same range of intensities, regardless of the end stimuli used to obtain these particular scale values. Thus we can provide a check on internal consistency, while at the same time extending the range of intensity over which we obtain a psychological scale.

Equal-appearing intervals—If the objects which we want to scale cannot be measured by a continuous physical dimension, then we must resort to other procedures. Suppose, for example, that we wanted to scale verbal ability in individuals as judged by other people; or we wanted to scale the "goodness of pattern" of several geometric patterns In these cases we are not able to tell the subject or rater to adjust the stimuli to provide equal intervals, because the stimuli are fixed, and cannot be adjusted.

In this case we can instruct the subject to give a number to each stimulus, so that the numbers he uses are spaced by equal intervals. Or, alternatively, we could have the subject sort the stimuli into adjacent categories, with the instruction that his sortings are to satisfy the interval requirements. The data would be in exactly the same form as with the method of category ranks, as shown in Table 3. The only difference lies in the instruction to the subject to use his categories as equal intervals rather than as ranks. With the assumption that he does so, however, it becomes legitimate to use the mean category value for each stimulus, rather than the median, as we suggested before.

To contrast the method of equal-appearing intervals with that of equisection, we might note that in the latter method stimuli are chosen or set by the subject to define a series of points on the attribute continuum, and the intervals between these points are then assumed to be equal. With equal-appearing intervals, however, we never have stimuli which define equal intervals as points on the continuum. Nor do the category values either used or assigned do so either, since they define a range of values, not points. Rather, the assumption is that each response category provides a range of values, an interval, which is equal to all other intervals. And it is also assumed, of course, that the intervals are in proper order and are contiguous.

Numerical category scales—The method of equal-appearing intervals is normally used where a large number of stimuli must be judged, and each subject rates or judges each stimulus just once. A similar (in fact, logi-cally identical) method is used where there are relatively few stimuli, but each stimulus is rated several times by each subject, on a numerical scale, with instructions to the subject to use the scale values as an interval scale. The term "category scale" is usually applied to this method, and we have called it the method of numerical category scales to distinguish it from those methods in which verbal, or even spatially arranged, categories are used.

As an illustration of the use of this scale, Figure 3 shows some data from an experiment by Torgerson (1960). For stimuli, 17 shades of neutral gray paper were used, and each was judged five times by each of 16 subjects. The stimuli were presented in random order, and the subjects rated each stimulus on an 11-point scale (0 through 10), and they were instructed to use the numerical scale as an interval scale. For one set of experiments, they judged lightness, with the larger numbers indicating more lightness, and for another set they judged darkness,

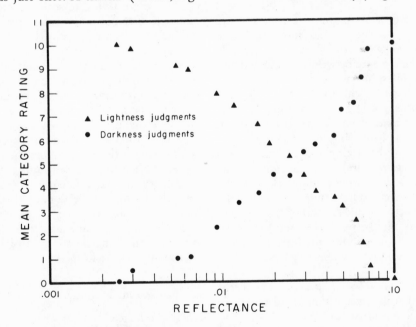

Figure 3. Results of a numerical category scaling experiment. In one case the subjects were asked to judge relative lightness, and in the other, relative darkness, each on an eleven-point scale. (After Torgerson, 1960). Courtesy of D. Van Nostrand Company, Inc.

with the larger numbers indicating more darkness. Figure 3 shows the mean category ratings as a function of reflectance, for each type of judgment. In this particular experiment, internal consistency was demonstrated by the fact that the function for the attribute of lightness is the inverse of the function for the attribute of darkness. This check, of course, is possible only where the same stimuli can be judged on two attributes which are themselves the inverse of each other.

Verbal rating scales—One last technique is worth mentioning briefly, and that is the verbal rating scale. The term "rating scale" is itself a very general term which can be used to describe any response scale used by subjects in a rating or judging task. A verbal rating scale differs from a method of equal appearing intervals or the numerical category scale only in that verbal labels are used as the responses. For example, we might have a seven-category scale for judging brightness: very very dark, very dark, dark, neutral, light, very light, very very light. If in summarizing the data we assign equally spaced numerals to these response categories, and use metric statistics, we are in effect assuming interval properties of the scale. The only essential difference between this method and other manifest-interval techniques lies in the kind of response scale used.

The usual grading scale, mentioned earlier as an example of an ordinal scale, is often treated as if it had interval properties, as if it were a verbal rating scale. This is done when arbitrary numbers are assigned to the grades for the purpose of making "grade-point" averages. The assumption is that the distance between an "A" and "B" is the same as the distance between "D" and "E"—precisely the assumption of the interval scale—when consecutive numbers are assigned to the grades.

Checks on internal consistency—Techniques of scale construction based on manifest properties of the data do not ordinarily include self-checking procedures for internal consistency as an inherent aspect of the technique. So with these techniques the internal consistency check must be provided by carrying out two or more experiments which should logically lead to the same resultant scale, either in whole or in part.

The Torgerson experiment, with judgments of lightness and of darkness, illustrates one method of providing a check on internal consistency, but obviously such a check depends both on the nature of the stimuli and on the nature of the attributes. There is, for example, no inverse attribute for pitch, for skill, or for most aptitudes.

The other easily used check on internal consistency is the one we mentioned for the equisection technique—namely, duplication of the experiment with different but overlapping ranges of stimuli. In the case of the loudness experiment we had a physical dimension which corresponded to the attribute, so we could select fixed end stimuli ahead of time and there was reasonable assurance that overlapping scale values would result. The problem is somewhat different with stimuli such as art objects, foods whose relative preference we are trying to scale, or sociability of people. Here, as we saw, the equal-appearing intervals technique is usually used, since we cannot give our subjects direct control over the stimuli. In this case an equivalent procedure to the consistency check used with equisection is possible. We can conduct subexperiments in which three or more stimuli are duplicated in different sets of stimuli. We then would have the same sort of check as before, where the scale values assigned to the stimuli are transformed so that the common ones from the different subexperiments coincide. If this can be done with three or more stimuli there is strong evidence that the interval property assumed for the responses is valid. Unfortunately this sort of internal check is seldom performed.

Latent-Interval Techniques

There are logically many ways to construct psychological scales with interval properties based on latent properties of the data—and in a sense the Coombs unfolding technique is an illustration. But in psychological scaling, essentially all techniques are based on the acceptance of manifest ordinal properties, with interval properties added by a further assumption about the statistical *distribution* of the scale values. And the common assumption is that psychological processes are distributed according to the normal distribution.

Over 100 years ago Fechner first constructed a psychological interval scale based on latent-interval properties. He integrated *jnd*'s to give a scale of sensory magnitude, using the assumption that all *jnd*'s are equal in sensation. This assumption made it possible to construct a scale with interval properties.

Thurstone (1927) extended the principle used by Fechner, to provide a much more general law. In effect Fechner had assumed that differences noted equally often constitute equal psychological differences, since a *jnd* is defined as a constant proportion of judgments that one stimulus is greater than another. But Fechner made no assumption about the distribution of the judgments. Thurstone's extension was to assume that the psychological process which leads to difference judgments is normally distributed. From this assumption psychological distance can be deduced if we know the proportion of times that one stimulus is chosen over another, since there is an invariant relation between probabilities and normal deviates or standard scores. Thus if we know the proportion of times that A is chosen over B, we can determine the interval distance between A and B by converting the proportion into the equivalent standard score from normal curve tables. Thurstone developed a fairly complete mathematical model based on this *Law of Comparative Judgment* (the name given to the normality-interval assumptions), but for our purposes, the important principle is that psychological distances with interval properties can be deduced from proportions of ordinal judgments.

Thus in all of the latent-interval techniques, the manifest data have ordinal properties and these are accepted as valid. With the assumption of the normal distribution of judgment or psychological process, interval properties are obtained for the psychological scale. The differences between the various techniques have to do with the nature of the manifest data.

Normalized ranks—The simplest procedure for obtaining a manifest-ordinal scale is to have several subjects rank order a set of stimuli. With the illustrative data of Table 1, we could then sum up the rankings to obtain generalized, or average, rank, but we pointed out that the stimuli should then be reranked to avoid the implication that the unequal numerical differences between successive sums have any interval meaning. The size of these differences can have no meaning, because only ordinal judgments were made, and we do not know the interval distance between successive ranks.

If we assume, however, that the stimuli are normally distributed in scale value, then we can construct an interval scale. The procedure to use is as follows: In our illustration we had five different stimuli to be ranked. If these stimuli are normally distributed, then our best working assumption is that each stimulus occupies 1/5 of the total continuum of possible values. In other words, the lowest ranked stimulus lies somewhere between 0 and 20 per cent of the total range of values, the second stimulus lies somewhere between 20 and 40 per cent, the third between 40 and 60 per cent, the fourth between 60 and 80 per cent, and the fifth between 80 and 100 per cent. Now we do not know exactly where each stimulus lies, but our best estimate is that it lies in the middle of its range of possible values. So we assume that the first stimulus is at the 10th percentile, the second at the 30th percentile, and so on to the last, which is at the 90th percentile. The standard score equivalent of each percentile is then determined from normal tables, and these values are accepted as our best estimate of the interval scale values. For example, the normalized rank for a rank of 1 is $+ 1.28$, which is the normal deviate equivalent of .90.

The ranks for each of the four raters in

Table 1 are shown as normalized ranks in Table 5, and now we can reasonably take the mean of these normalized ranks, since we are averaging values with interval properties. These mean normalized ranks are shown at the bottom of the table.

Since both positive and negative numbers make up the scale, it becomes hard to interpret. Often the numbers are transformed so that they are all positive. In the last line of the table this has been done, and in addition, the numbers have all been multiplied by 10, to give them more spread. In an interval scale all that we must preserve is the relative sizes of the distances between scale values, and this has been done with the transformation. The final scale is related to the original by the formula $Y = 10\,X + 11.925$.

In our example we had our subjects rate just five objects. If more objects are rated the same basic procedure is used, but the total continuum is simply divided into more steps. So, for example, if we had ten ranks, we would have divided the total range into ten equal parts, 0 to 10, 10 to 20, etc. And the midpoints of these ranges, 5, 15, 25, etc., would have been used to determine the normal deviate equivalent value. Otherwise the technique would be just as illustrated.

Normalized pair comparisons—The second technique we discussed for obtaining manifest-ordinal scales was pair comparisons, in which each object is paired with every other object in the set. A group of subjects is then required to indicate a preference for one object from each pair. The data from such a technique were shown in Table 2, where each cell shows the proportion of times each painting was chosen over each other painting. These data can be used to construct an interval scale with the normalizing assumption, if we convert each of the proportions into its equivalent standard score, and from these standard scores compute mean distances, in standard score units, between successive stimuli. Once again, as with normalized ranks, the manifest ordinal property of the data is accepted.

The rationale for the scale construction is as follows: First, consider each column in Table 6. The values in the first column show the normal deviate scores when each painting has been compared with the first painting. Since the painting against which each of seven paintings has been compared is constant for that one column, then, with the normal-interval assumption, the values in that column can be used directly as interval scale values for all of the paintings. A scale value of 0 is assigned to the first painting— the standard—quite arbitrarily, and this procedure is perfectly all right, since we are only constructing a scale with interval properties, and such a scale has no true or absolute zero point.

In a logical sense, one column of compari-

TABLE 5

THE NORMALIZED RANK PROCEDURE*

Raters	Joe	Bill	Andy	Jack	Sam
Foreman	.53	1.28	0	—.53	—1.28
Superintendent	0	.53	1.28	—1.28	—.53
Shop steward	.53	1.28	—.53	0	—1.28
Psychologist	0	.53	—.53	1.28	—1.28
Sum	1.06	3.62	.22	—.53	—4.37
Mean normalized rank	.265	.905	.055	—.132	—1.092
Transformed scale	14.575	20.975	12.475	10.600	1.000

* Each entry is the standard score equivalent of the rank given in Table 1. The transformed scale (Y) is related to the original scale (X) by the formula $Y = 10\,X + 11.925$.

son data is all that is necessary to construct the latent-interval scale. However, we could just as well use any column instead of the first, because in each column seven paintings have been compared to a single standard. In each column, however, the scale we construct would assign the value of 0 to the painting which had been used as the standard of comparison. Now, if the data were perfectly reliable, and the interval scale assumptions involved were valid, each of these eight scales would be exactly the same except for the arbitrary location of the zero point. Since the location of the zero value is quite arbitrary, we could simply change each set of scale values so that the same stimulus was given a value of 0. Then we could average the scale values for each stimulus to obtain a more general scale.

There is a major difficulty with this simple procedure, however, which is illustrated in Table 6, and that is that each column—with the eight different paintings used as standards—does not provide an actual scale value for each of the eight paintings, since in extreme cases one painting is chosen or preferred over one or two others all, or nearly all, of the time. In these cases standard scores are indeterminate. Thus we have eight different scales in the eight columns, but not all of the same stimuli are scaled in each column.

What we must do is determine the difference between each pair of adjacent stimuli by computing the average difference in scale value for all scales where both paintings of a pair had scale values. To illustrate, both paintings A and B have scale values in the first five columns, so we can obtain five estimates of the difference between A and B by using the scale values in these five columns. The average difference between scale values is, for these five columns, .592 standard score units.

In like manner, we determine the average difference in scale value between B and C, using the seven columns in which scale values occur for both of these stimuli. And so on, until we have scale value differences between all successive stimuli, the differences in each case being the mean of all the differences which occur for that pair of stimuli. These mean differences are shown at the right of Table 6.

The final scale values are then obtained by assuming the successive scale value differences as shown in the last column of Table 6 —and once again, we can shift these scale values to provide any zero point we wish. We actually can multiply the scale values as well, and there are theoretical reasons for multiplying by the square root of 2. It is probably just as well to leave the numbers in this

TABLE 6

NORMALIZED PAIR COMPARISONS, USING THE DATA FROM TABLE 2

		Paintings								Mean Difference	Scale Value
		A	B	C	D	E	F	G	H		
	A	0	−.52	−1.08	−1.55	−1.55	—	—	—		2.786
	B	.52	0	−.31	−.77	−1.18	−1.41	−1.41	—	.592	2.194
Paintings	C	1.08	.31	0	−.47	−.52	−1.08	−1.28	−1.55	.371	1.823
	D	1.55	.77	.47	0	−.47	−.36	−.92	−1.41	.392	1.431
	E	1.55	1.18	.52	.47	0	−.31	−.99	−1.28	.189	1.242
	F	—	1.41	1.08	.36	.31	0	−.36	−1.28	.276	.966
	G	—	1.41	1.28	.92	.99	.36	0	.77	.381	.585
	H	—	—	1.55	1.41	1.28	1.28	.77	0	.585	0

* The proportions were taken to be estimates of the probability that each painting would be chosen over each other painting, and the numbers here are the standard-score equivalents of these probabilities. At the right is shown the mean distance in standard score units between the paintings, and the final scale, with the least preferred painting assigned a value of zero.

form, however, since they are easily and directly interpretable back to the original proportions from which they were obtained.

The method of normalized pair comparisons provides an internal consistency check which is not possible with normalized ranks. It will be recalled that we could consider each column in Table 6 to provide an estimate of the scale values for all stimuli, but we then use the mean scale differences to obtain our final set of scale values. Each separate scale, however, should correspond to this average scale within the expected error of measurement, if the zero point of the scale is adjusted. If we use the average scale to predict each separate scale, we can convert the scale values back into expected proportions, and if these predictions do not correspond, again within error of measurement, we must reject the assumption that all scales are in fact the same. In such a case, there are many alternative models which can be used, the most common of which is to assume that the standard deviations are not equal. In other words, we keep the normality assumption, but we do not assume that the normal distribution for each stimulus has the same standard deviation. But it is not our purpose to go into this level of detail here.

Normalized category ranks—The third technique for obtaining manifest-*ordinal* scales is that of category ranks, and once again the data can be used to make a latent-*interval* scale if we make the normality assumption. The data which we will use are from Table 3, for the method of category ranks. However, data can just as well be used from the methods of equal-appearing intervals, numerical categories, or rating scales, if we assume that the only valid manifest property of the obtained data is the ordinal property.

Many techniques with different names have been suggested for making latent-interval scales based on category data. As Guilford (1954) points out, however, they are all basically the same. Saffir (1937) first used the method, basing his procedure on a technique developed by Thurstone and called the technique the method of *successive cate-*

gories. Guilford (1938) proposed a method which he called the method of *absolute scaling.* Attneave (1949) proposed what he called the method of *graded dichotomies,* and Garner and Hake (1951) described a method for constructing an *equal discriminability* scale. All of these methods, however, involve the same essential principles, depending primarily on the normality assumption to create a latent-interval scale from data with manifest-ordinal properties.

The first step in constructing a latent-interval scale is illustrated in Table 3 itself, where the lower of each pair of numbers in each cell is the cumulative proportion that each stimulus was ranked in the given category or lower. Thus these cumulative proportions must be considered to be the proportion of judgments falling below the upper category limit for each category rank. Naturally, all cumulative proportions are 1.00 for the highest category ranks, since each stimulus pattern was given a category rank by each of the 20 raters, and the proportions must sum to unity.

Now we can assume that these proportions are normally distributed, and can convert the cumulative proportions into standard scores from the normal curve tables. These values, shown in Table 7, are the assumed psychological scale values for the upper response category limits, and the last (fifth) category rank has no value because the normal curve deviate score for a proportion of 1.00 is at plus infinity.

We now have a scale value for the upper interval limit of each category rank, except in those cases where the cumulative proportion is at or near 1.00. (We have, as is customary, not used cumulative values above .95 or below .05 because of the high statistical error obtained with such proportions.) We can consider, however, that at each upper interval limit we also now have a scale value for each successive stimulus. Thus each row provides us with a set of stimulus scale values. We can obtain estimates of the average scale difference between successive stimuli from the columns in which both stimuli of the pair have actual values, and we can cumulate these average differences to obtain a final scale for the stimuli. The zero value can be assigned to any stimulus we choose. This calculation is illustrated in Table 7.

A check on internal consistency is provided in much the same manner as with normalized pair comparisons. We can use the average scale to compute the differences between stimuli at the upper interval limits, and then convert these back to cumulative proportions. Then we can compare these with the original proportions and decide whether the same psychological scale was operating for all stimuli. If not, then other models can be used, especially those which assume unequal standard deviations.

Manifest-Ratio Techniques

Any technique based on manifest-ratio properties of a subject's or rater's responses must make the parallel assumptions that the attribute in question actually has ratio properties and that subjects can directly perceive and describe these properties. Specifically, the ratio property requires that the attribute has an absolute zero, since without an absolute zero an expression of ratios is quite meaningless. . . .

In some form, then, manifest-ratio techniques require that a subject express a relation between two or more stimulus objects in a ratio form. The objects need not, of course, be what we would ordinarily call stimuli but could be people, although the ratio techniques have rarely been used with such objects.

Ratio production—Probably the oldest technique of this sort is ratio production. The method has frequently been called "fractionation," since a subject is required to produce one stimulus magnitude which is some specified fraction of another, but since the subject can just as well be asked to produce a stimulus which is a constant multiple of the other, the broader term, ratio production, is preferable.

As we have just indicated, the basic procedure is to give the subject a standard stimulus which presumably has the attribute under consideration, and then require that the subject produce another stimulus which bears some constant stated ratio to the standard. This method is, of course, similar to equisection in that the subject produces a stimulus (he could even produce a series of stimuli) which has some stated numerical relation to a standard. As with equisection, the method is amenable only to those psychological attributes in which there is an easily manipulable physical dimension which is a counterpart to the psychological attribute. Loudness has been the most frequently used attribute, and we shall use it to illustrate the method.

In its logically simplest form, we would start with a loud standard stimulus and require a subject to produce a stimulus which

TABLE 7

NORMALIZED CATEGORY RANKS, USING THE DATA FROM TABLE 3*

| Category | Stimulus Patterns | | | | | |
	1	2	3	4	19	20
1	00	−.25	−.13	−.52	−1.28	—
2	.84	.67	.25	.13	−1.28	−1.28
3	1.04	1.28	.67	.67	−.67	−.84
4	—	1.28	1.28	1.04	.38	.25
5	—	—	—	—	—	—
Mean difference		.060	.287	.187	.100	
Scale value	0	.060	.347	.534	10.310	10.410

* In this case we have used the cumulative proportions to give standard-score values.

is half as loud. If we arbitrarily assign a numeral, say, 100, to the standard, then the
numeral 50 would be assigned to that stimulus which the subject says is half as loud.
Then we would use that stimulus as a standard, and ask the subject to produce one
which is half as loud as it, and we would then
assign the numeral 25 to it. And so on to a
loudness of 12.5, 6.25, etc.

Actually, this logically simple procedure is
rarely used because of the possible experimental biases which could occur with the
successive decrease in loudness. So the usual
procedure, illustrated in Figure 4, is to use a

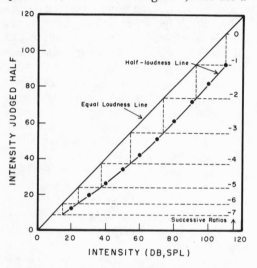

Figure 4. The ratio production method, as applied to half-loudness judgments. The points
show the mean half-loudness setting for each
value of sound intensity. When 110 db was presented, the mean setting was 95 db, etc. The line
drawn through these points enables us to estimate what would be the value set as half of
any given sound intensity. The dotted lines are
used to estimate the expected values of successive halvings, which are used to construct the
scale of Figure 5. Courtesy of D. Van Nostrand
Company, Inc.

series of fixed standards, say every 10 db.
Then each subject adjusts another stimulus
to sound half as loud as each standard. The
standard stimuli are used in random or counterbalanced order, and each of several sub-

jects may make several productions for each
standard. These various values are then
averaged to yield an average curve showing
the relation between the intensity of the
standard and the intensity judged to be half
as loud. This is the experimentally obtained
curve shown in Figure 4.

The psychological scale of loudness is then
constructed by interpolating to obtain successive half-loudness intensities. To illustrate,
we can arbitrarily assign a value of 100 to an
intensity of 110 db, and then we read from
the function in Figure 4 the intensity which
is judged, on the average, to be half as loud.
This intensity is assigned a scale value of 50,
and then we determine, by interpolation,
what intensity was judged half as loud as it.
That intensity is given a value of 25, and it
then is entered to determine what intensity
was judged half as loud as, etc., to intensities
as low as were experimentally used. The
loudness scale thus obtained, as a function of
intensity, is shown in Figure 5.

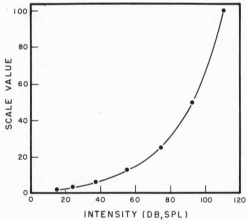

Figure 5. A loudness scale constructed from
the data of Figure 4, assuming half-loudness
judgments reflect halving of subjective intensity.
The upper point, at 110 db, is called 100. Then
the next point, set as one half of 110 db, is
plotted at 50, etc. (After Garner, 1954a). Courtesy of D. Van Nostrand Company, Inc.

The kinds of internal consistency checks which can be used with this procedure are primarily concerned with the ability of the subjects to use the ratio numbers correctly. We could, for example, run exactly this same experiment except that the subject is required to produce a stimulus twice as loud; or he could be required to produce stimuli one-third as loud, or even three times as loud. Each of these procedures, of course, should lead to the same loudness scale if subjects use the numbers correctly.

Magnitude estimation—With the ratio production technique, the subject is given a numerical value and is required to adjust stimuli to satisfy the criterion. With magnitude estimation, as with the manifest-interval techniques of equal-appearing intervals, numerical category scales, and rating scales, the stimuli are given and the subject is required to indicate, in this case always numerically, the relations between the stimuli.

There are two magnitude estimation procedures which can be used. The first is simply to present one stimulus at a time and require the subject to indicate its numerical value, with any modulus or unit of measurement he chooses. This procedure is a direct numerical rating procedure, and the scale values are simply the mean numerical values produced. The ratio properties of the scale depend entirely on the assumption that ratio properties were in fact used by the subjects.

The second procedure is to present one stimulus as a standard and assign to it a numerical value beforehand, which becomes the modulus, or unit of measure. Then other stimuli are presented, and the subject is required to state what numerical value should be assigned to each, given the standard modulus. The standard stimulus can be presented each time that another comparison stimulus is presented, or it may be presented only occasionally.

In order to provide a check on internal consistency, it is preferable to use at least two different standard stimuli, either with the same or different numerical modulus. Table 8 shows some illustrative data in which two different standard stimuli were used, each with the same numerical modulus. The stimuli were weights which were lifted. The values shown are the mean numerical values given by the subjects for each of the other weights.

TABLE 8

RESULTS OF A MAGNITUDE ESTIMATION EXPERIMENT IN SUBJECTIVE WEIGHT, USING A STANDARD*

Weight	Standard 90 g	Standard 190 g	Converted 190 g scale
20	10		
30	19		
40	29		
60	54		
70	68	21	68
→ 90	100	31	100
102	120	38	123
110	140	43	139
120	160	49	158
160	250	76	245
180	300	92	297
→ 190	320	100	323
220	400	128	413
280		190	613
350		260	839

* The first data column shows the median number assigned to each weight listed at the left, when a weight of 90 g was assigned the number 100. The next column shows the median number assigned to each weight when the standard was 190 g, again called 100. The final column shows the transformed scale from the 190 g data. Each number was multiplied by 100/31 to get a new value where 90 g again has the value 100. (After Stevens and Galanter, 1957.)

Each of these two sets of data can be used to construct a psychological scale of weight, or we can convert both of them to the same numerical modulus to construct a single composite scale. We simply multiply (or divide) all the numbers obtained with the second standard so that the numerical value of the second standard corresponds to its value when judged against the first standard. A ratio scale allows any multiplicative transformation, so this change is quite valid. Note, however, that we are not free to add or subtract a constant from either scale, since the ratio scale does not allow such a transformation. If we had to do so in order to make the two scales agree, we would have evidence that the numbers were not being used as ratios.

These two scales, transformed to the same-numerical modulus, are shown in Figure 6, and in our particular example, the two scales agree very well.

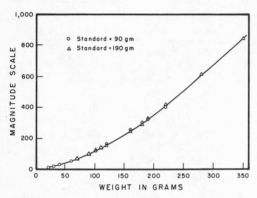

Figure 6.   A scale of subjective weight, based on magnitude estimation from Table 8. Two sets of points are from the two different standards, and the overlap of the two sets is a check on consistency. Courtesy of D. Van Nostrand Company, Inc.

The constant sum method—Metfessel (1947) suggested still a third technique for obtaining ratio scales, and this technique has come to be called the constant sum method. This technique is analogous to the method of pair comparisons, except that subjects make ratio rather than ordinal judgments.

The experimental situation is one in which we have a fixed number of stimuli which we want to scale on some attribute, and since the stimuli remain constant, it is not necessary that there be a physical dimension corresponding to the attribute. Each stimulus is paired with each other to form all possible pairs. The pairs are then presented to a subject one at a time, and he is required to assign numerical values to the two stimulus objects

of the pair. The restriction on his numerical assignment is that the sum of the two numbers used must be some constant stated by the experimenter, usually 100. Thus, to illustrate, a subject may say that stimulus A receives a value of 60, and B a value of 40. Now if a subject can divide a fixed sum this way, it implies that he can form ratios, and we are free to deduce that the numerical ratio between the scale values for stimuli A and B is 1.5 to 1. The subject makes such a judgment for every pair and he may make several judgments of each pair. In addition, several subjects will be used to give generality to the scale.

There are alternative ways of treating the data, and it is possible to use the data in their direct numerical form. Torgerson (1958), however, has suggested a procedure which is arithmetically very simple, and which keeps the rationale of the procedure quite similar to the treatment of data with normalized pair comparisons.

The essence of the procedure lies in the relation between logarithms and ratios. If we take logarithms of the numerical values on a ratio scale, then equal logarithmic differences are equivalent to what were originally equal ratios. Thus a series of numerical values on a ratio scale of 1, 2, 4, 8, and 16 become in logarithms, 0, 0.3, 0.6, 0.9, and 1.2. So if we convert our ratio numerals obtained from the data into logarithms, we can deal with numbers in which a constant difference always means a constant ratio, regardless of the actual values of the original numbers.

Our procedure, then, is to take each pair of numbers which a subject produces, express the numbers as a single ratio, and then convert this ratio into its equivalent logarithm. Thus the values of 60 and 40 assigned to A and to B, are expressed as a ratio of 1.5 to 1, with a logarithmic equivalent of 0.176. This value then represents the logarithmic *difference* between A and B, which is equivalent to the ratio.

For each pair of stimuli, we obtain the mean of all such logarithmic differences, and these means are entered into a table in Table 9. The value of 0 occurs on the diagonal be-

TABLE 9

THE CONSTANT SUM METHOD*

	Bill	Joe	Andy	Jack	Sam
Bill	0	−.71	−.66	−.88	−1.17
Joe	.71	0	−.15	−.36	−.59
Andy	.66	.15	0	−.07	−.22
Jack	.88	.36	.07	0	−.18
Sam	1.17	.59	.22	.18	0
Mean difference	.606	.182	.122	.206	
Log scale	1.116	.510	.328	.206	0
Ratio scale	13.06	3.24	2.12	1.67	1

* Each worker was paired with each other worker and the raters were to divide 100 so as to reflect the ratio of actual performance. The ratios were converted into logarithms, and the entry in each cell is the mean of the logs, reflecting the average ratio for the worker listed at the top to the worker listed at the side of the table. The mean difference between the columns is then made into a scale by successive addition (as in an interval scale), and the final scale is the antilog of each value.

cause it is assumed that if each stimulus were compared to itself the numerical values would be 50 and 50, giving a ratio of 1.0 and a logarithm of 0.

Now this table can be interpreted exactly as Table 6 was. Each column of the table gives a perfectly valid psychological scale, in which all stimuli have been compared with a single standard, but the standard is different in each column. Except for error of measurement, these scales should all be the same, although the zero point is different for each scale because of the different standard stimulus used. This is then an interval scale in logarithmic form. A change in the zero point here amounts to multiplication by a constant.

To obtain an average scale, we can, just as with normalized pair comparisons, compute the average difference between scale values for all pairs of stimuli, regardless of the standard. If some stimuli received all 100 points when compared to some others, then we have no usable scale difference, because the ratio is infinity. So we obtain the average only for the real pair differences, and then add up these differences to get the complete scale in logarithmic form. All that is now required is to reconvert these values back to numerical form. We can, of course, multiply these numbers by any constant value we choose.

Our internal consistency check lies in the fact that each stimulus was used both as a standard and as a comparison for every other stimulus. In other words, each stimulus serves as a modulus, and a change in modulus should not change the scale except for a multiplier constant. If the scales are not the same, then we know that our assumption of ratio properties is not valid.

A Latent-Ratio Technique

A scale with more powerful measurement properties presumes all the properties of the less powerful scale. Thus an interval scale also has the ordinal property, and a ratio scale has interval properties as well as ordinal properties. This fact suggests that a logical procedure for checking on the internal consistency of any scale is to show that the scale obtained is consistent with properties of a lower-order scale. To be more specific, suppose we have constructed a loudness scale with any of the three manifest-ratio techniques. It is quite possible to obtain a scale which is consistent within the same framework of measurement, but which might not be consistent with properties of a scale obtained with, say, a manifest-interval or a latent-interval technique. Since there are major differences in these techniques, particularly when latent procedures are involved, we might not always expect consistency between them, and to some extent the lack of consistency can be justified on the basis of the fundamentally different assumptions involved.

However, many of the manifest techniques are basically the same, and are applied to interval or to ratio scaling problems with the only change being the assumed ability of the subject to make use of scales with higher (but inclusive) properties. Thus the ratio production technique is exactly the same as the equisection technique except that in the latter case the subject is instructed to produce equal intervals, while in the former he is instructed to produce a given ratio. In similar fashion, the magnitude estimation technique is the same as the numerical category techniques (and even the method of equal appearing intervals, or rating scales).

In these cases of analogous techniques it would be reasonable to assume that a scale based on the ratio technique could accurately predict the scale based on its equivalent interval technique. Rarely, however, do these analogous procedures lead to the same psychological scale (see Stevens and Galanter, 1957), a fact which must raise a serious question concerning the validity of the manifest procedures. When such failures of agreement occur, we do not, of course, know which technique is at fault, or whether either technique is valid.

It is possible, however, as Stevens (1951) has shown logically, to produce a scale with ratio properties which does not require the same strong assumptions about the manifest properties of the responses as are necessary with manifest-ratio techniques. Thus a ratio scale can be constructed based on latent properties of data.

A technique was developed and used by Garner (1954a) for doing just this with loudness. First, we construct two loudness scales, the first based on ratio production (specifically, fractionation to half loudness), and the second based on equisection. Now, however, we do not make the assumption that the ratio of half was in fact used by the subjects, but

rather make the much weaker assumption that the ratio was the same for all judgments, but of unknown value. With this assumption, we can still determine a loudness function, but we do not know the ratio that was used. This function will be related to the true (latent) loudness function as

$$L = ab^x$$

where L is the true loudness function, a is an arbitrary unit of measurement, b is the value of the unknown ratio, and x is the value of the successive ratio. We can assign any value we choose to a, so we are left with a single unknown value on the right of this equation.

From the data of the equisection experiment we can also determine the loudness function except that we do not know the value of the intercept constant—the location of the zero point. In equation form, we know that

$$L = c(Y - d)$$

where L is as above, c is an arbitrary unit of measurement, Y is the loudness value assigned from the interval data, d the unknown intercept constant.

Now in reality we have only two unknown terms, the value of the ratio from the fractionation experiment and the value of the intercept from the equisection data. But we have two independent sets of data, and we can thus estimate these two unknown values so as to lead to the same loudness scale. We need not here go into the details of the arithmetic procedure used to provide the estimates, but what is important is that these estimates must satisfy the condition of a single loudness function. Thus this procedure, as with the Guttman and the Coombs techniques, has the check on internal consistency as its primary requirement, and a psychological scale is not formed unless the internal consistency check has shown the validity of the assumed attribute.

There have been relatively few attempts at using latent scaling techniques to construct ratio scales of psychological attributes. Michels (1954) has published a scale of brightness based on fractionation judgments, and Michels and Doser (1955) have done the same for a loudness scale. But their techniques, which we shall discuss at greater length a bit later, are more concerned with theorizing about the nature of the scale than with developing a method for constructing one.

Other Measurement Techniques

The problem of measurement in psychology is ubiquitous. To discuss techniques of psychological scaling requires considerable arbitrary selection, since the logical measurement problems associated with what we have called scaling occur in other areas of psychology as well.

Psychologists measure such things as intelligence, abilities, skills, attitudes, interests, and so on. All of these can be considered problems in the measurement of attributes, and yet there are some differences which led us to exclude them from our discussion.

We have discussed problems where there is little question about the existence of a psychological attribute. Our concern has been with how one would determine the scale properties of an attribute and then arrive at a set of numerals to assign to objects which elicit the attribute to a greater or lesser extent. Furthermore, we have restricted ourselves to those cases where the attribute can be defined as a single continuum.

We have not discussed measurement of such things as intelligence and ability, because these are usually defined in terms of multiple tasks where the measure makes no pretense of having scale properties assignable to an attribute. For example, a final examination in a course in psychology will have many items, and the final score will be the sum of the items correct. But all items do not measure the same attribute, and in fact most examinations are constructed to ensure that they do not, by deliberately including items that are uncorrelated. Such tests make the problems of measurement no less difficult and intriguing (see Gulliksen, 1950), but they are simply of a different kind.

On the other hand, many highly sophisti-

cated measurement techniques are concerned primarily with the establishment of the existence of underlying continua, or attributes. Factor analysis as a technique, for example, is less concerned with the measurement properties of an attribute than in discovering how many attributes are exhibited in a given number of persons and tests. The Lazarsfeld technique of *latent structure analysis* has been omitted for this reason also (perhaps incorrectly); it is more concerned with establishing the existence of attributes than with measuring their amounts (see Lazarsfeld's Chapter 10 in Stouffer, *et al.*, 1950; Torgerson, 1958).

THE RELATION OF RESPONSE TO ATTRIBUTE

We have discussed several techniques of psychological scaling—techniques which are quite different in procedure, but which differ also in the basic philosophy underlying them. Does it make no difference which technique we choose to use in scaling a particular attribute? Some psychologists would argue that any technique can lead to a scale which is valid, as long as we state what the particular operations were which led to it. But such a position is essentially defeatist, since it refuses to face the problem of the nature of the attribute itself, and the relation of the obtained scale to the attribute.

In particular, the difference in underlying philosophy between the manifest and the latent techniques is fundamental. The manifest techniques rely on the ability of a subject to describe his experience of an attribute using numbers with the proper measurement properties. The latent techniques make no such assumption, but on the contrary assume only that there is an attribute which affects the responses, although not in a simple one-to-one fashion.

Actually, there are many theoretical positions which have been taken on the relation of the manifest response to the attribute, and in this section we will discuss some of these positions. While such a discussion need not necessarily be part of a chapter on psychological scaling, the choice of technique cannot but depend on the assumptions which the experimenter makes concerning the relation of response to attribute. So, in a sense, these assumptions are part and parcel of the scaling problem.

To classify various theoretical positions, we will use Figure 7 as a framework to discuss

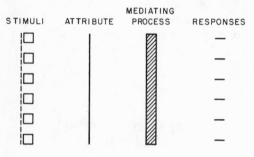

Figure 7. Schematic representation of some logical problems in psychological scaling. Scaling requires implicit or explicit assumptions about each of the steps represented. Courtesy of D. Van Nostrand Company, Inc.

the problem. We can consider four processes as critical for scaling an attribute. First, of course, there are the objects with which the attribute is presumed to correspond, but the attribute is not identical with the object. The object will have many properties, and even if it has a closely related physical dimension as one of its properties, there is no necessary reason why the scale values of the attribute should correspond to those of the physical dimension.

Second, we have the attribute itself. It exists as an abstraction from the object, but an abstraction which is directly experienced in most cases by a human subject or observer. It is the scale values of this attribute which we seek in psychological scaling, and as we have mentioned before, one of our major problems is to determine what measurement properties exist in this attribute. To ask this question is quite different from asking how the attribute is related to a physical dimension, or to the responses, because we want to know about the attribute itself, and we cannot determine whether, for example, the at-

tribute has a true or absolute zero by showing that it is related to a physical dimension which has an absolute zero.

Third, in Figure 7, we have a mediating process—some process which intervenes between the attribute and the response which reflects it. We have used the term "mediating process" as a general one, and in specific cases we might choose to call it an intervening variable, or hypothetical construct. But whatever it is called, we must consider the possibility of its operation. And more importantly, we must consider the possibility that it adds its own characteristics in relating the response to the attribute. In other words, if there is a mediating process, and we want to find out what the nature of the attribute is, then we will have to learn something about the nature of the mediating process as well.

Last, there is the response process itself, but by no means is this the least of our problems. If a response must be used to indicate the properties of the attribute, then we must be concerned about the properties of the response process itself. To illustrate, if the attribute has interval properties, then the response must also have at least these properties in order to have it correctly indicate the properties of the attribute. And it is not a foregone conclusion that the properties of numbers, as used by a human subject, necessarily have the ratio properties of the scale of number.

As we have mentioned before, nearly all psychologists seem to agree that responses can at least indicate ordinal properties of an attribute; that whatever distortions might be introduced by a mediating process or by peculiarities of the response process itself will be distortions of interval and ratio properties, not of the ordinal properties. Thus most theoretical positions have been primarily concerned with the interval and ratio properties of the attribute as evinced by the responses.

Response as Direct Indicator of Attribute

The simplest assumption which can be made about the relation between response and attribute is that the response directly and correctly indicates properties of the attribute. If a mediating process is assumed to exist it is also assumed to be bypassed or short-circuited by the response process. To say that this assumption is the simplest is not to say that it is the least complicated, because it is one of the most difficult to prove. Consequently, its validity is ordinarily of the face variety, i.e., it is valid by experimenter's fiat.

In recent years Stevens (1957)—and some of his coworkers—has been the major proponent of this position, although he has been concerned almost exclusively with psychophysical attributes, i.e., those sensory attributes for which there is a reasonable equivalent physical continuum such as brightness, loudness, etc. He has specifically argued for the use of manifest-ratio scaling techniques, and while in principle he accepts any of these methods as valid, his own recent work (Stevens, 1959) suggests a strong preference for the method of magnitude estimation.

This primary emphasis on a specific technique leaves some open questions, since we would expect that all techniques of the same logical class should be equally capable of leading to the same psychological scale. In other words, there should at least be generality with regard to technique.

Even further, as we pointed out earlier, a ratio scale should correctly predict interval properties; and if we accept the validity of manifest-ratio techniques, then we should also expect the equivalent manifest-interval techniques to provide the same psychological scale within the limits of the technique. But the manifest-interval techniques do not provide the required cross check.

The reason for this difficulty may lie in the problem of the nature and properties of the response process itself, since it cannot accurately indicate properties of an attribute unless it is used accurately, with properties at least as powerful as those of the attribute. We saw in Figure 3 that Torgerson's data showed an inverse relation between scales of darkness and scales of lightness when numerical category scaling was used. Torgerson also obtained judgments with the method of magnitude estimation. For both darkness and

lightness he obtained a scale quite different from that obtained with numerical category scaling, but the logarithm of the magnitude estimation scale was linearly related to the numerical category scale. Furthermore, the scales of lightness and of darkness obtained with magnitude estimations were related in a reciprocal rather than an inverse fashion. These results of Torgerson make clear that human subjects do not use numerical scales in the same way when they assign numerical categories rather than magnitude estimations. Furthermore, if we accept the results from each method on its own merits, we would have to conclude that the attribute of darkness is the inverse of the attribute of lightness in one case, while it is the reciprocal in the other.

These results make it clear that the validity of the required assumptions for manifest-ratio or for manifest-interval techniques are in considerable doubt. The minimum checks on the validity of the assumptions do not provide favorable results, and we can only conclude that it is not self-evident that the manifest techniques are valid.

Response as Indicator of Mediating Process

Most modern psychologists assume that the response is an indicator of some intervening variable or mediating process. Some, however, assume that the response is a relatively direct indicator of the intermediate process, and others that the response may be quite indirectly related. We shall discuss this first class of theories now, and the others later.

Correlated process—One of the most straightforward theories that the response is related to a mediating process states that the response is directly related to some process which is itself correlated with the attribute. There are many instances of this point of view in the literature on scaling of skills, attitudes, etc. For example, the halo effect is a description of the tendency to rate persons on one attribute according to their previous ratings on another attribute. De Soto (1961) has emphasized this tendency of people to rate other people or objects in a consistent simple ordering.

More specifically, again in the realm of psychophysical continua, Warren (1958) developed the *physical correlate* theory of judgment. Basically, he argues that the responses made by subjects do not indicate the properties of the attribute itself, but reflect instead the properties of a correlated physical dimension, with which the subject has had experience in using numbers.

He argues, for example, that where subjects have had direct experience in using a numerical scale, their manifest-ratio responses will be linearly related to the underlying physical continuum. Thus judged heaviness will be directly related to the physical scale of weight, because we all have experienced pounds and ounces. He presents evidence to show that this is so when the contaminating factor of size is ruled out. In like manner, judgments of sweetness will be directly related to physical concentration of the sweetener, since people have had experience with amounts of sugar. And judgments of distance or length will be directly related to the physical dimension for the same reason.

Most people have had no direct experience with the physical dimension of intensity, and thus cannot judge attributes such as brightness or loudness directly. But there is a physical dimension closely related to loudness and brightness with which people have had considerable experience, and that is distance. So Warren argues that a judgment of half-loudness or half-brightness is really a judgment of twice the equivalent distance, and presents data to show that judgment of brightness or loudness, and distance are related. In other words, a subject says that a given sound is half as loud as another, when its source seems twice as far away.

The evidence which Warren presents (see Warren, Sersen, and Pores, 1958, and Warren and Poulton, 1960) is convincing, and certainly suggests that subjects can *learn* to use numerals with ratio properties if they learn them along with a physical dimension which in fact has those properties. Whether they can ever transfer this skill to descriptions of an attribute with which they have had no direct numerical experience remains an open question.

Interacting process—Another point of view toward the relation of response to attribute is that there is a mediating process which constantly interacts with the attribute, so that the response to any stimulus object is a joint function of the attribute and the mediating process. While Helson and Michels did not describe their theoretical positions in exactly this form, it is one way of considering their approach.

Helson (1948, see also 1959) originally formulated his *adaptation-level* theory with primary concern for determining what stimulus conditions led to a judgment of "neutral" with a verbal rating scale technique. He argued that the adaptation level at any given instant was a weighted geometric mean of all stimuli, past and present, and their effects on the attribute being judged. The adaptation level will be constantly changing as new stimulus objects are experienced. The neutral judgment, whether the verbal label on a rating scale, or the middle value on a numerical scale, will always correspond to this adaptation level.

But Helson further argued that all other judgments are made relative to this adaptation level. He was concerned not with just the neutral judgment, but with all verbal or numerical judgments over the entire length of the scale. In other words he stated a theory regarding the relation between the responses and the attribute. This relation was made mathematically much more explicit by Michels and Helson (1949), who derived a relation between responses and stimulus intensity which shows a formal correspondence to Fechner's law, but with this important difference: Fechner assumed that the origin (in the mathematical sense) of the sensory attribute was the absolute threshold, while Michels and Helson argue that the origin is the adaptation level. More specifically, they argued that the first response category (on a categorical scale) corresponded to a stimulus magnitude 1-kth below the adaptation level (where k is the number of judgment categories below neutral), and that all other responses were adjusted to satisfy this requirement.

Michels (1954) carried this development further by interpreting fractionation judgments of brightness along the same lines, and later (Michels and Doser, 1955) by doing the same for loudness judgments. This is not the place to go into the exact mathematical formulation which Michels used, but the point of view expressed by Helson and by Michels about the relation between the response and the attribute is an important one.

It should be remembered that the adaptation level is constantly changing, and that it will be different for every set of experimental conditions. Thus to argue that the response is always relative to the adaptation level is to say that there is no invariant relation between response and stimulus object, or the underlying physical continuum. We can express this position either by arguing that the attribute scale is not stable, or by stating that the adaptation level is a mediating process which constantly interacts with the attribute (or possibly with the response continuum) so that we can never experimentally obtain an invariant relation between stimulus and response.

Certainly this relativistic position with regard to psychological scaling has considerable experimental backing, since most experiments on scaling do not show an invariant relation between response and the underlying physical dimension. Garner (1954b), for example, has shown that fractionation judgments obtained with the method of constant stimuli were almost completely dependent on the range of the comparison stimuli presented, i.e., on the context of the stimuli presented for judgment. It could still be possible, however, that there is a meaningful stable attribute, and that our problem is to determine what its properties are by attempting to carry out experimental operations which can take these response and judgment characteristics into account.

Response as an Indirect Indicator of Attribute

The third major position taken concerning the relation of response to attribute is that the response does not directly reflect properties of the attribute at all, even through a mediating process, but rather that the response is only indirectly related to the attribute. Thus we do not assume that the numerical properties of the response indicate the numerical properties of the attribute.

Essentially all latent techniques make this assumption. With normalized pair comparisons, for example, the subjects are not even required to make more than an ordinal judgment. And with normalized category ranks, even if the subjects actually used an interval response, this property is not assumed to hold when the scale values are determined. For example, subjects can use the numerical category scaling method, but the experimenter then assumes only the ordinal property in constructing his scale.

Even the technique which Garner (1954a) used to construct a loudness scale from equisection and fractionation judgments dropped the assumption that the stated numerical ratio for the fractionation settings was the true ratio.

Clearly, if the numerical properties of the responses are not considered adequate to reflect accurately the properties of the attribute, some assumptions must be made in order to get numerical properties back into the scale, and herein lies the crux of the problem with these indirect and latent techniques. When such assumptions are made, they must be validated before we can reasonably accept the psychological scale as meaningful. With a technique such as normalized ranks, no means is provided for checking on the validity of the normal assumption; but with most of the other techniques, such procedures are available. With normalized pair comparisons, for example, the ability to use the average scale to check back on each individual scale makes it possible to show when the normal assumption does not apply.

In a sense, these techniques aim to provide scale values for an attribute which is really a hypothetical construct. It may or may not "exist," but its assumed existence, with the stated properties, often allows one to integrate a large amount of data.

A SUMMARY EVALUATION

We have been unable to avoid evaluative comments both about the techniques we have discussed and about the various theoretical positions regarding the relation between response and attribute. It might be well, however, by way of a summary, to state explicitly what we consider to be the criteria by which techniques should be evaluated, and some opinions about the techniques.

A psychological scale, and even the attribute itself, is a concept, one which the experimenter uses because it provides meaning and generality, and it allows a larger body of data or facts to be integrated into fewer working principles. The whole role of such concepts in a science revolves around the idea of generality. Science does not search simply for data, or even for facts. Rather, it searches for facts which have some degree of generality, so that we do not have as many facts as there are possible events in the world. Generality can exist for many different kinds of things, and here is where we must look in evaluating the techniques: In how many different ways do the scales provide generality? While there are many different things over which we could expect generality, there are several which are of primary importance in evaluating scaling techniques.

Time—At a minimum a psychological scale must be invariant across time, but we have little problem in this regard, since most techniques which have survived have shown reasonable invariance when the experiment is simply repeated at another time.

Subjects—Once again, there is little difference between the techniques in this regard. Most of them make provision for obtaining data from several different subjects, so that we can be reasonably assured of invariance across a specified population.

Objects—We would like to find psychological scales which hold for all the stimuli or objects which are presumed to contain the attribute. That is to say the scale should be invariant in its properties regardless of the particular stimulus objects used to determine the scale.

In this regard, the manifest techniques show a real weakness. In fact, this is the real essence of the Helson and Michels position, that under changed stimulus conditions the manifest response itself will change, even for the same stimuli. Thus the scale of loudness we obtain with the fractionation technique depends on the particular stimuli which the subject encounters (Michels and Doser, 1955, and Garner, 1954*b*).

On the other hand, Jones (1960) has shown that the method of successive intervals (normalized category ranks) is invariant even when different specific stimuli are used in establishing the scale. He compared this method to manifest-interval techniques, but his conclusion might well be extended to other manifest techniques. Jones further showed invariance of the latent technique with changes in the actual response continuum used.

Method—In an earlier section we remarked that generality should be established with regard to responses, but in a broader sense we need to require generality with regard to method. A particular method usually specifies a class of responses, and while we can change the actual numerical values within the same basic method, we are more interested in generality across classes of responses rather than just across different possible numerical values.

Of greatest concern is that a psychological scale should be invariant with regard to methods which are logically equivalent, or where one method implies the possibility of another. If subjects can make ratio judgments, then they should also be able to make interval judgments with regard to the same attribute. But as we have seen we do not obtain the same psychological scale when these different techniques are used. It is in fact this very difficulty which has led many experimenters to search for the one "correct" technique. But a scale which is unique to a particular method is a concept so narrowly defined that it can have little general utility.

Garner (1958) has specifically argued for the use of a latent scale of loudness based on the discriminability criterion for exactly these reasons, since the criterion involved in most of the latent techniques has much greater generality from one method to another. Jones (1960) has supported this argument for stimulus materials which are not of the psychophysical variety. Actually, psychological scales based on latent properties of data show more correspondence to scales based on manifest-interval techniques than these do to scales based on manifest-ratio techniques.

Thus the available evidence suggests that the latent scales have greater generality than do the manifest scales, particularly those manifest scales which assume the ability of subjects to use ratio properties. Perhaps part of the reason lies in a remark we made earlier to the effect that the latent techniques require special assumptions; but the requirement of these assumptions is sufficiently obvious that most experimenters go to great pains to establish their validity.

In the ideal case, then, a scale should have generality over time, subjects, objects which elicit the attribute, and method. As we have suggested, the last, the problem of generality over different methods, is at present the greatest stumbling block to the development of psychological scaling. When we pointed out that the latent procedures seem to provide somewhat greater generality than the manifest techniques, we dodged a very real problem. We were unwilling to say that the techniques were more successful because they reflected actual processes inside people; that they really reflected the metric properties of attributes. We were unwilling to say this because we do not know whether the statement is true or not.

Ideally, a scale which has the greatest generality is the one that has the greatest correspondence with the internal attributes and mediating processes. Such a scale could only grow from a theory about how people make judgments about their experience, when the theory is applied to the procedure used in constructing the scale. It would be unfair to state that such a theory does not exist; the normality assumption used in most of the latent scaling procedures is really the first step toward such a theory. Lately many theories have been advanced about different aspects of the judgment process. So far little work has been done toward applying these theories to problems of scale construction. Meanwhile, as we have seen, many useful procedures have been developed for the psychologist to use if he has need to measure psychological processes.

REFERENCES

Abelson, R. P.
1960 "Scales derived by consideration of variance components in multi-way tables." In Psychological Scaling (Gulliksen, H., and Messick, S., eds.) New York: John Wiley & Sons, Inc.

Attneave, F.
1949 "A method of graded dichotomies for the scaling of judgments." Psychological Review 56:334–340.

Coombs, C. H.
1950 "Psychological scaling without a unit of measurement." Psychological Review 57:145–158.

De Soto, C. B.
1961 "The predilection for single orderings." Journal of Abnormal and Social Psychology 62:16–23.

Garner, W. R.
1954a "A technique and a scale for loudness measurement." Journal of the Acoustical Society of America 26:73–88.
1954b "Context effects and the validity of loudness scales." Journal of Experimental Psychology 48:218–224.

1958 "Advantages of the discriminability criterion for a loudness scale." Journal of the Acoustical Society of America 30:1005–1012.

Garner, W. R., and H. W. Hake.
1951 "The amount of information in absolute judgments." Psychological Review 58:446–459.

Garner, W. R., H. W. Hake, and C. W. Eriksen.
1956 "Operationism and the concept of perception." Psychological Review 63: 149–159.

Green, B. F.
1954 "Attitude measurement." In G. Lindzey (ed.), Handbook of Social Psychology. Reading, Mass.: Addison-Wesley Publishing Company.

Guilford, J. P.
1938 "The computation of psychological values from judgments in absolute categories." Journal of Experimental Psychology 22:34–42.
1954 Psychometric Methods. 2nd ed. New York: McGraw-Hill Book Company, Inc.

Gulliksen, H.
1950 Theory of Mental Tests. New York: John Wiley & Sons, Inc.

Guttman, L.
1950 Measurement and Prediction. (Stouffer, S. A., et al.) Chaps. 2, 3, 6, 8, and 9. Princeton, New Jersey: Princeton University Press.

Helson, H.
1948 "Adaptation-level as a basis for a quantitative theory of frames of reference." Psychological Review 55:297–313.
1959 "Adaptation-Level Theory." In Psychology: A Study of a Science. Vol. I. (Koch, S., ed.) New York: McGraw-Hill Book Company, Inc.

Jones, L. V.
1960 "Some invariant findings under the method of successive intervals." In Psychological Scaling (Gulliksen, H., and Messick, S., eds.) New York: John Wiley & Sons, Inc.

Kuffler, S. W., R. FitzHugh, and H. B. Barlow.
1957 "Maintained activity in the cat's retina in light and darkness." Journal of General Physiology 40:683–702.

Metfessel, M.
1947 "A proposal for quantitative reporting of comparative judgments." Journal of Psychology 24:229–235.

Michels, W. C.
1954 "An interpretation of the bril scale of subjective brightness." Journal of the Optical Society of America 44:70–74.

Michels, W. C., and B. T. Doser.
1955 "Rating scale method for comparative loudness measurements." Journal of the Acoustical Society of America 27: 1173–1180.

Michels, W. C., and H. Helson.
1949 "A reformulation of the Fechner law in terms of adaptation-level applied to rating-scale data." American Journal of Psychology 62:355–368.

Saffir, M. A.
1937 "A comparative study of scales constructed by three psychophysical methods." Psychometrika 2:179–198.

Stevens, S. S.
1951 "Mathematics, measurement, and psychophysics." In S. S. Stevens (ed.), Handbook of Experimental Psychology. New York: John Wiley & Sons, Inc.
1957 "On the psychophysical law." Psychological Review 64:153–181.
1959 "Cross-modality validation of subjective scales for loudness, vibration, and electric shock." Journal of Experimental Psychology 57:201–209.

Stevens, S. S., and E. H. Galanter.
1957 "Ratio scales and category scales for a dozen perceptual continua." Journal of Experimental Psychology 54:377–411.

Stouffer, S. A., L. Guttman, E. A. Suchman, P. F. Lazarsfeld, S. A. Star, and J. A. Clausen.
1950 Measurement and Prediction. Vol. IV. Princeton, New Jersey: Princeton University Press.

Thurstone, L. L.
1927 "A law of comparative judgment." Psychological Review 34:273–286.

Torgerson, W. S.
1958 Theory and Methods of Scaling. New York: John Wiley & Sons, Inc.
1960 "Quantitative judgment scales." In Psychological Scaling (Gulliksen, H., and Messick, S., eds.) New York: John Wiley & Sons, Inc.

Warren, R. M.
  1958 "A basis for judgments of sensory in-
        tensity." American Journal of Psychol-
        ogy 71:675–687.
Warren, R. M., and E. C. Poulton.
  1960 "Basis for lightness-judgment of
        grays." American Journal of Psychol-
        ogy 73:380–387.
Warren, R. M., E. A. Sersen, and E. B. Pores.
  1958 "A basis for loudness-judgments."
        American Journal of Psychology 71:
        700–709.

CHAPTER 3 Reliability and Validity Assessment in Attitude Measurement

GEORGE W. BOHRNSTEDT

Measurement is a sine qua non of any science. One must be able to obtain measures of all variables contained in a given theoretical statement if the validity of that statement is to be evaluated. In the social sciences the lack of measuring devices has been a most important deterrent to the development of an explanatory and predictive science. Unlike the physicist who can measure in grams, centimeters, and pounds of pressure per square inch, social scientists most often have had to be satisfied with instruments which at best merely rank individuals on a variable. In many cases, even very crude measuring devices have not been available.

Measurement has not improved quickly in the social sciences for a variety of reasons. Perhaps the most important reason is that the concepts which are at the foundation of the science often are not well-defined. Researchers often do not agree on the meaning of opaque concepts such as "alienation," "political efficacy," and "prejudice." Thus, several different measures have been constructed to

The author is grateful to Lowell Hargens and Anne Richardson for critical comments. The preparation of this paper has been made possible by the partial support of the author by the U.S. Office of Education (OE–5–10–292). This chapter was prepared especially for this volume.

tap each of these contents, but there is little evidence that measures which supposedly tap the same construct correlate highly with one another. That is, one might question the *validity* of the various measures. Are these instruments measuring what they purport to measure?

One must also be concerned about how *reliably* individuals are ordered by a given measuring instrument. Assuming individuals have not changed, are they ordered the same upon remeasurement? If not, the researcher can never be certain whether he knows the true ordering of individuals on the variable.

The need to evaluate the reliability and validity of one's measures should be readily apparent. In attitude measurement, there are several techniques for such evaluation. These techniques will be the substance of this chapter. Not all the important methods can be discussed in the detail needed for one who wants more than an introduction to these areas. Those wanting more detailed information are referred to Lord and Novick (1968), Horst (1966), and Gulliksen (1950).

While not all attitude measuring instruments are scales or scores based on several items, many of them are and we shall make this an assumption in this chapter. That is, one's scale is assumed to be the sum of several items rather than a single item. In making this assumption, much of what is said about reliability and validity becomes *item analysis*. Item analysis is the selection of an item for inclusion in one's scale or score based on the reliability and validity of the item. The details of item analysis are part of what is to be described in this chapter.

This chapter begins with an elementary discussion of measurement theory and continues with discussions of reliability and validity. It ends with a section relating reliability and validity to each other.

ERRORS IN MEASUREMENT

Measurement is the assignment of numbers to outcomes according to certain rules. Thus, one might arbitrarily assign the number 0 to all males and 1 to all females. Or, one might assign the number 0 to all persons 40 inches or shorter in height, 1 to those 41 to 50 inches in height, 2 to those 51 to 60 inches, and so on. These *rules of correspondence* are called functions. Notice in the latter example that the measurement is relatively crude. In fact, the original measure, height in inches, is several times more refined than the rule of correspondence used in the example. In doing research one should use the most refined measures available, since the better the measure, the more accurately the true underlying relationship between two variables can be assessed. Notice that whether inches or the more crude rule of correspondence is used, it can be said that the larger the number, the taller the person. This is not true for all levels of measurement. Thus, in the first example, the fact that males are zeroes says nothing about their relative standing compared to females (although some married men might quarrel with this assertion). Thus, for some rules of correspondence one can say no more than whether or not outcomes are in the same class (*nominal* scale measurement). In others, one only can say whether or not one outcome is greater than, less than, or equal to some other outcome (*ordinal* scale measurement).

In still others, one can say exactly how many units greater or fewer one outcome is compared to another (*interval* scale measurement). Finally, in a few cases one might in addition be able to say that one outcome is *n* times greater or less than another (*ratio* scale measurement). Some examples might help in understanding the distinction among these four *levels of measurement*. Assigning different numbers to represent the 50 states in the union is classification without ordering and is therefore only nominal measurement. Asking persons to choose three acquaintances and to order them by friendship level would be ordinal measurement. In interval and ratio scale measurement the intervals between the numbers are assumed to be equispaced. Thus, on a Fahrenheit temperature scale the difference between 25 and 26 degrees is the same as the difference between 30 and 31 degrees, i.e., one degree. Notice that where friends were ordered the difference in affection between friends 1 and 2 could be quite different from that between friends 2 and 3. That is, the intervals in ordinal measurement need not be equal. Ratio measurement differs from interval measurement in that ratio scales have true rather than arbitrary zero points. Fahrenheit and Centigrade scales are interval measures since they both have arbitrary zero points; neither represents an absolute lack of heat. The Kelvin temperature scale, however, does have an absolute zero point and is a ratio scale. When ratio measurement is possible one can speak of an outcome as being *n* times as great as or less than another. A boy 60 inches tall is twice as tall as a boy 30 inches in height. However, when discussing Fahrenheit temperatures one *cannot* speak of 60 degrees as twice as hot as 30 degrees. The reader interested in further pursuing the differences among these levels of measurement is referred to Stevens (1951).

The discussion which follows assumes at least interval measurement. Obviously, few variables in the social sciences can be measured on an interval scale and the reader may be wondering why then the material is presented at all. The reason is simple: *In science, one rarely can meet exactly the assumptions underlying the tools he uses.* And, unfortunately, usually the more powerful the tool is for making scientific inferences, the more difficult the assumptions are to meet. If a field is ever to advance, the researchers within it must try to build measuring devices which have characteristics that approach the assumptions underlying their use rather than to remain mathematical purists and throw up their hands. The latter approach is akin to scientific rigor mortis. Those social scientists who have taken the former approach have demonstrated that the results obtained from assuming interval data have been fruitful. Making this assumption allows one to estimate the *degree* of association between variables rather than having to be content with merely estimating whether or not some association exists.

By assuming interval measurement where only ordinal measurement exists, some measurement errors will occur. The result of errors generally is the attenuation of relations among variables. That is, one's apparent results will be more attenuated than they are in reality. Thus, it is unlikely that the decision to assume interval measurement when it does not exist will lead to the spurious overestimation of results.[1] Our discussion will now turn to a somewhat more mathematical treatment of measurement and errors in measurement.

A person's observed score X_i on an individual item can be thought of as a function of his true score, T_i plus error in measurement, e_i. The relation linking the observed score with the true score and error is defined then as

$$(1) \qquad X_i = T_i + e_i.$$

Then, the following assumptions are made

$$(2a) \qquad E(e_i) = 0$$
$$(2b) \qquad \rho_{T_i\, e_i} = 0$$
$$(2c) \qquad \rho_{T_i, e_j} = 0$$
$$(2d) \qquad \rho_{e_i, e_j} = 0.$$

E represents the expected value or "long-run" mean of the variable and ρ is the correlation between two variables in a population. Assumption 2a states that the expectation of the errors is zero. Positive errors and negative errors are made but they are expected to cancel each other out in the long run—they have a mean of zero. This fits with our intuition of what is meant by *random* error. Assumption 2b states that the true score for a given variable is assumed to be uncorrelated with its measurement error, and 2c states that the true scores in one variable are assumed to be uncorrelated with the errors in a second variable. Finally, 2d states that errors in variables are assumed to be uncorrelated with each other. From these assumptions several important results follow. First,

$$(3) \qquad E(X_i) = E(T_i).$$

That is, the expected value of the observed scores is the same as the expected value of the true scores. The importance of this relationship is that the mean of the observed scores (an observable) is an unbiased estimate of the mean of the true scores (an unobservable). Another important result is that

$$(4) \qquad \sigma^2_{X_i} = \sigma^2_{T_i} + \sigma^2_{e_i};$$

the variance of the observed scores is simply the sum of the variance of the true scores and the errors. Ordinarily, of course, the variance of sums is not the simple sum of the individual variances [see Formula (19)]; in this case, however, it is true since by 2b the true scores and errors are assumed to be uncorrelated. Using these definitions, assumptions and resulting theorems, we now can move on to a discussion of reliability theory.

RELIABILITY

When one has built a measuring instrument, he needs to know how reliably it orders individuals. If individuals cannot reliably be

---

[1] It is true that errors in measurement will attenuate the association between two variables. However, it is possible in the *k*-variable case to obtain partial correlations and regression coefficients which are inflated due to errors in measurement. See Blalock (1964, pp. 146–150) and Bohrnstedt (1969, pp. 126–128).

placed on the scale it is of no scientific utility, since results based on it are likely to be grossly in error. What is meant by reliability? Perhaps the best synonym is *consistency*. If no true change occurs in a given attitude an individual holds, does the attitude scale consistently yield the same ordering for him relative to others? If not, the scale is unreliable. Obviously, reliability is not an all-or-none matter—there are degrees of reliability.

Reliability is defined as a correlation coefficient. More precisely, reliability ($\rho_{XX'}$) is defined as the correlation between two parallel measures. Before discussing the rationale for this definition, consider the following. Suppose one has two measurements X and X' such that $X = T + e$, $X' = T + e'$, and $\sigma_e^2 = \sigma_{e'}^2$. Notice that both X and X' are functions of the same true score (T) and differ only because of different errors in measurement. The measures X and X' then are said to be parallel. The correlation between these two parallel measures indicates the reliability of measurement of the variable under study. Two immediate results which follow from the definition of parallel measures are

$$(5) \qquad E(X) = E(X')$$

and

$$(6) \qquad \sigma_X^2 = \sigma_{X'}^2.$$

Now the reliability of the measure is given as

$$(7) \qquad \rho_{XX'} = \frac{\sigma_{XX'}}{\sigma_X \sigma_{X'}}$$
$$= \frac{\sigma_T^2}{\sigma_X^2},$$

where $\sigma_{XX'}$ is the covariance between X and X'. Notice from (7) that the reliability of a measure is the ratio of true score to total variance. A proof of (7) can be found in Gulliksen (1950, pp. 13–14). Note further that $0 \leq \rho_{XX'} \leq 1.0$. The reliability will be zero when all of the true score variance is error. This is seen by noting that $\sigma_T^2 = \sigma_X^2 - \sigma_e^2$ [from (4)]; hence when all the observed score variance is error, i.e., $\sigma_X^2 = \sigma_e^2$, it follows that $\sigma_T^2 = 0$, and $\rho_{XX'} = 0$. It also is clear from this that the reliability will be unity when there is no error.

Although not proven here, it can be shown that if Y_1, Y_2, Y_3 ... are parallel measures and Z is another distinct random variable, then

$$(8) \qquad \rho_{Y_1, Y_2} = \rho_{Y_1, Y_3} = \rho_{Y_2, Y_3} = \cdots$$

and

$$(9) \qquad \rho_{Y_1, Z} = \rho_{Y_2, Z} = \rho_{Y_3, Z} = \cdots$$

The equalities in (8) indicate that the intercorrelations among all parallel items are the same. This suggests that the reliabilities of measurement are independent of which parallel forms are used *if* they are truly parallel. And (9) further indicates that the intercorrelations of all parallel tests with some other variable are all equal.

The Regression of True Scores on Observed Scores

One should be interested in how well the true scores can be predicted from the observed variables. It is proven by Lord and Novick (1968, p. 65) that

$$(10) \qquad \beta_{TX} = \rho_{XX'}$$

and

$$(11) \qquad \hat{T} = \rho_{XX'} X + (1 - \rho_{XX'}) \mu_x,$$

where β_{TX} is a regression coefficient, $\hat{T}$ is the predicted true score and X is the observed score. That is, the regression coefficient for predicting the true scores from the observed scores is just the reliability coefficient, and the intercept is 1 minus the reliability coefficient times the mean of the observed scores. It follows from (11) that when the reliability of a measure is high, much weight is placed on the observed scores and little on the group mean in predicting the true scores. However, when a measure is unreliable, less emphasis is placed on the observed scores and more placed on the group mean.

The dispersion of errors, called the standard error of measurement, is

$$(12) \qquad \sigma_e = \sigma_X \sqrt{1 - \rho_{XX'}}.$$

With it, one can construct confidence intervals around a person's true score. Notice from

(12) that the standard error of measurement approaches zero as the reliability of one's measure approaches unity, as would be expected. If one assumes that errors are normally distributed, it can be said that for all persons with a given *true* score, the probability is at least $1 - \alpha$ that the observed score will lie within plus or minus k times the standard error of measurement of the true score, where α is the probability of a Type I error (Du Bois, 1965, pp. 341–342), and k is a function of α. However, one cannot construct such an interval around the *observed* scores using the standard error of measurement (Gulliksen, 1950, pp. 17–22). It also is possible to compute the standard deviation *around the regression line* which is fit to the prediction of true from observed scores. This is the *standard error of estimate* and is

$$(13) \qquad \sigma_\epsilon = \sigma_x \sqrt{\rho_{xx'}} \sqrt{1 - \rho_{xx'}}.$$

It can be proven (Lord and Novick, p. 68) that, in general, the standard error of estimate is smaller than the standard error of measurement. This occurs because the latter measure in its derivation makes use of the group mean as well as the reliability, whereas the former makes use only of the reliability. A comparison of (12) and (13) shows they differ by a factor of $\sqrt{\rho_{xx'}}$, which must be less than or equal to unity. Hence (13) must be as small or smaller than (12). We have seen now how reliability is defined and how unreliability affects the prediction of an individual's true score. We now move on to a discussion of how unreliability affects the correlation between two variables.

Attenuation Due to Unreliability

As noted earlier, random error has the effect of reducing the relationship between two variables. It can easily be proven that

$$(14) \qquad \rho_{T_1 T_2} = \frac{\rho_{x_1 x_2}}{\sqrt{\rho_{x_1 x_1'} \rho_{x_2 x_2'}}}.$$

That is, the true correlation between variables, $\rho_{T_1 T_2}$, is reduced because of unreliability in the two variables. Since the reliabilities of X_1 and X_2 in (14) are necessarily less than or equal to unity, $\rho_{T_1 T_2}$ must be greater than or equal to $\rho_{x_1 x_2}$. The two will be equal only when $\rho_{x_1 x_1'} = \rho_{x_2 x_2'} = 1.00$. As an example, suppose $\rho_{x_1 x_2} = .5$, and $\rho_{x_1 x_1'} = .8$ and $\rho_{x_2 x_2'} = .8$. Substituting these figures into (14) yields $\rho_{T_1 T_2} = .5/\sqrt{.64} = .625$. One can see how unreliability affects the explanation of variance in one variable to another by looking at the coefficients of determination, i.e., by comparing $\rho_{T_1 T_2}^2$ and $\rho_{x_1 x_2}^2$. Since $\rho_{T_1 T_2}^2 = .39$ and $\rho_{x_1 x_2}^2 = .25$, unreliability accounts for roughly a 14 per cent decrease in explained variance. Unfortunately, many of our attitude scales have reliabilities even lower than .8, which may explain why correlations between these scales and other variables often are very low.

Whether or not researchers should correct observed correlations for attenuation, due to unreliability in the variables, has been the subject of considerable debate. There are several evaluations to be made. First $\rho_{T_1 T_2}$ is a population parameter, but in fact one must deal with samples, and samples yield only *estimates* of parameters. The estimate of $\rho_{T_1 T_2}$ can be particularly misleading since not only are the reliabilities in the denominator of the righthand side of (14) estimates themselves, but the observed correlation in the numerator also is an estimate. Thus, depending on how stable the estimate of each of the three parameters are, the value of $\rho_{T_1 T_2}$ could fluctuate substantially. Whether or not to correct for attenuation depends partly on the confidence one has in these estimates.

Moreover, when reporting results of a prediction study, one ordinarily would not correct for attenuation. Researchers are not usually interested in how well a measure *might* predict if it were reliable, but in how well it predicts in fact. However, in examining causal relationships and estimating the true causal relation between two variables, correction for attenuation would be in order, assuming good estimates of the parameters exist. To illustrate, if one were interested in *predicting* political activism among college students from a scale measuring attitude towards authority, correction for attenuation probably would not occur. In this case one wants to know if it can be determined who the activists will be and errors in measurement clearly will affect this determination. By contrast, if a researcher were interested in obtaining an estimate of how these two variables are theoretically related, i.e., in the absence of error, then, if he had confidence in his reliability estimates, he might correct for attenuation.

Types of Reliability and Their Measurement

To this point, only a general theoretical statement of reliability has been presented. Now specific ways of measuring reliability will be discussed. Generally, reliability measures are split into two major classes: measures of *stability* and measures of *equivalence*.

Measures of stability—A person's score on an attitude scale may vary somewhat from one measurement to another. The respondent may be temporarily distracted, misunderstand the meaning of an item, respond differently on different occasions because someone else is present, and so on. All these various sources of error will contribute to the unreliability of an attitude scale. The problem to be faced is how to evaluate the amount of unreliability in one's measures. A most popular way to evaluate unreliability has been to correlate persons' responses at one time with their responses at some later time. Reliability evaluated by correlating a measure across time is called a *measure of stability*, or *test-retest* reliability.

There are some obvious problems with a test-retest reliability estimate. Different results may occur depending upon the length of time between measurement and remeasure-

ment. The longer the time interval, the lower the reliability estimate. For one thing, when the time interval is short, persons may remember how they answered on the first administration of the items and thus may appear to be more consistent than they actually are. To handle this problem, some researchers modify the test-retest procedure by using a second form which parallels in content the one used for the first administration, although different items are used. When devising his measurement instrument, the researcher writes twice as many items to measure a given content domain. Half of the items are used in one form and the other half in a second form. If the forms truly are parallel, they should correlate exactly the same with any other variables. In addition, the mean and standard deviations of the two forms should be identical and the intercorrelations among the items should be the same in both versions. Obviously, it is very difficult, if not impossible, to meet these criteria and it should be clear from this that few "parallel forms" of tests actually are parallel. Nevertheless, it is possible through careful item selection to build two forms which are roughly parallel. If it is possible to do this, then the parallel forms can be correlated across time as a measure of reliability. Using parallel forms reduces the degree to which respondents' memory of their previous responses can cause spuriously high reliability estimates.

A second problem with test-retest reliability estimates is that individuals' true scores have a greater probability of actually changing, the longer the time interval between test and retest. It is clear that if individuals have truly changed, a low test-retest correlation does not necessarily mean that the reliability of the attitude scale is low. In a recent paper, Heise (1969) has shown that with three observations across time one can distinguish change from unreliability if the intervals between administrations are the same and if it can be assumed that the errors in measurement are uncorrelated across time. Without the use of parallel forms this last assumption would be very difficult to meet. The reliability coefficient is defined as

$$(15) \qquad \rho_{xx'} = \frac{\rho_{12}\rho_{23}}{\rho_{13}},$$

where the subscripts refer to the measurement period. Heise provides an example from Crowther (1965) where correlations between scores on the California Test of Mental Maturity test of intelligence at the third, sixth, and ninth grade are used to estimate the reliability of the CTMM. The correlations were $r_{12} = .56, r_{23} = .65,$ and $r_{13} = .52$. By formula (15) $r_{xx'} = .70$. Notice that $r_{xx'}$ is somewhat higher than any of the individual test-retest correlations, which demonstrates that some change has occurred on intelligence as measured by the CTMM.

In addition to getting a reliability estimate, the method yields coefficients which indicate the amount of change from Time 1 to Time 2, Time 2 to Time 3, and Time 1 to Time 3. Heise labels these coefficients s_{ij}, and they are shown to be $s_{12} = \rho_{13}/\rho_{23}, s_{23} = \rho_{13}/\rho_{12}$, and $s_{13} = \rho_{13}^2/\rho_{12}\rho_{23}$. For the above data, $s_{12} = .80, s_{23} = .93$, and $s_{13} = .74$, indicating the measured IQ is changing more between third and sixth grades than between sixth and ninth grades, which fits our expectations. Thus, Heise has provided a useful way to partition unreliability and change, if one has three measurements over time.

Another problem a researcher must face when using any test-retest procedure has been called the *reactivity* problem (Campbell and Stanley, 1963; Webb, Campbell, Schwartz, and Sechrest, 1966). Reactivity refers to the fact that a respondent's sensitivity or responsiveness to the variable under study may be enhanced by the measurement of that variable. Asking an individual about his political opinions at one time may heighten his interest in political affairs and cause him to discuss and read about politics and hence show change across time, whereas there would be no change in a person similar in all other respects but not surveyed. In this situation the test-retest correlation is lower because change

has occurred; not change due to some experimental variable, but change due to reactivity. There apparently is no easy solution to this problem.

Because of the problems inherent in the test-retest approach to reliability assessment, many researchers have abandoned measures of stability for what are called *measures of equivalence* and we now turn to a discussion of some of these methods.

Measures of equivalence—It is assumed that when several items are summed into a single attitude scale, the items are measuring the same underlying attitude. In this sense, each item can be thought of as a measure of the attitude. Reliability estimates which measure the equivalence of each item as an indicator of an underlying attitude are called, logically enough, *measures of equivalence*. The earliest variety of equivalence measures to appear were the *split-half* methods. In the split-half approach, the total number of items are divided into two halves and the half-tests are correlated to get an estimate of the reliability. For good reason, this approach to reliability generally has fallen into disuse. Some researchers used even versus odd items, others correlated the first half of the scale with the second, and so on. Obviously, each of these splits could yield different reliability estimates. Indeed, for a scale $2n$ items long, the total number of possible splits is $\frac{(2n!)}{2(n!)(n!)}$. For a 10-item scale, there are 126 possible splits, all different. Some will yield reliability estimates above the true reliability and others below. Thus, split-halves may be far from equivalent halves.

Most researchers who have used the split-half technique have generally applied the Spearman-Brown Prophecy formula to the obtained correlation between the two splits. This formula was derived independently by Spearman (1910) and Brown (1910). The formula was developed to discern the effect of increasing the length of a measure. As one might guess, the greater the number of independent measures one has of a phenomenon, the greater the reliability of a composite measure based on these measures. Spearman and Brown showed that the reliability of a scale which is n times longer than the original scale is

$$(16) \qquad \rho_{x_n x_n'} = \frac{n\rho_{xx'}}{1 + (n-1)\rho_{xx'}},$$

where $\rho_{x_n x_n'}$ is the reliability of the longer scale. However, while the Spearman-Brown Prophecy formula indicates that increasing the length of the scale increases its reliability, there is a point of diminishing returns. Figure 1 shows the increase in reliability as a function of increase in the length of the measure for different initial reliabilities. It is obvious that the higher the initial reliability, the less increase in reliability as a function of adding additional items. Nonetheless, when selecting items, Figure 1 can generally be useful in indicating how many items to retain in one's scale.

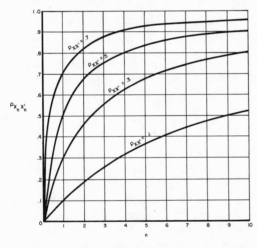

Figure 1. Diagram for Formula 14 showing increase in reliability as a function of increase in the length of scale (n) for different initial reliabilities.

The Spearman-Brown formula sometimes is used with split-half correlations to get an estimate of the reliability of the $2n$ item score. This point is subtle and needs some explanation. In computing a split-halved reliability, the whole test (both halves) must be given to all respondents. Thus, the correlation between the halves is the reliability estimate for a scale only one-half as long as the scale actually used. The Spearman-Brown Prophecy formula is then used to estimate the reliability of the full-length scale, which is $2n$ items in length. As an example, suppose a researcher has 16 items which are designed to tap feelings of political efficacy. He arbitrarily selects eight of the items, adds them into one score and the remaining eight into a second score and correlates them. A reasonable correlation between the two halves would be .65. However, the researcher wants to use the full 16-item scale as his measure and, therefore, uses the Spearman-Brown Prophecy formula with $n = 2$. Substituting $\rho_{xx'} = .65$ and $n = 2$ into (15) yields $\rho_{x_2 x_2'} = 2(.65)/(1 + .65) = .788$ and this is the reliability estimate of the 16-item attitude scale. Again, because of the arbitrary way in which the halves are chosen, this procedure is generally *not* recommended for determining reliability.

A second method of equivalence is based on the correlation of parallel forms with each other based on data collected at one point in time. As indicated when discussing test-retest methods, parallel forms are not arbitrary splits of items. It is assumed that each item in one form has an item which exactly parallels it in a second version. The use of parallel forms is limited only by the difficulty in constructing them. Unfortunately, it is practically impossible to find two completely parallel sets of items. For this reason, the method developed by Kuder and Richardson (1937) is the recommended approach for those who desire to compute a coefficient of equivalence.

This approach, called *internal consistency*, examines the covariance among *all* of the items simultaneously rather than that in a particular and arbitrary split. The Kuder-Richardson formulas and generalizations coming from them remain the most popular approach to reliability today. The original formulas were developed for dichotomous items only and were termed KR20 and KR21 respectively. For both formulas, Kuder and Richardson assumed that all items were parallel, and for KR21, that the proportion answering positively to *all* items was the same (sometimes called the "difficulty" of an item). Let n equal the number of dichotomous items in one's measure, p_i the proportion answering item i positively, and σ_X^2 the variance of the total scale, then

$$(17) \quad KR20 = \rho_{XX'} = \frac{n}{n-1} [1 - \frac{\sum\limits_{i=1}^{n} p_i q_i}{\sigma_X^2}]$$

and

$$(18) \quad KR21 = \rho_{XX'} = \frac{n}{n-1} [1 - \frac{\mu_X - \frac{\mu_X^2}{n}}{\sigma_X^2}],$$

where μ_X is the mean, $p_i q_i$ is the variance of the ith item $(q_i = 1 - p_i)$, and σ_X^2 the variance of the total score. Formula (17) is the more general and, hence, the more useful of the two formulas, and is the one which should be used in actual computations. As an example of the use of KR20, suppose one constructed a five-item scale to measure religiosity, where respondents were asked to show either agreement ('positive' response) or disagreement ('negative' response), and where agreement with an item is coded a 1 and disagreement a 0.

Now to compute $\rho_{XX'}$ we also need to know the variance of the total score, σ_X^2. This could be computed in two ways. First, simply add together the five-item responses for each individual into a single score and then compute the variance on this new variable. Or, compute the total score variance by knowing the item variances and covariances. Recall that for items scored $0 = 1$ the variance for item i is given by $\sigma_i^2 = p_i q_i$, where q_i is $1 - p_i$. Further, the covariance between any two items i and j is $\sigma_{ij} = p_{ij} - p_i p_j$ where p_{ij} is the proportion answering positively to both items i and j. Knowing the item variances and covariances one can compute the variance of the total score by the following theorem on the variance of sums of variables:

$$(19) \quad \sigma_X^2 = \sum_{i=1}^{n} \sigma_i^2 + 2 \sum_{i=1}^{n} \sum_{\substack{j=1 \\ i<j}}^{n} \sigma_{ij}.$$

Suppose that we computed the proportions, variances, and covariances for the five items and found the following:

	1	2	3	4	5	p_i	p_i^2
1	.09	.07	.05	.04	.08	.9	.81
2		.21	.11	.08	.14	.7	.49
3			.21	.07	.13	.7	.49
4				.24	.11	.6	.36
5					.16	.8	.64

The values in the main diagonal are the item variances and in the off-diagonal their covariances. To compute $\sum\limits_{i=1}^{n} \sigma_i^2$, which also is $\sum\limits_{i=1}^{n} p_i q_i$ in this case, we sum down the main diagonal, i.e., $.09 + .21 + .21 + .24 + .16 = .91$. Similarly, $2 \sum\limits_{i=1}^{n} \sum\limits_{j=1}^{n} \sigma_{ij}$ is simply twice the sum of the off-diagonal elements, i.e., $2(.07 + .05 + .04 + .08 + .11 + .08 + .14 + .07 + .13 + .11) = 2(.88) = 1.76$. Hence, $\sigma_X^2 = .91 + 1.76 = 2.67$. We saw above that $\sum\limits_{i=1}^{n} p_i q_i = .91$, which is simply another expression for the sum of the item variances. Substituting this information into (17) yields

$$\rho_{XX'} = 5/4[1 - \frac{.91}{2.67}] = .82.$$

That is, the reliability of this five-item scale is .82.

Several formulas which are generalizations of the Kuder-Richardson 20 formula have appeared over the years (Jackson and Ferguson, 1941; Hoyt, 1941; and Gulliksen, 1950), all with what appeared to be different assumptions. A common characteristic of all these formulas is that they allow one to compute a reliability estimate when items have k response categories rather than only two. However, Novick and Lewis (1967) demonstrated that all of these formulas were making the assumption that a given respondent's true score was exactly the same on all items or at least that his true scores on the items differed from one another by no more than a constant, a condition they call essential tau-equivalence. Thus, if one has two items a and b, they are essentially tau-equivalent if $T_a = T_b + c$, where c is a constant. Clearly if $c = 0$, the items are parallel by earlier definitions. Thus, tau-equivalence is a *less* restrictive assumption than the parallel items assumption since true scores can differ by a constant from item to item. What this means is that when items are tau-equivalent, KR20 and the generalizations from it are all equal to the reliability of the total score. To the degree that items are not tau-equivalent, these formulas tend to underestimate the reliability coefficient, though not seriously unless the items depart radically from tau-equivalence.

The generalization of KR20 which has gained the most popularity is called α by Cronbach (1951) and is[2]

$$(20) \qquad \alpha = \frac{n}{n-1}[1 - \frac{\sum_i \sigma^2_{Y_i}}{\sigma^2_X}].$$

Using data from a study by Ford, Borgatta, and Bohrnstedt (1969), we can show the use of α. A series of items were designed to measure the amount of competitiveness desired in a job by new college-level personnel hired by a large company. The following nine items were added into a single measure called *competitiveness desirability*:

1. Salary increases would be strictly a matter of how much you accomplished for the company.
2. The company is known to be involved in heavy competition.
3. Persons are supposed to "get the boot" if they don't make good and keep making good.
4. There are opportunities to earn bonuses.
5. Competition would be open and encouraged.
6. The supervisor might be highly critical.
7. There is emphasis on the actual production record.

---

[2] Not to be confused with the a referred to earlier which is the probability of a Type I error in statistical inference.

8. Salary increases would be a matter of how much effort you put in.
9. The rewards could be great, but many people are known to fail or quit.

Based on a sample of 869 males hired, the covariance matrix shown in Table 1 was obtained.

TABLE 1

COVARIANCE MATRIX FOR ITEMS IN "COMPETITIVENESS DESIRABILITY" SCORE ($N = 869$ MALES)

	1	2	3	4	5	6	7	8	9
1	.534	.115	.168	.085	.118	.090	.167	.144	.129
2		.411	.114	.062	.140	.080	.104	.065	.148
3			.814	.061	.118	.116	.177	.093	.272
4				.348	.087	.012	.103	.084	.054
5					.401	.072	.140	.123	.125
6						.465	.093	.052	.105
7							.645	.078	.127
8								.383	.093
9									.679

Note: The underlined values in the diagonal are the item variances.

tained. To compute α, we need $\sum_{i=1}^{k} \sigma^2_i$ which is simply the sum of the elements in the diagonal, i.e., $\sum_{i=1}^{9} \sigma^2_i = (.534 + .411 + \ldots + .679) = 4.68$. In addition, we need to compute σ^2_X, the variance of the total scale. The reader can verify from (19) that this variance is equal to the sum of the elements in the main diagonal plus twice the sum of the off-diagonal elements. We already have computed the sum of the diagonal. Now the sum of the off-diagonals is $\sum_{\substack{i=1 \\ i<j}}^{9} \sum_{j=1}^{9} \sigma_{ij} = (.115 + .168 + \ldots + .093) = 3.919$ and twice this sum is 7.828. Add to this the sum of the diagonal and one obtains $\sigma^2_X = 12.508$. Hence,

$$\alpha = 9/8(1 - 4.68/12.508) = .70.$$

That is, the internal consistency reliability estimate for the *competitiveness desirability* score is .70. Given this reliability estimate, we can now use (12) to compute the standard error of measurement. In this example it is $\sigma_e = \sqrt{12.508}\sqrt{1 - .70} = 1.94$. Again, if we assume that errors are normally distributed and want to be 99 per cent certain that all persons with true scores of T_X lie within k standard errors of measurement of T_X, we know from the theory of normal distributions that $k = 2.58$ (Hays, 1963, p. 289). Hence, if we choose $T_X = 15$, the lower and upper bounds of the confidence interval are $15 - (2.58)(1.94)$ and $15 + (2.58)(1.94) = 5.01$ or 9.99 and 20.01 respectively. That is, the probability is .99 that persons with a true score of 15 will have an observed score which lies between 9.99 and 20.01.

We also can substitute in (11) to obtain the regression equation for predicting an individual's true score from his observed score. In this example suppose $\mu_x = 18$, where μ_x is the mean for the scale, then the regression equation is

$$\hat{T} = .70X + (.3)(18)$$
$$= .70X + 5.4.$$

Someone with an observed score of 15 would have a predicted true score of $(.70)(15) + 5.4 = 15.9$. The standard error of estimate for this prediction equation is given as (13) and in this example is $\sqrt{12.508}\sqrt{.70}\sqrt{1 - .70} = 1.62$, which is the standard deviation of the errors around the line of regression.

In most attitude research we are not interested in the prediction of an individual's true score and for this reason usually only the reliability estimate itself is presented. However, the researcher should know that individual prediction is possible and for this reason the above example was computed.

We now move to a very brief discussion of item analysis.

Item Analysis and Reliability

Techniques for determining which items to retain in one's scales are called *item analysis*

techniques. Stated most simply, items are chosen which correlate most highly with the other items in the scale. Obviously, the items which correlate highest with each other also will correlate highest with a total scale score based on the summation of these same items. Perhaps the most straightforward item analysis procedure is the item-to-total correlation technique. One simply selects the items which have the highest correlations with the total score.

Much of item analytic theory in educational measurement is based on dichotomous rather than polychotomous items. Since the latter class of items is more important in attitude measurement, the item-to-total formulas for dichotomies usually presented in techniques of item analysis are omitted here. Most of the formulas omit the item under study from the total score because when it is included, the resultant item-to-total correlation is spuriously high (Zubin, 1934; Guilford, 1954; Henrysson, 1963). Recently, however, Cureton (1966) pointed out that the reliability of the total scale with the item omitted varies inversely with the reliability of the item omitted. Thus, Cureton suggests that the omitted item be replaced with a rationally equivalent (parallel) item in the total score. Doing this leaves the reliability of the total scale unchanged. Cureton also demonstrates that if we can assume that the scale is factorially homogeneous (unidimensional), then we need not actually replace the item under study with a rationally equivalent one. If $\rho_{i,x}$ is the *uncorrected* item-to-total correlation for the ith item, $S_i = \sigma_i/\sigma_x$, $\rho_{xx'}$ is the reliability of the total scale; then according to Cureton the *corrected* item-to-total correlation $\rho_{i,x'}$ for the ith item is

$$(21) \quad \rho_{i,x'} = \frac{\rho_{xx'} - \sqrt{\rho_{xx'}^2 - 4\rho_{xx'} \cdot S_i(\rho_{i,x} - S_i)}}{2S_i}.$$

Formula (21) is true for all items whether dichotomous or not. To use (21) we also need to know the formula for the uncorrected item-to-total correlations. It is

(22) $$\rho_{i,x} = \sum_j \sigma_{ij}/\sigma_i \sigma_x$$

where j takes on all values including i. Using the above information, we now can compute an example using (21). Looking back to Table 1, we will compute the item-to-total correlation for item 1. We begin by computing the uncorrected correlation. The numerator of (22) is simply $\sum_{j=1}^{9} \sigma_{ij} = .534 + .115 + \ldots + .129 = 1.55$. Substituting this in (22) we obtain

$$\rho_{1,x} = 1.55/\sqrt{.534}\sqrt{12.508} = .597$$

as the uncorrected item-to-total correlation. We saw earlier that $\rho_{xx'} = .70$. Computing $S_1 = \sqrt{.534} / \sqrt{12.508} = .206$, we now can compute the corrected correlation. It is:

$$\rho_{1,x'} = \frac{.70 - \sqrt{(.70)^2 - 4(.70)(.206)(.597 - .206)}}{2(.206)}$$
$$= .451$$

Notice that the uncorrected correlation is roughly .15 larger than the corrected one, which is not a trivial amount.

If one has a large item pool, the items with the best item-to-total correlations for his scale should be selected. However, one should recall three important points. First, as Figure 1 indicates, reliability is increased only slightly by adding items indefinitely so usually not more than 15 items in a single score would be used. Second, (21) assumes a single dimension underlying the items and as the number of items increases this assumption becomes less and less tenable. Third, the greater the number of items, the longer the time required to administer the scale. Thus, one can have too many as well as too few. Nonetheless, experience would indicate that the latter rather than the former is more likely to be the problem.

Although this discussion of reliability must necessarily be somewhat superficial, it should be sufficient to provide the researcher who wishes to construct an attitude scale with techniques for estimating the reliability of

his scale. Finally, it is important to realize the limitations of the particular method chosen. There is no way to determine the exact reliability of an instrument. One can only obtain estimates and these are only adequate to the degree that adequate samples are used and to the degree that the underlying assumptions of a particular estimation technique are met.

We now move on to a discussion of the second important consideration in deciding the worth of an attitude scale—its validity.

VALIDITY

Validity has several different meanings. However, a very general definition can be given: *Validity indicates the degree to which an instrument measures the construct which is under investigation.* Thus, a valid verbal intelligence test is one which measures verbal intelligence and not some other ability; a valid measure of sociability measures sociability only. This is an oversimplification, however, and validity can be broken into several types. The American Psychological Association (1966) in its *Standards for Educational and Psychological Tests and Manuals* lists three types: (1) content validity, (2) criterion-related validity, and (3) construct validity.

Content Validity

Content validity refers to the degree that the score or scale being used represents the concept about which generalizations are to be made. Although content validity is carefully considered in constructing achievement and proficiency tests, it has usually been ignored in the construction of attitude scales. Many researchers in the area of attitude measurement have been satisfied to devise a number of items on an ad hoc basis which they believe will measure what they want measured.

The researcher needs to search the literature carefully to determine how various authors have used the concept. Moreover, he should rely on his own observations and experiences and ask whether they yield any new facets to the concept under consideration. Whereupon, a series of items can be constructed which measure each of the substrata of the domain of content, a procedure referred to as *sampling from a domain of content*. One's measuring instruments show content validity to the degree that sampling from the domain of content is representative of all strata and to the degree that items constructed tap the subtleties of meaning within each of these strata.

For example, alienation is a concept which has received much attention. Seeman (1959) notes that it has been used in at least five different ways by theorists and researchers: powerlessness, meaninglessness, normlessness, isolation, and self-estrangement. Additionally, it is clear that alienation overlaps the "anomie" concept. A little thought yields other concepts which ought to be considered if one is to build a measure of alienation: apathy, dissension, estrangement, disenfranchisement, and so on. The point here is that alienation is used glibly by researchers although it has several different meanings. Conceptually, alienation is not unidimensional at all. What may be needed are several measures, each of which captures one of the various meanings attached to the concept of alienation. Perhaps content validity has been ignored because of the tremendously difficult job involved in building a scale or a set of scales which samples a domain of content. It should be clear, however, that ad hoc measures tell us little about how well the measure taps the various strata in the domain of content. Various researchers using the same term (e.g., alienation) may obtain different results in the prediction of dependent variables simply because they are really measuring several different facets of the construct. Remarks such as "Intelligence is what intelligence tests measure," represent an extreme in operationalism which if followed would impede the development of the social sciences as sciences. If a researcher develops a measure of alienation it is incumbent upon him to spell

out the rationale (theory and research) which justifies calling a scale built on a particular set of items, "alienation."

Content validity is not easy to achieve for most scores or scales since one ordinarily cannot enumerate all of the elements in his population (the domain) and then sample from them. Usually it is impossible to define the population with optimum rigor unless one happens to be constructing something like a spelling test where a dictionary can be used to enumerate the population. Therefore it is incumbent on the researcher to spell out how he has determined the boundaries of the domain under study. It is necessary to indicate how items utilized capture the various meanings given a concept by theorists who have investigated it. Additionally, logical gaps present in these two sources should be indicated.

There is no single statistical criterion which can be used to determine whether or not one has properly sampled from the domain of content. No single content validity coefficient can be computed. However, the researcher can take several precautions to help insure the representation of the various shades of meaning from within the domain.

First, the domain can be *stratified* into its major components. One simply lays out the most important and obvious meanings or facets of the concept, making as certain as possible that the stratification exhausts the meanings in the domain. One may decide to take one of the strata and further divide it into substrata if the stratum does not appear to represent a single dimension. Thus, powerlessness could be subdivided into political, economic, and familial powerlessness, and so on. The further one refines these subareas, the easier it will be to construct items later.

Second, several items can be written to capture the shades of meaning associated with each stratum and substratum. "Several" means no fewer than seven to ten items. One always can choose not to include an item in a scale after data are gathered but an item not included is lost forever. This is important since one often finds that several items did not behave in the way anticipated. If only five items are used to capture a given stratum and two items are omitted from the scale because item analysis indicates they do not correlate well with the others, a three-item scale must be built. As seen in the section on reliability, the number of items in a researcher's scale is important in the determination of the size of his reliability estimate. Rarely are three-item scales highly reliable. It may be discovered that what was thought to be a unidimensional concept is two-dimensional. Unfortunately, one might end up having only three items to measure one dimension and two items for the other. If one has ten items and finds a three-item cluster breaking from the other seven items, at least the main cluster still will contain seven items.

Third, one can cluster analyze the items after data have been collected to determine whether the items constructed to measure the meaning of a given stratum cluster together. *Determine whether the items in a stratum correlate higher with each other than they do with items in other strata.* The assumption made is as follows: If a set of items is really measuring some underlying trait or attitude, then the underlying trait causes the covariation among the items. The higher the correlations, the better the items are measuring the same underlying construct. One can proceed in the following ways: (1) Compute the average of the intercorrelations within a stratum and compare it with the average correlation of these same items with items included in the other strata. The within-cluster average correlation should be higher than the between-cluster average correlations. If the average correlation between clusters is higher than the average correlation within clusters, the items in one cluster, on the average, could be used to predict responses to items in the other stratum better than they could predict responses to the items in the stratum to which they belong! This would most certainly indicate that one or more of the items in the cluster do *not* belong to the stratum to which they were originally assigned. (2) Check the intercorrelations of

each item with each of the other items in the stratum and compare these to correlations for this item with the items in the other strata. If the item correlates somewhat higher within its own stratum than it correlates within other strata, it probably belongs where it is. If this is not the case, then locate the stratum with which, on the average, it is most highly correlated. That is, find out where the item fits best *statistically*. Now, however, it is necessary to determine that the content of the misplaced item agrees with that of the stratum to which it has been moved since it also must fit into the stratum *semantically*.

An item which correlates about equally well in two strata usually is not a good item. It is not good because it is at the boundary between two strata. Including it in either cluster will result in a somewhat higher correlation between the two scores than if it were simply omitted entirely. In summary, although content validity with a single coefficient cannot be demonstrated, statistical and logical procedures can be applied to help insure that items are content valid.

Criterion-related Validity

Criterion-related validity is ascertained by correlating one's measure with a direct measure of the characteristic under investigation. Criteria are generally divided into those which are *concurrent* and those which are *predictive*. An attitude scale designed to measure religious orthodoxy could be evaluated concurrently by inquiring about church attendance. Some instruments such as aptitude and achievement tests are designed for prediction purposes only. They may be used to predict success on the job or to predict success or failure in college, and so on. The question of what is concurrent and what is predictive is not always clear. However, predictive criteria are usually reserved for long-range forecasts.

It should be clear that a scale which has concurrent validity may not necessarily be predictively valid. Thus, a set of items which measures political beliefs may correlate highly with which party a person *believes* he will vote for in November. However, the scale may be correlated somewhat lower with actual behavior. Attitudes change through time and thus bear something less than a one-to-one relationship to behavior.

Whereas content validity is not demonstrable by a single coefficient, criterion-related validity is. As indicated above, all the researcher does is to correlate his scale with the criterion and this correlation coefficient is taken to be the validity coefficient. However, the validity coefficient can be attenuated by unreliability either in the scale or in the criterion itself. The method of correcting for unreliability is the correction for attenuation [Formula (14)]. Thus, if one's measure of religious orthodoxy has a reliability of .8, and the reliability of one's measure of religious services attendance is .9, and the two measures have a correlation of .6 with each other, the *estimated* true correlation between the two variables is $.6 / \sqrt{(.8)(.9)} = .71$. That is, the variance explained in church attendance by orthodoxy increases by roughly 14 per cent when unreliability in the two variables is taken into account $[(.71)^2 - (.60)^2 = .14]$. As indicated earlier, the corrected correlation is only an estimate of the true correlation between the variables since all of the components have sampling distributions. Nonetheless, when one does have large samples and good reliability estimates, the corrected correlation between a scale and a criterion can provide useful information about the validity of the scale.

Clearly, many of the constructs of interest in attitude research do *not* have a single criterion with which the validity of one's measure can be checked. Many times the "criterion" may be a worse measure of the construct than the scale which was constructed. This may well be the case with psychiatrists' ratings of personality characteristics, for example. Thus, one would not want to dismiss a scale as an invalid measure because of a near-zero correlation with a single criterion unless he were relatively convinced of the validity of the criterion it-

self. In the section which follows, we shall address ourselves to other methods of validation when no single "hard" criterion exists.

Construct Validity

"*Construct validity* is evaluated by investigating what qualities a test measures, that is, by determining the degree to which certain explanatory concepts or constructs account for performance on the test" (American Psychological Association, 1966, p. 13). The *APA Technical Recommendations* further indicate that studies of construct validity are done to validate the theory underlying the scale, score, or test constructed. The researcher validates his scales by investigating whether they confirm or deny the hypotheses predicted from a theory which is based on the constructs. One of the limitations of this approach is, of course, that inability to predict according to the hypotheses can result either from a lack of construct validity or an incorrect theory. We are not here concerned with this problem, however.

Construct validity was developed to replace the plethora of terms such as "face validity," "logical validity," "intrinsic validity," "factorial validity," and "trait validity" which had sprung up over the years. All of these concepts had different shades of meaning, but all were bound together by the notion that some underlying trait or construct accounted for the variance in one's measure. Unlike many constructs in the physical sciences, few in the social sciences are easily operationally defined. That is, there is no general acceptance of sets of operations as *the* definitions of constructs. When acceptance of operational definitions does not occur within a discipline, researchers sometimes are arrogant and say, "Anomie is what these five items measure." However, if only a few researchers in the science are willing to content themselves with the operational definition, chaos develops. Different researchers use the same construct name (e.g., 'anomie'), but each with somewhat different meaning. When this occurs, generalizations involving the construct are impossible to make since there really is no single construct under investigation but, instead, a multitude of constructs. Given that many of the constructs in the social sciences are not precisely specified, acceptance of operational definitions is unlikely. Thus, it is relatively rarely that one can correlate his measure with some *real* criterion variable to assess its validity. Instead, more indirect validation procedures are necessary and this points up the need for the concept of construct validity.

Because of the fallibility of any single criterion, we need to validate our measure of X by several *independent* measures, all of which supposedly measure X. Suppose, for example, that we are interested in constructing a scale to measure a respondent's degree of economic conservatism. We might construct ten items which inquire into views about government laissez-faire, government aid to education, and so on, to all of which individuals respond about themselves. However, to validate the scale constructed from these ten items we might ask that the three best friends of each respondent complete the items in the way they believe the respondent would complete them. A third measure might include a self-rating by the respondent of how similar his own personal philosophy is to that of several well-known individuals such as Ayn Rand, William Buckley, Hubert Humphrey, Wayne Morse, and so on. It might be suggested that the variance on the ten items is really due not to economic conservatism but instead to social class, or to intelligence. We can correlate our original measure of economic conservatism with the two independent measures of economic conservatism plus measures of social class and intelligence. Ideally, the three independent measures of economic conservatism would all correlate highly with each other and, additionally, the original measure would not correlate highly with the measures of social class and intelligence. If this occurred, we would be encouraged to accept the scale as a valid measure of economic conservatism. Suppose, however, that we found not only

high correlations among our three measures, but also observed high correlations of our scale with social class and intelligence. These latter correlations would not invalidate our scale *if* we should expect these correlations for theoretical reasons. That is, if political theory predicts a high positive correlation between economic conservatism and social class and it actually occurs, this too validates the measure. However, the correlations among the three measures of economic conservatism should be higher in each case than the scale's correlations with other variables, since they are measures of the *same* construct.

It should also be clear that a scale must not correlate too highly with measures of different content. This is an especially important requirement when developing a number of scales to measure the various facets in a multi-dimensional domain. If, for example, one finds five facets in the alienation domain, they should not correlate too highly with each other or it might be suspected that the concept is not multidimensional after all, and the items should be added into a single score. How does one determine when scales are too highly correlated with each other? If there are several independent measures of each of the five dimensions, the independent measures of the same construct should correlate more highly with each other than they do with any measure of any of the other constructs. An attempt to validate one's scales by examining a matrix of correlations in this manner has been developed by Campbell and Fiske (1959) and is called the *multitrait-multimethod approach* to construct validation. A detailed presentation of the method is presented in Chapter 4 and hence is not covered in depth here.

Briefly, Campbell and Fiske suggest two types of validation not explicitly mentioned in the *APA Technical Recommendations,* but which would fall under the heading of construct validity. The first type, *convergent validation,* is confirmation of a relationship by independent measurement procedures. For example, if one were interested in studying prejudice (say, in a laboratory setting), one might obtain self-ratings from a respondent on a series of items which measures attitudes towards minority groups and at the same time obtain ratings of prejudice from his three best friends. A third measure of prejudice might be a physiological reaction (say, blood pressure) to watching a movie where individuals from various ethnic and racial groups interact in a variety of situations (i.e., playing cards together, dating, and so on). These three separate measures of prejudice could then be correlated with each other. The higher the separate measures correlate with each other, the greater the convergent validity.

The second kind of validation procedure mentioned by Campbell and Fiske is *discriminant validation*. Discriminant validation needs to be established when one's domain is *not* unidimensional. It refers to the fact that scales which correlate too highly with one another may be measuring the *same* rather than *different* constructs. Thus, if one builds one measure and calls it "fatalism" and then another and calls it "anomie," he needs to demonstrate that these are different constructs by correlating the measures with one another and showing that the correlation is lower than the correlations between measures of the same construct. What can be done if the measures of different constructs correlate too highly? Again, the correlations of each item with each other item both within and across clusters should be checked. Items which correlate higher in another cluster probably belong in that cluster rather than in the one originally chosen.

Factor analysis also can be very useful in (a) determining the dimensionality of a domain and (b) selecting the items which fit best into the various strata of the domain. This technique provides the correlation of each item with each facet of the domain. (These facets are called "factors.") Items which correlate highly with a single factor are clearly to be preferred in construction of one's scales. The use of factor analysis in the validation of scales to measure attitudes toward education is shown in an article by

Kerlinger and Kaya (1959) which is reproduced here as Chapter 15.

Although the issue appears now to have been resolved, there was much controversy about the logical status of the construct validity concept after its appearance in the 1954 edition of the *Technical Recommendations*. In particular, Bechtoldt (1959), responding not only to the statement in the *Technical Recommendations,* but also to an extended discussion of the concept by Cronbach and Meehl (1955), held that operational definitions are necessary from a philosophical point of view and that introducing a term such as construct validity runs counter to an operational methodology. The reader interested in this debate is directed to the article by Bechtoldt and a reply to it by Campbell (1960).

THE RELATIONSHIP BETWEEN RELIABILITY AND VALIDITY

Although the verbal definitions of reliability and validity make quite clear the distinction between the two concepts, there are cases where this distinction is considerably blurred. This blurring occurs especially when internal consistency is considered to be reliability. It is clear that if one has n parallel items administered simultaneously, they provide several instant test-retests. Another aspect, however, is that all the correlations among these manifest variables are due to the correlations between each of the manifest variables and some underlying construct, trait, or factor. These latter correlations would indicate the validity of each item since they indicate the degree to which each item correlates with that which one wants to measure—the underlying construct. The relationship between these two perspectives hints at the existence of a close relationship between reliability and validity. As Lord and Novick (p. 68) demonstrate, the relation is given by

$$(23) \qquad \rho_{XT}^2 = \rho_{XX'}.$$

The square of the validity coefficient (where validity is defined as the correlation of an observed score with its true score) equals the reliability of the scale. Lord and Novick (p. 72) further note, however, that validity as determined by correlation of one's score with some other "outside" criterion can never exceed the correlation of an observed score with its true score. That is,

$$(24) \qquad \rho_{XZ} \leq \rho_{XT}\sqrt{\rho_{XX'}},$$

where Z is the criterion. The implication of (24) is clear: The correlation of a scale with some criterion can never exceed the square root of the reliability of the scale. Thus, if one has a measure with a low reliability, say, .64, that measure will never correlate greater than .8 with another variable. This demonstrates that reliability and validity go hand in hand. If one cannot reliably measure an attitude, he will never be able to predict actual behavior with it.

One should guard against being misled by Formula (23), however. It is *not* true that the validity of a scale can be determined merely by taking the square root of its reliability coefficient. There are several reasons for this. First, the square root of the left-hand side of (23) is the correlation of the scale with *whatever it is that the scale is measuring*. What is really being measured may or may not be that which one *wants* to measure. Stated differently, (23) says nothing about the content or construct validity of the scale. Second, we can obtain only an estimate of reliability, and if we use (23) to estimate validity the two estimates are totally dependent. It is incumbent upon the researcher to present *independent* validation, according to Campbell and Fiske. In fact, they suggest that the concept of independence is one way of distinguishing between reliability and validity. Validity is the correlation between measures of the same construct when the measures are maximally independent. Reliability reflects the degree of agreement among maximally similar methods.

To summarize, there is indeed an intimate relationship between reliability and validity, but validation procedures must be independent of those which establish the reliability of the scale.

SUMMARY

The goal of science is to explain relations among variables. The implementation of this goal is heavily dependent upon the ability of the researcher to measure his variables with as little error as possible. As was indicated, errors in measurement tend to distort relations among variables. Additionally, he needs to be concerned that his measures are valid, measuring that which they purport to measure. If hypothesized relations among variables are to be measured, the researcher needs to be certain that his measures of the variables are reliable and valid.

In this chapter, we have attempted to present several different ways in which concepts of reliability and validity are understood by researchers, and to present the ways in which reliability and validity can be estimated given these different meanings. Not all scientists will agree with the interpretations given here and the reader should recognize that there is still debate about the issues even though the American Psychological Association's *Technical Recommendations* (1954) did much to resolve such controversy. For example, an interesting comparison between the use of the term "validity" in 1951 and its use today can be made by reading Cureton (1951). Undoubtedly, the debate about the meanings of reliability and validity will continue for some time.

Finally, it should be acknowledged again that the discussion has necessarily been restricted, in the interests of comprehensiveness, to a somewhat superficial review of test construction procedures. Only the insightful researcher can build items which are both reliable and valid, and usually none of us can be satisfied with our first attempts at scale construction. Apparently, however, many researchers are satisfied with their "first-cut" instruments because many attitude scales are developed and used on a single sample. The careful researcher, however, ascertains the viability of the item by sampling and resampling within his population of respondents, replacing items in some cases and revising them in others until he is reasonably well satisfied that he has a viable scale. These cross-validation procedures can mean that years are spent in developing adequate measures. But adequate measures are a prerequisite for the demonstration of the utility of attitude measurement.

REFERENCES

American Psychological Association
1954 Standards for Educational and Psycho-
and logical Tests and Manuals. Washing-
1966 ton, D.C.: APA.
Bechtoldt, H. P.
1959 "Construct validity: A critique."
      American Psychologist 14:619–629.
Blalock, H. M. Jr.
1964 Causal Inferences in Nonexperimental
      Research. Chapel Hill: University of
      North Carolina Press.
Bohrnstedt, G. W.
1969 "Observations on the measurement of
      change." Pp. 113–133 in E. R. Borgatta
      (ed.), Sociological Methodology:1969.
      San Francisco: Jossey-Bass.
Brown, W.
1910 "Some experimental results in the cor-
      relation of mental abilities." British
      Journal of Psychology 3:296–322.
Campbell, D. T.
1960 "Recommendations for APA test stan-
      dards regarding construct, trait, or dis-
      criminant validity." American Psy-
      chologist 15:546–553.
Campbell, D. T., and D. W. Fiske.
1959 "Convergent and discriminant valida-
      tion by the multitrait-multimethod
      matrix." Psychological Bulletin 56:81–
      105.
Campbell, D. T., and J. C. Stanley.
1963 "Experimental and quasi-experimental
      designs for research on teaching." Pp.
      171–246 in N. L. Gage (ed.), Hand-
      book of Research on Teaching. Chi-
      cago: Rand McNally.
Cronbach, L. J.
1951 "Coefficient alpha and the internal

structure of tests." Psychometrika
      16:297–334.
Cronbach, L. J., and P. E. Meehl.
1955 "Construct validity in psychological
      tests." Psychological Bulletin 52:281–
      302.
Crowther, B.
1965 "A sociological analysis of achieve-
      ment correlates." Unpublished doctoral
      dissertation, Madison: University of
      Wisconsin.
Cureton, E. E.
1951 "Validity." Pp. 621–694 in E. F. Lind-
      quist (ed.), Educational Measurement.
      Washington, D.C.: American Council
      on Education.
1966 "Corrected item-test correlations." Psy-
      chometrika 31:93–96.
DuBois, P. H.
1965 An Introduction to Psychological Sta-
      tistics. New York: Harper and Row.
Ford, R. N., E. F. Borgatta, and G. W. Bohrn-
      stedt.
1969 "Use of the Work Components Study
      (WCS) with new college level em-
      ployees." Journal of Applied Psychol-
      ogy 53:367–376.
Guilford, J. P.
1954 Psychometric Methods (2nd edition).
      New York: McGraw-Hill.
Gulliksen, H.
1950 Theory of Mental Tests. New York:
      Wiley.
Guttman, L.
1953 "Reliability formulas that do not as-
      sume experimental independence."
      Psychometrika 18:225–239.
Hays, W. L.
1963 Statistics for Psychologists. New York:
      Holt, Rinehart, and Winston.
Heise, D. R.
1969 "Separating reliability and stability in
      test-retest correlations." American So-
      ciological Review 34:93–101.
Henrysson, S.
1963 "Correction of item-total correlations
      in item analysis." Psychometrika 32:
      435–441.
Horst, P.
1966 Psychological Measurement and Pre-
      diction. Belmont: Wadsworth.
Hoyt, C.
1941 "Test reliability estimated by analysis

of variance." Psychometrika 6:153–160.

Jackson, R. W. B., and G. A. Ferguson.
1941   Studies of the Reliability of Tests. Bulletin 12, Department of Educational Research. Toronto: University of Toronto.

Kerlinger, F. N., and E. Kaya.
1959   "The construction and factor analytic validation of scales to measure attitudes toward education." Educational and Psychological Measurement 19:13–29.

Kuder, G. F., and M. W. Richardson.
1937   "The theory of the estimation of test reliability." Psychometrika 2:135–138.

Lord, F. M., and M. R. Novick.
1968   Statistical Theories of Mental Test Scores. Reading: Addison-Wesley.

Novick, M. R., and C. Lewis.
1967   "Coefficient alpha and the reliability of composite measurements." Psychometrika 32:1–13.

Seeman, M.
1959   "On the meaning of alienation." American Sociological Review 24:783–791.

Spearman, C.
1910   "Correlation calculated with faulty data." British Journal of Psychology 3:271–295.

Stevens, S. S.
1951   "Mathematics, measurement, and psychophysics." In S. S. Stevens (ed.), Handbook of Experimental Psychology. New York: Wiley.

Webb, E. J., D. T. Campbell, R. D. Schwartz, and L. Sechrest.
1966   Unobtrusive Measures: Nonreactive Research in the Social Sciences. Chicago: Rand McNally.

Zubin, J.
1934   "The method of internal consistency for selecting test items." Journal of Educational Psychology 25:345–356.

CHAPTER 4

Convergent and Discriminant Validation by the Multitrait-Multimethod Matrix[1]

DONALD T. CAMPBELL AND DONALD W. FISKE

In the cumulative experience with measures of individual differences over the past 50 years, tests have been accepted as valid or discarded as invalid by research experiences of many sorts. The criteria suggested in this paper are all to be found in such cumulative evaluations, as well as in the recent discussions of validity. These criteria are clarified and implemented when considered jointly in the context of a multitrait-multimethod matrix. Aspects of the validational process receiving particular emphasis are these:

1) Validation is typically *convergent,* a confirmation by independent measurement procedures. Independence of methods is a

From Donald T. Campbell and Donald W. Fiske, "Convergent and discriminant validation by the multitrait-multimethod matrix." *Psychological Bulletin* 1959, *56,* 81–105. Copyright 1959 by the American Psychological Association, and reproduced by permission of the authors and publisher.

[1] The new data analyses reported in this paper were supported by funds from the Graduate School of Northwestern University and by the Department of Psychology of the University of Chicago. We are also indebted to numerous colleagues for their thoughtful criticisms and encouragement of an earlier draft of this paper, especially Benjamin S. Bloom, R. Darrell Bock, Desmond S. Cartwright, Loren J. Chapman, Lee J. Cronbach, Carl P. Duncan, Lyle V. Jones, Joe Kamiya, Wilbur L. Layton, Jane Loevinger, Paul E. Meehl, Marshall H. Segall, Thornton B. Roby, Robert C. Tryon, Michael Wertheimer, and Robert F. Winch.

common denominator among the major types of validity excepting content validity insofar as they are to be distinguished from reliability.

2) For the justification of novel trait measures, for the validation of test interpretation, or for the establishment of construct validity, *discriminant* validation as well as convergent validation is required. Tests can be invalidated by too high correlations with other tests from which they were intended to differ.

3) Each test or task employed for measurement purposes is a *trait-method unit,* a union of a particular trait content with measurement procedures not specific to that content. The systematic variance among test scores can be due to responses to the measurement features as well as responses to the trait content.

4) In order to examine discriminant validity, and in order to estimate the relative contributions of trait and method variance, *more than one trait* as well as *more than one method* must be employed in the validation process. In many instances it will be convenient to achieve this through a multitrait-multimethod matrix. Such a matrix presents all of the intercorrelations resulting when each of several traits is measured by each of several methods.

To illustrate the suggested validational

process, a synthetic example is presented in Table 1. This illustration involves three different traits, each measured by three methods, generating nine separate variables. It will be convenient to have labels for various regions of the matrix, and such have been provided in Table 1. The reliabilities will be spoken of in terms of three *reliability diagonals,* one for each method. The reliabilities could also be designated as the monotrait-monomethod values. Adjacent to each reliability diagonal is the *heterotrait-monomethod* triangle. The reliability diagonal and the adjacent heterotrait-monomethod triangle make up a *monomethod block.* A *heteromethod block* is made up of a *validity* diagonal (which could also be designated as monotrait-heteromethod values) and the two *heterotrait-heteromethod* triangles lying on each side of it. Note that these two heterotrait-heteromethod triangles are not identical.

In terms of this diagram, four aspects bear upon the question of validity. In the first place, the entries in the validity diagonal should be significantly different from zero and sufficiently large to encourage further examination of validity. This requirement is evidence of convergent validity. Second, a validity diagonal value should be higher than the values lying in its column and row in the heterotrait-heteromethod triangles. That is, a validity value for a variable should be higher than the correlations obtained between that variable and any other variable having neither trait nor method in common. This requirement may seem so minimal and so obvious as to not need stating, yet an inspection of the literature shows that it is frequently not met, and may not be met even when the validity coefficients are of substantial size. In Table 1, all of the validity values meet this requirement. A third common-sense desideratum is that a variable correlates higher with an independent effort to measure the same trait than with measures designed to get at different traits which happen to employ the same method. For a given variable, this involves comparing its values in the validity diagonals with its values in the heterotrait-monomethod triangles. For variables A_1, B_1, and C_1, this requirement is met to some degree. For the other variables, A_2,

TABLE 1

A Synthetic Multitrait-Multimethod Matrix

	Traits	Method 1			Method 2			Method 3		
		A_1	B_1	C_1	A_2	B_2	C_2	A_3	B_3	C_3
Method 1	A_1	(.89)								
	B_1	.51	(.89)							
	C_1	.38	.37	(.76)						
Method 2	A_2	.57	.22	.09	(.93)					
	B_2	.22	.57	.10	.68	(.94)				
	C_2	.11	.11	.46	.59	.58	(.84)			
Method 3	A_3	.56	.22	.11	.67	.42	.33	(.94)		
	B_3	.23	.58	.12	.43	.66	.34	.67	(.92)	
	C_3	.11	.11	.45	.34	.32	.58	.58	.60	(.85)

Note.—The validity diagonals are the three sets of italicized values. The reliability diagonals are the three sets of values in parentheses. Each heterotrait-monomethod triangle is enclosed by a solid line. Each heterotrait-heteromethod triangle is enclosed by a broken line.

A₃, etc., it is not met and this is probably typical of the usual case in individual differences research, as will be discussed in what follows. A fourth desideratum is that the same pattern of trait interrelationship be shown in all of the heterotrait triangles of both the monomethod and heteromethod blocks. The hypothetical data in Table 1 meet this requirement to a very marked degree, in spite of the different general levels of correlation involved in the several heterotrait triangles. The last three criteria provide evidence for discriminant validity.

Before examining the multitrait-multimethod matrices available in the literature, some explication and justification of this complex of requirements seems in order.

Convergence of Independent Methods: the Distinction between Reliability and Validity

Both reliability and validity concepts require that agreement between measures be demonstrated. A common denominator which most validity concepts share in contradistinction to reliability is that this agreement represent the convergence of independent approaches. The concept of independence is indicated by such phrases as "external variable," "criterion performance," "behavioral criterion" (American Psychological Association, 1954, pp. 13–15) used in connection with concurrent and predictive validity. For construct validity it has been stated thus: "Numerous successful predictions dealing with phenotypically diverse 'criteria' give greater weight to the claim of construct validity than do . . . predictions involving very similar behavior" (Cronbach and Meehl, 1955, p. 295). The importance of independence recurs in most discussions of proof. For example, Ayer, discussing a historian's belief about a past event, says "if these sources are numerous and independent, and if they agree with one another, he will be reasonably confident that their account of the matter is correct" (Ayer, 1954, p. 39). In discussing the manner in which abstract scientific concepts are tied to operations, Feigl speaks of their being "fixed" by "triangulation in logical space" (Feigl, 1958, p. 401).

Independence is, of course, a matter of degree, and in this sense, reliability and validity can be seen as regions on a continuum. (Cf. Thurstone, 1937, pp. 102–103.) Reliability is the agreement between two efforts to measure the same trait through maximally similar methods. Validity is represented in the agreement between two attempts to measure the same trait through maximally different methods. A split-half reliability is a little more like a validity coefficient than is an immediate test-retest reliability, for the items are not quite identical. A correlation between dissimilar subtests is probably a reliability measure, but is still closer to the region called validity.

Some evaluation of validity can take place even if the two methods are not entirely independent. In Table 1, for example, it is possible that Methods 1 and 2 are not entirely independent. If underlying Traits A and B are entirely independent, then the .10 minimum correlation in the heterotrait-heteromethod triangles may reflect method covariance. What if the overlap of method variance were higher? All correlations in the heteromethod block would then be elevated, including the validity diagonal. The heteromethod block involving Methods 2 and 3 in Table 1 illustrates this. The degree of elevation of the validity diagonal above the heterotrait-heteromethod triangles remains comparable and relative validity can still be evaluated. The interpretation of the validity diagonal in an absolute fashion requires the fortunate coincidence of both an independence of traits and an independence of methods, represented by zero values in the heterotrait-heteromethod triangles. But zero values could also occur through a combination of negative correlation between traits and positive correlation between methods, or the reverse. In practice, perhaps all that can be hoped for is evidence for relative validity, that is, for common variance specific to a trait, above and beyond shared method variance.

Discriminant validation—While the usual reason for the judgment of invalidity is low correlations in the validity diagonal—e.g., the Downey Will-Temperament Test [Symonds, 1931, p. 337ff]—tests have also been invalidated because of too high correlations with other tests purporting to measure different things. The classic case of the social intelligence tests is a case in point. (See below and also [Strang, 1930; R. Thorndike, 1936].) Such invalidation occurs when values in the heterotrait-heteromethod triangles are as high as those in the validity diagonal, or even where within a monomethod block, the heterotrait values are as high as the reliabilities. Loevinger, Gleser, and DuBois (1953) have emphasized this requirement in the development of maximally discriminating subtests.

When a dimension of personality is hypothesized, when a construct is proposed, the proponent invariably has in mind distinctions between the new dimension and other constructs already in use. One cannot define without implying distinctions, and the verification of these distinctions is an important part of the validational process. In discussions of construct validity, it has been expressed in such terms as "from this point of view, a low correlation with athletic ability may be just as important and encouraging as a high correlation with reading comprehension" (APA, 1954, p. 17).

The test as a trait-method unit—In any given psychological measuring device, there are certain features or stimuli introduced specifically to represent the trait that it is intended to measure. There are other features which are characteristic of the method being employed, features which could also be present in efforts to measure other quite different traits. The test, or rating scale, or other device, almost inevitably elicits systematic variance in response due to both groups of features. To the extent that irrelevant method variance contributes to the scores obtained, these scores are invalid.

This source of invalidity was first noted in the "halo effects" found in ratings (Thorndike, 1920). Studies of individual differences among laboratory animals resulted in the recognition of "apparatus factors," usually more dominant than psychological process factors (Tryon, 1942). For paper-and-pencil tests, methods variance has been noted under such terms as "test-form factors" (Vernon: 1957, 1958) and "response sets" (Cronbach: 1946, 1950; Lorge, 1937). Cronbach has stated the point particularly clearly: "The assumption is generally made . . . that what the test measures is determined by the content of the items. Yet the final score . . . is a composite of effects resulting from the content of the item and effects resulting from the form of the item used" (Cronbach, 1946, p. 475). "Response sets always lower the logical validity of a test . . . Response sets interfere with inferences from test data" (p. 484).

While E. L. Thorndike (1920) was willing to allege the presence of halo effects by comparing the high obtained correlations with commonsense notions of what they ought to be (e.g., it was unreasonable that a teacher's intelligence and voice quality should correlate .63) and while much of the evidence of response set variance is of the same order the clear-cut demonstration of the presence of method variance requires both several traits and several methods. Otherwise, high correlations between tests might be explained as due either to basic trait similarity or to shared method variance. In the multitrait-multimethod matrix, the presence of method variance is indicated by the difference in level of correlation between the parallel values of the monomethod block and the heteromethod blocks, assuming comparable reliabilities among all tests. Thus the contribution of method variance in Test A_1 of Table 1 is indicated by the elevation of $r_{A_1B_1}$ above $r_{A_1B_2}$, i.e., the difference between .51 and .22, etc.

The distinction between trait and method is of course relative to the test constructor's intent. What is an unwanted response set for one tester may be a trait for another who wishes to measure acquiescence, willingness to take an extreme stand, or tendency to attribute socially desirable attributes to oneself (Cronbach: 1946, 1950; Edwards, 1957; Lorge, 1937).

Multitrait-Multimethod Matrices in the Literature

Multitrait-multimethod matrices are rare in the test and measurement literature. Most frequent are two types of fragment: two methods and one trait (single isolated values from the validity diagonal, perhaps accompanied by a reliability or two), and heterotrait-monomethod triangles. Either type of fragment is apt to disguise the inadequacy of our present measurement efforts, particularly in failing to call attention to the preponderant strength of methods variance. The evidence of test validity to be presented here is probably poorer than most psychologists would have expected.

One of the earliest matrices of this kind was provided by Kelley and Krey in 1934. Peer judgments by students provided one method, scores on a word-association test the other. Table 2 presents the data for the four most valid traits of the eight he employed. The picture is one of strong method factors, particularly among the peer ratings, and al-

most total invalidity. For only one of the eight measures, School Drive, is the value in the validity diagonal (.16!) higher than all of the heterotrait-heteromethod values. The absence of discriminant validity is further indicated by the tendency of the values in the monomethod triangles to approximate the reliabilities.

An early illustration from the animal literature comes from Anderson's (1937) study of drives. Table 3 presents a sample of his data. Once again, the highest correlations are found among different constructs from the same method, showing the dominance of apparatus or method factors so typical of the whole field of individual differences. The validity diagonal for hunger is higher than the heteroconstruct-heteromethod values. The diagonal value for sex has not been *italicized* as a validity coefficient since the obstruction box measure was pre-sex-opportunity, the activity wheel post-opportunity. Note that the high general level of heterotrait-heteromethod values could be due either to correlation of methods variance between the two methods, or to correlated trait variance. On a priori grounds, however, the methods would seem about as independent as one would be likely to achieve. The predominance of an apparatus factor for the activity wheel is evident from the

TABLE 2

PERSONALITY TRAITS OF SCHOOL CHILDREN FROM KELLEY'S STUDY ($N = 311$)

		Peer Ratings				Association Test			
		A_1	B_1	C_1	D_1	A_2	B_2	C_2	D_2
Peer Ratings									
Courtesy	A_1	(.82)							
Honesty	B_1	.74	(.80)						
Poise	C_1	.63	.65	(.74)					
School Drive	D_1	.76	.78	.65	(.89)				
Association Test									
Courtesy	A_2	*.13*	.14	.10	.14	(.28)			
Honesty	B_2	.06	*.12*	.16	.08	.27	(.38)		
Poise	C_2	.01	.08	*.10*	.02	.19	.37	(.42)	
School Drive	D_2	.12	.15	.14	*.16*	.27	.32	.18	(.36)

TABLE 3

MEASURES OF DRIVES FROM ANDERSON'S DATA ($N = 50$)

		Obstruction Box			Activity Wheel		
		A_1	B_1	C_1	A_2	B_2	C_2
Obstruction Box							
Hunger	A_1	(.58)					
Thirst	B_1	.54	( )				
Sex	C_1	.46	.70	( )			
Activity Wheel							
Hunger	A_2	.48	.31	.37	(.83)		
Thirst	B_2	.35	.33	.43	.87	(.92)	
Post-Sex	C_2	.31	.37	.44	.69	.78	( )

Note.—Empty parentheses appear in this and subsequent tables where no appropriate reliability estimates are reported in the original paper.

fact that the correlation between hunger and thirst (.87) is of the same magnitude as their test-retest reliabilities (.83 and .92 respectively).

R. L. Thorndike's study (1936) of the validity of the George Washington Social Intelligence Test is the classic instance of invalidation by high correlation between traits. It involved computing all of the intercorrelations among five subscales of the Social Intelligence Test and five subscales of the George Washington Mental Alertness Test. The model of the present paper would demand that each of the traits, social intelligence and mental alertness, be measured by at least two methods. While this full symmetry was not intended in the study, it can be so interpreted without too much distortion. For both traits, there were subtests employing acquisition of knowledge during the testing period (i.e., learning or memory), tests involving comprehension of prose passages, and tests that involved a definitional activity. Table 4 shows six of Thorndike's ten variables ar-

TABLE 4

SOCIAL INTELLIGENCE AND MENTAL ALERTNESS SUBTEST INTERCORRELATIONS FROM THORNDIKE'S DATA ($N = 750$)

		Memory		Compre-hension		Vocabulary	
		A_1	B_1	A_2	B_2	A_3	B_3
Memory							
Social Intelligence (Memory for Names & Faces)	A_1	( )					
Mental Alertness (Learning Ability)	B_1	.31	( )				
Comprehension							
Social Intelligence (Sense of Humor)	A_2	.30	.31	( )			
Mental Alertness (Comprehension)	B_2	.29	.38	.48	( )		
Vocabulary							
Social Intelligence (Recog. of Mental State)	A_3	.23	.35	.31	.35	( )	
Mental Alertness (Vocabulary)	B_3	.30	.58	.40	.48	.47	( )

ranged as a multitrait-multimethod matrix. If the three subtests of the Social Intelligence Test are viewed as three methods of measuring social intelligence, then their intercorrelations (.30, .23, and .31) represent validities that are not only lower than their corresponding monomethod values, but also lower than the heterotrait-heteromethod correlations, providing a picture which totally fails to establish social intelligence as a separate dimension. The Mental Alertness validity diagonals (.38, .58, and .48) equal or exceed the monomethod values in two out of three cases, and exceed all heterotrait-heteromethod control values. These results illustrate the general conclusions reached by Thorndike in his factor analysis of the whole 10 × 10 matrix.

The data of Table 4 could be used to validate specific forms of cognitive functioning, as measured by the different methods represented by usual intelligence test content on the one hand and social content on the other. Table 5 rearranges the 15 values for this purpose. The monomethod values and the validity diagonals exchange places, while the heterotrait-heteromethod control coefficients are the same in both tables. As judged against these latter values, comprehension (.48) and vocabulary (.47), but not memory (.31), show some specific validity. This transmutability of the validation matrix argues for the comparisons within the heteromethod block as the most generally relevant validation data,

and illustrates the potential interchangeability of trait and method components.

Some of the correlations in Chi's (1937) prodigious study of halo effect in ratings are appropriate to a multitrait-multimethod matrix in which each rater might be regarded as representing a different method. While the published report does not make these available in detail because it employs averaged values, it is apparent from a comparison of his Tables IV and VIII that the ratings generally failed to meet the requirement that ratings of the same trait by different raters should correlate higher than ratings of different traits by the same rater. Validity is shown to the extent that of the correlations in the heteromethod block, those in the validity diagonal are higher than the average heteromethod-heterotrait values.

A conspicuously unsuccessful multitrait-multimethod matrix is provided by Campbell (1953, 1956) for rating of the leadership behavior of officers by themselves and by their subordinates. Only one of 11 variables (Recognition Behavior) met the requirement of providing a validity diagonal value higher than any of the heterotrait-heteromethod values, that validity being .29. For none of the variables were the validities higher than heterotrait-monomethod values.

A study of attitudes toward authority and nonauthority figures by Burwen and Campbell (1957) contains a complex multitrait-

TABLE 5

MEMORY, COMPREHENSION, AND VOCABULARY MEASURED WITH SOCIAL AND ABSTRACT CONTENT

		Social Content			Abstract Content		
		A_1	B_1	C_1	A_2	B_2	C_2
Social Content							
Memory (Memory for Names and Faces)	A_1	( )					
Comprehension (Sense of Humor)	B_1	.30	( )				
Vocabulary (Recognition of Mental State)	C_1	.23	.31	( )			
Abstract Content							
Memory (Learning Ability)	A_2	.31	.31	.35	( )		
Comprehension	B_2	.29	.48	.35	.38	( )	
Vocabulary	C_2	.30	.40	.47	.58	.48	( )

multimethod matrix, one symmetrical excerpt from which is shown in Table 6. Method variance was strong for most of the procedures in this study. Where validity was found, it was primarily at the level of validity diagonal values higher than heterotrait-heteromethod values. As illustrated in Table 6, attitude toward father showed this kind of validity, as did attitude toward peers to a lesser degree. Attitude toward boss showed no validity. There was no evidence of a generalized attitude toward authority which would include father and boss, although such values as the .64 correlation between father and boss as measured by interview might have seemed to confirm the hypothesis had they been encountered in isolation.

Borgatta (1954) has provided a complex multimethod study from which can be extracted Table 7, illustrating the assessment of two traits by four different methods. For all measures but one, the highest correlation is the apparatus one, i.e., with the other trait measured by the same method rather than with the same trait measured by a different method. Neither of the traits finds any consistent validation by the requirement that the validity diagonals exceed the heterotrait-heteromethod control values. As a most minimal requirement, it might be asked if the

sum of the two values in the validity diagonal exceeds the sum of the two control values, providing a comparison in which differences in reliability or communality are roughly partialled out. This condition is achieved at the purely chance level of three times in the six tetrads. This matrix provides an interesting range of methodological independence. The two "Sociometric by Others" measures, while representing the judgments of the same set of fellow participants, come from distinct tasks: Popularity is based upon each participant's expression of his own friendship preferences, while Expansiveness is based upon each participant's guesses as to the other participant's choices, from which has been computed each participant's reputation for liking lots of other persons, i.e., being "expansive." In line with this considerable independence, the evidence for a method factor is relatively low in comparison with the observational procedures. Similarly, the two "Sociometric by Self" measures represent quite separate tasks, Popularity coming from his estimates of the choices he will receive from others, Expansiveness from the number of expressions of attraction to others which he makes on the sociometric task. In contrast, the measures of Popularity and Expansiveness from the observations of

TABLE 6

ATTITUDES TOWARD FATHER, BOSS, AND PEER, AS MEASURED BY
INTERVIEW AND CHECK-LIST OF DESCRIPTIVE TRAITS

		Interview			Trait Check-List		
		A_1	B_1	C_1	A_2	B_2	C_2
Interview							
($N = 57$)							
Father	A_1	( )					
Boss	B_1	.64	( )				
Peer	C_1	.65	.76	( )			
Trait Check-List							
($N = 155$)							
Father	A_2	.40	.08	.09	(.24)		
Boss	B_2	.19	−.10	−.03	.23	(.34)	
Peer	C_2	.27	.11	.23	.21	.45	(.55)

TABLE 7

MULTIPLE MEASUREMENT OF TWO SOCIOMETRIC TRAITS ($N = 125$)

| | | Sociometric | | | | Observation | | | |
| | | by Others | | by Self | | Group Interaction | | Role Playing | |
		A_1	B_1	A_2	B_2	A_3	B_3	A_4	B_4
Sociometric by Others									
Popularity	A_1	( )							
Expansiveness	B_1	.47	( )						
Sociometric by Self									
Popularity	A_2	.19	.18	( )					
Expansiveness	B_2	.07	.08	.32	( )				
Observation of Group Interaction									
Popularity	A_3	.25	.18	.26	.11	( )			
Expansiveness	B_3	.21	.12	.28	.15	.84	( )		
Observation of Role Playing									
Popularity	A_4	.24	.14	.18	.01	.66	.58	( )	
Expansiveness	B_4	.25	.12	.26	.05	.66	.76	.73	( )

group interaction and the role playing not only involve the same specific observers, but in addition the observers rated the pair of variables as a part of the same rating task in each situation. The apparent degree of method variance within each of the two observational situations, and the apparent sharing of method variance between them, is correspondingly high.

In another paper by Borgatta (1955), 12 interaction process variables were measured by quantitative observation under two conditions, and by a projective test. In this test, the stimuli were pictures of groups, for which the S generated a series of verbal interchanges; these were then scored in Interaction Process Analysis categories. For illustrative purposes, Table 8 presents the five traits which had the highest mean communalities in the over-all factor analysis. Between the two highly similar observational methods, validation is excellent: trait variance runs higher than method variance; validity diagonals are in general higher than heterotrait values of both the heteromethod and monomethod blocks, most unexceptionally so for

Gives Opinion and Gives Orientation. The pattern of correlation among the traits is also in general confirmed.

Of greater interest because of the greater independence of methods are the blocks involving the projective test. Here the validity picture is much poorer. Gives Orientation comes off best, its projective test validity values of .35 and .33 being bested by only three monomethod values and by no heterotrait-heteromethod values within the projective blocks. All of the other validities are exceeded by some heterotrait-heteromethod value.

The projective test specialist may object to the implicit expectations of a one-to-one correspondence between projected action and overt action. Such expectations should not be attributed to Borgatta, and are not necessary to the method here proposed. For the simple symmetrical model of this paper, it has been assumed that the measures are labeled in correspondence with the correlations expected, i.e., in correspondence with the traits that the tests are alleged to diagnose. Note that in Table 8, Gives Opinion is the best projective

TABLE 8

INTERACTION PROCESS VARIABLES IN OBSERVED FREE BEHAVIOR, OBSERVED ROLE PLAYING AND A PROJECTIVE TEST ($N = 125$)

	Free Behavior					Role Playing					Projective Test				
	A_1	B_1	C_1	D_1	E_1	A_2	B_2	C_2	D_2	E_2	A_3	B_3	C_3	D_3	E_3
Free Behavior															
Shows solidarity A_1	( )														
Gives suggestion B_1	.25	( )													
Gives opinion C_1	.13	.24	( )												
Gives orientation D_1	−.14	.26	.52	( )											
Shows disagreement E_1	.34	.41	.27	.02	( )										
Role Playing															
Shows solidarity A_2	.43	.43	.08	.10	.29	( )									
Gives suggestion B_2	.16	.32	.00	.24	.07	.37	( )								
Gives opinion C_2	.15	.27	.60	.38	.12	.01	.10	( )							
Gives orientation D_2	−.12	.24	.44	.74	.08	.04	.18	.40	( )						
Shows disagreement E_2	.51	.36	.14	−.12	.50	.39	.27	.23	−.11	( )					
Projective Test															
Shows solidarity A_3	.20	.17	.16	.12	.08	.17	.12	.30	.17	.22	( )				
Gives suggestion B_3	.05	.21	.05	.08	.13	.10	.19	−.02	.06	.30	.32	( )			
Gives opinion C_3	.31	.30	.13	−.02	.26	.25	.19	.15	−.04	.53	.31	.63	( )		
Gives orientation D_3	−.01	.09	.30	.35	−.05	.03	.00	.19	.33	.00	.37	.29	.32	( )	
Shows disagreement E_3	.13	.18	.10	.14	.19	.22	.28	.02	.04	.23	.27	.51	.47	.30	( )

TABLE 9

MAYO'S INTERCORRELATIONS BETWEEN OBJECTIVE AND RATING MEASURES
OF INTELLIGENCE AND EFFORT ($N = 166$)

		Peer Ratings		Objective	
		A_1	B_1	A_2	B_2
Peer Rating					
Intelligence	A_1	(.85)			
Effort	B_1	.66	(.84)		
Objective Measures					
Intelligence	A_2	.46	.29	( )	
Effort	B_2	.46	.40	.10	( )

test predictor of both free behavior and role playing Shows Disagreement. Were a proper theoretical rationale available, these values might be regarded as validities.

Mayo (1956) has made an analysis of test scores and ratings of effort and intelligence, to estimate the contribution of halo (a kind of methods variance) to ratings. As Table 9 shows, the validity picture is ambiguous. The method factor or halo effect for ratings is considerable although the correlation between the two ratings (.66) is well below their reliabilities (.84 and .85). The objective measures share no appreciable apparatus overlap because they were independent operations. In spite of Mayo's argument that the ratings have some valid trait variance, the .46 heterotrait-heteromethod value seriously depreciates the otherwise impressive .46 and .40 validity values.

Cronbach (1949, p. 277) and Vernon (1957, 1958) have both discussed the multitrait-multimethod matrix shown in Table 10, based upon data originally presented by H. S. Conrad. Using an approximative technique, Vernon estimates that 61 per cent of the systematic variance is due to a general factor, that $21\frac{1}{2}$ per cent is due to the test-form factors specific to verbal or to pictorial forms of items, and that but $11\frac{1}{2}$ per cent is due to the content factors specific to electrical or to mechanical contents. Note that for the purposes of estimating validity, the interpretation of the general factor, which he estimates from the .49 and .45 heterotrait-heteromethod values, is equivocal. It could represent desired competence variance, representing components common to both electrical and mechanical skills—perhaps resulting from general industrial shop experience, common ability

TABLE 10

MECHANICAL AND ELECTRICAL FACTS MEASURED BY VERBAL AND PICTORIAL ITEMS

		Verbal Items		Pictorial Items	
		A_1	B_1	A_2	B_2
Verbal Items					
Mechanical Facts	A_1	(.89)			
Electrical Facts	B_1	.63	(.71)		
Pictorial Items					
Mechanical Facts	A_2	.61	.45	(.82)	
Electrical Facts	B_2	.49	.51	.64	(.67)

components, overlapping learning situations, and the like. On the other hand, this general factor could represent overlapping method factors, and be due to the presence in both tests of multiple choice item format, IBM answer sheets, or the heterogeneity of the Ss in conscientiousness, test-taking motivation, and test-taking sophistication. Until methods that are still more different and traits that are still more independent are introduced into the validation matrix, this general factor remains uninterpretable. From this standpoint it can be seen that 21½ per cent is a very minimal estimate of the total test-form variance in the tests, as it represents only test-form components specific to the verbal or the pictorial items, i.e., test-form components which the two forms do *not* share. Similarly, and more hopefully, the 11½ per cent content variance is a very minimal estimate of the total true trait variance of the tests, representing only the true trait variance which electrical and mechanical knowledge do *not* share.

Carroll (1952) has provided data on the Guilford-Martin Inventory of Factors STDCR and related ratings which can be rearranged into the matrix of Table 11. (Variable R has been inverted to reduce the number of negative correlations.) Two of the methods, Self Ratings and Inventory scores, can be seen as sharing method variance, and thus as having an inflated diagonal. The more independent heteromethod blocks involving Peer Ratings show some evidence of discriminant and convergent validity, with validity diagonals averaging .33 (Inventory × Peer Ratings) and .39 (Self Ratings × Peer Ratings) against heterotrait-heteromethod control values averaging .14 and .16. While not intrinsically impressive, this picture is nonetheless better than most of the validity matrices here assembled. Note that the Self Ratings show slightly higher validity diagonal elevations than do the Inventory scores, in spite of the much greater length and undoubtedly higher reliability of the latter. In addition, a method factor seems almost totally lacking for the Self Ratings, while

strongly present for the Inventory, so that the Self Ratings come off much the best if true trait variance is expressed as a proportion of total reliable variance (as Vernon [1958] suggests). The method factor in the STDCR Inventory is undoubtedly enhanced by scoring the same item in several scales, thus contributing correlated error variance, which could be reduced without loss of reliability by the simple expedient of adding more equivalent items and scoring each item in only one scale. It should be noted that Carroll makes explicit use of the comparison of the validity diagonal with the heterotrait-heteromethod values as a validity indicator.

Ratings in the Assessment Study of Clinical Psychologists

The illustrations of multitrait-multimethod matrices presented so far give a rather sorry picture of the validity of the measures of individual differences involved. The typical case shows an excessive amount of method variance, which usually exceeds the amount of trait variance. This picture is certainly not as a result of a deliberate effort to select shockingly bad examples: these are ones we have encountered without attempting an exhaustive coverage of the literature. The several unpublished studies of which we are aware show the same picture. If they seem more disappointing than the general run of validity data reported in the journals, this impression may very well be because the portrait of validity provided by isolated values plucked from the validity diagonal is deceptive, and uninterpretable in isolation from the total matrix. Yet it is clear that few of the classic examples of successful measurement of individual differences are involved, and that in many of the instances, the quality of the data might have been such as to magnify apparatus factors, etc. A more nearly ideal set of personality data upon which to illustrate the method was therefore sought in the multiple application of a set of rating scales in the assessment study of clinical psychologists (Kelly and Fiske, 1951).

TABLE 11
GUILFORD-MARTIN FACTORS STDCR AND RELATED RATINGS (N = 110)

	Inventory					Self Ratings					Peer Ratings				
	S	T	D	C	−R	S	T	D	C	−R	S	T	D	C	−R
Inventory															
S	(.92)														
T	.27	(.89)													
D	.62	.57	(.91)												
C	.36	.47	.90	(.91)											
−R	.69	.32	.28	−.06	(.89)										
Self Ratings															
S	.57	.11	.19	−.01	.53	( )									
T	.28	.65	.42	.26	.37	.26	( )								
D	.44	.25	.53	.45	.29	.31	.32	( )							
C	.31	.20	.54	.52	.13	.11	.21	.47	( )						
−R	.15	.30	.12	.04	.34	.10	.12	.04	.06	( )					
Peer Ratings															
S	.37	.08	.10	−.01	.38	.42	.02	.08	.08	.31	(.81)				
T	.23	.32	.15	.04	.40	.20	.39	.40	.21	.31	.37	(.66)			
D	.31	.11	.27	.24	.25	.17	.09	.29	.27	.30	.49	.38	(.73)		
C	.08	.15	.20	.26	−.05	.01	.06	.14	.30	.07	.19	.16	.40	(.75)	
−R	.21	.20	−.03	−.16	.45	.28	.17	.08	.01	.56	.55	.56	.34	−.07	(.76)

In that study, "Rating Scale A" contained 22 traits referring to "behavior which can be directly observed on the surface." In using this scale the raters were instructed to "disregard any inferences about underlying dynamics or causes" (p. 207). The Ss, first-year clinical psychology students, rated themselves and also their three teammates with whom they had participated in the various assessment procedures and with whom they had lived for six days. The median of the three teammates' ratings was used for the Teammate score. The Ss were also rated on these 22 traits by the assessment staff. Our analysis uses the Final Pooled ratings, which were agreed upon by three staff members after discussion and review of the enormous amount of data and the many other ratings on each S. Unfortunately for our purposes, the staff members saw the ratings by Self and Teammates before making theirs, although presumably they were little influenced by these data because they had so much other evidence available to them. (Kelly and Fiske, 1951, especially p. 64.) The Self and Teammate ratings represent entirely separate "methods" and can be given the major emphasis in evaluating the data to be presented.

In a previous analysis of these data (Fiske, 1949), each of the three heterotrait-monomethod triangles was computed and factored. To provide a multitrait-multimethod matrix, the 1452 heteromethod correlations have been computed especially for this report.[2] The full 66 × 66 matrix with its 2145 coefficients is obviously too large for presentation here, but will be used in analyses that follow. To provide an illustrative sample, Table 12 presents the interrelationships among five variables, selecting the one best representing each of the five recurrent factors discovered in Fiske's

[2] We are indebted to E. Lowell Kelly for furnishing the V.A. assessment date to us, and to Hugh Lane for producing the matrix of intercorrelations.

In the original report the correlations were based upon 128 men. The present analyses were based on only 124 of these cases because of clerical errors. This reduction in N leads to some very minor discrepancies between these values and those previously reported.

(1949) previous analysis of the monomethod matrices. (These were chosen without regard to their validity as indicated in the heteromethod blocks. Assertive—No. 3 reflected—was selected to represent Recurrent Factor 5 because Talkative had also a high loading on the first recurrent factor.)

The picture presented in Table 12 is, we believe, typical of the best validity in personality trait ratings that psychology has to offer at the present time. It is comforting to note that the picture is better than most of those previously examined. Note that the validities for Assertive exceed heterotrait values of both the monomethod and heteromethod triangles. Cheerful, Broad Interests, and Serious have validities exceeding the heterotrait-heteromethod values with two exceptions. Only for Unshakable Poise does the evidence of validity seem trivial. The elevation of the reliabilities above the heterotrait-monomethod triangles is further evidence for discriminant validity.

A comparison of Table 12 with the full matrix shows that the procedure of having but one variable to represent each factor has enhanced the appearance of validity, although not necessarily in a misleading fashion. Where several variables are all highly loaded on the same factor, their "true" level of intercorrelation is high. Under these conditions, sampling errors can depress validity diagonal values and enhance others to produce occasional exceptions to the validity picture, both in the heterotrait-monomethod matrix and in the heteromethod-heterotrait triangles. In this instance, with an N of 124, the sampling error is appreciable, and may thus be expected to exaggerate the degree of invalidity.

Within the monomethod sections, errors of measurement will be correlated, raising the general level of values found, while within the heteromethods block, measurement errors are independent, and tend to lower the values both along the validity diagonal and in the heterotrait triangles. These effects, which may also be stated in terms of method factors or shared confounded irrelevancies, operate

TABLE 12

RATINGS FROM ASSESSMENT STUDY OF CLINICAL PSYCHOLOGISTS ($N = 124$)

	Staff Ratings					Teammate Ratings					Self Ratings				
	A_1	B_1	C_1	D_1	E_1	A_2	B_2	C_2	D_2	E_2	A_3	B_3	C_3	D_3	E_3
Staff Ratings															
A_1 Assertive	(.89)														
B_1 Cheerful	.37	(.85)													
C_1 Serious	−.24	−.14	(.81)												
D_1 Unshakable Poise	.25	.46	.08	(.84)											
E_1 Broad Interests	.35	.19	.09	.31	(.92)										
Teammate Ratings															
A_2 Assertive	.71	.35	−.18	.26	.41	(.82)									
B_2 Cheerful	.39	.53	−.15	.38	.29	.37	(.76)								
C_2 Serious	−.27	−.31	.43	−.06	.03	−.15	−.19	(.70)							
D_2 Unshakable Poise	.03	−.05	.03	.20	.07	.11	.23	.19	(.74)						
E_2 Broad Interests	.19	.05	.04	.29	.47	.33	.22	.19	.29	(.76)					
Self Ratings															
A_3 Assertive	.48	.31	−.22	.19	.12	.46	.36	−.15	.12	.23	( )				
B_3 Cheerful	.17	.42	−.10	.10	−.03	.09	.24	−.25	−.11	−.03	.23	( )			
C_3 Serious	−.04	−.13	.22	−.13	−.05	−.04	−.11	.31	.06	.06	−.05	−.12	( )		
D_3 Unshakable Poise	.13	.27	−.03	.22	−.04	.10	.15	.00	.14	−.03	.16	.26	.11	( )	
E_3 Broad Interests	.37	.15	−.22	.09	.26	.27	.12	−.07	.05	.35	.21	.15	.17	.31	( )

strongly in these data, as probably in all data involving ratings. In such cases, where several variables represent each factor, none of the variables consistently meets the criterion that validity values exceed the corresponding values in the monomethod triangles, when the full matrix is examined.

To summarize the validation picture with respect to comparisons of validity values with other heteromethod values in each block, Table 13 has been prepared. For each trait and for each of the three heteromethod blocks, it presents the value of the validity diagonal, the highest heterotrait value involving that trait, and the number out of the

42 such heterotrait values which exceed the validity diagonal in magnitude. (The number 42 comes from the grouping of the 21 other column values and the 21 other row values for the column and row intersecting at the given diagonal value.)

On the requirement that the validity diagonal exceed all others in its heteromethod block, none of the traits has a completely perfect record, although some come close. Assertive has only one trivial exception in the Teammate-Self block. Talkative has almost as good a record, as does Imaginative. Serious has but two inconsequential exceptions and Interest in Women three. These traits stand

TABLE 13

VALIDITIES OF TRAITS IN THE ASSESSMENT STUDY OF CLINICAL PSYCHOLOGISTS,
AS JUDGED BY THE HETEROMETHOD COMPARISONS

	Staff-Teammate			Staff-Self			Teammate-Self		
	Val.	Highest Het.	No. Higher	Val.	Highest Het.	No. Higher	Val.	Highest Het.	No. Higher
1. Obstructiveness*	.30	.34	2	.16	.27	9	.19	.24	1
2. Unpredictable	.34	.26	0	.18	.24	3	.05	.19	29
3. Assertive*	.71	.65	0	.48	.45	0	.46	.48	1
4. Cheerful*	.53	.60	2	.42	.40	0	.24	.38	5
5. Serious*	.43	.35	0	.22	.27	2	.31	.24	0
6. Cool, Aloof	.49	.48	0	.20	.46	10	.02	.34	36
7. Unshakable Poise	.20	.40	16	.22	.27	4	.14	.19	10
8. Broad Interests*	.47	.46	0	.26	.37	6	.35	.32	0
9. Trustful	.26	.34	5	.08	.25	19	.11	.17	9
10. Self-centered	.30	.34	2	.17	.27	6	—.07	.19	36
11. Talkative*	.82	.65	0	.47	.45	0	.43	.48	1
12. Adventurous	.45	.60	6	.28	.30	2	.16	.36	14
13. Socially Awkward	.45	.37	0	.06	.21	28	.04	.16	30
14. Adaptable*	.44	.40	0	.18	.23	10	.17	.29	8
15. Self-sufficient*	.32	.33	1	.13	.18	5	.18	.15	0
16. Worrying, Anxious*	.41	.37	0	.23	.33	5	.15	.16	1
17. Conscientious	.26	.33	4	.11	.32	19	.21	.23	2
18. Imaginative*	.43	.46	1	.32	.31	0	.36	.32	0
19. Interest in Women*	.42	.43	2	.55	.38	0	.37	.40	1
20. Secretive, Reserved*	.40	.58	5	.38	.40	2	.32	.35	3
21. Independent Minded	.39	.42	2	.08	.25	19	.21	.30	3
22. Emotional Expression*	.62	.63	1	.31	.46	5	.19	.34	10

Note.—Val. = value in validity diagonal; Highest Het. = highest heterotrait value; No. Higher = number of heterotrait values exceeding the validity diagonal.

* Trait names which have validities in all three heteromethod blocks significantly greater than the heterotrait-heteromethod values at the .001 level.

out as highly valid in both self-description and reputation. Note that the actual validity coefficients of these four traits range from but .22 to .82, or, if we concentrate on the Teammate-Self block as most certainly representing independent methods, from but .31 to .46. While these are the best traits, it seems that most of the traits have far above chance validity. All those having ten or fewer exceptions have a degree of validity significant at the .001 level as crudely estimated by a one-tailed sign test.[3] All but one of the variables meet this level for the Staff-Teammate block, all but four for the Staff-Self block, all but five for the most independent block, Teammate-Self. The exceptions to significant validity are not parallel from column to column, however, and only 13 of 22 variables have .001 significant validity in all three blocks. These are indicated by an asterisk in Table 13.

This highly significant general level of validity must not obscure the meaningful problem created by the occasional exceptions, even for the best variables. The excellent traits of Assertive and Talkative provide a case in point. In terms of Fiske's original analysis, both have high loadings on the recurrent factor "Confident self-expression" (represented by Assertive in Table 12). Talkative also had high loadings on the recurrent factor of Social Adaptability (represented by Cheerful in Table 12). We would expect, therefore, both high correlation between them and significant discrimination as well. And even at the commonsense level, most psychologists would expect fellow psychologists to discriminate validly between assertiveness (nonsubmissiveness) and talkativeness. Yet in the Teammate-Self block, Assertive rated by self correlates .48 with

---

[3] If we take the validity value as fixed (ignoring its sampling fluctuations), then we can determine whether the number of values larger than it in its row and column is less than expected on the null hypothesis that half the values would be above it. This procedure requires the assumption that the position (above or below the validity value) of any one of these comparison values is independent of the position of each of the others, a dubious assumption when common methods and trait variance are present.

Talkative by teammates, higher than either of their validities in this block, .43 and .46.

In terms of the average values of the validities and the frequency of exceptions, there is a distinct trend for the Staff-Teammate block to show the greatest agreement. This can be attributed to several factors. Both represent ratings from the external point of view. Both are averaged over three judges, minimizing individual biases and undoubtedly increasing reliabilities. Moreover, the Teammate ratings were available to the Staff in making their ratings. Another effect contributing to the less adequate convergence and discrimination of Self ratings was a response set toward the favorable pole which greatly reduced the range of these measures (Fiske, 1949, p. 342). Inspection of the details of the instances of invalidity summarized in Table 13 shows that in most instances the effect is attributable to the high specificity and low communality for the self-rating trait. In these instances, the column and row intersecting at the low validity diagonal are asymmetrical as far as general level of correlation is concerned, a fact covered over by the condensation provided in Table 13.

The personality psychologist is initially predisposed to reinterpret self-ratings, to treat them as symptoms rather than to interpret them literally. Thus, we were alert to instances in which the self ratings were not literally interpretable, yet nonetheless had a diagnostic significance when properly "translated." By and large, the instances of invalidity of self-descriptions found in this assessment study are not of this type, but rather are to be explained in terms of an absence of communality for one of the variables involved. In general, where these self descriptions are interpretable at all, they are as literally interpretable as are teammate descriptions. Such a finding may, of course, reflect a substantial degree of insight on the part of these Ss.

The general success in discriminant validation coupled with the parallel factor patterns found in Fiske's earlier analysis of the three intramethod matrices seemed to justify an inspection of the factor pattern validity in this instance. One possible procedure would be to do a single analysis of the whole 66 × 66 matrix. Other approaches focused upon separate factoring of heteromethods blocks, matrix by matrix, could also be suggested. Not only would such methods be extremely tedious, but in addition they would leave undetermined the precise comparison of factor-pattern similarity. Correlating factor loadings over the population of variables was employed for this purpose by Fiske but while this provided for the identification of recurrent factors, no single over-all index of factor pattern similarity was generated. Since our immediate interest was in confirming a pattern of interrelationships, rather than in describing it, an efficient short cut was available: namely to test the similarity of the sets of heterotrait values by correlation coefficients in which each entry represented the size values of the given heterotrait coefficients in two different matrices. For the full matrix, such correlations would be based upon the N of the 22 × 21/2 or 231 specific heterotrait combinations. Correlations were computed between the Teammate and Self monomethods matrices, selected as maximally independent. (The values to follow were computed from the original correlation matrix and are somewhat higher than that which would be obtained from a reflected matrix.) The similarity between the two monomethods matrices was .84, corroborating the factor-pattern similarity between these matrices described more fully by Fiske in his parallel factor analyses of them. To carry this mode of analysis into the heteromethod block, this block was treated as though divided into two by the validity diagonal, the above diagonal values and the below diagonal representing the maximally independent validation of the heterotrait correlation pattern. These two correlated .63, a value which, while lower, shows an impressive degree of confirmation. There remains the question as to whether this pattern upon which the two heteromethod-heterotrait triangles agree is the same one found in common between the two mono-

method triangles. The intra-Teammate matrix correlated with the two heteromethod triangles .71 and .71. The intra-Self matrix correlated with the two .57 and .63. In general, then, there is evidence for validity of the intertrait relationship pattern.

DISCUSSION

Relation to Construct Validity

While the validational criteria presented are explicit or implicit in the discussions of construct validity (Cronbach and Meehl, 1955; APA, 1954), this paper is primarily concerned with the adequacy of tests as measures of a construct rather than with the adequacy of a construct as determined by the confirmation of theoretically predicted associations with measures of other constructs. We believe that before one can test the relationships between a specific trait and other traits, one must have some confidence in one's measures of that trait. Such confidence can be supported by evidence of convergent and discriminant validation. Stated in different words, any conceptual formulation of trait will usually include implicitly the proposition that this trait is a response tendency which can be observed under more than one experimental condition and that this trait can be meaningfully differentiated from other traits. The testing of these two propositions must be prior to the testing of other propositions to prevent the acceptance of erroneous conclusions. For example, a conceptual framework might postulate a large correlation between Traits A and B and no correlation between Traits A and C. If the experimenter then measures A and B by one method (e.g., questionnaire) and C by another method (such as the measurement of overt behavior in a situation test), his findings may be consistent with his hypotheses solely as a function of method variance common to his measures of A and B but not to C.

The requirements of this paper are intended to be as appropriate to the relatively atheoretical efforts typical of the tests and measurements field as to more theoretical efforts. This emphasis on validational criteria appropriate to our present atheoretical level of test construction is not at all incompatible with a recognition of the desirability of increasing the extent to which all aspects of a test and the testing situation are determined by explicit theoretical considerations, as Jessor and Hammond (1957) have advocated.

Relation to operationalism—Underwood (1957, p. 54) in his effective presentation of the operationalist point of view shows a realistic awareness of the amorphous type of theory with which most psychologists work. He contrasts a psychologist's "literary" conception with the latter's operational definition as represented by his test or other measuring instrument. He recognizes the importance of the literary definition in communicating and generating science. He cautions that the operational definition "may not at all measure the process he wishes to measure; it may measure something quite different" (p. 55). He does not, however, indicate how one would know when one was thus mistaken.

The requirements of the present paper may be seen as an extension of the kind of operationalism Underwood has expressed. The test constructor is asked to generate from his literary conception or private construct not one operational embodiment, but two or more, each as different in research vehicle as possible. Furthermore, he is asked to make explicit the distinction between his new variable and other variables, distinctions which are almost certainly implied in his literary definition. In his very first validational efforts, before he ever rushes into print, he is asked to apply the several methods and several traits jointly. His literary definition, his conception, is now best represented in what his independent measures of the trait hold *distinctively* in common. The multitrait-multimethod matrix is, we believe, an important practical first step in avoiding "the danger . . . that the investigator will fall into the trap of thinking that because he went from an artistic or literary conception . . . to the construction of items for a scale to measure it, he has validated his artistic conception" (Underwood, 1957, p. 55). In contrast with the *single operationalism* now dominant in psychology, we are advocating a *multiple operationalism*, a *convergent operationalism* (Garner, 1954; Garner, Hake, and Eriksen, 1956), a *methodological triangulation* (Campbell, 1953, 1956), an *operational delineation* (Campbell, 1954), a *convergent validation*.

Underwood's presentation and that of this paper as a whole imply moving from concept to operation, a sequence that is frequent in science, and perhaps typical. The same point can be made, however, in inspecting a transition from operation to construct. For any body of data taken from a single operation, there is a sub-infinity of interpretations possible; a sub-infinity of concepts, or combinations of concepts, that it could represent. Any single operation, as representative of concepts, is equivocal. In an analogous fashion, when we view the Ames distorted room from a fixed point and through a single eye, the data of the retinal pattern are equivocal, in that a sub-infinity of hexahedrons could generate the same pattern. The addition of a second viewpoint, as through binocular parallax, greatly reduces this equivocality, greatly limits the constructs that could jointly account for both sets of data. In Garner's (1954) study, the fractionation measures from a single method were equivocal—they could have been a function of the stimulus distance being fractionated, or they could have been a function of the comparison stimuli used in the judgment process. A multiple, convergent operationalism reduced this equivocality, showing the latter conceptualization to be the appropriate one, and revealing a preponderance of methods variance. Similarly for learning studies: in identifying constructs with the response data from animals in a specific operational setup there is equivocality which can operationally be reduced by introducing transposition tests, different operations so designed as to put to comparison the rival conceptualizations (Campbell, 1954).

Garner's convergent operationalism and our insistence on more than one method for measuring each concept depart from Bridgman's early position that "if we have more than one set of operations, we have more than one concept, and strictly there should be a separate name to correspond to each different set of operations" (Bridgman, 1927, p. 10). At the current stage of psychological progress, the crucial requirement is the demonstration of some convergence, not complete congruence, between two distinct sets of operations. With only one method, one has no way of distinguishing trait variance from unwanted method variance. When psychological measurement and conceptualization become better developed, it may well be appropriate to differentiate conceptually between Trait-Method Unit A_1 and Trait-Method Unit A_2, in which Trait A is measured by different methods. More likely, what we have called method variance will be specified theoretically in terms of a set of constructs. (This has in effect been illustrated in the discussion above in which it was noted that the response set variance might be viewed as trait variance, and in the rearrangement of the social intelligence matrices of Tables 4 and 5.) It will then be recognized that measurement procedures usually involve several theoretical constructs in joint application. Using obtained measurements to estimate values for a single construct under this condition still requires comparison of complex measures varying in their trait composition, in something like a multitrait-multimethod matrix. Mill's joint method of similarities and differences still epitomizes much about the effective experimental clarification of concepts.

The evaluation of a multitrait-multimethod matrix—The evaluation of the correlation matrix formed by intercorrelating several trait-method units must take into consideration the many factors which are known to affect the magnitude of correlations. A value in the validity diagonal must be assessed in the light of the reliabilities of the two measures involved: e.g., a low reliability for Test A_2 might exaggerate the apparent method variance in Test A_1. Again, the whole approach assumes adequate sampling of individuals: the curtailment of the sample with respect to one or more traits will depress the reliability coefficients and intercorrelations involving these traits. While restrictions of range over all traits produces serious difficulties in the interpretation of a multitrait-multimethod matrix and should be avoided whenever possible, the presence of different degrees of restriction on different traits is the more serious hazard to meaningful interpretation.

Various statistical treatments for multitrait-multimethod matrices might be developed. We have considered rough tests for the elevation of a value in the validity diagonal above the comparison values in its row and column. Correlations between the columns for variables measuring the same trait, variance analyses, and factor analyses have been proposed to us. However, the development of such statistical methods is beyond the scope of this paper. We believe that such summary statistics are neither necessary nor appropriate at this time. Psychologists today should be concerned not with evaluating tests as if the tests were fixed and definitive, but rather with developing better tests. We believe that a careful examination of a multitrait-multimethod matrix will indicate to the experimenter what his next steps should be: it will indicate which methods should be discarded or replaced, which concepts need sharper delineation, and which concepts are poorly measured because of excessive or confounding method variance. Validity judgments based on such a matrix must take into account the stage of development of the constructs, the postulated relationships among them, the level of technical refinement of the methods, the relative independence of the methods, and any pertinent characteristics of the sample of Ss. We are proposing that the validational process be viewed as an aspect of an ongoing program for improving measuring procedures and that the "validity coefficients" obtained at any one stage in the process be interpreted in terms of gains over preceding stages and as indicators of where further effort is needed.

The design of a multitrait-multimethod matrix—The several methods and traits included in a validational matrix should be selected with care. The several methods used to measure each trait should be appropriate to the trait as conceptualized. Although this view will reduce the range of suitable methods, it will rarely restrict the measurement to one operational procedure.

Wherever possible, the several methods in one matrix should be completely independent of each other: there should be no prior reason for believing that they share method variance. This requirement is necessary to permit the values in the heteromethod-heterotrait triangles to approach zero. If the nature of the traits rules out such independence of methods, efforts should be made to obtain as much diversity as possible in terms of data-sources and classification processes. Thus, the classes of stimuli *or* the background situations, the experimental contexts, should be different. Again, the persons providing the observations should have different roles *or* the procedures for scoring should be varied.

Plans for a validational matrix should take into account the difference between the interpretations regarding convergence and discrimination. It is sufficient to demonstrate convergence between two clearly distinct methods which show little overlap in the heterotrait-heteromethod triangles. While agreement between several methods is desirable, convergence between two is a satisfactory minimal requirement. Discriminative validation is not so easily achieved. Just as it is impossible to prove the null hypothesis, or that some object does not exist, so one can never establish that a trait, as measured, is differentiated from all other traits. One can only show that this measure of Trait A has little overlap with those measures of B and C, and no dependable generalization beyond B and C can be made. For example, social

poise could probably be readily discriminated from aesthetic interests, but it should also be differentiated from leadership.

Insofar as the traits are related and are expected to correlate with each other, the monomethod correlations will be substantial and heteromethod correlations between traits will also be positive. For ease of interpretation, it may be best to include in the matrix at least two traits, and preferably two sets of traits, which are postulated to be independent of each other.

In closing, a word of caution is needed. Many multitrait-multimethod matrices will show no convergent validation: no relationship may be found between two methods of measuring a trait. In this common situation, the experimenter should examine the evidence in favor of several alternative propositions: (*a*) Neither method is adequate for measuring the trait. (*b*) One of the two methods does not really measure the trait. (When the evidence indicates that a method does not measure the postulated trait, it may prove to measure some other trait. High correlations in the heterotrait-heteromethod triangles may provide hints to such possibilities.) (*c*) The trait is not a functional unity, the response tendencies involved being specific to the nontrait attributes of each test. The failure to demonstrate convergence may lead to conceptual developments rather than to the abandonment of a test.

SUMMARY

This paper advocates a validational process utilizing a matrix of intercorrelations among tests representing at least two traits, each measured by at least two methods. Measures of the same trait should correlate higher with each other than they do with measures of different traits involving separate methods. Ideally, these validity values should also be higher than the correlations among different traits measured by the same method.

Illustrations from the literature show that these desirable conditions, as a set, are rarely met. Method or apparatus factors make very large contributions to psychological measurements.

The notions of convergence between independent measures of the same trait and discrimination between measures of different traits are compared with previously published formulations, such as construct validity and convergent operationalism. Problems in the application of this validational process are considered.

REFERENCES

American Psychological Association.
1954 "Technical recommendations for psychological tests and diagnostic techniques." Psychological Bulletin Supplement 51 Part 2:1–38.

Anderson, E. E.
1937 "Interrelationship of drives in the male albino rat. I. Intercorrelations of Measures of Drives." Journal of Comparative Psychology 24:73–118.

Ayer, A. J.
1956 The Problem of Knowledge. New York: St. Martin's Press.

Borgatta, E. F.
1954 "Analysis of social interaction and sociometric perception." Sociometry 17: 7–32.
1955 "Analysis of social interaction: Actual, role-playing, and projective." 51:394–405.

Bridgman, P. W.
1927 The Logic of Modern Physics. New York: Macmillan.

Burwen, L. S., and D. T. Campbell.
1957 "The generality of attitudes toward authority and nonauthority figures." Journal of Abnormal and Social Psychology 54:24–31.

Campbell, D. T.
1953 A Study of Leadership Among Submarine Officers. Columbus: Ohio State University Research Foundation.
1954 "Operational delineation of 'what is learned' via the transposition experiment." Psychological Review 61:167–174.
1956 Leadership and Its Effects Upon the Group. Monogr. No. 83. Columbus: Ohio State University Bureau of Business Research.

Carroll, J. B.
1952 "Ratings on traits measured by a factored personality inventory." Journal of Abnormal and Social Psychology 47: 626–632.

Chi, P. L.
1937 "Statistical analysis of personality rating." Journal of Experimental Education 5:229–245.

Cronbach, L. J.
1946 "Response sets and test validity." Educational and Psychological Measurement 6:475–494.
1949 Essentials of Psychological Testing. New York: Harper.
1950 "Further evidence on response sets and test design." Educational and Psychological Measurement 10:3–31.

Cronbach, L. J., and P. E. Meehl.
1955 "Construct validity in psychological tests." Psychological Bulletin 52:281–302.

Edwards, A. L.
1957 The Social Desirability Variable in Personality Assessment and Research. New York: Dryden.

Feigl, H.
1958 "The mental and the physical." In H. Feigl, M. Scriven and G. Maxwell (eds.), Minnesota Studies in the Philosophy of Science. Vol. II. Concepts, Theories and the Mind-body Problem. Minneapolis: University of Minnesota Press.

Fiske, D. W.
1949 "Consistency of the factorial structures of personality ratings from different sources." Journal of Abnormal and Social Psychology 44:329–344.

Garner, W. R.
1954 "Context effects and the validity of loudness scales." Journal of Experimental Psychology 48:218–224.

Garner, W. R., H. W. Hake, and C. W. Ericksen.
1956 "Operationism and the concept of perception." Psychological Review 63: 149–159.

Jessor, R., and K. R. Hammond.
1957 "Construct validity and the Taylor Anxiety Scale." Psychological Bulletin 54:161–170.

Kelley, T. L., and A. C. Krey.

1934   Tests and Measurements in the Social Sciences. New York: Scribner.

Kelly, E. L., and D. W. Fiske.
1951   The Prediction of Performance in Clinical Psychology. Ann Arbor: University of Michigan Press.

Loevinger, J., G. C. Gleser, and P. H. DuBois.
1953   "Maximizing the discriminating power of a multiple-score test." Psychometrika 18:309–317.

Lorge, I.
1937   "Gen-like: Halo or reality?" Psychological Bulletin 34:545–546.

Mayo, G. D.
1956   "Peer ratings and halo." Educational and Psychological Measurement 16: 317–323.

Strang, R.
1930   "Relation of social intelligence to certain other factors." School and Society 32:268–272.

Symonds, P. M.
1931   Diagnosing Personality and Conduct. New York: Appleton-Century.

Thorndike, E. L.

1920   "A constant error in psychological ratings." Journal of Applied Psychology 4:25–29.

Thorndike, R. L.
1936   "Factor analysis of social and abstract intelligence." Journal of Educational Psychology 27:231–233.

Thurstone, L. L.
1937   The Reliability and Validity of Tests. Ann Arbor: Edwards.

Tryon, R. C.
1942   "Individual differences." In F. A. Moss (ed.), Comparative Psychology. (2nd ed.) New York: Prentice-Hall. Pp. 330–365.

Underwood, B. J.
1957   Psychological Research. New York: Appleton-Century-Crofts.

Vernon, P. E.
1957   "Educational ability and psychological factors." Address given to the Joint Education-Psychology Colloquium. University of Illinois, March 29, 1957.
1958   Educational Testing and Test-form Factors. Princeton: Educational Testing Service. (Res. Bull. RB-58-3.)

SECTION **II**   **Early Self-Report Techniques**

Overview

From his extensive experience with measurement of abilities and traits Thurstone proposed a method for the measurement of attitude. Statements of opinion were said to symbolize attitudes and attitudes could be measured by developing scales of opinion statements. With such scales individuals could be differentiated with respect to attitudes in much the same way that individual differences in intelligence, abilities, or traits could be ascertained. Thus, early in the history of attitude measurement Thurstone took a position favoring use of self-report specimens. Perhaps due to the high regard psychologists held for Thurstone and the growing popularity of operationalism among psychologists the Thurstone technique became quickly established. It is important to note also that his scaling procedure incorporated established techniques from psychophysics. Early statements of the rationale and technique are contained in Chapter 5 and with co-author Chave in Chapter 6.

The Thurstone method of attitude scaling contained several unverified statistical assumptions and the method was quite laborious to use. In 1932 Likert published a monograph which attempted to deal with both these matters. He proposed a simpler method which did not require the unverified statistical assumption. Excerpts from the monograph are presented as Chapter 7 and are sufficient to convey the nature of Likert's proposal.

Whether the Likert method is an adequate, perhaps superior, alternative to the Thurstone method has been a point of discourse since Likert's monograph appeared. Unfortunately, as is often the case in such matters, there is little empirical evidence that may be introduced into the discourse. Seiler and Hough have undertaken a search for such empirical evidence as exists and their findings are discussed in Chapter 8. While there is clearly a need for further research before the issue can be settled, two matters do seem settled: 1) "the Likert method of *scoring* an attitude scale, of any given number of items, consistently produces more reliable results than the Thurstone method of *scoring* the scale" (p. 171); and 2) the Likert method of scale construction and scoring requires fewer items to produce the same reliability as the Thurstone method.

A colleague once remarked that without the two world wars social psychology would have died in infancy. Whether this statement is true or not, it was while assigned to the Department of the Army that sociologist Louis Guttman developed a method of scale construction which rests upon assumptions quite different from either Thurstone's or Likert's and has a much greater versatility. While its popularity is greatest among attitude researchers it is appropriate for scaling many other object universes.

One of the limitations of both the Thurstone and Likert methods is that identical scores may be arrived at in more than one way. Thus, persons with the same attitude score on either a Thurstone or Likert scale, may not be said to have the same attitude. The Guttman scaling method overcomes this limitation. By knowing a person's score on a perfect Guttman scale it is possible to reproduce the person's entire pattern of responses to the scale items. This is so because the items are ordered by difficulty level and the scale score represents the level at which failure (non-endorsement) occurred. Unfortunately, perfect Guttman scales never occur in practice. It is necessary, therefore, to estimate the error of reproducibility. In Chapter 9 Guttman presents the rationale for his method of scale construction and Chapter 10 is a presentation of the technique of scale construction he developed and published while at Cornell University.

Since the first presentation of the Guttman scale construction procedures considerable effort has been directed toward expanding, modifying and refining the method and toward developing more efficient and simpler techniques of scale construction. Chapter 11 by Dotson and Summers is a brief summary of the most important efforts to elaborate Guttman scaling techniques.

Chapter 12 presents the scale-discrimination developed by Edwards and Kilpatrick. It is a "new" technique only in the sense that it combines the Thurstone, Likert and Guttman methods. Arguing that Thurstone and Likert methods provide a basis for selecting items to be included in a scale while Guttman's method allows items to be evaluated, they present a procedure for screening items first by the Thurstone method of judges and then subjecting items retained to Likert selection criteria. Those items meeting both sets of criteria are finally examined for reproducibility.

CHAPTER 5   Attitudes Can Be Measured[1]

L. L. THURSTONE

THE POSSIBILITY OF MEASURING ATTITUDE

The purpose of this paper is to discuss the problem of measuring attitudes and opinions and to offer a solution for it. The very fact that one offers a solution to a problem so complex as that of measuring differences of opinion or attitude on disputed social issues makes it evident from the start that the solution is more or less restricted in nature and that it applies only under certain assumptions that will, however, be described. In devising a method of measuring attitude I have tried to get along with the fewest possible restrictions because sometimes one is tempted to disre-

Reprinted from the *American Journal of Sociology*, Volume XXXIII (January, 1928), 529–554 by L. L. Thurstone by permission of The University of Chicago Press, Chicago, Illinois.

[1] This is one of a series of papers by the staff of the Behavior Research Fund, Illinois Institute for Juvenile Research, Chicago. Series B No. 110.

The original manuscript for this paper has enjoyed a great deal of friendly criticism, some of which turns on matters of terminology and some on the assumptions which are here stated. In order to keep this paper within reasonable length, the description of the detailed psychophysical methods used and the construction of several attitude scales are reserved for separate publication. This paper concerns then only an outline of one solution to the problem of measuring attitude.

gard so many factors that the original problem disappears. I trust that I shall not be accused of throwing out the baby with its bath.

In promising to measure attitudes I shall make several common-sense assumptions that will be stated here at the outset so that subsequent discussion may not be fogged by confusion regarding them. If the reader is unwilling to grant these assumptions, then I shall have nothing to offer him. If they are granted, we can proceed with some measuring methods that ought to yield interesting results.

It is necessary to state at the very outset just what we shall here mean by the terms "attitude" and "opinion." This is all the more necessary because the natural first impression about these two concepts is that they are not amenable to measurement in any real sense. It will be conceded at the outset that an attitude is a complex affair which cannot be wholly described by any single numerical index. For the problem of measurement this statement is analogous to the observation that an ordinary table is a complex affair which cannot be wholly described by any single numerical index. So is a man such a complexity which cannot be wholly represented by a single index. Nevertheless we do not hesitate to say that we measure the table. The context usually implies what it is about the table that we propose to measure. We say without hesitation that we measure a man when we take some anthropometric measurements of him. The context may well imply without explicit declaration what aspect of the man we are measuring, his cephalic index, his height or weight or what not. Just in the same sense we shall say here that we are measuring attitudes. We shall state or imply by the context the aspect of people's attitudes that we are measuring. The point is that it is just as legitimate to say that we are measuring attitudes as it is to say that we are measuring tables or men.

The concept "attitude" will be used here to denote the sum total of a man's inclinations and feelings, prejudice or bias, preconceived notions, ideas, fears, threats, and convictions about any specified topic. Thus a man's attitude about pacifism means here all that he feels and thinks about peace and war. It is admittedly a subjective and personal affair.

The concept "opinion" will here mean a verbal expression of attitude. If a man says that we made a mistake in entering the war against Germany, that statement will here be spoken of as an opinion. The term "opinion" will be restricted to verbal expression. But it is an expression of what? It expresses an attitude, supposedly. There should be no difficulty in understanding this use of the two terms. The verbal expression is the *opinion*. Our interpretation of the expressed opinion is that the man's *attitude* is pro-German. An opinion symbolizes an attitude.

Our next point concerns what it is that we want to measure. When a man says that we made a mistake in entering the war with Germany, the thing that interests us is not really the string of words as such or even the immediate meaning of the sentence merely as it stands, but rather the attitude of the speaker, the thoughts and feelings of the man about the United States, and the war, and Germany. It is the attitude that really interests us. The opinion has interest only in so far as we interpret it as a symbol of attitude. It is therefore something about attitudes that we

want to measure. We shall use opinions as the means for measuring attitudes.[2]

There comes to mind the uncertainty of using an opinion as an index of attitude. The man may be a liar. If he is not intentionally misrepresenting his real attitude on a disputed question, he may nevertheless modify the expression of it for reasons of courtesy, especially in those situations in which frank expression of attitude may not be well received. This has led to the suggestion that a man's action is a safer index of his attitude than what he says. But his actions may also be distortions of his attitude. A politician extends friendship and hospitality in overt action while hiding an attitude that he expresses more truthfully to an intimate friend. Neither his opinions nor his overt acts constitute in any sense an infallible guide to the subjective inclinations and preferences that constitute his attitude. Therefore we must remain content to use opinions, or other forms of action, merely as indices of attitude. It must be recognized that there is a discrepancy, some error of measurement as it were, between the opinion or overt action that we use as an index and the attitude that we infer from such an index.

But this discrepancy between the index and "truth" is universal. When you want to know the temperature of your room, you look at the thermometer and use its reading as an index of temperature just as though there were no error in the index and just as though there were a single temperature reading which is the "correct" one for the room. If it is desired to ascertain the volume of a glass paper weight, the volume is postulated as an attri-

---

[2] Professor Faris, who has been kind enough to give considerable constructive criticism to the manuscript for this paper, has suggested that we may be measuring opinion but that we are certainly not measuring attitude. It is in part a terminological question which turns on the concept of attitude. If the concept of attitude as here defined is not acceptable, it may be advisable to change the terminology provided that a distinction is retained between (1) the objective index, which is here called the statement or opinion, and (2) the inferred subjective inclination of the person, which is here called the attitude variable.

bute of the piece of glass, even though volume is an abstraction. The volume is measured indirectly by noting the dimensions of the glass or by immersing it in water to see how much water it displaces. These two procedures give two indices which might not agree exactly. In almost every situation involving measurement there is postulated an abstract continuum such as volume or temperature, and the allocation of the thing measured to that continuum is accomplished usually by indirect means through one or more indices. Truth is inferred only from the relative consistency of the several indices, since it is never directly known. We are dealing with the same type of situation in attempting to measure attitude. We must postulate an attitude variable which is like practically all other measurable attributes in the nature of an abstract continuum, and we must find one or more indices which will satisfy us to the extent that they are internally consistent.

In the present study we shall measure the subject's attitude as expressed by the acceptance or rejection of opinions. But we shall not thereby imply that he will necessarily *act* in accordance with the opinions that he has indorsed. Let this limitation be clear. The measurement of attitudes expressed by a man's opinions does not necessarily mean the prediction of what he will do. If his expressed opinions and his actions are inconsistent, that does not concern us now, because we are not setting out to predict overt conduct. We shall assume that it is of interest to know what people *say* that they believe even if their conduct turns out to be inconsistent with their professed opinions. Even if they are intentionally distorting their attitudes, we are measuring at least the attitude which they are trying to make people believe that they have.

We take for granted that people's attitudes are subject to change. When we have measured a man's attitude on any issue such as pacifism, we shall not declare such a measurement to be in any sense an enduring or constitutional constant. His attitude may change, of course, from one day to the next, and it is our task to measure such changes, whether they be due to unknown causes or to the presence of some known persuasive factor such as the reading of a discourse on the issue in question. However, such fluctuations may also be attributed in part to error in the measurements themselves. In order to isolate the errors of the measurement instrument from the actual fluctuation in attitude, we must calculate the standard error of measurement of the scale itself, and this can be accomplished by methods already well known in mental measurement.

We shall assume that an attitude scale is used only in those situations in which one may reasonably expect people to tell the truth about their convictions or opinions. If a denominational school were to submit to its students a scale of attitudes about the church, one should hardly expect intelligent students to tell the truth about their convictions if they deviate from orthodox beliefs. At least, the findings could be challenged if the situation in which attitudes are expressed contains pressure or implied threat bearing directly on the attitude to be measured. Similarly, it would be difficult to discover attitudes on sex liberty by a written questionnaire, because of the well-nigh universal pressure to conceal such attitudes where they deviate from supposed conventions. It is assumed that attitude scales will be used only in those situations that offer a minimum of pressure on the attitude to be measured. Such situations are common enough.

All that we can do with an attitude scale is to measure the attitude actually expressed with the full realization that the subject may be consciously hiding his true attitude or that the social pressure of the situation has made him really believe what he expresses. This is a matter for interpretation. It is something probably worth while to measure an attitude expressed by opinions. It is another problem to interpret in each case the extent to which the subjects have expressed what they really believe. All that we can do is to minimize as far as possible the conditions that prevent our subjects from telling the truth, or else to adjust our intepretations accordingly.

When we discuss opinions, about prohibition for example, we quickly find that these opinions are multidimensional, that they cannot all be represented in a linear continuum. The various opinions cannot be completely described merely as "more" or "less." They scatter in many dimensions, but the very idea of measurement implies a linear continuum of some sort such as length, price, volume, weight, age. When the idea of measurement is applied to scholastic achievement, for example, it is necessary to force the qualitative variations into a scholastic linear scale of some kind. We judge in a similar way such qualities as mechanical skill, the excellence of handwriting, and the amount of a man's education, as though these traits were strung out along a single scale, although they are of course in reality scattered in many dimensions. As a matter of fact, we get along quite well with the concept of a scale in describing traits even so qualitative as education, social and economic status, or beauty. A scale or linear continuum is implied when we say that a man has more education than another, or that a woman is more beautiful than another, even though, if pressed, we admit that perhaps the pair involved in each of the comparisons have little if anything in common. It is clear that the linear continuum which is implied in a "more or less" judgment may be conceptual, that it does not necessarily have the physical existence of a yardstick.

And so it is also with attitudes. We do not hesitate to compare them by the "more and less" type of judgment. We say about a man, for example, that he is more in favor of prohibition than some other, and the judgment conveys its meaning very well with the implication of a linear scale along which people or opinions might be allocated.

THE ATTITUDE VARIABLE

The first restriction on the problem of measuring attitudes is to specify an attitude variable and to limit the measurement to that. An example will make this clear. Let us consider the prohibition question and let us take as the attitude variable the degree of restriction that should be imposed on individual liberty in the consumption of alcohol. This degree of restriction can be thought of as a continuum ranging from complete and absolute freedom or license to equally complete and absolute restriction, and it would of course include neutral and indifferent attitudes.

In collecting samples from which to construct a scale we might ask a hundred individuals to write out their opinions about prohibition. Among these we might find one which expresses the belief that prohibition has increased the use of tobacco. Surely this is an opinion concerning prohibition, but it would not be at all serviceable for measuring the attitude variable just mentioned. Hence it would be irrelevant. Another man might express the opinion that prohibition has eliminated an important source of government revenue. This is also an opinion concerning prohibition, but it would not belong to the particular attitude variable that we have set out to measure or scale. It is preferable to use an objective and experimental criterion for the elimination of opinions that do not belong on the specified continuum to be measured, and I believe that such a criterion is available.

This restriction on the problem of measuring attitudes is necessary in the very nature of measurement. It is taken for granted in all ordinary measurement, and it must be clear that it applies also to measurement in a field in which the multidimensional characteristics have not yet been so clearly isolated. For example, it would be almost ridiculous to call attention to the fact that a table cannot be measured unless one states or implies what it is about the table that is to be measured; its height, its cost, or beauty or degree of appropriateness or the length of time required to make it. The context usually makes this restriction on measurement. When the notion of measurement is applied to so complex a phenomenon as opinions and attitudes, we must here also restrict ourselves to some specified or implied continuum along which the measurement is to take place.

In specifying the attitude variable, the first requirement is that it should be so stated that one can speak of it in terms of "more" and "less," as, for example, when we compare the attitudes of people by saying that one of them is more pacifistic, more in favor of prohibition, more strongly in favor of capital punishment, or more religious than some other person.

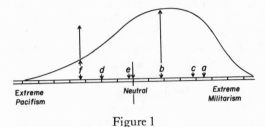

Extreme
Pacifism   Neutral   Extreme
                                                 Militarism

Figure 1

Figure 1 represents an attitude variable, militarism–pacifism, with a neutral zone. A person who usually talks in favor of preparedness, for example, would be represented somewhere to the right of the neutral zone. A person who is more interested in disarmament would be represented somewhere to the left of the neutral zone. It is possible to conceive of a frequency distribution to represent the distribution of attitude in a specified group on the subject of pacifism–militarism.

Consider the ordinate of the frequency distribution at any point on the base line. The point and its immediate vicinity represent for our purpose an attitude, and we want to know relatively how common that degree of feeling for or against pacifism may be in the group that is being studied. It is of secondary interest to know that a particular statement of opinion is indorsed by a certain proportion of that group. It is only to the extent that the opinion is representative of an attitude that it is useful for our purposes. Later we shall consider the possibility that a statement of opinion may be scaled as rather pacifistic and yet be indorsed by a person of very pronounced militaristic sympathies. To the extent that the statement is indorsed or rejected by factors other than the attitude-variable that it represents, to that extent the statement is useless for our purposes. We

shall also consider an objective criterion for spotting such statements so that they may be eliminated from the scale. In our entire study we shall be dealing, then, with opinions, not primarily because of their cognitive content but rather because they serve as the carriers or symbols of the attitudes of the people who express or indorse these opinions.

There is some ambiguity in using the term attitude in the plural. An attitude is represented as a point on the attitude continuum. Consequently there is an infinite number of attitudes that might be represented along the attitude scale. In practice, however, we do not differentiate so finely. In fact, an attitude, practically speaking, is a certain narrow range or vicinity on the scale. When a frequency distribution is drawn for any continuous variable, such as stature, we classify the variable for descriptive purposes into steps or class intervals. The attitude variable can also be divided into class intervals and the frequency counted in each class interval. When we speak of "an" attitude, we shall mean a point, or a vicinity, on the attitude continuum. Several attitudes will be considered not as a set of discrete entities, but as a series of class intervals along the attitude scale.

A FREQUENCY DISTRIBUTION OF ATTITUDES

The main argument so far has been to show that since in ordinary conversation we readily and understandably describe individuals as more and less pacifistic or more and less militaristic in attitude, we may frankly represent this linearity in the form of a unidimensional scale. This has been done in a diagrammatic way in Figure 1. We shall first describe our objective and then show how a rational unit of measurement may be adopted for the whole scale.

Let the base line of Figure 1 represent a continuous range of attitudes from extreme pacifism on the left to extreme militarism on the right.

If the various steps in such a scale were defined, it is clear that a person's attitude on militarism–pacifism could be represented by a point on that scale. The strength and direction of a particular individual's sympathies might be indicated by the point *a*, thus showing that he is rather militaristic in his opinions. Another individual might be represented at the point *b* to show that although he is slightly militaristic in his opinions, he is not so extreme about it as the person who is placed at the point *a*. A third person might be placed at the point *c* to show that he is quite militaristic and that the difference between *a* and *c* is very slight. A similar interpretation might be extended to any point on the continuous scale from extreme militarism to extreme pacifism, with a neutral or indifference zone between them.

A second characteristic might also be indicated graphically in terms of the scale, namely, the range of opinions that any particular individual is willing to indorse. It is of course not to be expected that every person will find only one single opinion on the whole scale that he is willing to indorse and that he will reject all the others. As a matter of fact we should probably find ourselves willing to indorse a great many opinions on the scale that cover a certain range of it. It is conceivable, then, that a pacifistically inclined person would be willing to indorse all or most of the opinions in the range *d* to *e* and that he would reject as too extremely pacifistic most of the opinions to the left of *d*, and would also reject the whole range of militaristic opinions. His attitude would then be indicated by the average or mean of the range that he indorses, unless he cares to select a particular opinion which most nearly represents his own attitude. The same sort of reasoning may of course be extended to the whole range of the scale, so that we should have at least two, or possibly three, characteristics of each person designated in terms of the scale. These characteristics would be (1) the mean position that he occupies on the scale, (2) the range of opinions that he is willing to accept, and (3) that one opinion which he selects as the one which most nearly represents his own attitude on the issue at stake.

It should also be possible to describe a

group of individuals by means of the scale. This type of description has been represented in a diagrammatic way by the frequency outline.

Any ordinate of the curve would represent the number of individuals, or the percentage of the whole group, that indorses the corresponding opinion. For example, the ordinate at *b* would represent the number of persons in the group who indorse the degree of militarism represented by the point *b* on the scale. A glance at the frequency curve shows that for the fictitious group of this diagram militaristic opinions are indorsed more frequently than the pacifistic ones. It is clear that the area of this frequency diagram would represent the total number of indorsements given by the group. The diagram can be arranged in several different ways that will be separately discussed. It is sufficient at this moment to realize that, given a valid scale of opinions, it would be possible to compare several different groups in their attitudes on a disputed question.

A second type of group comparison might be made by the range or spread that the frequency surfaces reveal. If one of the groups is represented by a frequency diagram of considerable range or scatter, then that group would be more heterogeneous on the issue at stake than some other group whose frequency diagram of attitudes shows a smaller range or scatter. It goes without saying that the frequent assumption of a normal distribution in educational scale construction has absolutely no application here, because there is no reason whatever to assume that any group of people will be normally distributed in their opinions about anything.

It should be possible, then, to make four types of description by means of a scale of attitudes. These are (1) the average or mean attitude of a particular individual on the issue at stake, (2) the range of opinion that he is willing to accept or tolerate, (3) the relative popularity of each attitude of the scale for a designated group as shown by the frequency distribution for that group, and (4) the degree of homogeneity or heterogeneity in the attitudes of a designated group on the issue as shown by the spread or dispersion of its frequency distribution.

This constitutes our objective. The heart of the problem is in the unit of measurement for the base line, and it is to this aspect of the problem that we may now turn.

A UNIT OF MEASUREMENT FOR ATTITUDES

The only way in which we can identify the different attitudes (points on the base line) is to use a set of opinions as landmarks, as it were, for the different parts or steps of the scale. The final scale will then consist of a series of statements of opinion, each of which is allocated to a particular point on the base line. If we start with enough statements, we may be able to select a list of twenty or thirty opinions so chosen that they represent an evenly graduated series of attitudes. The separation between successive statements of opinion would then be uniform, but the scale can be constructed with a series of opinions allocated on the base line even though their base line separations are not uniform. For the purpose of drawing frequency distributions it will be convenient, however, to have the statements so chosen that the steps between them are uniform throughout the whole range of the scale.

Consider the three statements a, c, and d, in Figure 1. The statements c and a are placed close together to indicate that they are very similar, while statements c and d are spaced far apart to indicate that they are very different. We should expect two individuals scaled at c and a respectively to agree very well in discussing pacifism and militarism. On the other hand, we should expect to be able to tell the difference quite readily between the opinions of a person at d and another person at c. The scale separations of the opinions must agree with our impressions of them.

In order to ascertain how far apart the statements should be on the final scale, we submit them to a group of several hundred people who are asked to arrange the statements in order from the most pacifistic to the most militaristic. We do not ask them for their own opinions. That is another matter entirely. We are now concerned with the construction of a scale with a valid unit of measurement. There may be a hundred statements in the original list, and the several hundred persons are asked merely to arrange the statements in rank order according to the designated attitude variable. It is then possible to ascertain the proportion of the readers who consider statement a to be more militaristic than statement c. If the two statements represent very similar attitudes we should not expect to find perfect agreement in the rank order of statements a and c. If they are identical in attitude, there will be about 50 per cent of the readers who say that statement a is more militaristic than statement c, while the remaining 50 per cent of the readers will say that statement c is more militaristic than statement a. It is possible to use the proportion of readers or judges who agree about the rank order of any two statements as a basis for actual measurement.

If 90 per cent of the judges or readers say that statement a is more militaristic than statement b ($p_{a>b} = .90$) and if only 60 per cent of the readers say that statement a is more militaristic than statement c ($p_{a>c} = .60$) then clearly the scale separation $(a - c)$ is shorter than the scale separation $(a - b)$. The psychological scale separation between any two stimuli can be measured in terms of a law of comparative judgment which the writer has recently formulated.[3]

The detailed methods of handling the data will be published in connection with the construction of each particular scale. The practical outcome of this procedure is a series of statements of opinions allocated along the base line of Figure 1. The interpretation of the base-line distances is that the apparent difference between any two opinions will be equal to the apparent difference between any other two opinions which are spaced equally far apart on the scale. In other words, the

---

[3] For a more detailed discussion of this law see my article "The Law of Comparative Judgment," *Psych Rev.* (July, 1927). For the logic of the psychological S-scale see "Psychophysical Analysis," *Amer. J. Psych.* (July, 1927).

shift in opinion represented by a unit distance on the base line seems to most people the same as the shift in opinion represented by a unit distance at any other part of the scale. Two individuals who are separated by any given distance on the scale *seem* to differ in their attitudes as much as any other two individuals with the same scale separation. In this sense we have a truly rational base line, and the frequency diagrams erected on such a base line are capable of legitimate interpretation as frequency surfaces.

In contrast with such a rational base line or scale is the simpler procedure of merely listing ten to twenty opinions, arranging them in rank order by a few readers, and then merely counting the number of indorsements for each statement. That can of course be done provided that the resulting diagram be not interpreted as a frequency distribution of attitude. If so interpreted the diagram can be made to take any shape we please by merely adding new statements or eliminating some of them, arranging the resulting list in a rough rank order evenly spaced on the base line. Allport's diagrams of opinions[4] are not in any sense frequency distributions. They should be considered as bar-diagrams in which are shown the frequency with which each of a number of statements is indorsed. Our principal contribution here is an improvement on Allport's procedure. He is virtually dealing with rank orders, which we are here trying to change into measurement by a rational unit of measurement. Allport's pioneering studies in this field should be read by every investigator of this problem. My own interest in the possibility of measuring attitude by means of opinions was started by Allport's paper, and the present study is primarily a refinement of his statistical methods.

The unit of measurement for the scale of attitudes is the standard deviation of the dispersion projected on the psychophysical scale of attitudes by a statement of opinion, chosen as a standard. It is a matter of indifference

which statement is chosen as a standard, since the scales produced by different standard statements will have proportional scale values. This mental unit of measurement is roughly comparable to, but not identical with, the so-called "just noticeable difference" in psychophysical measurement.

A diagram such as Figure 1 can be constructed in either of at least two different ways. The area of the frequency surface may be made to represent the total number of votes or indorsements by a group of people, or the area may be made to represent the total number of individuals in the group studied. Allport's diagrams would be made by the latter principle if they were constructed on a rational base line so that a legitimate area might be measured. Each subject was asked to select that one statement in the list most representative of his own attitude. Hence at least the sum of the ordinates will equal the total number of persons in the group. I have chosen as preferable the procedure of asking each subject to indorse all the statements with which he agrees. Since we have a rational base line, we may make a legitimate interpretation of the area of the surface as the total number of indorsements made by the group. This procedure has the advantage that we may ascertain the range of opinion which is acceptable to each person, a trait which has considerable interest and which cannot be ascertained by asking the subject to indorse only one of the statements in the list. The ordinates of the frequency diagram can be plotted as proportions of the whole group. They will then be interpreted as the probability that the given statement will be indorsed by a member of the group. In other words, the frequency diagram is descriptive of the distribution of attitude in the whole group, and at each point on the base line we want an ordinate to represent the relative popularity of that attitude.

THE CONSTRUCTION OF AN ATTITUDE SCALE

At the present time three scales for the mea-

---

[4] Floyd H. Allport, and D. A. Hartman, "Measurement and Motivation of Atypical Opinion in a Certain Group," *American Political Science Review*, XIX (1925), 735–60.

surement of opinion are being constructed by the principles here described.[5] These three scales are planned to measure attitudes on three different variables, namely, pacifism-militarism, prohibition, and attitude toward the church. All three of these scales are being constructed first by a procedure somewhat less laborious than the direct application of the law of comparative judgment, and if consistent results are obtained the method will be retained for other scales.

The method is as follows. Several groups of people are asked to write out their opinions on the issue in question, and the literature is searched for suitable brief statements that may serve the purposes of the scale. By editing such material a list of from 100 to 150 statements is prepared expressive of attitudes covering as far as possible all gradations from one end of the scale to the other. It is sometimes necessary to give special attention to the neutral statements. If a random collection of statements of opinion should fail to produce neutral statements, there is some danger that the scale will break in two parts. The whole range of attitudes must be fairly well covered, as far as one can tell by preliminary inspection, in order to insure that there will be overlapping in the rank orders of different readers throughout the scale.

In making the initial list of statements several practical criteria are applied in the first editing work. Some of the important criteria are as follows: (1) the statements should be as brief as possible so as not to fatigue the subjects who are asked to read the whole list. (2) The statements should be such that they can be indorsed or rejected in accordance with their agreement or disagreement with the attitude of the reader. Some statements in a random sample will be so phrased that the reader can express no definite indorsement or rejection of them. (3) Every statement should be such that acceptance or rejection of the statement does indicate something regarding the reader's attitude about the issue in question. If, for example, the statement is made that war is an incentive to inventive genius, the acceptance or rejection of it really does not say anything regarding the reader's pacifistic or militaristic tendencies. He may regard the statement as an unquestioned fact and simply indorse it as a fact, in which case his answer has not revealed anything concerning his own attitude on the issue in question. However, only the conspicuous examples of this effect should be eliminated by inspection, because an objective criterion is available for detecting such statements so that their elimination from the scale will be automatic. Personal judgment should be minimized as far as possible in this type of work. (4) Double-barreled statements should be avoided except possibly as examples of neutrality when better neutral statements do not seem to be readily available. Double-barreled statements tend to have a high ambiguity. (5) One must insure that at least a fair majority of the statements really belong on the attitude variable that is to be measured. If a small number of irrelevant statements should be either intentionally or unintentionally left in the series, they will be automatically eliminated by an objective criterion, but the criterion will not be successful unless the majority of the statements are clearly a part of the stipulated variable.

When the original list has been edited with these factors in mind, there will be perhaps 80 to 100 statements to be actually scaled. These statements are then mimeographed on small cards, one statement on each card. Two or three hundred subjects are asked to arrange the statements in 11 piles ranging from opinions most strongly affirmative to those most strongly negative. The detailed instructions will be published with the description of the separate scales. The task is essentially to sort out the small cards into 11 piles so that they *seem* to be fairly evenly spaced or graded. Only the two ends and the middle pile are labelled. The middle pile is indicated for neutral opinions. The reader must decide

---

[5] Three attitude scales are now in course of preparation by Mr. E. J. Chave, of the Divinity School, University of Chicago, on attitudes toward the church, [Ed. note: see Chapter 6] and by Mr. Daniel Droba on attitudes about pacifism-militarism. [Ed. note: see Chapter 7]...

for each statement which of five subjective degrees of affirmation or five subjective degrees of negation is implied in the statement or whether it is a neutral opinion.

When such sorting has been completed by two or three hundred readers, a diagram like Figure 2 is prepared. We shall discuss it with the scale for pacifism–militarism as an example. On the base line of this diagram are represented the 11 apparently equal steps of the attitude variable. The neutral interval is the interval 5 to 6, the most pacifistic interval from 0 to 1, and the most militaristic interval from 10 to 11. This diagram is fictitious and is drawn to show the principle involved. Curve A is drawn to show the manner in which one of the statements might be classified by the three hundred readers. It is not classified by anyone below the value of 3, half of the readers classify it below the value 6, and all of them classify it below the value 9. The scale value of the statement is that scale value below which just one-half of the readers place it. In other words, the scale value assigned to the statement is so chosen that one-half of the readers consider it more militaristic and one-half of them consider it less militaristic than the scale value assigned. The numerical calculation of the scale value is similar to the calculation of the limen by the *phi-gamma* hypothesis in psychophysical measurement.

It will be found that some of the statements toward the ends of the scale do not give complete ogive curves. Thus statement C is incomplete in the fictitious diagram. It behaves as though it needed space beyond the arbitrary limits of the scale in order to be completed. Its scale value may, however, be determined as that scale value at which the *phi-gamma* curve through the experimental proportions crosses the 50 per cent level, which is at c. Still other statements may be found, such as D, which have scale values beyond the arbitrary range of the scale. These may be assigned scale values by the same process, though less accurately.

The situation is different at the other end of the scale. The statement E has a scale value at e, but owing to the limit of the scale at the point 11 the experimental proportion will be 1.00 at that point. If the scale continued beyond the point 11 the proportions would continue to rise gradually as indicated by the dotted line. The experimental proportions are all necessarily 1.00 for the scale value 11, and hence these final proportions must be ignored in fitting the *phi-gamma* curves and in the location of the scale values of the statements.

THE VALIDITY OF THE SCALE

a) The scale must transcend the group measured—One crucial experimental test must be applied to our method of measuring attitudes before it can be accepted as valid. A measuring instrument must not be seriously affected in its measuring function by the object of measurement. To the extent

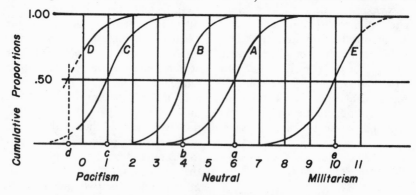

Figure 2

that its measuring function is so affected, the validity of the instrument is impaired or limited. If a yardstick measured differently because of the fact that it was a rug, a picture, or a piece of paper that was being measured, then to that extent the trustworthiness of that yardstick as a measuring device would be impaired. Within the range of objects for which the measuring instrument is intended, its function must be independent of the object of measurement.

We must ascertain similarly the range of applicability of our method of measuring attitude. It will be noticed that the *construction* and the *application* of a scale for measuring attitude are two different tasks. If the scale is to be regarded as valid, the scale values of the statements should not be affected by the opinions of the people who help to construct it. This may turn out to be a severe test in practice, but the scaling method must stand such a test before it can be accepted as being more than a description of the people who construct the scale. At any rate, to the extent that the present method of scale construction is affected by the opinions of the readers who help to sort out the original statements into a scale, to that extent the validity or universality of the scale may be challenged.

Until experimental evidence may be forthcoming on this point, we shall make the assumption that the scale values of the statements are independent of the attitude distribution of the readers who sort the statements. The assumption is, in other words, that two statements on a prohibition scale will be as easy or as difficult to discriminate for people who are "wet" as for those who are "dry." Given two adjacent statements from such a scale, we assume that the proportion of "wets" who say that statement *a* is wetter than statement *b* will be substantially the same as the corresponding proportion for the same statements obtained from a group of "drys." Restating the assumption in still another way, we are saying that it is just as difficult for a strong militarist as it is for a strong pacifist to tell which of two statements

is the more militaristic in attitude. If, say, 85 per cent of the militarists declare statement *A* to be more militaristic than statement *B*, then, according to our assumption, substantially the same proportion of pacifists would make the same judgment. If this assumption is correct, then the scale is an instrument independent of the attitude which it is itself intended to measure.

The experimental test for this assumption consists merely in constructing two scales for the same issue with the same set of statements. One of these scales will be constructed on the returns from several hundred readers of militaristic sympathies and the other scale will be constructed with the same statements on the returns from several hundred pacifists. If the scale values of the statement are practically the same in the two scales, then the validity of the method will be pretty well established.[6] It will still be necessary to use opinion scales with some discretion. Queer results might be obtained with the prohibition scale, for example, if it were presented in a country in which prohibition is not an issue.

b) An objective criterion of ambiguity— Inspection of the curves in Figure 2 reveals that some of the statements of the fictitious diagram are more ambiguous than others. The degree of ambiguity in a statement is immediately apparent, and in fact it can be definitely measured. The ambiguity of a statement is the standard deviation of the best fitting *phi-gamma* curve through the observed proportions. The steeper the curve, the smaller is the range of the scale over which it was classified by the readers and the clearer and more precise is the statement. The more gentle the slope of the curve, the more ambiguous is the statement. Thus of the two statements *A* and *B* in the fictitious diagram the statement *A* is the more ambiguous.

---

[6] The neutrality point would not necessarily be represented by the same statement for both militarists and pacifists, but the scale separations between all pairs of statements should be practically the same for the two conditions of standardization.

In case it should be found that the *phi-gamma* function does not well describe the curves of proportions in Figure 2, the degree of ambiguity may be measured without postulating that the proportions follow the *phi-gamma* function when plotted on the attitude scale. A simple method of measuring ambiguity would then be to determine the scale distance between the scale value at which the curve of proportions has an ordinate of .25 and the scale value at which the same curve has an ordinate of .75. The scale value of the statement itself can also be defined, without assuming the *phi-gamma* function, as that scale value at which the curve of proportions reaches .50. If no actual proportion is found at that value, the scale value of the statement may be interpolated between the experimental proportions immediately above and below the .50 level. In scaling the statements whose scale values fall outside the ten divisions of the scale, it will be necessary to make some assumption regarding the nature of the curve, and it will probably be found that for most situations the *phi-gamma* function will constitute a fairly close approximation to truth.

c) An objective criterion of irrelevance— Before a selection of statements can be made for the final scale, still another criterion must be applied. It is an objective criterion of irrelevance. Referring again to Figure 1, let us consider two statements that have identical scale values at the point *f*. Suppose, further, that these two statements are submitted to the group of readers represented in the fictitious diagram of Figure 1. It is quite conceivable, and it actually does happen, that one of these statements will be indorsed quite frequently while the other statement is only seldom indorsed in spite of the fact that they are properly scaled as implying the same degree of pacifism or militarism. The conclusion is then inevitable that the indorsement that a reader gives to these statements is determined only partly by the degree of pacifism implied and partly by other implied meanings which may or may not be related to the attitude variable under consideration.

Now it is of course necessary to select for the final attitude scale those statements which are indorsed or rejected primarily on account of the degree of pacifism–militarism which is implied in them and to eliminate those statements which are frequently accepted or rejected on account of other more or less subtle and irrelevant meanings.

An objective criterion for accomplishing this elimination automatically and without introducing the personal equation of the investigator is available. It is essentially as follows: Assume that the whole list of about one hundred statements has been submitted to several hundred readers for actual voting. These need not be the same readers who sorted the statements for the purpose of scaling. Let these readers be asked to mark with a plus sign every statement which they indorse and to reject with a minus sign every statement not to their liking.

If we want to investigate the degree of irrelevance of any particular statement which, for example, might have a scale value of 4.0 in Figure 3, we should first of all determine

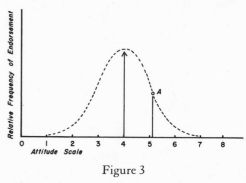

Figure 3

how many readers indorsed it. We find, for example, that 260 readers indorsed it. Let this total be represented on the diagram as 100 per cent, and erect such an ordinate at the scale value of this statement. We may now ascertain the proportion of these 260 readers who *also* indorsed each other statement. If the readers indorse and reject the statements largely on the basis of the degree of pacifism–militarism implied, then those readers who indorse statements in the vicinity of 4.0 on the scale will not often indorse statements that are very far away from that point on the scale. Very few of them should indorse a statement which is scaled at the point 8.0, for example. If a large proportion of the 260 readers who indorse the basic statement scaled at 4.0 should also indorse a statement scaled at the point 8.0, then we should infer that their voting on these two statements has been influenced by factors other than the degree of pacifism that is implied in the statements. We can represent this type of analysis graphically.

Every one of these other statements will be represented by a point on this diagram. Its x-value will be the scale value of the statement, and its y-value will be the proportion of the 260 readers who indorsed it. Thus, if out of the 260 readers who indorsed the basic statement there were 130 who also indorsed statement No. 14, which has a scale value of, say, 5.0, then statement No. 14 will be represented at the point A on Figure 3.

If the basic statement, the degree of irrelevance of which is represented in Figure 3, is an ideal statement, one which people will accept or reject primarily because of the attitude on pacifism which it portrays, then we should expect the one hundred statements to be represented by as many points hovering more or less about the dotted line of Figure 3. The diagram may of course be more contracted or spread out, but the general appearance of the plot should be that of Figure 3. If, on the other hand, the basic statement has implications that lead to acceptance or rejection quite apart from the degree of pacifism which it conveys, then the proportion of the indorsements of the statements should not be a continuous function of their scale distance from the basic statement. The one hundred points might then scatter widely over the diagram. This inspectional criterion of irrelevance is objective and it can probably be translated into a more definite algebraic form so as to eliminate entirely the personal equation of the investigator.

Two other objective criteria of irrelevance have been devised. They will be described in connection with the attitude scales now being constructed.

SUMMARY OF THE SCALING METHOD

The selection of the statements for the final scale should now be possible. A shorter list of 20 or 30 statements should be selected for actual use. We have described three criteria by which to select the statements for the final scale. These criteria are:

1. The statements in the final scale should be so selected that they constitute as nearly as possible an evenly graduated series of scale values.

2. By the objective criterion of ambiguity it is possible to eliminate those statements which project too great a dispersion on the attitude continuum. The objective measure of ambiguity is the standard deviation of the best fitting *phi-gamma* curve as illustrated in Figure 2.

3. By the objective criteria of irrelevance it is possible to eliminate those statements which are accepted or rejected largely by factors other than the degree of the attitude-variable which they portray. One of these criteria is illustrated in Figure 3.

The steps in the construction of an attitude scale may be summarized briefly as follows:

1. Specification of the attitude variable to be measured.

2. Collection of a wide variety of opinions relating to the specified attitude variable.

3. Editing this material for a list of about one hundred brief statements of opinion.

4. Sorting the statements into an imaginary scale representing the attitude variable. This should be done by about three hundred readers.

5. Calculation of the scale value of each statement.

6. Elimination of some statements by the criterion of ambiguity.

7. Elimination of some statements by the criteria of irrelevance.

8. Selection of a shorter list of about 20 statements evenly graduated along the scale.

MEASUREMENT WITH AN
ATTITUDE SCALE

The practical application of the present measurement technique consists in presenting the final list of about 25 statements of opinion to the group to be studied with the request that they check with plus signs all the statements with which they agree and with minus signs all the statements with which they disagree. The score for each person is the average scale value of all the statements that he has indorsed. In order that the scale be effective toward the extremes, it is advisable that the statements in the scale be extended in both directions considerably beyond the attitudes which will ever be encountered as mean values for individuals. When the score has been determined for each person by the simple summation just indicated, a frequency distribution can be plotted for the attitudes of any specified group.

The reliability of the scale can be ascertained by preparing two parallel forms from the same material and by presenting both forms to the same individuals. The correlation between the two scores obtained for each person in a group will then indicate the reliability of the scale. Since the heterogeneity of the group affects the reliability coefficient, it is necessary to specify the standard deviation of the scores of the group on which the reliability coefficient is determined. The standard error of an individual score can also be calculated by an analogous procedure.

The unit of measurement in the scale when constructed by the procedure here outlined is not the standard discriminal error projected by a single statement on the psychological continuum. Such a unit of measurement can be obtained by the direct application of the law of comparative judgment, but it is considerably more laborious than the method here described. The unit in the present scale is a more arbitrary one, namely, one-tenth of the range on the psychological continuum which covers the span from what the readers regard as extreme affirmation to extreme negation in the particular list of statements with which we start. Of course the scale values can be determined with reliability to fractional parts of this unit. It is hoped that this unit may be shown experimentally to be proportional to a more precise and more universal unit of measurement such as the standard discriminal error of a single statement of opinion.

It is legitimate to determine a central tendency for the frequency distribution of attitudes in a group. Several groups of individuals may then be compared as regards the means of their respective frequency distributions of attitudes. The differences between the means of several such distributions may be directly compared because of the fact that a rational base line has been established. Such comparisons are not possible when attitudes are ascertained merely by counting the number of indorsements to separate statements whose scale differences have not been measured.

In addition to specifying the mean attitude of each of several groups, it is also possible to measure their relative heterogeneity with regard to the issue in question. Thus it will be possible, by means of our present measurement methods, to discover for example that one group is 1.6 more heterogeneous in its attitudes about prohibition than some other group. The heterogeneity of a group is indicated perhaps best by the standard deviation of the scale values of all the opinions that have been indorsed by the group as a whole rather than by the standard deviation of the distribution of individual mean scores. Perhaps different terms should be adopted for these two types of measurement.

The tolerance which a person reveals on any particular issue is also subject to quantitative measurement. It is the standard deviation of the scale values of the statements that he indorses. The maximum possible tolerance is of course complete indifference, in which all of the statements are indorsed throughout the whole range of the scale.

If it is desired to know which of two forms of appeal is the more effective on any particular issue, this can be determined by using the scale before and after the appeal. The difference between the individual scores, before and after, can be tabulated and the average shift in attitude following any specified form of appeal can be measured.

The essential characteristic of the present measurement method is the scale of evenly graduated opinions so arranged that equal steps or intervals on the scale *seem* to most people to represent equally noticeable shifts in attitude.

CHAPTER **6**   **The Scale Values**

CHAPTER **6**   **The Scale Values**

L. L. THURSTONE AND E. J. CHAVE

*   *   *

AN OBJECTIVE CRITERION OF IRRELEVANCE

We have tried to devise objective checks on our procedures wherever possible, and in the present experiments we have even retained intentionally a number of statements of opinion which were clearly ambiguous or otherwise unsuitable for an attitude scale in order to see to what extent they could be eliminated by objective methods. We should hardly expect to be able to construct a workable attitude scale entirely by the mechanical application of objective rules. Some latitude will probably always be given to the judgment of the investigator, but our methods will be successful to the extent that the individual judgments of an investigator about material of this sort can be checked objectively. In the present study we retained some material which would have been eliminated by inspection at the very start just in order to test the validity of the several objective criteria.

The criterion of ambiguity is concerned with the spread of a statement over the sub-

Reprinted from *The Measurement of Attitudes* (pp. 45–56) by L. L. Thurstone and E. J. Chave by permission of The University of Chicago Press. Copyright 1929 by the University of Chicago. All rights reserved. Published September 1929.

jective scale of equal-appearing intervals. If the three hundred subjects place a statement of opinion in widely different intervals on the subjective scale, the Q-value of the statement will be large and the statement will therefore be judged by this objective criterion to be ambiguous. It has widely different meanings along the attitude scale when it is read by different subjects. Clearly such statements should be eliminated. Often it is possible to tell by inspection that a statement will have a large Q-value. It should be noted that the Q-value of a statement of opinion does not reflect the actual opinions held by the subjects on the issue in question. They sort the statements merely in accordance with the attitude that they read into the statements without thereby expressing their own attitudes.

The criterion of irrelevance, on the other hand, is concerned with the records of actual votes. The whole list of 130 statements was mimeographed and presented to three hundred subjects with the request that they check the statements that they indorsed or agreed with, and that they leave blank the statements which they did not care to indorse. It was then possible to study the returns for internal consistency. If we find considerable inconsistency, we might attribute it to the carelessness of the subjects in making their check marks more or less at random, or we might attribute it to defects in the statements themselves. In the present experiments we found a certain amount of inconsistency throughout the whole list, and it can undoubtedly be attributed at least in part to the subjects themselves. But the inconsistencies vary with the statement that is chosen as a basis of comparison with all the rest, and such differences are due primarily no doubt to defects in the statements themselves. We have so regarded them and we have devised a criterion of irrelevance which can be used further to eliminate the unsuitable statements from the scale.

This criterion is constructed as follows: Suppose that a statement of low ambiguity is properly scaled at the point 6. If a subject has an attitude which is also scaled properly at the point 6, then we should expect him to check that statement. Another subject who is scaled at the point 12 should be less likely to check that statement, and similarly there should be a low probability that a subject at the point zero will check the statement at 6 on the scale.

In order to make this type of analysis quantitative we have devised a rather crude index of similarity which is based on the voting of any large group of subjects. The index of similarity for any pair of statements is based on three facts, namely, n_a = the total number of subjects who indorse statement a in the comparison; n_b = the total number of subjects who indorse statement b in the comparison; n_{ab} = the total number of subjects who indorse both a and b.

If the two statements a and b are practically identical in the attitudes they reflect, then we should expect to find that those subjects who indorse statement a will also indorse statement b. This factor, n_{ab}, will therefore be in the numerator of the index of similarity. On the other hand, the statements vary considerably in intrinsic popularity even when they are scaled at identical points on the scale. The more popular a statement is, the larger will be the number of people who indorse it and any other statement. In order to reduce the index of similarity to the same basis of popu-

larity for all statements, the number of subjects who indorse both statements is divided by the product of the number of total indorsements for each of the two statements so that the index of similarity becomes

$$\frac{n_{ab}}{n_a \cdot n_b}.$$

If we tabulate the indices for statement a with each of all the other statements in turn, we shall have the common factor $1/n_a$ which may be disregarded since it is a constant. We shall then have

Index of similarity[1] for statement

$$a = C_a = \frac{n_{ab}}{n_b}.$$

This index is written for the comparison of statement a with each of the others. It is evident that the maximum possible value for this index is unity and its minimum value is zero. If all of the people who indorse statement a also indorse statement k, then the index of similarity is unity as it should be because the two statements are then evidently very similar in the attitudes reflected. If, on the other hand, none of those who indorse statement a also indorse statement k, then the index is zero and this is reasonable because the two statements are then evidently very different in the attitudes which they describe.

In Figure 10 we have a graphical representation of the indices of similarity for statement 96 with each of the other statements, plotted against the scale-value of each statement. The scale-value of statement 96 is indicated by the small arrow on the top line of the diagram. Its index of similarity with itself under ideal conditions would be unity. It is immediately apparent that the indices for statement 96 and each of the other statements are very low for those statements which are distant from statement 96. This is to be expected. In other words, those who indorsed statement 96, which is scaled at 10.5, do not often indorse statements which

---

[1] Since the completion of this monograph the index of similarity has been developed in a better and more correct form. . . .

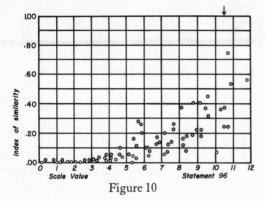

Figure 10

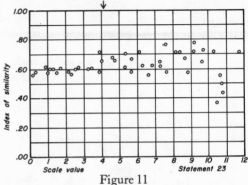

Figure 11

are scaled in the four or five class-intervals at the other end of the scale. The indices are higher when the second statement approaches the scale-value of statement 96. Every small circle in this diagram represents the index of similarity between statement 96 and a second statement, and it is placed immediately above the scale-value of that second statement.

The criterion of irrelevance is the appearance of the whole diagram. If the indices of similarity are relatively high near the scale-value of the first or common statement and relatively low for statements that are distant from the first or common statement, then the first statement is considered to be satisfactory. It means merely that the people who indorse statement 96 are not so likely to indorse statements that are scaled distant from the scale-value of 96. The appearance of Figure 10 is considered to be satisfactory and therefore statement 96 is retained.

We may turn next to a similar analysis for a statement that was discarded by the criterion of irrelevance. Figure 11 shows the indices of similarity for statement 23. The scale-value of this statement is also indicated by a small arrow on the top line of the diagram. Consider the small circle to the extreme left of this diagram. It is the index of similarity between statement 23 and statement 101, which has a scale-value of 0.02. The index is 0.56. The other circles are located in a similar manner and represent the degree of

similarity between statement 23 and each of the other statements.

Note that the people who indorse statement 23 are just as likely to indorse statements at either extreme of the scale as the statements that are scaled near to statement 23. The points scatter more or less horizontally on the diagram. This indicates clearly that there is something fundamentally wrong with statement 23 as an index of a particular attitude on the scale. In other words, if a man indorses this statement we can say nothing about his attitude toward the church because he is likely to indorse not only statements in the class-interval 4–5 but also at either or both extremes of the scale as far as one can judge by statement 23. The indorsement of this statement therefore does not help us in allocating the subject to a point on the scale.

We then turn back to the original statement and we find that it reads as follows: "I am interested in a church that is beautiful and that emphasizes the aesthetic side of life." We can now see why this statement is irrelevant to the attitude variable that we are attempting to measure. The pious church member can certainly indorse this statement conscientiously. Of course he is interested in a church that is beautiful. But the most outspoken atheist can also indorse the statement because he may very well be interested in beautiful buildings, including beautiful churches, and he may very well also be interested in church music even though he does not take at all seriously the religious functions of the church. The attitude reflected by the indorsement of statement 23 is therefore not valid as an index of the attitude variable which is implied in the list of statements as a whole. The fact that the indices of Figure 11 spread more or less horizontally across the whole scale constitutes the objective reason for discarding statement 23.

We may now review more briefly a few additional specimens showing the criterion of irrelevance for other statements. In Figure 12 the indices of similarity have been plotted

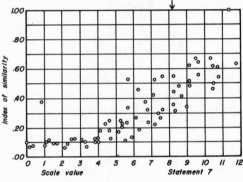

Figure 12

for statement 7. This statement is scaled at 8.2 and the indices fall to very low values at the other end of the scale. This statement is therefore retained in the final scale.

Figure 13 shows a similar plot for statement 113 in which the indices of similarity

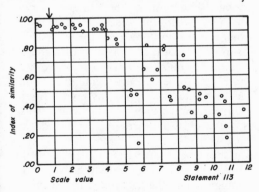

Figure 13

fall to rather low values for second statements in the upper half of the scale. The indices are all above 0.90 for the first few class-intervals. The statement is therefore retained for the final scale.

Figure 14 contains a similar plot for statement 49. Here again the indices spread more

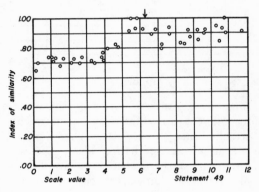

Figure 14

or less horizontally across the whole scale and therefore statement 49 is discarded. We turn to the original statement. It reads as follows: "I do not think one has to belong to the church to be religious." It is quite possible for a pious church member to indorse this statement. It also is possible for the non-religious person to indorse it as a statement of fact even though he may have no interest in either the church or in religion. It is to be expected that the proportion of indorsements of this statement should be higher at the anti-end of the scale and this is what we find in Figure 14, but the discrimination is by no means sufficient. The indices have roughly the same level clear across the scale and the statement is therefore discarded.

Figure 15 shows a satisfactory discrimination for statement 50 because the indices are above 0.90 in the vicinity of the scale-value of statement 50, indicated by the small arrow, and they fall to rather low values at the other end of the scale. The statement is therefore retained.

Figure 16 shows the plot for statement 9, which is discarded because the indices of

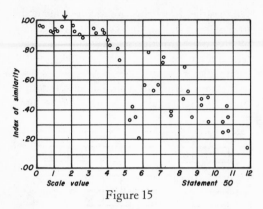

Figure 15

similarity do not show sufficient variation for the different parts of the scale. The statement actually reads: "I don't believe church-going will do anyone any harm." Here again we can readily imagine that the pious church member will acknowledge the truth of the

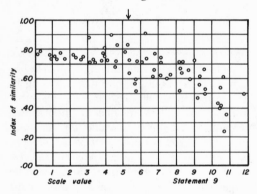

Figure 16

statement. The strong anti-church voter may also be willing to acknowledge that church-going will not do anyone any harm. The latter group do not so readily indorse the statement as the former, but inspection of the diagram indicates clearly that the discrimination is unsatisfactory. People all over the scale indorse this statement although they may have quite different feelings or ideas in doing so. The mere indorsement of this statement does not help us in locating the voter on the scale. The statement is therefore judged to be irrelevant to the scale, which is represented by the whole list of statements.

It would undoubtedly be possible to quantify the criterion of irrelevance still further. It seems better to delay further quantification until a more generalized rational formulation has been completed.

We have brought to bear on the selection and allocation of the statements of opinion two objective criteria, namely the criterion of ambiguity, the Q-value, which is based on the degree of uniformity in the sorting of the statements, and the criterion of irrelevance, which is based on the consistency of the actual voting, or indorsing. These two parts of our experiments were carried out on two different groups of subjects.

We have found that a statement may be sorted quite uniformly by all the subjects and still be declared unsuitable by the criterion of irrelevance. This may be explained as follows: When we read a statement and then judge the attitude which it would ordinarily represent, we may agree fairly well and thereby assign a low Q-value to the statement. When we are asked to indorse the statement, we may find that people of widely different attitudes find widely different reasons for indorsing it. This is especially likely to happen when a statement can be read either as an expression of attitude or as an expression of fact. For example, the churchman is not likely to volunteer the statement, "Church-going will not do anyone any harm." A person who volunteers that statement spontaneously is not likely to be a devoted churchman. The situation is quite different when the statement is made by someone else and presented for indorsement as to whether it is true or false. In such a situation the churchman may acknowledge the statement to be true even though he would not naturally so express his own attitudes. This distinction between that which we say spontaneously in expressing our attitudes and that which we are willing to acknowledge or indorse when stated by someone else probably accounts for the fact that the criterion of ambiguity and the criterion of irrelevance do not always eliminate the same statements.

Ideally, the scale should perhaps be constructed by means of the voting only. It may be possible to formulate the problem so that the scale values of the statements may be extracted from the records of actual voting. If that should be possible, then the present procedure of establishing the scale-values by sorting will be superseded.

INFORMAL CRITERIA FOR THE SELECTION OF OPINIONS

As a result of our work on the present attitude scale we have formulated a list of informal criteria which will be used in the construction of future attitude scales. By these criteria it is seen that many of the opinions in the present experimental scale are defective, and it is our plan to start the construction of an improved attitude scale which shall be free as far as possible from the defects that we can now describe, but these criteria were not clearly formulated when the original material for the present experiments was compiled.

The following is a list of some informal criteria for the selection of opinions in the construction of an attitude scale. The list is certainly not complete and it may very well be decided that some of the following characteristics are not defects.

1. As far as possible, the opinions should reflect the present attitude of the subject rather than his attitudes in the past. By wording the opinions in the present tense one avoids the situation in which a subject might indorse two conflicting opinions, one referring to his past attitude and one to his present attitude. The scale-value of the subject should naturally describe his present attitude.

2. It has been found that double-barreled statements tend to be ambiguous. The material should be edited so that each opinion expresses as far as possible only one thought or idea. The subject is confused in reading a double statement in which he might want to indorse one idea but not the other. Example: "I believe in the ideals of the church but I am tired of denominationalism." Perhaps this statement would serve better if it were divided into two opinions.

3. One should avoid statements which are evidently applicable to a very restricted range of indorsers. Example: "I go to church because I enjoy good music. I am in the choir and get musical training and chorus-singing." The first sentence can be indorsed by a fairly wide group of indorsers, but the second statement can be indorsed only by those who happen to be members of a church choir. It is probably not worth while to include opinions which are so restricted by factual qualifications in an attitude scale. What we want to measure is attitude and in doing so we should avoid so marked an influence on the range of possible indorsers. The foregoing statement would probably be much improved for our purposes if only the first sentence were retained for scaling.

4. Each opinion selected for the attitude scale should preferably be such that it is not possible for subjects from both ends of the scale to indorse it. Such opinions will be canceled by the objective criteria, but when this defect is conspicuous the statement might as well be discarded at the start. On the other hand, there will probably always be a certain number of opinions in a list which have this defect and which are not recognized when read by the investigator. Later, when they are discarded by the objective criteria it is usually easy to see why it is that these statements are eliminated. In other words, it is easier to have the objective basis for discarding a statement and then to see why it should have been discarded by inspection than to spot these defective statements in the reading of the original whole list of statements.

5. As far as possible the statements should be free from related and confusing concepts. In the present material we have a number of statements which mention "true religion" and "the religion of Jesus." These statements are likely to be difficult to interpret because, in addition to the assertions about the church, these statements involve also additional though related concepts which might as well be avoided wherever possible. Example: "I

think the church allows denominational differences to appear larger than true religion." A statement of this type can just as well be written directly with reference to the alleged overemphasis of denominational differences by the churches without involving the uncertainties of interpretation of the phrase, "true religion."

6. Other things being equal, slang may be avoided except where it serves the purpose of describing an attitude more briefly than it could otherwise be stated. For example, to say that most sermons are "all bunk" may be justified if it should be considered a natural way of expressing an attitude which is to be represented on the scale.

CHAPTER **7** **A Technique for the Measurement of Attitudes**

RENSIS LIKERT

INTRODUCTION

Attempts to measure the traits of character and personality are nearly as old as techniques for the measurement of intellectual capacity, yet it can scarcely be claimed that they have achieved a similar success. Part, at least, of the difficulty has lain in the statistical difficulties which are encountered when everyday aspects of social behavior, ordinarily handled as qualitative affairs, are treated from the mathematical point of view. The present study, although part of a larger investigation undertaken in 1929 by Gardner Murphy, aims primarily at the solution of a technical problem which has arisen in relation to the quantitative aspects of the study of social attitudes.

The history and present status of research upon personality traits in general, and social attitudes in particular, have been so thoroughly surveyed by Murphy (21, pp. 381–386, and 22, pp. 558–690), Bain (4), Vetter (41), Katz and Allport (16), Watson (43), and others, that no useful purpose would be served in attempting such a study here.

Excerpted from A Technique for the Measurement of Attitudes, *Archives of Psychology*, 1932, No. 140, with permission of the author and the Trustees of Columbia University in the City of New York. The bibliography is reproduced intact for the benefit of the reader.

Nevertheless, among the hundreds of efforts to measure social attitudes during the last few years, the careful procedures developed by Thurstone (34,38) have naturally and rightly received special attention. These are characterized by a special endeavor to equalize the step-intervals from one attitude to the next in the attitude scale, using the familiar methods of psychophysics for such determinations. The Thurstone methods have been shown to yield a satisfactory reliability, and, in terms of correlations between scores and case histories as evaluated by judges, a satisfactory validity (29).

Many obvious affinities appear between the present study and those of Thurstone, yet in a sense the present report constitutes a radical departure from the concepts which Thurstone has published, as, for example, in the use of judges.

A number of statistical assumptions are made in the application of his attitude scales, —e.g., that the scale values of the statements are independent of the attitude distribution of the readers who sort the statements (38, p. 92),—assumptions which, as Thurstone points out, have not been verified. The method is, moreover, exceedingly laborious. It seems legitimate to inquire whether it actually does its work better than the simpler scales which may be employed, and in the same breath to ask also whether it is not possible to construct equally reliable scales without making unnecessary statistical assumptions. Since so much is being published about attitude measurement, it seems worth while to raise these questions and to report on some results relative to the problem. It is feared that some will mistakenly interpret this article as an "attack" on Thurstone's methods. I therefore wish to emphasize in the strongest terms that I am simply endeavoring to call attention to certain problems of method, and that I am very far from convinced that the present data close the question.

* * *

PROCEDURE

The project conceived in 1929 by Gardner Murphy and the present writer aimed first of all to present a wide array of problems having to do with these five major "attitude areas": international relations, race relations, economic conflict, political conflict and religion. The attitude areas best covered in the questionnaire are those of race relations, international relations, and economic conflict.

The method by which the questionnaire was constructed was as follows: Having determined to study intensively the matter of international, interracial and economic attitudes, and, to a minor degree, political and religious attitudes, among large numbers of college students at typical American universities, a survey was made of the questionnaires already administered by other psychologists for these purposes. Among those which proved especially helpful were those of G. B. Neumann (23), C. W. Hunter (15) and R. W. George (9). In addition, about two hundred newspapers and magazines were rapidly surveyed during the autumn of 1929, declarations of opinion being culled for consideration, special emphasis being given to the more dogmatic types of opinion frequently found in editorials. A small number of questions were included from books, addresses and pamphlets, and a number were made up by the experimenters. Wherever it was possible to use questionnaire material which had previously been extensively tried out, and where, in a sense, "norms" were available, we preferred to use the questions exactly as they stood. In a few cases, it was necessary to abbreviate and simplify the questions in order to make sure that only one issue was involved and that ambiguity was avoided. In those instances in which we made up our own questions, we sought to emphasize simplicity, clarity, and brevity.

Without exception, the questions were presented in such a form as to permit a "judgment of value" rather than a "judgment of fact." Phrases such as "The United States should," or "We ought to," or "No man should be allowed," constantly reappeared. In a few instances it may seem on first inspection that a question has to do with a question of fact, but closer analysis will reveal the highly arbitrary character of such "facts." Perhaps the least desirable of all the questions used was the following: "Is war at present a biological necessity?" Such a question appears to many minds to be categorically a factual one; for example, from a neo-Malthusian point of view it may be regarded as capable only of an affirmative answer. The term "necessity," however, refers here more to the student's attitudes toward various wants than to any of those types of necessity which are discussed by physicists or logicians. This is not offered in defense of the use of this particular item, which is regarded as one which should have been omitted; this explanation is offered only to make clear that at least in the great majority of cases and, we hope, in all, the inquiry has to do with the wants, desires, conative dispositions of the subjects, not with their opinions regarding matters of fact.

* * *

Through collaboration with instructors, the attitudes tests were given to undergraduates (chiefly male) in nine universities and colleges extending from Illinois to Connecticut and from Ohio and Pennsylvania to Virginia. (The names of the institutions cannot appropriately be printed here, only the Columbia College data, Group D, being identified.) The total number of individuals participating was somewhat above 2000 but the data here intensively analyzed were derived from only 650* persons. The attitudes test, called a Survey of Opinions, was first given in the late fall of 1929 (to all groups except Group C and Group F which were given the test in 1931) and, by arrangement with instructors, a retest given 30 days later. Some items from the first test and many new items were included in this second test. The first test required on the average about 40 minutes and the retest a slightly longer time.

The kind of questionnaire material to be reported here falls into four main classes. In the first, questions were to be answered by a Yes, a question mark, or a No, as for example, "Do you favor the early entrance of the United States into the League of Nations?" YES ? No. Next came a series of multiple-choice questions in which one of five possible answers was to be selected, for example: "Using the term 'armaments' to mean equipment devised for war rather than for police purposes, our policy should be to favor: (a) absolute and immediate disarmament of all nations, (b) rapid and drastic reduction of the armaments of all nations, (c) slow but steady reduction of all armaments, (d) maintenance for a long time of approximately the present military and naval strength of all the powers, (e) our free military and naval expansion unembarrassed by agreements with other nations." Third, there was a series of propositions to be responded to by the words (a) *strongly approve,* (b) *approve,* (c) *undecided,* (d) *disapprove,* (e) *strongly disapprove;* for example: "All men who have the opportunity should enlist in the Citizens Military Training Camps." Fourth, a series of abbreviated newspaper

* These 650 cases represent a random sample from seven of the groups comprised in the study. . . . Of course, only those individuals were used for whom we have complete data.

narratives about social conflicts, terminating in a sentence describing the *outcome* of this conflict, the student being asked to indicate his response to this outcome; for example: "A group of Japanese truck-farmers in Southern California, through their industry and lower standards of living, are able to undersell their American competitors. The American farmers insist that IT IS THE DUTY OF ALL WHITE PEOPLE TO PURCHASE ONLY FROM WHITE FARMERS." This last form of question makes use of the same set of five responses mentioned above, *strongly approve, approve, undecided, disapprove,* and *strongly disapprove.*

* * *

RESULTS

The *Sigma* Method of Scoring

In order to compare one type of statement with another such as the "multiple choice" with the "strongly approve," it was necessary to devise some technique whereby they might be made comparable. In attempting to work out such a technique, it was noticed that a great number of the five-point statements, i.e. the "multiple choice" or "strongly approve" statements (in each case the subject being offered five alternatives from which to choose), yielded a distribution resembling a normal distribution (see Table 1).

On the basis of this experimental evidence and upon the results of others (8, pp. 542–548 and 28, pp. 71–91), it seems justifiable for experimental purposes to assume that attitudes are distributed fairly normally and to use this assumption as the basis for combining the different statements. The possible dangers inherent in this assumption are fully realized. This assumption is made simply as part of an experimental approach to attitude measurement. It is a step which it is hoped subsequent work in this field will either make unnecessary or prove justifiable. Perhaps this assumption is not correct; its correctness or incorrectness can best be determined by further experiment.

TABLE 1

PERCENTAGE OF INDIVIDUALS CHECKING THE DIFFERENT ALTERNATIVES.
COMPUTED FROM A SAMPLE OF 100 CASES, ALL MALE, FROM A SINGLE UNIVERSITY

Multiple Choice Statements

Scale	Statement Number	Alternatives				
		a	*b*	*c*	*d*	*e*
Negro	7	1	1	3	8	87
Negro	8	29	42	26	3	0
Imperialism	3	11	43	27	15	4

Strongly Approve Statements

		Alternatives				
		Strongly Approve	Approve	Un-decided	Dis-approve	Strongly Disapprove
Internationalism	16	13	43	21	13	10
Negro	9	3	17	14	44	22
Imperialism	5	32	52	10	5	1
Negro	10	24	49	17	7	3
Imperialism	6	10	27	17	35	11

The percentage of individuals that checked a given position on a particular statement was converted into *sigma* values. This was done for each of the five-point statements which in our opinion had to do with internationalism. Table 22 of Thorndike's tables (30) greatly facilitated this calculation. These tables assume that 100 per cent of the cases fall between −3 and +3 *sigma*. The values given in the table are the average *sigma* values of intervals represented by the stated percentages, the origin considered to be at the mean. The *sigma* deviations were always taken from the mean and the positive value was assigned to the end which seemed to favor internationalism, the negative being assigned to the end which favored nationalism. To avoid using negative values the arbitrary zero may be placed at −3 *sigma* rather than at the mean. These signs were designated in an arbitrary fashion and then verified objectively. . . . The *sigma* values were computed from percentages obtained from a sample of 100 cases, all male, selected from one particular university. Table 2 shows the

percentage of individuals checking each of the different alternatives and the corresponding *sigma* values for statement number 16 of the Internationalism scale.

The statements selected were checked for internal consistency or "clustering," by finding the reliability, using odd statements vs. even statements. The 14 five-point statements used yielded moderately high reliabilities when tried on three different groups with between 30 and 35 subjects in each group. Two of these groups were from the same university, the third was from another university in an entirely different geographical area. These results indicate a "cluster" or attitude variable which we are justified in treating as a unit, so far as these three groups are concerned. The reliabilities obtained for these groups are given in Table 3. These results and the following considerations seem to justify the statement that the *sigma* scoring technique is the most satisfactory now available for attitude measurement. It not only seems to avoid many of the shortcomings of existing methods of attitude measurement,

TABLE 2

DATA FOR STATEMENT NUMBER 16 OF THE INTERNATIONALISM SCALE

Alternative	Strongly Approve	Approve	Un-decided	Dis-approve	Strongly Disapprove
Percentage checking	13%	43	21	13	10
Corresponding *sigma* value	−1.63	− .43	+ .43	+ .99	+1.76
Corresponding 1 to 5 value	1	2	3	4	5

but at the same time retains most of the advantages present in methods now used.

In the first place, the *sigma* scoring method meets the requirement stated by Thurstone (38, p. 56):

Ideally, the scale should perhaps be constructed by means of the voting only. It may be possible to formulate the problem so that the scale values of the statements may be extracted from the records of actual voting. If that should be possible, then the present procedure of establishing the scale-values by sorting will be superseded.

Further, it avoids the difficulties encountered when using a judging group to construct the scale. A number of these difficulties have been pointed out by Rice (27). The following quotation deals with one of the major shortcomings of any technique employing a judging group (27, pp. 190–191):

TABLE 3

RELIABILITY COEFFICIENTS—SIGMA SCORING
METHOD—FOURTEEN STATEMENTS DEALING WITH
INTERNATIONALISM

Odds vs. Evens (7 items vs. 7 items)			
Group	N	Raw	Corrected
A	30	.76	.86
B	32	.79	.88
F	33	.75	.86

The difficulties of building scales similar to Thurstone's and applying them to the measurement of the attitudes of social groups, become increasingly difficult once we leave the classroom, the discussion club and the other small, comparatively infrequent and highly selected groups that enjoy having experiments tried upon them. Such groups already have developed ways of making their attitudes articulate. It is the more numerous work-a-day groupings of society, which are inaccessible to his controlled measurements, about whose attitudes the social scientist is in the most need of information. Students may be required, good natured academicians may be cajoled, and sundry needy persons may be paid to sort cards containing propositions into eleven piles. But it is difficult to imagine securing comparable judgments, or satisfactory measurements in the final application, from bricklayers, businessmen, Italian-Americans, nuns, stevedores, or seamstresses. And, unless the scale itself is based upon equal-seeming differences to a random sample of the group which is to be measured, its validity—the degree to which it measures that which it purports to measure—becomes open to question.

Another decided advantage of the *sigma* technique is that it yields reliabilities as high as those obtained by other techniques, with fewer items. This is possible because it uses an approach to the problem somewhat different from that conventionally used. Previously attempts have been made to find the scale value of each particular statement along a continuum; a person's score being then determined by the scale value of the statements that he accepts. In this study, however, each statement becomes a scale in itself and a person's reaction to each statement is given a score. These scores are then combined by using a median or a mean. Eggan's study reported by Thurstone (35) lends further evidence to support the method presented here.

In contemplating this method of measuring attitudes it is well to realize that the stronger the generic set toward one extreme or the other extreme of an attitude continuum, the more it influences the specific reactions. When the generic set is not strong then the specific items themselves largely determine the reaction. In the latter case, however, the reaction is seldom very intense but rather mildly pro or con. That is, the individual's reactions, so far as that particular attitude is concerned, do not deviate widely from the average.

The *sigma* technique also yields scores the units of which are equal throughout the entire range. Likewise, the same kinds of measures can be obtained with it as are obtained with other techniques now in existence (38). Thus it is possible to obtain the most typical measure of an individual's attitude and also the range or dispersion of his attitude.

Needless to say the construction of an attitude scale by the *sigma* method is much easier than by using a judging group to place the statements in piles from which the scale values must be calculated.

Among the excellent characteristics of Thurstone's method of attitude construction (38) are the objective checks which he has devised for ambiguity and irrelevance. Similar objective checks can be applied to the *sigma* technique, if desired.

*   *   *

The Simpler Method of Scoring

Although the *sigma* technique seems to be quite satisfactory for the intended use, it was decided to try a simpler technique to see if it gave results comparable with the *sigma* technique. If it did, the simpler method would save considerable work in a general survey type of study of this kind. The simpler technique involved the assigning of values of from 1 to 5 to each of the five different positions on the five-point statements. The 1 end was always assigned to the negative end of the *sigma* scale, and the 5 end to the positive end of the *sigma* scale. (See Table 2.)

After assigning in this manner the numerical values to the possible responses, the score for each individual was determined by finding the average of the numerical values of the positions that he checked. Actually, since the number of statements was the same for all individuals, the sum of the numerical scores rather than the mean was used. The reliability of odds vs. evens for this method yielded essentially the same values as those obtained with the *sigma* method of scoring. The scores obtained by this method and the *sigma* method correlated almost perfectly as will be seen in Table 4.

TABLE 4

COEFFICIENTS OF CORRELATION BETWEEN SCORES OBTAINED BY THE SIGMA METHOD, THE 1–5 METHOD, AND THE 1–7 METHOD

Group	N	International (15 Statements)			Negro (10 Statements)
		σ vs. 1–5	1–5 vs. 1–7	σ vs. 1–7	σ vs. 1–5
A	30	.991	.990		.987
B	32	.995	.993		.992
F	33	.995	.990	.997	

The same results were obtained when the values of 1, 3, 4, 5 and 7 were assigned to the different positions corresponding respectively to 1, 2, 3, 4 and 5. In the former case, it will be noted that the extremes were given slightly greater weight. This method likewise correlated very highly with the *sigma* method and with the 1 to 5 method as shown in Table 4.

These results seem to justify the use of the simpler methods of scoring since they yield almost identical results with the *sigma* method and similarly do not involve any of the errors likely to be present in any technique in which experts, judges, or raters are used.

* * *

Comparison of the Simpler Method with the Thurstone Method of Scoring

Two groups, C and F, were given the Thurstone-Droba War scale (6) as well as the Survey of Opinions. Table 8 shows the reliability coefficients obtained for the Thurstone scale and for the Internationalism scale, derived from the Survey of Opinions, for these two groups. The reliability coefficients of the Thurstone test, obtained by correlating Form A against Form B, were respectively .78 and .74 for the two groups. The reliability for the two forms combined, as determined by the Spearman-Brown formula, becomes .88 and

.85, respectively. The same reliability is obtained by the present Internationalism scale with 24 items as is obtained by combining both forms of the Thurstone-Droba scale with a total of 44 items. Thus using the method here described, a measure of a person's attitude as reliable as that obtained by the Thurstone method is secured by asking him to react to one-half as many items. The coefficients of correlation between the Internationalism scale and the Thurstone-Droba scale are also given in Table 8.

In view of the fact that the method presented here when compared with the Thurstone method gave evidence of yielding the same reliability with fewer items, or higher reliabilities with the same number of items, it was decided to try the 1 to 5 method of scoring upon the Thurstone-Droba War scale to see how it would compare with Thurstone's method of scoring. Using Group C each individual was asked to indicate whether he strongly agreed, agreed, was undecided, disagreed, or strongly disagreed with each statement in the Thurstone-Droba War scale, Forms A and B.

Four statements in each form were not used in the scoring because it was found virtually impossible to determine whether to assign a value of 1 or 5 to the "strongly agree" alternative. An illustration of such a statement is number 5 in Form A: "Compulsory military training in all countries should be

TABLE 8

COMPARISON OF THE THURSTONE-DROBA WAR SCALE AND THE INTERNATIONALISM SCALE

| Group | N | Reliability Coefficients Thurstone-Droba Scale | | Reliability Coefficients of Internationalism Scale | Internationalism Scale vs. Thurstone-Droba Scale | |
		Form A vs. B 22 Items vs. 22	Corrected A & B 44 Items	24 Items	Raw	Corrected For Attenuation
C	54	.78	.88	.88	.71	.81
F	32	.74	.85	.88	.65	.75

reduced but not eliminated." It is impossible to tell whether a person is agreeing or disagreeing with the "reduction" aspect of this statement or the "not eliminated" aspect. A person who strongly opposes compulsory military training would disagree or strongly disagree with the *"not eliminated"* aspect, whereas a person who favors compulsory military training would disagree or strongly disagree with the *"reduction"* aspect of the statement. Obviously for the 1 to 5 method of scoring the statement is double-barreled and of little value because it does not differentiate persons in terms of their attitudes. Persons at either extreme of the attitude continuum can readily check the same alternative.

Another illustration of a statement that could not be used is number 17 of Form B: "Wars often right tremendous wrongs." This might be treated as a statement concerning fact, and could well be agreed with or disagreed with by a person regardless of his attitude. The other statements that were not used follow:

Form A, statements 8, 10 and 17.
Form B, statements 5, 10 and 20.

The criterion of internal consistency . . . was used as an objective check to see (1)

whether the numerical values were properly assigned and (2) whether each statement differentiated the extremes in the manner expected.

The results expected were obtained and are shown in Table 9. The 1 to 5 method of scoring with fewer items used on each form yielded as high a reliability coefficient for *one* form as the Thurstone method did for the *two* forms combined. The most plausible explanation for this higher reliability obtained by the 1 to 5 method has already been suggested on pages 153–154.

The two methods of scoring correlate quite highly, namely .83, which when corrected for attenuation becomes .92. It is possible that if the same statements had been used in both methods, rather than four less in each form on the 1 to 5 scoring, a still higher coefficient of correlation between the two methods would have been obtained.

BIBLIOGRAPHY

1. Allport, F. H., and D. A. Hartman.
    1925 "The measurement and motivation of atypical opinion in a certain group." American Political Science Review 19:735–760.

TABLE 9

COMPARISON OF THE THURSTONE AND THE 1 TO 5 METHOD OF SCORING THE
THURSTONE-DROBA WAR SCALE DATA FROM GROUP "C" (N = 54)

	Form A vs. B	
	Raw	Corrected
Thurstone-Droba scale scored 1–5 method (18 questions only used in each form instead of 22)	(18 vs. 18) .88	(36 items) .94
Regular Thurstone scoring	(22 vs. 22) .78	(44 items) .88

COEFFICIENT OF CORRELATION BETWEEN THE TWO METHODS

	Raw	Corrected for Attenuation
Thurstone scale (44 items) vs. 1–5 scoring of Thurstone scale (36 items)	.83	.92

2. Allport, G. W.
   1929 "The composition of political attitudes." American Journal of Sociology 35:220–238.
3. Allport, G. W., and P. E. Vernon.
   1930 "The field of personality." Psychological Bulletin 27:677–730.
4. Bain, R.
   1930 "Theory and measurement of attitudes and opinion." Psychological Bulletin 27:357–379.
5. Chave, E. J., and L. L. Thurstone.
   1931 The Measurement of Social Attitudes. Attitude Toward God, Scale No. 22. Chicago: University of Chicago Press.
6. Droba, D. D.
   1930 The Measurement of Social Attitudes. Attitude Toward War. Chicago: University of Chicago Press.
7. Filter, R. O.
   1921 "An experimental study of character traits." Journal of Applied Psychology 5:297–317.
8. Folsom, J. K.
   1931 Social Psychology. New York: Harper.
9. George, R. W.
   1925 "A comparison of Pressey X–0 scores with liberal-conservative attitudes." Master's essay in Columbia University Library.
10. Hartmann, G. W.
   1928 "Precision and accuracy." Archives of Psychology No. 100.
11. Hartshorne, H., and M. A. May.
   1928 Studies in Deceit. New York: Macmillan.
12. Hartshorne, H., M. A. May, and J. B. Maller.
   1929 Studies in Service and Self-control. New York: Macmillan.
13. Hartshorne, H., M. A. May, and F. K. Shuttleworth.
   1930 Studies in the Organization of Character. New York: Macmillan.
14. Hinckley, E. D.
   1930 A Scale for Measuring Attitude Toward the Negro. Chicago: University of Chicago Press.
15. Hunter, C. W.
   1927 "A comparative study of the relationship existing between the white race and the Negro race in the State of North Carolina and in the City of New York." Master's essay in Columbia University Library.
16. Katz, D., F. H. Allport, and M. B. Jenness.
   1931 "Students' attitudes; a report of the Syracuse University Reaction Study." Syracuse: Craftsman Press.
17. Kulp, D. H., II, and H. B. Davidson.
   1931 "Can Neumann's 'Attitude Indicator' be used as a test?" Teachers College Records 32:332–337.
18. Maller, J. B.
   1932 Character and Personality Tests. New York: Teachers College.
19. Mathews, C. O.
   1929 "The effect of the order of printed response words on an interest questionnaire." Journal of Educational Psychology 20:128–134.
20. Moore, H. T.
   1925 "Innate factors in radicalism and conservatism." Journal of Abnormal and Social Psychology 20:234–244.
21. Murphy, G.
   1929 An Historical Introduction to Modern Psychology. New York: Harcourt, Brace and Company.
22. Murphy, G., and L. B. Murphy.
   1931 Experimental Social Psychology. New York: Harper.
23. Neumann, G. B.
   1927 A Study of International Attitudes of High School Students. Teachers College Contributions to Education No. 239.
24. Newcomb, T. M.
   1929 The Consistency of Certain Extrovert-introvert Behavior Patterns in 51 Problem Boys. Teachers College Contributions to Education No. 382.
25. Porter, E.
   1926 "Student opinion on war." Doctoral dissertation in University of Chicago Library.
26. Rice, S. A.
   1930 "Report, Inst. of methods of rural

sociological research." United States Department of Agriculture 11–20.

27. Rice, S. A.
    1930 "Statistical studies of social attitudes and public opinion." In Rice, S. A. (ed.), Statistics in Social Studies. Pp. 171–192. Philadelphia: University of Pennsylvania Press.

28. Rice, S. A.
    1928 Quantitative Methods in Politics. New York: Knopf.

29. Stouffer, S. A.
    1930 "An experimental comparison of statistical and case history methods of attitude research." Doctoral dissertation in University of Chicago Library.

30. Thorndike, E. L.
    1913 An Introduction to the Theory of Mental and Social Measurements. Second Edition. New York: Teachers College.

31. Thurstone, L. L.
    1927 "A law of comparative judgment." Psychological Review 34:273–286.

32. Thurstone, L. L.
    1928 "An experimental study of nationality preferences." Journal of General Psychology 1:405–425.

33. Thurstone, L. L.
    1930 "A scale for measuring attitude toward the movies." Journal of Educational Research 22:89–94.

34. Thurstone, L. L.
    1928 "Attitudes can be measured." American Journal of Sociology 33: 529–554.

35. Thurstone, L. L.
    1930 "Commentary." In Rice, S. A. (ed.), Statistics in Social Attitudes. Pp. 192–196. Philadelphia: University of Pennsylvania Press.

36. Thurstone, L. L.
    1928 "The measurement of opinion." Journal of Abnormal and Social Psychology 22:415–430.

37. Thurstone, L. L.
    1929 "Theory of attitude measurement." Psychological Review 36:222–241.

38. Thurstone, L. L., and E. J. Chave.
    1929 The Measurement of Attitude. Chicago: University of Chicago Press.

39. Trow, W. C.
    1923 "The psychology of confidence." Archives of Psychology No. 67.

40. Trow, W. C.
    1925 "Trait consistency and speed of decision." School and Society 21: 538–542.

41. Vetter, G. B.
    1930 "The measurement of social and political attitudes and the related personality factors." Journal of Abnormal and Social Psychology 25:149–189.

42. Wang, C. K. A., and L. L. Thurstone.
    1930 The Measurement of Social Attitudes. Scale No. 21, Forms A, B. Attitude Toward Birth Control. Chicago: University of Chicago Press.

43. Watson, G.
    1932 "Measures of character and personality." Psychological Bulletin 29:147–176.

CHAPTER 8

Empirical Comparisons of the Thurstone and Likert Techniques

LAUREN H. SEILER AND RICHARD L. HOUGH

Two of the most important and enduring methods of attitude-scale construction were introduced by Louis Thurstone and Rensis Likert. Despite more recent innovations, such as Guttman scaling, their methods remain in heavy use, and the discourse over the advantages of one vis-à-vis the other still continues. This paper is concerned with analyzing the attempts that were made to establish directly and empirically the comparative validity, reliability, and efficiency of the Thurstone and Likert techniques of attitude-scale construction.

The Thurstone method grew out of the efforts of psychophysicists of the late nineteenth and early twentieth centuries to relate psychological judgments to physical continua, using the method of paired comparisons.[1] Thurstone's (1927) "law of comparative judgment" proposed the rationale for the placement of psychological stimuli along a continuum independent of any underlying physical order. This represented an important advance in the development of psychological measurement, in that the basis for the psychological continuum was no longer directly bound to physical sensations.

As a direct outgrowth of these earlier efforts, Thurstone and Chave (1929) produced their classic work on the measurement of attitudes, in which they suggested a shorter and easier alternative to the method of paired comparisons. This simpler method is most commonly known as the Thurstone method, or the method of equal-appearing intervals. This method is fully described in Thurstone and Chave's article in this book (Chapter 6). Even at the time they proposed it, however, Thurstone and Chave did not consider this procedure to be the ultimate in the construction of an attitude scale. They suggested that "ideally, the scale would perhaps be constructed by means of voting only" (pp. 146–147 in this volume).

In 1932, Likert reported what he thought to be a simpler method of attitude-scale construction, one that did use voting only.[2] Since

---

This chapter was prepared especially for this volume.

[1] For example, in the exploration of the relation of psychological judgments to the physical continuum of weight, a subject was asked to rank-order ten objects. The method of paired comparisons had the subject compare every possible pair of objects and state which of the two he held at the time was heavier. This procedure produces $n(n-1)/2$ comparisons, or for 10 objects, 45 comparisons; while for 50 objects, 1,225 comparisons are needed.

[2] Actually, he produced two methods, the "*sigma* method" and the "1–2–3–4–5 method." The latter proved to be simpler and highly correlated with the *sigma* method (Likert, 1932). The 1–2–3–4–5 method is the one currently known as the Likert method, or the method of summated ratings. For a fuller discussion, see Chapter 7.

that time, a discourse has continued; whether or not the Likert method is an adequate or superior alternative to the Thurstone method.

Although conceptual and theoretical comparisons of the two are extensive, there have been few attempts to test their relative characteristics empirically, and no recent attempts to summarize such comparisons. This paucity of direct empirical comparisons is surprising. McNemar (1946) found that between the inception of attitude measurement and the date of his paper, over 800 papers, articles, and books had been written concerning attitude measurement and public opinion. The rate of production has certainly not declined in the years that have followed. Nevertheless, after a thorough literature search for studies using the construction and/or administration of both the Thurstone and Likert scales as the basis for a direct empirical comparison of the two methods, only eight articles were found. Herein, these studies will be described in chronological order and then evaluated in terms of the relative advantages of one method over the other.

THE LIKERT COMPARISON

The first empirical comparison of the Thurstone and Likert methods was made by Likert at the time he proposed his method of scale construction (Likert, 1932),[3] excerpted in Chapter 7 in this volume. He pointed out that the Thurstone method "is . . . exceedingly laborious," (p. 149). Furthermore, he went on, "It seems legitimate to inquire whether it actually does its work better than the simpler scales which may be employed, and in the same breath to ask also whether it is not possible to construct equally reliable scales without making unnecessary statistical assumptions" (pp. 149–150). However he concluded, "I am very far from convinced that the present data close the question" (p. 150). [Pages refer to this volume.] Even more

specifically, Edwards and Kenney (1946) point out the four main hypotheses Likert makes regarding his method of summated ratings:

(1) "it avoids the difficulties encountered when using a judging group to construct the scale" (Murphy and Likert, 1938, p. 42); (2) "the construction of an attitude scale by the sigma method is much easier than by using a judging group to place the statements in piles from which the scale values must be calculated" (Murphy and Likert, 1938, p. 43); (3) "it yields reliabilities as high as those obtained by other techniques with fewer items" (Murphy and Likert, 1938, pp. 42–43); (4) it gives results which are comparable to those obtained by the Thurstone technique. More generally, the method of summated ratings "seems to avoid many of the shortcomings of existing methods of attitude measurement, but at the same time retains most of the advantages present in methods now used" (Murphy and Likert, 1938, p. 42). These claims, it should be noted, have been vigorously contested, notably by Bird (1940) and Ferguson (1941). (Edwards and Kenney, 1946, p. 75).

Taking a pragmatic orientation, hypothesis (1) states that the Likert method avoids the difficulties of using judges. If this is true, it should be reflected by higher reliabilities, higher validities, higher equivalencies between scales, and decreased expenditures of time and money. Therefore, hypothesis (1) may be subsumed under the three that follow it. In summation, the three remaining hypotheses state, very generally, that the Likert method is equally or more reliable, equally or more valid, and easier to construct than the Thurstone method. Each of these hypotheses is open to direct empirical verification. Hence we will use them as the basis for reviewing the empirical comparisons of the two methods.

To test the above hypotheses, Likert (1932) used data gathered from a research project he began in 1929 in conjunction with Gardner Murphy. For the main body of the research, questions were gathered in five attitude areas, i.e., international relations, race

---

[3] Another discussion of these same comparisons may be found in Murphy and Likert (1938).

relations, economic conflict, political conflict, and religion. Three scales were produced from the items they gathered, i.e., an internationalism scale (24 items), an imperialism scale (12 items), and a Negro scale (15 items). Subsequently, questionnaires containing the three scales were administered to more than two thousand students at nine universities. Of these two thousand questionnaires, 650 were randomly selected for intensive analysis.[4] In addition, the Thurstone-Droba war scale (Droba, 1930) was administered to two of the nine groups of university students.

With these data, Likert contrasted the Thurstone and Likert methods of scale construction in two ways. First, he compared the reliabilities of two scales which were independently produced by the two techniques of *scale construction;* the Likert internation-

---

[4] A procedure that seems to make little sense in an age of computer technology, but which provided a substantial savings in time in a period when all calculations were computed with only the aid of a desk calculator.

alism scale was compared to the Thurstone-Droba war scale. Second, he compared the reliabilities produced by the two techniques when *scoring* the same scale (the Thurstone-Droba war scale). To make the first comparison between the reliabilities of the internationalism scale and the Thurstone-Droba war scale (form A and form B, 22 items each), data was utilized from groups C and F to whom both scales had been administered. Table 1 summarizes these findings.

One notes that the split-half reliability of the internationalism scale (for the two groups who completed both the internationalism scale and the Thurstone-Droba war scale) was the same for each group—.88 (corrected for attenuation by the Spearman-Brown formula). By comparison, the reliabilities for the same two groups on the Thurstone-Droba war scale were .88 and .85 (corrected). Using about half as many items, the Likert technique produced a scale with a split-half reliability equal to that of the Thurstone scale, or it produced a higher reli-

---

TABLE 1

LIKERT'S COMPARISON OF RELIABILITY COEFFICIENTS: THURSTONE-DROBA WAR SCALE (FOR TWO GROUPS) AND THE INTERNATIONALISM SCALE (INDICATING THE RANGE FOR ALL NINE GROUPS AND FOR TWO GROUPS)

Likert's Group	N	Reliability coefficients Thurstone-Droba war scale		Reliability coefficients (corrected) internationalism scale. (24 items; 12 vs. 12; odds vs. evens)
		Form A vs. B (22 vs. 22)	Corrected A and B (44)	
C	54	.78	.88	.88
F	32	.74	.85	.88
G (group with highest reliability)	100	a	a	.90
A (group with lowest reliability)	30	a	a	.84

a Likert did not gather this data.

ability using the same number of items. The interpretation given to these findings is that it is certainly *possible* to construct an attitude scale by the Likert method that will yield reliabilities as high or higher than those produced by the Thurstone method.

Likert also found that these two independently produced scales correlated at .67 (or .78 corrected). Nevertheless, it would be incorrect to interpret these data as indicating that the two methods produced equally valid scales for the reason that, initially, they were not produced to measure the same thing. To note later that they seem to measure the same thing is a post hoc analysis that cannot be considered a test of convergent validation.[5] However, Likert did find all three of his scales correlated among themselves (.34 to .63 uncorrected). He noted that this probably indicated the presence of a common factor in all of them.

Likert's second comparison dealt with the scoring procedures utilized by the two methods. One of the groups, Group C, was given the Thurstone-Droba war scale for a second time. However, the instructions were changed so that the subjects were asked to indicate their attitudes by the Likert method.[6] Table 2 summarizes these findings. In general, Likert found that the Likert method of scoring produced a higher reliability than the Thurstone method of scoring for the same scale. He explained this by noting that in the Likert scoring procedure, "each statement becomes a scale in itself" (pp. 153–154 in this volume). He also found that the two methods of scoring the same scale were highly correlated—.92 (corrected). This high correlation indicates that one method of scoring is as valid as the other. No consideration, however, is given to the question of how valid either score may be in an absolute sense.

That is, no consideration is given to whether the scales actually measure what they purport to measure.

TABLE 2

Likert's Comparison of Thurstone and Likert Scoring Techniques on Form A and Form B of the Thurstone-Droba War Scale (Group C Only) $N = 54$

| | Form A versus Form B | |
	Raw	Corrected
	(18 vs. 18)	(36)
Likert scoring of the Thurstone-Droba war scale (using 18 items vs. 18 items—not 22 vs. 22).	.88	.94
	(22 vs. 22)	(44)
Thurstone scoring of the Thurstone-Droba war scale (22 items vs. 22 items).	.78	.88

| Correlation coefficients between the two methods | | |
	Raw	Corrected
Correlation between the Likert and Thurstone scoring methods. (Thurstone, 44 items; Likert, 36 items).	.83	.92

THE LIKERT, ROSLOW, AND MURPHY COMPARISON

To further substantiate Likert's hypothesis that the Likert scoring procedure yields more reliable results than the Thurstone scoring procedure when applied to a Thurstone scale, Likert, Roslow, and Murphy (1934) selected ten attitude scales that had been constructed by the Thurstone procedure. They then sought to determine whether the Likert "method of scoring the [scales] would consistently prove to be satisfactory." (p. 228) The scales measured attitudes toward birth control, the Chinese, Communism, evolution, Germans, God (2), Negroes, and war (2). The authors do not explain their motivation for selecting these particular scales.

Each of the ten Thurstone scales consisted of two parallel forms, a total of 20 scales in

---

[5] For a full explanation of the concept of convergent validation, see Chapter 4 in this book by Campbell and Fiske.

[6] Likert found that for each form of the Thurstone-Droba war scale, four items could not be meaningfully scored using the Likert method. Therefore, he excluded these items leaving 18 items in each form of the scale. For a full description, see Likert (Chapter 7, pp. 155–156 in this book).

all. For each of these 20 scales, a modified scale (suitable for Likert scoring) was constructed. As Likert (1932) noted, some items selected for a Thurstone scale are not suitable for a Likert scale.[7] Therefore, to modify each of the Thurstone scales, between one and six items were excluded. In this manner, a total of 20 scales suitable for Likert scaling were derived from the 20 Thurstone scales—a total of 40 scales. However, it should be pointed out that only the 20 Thurstone scales were administered to respondents. The Likert scales were formed after the questionnaires had been filled out by simply scoring the questionnaires according to the Likert method and excluding those items which were not desired.

These scales were administered to 12 groups of male university students in New York as well as to one group of male high school seniors—presumably also in New York (13 groups in all). However, not all attitude scales were administered to all groups. Both parallel forms of a single attitude scale were administered to as few as one student group and to as many as seven. Some groups completed as few as the parallel forms of only one scale, while other groups completed as many as the parallel forms of five scales.

The students were directed as follows: "If you agree with a statement, put a plus [mark]; if you strongly agree with a statement, put a plus with a circle around it; if you disagree with a statement, put a minus [mark]; if you strongly disagree with a statement, put a minus with a circle around it; if you are undecided, put a question mark." After the students had indicated their reactions, the scales were then scored by the

Thurstone and Likert methods. In scoring the scales by the Thurstone method, each plus mark was considered an endorsement; minuses and question marks were considered non-endorsements. In scoring by the Likert method, the direction of the item was first determined. Specifically the researchers asked: Does a response of + (strongly agree) indicate a favorable or an unfavorable attitude? Then, numerical weights (1-2-3-4-5) were assigned to each response in the usual Likert fashion.

Table 3 presents results typical of those obtained. In general, the Likert method of scoring consistently produced higher reliabilities than the Thurstone method. Out of 27 comparisons, only once did the Thurstone method produce a scale with a reliability equal to the Likert method, and never a higher reliability.[8] Furthermore, the authors concluded, "The scores obtained by the two methods correlate highly, indicating that they are measuring essentially the same thing" (p. 237). These findings add strong support to Likert's hypothesis that when scoring a scale constructed by the Thurstone procedure, the Likert scoring method yields more reliable results than the Thurstone method. Since the two methods are highly correlated, they are almost equivalent—in other words, equally valid.

THE FERGUSON COMPARISON

Ferguson suggested that the conclusions

---

[7] Likert discovered that some double-barreled items made it impossible to determine whether to assign a value of 1 or 5 to the "strongly agree" alternative. For example, persons strongly opposing and strongly favoring compulsory military training could both strongly agree with the statement: "Compulsory military training in all countries should be reduced but not eliminated." Two people with opposing attitudes could both agree with the statement, depending on to which part of the statement ("not eliminated" or "reduced") the person is responding.

[8] One possible explanation for these findings might be that it is the more unreliable items of the Thurstone scale (those items that tend to fall around the neutral categories) that are most often excluded from the scale when it is scored by the Likert method. "In general, those statements whose scale values in the Thurstone method of scoring fell in the middle of the scale (5.0 to 6.0) were the statements that were found to be unsatisfactory. . . ." (Likert, Roslow and Murphy, 1934, p. 231) To the extent that the more unreliable items are excluded from Likert scoring, the scale as a whole becomes more reliable. If this were indeed the case, one would expect that when many unreliable items were excluded, the Likert scoring would compare more favorably to the Thurstone method than when only one or a few unreliable items were excluded, and vice versa. After looking at the data, this does not appear to be the case. Therefore, we reject this alternative hypothesis.

TABLE 3

EXAMPLES AND SUMMARY OF LIKERT, ROSLOW, AND MURPHY'S 1934 COMPARISON
OF RELIABILITY FOR THE THURSTONE AND LIKERT METHOD OF SCORING

Attitude scale	Group	N	Reliability Coefficients				Absolute value of corre-lation between the two methods	Number of Items	
			Thurstone method		Likert method			Thurstone method	Likert method
			Obtained	Corrected	Obtained	Corrected			
			A vs. B	A + B	A vs. B	A + B			
Birth control	G&H	56	.87	.93	.91	.95	.88	20	19
German	H	26	.42	.59	.67	.80	.85	20	17
Communism	L	61	.87	.93	.95	.97	.93	20	17
Median values	...	54	.76	.86	.85	.92	.88	20	16

Likert (1932) derived from his data were par-tially unfounded. Since the Likert, Roslow, and Murphy paper (1934) was an extension of Likert's work, Ferguson's criticisms are applicable to both papers. Ferguson argued that "in attempting to shorten this laborious procedure (the Thurstone procedure), Likert (1932) presented a technique which accord-ing to him did away with the need for a judg-ing group " (1941, p. 51). However, while he noted, as did Likert, that increasing the num-ber of possible responses in the scale increases the reliability, this demonstration of in-creased reliability does not obviate the need for a judging group. To make his point, Ferguson argued: "Likert used a scale which was constructed by the Thurstone equal-appearing interval method. Since the state-ments had been sifted through the sorting procedure, it would seem unjustifiable to conclude that Likert's method did away with the need for a judging group" (p. 51).[9]

Ergo, the Likert method of scale construction was not demonstrated to be an equal or su-perior alternative to the Thurstone method.

Ferguson then went on to suggest that to test Likert's hypotheses, "One should com-pare scales constructed (independently of the Thurstone method) by the Likert technique with those constructed by the equal-appear-ing interval method" (p. 52). Ferguson im-plemented the above suggestion by saying: "A more adequate test can be provided by re-scaling items using Thurstone's method in scales constructed by Likert's technique. If Likert's technique does away with the need for a judging group, the two methods of treating the statements should give the same results" (p. 52). [The inconsistency between the logic of Ferguson's criticism of Likert's

[9] While Ferguson's criticism seems valid and impor-tant, one should note that it applies *only* to the procedure of comparing scales first constructed by the Thurstone method and then scored by both methods. This is the procedure followed by Likert (1932) in his comparison of Thurstone and Likert scorings for the Thurstone-Droba war scale; also, by Likert, Roslow, and Murphy

in comparing the reliabilities of Thurstone and Likert scorings of 10 original Thurstone scales. As noted above, these procedures compare only the scoring method, not the scale-construction methods. The criticism does *not* apply to the comparison Likert made between his inde-pendently derived internationalism scale and the Thur-stone-Droba war scale, a point that Ferguson (1941) and Edwards and Kenney (1946) fail to note. This com-parison, however, also fails to meet Ferguson's and Ed-wards and Kenney's suggestions for a more adequate comparison, since the two scales do not expressly claim to be measures of the same attitude.

conclusions and the means of implementing his own suggestion is pointed out by Edwards and Kenney (1946)].

To make his comparison, Ferguson selected the Minnesota Scale for the Survey of Opinions (Rundquist and Sletto, 1936). Five scales were used: morale, family, law, economic conservation, and education. The questionnaire was administered to one hundred subjects. After the subjects had completed the questionnaire, they were asked to rate each of the scales, i.e., to place the items of each scale on an eleven-point continuum from favorable to unfavorable (like judges in the Thurstone procedure). Scale and Q values were then computed in plotting each of the statements onto its scale. Ferguson found that of the five scales, only one—economic conservation—had scale values more or less equally spread across the continuum. The other four contained statements that "represent only very favorable or very unfavorable attitudes on that continuum." For example, "in the morale scale there are seven statements scaled between 7 and 8, but only two between 3 and 4. In the family scale, there are eight statements between 7 and 8 and none between 3 and 6" (pp. 56–57).

Ferguson also points out, "If a person agrees with a statement scaled near 7 or 8, theoretically he should agree with all those clustering around that same value; so that if there are not equal numbers of statements at other positions, the scale is artificially weighted" (p. 57). He then makes this somewhat dubious concluding statement:

Since the scale for economic conservation has the most adequate distribution of statements along the continuum (but also the highest Q values), the scores as determined by the two methods were correlated with each other and found to be .70, which amply confirms the conclusion that Likert's technique for the construction of attitude scales does not obviate the need for a judging group. (p. 57)

In summary, Ferguson raised an important question about the adequacy of most previous comparisons.[10] He pointed out that previous studies had compared only the scoring procedures, not the entire attitude-scale construction methods. Unfortunately, his research design was poorly suited to the task he proposed.

THE EDWARDS AND KENNEY COMPARISON

As noted before, Edwards and Kenney (1946) summarized Likert's comparison concerning the favorability of the Likert method over the Thurstone method into four hypotheses: (1) it avoids the difficulties produced by using a separate judging group, (2) it is easier, (3) it is equally or more reliable, and (4) it gives results that are equally or more valid. As mentioned previously, from the pragmatic orientation we have taken in this paper, hypothesis (1) was subsumed under the three following ones.

As also noted before, Edwards and Kenney were in agreement with Ferguson's (1941) criticism of Likert: "Since the statements (used by Murphy and Likert) had been sifted through the sorting procedure (Thurstone's), it would seem unjustifiable to conclude that Likert's method did away with the need for a judging group" (Ferguson, 1941, p. 52). Edwards and Kenney, furthermore, agreed with Ferguson's suggestion for a more adequate test: "To test this point adequately one should compare scales constructed (independently of the Thurstone method) by the Likert technique with those constructed by the equal-appearing interval method." (p. 52).[11]

However, where Ferguson did not implement his own suggestion to the fullest, Edwards and Kenney did. They state that, "A valid comparison of the Thurstone and Likert techniques, we believe, must start with an original set of items, not with items already

---

[10] See footnote 9.

[11] Edwards and Kenney, like Ferguson, ignore the comparison Likert made of the Thurstone-Droba war scale with the Likert internationalism scale. (See footnote 9.)

sifted by the Thurstone procedure and then scored by Likert's method, and not with items sifted by the Likert procedure and then scaled by the Thurstone technique." (Edwards and Kenney, 1946, p. 79).

Therefore Edwards and Kenney randomly divided 72 students into two equal groups. One group was asked to judge statements according to the Thurstone procedure, while the other group was asked to give Likert-type responses to the same statements. The statements were the entire pool of items originally used by Thurstone and Chave in their construction of a scale measuring attitudes toward the church. Two days later, the first group gave Likert responses to the same statements, and the second group acted as Thurstone judges. Using these data, the typical procedures were employed in forming two equivalent Thurstone scales of 20 items each and one Likert scale of 25 items. Of the 25 items used in the Likert scale, 5 were also used in one or the other Thurstone scale. Then, 80 newly selected students were randomly assigned to two approximately equal groups. The first group completed a questionnaire containing the two Thurstone scales immediately followed by the Likert scale. The procedure was reversed for the second group.

Edwards and Kenney found that the Likert scale produced a split-half reliability of .94, while the Thurstone scales produced a parallel-forms reliability of .88 (uncorrected). They also found that form A correlated .72 with the Likert scale (.79 corrected) and that form B correlated .92 with the Likert scale (1.00 corrected). Therefore they concluded that "*it is possible* to construct scales by the two methods which will yield comparable scores. This is the question we set out to answer" (p. 82).

From the data, Edwards and Kenney also concluded that:

(1) scales constructed by the Likert method will yield higher reliability coefficients with fewer items than scales constructed by the Thurstone method. (2) What evidence we do have (and it is subjective) seems to indicate that the Likert

technique is less time-consuming and less laborious than the Thurstone technique. (3) It is true that Likert-selected items tend to be those which would fall at one or the other extreme on the Thurstone continuum, if scaled according to the Thurstone technique. But the implication of this finding is more theoretical than practical as far as the need for a judging group is concerned. The important problem is whether scores obtained from the two differently constructed scales are comparable and the evidence at hand indicates that they are. As far as we can determine there is nothing of a practical nature to indicate that a judging group, in the Thurstone sense, is a prerequisite for the construction of an adequate attitude scale. (Pp. 82–83).

THE EYSENCK AND CROWN COMPARISON

In 1949, Eysenck and Crown reported certain of their findings on research they had done during the previous three years. Although much of the research is beyond the scope of this paper, they did construct an attitude scale to measure anti-Semitism. Initially, they followed the Thurstone procedure in gathering 150 items from "written and spoken comments on the Jews, from periodicals, students, and nonacademic respondents." (p. 49). Eighty persons, mainly nonacademic, then judged the items, placing them along an eleven-point continuum of favorableness to Jews. After the scale was administered in Thurstone fashion to two hundred university students, the split-half reliability was found to be .83 (corrected).[12] Since they considered this reliability unsatisfactory, Eysenck and Crown decided to readminister the scale, requesting Likert-type responses from a second group of two hundred students. The split-half reliability was .90 (corrected). Thus, the Likert scoring procedure was again

---

[12] Eysenck and Crown's procedure is somewhat different from the original Thurstone procedure. They constructed only one scale and then calculated a split-half reliability, as is commonly done with Likert scales. They did not construct two parallel-form scales and then calculate a parallel-forms reliability. . . .

shown to yield a higher reliability than Thurstone's.

As Eysenck and Crown pointed out, "this is not strictly speaking a comparison between Thurstone and Likert scales . . . it is a comparison between Thurstone and Likert methods of scoring items selected according to the Thurstone method" (1949, p. 51). As such, this is a replication of one of the two comparisons made by Likert (1932) and of the comparison by Likert, Roslow, and Murphy (1934); nevertheless, the content (anti-Semitism) is not borrowed from the preceding studies.

Eysenck and Crown also give some consideration to the problem of validity. However, this is of little concern here because only subjective impressions were obtained, i.e., the interviewers' previous knowledge of the respondents' attitudes was compared with the respondents' scale scores (two measures which are not wholly independent). Furthermore, they make no comparison, even subjectively, between the interviewers' assessments of the respondents' anti-Semitism and either the Thurstone or Likert scale scores.

THE BANTA COMPARISON

In 1961, Banta published a summary of research he had recently conducted. Much of his research is unrelated to the purpose of this writing; he did, however, raise a significant question: under what practical conditions will different methods of scoring identical attitude scales *not* produce similar results? Extending this question poses another equally important one: under what conditions will different techniques of attitude-scale construction not yield scales that produce similar results?

Banta was "concerned with measuring social attitudes where the ambiguity of the referent in the attitude questionnaire is deliberately varied" (1961, p. 543).[13] He hypothesized that the more ambiguous the referent of the attitude scale, the less correlated different methods of scoring a particular attitude scale would be.

To implement his ideas, Banta used three 20-item questionnaires, one measuring attitudes toward President Eisenhower, one toward college fraternities, and one toward people in general. According to Banta, the referent ambiguity of the three scales increases respectively. The three questionnaires were administered to three sets of students. Each set of students completed each questionnaire three different times, following a different set of instructions each time. Thurstone and Likert scoring procedures constituted two of the three sets of instructions. Thus, each student completed nine questionnaires. Later, in the analysis, ordering effects were ruled out.

For the purpose of this paper it is of interest to note that under all conditions of attitude-scale referent ambiguity, the Thurstone and Likert methods were highly correlated, although the pattern did tend to follow Banta's predictions. In the order of increasing ambiguity, the Thurstone and Likert scoring methods correlated .89 (President Eisenhower), .89 (college fraternities), and .72 (people in general).[14] As far as the comparison of Thurstone and Likert scoring is concerned, Banta's results seem inconclusive. Even if the results had been more striking, certain of Banta's procedures are questionable. It would be difficult to generalize his findings with confidence.

First, he reduces the possible Thurstone scale values from 11 to five. Since others have pointed to the fewer number of steps in the Thurstone scoring as the reason for its being less reliable than the Likert method, it would seem unwise to reduce the number of steps still further.

Second, Banta compares scales that were constructed to suit different scoring tech-

---

[13] It is of particular importance to note that Banta was concerned with variations in the ambiguity of the referents of attitude scales, i.e., the scale taken as a whole. He is not dealing with variations in the ambiguity of the items that make up the scale.

[14] Although these data are not in strong support of Banta's hypotheses, they should not be taken as representative of his findings. It would not be fair to judge Banta's conclusions on what is presented here, since only a small portion of his results are covered in this paper.

niques. Of his three scales, one was con-structed to be scored by the Thurstone method, one by the Likert method, and one by a third method that is outside the concerns of this discussion. Other authors have cau-tioned against the scoring of an attitude scale by one technique when the scale was con-structed by a second technique. Ferguson, for one, points out that items selected for Likert scales are often not suited to Thurstone scor-ing because Likert items usually do not fall into the neutral categories of the Thurstone scale.

Third, and most important, Banta seems to be insensitive to the difference between *attitude-scale* referent ambiguity and *item* ambiguity. Because he makes no mention of it, we must assume that he did not determine Q values (or some similar measure of item ambiguity) for the items in the three scales. Hence he does not demonstrate that it is the ambiguity of the attitude-scale referent that varies, rather than the ambiguity of the par-ticular items in each scale.[15] Therefore, either item ambiguity or attitude-scale referent am-biguity could produce his results.

In brief summary, Banta has raised an im-portant pragmatic question, i.e., when will the Thurstone and Likert methods not yield similar results? Scientific knowledge often advances only after pertinent questions have been raised. We should not, therefore, mini-mize the importance of this question. Never-theless, from the data that are presented, it does not seem that any answers have been provided.

THE BARCLAY AND WEAVER COMPARISON

From the time of the Edwards and Kenney (1946) research, two significant questions had received no empirical consideration. The first concerned the relative efficiency of the

---

[15] A more suitable research design to test for attitude-scale referent ambiguity, while holding item ambiguity constant, would be to use a single scale of, say, 20 items, varying the attitude-scale referent while holding the rest of the item constant; "*President Eisenhower* is friendly," would be varied to "*people in general* are friendly," etc.

two methods. Which of them would yield a satisfactory attitude scale in the least amount of time? The second question was, Which method would yield the more valid attitude scale, as determined by the correla-tion between the attitude-scale score and appropriate external criteria? Barclay and Weaver (1962) addressed themselves to the first of these two questions. Poppleton and Pilkington (1964) dealt with the second.

Barclay and Weaver compared two aspects of the Thurstone and Likert methods. Both comparisons have potential importance. First, they compared the reliability of scales con-structed by the Thurstone and Likert tech-niques from a common pool of items. This was the first study to utilize such a pool of items gathered specifically for the purpose. In other words, this was the first reported comparison of scales constructed by the two methods in which the authors started from scratch. Second, they compared the relative efficiency of the two methods. As Barclay and Weaver put it, "The question of the relative efficiency of the two techniques has never been fully resolved. It is the purpose of this study to get further evidence on the matter." (1962, p. 109).

To implement these two comparisons, they gathered a pool of 250 statements on Hawaii from tourists and military visitors to the is-lands. From these items they constructed four attitude scales: "Two were constructed using the original technique devised by Thurstone and Chave (1929), the other two using the technique devised by Likert (1932), and modified by Edwards and Kenney (1946)" (p. 109).

To construct two parallel-form Thurstone scales, they selected one hundred seniors, graduate students, instructors, and professors to act as judges. The judges followed the usual procedures for sorting the statements. Later, Q tests and the other procedures sug-gested by Thurstone were followed for the selection of items. The two Thurstone scales were then administered to a single group of 46 tourists. To control for sample composi-tion, the entire pool of items (a nine-page questionnaire) was also given to the same respondents. In this manner, the tourists served as Thurstone respondents as well as judges and Likert respondents. In addition to the tourists, the questionnaire was administered to 29 students who acted as Likert respondents, but did not fill out the Thurstone questionnaire.

Barclay and Weaver found the reliability coefficient for the Thurstone scales to be .66 (uncorrected). For the Likert method, the reliability coefficient was .97 (uncorrected). The probability of obtaining these results by chance alone is .01. In order to assess the comparative efficiency of the two methods, Barclay and Weaver kept a careful log of the time spent on the various activities required for the construction of the scales. The entire construction time of the Thurstone scales took 8,049 minutes. The Likert method took 5,620 minutes—excepting the following: "Since the same items were to be used in the construction of both scales, the time involved in compiling them was not charged to either method" (p. 111). Thus, "The time differential in favor of the Likert technique is 2,429 minutes (40 hours and 29 minutes), and represents 43.2 per cent of the time taken by Likert technique. [sic] This indeed is a considerable advantage" (p. 116).

Barclay and Weaver conclude: "None of the studies published earlier had ever settled the question of which method consumed the more time, so this research was so designed as to provide a definite answer to this problem. This it has done" (p. 119).

Perhaps a more conservative conclusion regarding their findings is in order. First, their procedure for comparing the relative efficiency of the two methods is technologically outmoded. Seashore and Hevner (1933) and Jurgensen (1943)—among others—have suggested methods for speeding up the process of Thurstone scale construction. Further, there seems to be little need for future comparisons of efficiency to be handcuffed by hand computations. The determination of Q values, scale values, and other computations can all be calculated by computers. With their use and the use of optical scanning devices—as shown by Webb (1951)—the hand-

processing of data has been virtually outmoded.

Several technical errors further reduce the value of their conclusion. As pointed out previously, they did not add the time spent gathering the original pool of items to either method. In effect, they subtracted a constant from the length of time spent to construct each scale. This has the effect of inflating the percentage time difference between the two methods.[16]

Their conclusion regarding the number of judges required ignores previous research. They state that "the very nature of the Thurstone technique requires the use of a moderately large number of persons to judge the entire set of attitude statements" (p. 109). Edwards (1957), after reviewing research by Nystrom (1933), Ferguson (1939), Rosander (1936), Uhrbrock (1934), and Edwards and Kenney (1946), concluded: "The evidence points to the conclusion that a relatively small number of judges can be used to obtain reliable scale values for statements using the method of equal-appearing intervals" (p. 94–95).

Finally, Barclay and Weaver selected an unequal number of persons to act as Thurstone and Likert judges. They used one hundred persons as Thurstone judges and 75 persons as Likert judges. From our analysis of their results, this inequity seems to account for approximately 700 minutes of the 2,429-minute time difference. Therefore, we must conclude that the Barclay and Weaver comparison concerning the relative efficiency of the two methods is not fully satisfactory. In view of more recent developments in data-processing techniques, the significance of such comparisons using time as a criterion is dubious.

THE POPPLETON-PILKINGTON COMPARISON

The most recent comparison between the two methods was made by Poppleton and Pilk-

---

[16] To take an extreme case, for example, 20 is 200 per cent of 10. If we subtract 5 from each figure, we find that 15 is 300 per cent of 5.

ington (1964). They constructed two parallel forms of a scale measuring religious attitudes, using the Thurstone method for the compilation of statements. In a preliminary survey, questionnaires were administered to 120 subjects. After an item analysis, two final scales were produced, each consisting of 22 items.

These two scales were then administered to two groups of 60 subjects each. One group was given form A; three weeks later they were given form B. The second group was given form B, followed by form A three weeks later. All subjects were asked to respond "strongly agree," "agree," "uncertain," "disagree," or "strongly disagree" to each of the 22 items.

The questionnaire was then scored by different methods: (1) "ordinary Thurstone scoring on items which were endorsed;" (2) "Likert scoring. Response categories were weighted 5-4-3-2-1, and the weights reversed at the midpoint of the scale" (p. 37). Two other scoring methods were utilized but are not reported here since they are outside the scope of this paper.

Poppleton and Pilkington's comparison of reliability is found in Table 4. In general, they found that the Likert method of scoring an attitude scale constructed by the Thurstone method was more reliable than the Thurstone method, the reliability coefficients being .95 versus .85 (uncorrected).

To analyze the validity of their attitude-scale scores, they selected five sorts of religious behavior to serve as criteria against which the scale scores could be compared, and obtained self-report measures on them. The attitude scores as obtained by the two methods were correlated with the self-reported religious behaviors. Table 5 summarizes their findings.

The Likert method was slightly more valid in four out of the five criteria, and the Thurstone method slightly more valid on one criterion. Inasmuch as the purpose of their paper was to assess the comparative reliabilities and validities of four scoring methods, and since none of the four methods consistently produced either the highest or lowest validity, they concluded that none of the four methods was demonstrated to be clearly superior to the others.

From Poppleton and Pilkington's data, we may conclude that the Thurstone and Likert methods yield approximately equal validities and that the predictive validity of both methods is reasonably high. However, for validity comparisons, it is desirable that the scales being compared have similar reliability coefficients. The reliability and validity of an attitude scale are not independent of each other. (Cf. Bohrnstedt, Chapter 3 of this volume.) More specifically, since the Thurstone scale was less reliable than the Likert scale, the authors did not fully compare the validity of the two methods for a given level of reli-

TABLE 4

POPPLETON AND PILKINGTON'S COMPARISON OF THE RELIABILITY
BETWEEN THE THURSTONE AND LIKERT SCORING METHODS ($N = 120$)

	Form A	Form B	Pearson product moment correlation (parallel forms reliability coefficient)
Thurstone scoring			.85
Mean	4.9	4.6	
Standard Deviation	1.2	2.0	
Likert scoring			.95
Mean	63.0	66.4	
Standard Deviation	14.3	13.4	

TABLE 5

POPPLETON AND PILKINGTON'S COMPARISON OF CRITERION VALIDITY BETWEEN
THE THURSTONE AND LIKERT METHODS ($N = 120$)

Criterion	Pearson product moment correlation (criterion validity coefficient)	
	Thurstone method	Likert method
Active church membership	.84	.86
Church attendance (twice or more per month)	.74	.79
Private daily prayers	.72	.73
Membership in student religious group	.60	.55
Expression of some form of religious belief	.93	.96

ability.[17] Although the criticism is a minor one, it is somewhat difficult to generalize their findings, since their comparison is more or less limited to their data.

CONCLUSION

In comparing the Likert and Thurstone methods, Likert initially proposed three hypotheses about his method of attitude scaling versus the Thurstone method: namely, that his (Likert's) method was (1) faster, (2) equally or more reliable, and (3) equally or more valid. Although some research has been done on each of the three hypotheses, the empirical coverage varies both in quality and quantity. Certain questions may be considered as answered; others, that have received too little empirical attention, cannot yet be considered answered; still others, while not answered, do not seem sufficiently important to warrant future consideration; and a final group of questions still needs to be raised.

Two issues appear to be empirically settled. First, the Likert method of *scoring* an attitude scale, of any given number of items, consistently produces more reliable results than the Thurstone method of scoring the scale, (Likert, 1932; Likert, Roslow, and Murphy 1938; Ferguson, 1941). The evidence further

indicates that the method of scale *construction* does not alter the consistently superior reliability of Likert scoring. Therefore, if a major consideration in the construction of an attitude scale is high reliability, the Likert method of scoring is preferable to Thurstone's, whether the scale itself has been constructed by the Thurstone or the Likert method.[18]

Second, it has been demonstrated that if one constructs *and* scores a scale by the Likert method, 20 or 25 items are usually enough to produce a reliability coefficient of .90 or more, which, as a rule of thumb, is considered sufficiently high. However, a 20- or 25-item scale constructed and scored by the Thurstone method is usually not sufficiently long to achieve a .90 reliability coefficient. To achieve that level of reliability (.90), a scale scored by the Thurstone method needs to contain approximately 50 items.

One question that needs further study is the length of time it takes to construct a Thurstone or a Likert scale, especially utilizing computer technology. Although the time of scale construction is not of primary importance when deciding which method to use, realistic estimates of just how long con-

---

[17] As the Spearman-Brown Formula indicates, reliability is related to the number of items in an attitude scale. Therefore, to produce scales with greater similarity in their reliability coefficients, one need only adjust the number of items in each scale.

[18] Using Likert scoring on scales produced by the Thurstone technique has the disadvantage of mixing theoretical models. Such theoretical eclecticism is best avoided. Nevertheless, to cite precedents, other authors —Eysenck and Crown (1949) and Castle (1953)— have mixed the very same theoretical models in empirical searches for scales with improved reliability.

struction does take would be helpful in planning research time allotments and for pedagogical purposes. While many researchers have suggested that Likert's method of construction is faster than Thurstone's—Likert; Edwards and Kenney; and Barclay and Weaver—no known data indicate the actual amount of time it takes to construct a Thurstone or a Likert scale.

Some questions seem to warrant little future attention. One such, constructing scales by the Likert method and scoring them by the Thurstone method, as done by Ferguson, was shown to be unsatisfactory by the same author. Another, comparing the time of scale construction using Thurstone's original procedures, as done by Barclay and Weaver, has been superseded by many manual time-saving innovations (see Edwards (1957), Chapters 4 and 6), as well as by computer usage.

Finally, certain questions have not been studied as yet. For example, Fishbein (1967) suggests that the Thurstone and Likert techniques are theoretically different and not amenable to combinative endeavors. Nevertheless, the data indicate that the Likert scoring of Thurstone scales increases the reliability of the scales. Whether or not a theoretical rationale can be given to this useful, pragmatic procedure remains to be seen. Also, there has been no empirical comparison of the test-retest reliabilities of Thurstone and Likert scales. Nor has there been any empirical comparison of the criterion validity of scales constructed by the two techniques. This is not to say that the test-retest reliability and criterion validity have never been determined for scales constructed by the Thurstone and Likert techniques. However, there are no studies in the literature that *compare* the test-retest reliability or the criterion validity of the two techniques.

In conclusion, we might note that one cannot directly compare the Thurstone and Likert methods. One can only compare scales that have been constructed and scored by one method to scales constructed and scored by the other method. Therefore, a single comparison of a few scales, (or a few comparisons of several scales) is hardly sufficient to allow unqualified generalizations. In order for the above questions to be answered, many comparisons must be made by numerous researchers, using scales from many attitude areas.

Our analysis has attempted to show that there have been few actual tests of the hypotheses Likert originally set forth. While many persons hold opinions about the relative pragmatic value of the aforementioned two methods of attitude scaling, these opinions are based, to a large extent, on speculation.

BIBLIOGRAPHY

Barclay, John E., and Herbert B. Weaver.
  1962 "Comparative reliabilities and the ease of construction of Thurstone and Likert attitude scales." The Journal of Social Psychology 58:109–120.
Banta, Thomas J.
  1961 "Social attitudes and response styles." Educational and Psychological Measurement 21:543–557.
Bird, C.
  1940 Social Psychology. New York: Appleton-Century.
Campbell, Donald T., and Donald W. Fiske.
  1959 "Convergent and discriminant validation by the multitrait-multimethod matrix." Psychological Bulletin 56:81–105.
Castle, P. F. C.
  1953 "A note on the scale-product technique of attitude scale construction." Occupational Psychology 27:104–109.
Droba, D. D.
  1930 The Measurement of Social Attitudes: Attitude Toward War. Chicago: University of Chicago Press.
Edwards, Allen L.
  1957 Techniques of Attitude Scale Construction. New York: Appleton-Century-Crofts, Inc.
Edwards, Allen L., and Kathryn Claire Kenney.
  1946 "A comparison of the Thurstone and Likert techniques of attitude scale construction." Journal of Applied Psychology 30:72–83.

Eysenck, H. J., and S. Crown.
1949 "An experimental study in opinion-attitude methodology." International Journal of Opinion and Attitude Research 3:47–86.

Ferguson, Leonard W.
1939 "The requirements of an adequate attitude scale." Psychological Bulletin 36:665–673.

Ferguson, Leonard W.
1941 "A study of the Likert technique of attitude scale construction." Journal of Social Psychology 13:51–57.

Fishbein, Martin.
1967 "A consideration of beliefs, and their role in attitude measurement." Pp. 257–266 in Martin Fishbein (ed.), Readings in Attitude Theory and Measurement. New York: Wiley.

Guilford, J. P.
1954 Psychometric Methods, 2nd ed. London: McGraw-Hill.

Jurgensen, C. E.
1943 "A nomograph for rapid determination of medians." Psychometrika 8: 265–269.

Likert, Rensis.
1932 "A technique for the measurement of attitudes." Archives of Psychology 22: 1–55.

Likert, Rensis, Sydney Roslow and Gardner Murphy.
1934 "A simple and reliable method of scoring the Thurstone attitude scales." Journal of Social Psychology 5:228–238.

McNemar, Quinn.
1946 "Opinion-attitude methodology." Psychological Bulletin 43:298–374.

Murphy, G., and Rensis Likert.
1938 Public Opinion and the Individual. New York: Harper.

Nystrom, G. H.
1933 "The measurement of Filipino attitudes toward America by the use of the Thurstone technique." Journal of Social Psychology 4:242–252.

Poppleton, Pamela K., and G. Pilkington.
1964 "A comparison of four methods of scoring an attitude scale in relation to its reliability and validity." British Journal of Social and Clinical Psychology 3:36–39.

Rosander, A. C.
1936 "The Spearman-Brown Formula in attitude scale construction." Journal of Experimental Psychology 19:486–495.

Rundquist, E. A., and R. F. Sletto.
1936 Personality in the Depression. Minneapolis: University of Minnesota Press.

Seashore, R. H., and Kate Hevner.
1933 "A time saving device for the construction of attitude scales." Journal of Social Psychology 4:366–372.

Thurstone, Louis L.
1927 "A law of comparative judgment." Psychological Review 34:273–286.

Thurstone, Louis L., and E. J. Chave.
1929 The Measurement of Attitude: A Psychological Method and Some Experiments With a Scale for Measuring Attitude Toward Church. Chicago: University of Chicago Press.

Uhrbrock, R. S.
1934 "Attitudes of 4,430 employees." Journal of Social Psychology 5:365–377.

Webb, Sam C.
1951 "A generalized scale for measuring interest in natural science subjects." Educational and Psychological Measurement 11:456–569.

CHAPTER 9

A Basis for Scaling Qualitative Data*

LOUIS GUTTMAN

1. Introduction

In a great deal of research in the social and psychological sciences, interest lies in certain large classes of qualitative observations. For example, research in marriage is concerned with a class of qualitative behavior called marital adjustment, which includes an indefinitely large number of interactions between husband and wife. Public opinion research is concerned with large classes of behavior like expressions of opinion by Americans about the fighting ability of the British. Educational psychology deals with large classes of behavior like achievement tests.

It is often desired in such areas to be able to summarize data by saying, for example, that one marital couple is better adjusted than another marital couple, or that one person has a better opinion of the British than has another person, or that one student has a greater knowledge of arithmetic than has another student. There has been considerable discussion concerning the utility of such orderings of persons. It is not our intention in this paper to review such discussions, but instead to present a rather new approach to the problem which seems to afford an adequate basis for quantifying qualitative data.

This approach has been used successfully for the past year or so in investigating morale and other problems in the United States Army by the Research Branch of the Morale Services Division of the Army Service Forces. While this approach to quantification leads to some interesting mathematics, no knowledge of this mathematics is required in actually analyzing data. Simple routines have been established which require no knowledge of statistics, which take less time than the various manipulations now used by various investigators (such as critical ratios, biserial correlations, factor analysis, etc.), and which give a complete picture of the data not afforded by these other techniques. The word "picture" might be interpreted here literally, for the results of the analysis are presented and easily assimilated in the form of a "scalogram," which at a glance gives the configuration of the qualitative data.

Description of the practical procedures, as well as the mathematical analysis, must be postponed to other papers. The present paper is devoted to a non-technical discussion of what we mean by a scale.

From Louis Guttman, "A basis for scaling qualitative data," *American Sociological Review*, 1944, 9, 139–150. Copyright 1944 by the American Sociological Association, and reproduced by permission of the author and publisher.

* Presented to the Thirty-eighth Annual Meeting of the American Sociological Society, New York December 4, 1943.

2. The Notions of Variable, Function, and Simple Function

First, a word about what is meant by a variable, whether qualitative or quantitative. We use the term in its conventional logical or mathematical sense, as denoting a set of values. These values may be numerical (quantitative) or non-numerical (qualitative).[1] We shall use the term "attribute" interchangeably with "qualitative variable." The values of an attribute (or of a quantitative variable, too, for that matter) may be called its *subcategories*, or simply *categories*.

An example of an attribute is religion. A person may have the value "Catholic," "Buddhist," "Jewish," "Mormon," "atheist," or some other value of this variable. There is no particular intrinsic ordering among these values. Another example is expression of an opinion. A person may say, "I like the British," "I don't like the British," or "I don't know whether or not I like the British." Another example is, a person may be observed to smile at another person upon meeting him, or he may be observed not to smile.

Quantitative variables are readily recognized and need no discussion here.

---

[1] In conventional courses in undergraduate college mathematics it is not ordinarily pointed out that a great deal of mathematics deals with purely qualitative variables. Notions of metrics and quantitative variables can be arrived at by sequences of qualitative classifications. In fact, this is the manner in which our approach to scaling derives a scale ordering.

The reader who is interested might look at a recent departure in textbooks for an introductory course in college mathematics (M. Richardson, *Fundamentals of Mathematics*, Macmillan, 1941). This book gives a simple, entertaining, and mature introduction to the foundations of mathematics. Its emphasis is on understanding, rather than on manipulation. It covers fundamental topics like point sets, the concept of number, and others that are rarely mentioned in ordinary undergraduate curricula and yet are mainstays of mathematical theory. It is only that most of us have been exposed exclusively to certain algebraic manipulations that we conceive such manipulations to be the essence of mathematics. A more sophisticated view is to regard mathematics as unveiling necessary relationships that arise from classifications. Much useless discussion of mathematics as a "tool" in social research could be saved by recognition of the fact that qualitative classifications lead to just as rigorous implications as do quantitative.

A variable y is said to be a single-valued function of a variable x if to each value of x there corresponds a single value of y. Thus, if y has the distinct values $y_1, y_2, \ldots, y_m$, and if x has the distinct values, $x_1, x_2, \ldots, x_n$, where m and n may be different, y is called a single-valued function of x if a table of correspondence can be set up like, for example, the following:

x	x_1	x_2	x_3	$\cdots$	x_n
y	y_3	y_5	y_{m-2}	$\cdots$	y_2

For each value of x there is one and only one value of y. (The converse need not hold: for the same value of y there may be two or more values of x.) Obviously, if y is to be a single-valued function of x, then we must have $m \leqq n$.

In particular, suppose y is an attribute, say like the above attribute about expression of liking for the British. Then $m = 3$, and we may denote by y_1 the statement, "I like the British"; by y_2, the statement, "I don't like the British"; and by y_3, "I don't know whether or not I like the British." If x is a quantitative variable which takes on more than m values $(n > m)$, and if we can divide the x values into m intervals which will have a one-to-one correspondence with the values of y, then we shall say the attribute y is a *simple* function of x. For example, suppose x takes on the ten values 0, 1, 2, 3, 4, 5, 6, 7, 8, 9. Then the correspondence table might be as follows:

x	0	1	2	3	4	5	6	7	8	9
y	y_1	y_1	y_1	y_3	y_3	y_2	y_2	y_2	y_2	y_2

Or we might show this graphically by plotting the x values on a straight line, and cutting it into intervals:

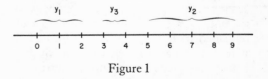

Figure 1

For statistical variables, another representation is in terms of a bar chart of frequencies, and this is what we use for convenience in §10 and §11 below.

3. The Definition of Scale

For a given population of objects, the multivariate frequency distribution of a universe of attributes will be called a *scale* if it is possible to derive from the distribution a quantitative variable with which to characterize the objects such that each attribute is a simple function of that quantitative variable. Such a quantitative variable is called a scale variable.

Perfect scales are not to be expected in practice. The deviation from perfection is measured by a *coefficient of reproducibility,* which is simply the empirical relative frequency with which the values of the attributes do correspond to the proper intervals of a quantitative variable. In practice, 85 per cent perfect scales or better have been used as efficient approximations to perfect scales.

A value of a scale variable will be called a *scale score,* or simply a *score.* The ordering of objects according to the numerical order of their scale scores will be called their scale order.

Obviously, any quantitative variable that is an increasing (or decreasing) function of a scale variable is also a scale variable. For example, in the illustration in §2, consider x to be a scale variable. Any constant could be subtracted from or added to each of the x scores, and y would remain a simple function of the transformed x. Thus, the scores 0, 1, 2, 3, 4, 5, 6, 7, 8, 9 could be replaced by the respective scores −5, −4, −3, −2, −1, 0, 1, 2, 3, 4. Or the x scores could be multiplied by any constant, or their square roots or logarithms could be taken—any transformation, continuous or discontinuous, could be used, as long as the rank order correlation between the original x and the transformed variable remained perfect. All such transformations will yield scale variables, each of which is equally good at reproducing the attributes.

Therefore, the problem of metric is of no particular importance here for scaling. For certain problems like predicting outside variables from the universe of attributes, it may be convenient to adopt a particular metric like a least squares metric, which has convenient properties for helping analyze multiple correlations. The interesting mathematics involved here will be discussed in another paper. However, it must be stressed that such a choice of metric is a matter of convenience; any metric will predict an outside variable as accurately as will any other.

In practice, the rank order has been used as a scale variable. (It is in fact a least squares metric for a rectangular distribution of scale scores.)

4. The Universe of Attributes[2]

A basic concept of the theory of scales is that of the universe of attributes. In social research, a universe is usually a large class of behavior such as described in the introduction above. The universe is the concept whose scalability is being investigated, like marital adjustment, opinion of British fighting ability, knowledge of arithmetic, etc. The universe consists of all the attributes that define the concept. Another way of describing the universe is to say it consists of all the attributes of interest to the investigation which have a common content, so that they are classified under a single heading which indicates that content.

For ease in focusing, let us take an example from opinion research where it is desired to observe the population of individuals in a standardized manner by a checklist of questions. The behavior of interest to the investigation is responses of individuals to such questions. Suppose the universe of attributes

---

[2] The words *population* and *universe* are ordinarily used interchangeably in statistical literature. For scales, it is necessary to refer both to a complete set of objects and to a complete set of attributes, so it will be convenient to reserve *population* for the former, and *universe* for the latter. In social research, the objects are usually people, so that *population* is appropriate for them.

consists of all possible questions which could be asked in such a list concerning the fighting ability of the British. Such questions might be: "Do you think the British Army is as tough as the German Army?"; "Do you think the R.A.F. is superior to the Luftwaffe?"; etc. (We do not pause here for problems of wording, interpretation, and the like. The reader is urged rather to focus on the general outline we are trying to establish.) There may be an indefinitely large number of such questions which belong in the universe; and in a particular investigation, ordinarily only a sample of the universe is used.

An attribute belongs to the universe by virtue of its content. The investigator indicates the content of interest by the title he chooses for the universe, and all attributes with that content belong in the universe. There will, of course, arise borderline cases in practice where it will be hard to decide whether or not an item belongs in the universe. The evaluation of the content thus far remains a matter that may be decided by consensus of judges or by some other means. This has been recognized before, although it need not be regarded as a "sin against the Holy Ghost of pure operationalism."[3] It may well be that the formal analysis for scalability may help clarify uncertain areas of content. However, we have found it most useful at present to utilize informal experience and consensus to the fullest extent in defining the universe.

An important emphasis of our present approach is that a criterion for an attribute to belong in the universe is *not* the magnitude of the correlations of that item with other attributes known to belong in the universe. It will be seen (in §10 below) that attributes of the same type of content may have any size of intercorrelations, varying from practically zero to unity.[4]

[3] Clifford Kirkpatrick, "A Methodological Analysis of Feminism in Relation to Marital Adjustment," *American Sociological Review*, June 1939, 4:325–334.

[4] That correlations are no criterion for content has been quite well known. See, for example, R. F. Sletto, *Construction of Scales by the Criterion of Internal Consistency*, Sociological Press, Hanover, N. H., 1937.

5. The Population of Objects

Defining the universe of attributes is a problem similar to the standard problem of defining the population of objects or individuals[5] of interest to the investigation. An investigator must always delimit the population with which he is working. For example, in the case of opinion about the British as fighters, he must decide *whose* opinions he wishes to ascertain. Is he interested in everyone in the world, or just in everyone in the United States? Is he interested in everyone in the United States, or just in adults? If just in adults, how is an adult to be defined? Here, too, decisions will sometimes be difficult as to whether a particular individual belongs in a population or not, and decisions must be made somehow before the investigation begins, else the investigator will not know whom to observe.

6. Methods of Observation

Let us assume that somehow we have a universe of attributes and a population of individuals defined. Next, observations are made as to the behavior of the population with respect to the universe. (In practice this will often be done only with samples. A sample of individuals from the population will have their behavior observed on a sample of attributes from the universe.) How the observations are to be made is of no concern to us here. In opinion research and other fields, questionnaires and schedules have been used. But any technique of observation which yields the data of interest to the investigation may be used. Such techniques for the social and psychological sciences might be case histories, interviews, introspection, and any other technique from which observations may be recorded. The important thing is not how the observations were obtained, but that the observations be of central interest to the investigation.

[5] For convenience, since the examples in this paper concern populations of human beings, we shall talk entirely in terms of such populations.

Use of a questionnaire implies that the investigator is interested in a certain type of universe of verbal behavior. Participant observation may imply that the investigator is interested in a certain type of universe of nonverbal behavior. Such distinct universes may each be investigated separately. It may often be of interest to see how well one universe correlates with another, but such a correlation cannot be investigated until each universe is defined and observed in its own right.

The examples of scales to be given later in this paper happen to comprise observations made by means of questionnaires. It should not be inferred, however, that scaling refers only to that technique. *Scaling analysis is a formal analysis, and hence applies to any universe of qualitative data of any science, obtained by any manner of observation.*

7. The Purpose of Scaling

Obviously it is very clumsy to record the large number of observations ordinarily involved in a universe of attributes for a population of individuals. The recording requires a table with one row for each individual and one column for each attribute. (The table may theoretically be indefinitely large.) It would be convenient if we could represent the observations in a more compact manner which would enable us to reproduce such a table whenever desired. A compact representation, if it could be obtained, would have two great advantages: first, a mnemonic advantage, for a compact representation would be easier to remember than would be a large table; and second, if it were desired to relate the universe to other variables it would be easier to do so by means of the compact representation than by using the large multivariate distribution of the attributes in the universe. From these are derived other advantages which will become apparent as the reader's familiarity with scales grows.

A particularly simple representation of the data would be to assign to each individual a numerical value and to each category of each attribute a numerical value such that, given

the value of the individual and the values of the categories of an attribute, we could reproduce the observations of the individual on the attribute. This will be possible only for restricted types of data, where each attribute in the universe can be expressed as a simple function of the same quantitative variable, that is, where the universe of attributes forms a *scale* for the population of individuals.

8. An Example of a Dichotomous Scale

As may be expected, the universe of attributes must form a rather specialized configuration for the population of individuals if it is to be scalable. Before describing a more general case, let us give a little example. (A sociological interpretation of this apparently mathematical example is given in §15 below.) Consider a mathematics test composed of the following problems:

(a) If r is the radius of a circle, then what is its area?

(b) What are the values of x satisfying the equation

$$ax^2 + bx + c = 0?$$

(c) What is de^x/dx?

If this test were given to the population of members of the American Sociological Society, we would perhaps find it to form a scale for that population. The responses to each of these questions might be reported as a dichotomy, right or wrong. There are $2 \times 2 \times 2 = 8$ possible types for three dichotomies. Actually, for this population of sociologists we would probably find only four of the possible types occurring. There would be the type which would get all three questions right, the type which would get the first and second questions right, the type which would get only the first question right, and the type which would get none of the questions right. Let us assume that this is what would actually happen. That is, we shall assume the other four types, such as the type getting the first and the third questions right but the second question wrong, would not occur. In such a case, it is possible to assign to the population a set of numerical values like 3, 2, 1, 0. Each member of the population will have one of these values assigned to him. This numerical value will be called the person's score. From a person's score we would then know precisely to which problems he knows the answers and to which he does not know the answer. Thus a score of 2 does not mean simply that the person got two questions right, but that he got two particular questions right, namely, the first and second. A person's behavior on the problems is reproducible from his score. More specifically, each question is a *simple function* of the score as is shown in §10 below.

9. The Meaning of "More" and "Less"

Notice that there is a very definite meaning to saying that one person knows more mathematics than another with respect to this sample. For example, a score of 3 means more than a score of 2 because the person with a score of 3 knows everything a person with a score of 2 does, and more.

There is also a definite meaning to saying that getting a question right indicates more knowledge than getting the same question wrong, the importance of which may not be too obvious. People who get a question right all have higher scale scores than do people who get the question wrong. As a matter of fact, we need no knowledge of which is a right answer and which is a wrong answer beforehand to establish a proper order among the individuals. For convenience, suppose the questions were given in a "true-false" form,[6] with suggested answers $2\Pi r$, $(-b \pm \sqrt{b^2 - 4ac}) / 2a$, and xe^{x-1} for the respective questions. Each person records either a T or an F after each question, according as he believes the suggested answers to be true or false. If the responses of the population form a scale, then we do not have to know which

are the correct answers in order to rank the respondents (only we will not know whether we are ranking them from high to low or from low to high). By the scale analysis, which essentially is based on sorting out the joint occurrences of the three items simultaneously, we would find only 4 types of persons occurring. One type would be $F_1T_2F_3$, where the subscripts indicate the questions; that is, this type says F to question 1, T to question 2, and F to question 3. The other three types would be $F_1T_2T_3$, $F_1F_2T_3$, and $T_1F_2T_3$. These types could be shown in a chart (a "scalogram") where there is one row for each type of person and one column for each category of each attribute. Without going into details, the scale analysis would establish an order among the rows and among the columns which would finally look like this:

Figure 2

Or, alternatively, both rows and columns might be completely reversed in order. Each response to a question is indicated by a check mark. Each row has three checkmarks because each question is answered, either correctly or incorrectly. The "parallelogram" pattern in the chart[7] is necessary and sufficient for a set of *dichotomous* attributes to be expressible as simple functions of a single quantitative variable.

From this chart we can deduce that F_1, T_2, and F_3, are all correct answers, or are all incorrect answers. That is, if we were now told

---

[6] We shall assume that no one gets an answer right by guessing. In a later paper it will be shown how scale analysis can actually pick out responses that were correct merely by guessing. But for this, much more than three items are necessary.

[7] Such a chart, where one column is used for each *category* of each attribute, we call a *scalogram*. The scalogram boards used in practical procedures are simply devices for shifting rows and columns to find a scale pattern if it exists.

that F_1 is a correct answer, we would immediately know that T_2 and F_3 are also correct answers. This means that we can order the men according to their knowledge even if we do not know which are the correct answers and which are the incorrect answers, only we do not know whether we are ordering them from highest to lowest or from lowest to highest. Except for direction, the ordering is a purely formal consequence of the configuration of the behavior of the population with respect to the items. The importance of this fact will become more apparent in more complicated cases where the attributes are not dichotomous but have more than two categories. We do not take the space here to expand on this point, but merely state that the scale analysis automatically decides, for example, where an "undecided" response to a public opinion poll questionnaire belongs, whether it is above "yes," below "no," in between, equivalent to "yes," or equivalent to "no."

10. The Bar Chart Representation

Another way of picturing the dichotomous scale of the sample of three items would be as follows: suppose that 80 per cent of the population got the first question right, 40 per cent got the second question right, and 10 per cent got the third question right. The univariate distributions of the three respective items could be shown by the bar chart in Figure 3.

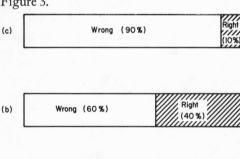

Figure 3

The bars show the percentage distributions for the respective questions. The multivariate distribution for the three questions, *given that they form a scale for the population,* can also be indicated on the same chart, since all those who are included in the group getting a harder question right are also included in the group getting an easier question right. Thus, we could draw the bar chart over again, but connect the bars with dashed lines in the fashion shown in Figure 4. Here we

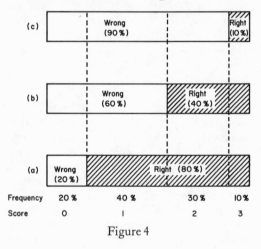

Figure 4

can see how the three questions are simple functions of the scores. From the marginal frequencies of the separate items, *together with the fact that the items form a scale,* we are enabled to deduce that 10 per cent of the people got a score of 3. The 10 per cent who got the hardest question right are included in those who got the easier questions right. This is indicated by the dashed line on the right, between the scores 2 and 3, which carries the same 10 per cent of the people (those with a score of 3) through the three bars. The 40 per cent who got the second question right include the 10 per cent who got the hardest question right and 30 per cent out of those who got the hardest question wrong, but all 40 per cent got the easiest question right. This leaves us 30 per cent who got just the first and second questions right. And so on. Thus we can think of an ordering of the persons along a horizontal axis, and each item can be thought of as a *cut* on that axis. All those above the cutting point get the question right and all those below the cutting point get the question wrong. Thus there is a one-to-one correspondence between the categories of an item and segments of the axis. Or we can say that each attribute is a simple function of the rank order along the axis.

It is because all the items in the sample can be expressed as simple functions of the same ordering of persons that they form a scale. Each item is perfectly correlated with or reproducible from the ordering along the axis. However, the point correlations between the items are not at all perfect. For example, the four-fold table between the second and third items is as follows:

Question (b)

Right Wrong

		Right	Wrong	
	Right	10	0	10
Question (c)				
	Wrong	30	60	90
		40	60	100

The point correlation between the two items is .41. As a matter of fact, the point correlation between two dichotomous items may be anything from practically zero to unity, and yet they may both be perfect functions of the same quantitative variable. That this may be paradoxical might be explained by inadequate treatment of qualitative variables in conventional courses and textbooks on statistics.[8]

---

[8] *Technical Footnote.* A tetrachoric coefficient for the four-fold table above, assuming a bivariate normal distribution, would be unity. However, this is *not* the correlation between the items. It does not tell how well one can predict one item from the other. The tetrachoric expresses instead the correlation between two quantitative variables of which the items are functions, provided the assumptions of normality are true. The reason the tetrachoric is unity in this case is that the quantitative varia-

An important feature of this four-fold table is the zero frequency in the upper right-hand corner cell. Nobody who got the third question right got the second question wrong. Such a zero cell must always occur in a four-fold table between two dichotomous items which are simple functions of the same quantitative variable.

11. Another Example of a Scale

Now let us give an example of a more complicated scale. Suppose we were interested in finding out how much desire soldiers may express now about going back to school after the war is over. Suppose that out of the universe of attributes which define this desire we select the following sample of four questions to be presented on a questionnaire.
1. If you were offered a good job, what would you do?
   (a) I would take the job
   (b) I would turn it down if the government would help me go to school
   (c) I would turn it down and go back to school regardless
2. If you were offered some kind of job, but not a good one, what would you do?
   (a) I would take the job
   (b) I would turn it down if the government would help me go to school
   (c) I would turn it down and go back to school regardless
3. If you could get no job at all, what would you do?
   (a) I would not go back to school
   (b) If the government would aid me, I would go back to school
   (c) I would go back to school even without government aid
4. If you could do what you like after the war is over, would you go back to school?

---

bles of which the items are functions are one and the same variable, namely, the scale variable. Notice, however, that the distribution of the scale variable according to the rank order is not at all normal. One of the contributions of scaling theory is to do away with untested and unnecessary hypotheses about normal distributions. It is the point correlation that is involved in the mathematical analysis of scaling, not the tetrachoric.

(a) Yes

(b) No

Let us suppose the responses of the men to these questions form a scale in the manner shown in Figure 5.

We now know how to read such a chart. 10 per cent of the men said they would turn down a good job to go back to school; 20 per cent said they would turn down a good job only if the government aided them; 70 per cent said they would take a good job; and so on. The 10 per cent who said they would turn down a good job are included in the 20 per cent who said they would turn down some kind of a job, and the 20 per cent are included in the 25 per cent who said they would go back to school if they got no job at all, and these 25 per cent are included in the 50 per cent who said they would like to go back to school.

For three trichotomous and one dichotomous questions there are $3 \times 3 \times 3 \times$

$2 = 54$ possible types. In order for these to form a scale, it can be shown that at most eight types can occur. The chart shows the eight types, which have been scored from 0 through 7. The chart shows the characteristics of each type. For example, the type with the score 3 includes all men with the following four values: they say that they would take a good job if it were offered to them rather than go back to school; that they would turn down some kind of job if the government would aid them to go back to school; that they would go back to school if the government would aid them if they could get no job at all; and that they would like to go back to school. Thus, by reading the categories crossed by the dashed lines which enclose each type, we can read off the characteristics of the type.

Notice that each of the four attributes is a simple function of the scale scores. For example, the "good job" question has its

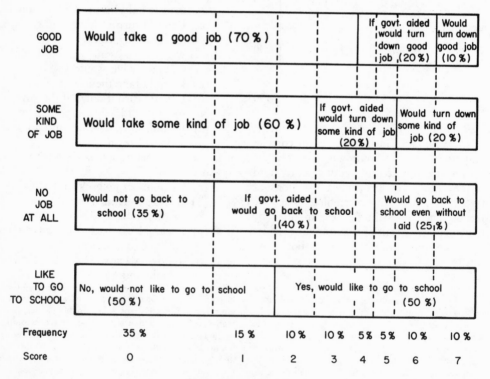

Figure 5

categories correspond with the following three intervals of the scale scores: 0-3, 4-6, 7.

The question might be raised as to how often will scales be found in practice. Isn't even a fair approximation to a structure like that in the above chart too much to hope for to be found in real life? Towards an answer to this, we can only cite thus far our experience with research in the Army. Literally dozens of sufficiently perfect scales have been found in various areas of attitude, opinion, and knowledge. The example given above of desire to go to school is a fictitious version of a set of similar questions that have actually proved scalable for the Army. Many varieties of data have been found scalable, and many have not. Those data which proved scalable could then be related to other variables very easily. Those that were not scalable required a more complicated analysis to handle them properly.

12. On Sampling the Universe of Attributes

An important property of a scalable universe is that the ordering of persons based on a sample of items will be essentially that based on the universe. If the universe is a scale, what the addition of further items would do would be merely to break up each type given by the sample into more differentiated types. But it would not interchange the order of the types already in the sample. For example, in Figure 5 above, type 6 would always have a higher rank order than type 5. People in type 6 might be ordered within the type into more subcategories; people within type 5 might be ordered into more subcategories; but all subcategories within 6 would remain of higher rank than all those in type 5. This may be seen in reverse, for example, by deleting one of the questions and noticing that all that is accomplished is to collapse the number of types to a smaller number so that two neighboring types may now become indistinguishable; but any types two steps apart would still remain in the same order with respect to each other.

Hence, we are assured that if a person ranks higher than another person in a sample of items, he will rank higher in the universe of items. This is an important property of scales, that *from a sample of attributes we can draw inferences about the universe of attributes.*

One of the criteria for selecting a sample of items is to choose a sample with enough categories to provide a desired amount of differentiation between individuals. Thus if individuals are desired to be differentiated say only into 10 groups, items should be chosen which will yield 10 types.[9] The shape of the distribution of the rank orders in a sample of attributes will of course depend upon the sample. One sample of attributes may give one shape distribution; another sample may give another shape distribution. This need not be a matter of concern, since our primary interest lies in the ordering of people, not the relative frequency of each position.

It might be asked how can one know the universe forms a scale if all one knows is a sample from the universe. At present it seems quite clear that in general the probability of finding a sample of attributes to form a scale by chance for a sample of individuals is quite negligible, even if there are as few as three dichotomous items in the sample and as many as one hundred individuals.[10] It seems quite safe to infer in general that if a sample

[9] We are of course not considering problems of reliability in the sense of repeated observations of the same attributes. For convenience, we are tacitly assuming perfect reliability.

[10] *Technical Footnote.* To work out the complete probability theory would require two things: first, a definition of a sampling process for selecting items, and second, a definition of what is meant by a scale not existing. A definition of the sampling process is difficult because items are ordinarily developed intuitively. Stating a null hypothesis that a scale does not exist leads to many possible analytical formulations, for different limiting conditions may be imposed upon the multivariate distribution of the items. For example, should the marginal frequencies be considered fixed in all samples, should the bivariate frequencies be considered fixed, etc.? These are questions which may become clearer as the theory of scaling develops, and in return may clarify our conceptions of what observation of social phenomena implies.

of attributes is selected without knowledge of their empirical interrelationships and is found to form a scale for any sizeable random sample of individuals, then the universe from which the attributes are selected is scalable for the entire population of individuals.

13. Scaling and Prediction

It is important to distinguish between two closely related topics, scaling and prediction. Finding that a universe of attributes is scalable for a population means that it is possible to derive a quantitative variable from the multivariate distribution such that each attribute is a simple function of that variable. We might phrase this otherwise by saying that each attribute is (perfectly) predictable from the quantitative variable.

This is the converse of the ordinary problem of prediction. In an ordinary problem of prediction, there is an outside variable, independently defined, that is to be predicted *from the attributes*. For example, it might be desired to predict the income of a student five years after he graduates from college, from his present knowledge of mathematics. To do this, an experimental sample would have to be obtained where salaries five years after college are known for each person and where responses to each item on the mathematics test are known. If the criterion of least-squares is adopted, then the best prediction on the basis of the sample would be the multiple regression of income on the three items in the sample. The multivariate distribution of the three items and the outside variable would give the necessary data for computing the regression, curvilinear or linear, which would be best for predicting the outside variable. If we wished to predict some other outside variable from the same items, a new multiple regression would have to be worked out from the multivariate distribution of the three items and the new outside variable. In general, the first of these regressions would ordinarily be expected to differ from the second. In general, weights to be used to predict one outside variable from a

set of attributes will differ from those used to predict another outside variable; a new multiple regression must be worked out for each outside variable.

This emphasizes an important property of scales. If the items have a multivariate distribution that is scalable, it can easily be seen that no matter what the outside variable may be, the same prediction weights may be given to the items. The correlation of any outside variable with the scale scores is precisely the same as the multiple correlation of that outside variable with the items in the scale. Thus we have an outstanding property of scaling, namely, that *it provides an invariant quantification of the attributes for predicting any outside variable*. No matter what prediction purpose is to be served by the attributes, the scale scores will serve that purpose.

14. On "Item Analysis"

Let us repeat the distinction just made. In scaling we reproduce the attributes from a quantitative variable. In prediction, we predict a variable from the attributes. This is a sharp difference which enables us to avoid much of the confusion that seems to prevail in the previous literature on scale construction. It seems to have been felt that items in a universe are merely stepping stones from which to obtain scores. It seems to have been felt that it was an embarrassing deficiency to lack a particular variable to predict from the items—that as a necessary evil one had to resort to methods of internal consistency to derive scores.

This accounts for current "item analysis" approaches to scaling. These use procedures that are typically as follows. A trial set of weights is assigned the categories, yielding a trial set of scores. Then each item is examined to see how well it by itself discriminates between these scores, that is, how well the scores can be predicted *from the item*. Those items which individually discriminate best are retained, and the others eliminated.

The misleading character of such procedures can be seen by inspection of the examples of scales in §10 and §11 above. We have pointed out that the intercorrelations between attributes in a scale can be as close to zero as one pleases. It can also easily be seen that the correlation ratio of the scale *scores* with any single item can also be as close to zero as one pleases. The predictability of the scale variable from an attribute does not tell whether or not the attribute is predictable from the scale variable.

The use of the "item analysis" procedures in connection with scales seems to be an unfortunate carry-over from the problem of ordinary prediction of an outside variable. In such a prediction problem, the items are truly but stepping stones to enable predictions to be made. It is known[11] that item analysis affords a first approximation to multiple correlation (or the discriminant function), and an item is of interest only insofar as it aids in the multiple regression.

Our emphasis for scaling is quite different. In scaling, we are interested in each and every attribute in the universe on its own merits. If we were not, we would not work with the universe. The attributes are the important things; and if they are scalable, then the scores are merely a compact framework with which to represent them.

If a compact framework is found, it has the additional important property of being an efficient device for predicting any outside variable in the best manner possible from the given universe of attributes.

15. The Relativity of Scales

An interesting problem associated with scales is: why does a universe form a scale for a given population? For example, take the sample of three mathematics questions given above. Why should these three questions be scalable? There is no necessary logical reason why a person must know the area of a

circle before he can know what a derivative is, and in particular the derivative of e^x. The reason for a scale emerging in this case seems largely cultural. Our educational system is such that the sequence with which we learn our mathematics in our high schools and colleges is first to get things such as areas of circles, then algebra, and then calculus. And the amount of drill that we have on each of these topics is probably also in that order. It would be quite possible, however, for the proverbial "man from Mars" to come to this earth and study calculus without having to learn the area of a circle, so that he might not be a scale type, according to the scale presented above; or a student may have had some personal incident which somehow impressed upon him with great force the derivative of e^x, but in the ordinary course of circumstances would have forgotten it even more readily than he forgot the area of a circle.

The scale analysis will pick out such deviants or non-scale types. Of course, if these non-scale types are too numerous, we shall not say that a scale exists. In practice we find scales, although never perfect scales, only because there has been sufficient uniformity of experience for the population of individuals so that the attributes mean essentially the same thing to the different individuals. As a matter of fact a study of the deviants is an interesting by-product of the scale analysis. Scale analysis actually picks out individuals for case studies.

A universe may form a scale for a population at a given time and may not at a later time. For example, the items in the scale of expression of desire of American soldiers to go back to school after the war may not prove to be scalable if they were asked once more at the close of the war.

A universe may form a scale for one population of individuals, but not for another. Or the attributes may form scales for two populations in different manners. For example, a sample of items of satisfaction with Army life which formed a scale for combat outfits in the Air Force did not form a scale

[11] See, for example, Louis Guttman, "An Outline of the Statistical Theory of Prediction," in Paul Horst, *et al.*, *The Prediction of Personal Adjustment*, Social Science Research Council, 1941.

for men in the technical schools of the Air Force. The structure of camp life for these two groups was too different for the same items to have the same meaning in both situations.

If a universe is scalable for one population but not for another population, or forms a scale in a different manner, we cannot compare the two populations in degree and say that one is higher or lower on the average than another with respect to the universe. They differ in more than one dimension, or in kind rather than in degree. It is only if two groups or two individuals fall into the same scale that they can be ordered from higher to lower. A similar consideration holds for comparisons in time. An important contribution of the present theory of scaling is to bring out this emphasis quite sharply.

16. Summary

1. The multivariate frequency distribution of a universe of attributes for a population of objects is a scale if it is possible to derive from the distribution a quantitative variable with which to characterize the objects such that each attribute is a simple function of that quantitative variable.
2. There is an unambiguous meaning to the order of scale scores. An object with a higher score than another object is characterized by higher, or at least equivalent, values on each attribute.
3. There is an unambiguous meaning to the order of attribute values. One category of an attribute is higher than another if it characterizes objects higher on the scale.
4. It can be shown that if the data are scalable, the orderings of objects and of categories are in general unique (except for direction). Both orderings emerge from analysis of the data, rather than from a priori considerations.
5. The predictability of any outside variable from the scale scores is the same as the predictability from the multivariate distribution with the attributes. The zero order correlation with the scale score is equivalent to the multiple correlation with the universe. Hence, *scale scores provide an invariant quantification of the attributes for predicting any outside variable whatsoever*.
6. Scales are relative to time and to populations.
    a. For a given population of objects, a universe may be scalable at one time but not at another, or it may be scalable at two periods of time but with different orderings of objects and categories.
    b. A universe may be scalable for one population but not for another, or it may be scalable for two populations but with different orderings of objects and categories.
    c. Comparisons with respect to degree can be made only if the same scaling obtains in both cases being compared.
7. From the multivariate distribution of a sample of attributes for a sample of objects, inferences can be drawn concerning the complete distribution of the universe for the population.
    a. The hypothesis that the complete distribution is scalable can be adequately tested with a sample distribution.
    b. The rank order among objects according to a sample scale is essentially that in the complete scale.
    c. The ordering of categories in a sample scale is essentially that in the complete scale.
8. Perfect scales are not found in practice.
    a. The degree of approximation to perfection is measured by a *coefficient of reproducibility*, which is the empirical relative frequency with which values of the attributes do correspond to intervals of a scale variable.
    b. In practice, 85 per cent perfect scales or better have been used as efficient approximations to perfect scales.
9. In imperfect scales, scale analysis picks out deviants or non-scale types for case studies.

CHAPTER **10**   The Cornell Technique for Scale and
Intensity Analysis[1]

LOUIS GUTTMAN

* * *

The Cornell technique is a procedure for testing the hypothesis that a universe of qualitative data is a scale for a given population of people, using the scalogram approach. It may also be used to test the hypothesis that the data form a quasi-scale. Of the several techniques now available for scalogram analysis,[3]

the one to be described here seems to be among the simplest and most convenient for general use. It requires no special equipment and involves only very simple clerical procedures which can readily be carried out by persons unskilled in statistics.

The various techniques just referred to, all do the same job since they follow the same scalogram theory; they differ only in how the work is arranged. The initial steps are common to all. First, the universe of content to be studied is defined. In an attitude or opinion study, this means deciding on the general content of the questions to be asked. Second, the population of people is defined. In an attitude or opinion survey, this means that the class of people to be interviewed is delimited.

Next come two kinds of sampling problems. One kind is the ordinary problem of random sampling of people, and the other is the sampling of items. For these two sampling problems, it is helpful to distinguish between the pre-test stage of a study and the final survey. Many fewer people can be used in a pre-test than must be used in the final survey, but fewer items can be used in the

---

Excerpts from Louis Guttman, "The Cornell technique for scale and intensity analysis," *Educational and Psychological Measurement*, 1947, 7, 247–280. Reproduced by permission of the author and publisher.

[1] A paper presented to the Conference on Measurement of Consumer Interest, University of Pennsylvania, May 17–18, 1946.

[2] [deleted]

[3] The first technique employed laborious least squares computations. See Louis Guttman, "The Quantification of a Class of Attributes: A Theory and Method of Scale Construction" in P. Horst *et al., The Prediction of Personal Adjustment*, Social Science Research Council, 1941, pp. 319–348. The standard procedure used by the Research Branch involves the use of scalogram boards especially invented for this purpose by the writer; these boards are simple to build and to operate, and a description of them will be in the forthcoming publication. A tabulation technique has been devised by another member of the Research Branch; see Ward H. Goodenough, "A Technique for Scale Analysis," *Educational and Psychological Measurement, 4* (1944), 179–190. The Cornell technique was devised by the writer at first for teaching purposes, and has proved to be very useful for general research purposes. A brief statement of the procedure as carried out on IBM equipment has already been

noted in E. William Noland, "Worker Attitude and Industrial Absenteeism: A Statistical Approach," *American Sociological Review, 10* (1945), 503–510.

final survey than must be used in the pre-test.

In the pre-test for a survey, about one hundred persons will usually constitute an adequate sample of the population to test the hypothesis of scalability. If the hypothesis is accepted, the items can then be used in the final study of the usual 3,000 or so people to obtain reliable proportions at each scale rank.

The other sampling problem is of quite a different nature; it consists of sampling the universe of content. In an attitude or opinion survey, this is done by constructing some questions which contain the required general content. In a pre-test, about a dozen questions usually can constitute an adequate sampling of the content. Since questions are constructed by the research workers, they do not fall into any standard random sampling scheme, and standard random sampling theory does not apply here. Instead, it is shown by the theory of scale analysis that *almost any* sample of about a dozen questions from the universe is adequate to test the hypothesis that the universe is scalable, provided the range of content desired is covered by the questions. If the hypothesis is accepted that the universe is scalable, then fewer questions can be used in the final study if fewer ranks are actually needed for the purposes of the final research.

Having defined the universe of content and the population of people, and having drawn a sample from each, the fifth step is to observe each person in the sample on each item or question in the sample. In an attitude or opinion survey where a questionnaire is used, this involves having the people indicate their answers to each question of the questionnaire.

The hypothesis of scalability—The problem now is to test the hypothesis, on the basis of the pre-test sample data, that the entire universe of items forms a scale for the entire population of people. Let us review what this hypothesis implies in order to see what the technique of analysis is trying to do.

The universe is said to be scalable for the population if it is possible to rank the people

from high to low in such a fashion that from a person's rank alone we can reproduce his response to each of the items in a simple fashion.[4] It is understood that a perfect scale is not to be expected in practice. Data have been considered sufficiently scalable if they are about 90 per cent reproducible, and if certain other conditions (to be explained later) are satisfied. For clarity, though, let us consider first a hypothetical perfect scale.

Suppose that a question from the universe is asked of a population concerning a certain political issue and that the responses are as follows:

Agree	60%
Undecided	10
Disagree	30
	100%

If "Agree" means a more favorable opinion than "Undecided," if "Undecided" is more favorable than "Disagree," and if the universe is perfectly scalable, then the following must be true. The highest 60 per cent of the people must be those who said "Agree"; the next highest 10 per cent must be those who said "Undecided"; and the lowest 30 per cent must be those who "Disagree." If another question from this scalable universe is asked and the responses are 20 per cent "Yes" and 80 per cent "No," and if "Yes" means a more favorable attitude than "No," then the top 20 per cent of the people must be those who said "Yes" and the bottom 80 per cent must be those who said "No." From the rank of a person, we can now deduce what his response must be to each of these two questions. Any person in the top 20 per cent of the population must have said "Agree" to the first question and "Yes" to the second question. Any person lower than the top 20 per cent but not lower than the top 60 per cent said "Agree" to the first question and "No" to the second question. Any person below the

---

[4] For a basic discussion of the theory of scales, see Louis Guttman, "A Basis for Scaling Qualitative Data," [Chapter 9 in this volume].

top 60 per cent but not below the top 70 per cent said "Undecided" to the first question and "No" to the second, and the rest of the people, the bottom 30 per cent, said "Disagree" to the first question and "No" to the second.

The various techniques for scalogram analysis are devices to find the rank order for the people which will best reproduce their responses to each of the items in this fashion. If the universe were a perfect scale, all of the techniques would involve little work and there would not be much to choose between them. It is the presence of imperfect reproducibility that raises the problem of technique.

The Cornell technique works by successive approximations. Usually just two approximations suffice to reject or accept the hypothesis of scalability. A first trial rank order for the people is established by a simple scoring scheme. For illustrative purposes, let us work out an actual case in detail. This illustration is not to be taken as a model of perfect research, but rather only to provide an example of the steps to be followed.

An example of the Cornell technique—It was desired to find out if the students in a certain class in race relations had a scalable attitude toward one of their textbooks, *A Nation of Nations*, by Louis Adamic. A questionnaire with seven questions was made out and administered to the class of 50 students. Both the number of questions and the number of students were smaller than those ordinarily used in a pre-test; they were used here only because these smaller numbers permit displaying the full data.

The seven questions were as follows:

A Nation of Nations

Questions

1. *A Nation of Nations* does a good job of analyzing the ethnic groups in this country.

    Strongly agree   Agree   Undecided
    __   4 __   3 __   2

    Disagree   Strongly disagree
    __   1 __   0

2. On the whole, *A Nation of Nations* is not as good as most college textbooks.

    Strongly agree   Agree   Undecided
    __   0 __   1 __   2

    Disagree   Strongly disagree
    __   3 __   4

3. Adamic organizes and presents his material very well.

    Strongly agree   Agree   Undecided
    __   4 __   3 __   2

    Disagree   Strongly disagree
    __   1 __   0

4. As a sociological treatise, Adamic's book does not rate very high.

    Strongly agree   Agree   Undecided
    __   0 __   1 __   2

    Disagree   Strongly disagree
    __   3 __   4

5. Adamic does not discuss any one group in sufficient detail so that a student can obtain a real insight into problems of ethnic group relations in this country.

    Strongly agree   Agree   Undecided
    __   0 __   1 __   2

    Disagree   Strongly disagree
    __   3 __   4

6. By providing a panorama of various groups, *A Nation of Nations* lets the student get a good perspective on ethnic group relations in this country.

    Strongly agree   Agree   Undecided
    __   4 __   3 __   2

    Disagree   Strongly disagree
    __   1 __   0

7. *A Nation of Nations* is good enough to be kept as a textbook for this course.

    Strongly agree   Agree   Undecided
    __   4 __   3 __   2

    Disagree   Strongly disagree
    __   1 __   0

Content Scale Analysis

We now describe, step by step, how the analysis of the responses is carried out by the Cornell technique:

(1) Weights for the first trial are assigned to each category of each question, using the successive integers beginning with zero. In this example, since each set of answers has five categories, the weights range from 0 to 4. In each question, the higher weights are assigned to the categories judged to express a more favorable attitude. This judging of ranks of categories is not to be regarded as final; the consequent analysis will either verify the judging or determine how to revise it.

(2) A total score is obtained for each person by adding up the weights of the categories he falls into. In our example, since the maximum weight for each person is four, and the total number of questions is seven, the total scores can range from zero to 28.

(3) The questionnaires are shuffled into rank order according to the total scores. In our example, we have arranged them from high to low.

(4) A table is prepared, like Table 1 below, with one column for each category of each question and one row for each person. Since each of our questions has five categories, and since there are seven questions, we have 35 columns in our table. There are 50 students, so we have 50 rows. The first five columns are for the five categories of the first question, the second five columns for the five categories of the second question, etc.

(5) The response of each person to each question is indicated on the table by placing an X in his row in the column for each category into which he falls. In our example, we have labeled the columns according to the questions and the weights of the categories. The first person is the one with the highest score, which is 28. He had checked the response weighted 4 in each of the questions, so he has seven Xs in his row, each under the respective columns for the categories with weight 4. There were two persons with a score of 25. The arrangement of people with the same score is arbitrary. Of the two persons in our example with a score of 25, the one placed first had a response of 4 to the first two questions, a response of 3·to the third question, of 4 to the fourth question, of 3

to the fifth and sixth questions, and of 4 to the seventh question. Similarly, the Xs in Table 1 indicate the response of each of the remaining persons to each question. Every person answers every question[5] so that there are seven Xs in each row. *Table 1 gives a complete record of all the data obtained by the survey with respect to this area.*

(6) At the bottom of Table 1 are the frequencies of response for each category. Category 4 of question 1 had nine people in it, whereas category 3 of the same question had 27 people, etc. The sum of the frequencies of the five categories in each question is always the total number of people in the sample, which in this case is 50.

(7) Now we come to the test for scalability. If the universe is a scale and if the order in which we have placed the people is the scale rank order, then the pattern of Xs in Table 1 must be of a particularly simple kind. Let us consider the first question in the table. If response 4 is higher than response 3, and if 3 is higher than 2, and if 2 is higher than 1 (response 0 happens to have no frequency in this case), then the nine people in category 4 should be the top nine people. Actually, six of them are the top six and the other three scatter farther down the column. Similarly, the 27 people in category 3 should be below the first nine people and should go down to the thirty-sixth person ($36 = 9 + 27$). Again, this is not perfectly true for our data. A similar examination for the other items shows that there is a substantial error of reproducibility in their present form. The approximate number of errors need not be counted at this stage, since it is evidently more than 15 per cent of all the 350 responses ($350 = 7 \times 50$, the number of questions times the number of people) in Table 1.

(8) It has seldom been found that an item with four or five categories will be sufficiently reproducible if the categories are regarded

---

[5] If people sometimes fail to respond to a question, then another category is added entitled "No Answer," which is weighted and treated like any other category for that question. In the present example, there were no "No Answers."

as distinct. One reason for this is the verbal habits of people. Some people may say "Strongly Agree" where others may say "Agree," whereas they have essentially the same position on the basic continuum but differ on an extraneous factor of verbal habits. By combining categories, minor extraneous variables of this kind can be minimized. By examining the overlapping of the Xs within the columns of each question, it can be determined how best to combine the categories so as to minimize the error of reproducibility for the combinations. In question 2, for example, categories 4 and 3 seem to intertwine, so they are combined. Similarly, in the same question, categories 1 and 0 seem to intertwine, so they are combined. In question 4, on the other hand, we combine categories 3, 2, and 1, leaving categories 4 and 0 separate. The way to combine categories is determined for each question separately. The combinations decided upon for this example on the basis of Table 1 are given in Table 2.

If it is desired to keep many scale types, then as little combination as possible should be done. However, if not many scale types are desired, the categories may be combined as far as one wishes even though this may not raise reproducibility. There is no harm in combining categories that could otherwise remain distinct with respect to scale error; all that is lost by such a combination is one scale type. On the other hand, categories may *require* combination in order to reduce error; they should be combined in the manner indicated by Table 1 and not arbitrarily.

(9) A second trial rank order for the people can now be established on the basis of the combined categories. This is done by reassigning weights. Since the first question now has three categories (that is, three combinations), these are assigned the weights 0, 1, and 2. Question 2 now has two categories. These could be assigned the weights 0 and 1. In the present example the weights 0 and 2 are used instead, since keeping the range of weights relatively constant from item to item often helps to establish a better ranking

for the people when there is error of reproducibility present.[6]

(10) Each person is now given a new score which represents his second trial rank order. This is done by re-scoring his questionnaire according to the new weights. This re-scoring is easily done from Table 1. Using a strip of paper which is as wide as the Table, the new weights for the old categories can be written directly on the edge of the strip. Placing the strip across the row for a person, the weights are added according to where the Xs lie. For our example, the strip would have for its first five columns the weights 2, 1, 0, 0, 0, weight 2 being placed in the column which was the old category 4, the weight 1 in the column which was the old category 3, and the 0s being in the old columns 2, 1, and 0 which are now combined. For question 2, the strip would have for the five columns the weights 2, 2, 0, 0, 0. Similarly, the new weights for the other questions can be written down to be used over the old columns of Table 1. The person who was formerly first on Table 1, with a score of 28, now has a score of $2 + 2 + 2 + 2 + 2 + 2 + 2 = 14$. The second person in Table 1 also gets a score of 14. The third person in Table 1 now gets a score of $2 + 2 + 2 + 1 + 2 + 2 + 2 = 13$; and so on for each person.

(11) The people are now shifted into the rank order of their new scores, and Table 3 is prepared from the combined data just as Table 1 was prepared from the original data. Question 1 now has three columns, question 2 has two columns, etc. The data of Table 1 are modified to fit Table 3 according to the combinations indicated in Table 2. The columns of Table 3 now refer to the combined categories, and the scores of Table 3 are the second trial scores just obtained in the preceding step.

(12) The error of reproducibility in Table 3 seems much smaller than in Table 1, and we shall now count up the actual errors. This

---

[6] In a perfect scale, *any* set of weights, provided they have the proper rank order for the categories, will yield a perfect rank ordering for the people.

TABLE 1

A NATION OF NATIONS

First Trial: Content

Score	1					2					3					4					5					6					7				
	4	3	2	1	0	4	3	2	1	0	4	3	2	1	0	4	3	2	1	0	4	3	2	1	0	4	3	2	1	0	4	3	2	1	0
28	x					x					x					x					x					x					x				
25	x					x						x				x						x					x				x				
25	x					x																x				x					x				
24	x						x					x						x				x					x				x				
23	x						x					x				x							x					x			x				
23	x						x					x										x						x				x			
23	x							x				x						x				x				x						x			
22			x					x				x					x						x					x				x			
21		x					x					x					x					x				x						x			
21		x					x					x					x					x					x					x			
21		x										x						x				x					x					x			
21					x			x				x						x				x					x				x			
20		x						x					x					x				x						x			x			
20		x						x				x							x				x				x					x		
20		x					x					x							x			x						x				x		
20		x							x				x							x		x						x					x	
19			x				x					x						x				x				x						x			
19	x							x				x								x				x			x				x			
18		x					x											x				x					x				x			
18		x					x						x					x				x					x				x			
18		x					x						x					x					x					x			x			
18		x					x						x					x				x					x					x		
17		x					x					x					x					x										x			
17		x					x											x				x							x			x			
16		x								x		x			x					x					x		x				x				

TABLE 1—(Continued)

Score	1					2					3					4					5					6					7				
	4	3	2	1	0	4	3	2	1	0	4	3	2	1	0	4	3	2	1	0	4	3	2	1	0	4	3	2	1	0	4	3	2	1	0
16	x																										x					x				
16	x					x																					x						x		
16	x					x					x													x			x		x				x		
15	x										x							x			x								x					x	
15											x						x							x					x						
15			x								x								x						x			x					x		
14	x												x				x								x					x					x
14				x					x									x									x								
13									x											x			x						x					x	
13	x							x				x					x				x					x						x			
12											x									x				x					x			x			
12	x																		x		x								x					x	
11								x												x				x						x		x			
11															x				x				x							x		x			
10				x					x										x				x				x							x	
9	x								x											x					x					x	x				
8						x								x				x							x	x					x				
7	x								x		x								x					x					x		x				
7	x					x								x		x									x			x						x	
6				x					x										x				x				x				x				
5				x					x		x									x			x			x			x			x			
5	x								x						x					x			x						x			x			
4				x						x	x			x						x					x					x				x	
Freq.	9	27	2	12	0	8	24	0	13	5	10	25	8	7	0	3	7	16	14	10	3	14	5	21	7	9	21	7	12	1	11	19	5	11	4

TABLE 2

COMBINATIONS OF CATEGORIES

Question	Combinations
1	(4) (3) (2,1,0)
2	(4,3) (2,1,0)
3	(4,3,2) (1,0)
4	(4) (3,2,1) (0)
5	(4,3,2) (1,0)
6	(4,3) (2,1,0)
7	(4) (3) (2,1,0)

is done by establishing *cutting points* in the rank order of the people which separate them according to the categories in which they would fall if the scale were perfect. For question 1, which has three categories, we need two cutting points. The first seems to fall between the last person with score 12 and the first person with score 11. All people above this cutting point should be in category 2, and all people below should not be in category 2. Since there is one person in category 2 below this point, we have one error for category 2. A second cutting point is needed to separate category 1 from category 0; since these two categories overlap somewhat, its exact location is not essential since moving it slightly up or down will not change the amount of error. It should be placed so as to minimize the error, but this may be done in several adjacent ways. One way is to place the cutting point between the second and third persons with score 4. Below this point we find three errors in category 1, and above this, we find five errors in category 0. The total number of errors in question 1 is 1 + 3 + 5 = 9. Since there are 50 responses to question 1, this means 18 per cent error. This error could be reduced, of course, by combining the last two columns and leaving question 1 as a dichotomy. Then there would be only the one error in the first column. Such a further dichotomization need not be done if there is relatively little error in the other questions so that the error over all questions is not much more than 10 per cent.

Question 2 has two categories in the second trial, and the cutting point which will minimize the error is between the last two scores 6, which makes two errors in the first column and four errors in the second column of question 2. Similarly, question 3 has a cutting point between the last score 2 and the first score 1, leaving three errors in its second column. Question 4 gets two cutting points, questions 5 and 6 one cutting point, and question 7 two cutting points. The total number of errors in the whole of Table 3 is 40, which is 11 per cent of all the responses. We can, therefore, conclude in view of the fact that much of the error occurs in question 1 and could be eliminated by combining two categories in that question, that this area is scalable. From a person's rank order, we can reproduce his response to each question *in terms of combined categories* with 89 per cent accuracy (or better, if we combine the last two columns of question 1).

(13) The per cent reproducibility alone is not sufficient to lead to the conclusion that the universe of content is scalable. The frequency of responses to each separate item must also be taken into account for a very simple reason. Reproducibility can be artificially high simply because one category in each item has a very high frequency. It can be proved that the reproducibility of an item can never be less than the largest frequency of its categories, regardless of whether the area is scalable or not. For example, question 3 in Table 3 has quite an extreme kind of distribution. Forty-three students are in one category, and seven in the other. Under no circumstances, then, could there be more than seven errors made on this item, regardless of whether or not a scale pattern existed. Or again, question 4 in Table 3 has 37 cases in its modal category and 13 cases in the other two categories. Under no circumstances, then, could item 4 have more than 13 errors. Clearly, the more evenly the frequencies are distributed over the categories of a given item, the harder it is for reproducibility to be spuriously high. Questions 5 and 6 in Table 3 each have high reproducibility, each having five errors; these are not artificially high because question 5 has only 28 cases in its more

frequent category and question 6 has 30 cases for its modal frequency. The maximum possible error for question 5 is 22, and for question 6 it is 20. The scale pattern represents quite a substantial reduction from this maximum error. An empirical rule for judging the spuriousness of scale reproducibility has been adopted to be the following: no category should have more error in it than non-error. Thus, the category with weight 2 in question 1 (Table 3) has eight non-errors and one error; category with weight 1 in this same question has 24 non-errors and three errors; category 0 has nine non-errors and five errors. Thus question 1 fits this rule. Question 3 comes perilously near to not fitting the rule. While the first column of question 3 (in Table 3) has no error, the second column has three errors compared to four non-errors. Similarly, the first column of question 4 has one error compared to two non-errors. It is because evenly distributed questions like 5 and 6 have little error and because the errors in the other questions, like in 3 and 4, are not too widely displaced from where they ought to be, that we consider this area to be scalable.

In constructing a sample of items to be used in a test for scalability, at least some of the items should be constructed, if at all possible, to obtain a uniform distribution of frequencies. Such items afford a good test of scalability. However, items with non-uniform frequencies are also needed in order to get differentiated scale types, so both kinds of items must be used. The more categories that are retained in an item, the sharper is the test for scalability, because error—if it really should be there—has a better possibility to appear when there are more categories.

Intensity Analysis

Separating "favorable" from "unfavorable" people—Since the expression of opinion about the textbook, *A Nation of Nations*, is sufficiently scalable, it is meaningful to say the one student likes the book better than another. There is a meaningful rank ordering of the students according to their opinion of the book. This ordering is expressed by the scale scores assigned in the second trial. A student with a higher score than another says the same or better things about the book (within scale error).

There is a further question that is of interest to the research worker. Given that the individuals can be ranked according to their degree of favorableness, is there a cutting point in this rank order such that we can say that all people to the right of the point are "favorable" and all people to the left are "unfavorable"? One person may be more favorable than another, yet both may be favorable. Obtaining just a rank order does not distinguish between being favorable and being unfavorable; it merely reflects being *more* favorable and *less* favorable and does not tell if a point is reached beyond which being *less* favorable actually means being "unfavorable."

An objective answer to this problem is provided by the use of the *intensity function*.

The theory of intensity analysis will be explained in detail in the forthcoming publication on the work of the Research Branch. For our purposes, all we need to know is that it provides a solution to the traditional problem of question "bias." No matter how questions are worded or "loaded," use of the intensity function will yield the same proportion of the group as favorable and unfavorable. The intensity function provides an invariant zero point for attitudes and opinions.

There are several techniques for obtaining intensity in a questionnaire, as will be discussed in the volumes to be published on the work of the Research Branch. . . . The first is the *fold-over* technique, and the second is the *two-part* technique. The fold-over technique is theoretically less justifiable than the two-part technique. However, it does have some practical advantages in some cases. [Ed. note: The *fold-over* technique is the only one discussed in these excerpts.]

The fold-over technique—The fold-over technique consists simply of re-scoring the content questions in order to obtain an in-

TABLE 3

A Nation of Nations
Second Trial: Content

Score	1			2		3		4			5		6		7		
	2	1	0	2	0	2	0	2	1	0	2	0	2	0	2	1	0
14	×			×		×		×			×		×		×		
14	×			×		×		×			×		×		×		
13	×			×		×			×		×		×		×		
13	×			×		×			×		×		×		×		
13	×			×		×			×		×		×		×		
13	×			×		×			×		×		×		×		
12	×			×		×			×		×		×			×	
12	×			×		×			×		×		×			×	
11		×		×		×			×		×		×			×	
11		×		×		×			×		×		×			×	
11		×		×		×			×		×		×			×	
11			×	×		×			×		×		×		×		
11		×		×		×			×		×		×			×	
11		×		×		×			×		×		×			×	
11		×		×		×			×		×		×			×	
11	×			×		×			×		×			×	×		
10		×			×	×			×		×		×		×		
10		×		×		×			×			×	×		×		
10		×		×		×			×			×	×		×		
9		×		×		×			×		×			×		×	
9		×		×		×			×		×			×		×	
9		×		×		×			×			×	×			×	
9		×		×		×			×			×	×			×	
9		×		×		×			×			×	×			×	
9		×			×	×			×		×		×			×	

TABLE 3—(Continued)

Score	7/0	7/1	7/2	6/0	6/2	5/0	5/2	4/0	4/1	4/2	3/0	3/2	2/0	2/2	1/0	1/1	1/2
8	x				x	x			x	x		x		x		x	
7		x		x		x			x	x		x		x		x	
7		x			x	x		x	x	x		x	x		x	x	
7		x			x	x			x		x	x	x		x		
6	x			x		x			x			x		x			
6	x			x	x	x			x			x		x		x	
6	x			x	x	x			x			x		x		x	
6						x	x		x			x		x		x	
5	x	x		x		x			x		x	x	x		x		
4	x			x		x			x				x		x		
4	x			x		x			x			x			x		
4	x				x	x			x		x	x	x				
3	x			x		x		x				x			x		
3	x			x	x	x		x				x	x	x	x		
3	x			x		x			x			x	x		x		
2	x			x		x		x					x		x	x	
2	x			x		x		x			x		x				
2	x			x		x		x			x		x		x		
1	x	x		x		x		x	x		x		x		x	x	
1	x			x		x		x	x		x		x		x		
1	x			x		x		x					x		x		
0	x			x		x		x			x		x		x		
Freq.	20	19	11	20	30	28	22	10	37	3	7	43	18	32	14	27	9

TABLE 4

A NATION OF NATIONS

Intensity

Score	1			2			3			4			5			6			7		
	2	1	0	2	1	0	2	1	0	2	1	0	2	1	0	2	1	0	2	1	0
14	x			x			x			x			x			x			x		
12	x x			x x x x			x			x x				x		x x x				x	
11		x			x		x				x		x x x x x x			x x x x			x x x x x x x x x		
11	x x x			x				x		x				x		x x x						
11					x		x					x	x x x x x				x					
11		x						x		x x		x			x x x x						
10				x x x				x			x	x x x				x		x x x		
10		x x x						x x x						x				x		
10					x x					x x			x							x	
9								x x x x x x x x x x x x x x x x x			x x x x x				x		x x x x			x x x x x x x		
9					x x x x x x x x x x													
9							x x x			x x			x x x x				x x x x			x		
9										x x x x x				x		x x x x x						
9											x			x x x			x				x	
9				x x x x x x x x x x x x							x			x						
8										x						x x x x				x x		
8		x x		x x							x			x							x	
8				x x							x x			x				x		x x		
8		x		x x x x x x x x x x x x													
8		x			x				x		x				x						
7	x x							x		x				x				x		x	
7									x			x			x						x x	
7									x			x		x								x

TABLE 4—(*Continued*)

Score	1			2			3			4			5			6			7		
	2	1	0	2	1	0	2	1	0	2	1	0	2	1	0	2	1	0	2	1	0
Freq.	9	39	2	13	37	0	10	32	8	13	21	16	10	35	5	10	33	7	15	30	5

tensity score. This is easily done for the form of question used to study opinions about *A Nation of Nations*. The following weights are assigned to the check list of answers: "Strongly agree" and "Strongly disagree" receive a weight of 2; "Agree" and "Disagree" receive a weight of 1; and "Undecided" receives a weight of 0.[7] Thus the apparently more intense responses receive higher weights, and the apparently less intense responses receive lower weights, regardless of whether the responses appear to be "favorable" or "unfavorable."

Weighting the responses in this way means that in order to obtain an intensity score, we are in fact combining opposite ends of the check list, so that there are but three (combined) intensity categories per question. Intensity, as obtained in this fashion, is not in general scalable. Instead, it forms what is called a quasi-scale. In a quasi-scale, there is no perfect relationship between a person's response to each question and his score on all the questions; instead, there is a gradient. The higher a person's score, the more *likely* he is to give a high response to each item, but there is not the high certainty that exists in the case of a scale. This can be seen in our example of Adamic's textbook. Arranging the data into a scalogram according to total intensity score, we obtain the configuration shown in Table 4. Each question now has three categories which represent the three intensity steps. There is a density gradient of responses. There are no clear-cut streaks in the category columns but, instead, gradually tapering densities that blend from one category into the next. Combining categories still will not yield a scalable pattern.

According to the basic theory of intensity analysis, intensity should be a perfectly scalable variable. The equations of scale analysis show that there is a second component in every scale of content which is a U- or J-shaped function of the scale scores. This

component has been identified as the intensity function of the content scale. What we are trying to do is to obtain this intensity by direct empirical methods. The fact that our observed intensity is not perfectly scalable shows that it is not the pure intrinsic intensity we are seeking. No perfect way has yet been found for obtaining intensity, but satisfactory results are obtainable even with imperfect intensity techniques. Instead of a perfect intensity function, we will get one that can have considerable error in its relationship to the content scale scores.

Plotting intensity against content—The empirical intensity function is obtained by plotting the intensity scores just obtained against the content scores obtained from the previous section from the second content trial. The scattergram is shown in Table 5. The frequency in boldface in each column of Table 5 corresponds to the position of the median intensity for the respective columns. If the pure intrinsic intensity were being measured by our technique, there would be no scatter about these medians at all, but intensity would be a perfect U- or J-shaped function of the content scores. Despite the presence of error, however, the approximate shape of the true intensity function is clear from the shape of the curve along which the columnar medians lie. The curve descends from the right, or the more favorable content scores, reaches its low point at the next to the last interval to the left (contents scores 3–5), and then rises again at the last interval to the left. The content scores 3–5, then, must be the approximate interval which contains the zero-point of the attitude. Students to the left of this interval can be said to have *negative* attitudes and students to the right can be said to have *positive* attitudes toward the textbook. Students in the 3–5 interval cannot be divided into positives and negatives without the aid of additional questions which will help to differentiate more precisely between their ranks.

On the basis of Table 5, we can conclude, then, that about 8 students did not like the textbook, 35 students did like the textbook,

---

[7] These weights can be written on a strip of paper to be put over Table 1 and added up there to obtain an intensity score for each person.

TABLE 5

A NATION OF NATIONS
Scattergram of Intensity and Content

Intensity	Content (Second Trial)							Total
	0–2	3–5	6–8	9–10	11	12–13	14	
14							1	1
13								0
12	1							1
11				1		2	1	4
10					1	2		3
9	4	1	1		1	1		8
8	2	1	1	2				6
7	1	1	4	2	4	1		13
6		1	3	4	2			10
5		1						1
4		1			1			2
3		1						1
Total	8	7	9	9	9	6	2	50

while 7 students were in between these. This division of the students into those with favorable and those with unfavorable attitudes does not depend upon the particular way we worded our questions. The same intensity curve, with the same proportion to the right and to the left of the zero-point would have been obtained if we had used other questions or other wordings, provided only that these other questions were scalable with the present questions. Proof of this invariant property of the intensity function is given in the forthcoming volumes on the Research Branch's work.

Need for larger sample of people—An important caution must be sounded here. The example we are working with must be regarded as a highly fortunate one in one sense for the purposes of this exposition. It is rare indeed to find as low error as we have in the intensity function so that the intensity curve and zero-point show out quite clearly on the basis of our small sample of 50 cases. In general this will be far from the case. To perform an intensity analysis safely, when there is a substantial error present—which is the usual case—ordinarily from one to three thousand cases are needed to obtain stable medians. To perform the scalogram analysis, it is also safer to use more than 50 cases. A hundred cases is a desirable minimum to use in the pre-test, as well as a dozen or so items instead of seven as we have used in our illustrative example. If the pre-test has established that the universe of items is scalable, the final study should be done on the usual number of cases used in opinion surveys if reliable results with respect to intensity are to be obtained. The hypothesis of scalability can be tested in a pre-test on relatively few people because of its specialized character. However, *proportions* of the population at any given rank or on one side of the zero-point are subject to ordinary sampling error; larger samples of people must be used for reliable results with respect to them.

Drawbacks to the fold-over technique— The fold-over technique for intensity has two theoretical drawbacks to it, as well as some practical ones. First, the intensity scores obtained thereby are not experimentally independent of the content scores because exactly the same answers are used for both of the scores. This may give rise to some spuriousness in the relationship between the two. Second, it assumes that "Strongly agree" and "Strongly disagree" are approximately equal in intensity and opposite in direction, and similarly for "Agree" and "Disagree," while it is assumed that "Undecided" approximately straddles the zero-point. These assumptions need not be true at all. In fact, the occasional falsity of these assumptions is one contribution to error in the obtained intensity scores.

If the assumptions were true, life would be much easier for research workers. It would not be necessary to ask a series of questions in order to obtain a zero interval because the "Undecided" category for any question would provide such an interval. But, unfortunately, it is clear that in a series of questions on the same issue, the people who are "Undecided" on one question can all be "Agreed"

on another question. It is just because we cannot interpret the bias of a question by looking at its content that such a technique like that of the intensity function is needed.

While the fold-over technique does have these two theoretical drawbacks, it does seem to average out the errors involved in violating the above assumptions and to provide a proper U- or J-shaped curve in many cases.

A practical disadvantage to the fold-over technique has been found in the case of man-in-the-street interviews, where people would avoid the "strongly" categories almost completely, so that not much differentiation in intensity could be obtained. In such a case, a two-part technique is necessary. An advantage of the fold-over over the two-part technique is that it takes less space and time in administering questionnaires.

* * *

CHAPTER 11 Elaboration of Guttman Scaling Techniques

LOUIS E. DOTSON AND GENE F. SUMMERS

Since the earlier work of Guttman, the unidimensional scale has found widespread use by sociologists and social psychologists. Its utility is suggested not only by the number of behavioral scientists who have employed it but by the number of diverse measuring tasks to which it has been adapted. Although two decades have passed since its development, it is perhaps still too early to evaluate accurately its contribution to sociology and social psychology. It is certainly true that the Guttman technique permits the treatment of qualitative data without the somewhat questionable conversion to quantitative data found in some scaling techniques. Thus researchers may have been able to minimize erroneous interpretations by avoiding misleading measurement assumptions. But more important to the development of behavioral science, the Guttman model contains a built-in mechanism (the coefficient of reproducibility) through which one is forced to examine the internal consistency among the items composing the scale. This mechanism forces attention upon what is actually being measured. Although on occasion "sterile" measures have resulted despite tests of internal consistency, generally, requirements of re-

producibility have resulted in greater conceptual clarity. It is difficult indeed to examine the internal consistency of a set of items without concern for what is really being measured, or at least for what is being varied over the items to account for the variation in item response frequencies. Greater conceptual clarity should also result from the requirement that each time a scale is used its internal consistency must be reexamined. Thus, when a set of items scales for one group but not for another, or scales for a particular group at time 1 but not at time 2, one must explain why. Furthermore, the Guttman technique has provided a model for the organization of collective and other nonattitudinal data (Riley *et al.*, 1954) and considerable effort has been stimulated to refine the original Guttman scaling procedure.

Most refinements in Guttman scaling since the late 1940s have centered around techniques for assessing a scale (i.e., techniques to determine more precisely the extent to which a set of items scales satisfactorily) and the mechanics of scale construction utilizing electronic data-processing equipment. Although there appears to have been more work dealing with criteria for the recognition of error than with criteria for the prevention of error in scale construction, important de-

This chapter was prepared especially for this volume.

velopments have occurred. From among them, we have selected for discussion: (1) the mechanics of Guttman scaling, (2) the placement of error types, (3) methods of estimating internal consistency, (4) significance tests, and (5) the intensity function.

THE MECHANICS OF GUTTMAN SCALING

The basic notion of the Guttman or cumulative scale is that an internal relationship exists among the items forming the scale such that a person who endorses or agrees with an item of a given scale position will endorse all items below it in the scale. If it is known that a person endorsed three items of a four-item scale, it is also known which three items he endorsed. Likewise, all individuals endorsing only three items will endorse the same three. Thus, it is possible to order individuals into relative categories or positions defined by the position of the items endorsed. Of course, these qualities of the Guttman scale deteriorate as the internal consistency decreases.

A number of techniques have been devised for constructing Guttman scales. In earlier work, the scalogram board technique was used (Suchman, 1950a). This procedure made use of a board consisting of a series of movable slats on which was placed buckshot, which represented the responses of subjects to each item. The slats could be manipulated in such fashion that the internal consistency of the items composing the scale could be visually determined. Other techniques, including the Cornell technique (Guttman, 1947), the least-squares method (Guttman, 1941), and the cross-tabulation technique (Toby and Toby, 1954) have been developed, as have various modifications for use with electronic data-processing equipment and computers. Some techniques employ arbitrarily assigned weights, which are summed to obtain a scale score for each subject; others do not. Weights may be used, but nothing is gained in the process.

Stouffer is given credit for the development of a technique that does not use a weighting system. Cutting points for dichotomously treated, multiple-response items are determined in this technique by cross-tabulating each item with all other items. It was developed for use on an electronic card-sorter but can be readily adapted for use with computers. Because of its simplicity, this method, with some modification, is summarized below. (For a more detailed presentation see Toby and Toby, 1954).

In this technique, as in others used for constructing Guttman scales, the rank order of the items should be predicted before the data are examined. The most difficult (or least favorable) item should be assigned rank 1, the second most difficult, rank 2, ..., and the least difficult, rank n. In this way, confidence in a scale is increased to the extent that the prediction of the rank order of items is supported by the data. To check on the prediction of rank order, ascertain the frequency of response to each answer category for each item. For example, if each item has five response alternatives of strongly agree, agree, undecided, disagree, and strongly disagree, determine the distribution of responses to each item and convert these to cumulative percentages from the most positive to the most negative. In the next step this information will be useful in choosing the cutting points of multiple-choice items that are treated as dichotomous items. When the items are truly dichotomous, e.g., yes-no, agree-disagree, the cumulative percentages can be determined directly.

The next step is to decide what shall be considered an endorsement ($+$) of each item. Generally, for an item with the five response alternatives above, checking either "strongly agree" or "agree" would be interpreted as endorsement ($+$). Checking any of the remaining alternatives would be considered nonendorsement ($-$) of the item. With truly dichotomous items this is a very simple matter; with multiple-choice items it is not.

The cutting point for an item is the point within the ordered alternatives that separates endorsement from nonendorsement. In the illustration just presented, the cutting point is between "agree" and "undecided." There are times when one may wish to shift the cutting point. This shifting obviously changes the proportion of respondents endorsing the item. By moving the cutting point downward, the percentage of endorsement is increased; by shifting it upward, the percentage is decreased.

There are basically two reasons for electing to shift the item cutting point. First, it may be desirable to change the marginal distribution of items. For example, the distribution may be 20, 30, 60, 80 per cent endorsement, with the cutting point between "agree" and "undecided" for all items. By shifting the cutting point on the 30 per cent item to include "undecided" as an endorsement, the item may be made into a 40 per cent item. This is a preferred marginal distribution for reasons to be outlined below. Second, by shifting the cutting point of an item it is sometimes possible to make an unscalable item scalable.

Maintaining as closely as possible a constant response cutting point (e.g., between the responses of "agree" and "undecided" in the above set of alternatives), the researcher should select items that maximize the distance between item marginals (the proportion of respondents endorsing the item). For example, a four-item scale should contain items that approximate marginals of 20, 40, 60, and 80 per cent. The farther apart the marginals, the less likely a reversal of the order of the items from the pretest to the final study or on any two applications of the scale. In addition, items with extreme marginals should be avoided. Items necessarily have reproducibilities equal to the modal response (either + or −). Thus, items with marginals of greater than 80 per cent or less than 20 per cent might cause one to place undue confidence in the scalability of the universe of content being considered.

With the trial set of items selected, each item should be run against every other item in order to determine if the items fit one another sufficiently to be compatible with the Guttman model. In the case of a perfect

relationship between two items, one of which is more difficult to endorse, all subjects endorsing the item with the smaller marginal (the more difficult item) should also endorse the less difficult item. The extent to which the items meet this perfect relationship is reflected in the "error cell" of each four-fold table (see Figure 1). No error cell should

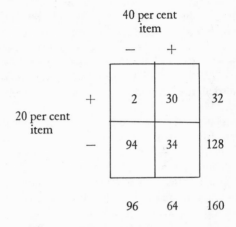

Figure 1. Four-fold table of two items.

contain more than 10 per cent of the total number of respondents. Further, the cells on the major diagonal (++) and (−−) of each table should contain at least twice as many cases as are found in the error cell (Toby and Toby, 1954). The item error is the proportion of respondents endorsing the more difficult item but failing to endorse the easier item.

Once the cutting point for each item and the item error have been established, the response patterns need to be obtained. This is accomplished by determining each subject's response to all items. The sequence of observations begins with the least frequently endorsed item and continues with items in descending order of difficulty. If a cardsorter is used, and the items are treated dichotomously, the first pass of the cards through the machine will result in two stacks of cards —one representing subjects who endorsed the item (+) and the other representing those who did not (−). Each stack is then run on the item second in the order of difficulty. This may generate four stacks representing those who (1) endorsed the most difficult item and the next most difficult one $(++)$, (2) endorsed the most difficult item but not the second $(+-)$, (3) did not endorse the first but did endorse the second $(-+)$, and (4) did not endorse either item $(--)$. Each of these stacks is then run on the item with the third lowest frequency of endorsement, which could generate eight response patterns: (1) $+++$, (2) $++-$, (3) $+-+$, (4) $+--$, (5) $-++$, (6) $-+-$, (7) $--+$, and (8) $---$. The procedure is continued until all items composing the scale are examined.

The number of possible response patterns is a function of the number of items. For dichotomous items the number of possible response patterns is 2^n, where n equals the number of items. A four-item scale then may produce 16 response patterns (2^4) and an eight-item scale may produce 256 (2^8). However, of the number of possible response patterns, only $n + 1$ are perfect or pure types, i.e., response patterns indicating a consistency of response such that if an item of a given scale position is endorsed, all items below it in the scale are also endorsed. For example, in a four-item scale, the response patterns $++++$, $-+++$, $--++$, $---+$, and $----$ are pure types. The other patterns that may be found which fail to show the response consistency are nonscale or error types.

THE PLACEMENT OF ERROR TYPES

In reality, the perfect scale is only approximated. Since there are inevitably some response patterns that are nonscale types, they must be assigned to perfect or pure response patterns. Several methods are available for classifying nonscale responses.

The first criterion to use in this procedure is that of minimizing error. In a strict sense the error has already been committed by the respondent when he deviated in his response pattern from the pure scale type. The prob-

lem then is to place his response pattern in one of the pure scale types and to do so in such a way that he is "charged" with the least amount of error for his deviation. For example, the pattern $-+--$ (most difficult to least difficult from left to right) could be assigned only to scale type 0 $(----)$ using this criterion. Any other assignment would involve two or more errors. If it were placed in scale type 1 $(---+)$, two errors associated with items 2 and 4 would be assumed. If it were placed in scale type 2, it would contain three errors involving items 2, 3, and 4.

The minimum error criterion will resolve the problem of classifying nonscale responses where there is but one possible assignment. However, there are patterns that may be classified in two or more scale types using this criterion. The response $+-++$ could be considered as either scale type 2 $(--++)$, with an error associated with the first item, or scale type 4 $(++++)$, with the second item accounting for one error.

For those cases where the minimum error criterion assigns a response pattern to two or more scale types, several solutions have been developed. Where there is reason to suspect systematic response error on the items with the smallest and largest marginals, the middle weighting technique, which gives more weight to the middle items, might be used. The decision regarding the placement of responses ambiguously classified by the minimum error criterion is determined by responses to the middle items. For example, the pattern $+-++$ could be placed in either scale type 2 or 4 with one error. If it were placed in scale type 2, item 1, an extreme item, would account for the error. An assignment to scale type 4 would place the error on item 2. If the item analysis described above had indicated that item 1 was subject to considerable error, assuming a greater probability of error in item 1 than in item 2 would be justified. Therefore, the decision would be made, on the basis of the greater reliability of item 2, to assign the response pattern to scale type 2, thus giving greater weight to the middle item (Henry, 1952).

A second solution to the ambiguous classification is the extreme weighting technique. Supposedly this practice may be used when the middle items are suspect. In the above example, the response $+-++$ would be placed in scale type 4 when the extreme weighting technique is used because of different assumptions regarding the location of error (Henry, 1952).

An alternative solution, the distribution of perfect scale types method, perhaps has become the most frequently used technique for classifying patterns that are assigned to two or more scale types by the minimum error solution. This method is reported "to predict the 'Modified Latent Distance' solutions much more efficiently . . ." (Henry, 1952, p. 105) than either the extreme weighting or the middle weighting techniques and is considerably less complex than the modified latent distance technique developed by Lazarsfeld.

The distribution of perfect scale types solution is to choose from among those scale types designated by the minimum error criterion, i.e., the scale type with the largest frequency. The assignment is made to this scale type if the difference between frequencies of the two pure types is statistically significant (chi-square, 1 d.f., .10 level) (Henry, 1952). In the example above, the pattern $+-++$ could be placed in scale types 2 or 4 with one error. If scale type 2 contained 98 cases and scale type 4 had 32, the pattern would be classified as scale type 2, since it occurred with greater frequency. When this technique is used, the nonscale type is assigned to the pure type from which it has the greater probability of deviating.

Another solution to the problem of classifying nonscale types when the minimum error criterion is ambiguous is the middle-class assignment technique, suggested by Borgatta and Hays (1952). This technique places an ambiguous response pattern midway between the two most extreme classes indicated by the minimum error criterion. Borgatta and Hays indicate that caution should be used

with each of the above arbitrary techniques for the classification of nonscale response patterns; they recommend the more complex latent distance analysis where possible.

METHODS OF ESTIMATING INTERNAL CONSISTENCY

Estimating the internal consistency of a set of items follows the placement of nonscale types. As a method of estimating the degree of internal consistency, Guttman (1950) proposed the coefficient of reproducibility, $\left(1 - \dfrac{\text{total placement error}}{\text{respondents} \times \text{items}}\right)$, and somewhat arbitrarily set a minimum of .90 as necessary for assuming unidimensionality. According to this standard, the amount of error tolerated is not to exceed 10 per cent.

The coefficient of reproducibility has been and continues to be the most frequently used estimate of internal consistency, although its limitations are recognized. As demonstrated by Menzel (1953) and Borgatta (1955), it fails to approximate zero in the absence of any internal consistency. To understand this weakness it is necessary only to realize that a single item can have no more error than its modal response. For example, an item endorsed by 80 per cent of the respondents can have a maximum of 20 per cent error. Thus, a set of items with no internal consistency will necessarily have some reproducibility according to the Guttman estimate.

Reasoning that reproducibility is a function of (a) extreme items, (b) extreme individuals, and (c) the scalability of the items for the respondents, Menzel proposed as a more satisfactory measure the coefficient of scalability, $\left(1 - \dfrac{\text{total placement error}}{\text{maximum error}}\right)$. Maximum error is computed on the basis of the difference between total responses and the sum of the modal categories of either items or subjects. The smaller of the two differences is used in estimating maximum error, apparently to avoid overestimating internal consistency. Menzel suggests that the lower limit of a satisfactory coefficient of scalability will lie somewhere between .60 and .65.

Menzel's coefficient of scalability is a dubious improvement over the coefficient of reproducibility, since it possesses the same limitations. As demonstrated by Borgatta, Menzel's index also fails to approximate zero in the absence of a common content among the items.

Borgatta proposed the error ratio as a substitute. This index varies from zero to one and may be compared with error ratios of other scales. The error ratio is the "ratio of errors in the scale to the maximum number of errors for a scale of the same marginal frequencies" (Borgatta, 1955, p. 99). The maximum number of errors is computed by utilizing the law of independent probabilities to determine the expected frequencies for each nonscale type from the marginals of each item. Thus, to determine the expected frequency for scale type 4 $(++++)$ in a four-item scale with marginals of 20, 40, 60, and 80 per cent, the marginals are multiplied $(.20 \times .40 \times .60 \times .80)$ to obtain the expected proportion in the scale type (in this case .0384), which is then multiplied by the number of respondents. For nonscale types the expected frequency must be multiplied by the number of errors of assignment in order to determine the sum of the errors of assignment for the expected distribution. This sum is used as the maximum number of errors. For example, in a four-item scale with marginals (the proportion of $+$ responses) of 20, 40, 60, and 80 per cent, the expected frequency for response pattern $-+--$ is determined by multiplying the proportion of $-$ responses (.80) for the first item by the proportion of $+$ responses (.40) for the second item, by the proportion of $-$ responses (.40) for the third item, by the proportion of $-$ responses (.20) for the fourth item. This product (.026) is then multiplied by the total number of respondents (N) to determine the number of respondents expected to have the nonscale type $-+--$. The expected frequency must then be multiplied by the number of errors of placement. In this case the

pattern $-+--$ can be assigned to scale type 0 $(----)$ with one error. Thus the total number of errors of placement expected for this response pattern, assuming an N of 2000 is:

$$(.80)(.40)(.40)(.20) = .026$$
$$.026 \times 2000 \qquad = 52$$
$$52 \times 1 \qquad = 52 .$$

This procedure is carried out for each nonscale type, and the sum of the errors of placement expected for nonscale types is used as the maximum number of errors in computing the error ratio,

$$\frac{\text{number of errors}}{\text{maximum number of errors}},$$

where the number of errors is the sum of observed placement errors. Thus the error ratio will be 1.00 when the number of errors of placement is equal to the maximum number of errors and 0.00 when there are no placement errors. Therefore, the lower the ratio the greater the internal consistency.

The error ratio appears to be a definite improvement over the coefficient of reproducibility and the coefficient of scalability. However, the error ratio should be used perhaps with the Guttman measure for the benefit of those unfamiliar with Borgatta's index.

SIGNIFICANCE TESTS

None of the above estimates of internal consistency—the coefficient of scalability, the coefficient of reproducibility, and the error ratio —is a test of statistical significance. The problem of data stability or the question of whether or not the observed patterns are the result of chance has not been met satisfactorily, even though a number of behavioral scientists have devoted their energies to finding a solution. Notable among those seeking satisfactory solutions are Sagi (1959), Goodman (1959), Schuessler (1961), and Chilton (1966). The problem has been approached in a variety of ways—from the standpoint of a chi-square test of significance (Schuessler) to the demonstration through computer-generated data that coefficients of reproducibility are normally distributed (Chilton). As indicated by Sagi and by Chilton, these tests must be made prior to the purification of a scale. Primarily they serve as devices for determining the feasibility of further efforts to develop a scale from a set of items. Sampling distributions for these indexes is one of the aspects of Guttman scaling which has not yet been developed. The clarification of such sampling distributions is needed and will be an important contribution to our knowledge of attitude measurement when these distributions are established.

THE INTENSITY FUNCTION

Guttman (1954) conceived of two methods for ordering individuals along a content continuum. One method, which is conventionally utilized and is implicit above, makes use of the observed response marginals of selected items from an attitude universe to obtain cutting points or to establish content ranks. The second method utilizes bending points of the regressions of higher principal components of scalable attitudes to obtain the various cutting points.

Working primarily from a mathematical model, four psychological variables—content, intensity, closure, and involution—have been posited as principal components of scalable attitudes. Intensity, the second component, is thought to function as a means of obtaining a dichotomy of respondents along a content continuum into positive and negative attitudes. The third component, tentatively identified as closure, is thought to discriminate further among respondents within the positive-negative dichotomy. Thus it is thought that the function of the third component serves to place respondents into positions of extreme positive, mild positive, mild negative, and extreme negative. Each higher principal component presumably provides further objective and theoretically meaningful cutting points.

Guttman's mathematical analysis posits an infinite number of principal components for perfect scales. The same mathematical analysis, using the criterion of maximizing internal consistency, in the least-squares sense, also predicts the type of curve obtained when the regression of one component is plotted upon the original rank order of perfect scales. For perfect scales, the first best solution yields a linear relationship. The second best solution establishes the second component, which yields a U-shaped curve and a single point of inflection. An additional bending point is obtained for each successive solution or higher component.

Although Guttman reports a degree of success in testing closure and involution as empirical referents of the third and fourth mathematical components, subsequent research suggests that these and other posited component variables fail to meet the criteria set forth by the mathematical model (Henry, 1957; Riland, 1959; Dotson, 1962). However, content and intensity are generally established. The first component is that of content for a specific attitude universe. For example, the attitude among southern whites toward the segregation of Negroes might be such a scalable universe of content. The second component is generally thought to be the intensity with which the attitude is held. When attitude intensity is plotted against its content rank, a U-shaped curve should be obtained, with the most negative and the most positive respondents evidencing high intensity. Empirical research suggests that the bending point of the intensity curve indicates a "point of indifference," or a zero point, on the underlying rank order. Further, Guttman (1954) holds that the point of inflection separates respondents into positive or negative scale types, depending upon which side of the zero point they are located.

Brim takes a different position, suggesting that "content responses to attitude questions are based on a class of P1 expectations which refer to probabilities about satisfaction to be gained from various states of affairs" (1955, p. 74). He feels that intensity or "strength of feeling is the equivalent of a P2 estimate that the first expectation is correct" (p. 74). Brim suggests that the bending point of the intensity curve indicates those respondents who do not know whether they would be satisfied or dissatisfied by the state of affairs with which the items deal. Thus, respondents falling in scale types on one side of the zero point are defined as those who estimate the probability of satisfaction as greater than 50 per cent. Those falling on the other (negative) side are defined as those who estimate the probability of satisfaction as less than 50 per cent. We do not attempt to resolve the issue between Brim and Guttman. Rather, we take the position of Henry:

Whether one maintains that the zero point defines those who don't know what their probable satisfaction would be—hence estimate it 50–50 according to some "equiprobable through ignorance" principle—or that it defines those who don't care or are indifferent, it still seems a useful objective technique for separating the favorables from the unfavorables (1957, p. 26).

Measures of intensity may be obtained by either the foldover technique or the two-part technique, neither of which forms scales in the Guttman sense (Suchman, 1950b). The foldover technique involves the use of items that measure both the content and intensity dimensions simultaneously. To obtain intensity scores by this technique, using items consisting of six response categories, the extreme positive and the extreme negative response categories are combined or "folded over" to form highest intensity values, the middle positive and middle negative categories are combined to form a lower intensity score, and the least positive and least negative responses are folded over to form the lowest intensity value. Arbitrary weights, e.g., 2, 1, and 0, are then assigned to the three intensity categories respectively. In this manner each respondent is given an intensity score for each item. The separate intensity scores are then summed for each individual.

The two-part technique employs a separate intensity question for each content question. For example, following a content item an intensity question such as, "How strongly do you feel about X?" is asked. Response alter-

natives of the nature (1) "very strongly," (2) "fairly strongly" and (3) "not so strongly" are utilized, and arbitrary weights are assigned and summed for each respondent as in the foldover technique. Of the two methods, the foldover technique has the quality of saving space on a questionnaire; however, the two-part technique provides greater rigor of measurement because of the independence of the content and intensity measure.

The cross-tabulation of intensity and content scores for all respondents functions to locate the point of indifference or zero point on the content continuum. With the respondents placed into scale types defined by cutting points obtained through observation of response marginal to content items, the median intensity rank is computed for each content rank. The curve of these medians is used as an approximation of the intrinsic second component regression curve. "Medians are used, rather than arithmetic means or similar averages, because medians are independent of any metric apart from rank order" (Suchman, 1950b, p. 220).

The values for the plotted points are determined in the following manner:

The cumulative percentages are computed for the total frequencies of both content and intensity, cumulating from negative to positive on content and from low to high on intensity. To determine the content value to be plotted we compute the mid-point of the interval of percentiles for each content rank. The intensity value to be plotted is the median intensity percentile for the content rank . . . (Suchman, 1950b, p. 221).

The general formula used for determining the median of grouped data is applicable:

$$\text{Median} = l_{\widetilde{x}} + \left(\frac{N/2 - \text{cum } f_{\widetilde{x}}}{f_{\widetilde{x}}} \right)(i),$$

where $l_{\widetilde{x}}$ is the lower limit of the interval containing the median, N is the number of cases included in the analysis, cum $f_{\widetilde{x}}$ is the cumulative sum of the absolute frequencies up to but not including the interval containing the median, $f_{\widetilde{x}}$ is the absolute frequency in the interval containing the median, and i is the size of the interval.

Table 1 and Figure 2 are presented for clarification. To compute the median intensity score for scale type 0 in Table 1, the values to be substituted in the formula are:

$$\text{Median} = 49 + \left(\frac{209/2 - 68}{51}\right)(69 - 49)$$
$$= 49 + (.71)(20)$$
$$= 63.$$

This median intensity value then is plotted for the midpoint of content rank 0 in Figure 2. When the median intensity value is plotted for each of the content ranks, a U- or J-shaped regression curve is obtained (Figure 2). The zero point or zone of indifference in Figure 2 is located in scale type 2. Thus scale types 0 and 1 are defined as negative and scale types 3 and 4 are defined as positive.

The procedure above makes use of the regression of intensity on content to identify the zone of indifference. A more precise lo-

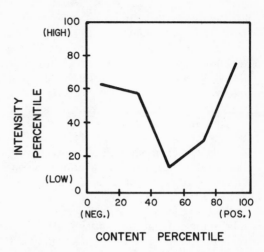

Figure 2. The regression of intensity on content for the data in Table 1.

cation of the zero point may be obtained by what Guttman calls the arrowhead technique, which is determined by the regression

TABLE 1

DISTRIBUTION OF INTENSITY BY CONTENT RANK

Intensity	Content					Total Frequency	Cumulative Percentage
	0	1	2	3	4		
8	48	74	2	12	115	251	100
7	42	63	2	17	38	162	81
6	51	123	5	40	44	263	69
5	16	85	6	39	32	178	49
4	21	48	36	58	13	176	35
3	11	16	42	59	16	144	22
2	7	2	41	42	5	97	11
1	4	1	14	6	2	27	4
0	9	0	4	6	3	22	2
Total frequency	209	412	152	279	268	1320	
Cumulative percentage	16	47	59	80	100		
Midpoint of content percentiles	8	32	53	70	90		
Median of intensity percentiles	63	58	15	28	75		

of content on intensity. "The estimate used is the median content percentile of the subgroup with the lowest intensity rank (choosing, say not less than 100 people for this lowest intensity group, to maintain sampling reliability)" (Guttman, 1954, p. 232).

Using the same general formula above for determining the median of grouped data, the zero point for the data in Table 1 is determined by first combining the lowest intensity ranks to provide a sufficient number of observations. By combining the original intensity ranks 0, 1, and 2, 146 subjects are placed in the lowest intensity category. The median falls in the content rank containing the 73rd case. By summing across content ranks, the median is found to fall in content rank 2. The median content percentile for the lowest intensity rank, in this case, is then arrived at as follows:

Cumulative % of Content Rank 1 +

$$\cfrac{\left[\left(\cfrac{\begin{array}{c}\text{Total freq. of}\\ \text{lowest intensity}\\ \text{rank}\end{array}}{2}\right) - \left(\begin{array}{c}\text{Cum. Freq. of}\\ \text{Content Ranks}\\ \text{0 and 1 for the}\\ \text{lowest intensity}\\ \text{rank}\end{array}\right)\right]}{\begin{array}{c}\text{Frequency of content rank 2}\\ \text{for the lowest intensity rank}\end{array}}$$

$$\left[\left(\begin{array}{c}\text{Cum. % of}\\ \text{content}\\ \text{rank 2}\end{array}\right) - \left(\begin{array}{c}\text{Cum. % of}\\ \text{content}\\ \text{rank 1}\end{array}\right)\right]$$

or

$$47 + \left(\frac{146/2 - 23}{59}\right)(59 - 47)$$
$$= 47 + (.85)(12)$$
$$= 57.$$

Thus for these data the zero point is located at the 57th percentile, and it may be concluded that approximately 57 per cent of the respondents were negative and 43 per cent positive in their attitude.

The cutting point or zero point as defined by the intensity function has the quality of invariance, i.e., it is not dependent on the sample of items used. The invariance of the zero point has been empirically demonstrated by comparing the intensity analyses of two sets of items from the same universe of content. Although one set of items was negatively biased and the other set positively biased, the same intensity curve was obtained for both sets of data (Suchman, 1950b).

The bending point of the intensity curve has the quality of invariance in that either the content or intensity metric may be expanded or contracted "and the bending point will remain at the same percentile as ever" (Guttman, 1954, p. 233). A zero point, however, may be expected to vary from one study population to another and to vary for one population over time. Therefore, intensity analysis is useful in comparing two study populations and in measuring change within a single population over time.

Several years have elapsed since Guttman first developed the theory of principal components of scalable attitudes. During this time little has been accomplished with respect to the isolation and identification of empirical referents for the third and fourth components. The years ahead may prove that the Guttman model produces no further fit with the empirical world; however, the usefulness of intensity and its fit to the mathematical model show promise of the validity and value of the entire model. The bending points of each of the higher component's regression curves are thought to have the same quality of invariance as the bending point of the intensity curve. Further, the model is most precise with respect to relationship among the bending points of a set of components (Guttman, 1954). Thus the researcher is provided with criteria for accepting or rejecting variables as empirical third and fourth components of scalable attitudes. Future research in component theory may be very rewarding. Certainly, the potential benefits that identification of correlates of the components offers for refining qualitative measurement in attitude and nonattitude areas are great indeed.

REFERENCES

Borgatta, Edgar F.
1955 "An error ratio for scalogram analysis." Public Opinion Quarterly 19 (Spring):96–100.

Borgatta, Edgar F., and D. G. Hays.
1952 "Some limitations on the arbitrary classification of non-scale response patterns in a Guttman scale." Public Opinion Quarterly 16 (Spring):410–416.

Brim, Orville G., Jr.
1955 "Attitude content—intensity and probability expectations." American Sociological Review 20 (February):68–76.

Chilton, Roland J.
1966 "Computer generated data and the statistical significance of scalogram." Sociometry 29 (June):175–181.

Dotson, Louis.
1962 "An empirical study of attitude-component theory." Public Opinion Quarterly 26 (Spring):227–235.

Goodman, Leo A.
1959 "Simple statistical methods for scalogram analysis." Psychometrika 24 (March):29–43.

Guttman, Louis.
1941 "The quantification of a class of attributes: a theory and method of scale construction." Pp. 319–348 in P. Horst et al. The Prediction of Personal Adjustment. New York: Social Science Research Council.
1947 "The Cornell technique for scale and intensity analysis." Educational and Psychological Measurement 7 (Summer):247–280.
1950 "The basis for scalogram analysis." In Samuel A. Stouffer et al.,Measurement and Prediction. Princeton: Princeton University Press, 60–90.
1954 "The principal components of scalable attitudes." Pp. 216–257 in Paul F. Lazarsfeld (ed.), Mathematical Thinking in the Social Sciences. Glencoe, Illinois: The Free Press.

Henry, Andrew F.
1952 "A method of classifying non-scale response patterns in a Guttman scale." Public Opinion Quarterly 16 (Spring): 94–106.
1957 "An empirical study of attitude components." Social Forces 36 (October): 26–31.

Menzel, Herbert.
1953 "A new coefficient for scalogram analysis." Public Opinion Quarterly 17 (Summer):268–280.

Riland, Lane H.
1959 "Relationship of the Guttman components of attitude intensity and personal involvement." Journal of Applied Psychology 43 (August): 279–284.

Riley, Matilda White, John W. Riley, Jr., and Jackson Toby.
1954 Sociological Studies in Scale Analysis. New Brunswick, New Jersey: Rutgers University Press.

Sagi, Phillip C.
1959 "A statistical test for a coefficient of reproducibility." Psychometrika 24 (March):19–27.

Schuessler, Karl F.
1961 "A note on statistical significance of scalogram." Sociometry 24 (September):312–318.

Suchman, Edward A.
1950a "The scalogram board technique for scale analysis." Pp. 91–121 in S. A. Stouffer, et al., Studies in Social Psychology in World War II. Measurement and Prediction. Vol. 4. Princeton: Princeton University Press.
1950b "The intensity component in attitude and opinion research." Pp. 213–276 in S. A. Stouffer, et al., Studies in Social Psychology in World War II. Vol. 4 Measurement and Prediction. Princeton: Princeton University Press.

Toby, Jackson, and Marcia L. Toby.
1954 "A method of selecting dichotomous items by cross-tabulation." Pp. 339–355 in M. Riley, et al.,Sociological Studies in Scale Analysis. New Brunswick, New Jersey: Rutgers University Press.

CHAPTER 12

A Technique for the Construction of Attitude Scales

ALLEN L. EDWARDS AND FRANKLIN P. KILPATRICK

Earlier articles (3, 6) have reviewed the various methods which have been used in the construction of attitude scales: the method of equal appearing intervals developed by Thurstone (16), the method of summated ratings developed by Likert (14), and the method of scale analysis developed by Guttman (9). The method of equal appearing intervals and the method of summated ratings are similar in that both provide techniques for selecting from an initial large number of items, a set of items which constitutes the measuring instrument. Scale analysis differs from these two methods in that it is concerned with the evaluation of a set of items, *after* the items have been selected in some fashion or another.

In the method of equal appearing intervals, items of opinion are sorted by a judging group into 9 or 11 categories constituting a continuum ranging from unfavorable to favorable. The scale value of each item is found by locating the point on the continuum

From Allen L. Edwards and Franklin P. Kilpatrick, "A technique for the construction of attitude scales," Journal of Applied Psychology, 1948, *32*, 374–384. Copyright 1948 by the American Psychological Association, and reproduced by permission of the authors and publisher.

above which and below which 50 per cent of the judges place the item. The spread of the judges' rating is measured by Q, the interquartile range. A high Q value for an item indicates that the judges are in disagreement as to the location of the item on the continuum and this, in turn, is taken to mean that the item is ambiguous. Both Q and scale values are used in selecting items for the attitude test. Approximately 20 items with scale values equally spaced along the continuum and with low Q values are selected for the test. Scores on the test are determined by finding the median of the scale values of the items with which a subject agrees.

In the method of summated ratings, items are selected by a criterion of internal consistency. Subjects check whether they strongly agree, agree, are undecided, disagree, or strongly disagree with each item. Numerical weights are assigned to these categories of response using the successive integers from 0 to 4, the highest weight being consistently assigned to the category which would indicate the most favorable attitude. A high and low group are selected in terms of total scores based upon the sum of the item weights. The responses of these two groups are then compared on the individual items and the 20 or so most discriminating items are selected for the attitude test. A subject's score on this test is determined by summing the weights assigned to his responses to the 20 items.

In scale analysis, a complete set of items is tested to determine whether they, as a group, constitute a scale in the sense that from the rank order score it is possible to reproduce a subject's response to the individual items. The degree to which this is possible is expressed by a coefficient of reproducibility.[1] Although ordinarily Guttman uses 10 to 12 items, to give a simple explanation of this coefficient let us suppose that we have but 3 items, each with but 2 categories of response, agree and disagree. We shall assume that the agree response, in each instance, represents a favorable attitude and the disagree response an unfavorable attitude. A weight of 0 is assigned to the disagree response and a weight of 1 is assigned to the agree response. Let us also suppose that for the first item we have in our sample 10 subjects with weights of 1 and 90 with weights of 0; for the second item we have 20 subjects with weights of 1 and 80 with weights of 0; and for the third item we have 40 with weights of 1 and 60 with weights of 0.

In the case of perfect reproducibility, the 10 subjects with weights of 1 on the first item will be the 10 subjects with the highest rank order scores. These 10 subjects will also be included in the 20 who have weights of 1 on the second item and these 20, in turn, will be included in the 40 who have weights of 1 on the third item. It would also be true that only 4 patterns of item response would occur, if the set of items were perfectly reproducible. For the sample at hand, these patterns and the scores associated with them would be: AAA-3; DAA-2; DDA-1; DDD-0. Since all responses could be perfectly predicted from the scores, the coefficient of reproducibility, in this instance, would be 100 per cent. Perfect reproducibility is seldom found, how-

ever, and in practice a coefficient of 85 per cent or higher is believed satisfactory for judging a set of items to be a scale.[2] Various techniques for computing the coefficient of reproducibility have been developed and are described in the articles by Festinger (7), Clark and Kreidt (2), and Guttman (11, 12).

Scale analysis, in the sense mentioned above, thus becomes a technique *secondary* to the problem of item selection.[3] The important problem is to obtain a set of items which the investigator may have some assurance will scale when a particular technique of testing for scalability is applied. Up to the present time, the problem of item selection in scale analysis seems to have been left largely to the intuition and experience of the investigator. The only practical rules suggested are that one should simply rephrase the same question in slightly different ways (7, p. 159) or that one should look for items with as homogeneous content as possible (12, p. 461). This latter suggestion indicates that if we are interested in the problem of attitude toward the Negro, we should break this universe of content down into sub-universes constituting perhaps such areas as attitude toward the Negro in public eating places, attitude toward the Negro as a resident in the community, attitude toward the Negro as a voter, attitude toward the Negro as an employer, attitude toward the Negro in public conveyances, and so on. But even here, we find that attitude toward the Negro, let us say, in public conveyances can be broken down into areas of content even more homogeneous by enumerating the specific conveyances: streetcars, busses, trains, planes, and so on. Each of

---

[1] This statistic is explained in the articles by Clark and Kreidt (2), Edwards and Kilpatrick (6), Festinger (7), and Guttman (9, 11, 12).

[2] There are other criteria to be applied in determining whether a set of items constitutes a scale in addition to the coefficient of reproducibility (10, 12). Little has been published, however, in which these criteria have been applied empirically to a concrete set of data. . . . The coefficient of reproducibility has been stressed in all of Guttman's publications, perhaps for the reason that it is considered a primary and necessary condition but an insufficient condition for a scale.

[3] This is not to deny the importance of the theory underlying scale analysis.

these areas of content might possibly be broken down into still more homogeneous areas. Eventually, we may end up, as Festinger suggests, with multiple rephrasings of the same question, and our two rules are thus but one (7, p. 159).

Obviously, any technique which enables us to select a set of items from the large number of possible items, with some assurance that the set of items selected will, in turn, meet the requirements of scale analysis would be of great value. In this paper, a technique which has proved successful in doing this is described. For reasons which will become clear as we proceed, we have called this technique the scale-discrimination method of attitude scale construction (5).

THE SCALE-DISCRIMINATION TECHNIQUE

The scale-discrimination method is based upon preliminary investigations which showed that the cutting point[4] of an item is related to the Thurstone scale value of the item and that the reproducibility[5] of an item is related to the discriminatory power of the item (6). The discriminatory power of an item, it has also been shown, is not, as might seem at first glance, merely a function of the item's scale value. It can easily be demonstrated that items with comparable Thurstone scale and Q values may differ tremendously in their power to differentiate between those with favorable and those with unfavorable attitudes.[6]

---

[4] The cutting point of an item marks the place in the rank order scores of the subjects where the most common response shifts from one category (agree) to the next (disagree). Between cutting points, in a *perfect* scale, all responses would fall in the same category.

[5] The reproducibility of an item is measured by degree to which responses to the item can be reproduced from the rank order scores of the subjects.

[6] For example, the extreme item: "All Republicans should be executed" would undoubtedly show a scale value at one extreme of the continuum and a definitely low Q value. But this item will not differentiate between those with favorable and unfavorable attitudes toward Republicans for the obvious reason that both groups would probably react in the same fashion to the item.

Statements of opinion concerning science were collected from a variety of sources. Books and essays were consulted. Individuals were asked to express their opinions in brief written statements. We eventually collected 266 statements of opinion about science. In editing these items, particular attention was paid to eliminating those items which: (1) were liable to be endorsed by individuals with opposed attitudes; (2) were factual or could be interpreted as such; (3) were obviously irrelevant to the issue under consideration; (4) appeared likely to be endorsed by everyone or by no one; (5) seemed to be subject to varying interpretations for any reason; (6) contained a word or words not common to the vocabularies of college students. Also, due to emphasis upon the matter during both the collecting and editing of the statements, most of the 155 statements finally selected expressed a clear-cut favorable or unfavorable opinion about science.

Thirteen other items, which might be called "control" items, were added to the original 155. These 13 items were added to determine how they would fare at various stages of the scale-discrimination method. Of the 13 items, we judged that 7 were "neutral" items in the Thurstone sense; 2 were items which could possibly be interpreted as factual; 1 was believed to be too extreme for many endorsements; 1 was judged ambiguous because the words "scientific holiday" could be interpreted as meaning a moratorium or as meaning a celebration; 1 was judged ambiguous because more than one dimension was involved; and 1 was judged irrelevant. Thus there were 168 items in all which were used in testing the scale-discrimination method of scale construction.[7]

Determining Scale and Q Values of the Items

Envelopes numbered 1 through 110 were prepared. In each envelope we placed a set of

---

[7] It should be emphasized that the inclusion of the "control" items mentioned is not to be considered part of the scale-discrimination procedure.

3×5 cards lettered A, B, C, D, E, F, G, H, I, and a pack of slips of paper approximately 2×4 inches in size. On each slip of paper one of the 168 items was printed along with the number of the item. In each case the pack of slips was shuffled so that the items would be arranged in no set order. The envelopes were given to an elementary psychology class along with a set of instructions describing the Thurstone sorting procedure and the members of the class were asked to sort the items in accordance with the instructions.

The item sortings of each subject were examined and we discarded those subjects whose sortings showed obvious reversals of the continuum or failure to carry out instructions. On this basis we were left with 82 completed sets of judgments.

Frequencies of judgments in each of the 9 categories for each item were tabulated, translated into cumulative frequencies, and then into cumulative proportions.[8] An ogive was plotted for each item with cumulative proportions on the axis of ordinates and scale values on the axis of abscissas. Scale values were read to two decimal places (the second decimal place being merely an approximation) by dropping a perpendicular to the baseline of scale values at the point where the cumulative proportion curve crossed the 50 per cent mark. In a similar fashion Q values were determined by dropping perpendiculars at the 25th and 75th per cent levels, Q being the scale distance between these two points or the interquartile range.[9]

The 168 items were then plotted in a bi-variate distribution according to scale and Q values, the scale values being plotted on the baseline. The distribution of scale values was bimodal in shape. There were very few items in the "neutral" section (none at all in between 5.0 and 5.9), the modal categories being 1.0 to 1.9 and 7.0 to 7.9. The Q values of the 7 items which did fall in the "neutral" scale interval (4.0 to 4.9) were quite low, 6 of the 7 falling well below the median Q value for all 168 items. All 7 of these items were "control" items, described previously.

A line was drawn through the distribution at approximately the median Q value of all the items, 1.29. All items with Q values above this point were rejected. We worked from here on with the remaining 83 items or with approximately the 50 per cent of the initial set of items with the least degree of ambiguity as measured by Q. One of the "neutral" control items was eliminated by this standard and 6 were acceptable. These 6 items all had scale values between 4.0 and 4.9. No items at all had been found in the scale interval 5.0 to 5.9 and the Q criterion eliminated all items in the interval 3.0 to 3.9. One of the 2 factual items was rejected by the Q criterion and the ambiguous item with the words "scientific holiday" was also eliminated. The remaining 10 "control" items would have to be judged acceptable by the Q criterion.

Item Analysis

The 83 items were prepared in a form suitable for Likert type reactions. Each item was followed by a 6 point forcing scale (strongly agree, agree, mildly agree, mildly disagree, disagree, strongly disagree). Subjects were instructed to check for each item the one expression which most nearly described their own attitude with respect to the item. In all, 355 subjects filled out the questionnaire: 245 from sociology, psychology, and speech classes at the University of Washington; 60 from a local junior college; and 50 from a police school. Of these 355 papers, 346 were usable, 9 of them being incomplete or having more than one answer for a single item.

---

[8] This task was most laborious. Almost 14,000 slips of paper had to be sorted and then tabulated. Some judging technique similar to that used by Ballin and Farnsworth (1) or Seashore and Hevner (15) would reduce much of this labor, but even here the task is not simple. Various methods which simplify the judging process are now being tried and will be reported upon in another paper.

[9] This operation was simplified by setting up a master chart with the cumulative proportions on the Y axis and the scale values on the X axis. This chart was then taped to a ground-glass plate which fitted over an enclosed wooden box containing a 100 watt bulb. Tracing paper could then be placed over this chart and the ogives for the individual items quickly drawn.

Scoring was done in the usual Likert fashion, weights of 0 through 5 being assigned to the 6 response categories, the weight of 5 being given to the strongly agree response in the case of items expressing a favorable opinion about science, and to the strongly disagree response in the case of items expressing an unfavorable opinion about science. For the 6 items in the scale interval, 4.0 to 4.9, the direction of the weights was assigned on the basis of whether the scale value of the item was larger or smaller than 4.5. Response weights on the 83 individual items were summated for each subject and a frequency distribution plotted for the resulting scores. The obtained range of scores was only 64 per cent of the possible range (140–405 obtained, 0–415 possible) with considerable bunching at the upper (favorable) end of the distribution.

Two criterion groups were chosen, approximately the upper and lower 27 per cent, in terms of total scores. The range of scores for the lower 94 papers was from 140 to 300 and the upper 94 papers had scores ranging from 343 to 405. The 83 items were then subjected to item analysis. For each item, frequencies in each of the response categories for the high and for the low group were tabulated. The 6 categories were then reduced to 2 by combining categories 0, 1, 2, 3, and 4.[10] From the resulting 2 × 2 tables, *phi* coefficients were calculated.[11] The *phi* coefficients ranged in size from .16 to .78.

Next the 83 items were plotted in a bivariate distribution with *phi* values on the Y axis and scale values on the X axis.[12] The 4 items

---

[10] This grouping was necessary because our subjects gave predominantly favorable responses to the items. If our universe of content had been attitude toward labor unions, we would expect a more symmetrical distribution of responses and consequently a different grouping of categories.

[11] The nomographs by Guilford (8) or the tables prepared by Jurgensen (13) make these calculations quite simple.

[12] A plot of *phi* values against Q values indicated no discernible relationship, the variability within columns being approximately the same as the total variability. This would indicate that in the procedure followed here, the scale-discrimination procedure, the *phi* analysis adds to the process of item selection when items with com-

with the highest *phi* coefficients were selected from each half-scale interval; due to the previously mentioned gaps in the scale continuum, this involved only the intervals from .5 to 2.5 and from 6.5 to 8.0. No items were selected from the "neutral" control items in the scale interval 4.0 to 4.9. The 28 items thus selected were assigned to Forms A and B of the questionnaires by alternating scale values between the two forms.

The final scales then consisted of 14 items each, with the items very closely equated as to Thurstone scale values, Q values, and *phi* values. For Forms A and B, respectively, the mean scale values of the 14 items were 3.85 and 3.91; the mean Q values were .90 and .92. *Phi* coefficients of the items in Form A ranged from .58 to .78 with a median value of .65; for Form B they ranged from .58 to .76 with a median value of .66. Only 1 of the remaining 10 "control" items had a *phi* value above .58. This was one of the 6 "neutral" items and it had a *phi* value of .61. The other "control" items would be rejected by the *phi* criterion.

RELIABILITY AND REPRODUCIBILITY OF THE SCALE

The reliability coefficient of the two forms of the scale, 14 items versus 14 items, based upon the responses of 248 new subjects was .81, uncorrected. For both forms of the test the range of scores was quite restricted, 30 to 70 in each case with possible ranges from 0 to 70. Within this restricted range, bunching at the upper, or favorable, end was present. The mean score for Form A was 58.22 and the standard deviation was 7.33. For Form B the mean was 57.20 and the standard deviation was 7.79.

Scale analysis based upon the performance of a sample of 87 subjects drawn from the larger group of 248 subjects was carried out with both forms of the test by the Cornell

---

parable Q values are used. We have, it may be recalled, already eliminated the 50 per cent of the items with the highest Q values. The relationship between the discriminatory power of an item and Q value when this is not the case is described in another paper (4).

technique (11). A coefficient of reproducibility of 87.5 per cent was obtained for Form A and a coefficient of reproducibility of 87.2 per cent was obtained for Form B. Response categories in each instance were dichotomized. Cutting points were established and we observed Guttman's rule that "no category should have more error than non-error" (11, p. 17). The range of modal response categories was from .51 to .82 for Form A. The mean value of the modal categories, .57, which is the minimum value[13] of the coefficient of reproducibility for this set of items with the sample at hand, may be compared with the observed coefficient of reproducibility of 87.5 per cent. For Form B the range of the modal categories was from .52 to .67. The mean value, which again is the lower limit of the coefficient of reproducibility, was .57, whereas the observed value of the coefficient of reproducibility was 87.2 per cent.

The two observed values of the coefficient of reproducibility are sufficiently high to constitute evidence that but a single dominant variable is involved in the sets of items or that, in other words, unidimensionality is present. Such sets of items are said to be scalable or to constitute a scale. The coefficients of reproducibility also mean that it is possible to reproduce item responses from rank order scores with the accuracy indicated by the value of the coefficients.

The error of reproducibility which is present is simply 1.00 minus the observed coefficient of reproducibility. If the error of reproducibility can be assumed to be random, then these sets of items possess an important property: the simple correlation between rank order scores and an external criterion will be equal to the multiple correlation between the items and the external criterion (10). This, in turn, means that efficiency of prediction is maximized by the simple correlation.

It would also be true in the case of sets of items which meet the criteria demanded of scales[14] that the interpretation of the rank order scores is unambiguous and that it is possible to make meaningful statements about one subject being higher (more favorable) than another on the variable in question.[15] This would not be true of a test involving more than one variable. Suppose, for example, a test involves two variables. Then a subject might obtain a given score by being high on one variable and low on the other. Another subject might obtain the same score by being high on the second variable and low on the first. From the rank order scores alone it would be impossible to tell the relative positions of the subjects on the two variables, and the interpretation of the composite score is ambiguous. Statements of "higher and lower than" might be made, but we would not know what the "higher and lower than" referred to, for by increasing or decreasing the number of items related to either variable, the rank order scores of the subjects could be altered.[16] This would not be true of a test in which the items all belong on a single continuum, that is, a test which is unidimensional. In such a test, increasing the number of items would not shift the rank order scores of the subjects.

SUMMARY

The method of scale construction described in this paper has been called the scale-discrimination method because it makes use of Thurstone's scaling procedure and retains Likert's procedure for evaluating the discriminatory power of the individual items. Furthermore, the items selected by the scale-discrimination method have been shown, in the case described, to yield satisfactory coeffi-

---

[13] This is the lower limit because the reproducibility of any single item cannot be less than the frequency in the modal category. The method of computing the minimum value of the coefficient assumes independence of the items. See Guttman (12).

[14] See footnote 2.

[15] In the case of perfect scales, where the coefficient of reproducibility is unity, it also follows that an individual with a low rank order score will not have given a more favorable response to any item than any person with a higher rank order score.

[16] We do not mean to imply by this discussion that multidimensional scales are without value.

cients of reproducibility and to meet the requirements of Guttman's scale analysis. The scale-discrimination method is essentially a synthesis of the methods of item evaluation of Thurstone, Likert, and Guttman. It also possesses certain advantages which are not present in any of these methods considered separately.

The scale-discrimination method, for example, eliminates the least discriminating items in a large sample, which Thurstone's method alone fails to do. The unsolved problem in the Thurstone procedure is to select from within each scale interval the most discriminating items. Items within any one scale interval may show a high degree of variability with respect to a measure of discrimination. For example, we found within a single interval items with *phi* values ranging from .24 to .78. That Thurstone's criterion of Q does not aid materially in the matter of selecting discriminating items is indicated by the plot of *phi* values against Q values, *after* the 50 per cent of the items with the highest Q values had already been rejected. Under this condition, items with Q values from 1.00 to 1.09 had *phi* coefficients ranging from .32 to .76. Thurstone's method also, by the inclusion of "neutral" items, tends to lower reliability and to decrease reproducibility of the set of items finally selected (6).

Thus when selecting items by Thurstone's technique alone, we have no basis for making a choice between items with comparable scale and Q values, and yet these items are not equally valuable in the measurement of attitude. By having available some measure of the discriminatory power of the items, the choice becomes objective as well as advantageous as far as the scale itself is concerned.[17]

The advantage of the scale-discrimination method over the Guttman procedure lies essentially in the fact that we have provided an objective basis for the selection of a set of items which are then tested for scalability. It

---

[17] Additional research may indicate that the Thurstone scaling procedure is not necessary. See, however, the articles by Edwards and Kilpatrick (6) and Clark and Kreidt (2).

may happen that not always will the scale-discrimination method yield a set of items with a satisfactory coefficient of reproducibility. But this is not an objection to the technique any more than the fact that not always will a set of intuitively selected items scale. Rather, it seems that the scale-discrimination method offers greater assurance of scalability than any intuitive technique such as applied by Guttman. Furthermore, the set of items selected by the scale-discrimination technique provides a wider range of content than do the intuitive Guttman items. In the scale-discrimination method, we obtain items which are not essentially multiple phrasings of the same question as is often true when the selection of a set of items to be tested for scalability is left to the experience of the investigator (7, p. 159).

Several different areas of content are now being studied by variations of the scale-discrimination method and the results of these researches should provide additional evidence concerning the relationship between the scale-discrimination method and scale analysis.

REFERENCES

1. Ballin, M., and P. R. Farnsworth.
   1941 "A graphic rating method for determining the scale values of statements in measuring social attitudes." Journal of Social Psychology 13:323–327.
2. Clark, K. E., and P. H. Kreidt.
   1947 "An application of Guttman's new scaling techniques to an attitude questionnaire." Educational and Psychological Measurement, 1948 8, Summer, No. 2.
3. Edwards, A. L., and K. C. Kenney.
   1946 "A comparison of the Thurstone and Likert techniques of attitude scale construction." Journal of Applied Psychology 30:72–83.
4. Edwards, A. L.
   1946 "A critique of 'neutral' items in attitude scales constructed by the method of equal appearing intervals." Psychological Review 53: 159–169.

5. Edwards, A. L., and F. P. Kilpatrick.
   1947 "The scale-discrimination method for measuring social attitudes." American Psychologist 2:332.
6. Edwards, A. L., and F. P. Kilpatrick.
   1948 "Scale analysis and the measurement of social attitudes." Psychometrika 13, June.
7. Festinger, L.
   1947 "The treatment of qualitative data by 'scale analysis.'" Psychological Bulletin 44:149–161.
8. Guilford, J. P.
   1941 "The phi coefficient and chi-square as indices of item validity." Psychometrika 6:11–19.
9. Guttman, L.
   1944 "A basis for scaling qualitative data." American Sociological Review 9:139–150.
10. Guttman, L.
   1945 Questions and Answers About Scale Analysis. Research Branch, Information and Education Division, Army Service Forces, Report D-2.
11. Guttman, L.
   1946 "The Cornell technique for scale and intensity analysis." Mimeographed.
12. Guttman, L.
   1947 "On Festinger's evaluation of scale analysis." Psychological Bulletin 44:451–465.
13. Jurgensen, C. E.
   1947 "Table for determining phi coefficients." Psychometrika 12:17–29.
14. Likert, R.
   1932 "A technique for the measurement of attitudes." Archives of Psychology. New York. No. 140.
15. Seashore, R. H., and K. Hevner.
   1933 "A time-saving device for the construction of attitude scales." Journal of Social Psychology 4:366–372.
16. Thurstone, L. L., and E. J. Chave.
   1929 The Measurement of Attitude. Chicago: University of Chicago Press.

SECTION **III**   **Recent Developments
in Self-Report Techniques**

Overview

The Semantic Differential was not developed for the purpose of measuring attitudes. Rather the initial intent of Osgood and associates was to explore the dimensions of meaning. This effort was encouraged by the development of computers to aid in the tedious calculations of factor analysis. "One of the significant by-products of our work in experimental semantics, we believe, has been a new approach and rationale for attitude measurement." (p. 227).

The Semantic Differential measures individuals' reactions to semantic objects. This is done by obtaining ratings of the object on a number of simple rating scales defined by bipolar adjectives; e.g., GOOD-BAD, PRETTY-UGLY, HOT-COLD. Ratings of each object are correlated and factor analyzed to determine the dimensions of meaning attributed to the object. Many replications of this procedure established the stability to three dimensions: 1) Evaluative, 2) Potency, and 3) Activity. Since attitude clearly involves an evaluative response with respect to an attitude object, the application of the Semantic Differential to attitude measurement was initiated with enthusiasm.

Chapter 13 contains excerpts from *The Measurement of Meaning* by Osgood, Tannenbaum, and Suci which indicate their interpretation of the feasibility of the Semantic Differential for attitude measurement. Since its development the Semantic Differential has had phenomenal popularity among attitude researchers. Somewhat surprisingly no one has previously summarized and critically examined its use as an attitude measurement method. At the Editor's request David R. Heise prepared a critical review which appears as Chapter 14. This is the only comprehensive review available to date and will be especially helpful to persons interested in using the Semantic Differential.

How does one know whether the items selected for a self-report attitude instrument reflect the attitude they are supposed to tap? Or, more simply, how may one establish whether they all reflect the same attitude dimension, whatever it may be? The content or logical validity of items for a multi-item scale is generally done on an a priori basis, prima facie. Chapters 15 and 16 present two methods for establishing valid operational definitions of multi-item scales. Kerlinger and Kaya demonstrate the utility of factor analysis to test the unidimensionality of the items which are candidates for inclusion in a scale. Lingoes presents a computer procedure for selecting unidimensional items sets from a pool of dichotomous items which may then be treated as a Guttman scale.

Traditionally, attitude measurement has meant locating individuals along a single attitude continuum, usually an evaluative dimension. Great effort was expended in developing unidimensional scales. It was customary to think of people as more or less favorable, pro or con, positive or negative with respect to an attitude object. Recently, however, attention has been turned to studying how attitude objects are located in a multidimensional space. The development is rich in promise though its progress has been slow due, perhaps, to the technical skills required to enter the arena of multidimensional scaling. John Ross has prepared a very lucid as well as technically accurate introduction to multidimensional scaling of attitudes (Chapter 17). It is clear that multidimensional scaling need not be limited to self-report data. And as Ross points out, it potentially may clarify the theoretical aspects of attitude while improving the measurement of attitudes.

Another recent noteworthy development in attitude measurement is the Social Judgment-Involvement Approach (Chapter 18) of Sherif and Sherif which is based on findings from the experimental study of judgment—psychophysical and social— and on findings about self- or ego-involvement. It offers both a theoretical framework of attitudes grounded solidly on experimental research and an intriguing technique of measurement. As such it deserves serious consideration by attitude researchers.

The critical evaluation of the self-report approach to attitude measurement by Webb and Salancik in Chapter 19 calls attention to a number of its limitations. These range from pragmatic considerations of field work to ontological and epistemological matters. The criticisms are wholly consistent with the purpose of this volume as presented in the Introduction and prepare the reader for the remaining sections.

CHAPTER 13 Attitude Measurement

CHARLES E. OSGOOD, GEORGE J. SUCI
AND PERCY H. TANNENBAUM

One of the significant by-products of our work in experimental semantics, we believe, has been a new approach and rationale for attitude measurement. It has been feasible to identify "attitude" as one of the major dimensions of meaning-in-general and thus to extend the measurement procedures of the semantic differential to an important area of social psychology. In working in this area with the differential we have also found evidence for a general principle governing some aspects of cognitive processes—a *principle of congruity*. Although the operation of this principle is not necessarily limited to the attitudinal dimension of the meaning space, we first encountered it in connection with research on attitude measurement and will therefore introduce it in this context.

A Definition of Attitude

Despite a plethora of definitions of "attitude" in contemporary social science, some consensus and agreement is evident, particularly

From Charles E. Osgood, George J. Suci, and Percy H. Tannenbaum, *The Measurement of Meaning*, pages 189–199. Copyright 1957 by the University of Illinois Press, and reproduced by permission of the authors and publisher.

with respect to the major properties that attitudes are assumed to possess. Most authorities are agreed that attitudes are learned and implicit—they are inferred states of the organism that are presumably acquired in much the same manner that other such internal learned activity is acquired. Further, they are predispositions to respond, but are distinguished from other such states of readiness in that they predispose toward an *evaluative* response. Thus, attitudes are referred to as "tendencies of approach or avoidance," or as "favorable or unfavorable," and so on. This notion is related to another shared view —that attitudes can be ascribed to some basic bipolar continuum with a neutral or zero reference point, implying that they have both direction and intensity and providing a basis for the quantitative indexing of attitudes. Or, to use a somewhat different nomenclature, attitudes are implicit processes having reciprocally antagonistic properties and varying in intensity.

This characterization of attitude as a learned implicit process which is potentially bipolar, varies in its intensity, and mediates evaluative behavior, suggests that attitude is part—to some authorities, the paramount part—of the internal mediational activity that operates between most stimulus and response patterns. This identification of attitude with anticipatory mediating activity has been made most explicit by Doob (1947), who, casting attitude within the framework of Hullian behavior theory, identified it with the "pure stimulus act" as a mediating mechanism.

Still lacking, however, is an identification and localization of attitude per se within this general system of mediational activity. Our work in semantic measurement appears to suggest such an identification: If attitude is, indeed, some portion of the internal mediational activity, it is, by inference from our theoretical model, part of the semantic structure of an individual, and may be correspondingly indexed. The factor analyses of meaning may then provide a basis for extracting this attitudinal component of meaning.

In all of the factor analyses we have done to date . . . a factor readily identifiable as evaluative in nature has invariably appeared; usually it has been the dominant factor, that accounting for the largest proportion of the total variance. Despite different concepts and different criteria for selecting scales, high and restricted loadings on this factor were consistently obtained for scales like *good-bad*, *fair-unfair*, and *valuable-worthless*, while scales which were intuitively non-evaluative in nature, like *fast-slow*, *stable-changeable*, and *heavy-light*, usually had small or negligible loadings on this factor. It seems reasonable to identify attitude, as it is ordinarily conceived in both lay and scientific language, with the evaluative dimension of the total semantic space, as this is isolated in the factorization of meaningful judgments.

In terms of the operations of measurement with the semantic differential, we have defined the *meaning* of a concept as its allocation to a point in the multidimensional semantic space. We then define *attitude* toward a concept as the projection of this point onto the evaluative dimension of that space. Obviously every point in semantic space has an evaluative component (even though the component may be of zero magnitude, when the evaluative judgments are neutral), and, therefore, every concept must involve an attitudinal component as part of its total meaning. This does not imply that the evaluative or attitudinal dimension is necessarily stable in orientation with respect to other dimensions of the space; . . . depending upon the concept or set of concepts being judged, "purely" evaluative scales, like *good-bad*, may rotate so as to correspond in alignment with the potency factor, the sensory adiency factor, and so on. In other words, the kind of evaluation may shift with the frame of reference determined by the concepts (e.g., political, aesthetic, and so on).

Measurement Procedure with the Semantic Differential

Following the definition and rationale above, to index attitude we would use sets of scales which have high loadings on the evaluative factor across concepts generally and negligible loadings on other factors, as determined from our various factor analytic studies. Thus, scales like *good-bad*, *optimistic-pessimistic*, and *positive-negative* should be used rather than scales like *kind-cruel*, *strong-weak*, or *beautiful-ugly* because the latter would prove less generally evaluative as the concept being judged is varied. However, since the concept-by-concept factoring work on which the present rationale is based was not done at the time most of the attitude measurement reported here was undertaken, we have not always satisfied this ideal criterion. For purposes of scoring consistency, we have uniformly assigned the unfavorable poles of our evaluative scales (e.g., *bad, unfair, worthless*, etc.) the score "1" and the favorable poles (*good, fair, valuable*) the score "7"—this regardless of the presentation of the scales to subjects in the graphic differential, where they should be randomized in direction. We then merely sum over all evaluative ratings to obtain the attitude "score." A more refined method would be to weight each scale in terms of its evaluative factor loading for the concepts being judged, but this would be extremely laborious and, if the scales are "purely" evaluative as defined above, would probably add little to the precision of the instrument. It should also be noted that in practice we usually include a considerable number of scales representing other factors—this is done both to obscure somewhat the purpose of the measurement and to provide additional information on the meaning of the concept as a whole, aside from the attitude toward it.

The major properties of attitude that any measurement technique is expected to index are readily accommodated by this procedure. *Direction* of attitude, favorable or unfavorable, is simply indicated by the selection of polar terms by the subject; if the score falls more toward the favorable poles, then the attitude is taken to be favorable, and vice versa. A score that falls at the origin, defined by "4" on the scales, is taken as an index of neutrality of attitude. *Intensity* of attitude is indexed by how far out along the evaluative dimension from the origin the score lies, i.e., the polarization of the attitude score. Although on a single scale there are only three levels of intensity, "slightly," "quite," and "extremely" in either direction, summing over several evaluative scales yields finer degrees of intensity. If six scales are used, for example, we have a range of possible scores from six (most unfavorable), through 24 (exactly neutral), to 42 (most favorable), there being 18 degrees of intensity of attitude score in each direction. On the basis of earlier work (see Katz, 1944; Cantril, 1946) it is assumed that a neutral rating is one of least intensity in terms of attitude. *Unidimensionality* of the attitude scale is provided automatically in the factor analytic procedures from which the scales are selected. If the scales used are selected on the basis that they all have high and pure loadings on the same factor—ideally maintaining this consistency across various factor analyses—unidimensionality must obtain. In other words, factor analysis is itself a

method for testing the dimensionality of the items or scales entering into a test.

Evaluation of the Differential as a Measure of Attitude

Reliability—Test-retest reliability data have been obtained by Tannenbaum (1953). Each of six concepts (LABOR LEADERS, THE CHICAGO TRIBUNE, SENATOR ROBERT TAFT, LEGALIZED GAMBLING, ABSTRACT ART, and ACCELERATED COLLEGE PROGRAMS) was judged against six evaluative scales (*good-bad, fair-unfair, valuable-worthless, tasty-distasteful, clean-dirty,* and *pleasant-unpleasant*) by 135 subjects on two occasions separated by five weeks. Attitude scores were computed by summing over the six scales, after realignment according to a constant evaluative direction. The test-retest coefficients ranged from .87 to .93, with a mean r (computed by z-transformation) of .91. Additional reliability data, which confirm this, were obtained in another study and are given in Table 31.

Validity—The evaluative dimension of the semantic differential displays reasonable face-validity as a measure of attitude. For example, Suci (1952) was able to differentiate between high and low ethnocentrics, as determined independently from the E-scale of the Authoritarian Personality studies, on the basis of their ratings of various ethnic concepts on the evaluative scales of the differential. Similarly, evaluative scale ratings were found to discriminate in expected ways between shades of political preference, by Suci in his study of voting behavior and by Tannenbaum and Kerrick in their pictorial political symbolism study. However, unlike the measurement of meaning in general, in the case of attitude we have other, independently devised measuring instruments which have been used and against which the present technique can be evaluated. We report two such comparisons, the first with Thurstone scales and the second with a Guttman-type scale.

Comparison with Thurstone scales—Each of three concepts (THE NEGRO, THE CHURCH, and CAPITAL PUNISHMENT) was rated against a series of scales, including five purely evaluative ones (*fair-unfair, valuable-worthless, pleasant-unpleasant, clean-dirty,* and *good-bad*). In addition, subjects indicated their attitudes on Thurstone scales specifically designed to scale these attitude objects—the standard scale for the Church, Form B of the Negro scale, and Form A of the Capital Punishment scale (see Thurstone, 1931). Subjects were divided into two groups for testing purposes: one group (N = 23) was given the semantic differential form first, followed approximately one hour later by the Thurstone tests, and the other group (N = 27) had the reverse order. Two weeks after this initial session, the subjects again took both tests, except that this time their respective orders were reversed. The latter session was run to obtain reliability information on both types of attitude measuring instruments. Columns (1) and (2) of Table 31 present the product-moment correlations between the semantic differential (s) and Thurstone (t) scale scores for each of the three objects of judgment, on the initial test session ($r_{s_1 t_1}$) and on the second test session ($r_{s_2 t_2}$); columns (3) and (4) present the test-retest reliability coefficients for the Thurstone scales ($r_{t_1 t_2}$) and for the evaluative scores on the differential ($r_{s_1 s_2}$), again for each of the three concepts judged. It may be seen that the reliabilities of the two instruments are both high and equivalent. The correlation between the semantic differential scores and the corre-

sponding Thurstone scores is significantly greater than chance (p < .01) in each case, and in no case is the across-techniques correlation significantly lower than the reliability coefficient for the Thurstone test. The differences in the between-techniques correlations from first to second testing sessions are well within chance limits. It is apparent, that, that whatever the Thurstone scales measure, the evaluative factor of the semantic differential measures just about as well. Indeed, when the six validity coefficients are corrected for attenuation, each is raised to the order of .90 or better.

Comparison with a Guttman scale—Recently, an opportunity to test the validity of the evaluative factor of the differential as a measure of attitude against a scale of the Guttman type arose. A 14-item Guttman-type scale (reproducibility coefficient: .92) had been developed, at the expense of some time and labor, to assess the attitudes of farmers toward the agricultural practice of crop rotation. At approximately the same time, the semantic differential was being used in connection with a series of television programs dealing with agricultural practices, and one of the concepts included was CROP ROTATION. Although these studies were conducted independently, 28 subjects were found who had been exposed to both testing instruments. The Guttman scale had been administered first in all cases and the time between the two tests varied considerably, from only three days to almost four weeks. With attitude scores on the differential obtained by summing over the three evaluative scales used

TABLE 31

VALIDITY AND RELIABILITY COEFFICIENTS FOR SEMANTIC DIFFERENTIAL
ATTITUDE SCORES (S) AND THURSTONE SCALE SCORES (T)

	(1)	(2)	(3)	(4)
Attitude Object	$r_{s_1 t_1}$ *	$r_{s_2 t_2}$	$r_{t_1 t_2}$	$r_{s_1 s_2}$
The Church	.74	.76	.81	.83
Capital Punishment	.81	.77	.78	.91
The Negro	.82	.81	.87	.87

* The subscripts 1 and 2 refer to the first and second testing, respectively.

(*good-bad, fair-unfair,* and *valuable-worth-less*), the rank order correlation between the two instruments was highly significant (*rho* = .78; p < .01). Again we may say that the Guttman scale and the evaluative scales of the differential are measuring the same thing to a considerable degree.

The findings of both of these studies support the notion that the evaluative factor of the semantic differential is an index of attitude. It is, moreover, a method of attitude assessment that is relatively easy to administer and easy to score. Although it does not tap much of the *content* of an attitude in the denotative sense (e.g., the specific reactions which people having various attitudes might make, the specific statements that they might accept), it does seem to provide an index to the location of the attitude object along a general evaluative continuum. That the semantic differential *in toto* may provide a richer picture of the meaning of the attitude object than just the evaluative dimension is a point to which we return momentarily.

The Question of Generalized Attitude Scales

It is apparent that the semantic differential may be used as a generalized attitude scale. Using exactly the *same* set of evaluative scales, we have seen that correlation between our scores and those obtained with specific Thurstone scales are *equally* high for such diverse attitude objects as WAR, NEGRO, and CAPITAL PUNISHMENT. If we were careful to select as our evaluative scales those which maintain high and pure loading on the evaluative factor regardless of the concept class being judged, it is probable that such high correlations with standard attitude-measuring instruments would be obtained regularly. The question, however, is whether the use of generalized attitude scales is justified and valuable.

Attitude scales of the generalized type were introduced some two decades ago by Remmers and his associates (see Remmers, 1934; Remmers and Silance, 1934) in an attempt to overcome the laborious work involved in developing scales by the Thurstone equal-appearing-interval technique. The same basic procedure was followed, but instead of having statements referring to single attitude objects, they were couched in terminology designed to be applicable to a variety of objects. A number of such "master" scales were developed, each applicable to a particular class of objects—e.g., a scale for attitude toward any social institution, toward any proposed social action, and so forth. Most of these master scales were fairly reliable (median coefficient, .70) and, on the whole they compared favorably with specific Thurstone scales.

These Remmers scales were criticized on many grounds and from many quarters, however: that generalized statements cannot apply with equivalent meaning to different attitude objects (see Krech and Crutchfield, 1948; Clark, 1953), that generality is achieved with a loss of detailed information about the structure of the attitude (see Campbell, 1953), that subjects are responding to the abstracted symbol and not in terms of the content of the issue as such (see Newcomb, 1941), and so on. All of these arguments, in one way or another, aim at the question of validity, as does McNemar's (1946) scathing criticism based on lack of correlation in some cases with Thurstone scales; for example, Dunlap and Kroll (1939) found that a generalized scale correlated only .28 with [the] specific Droba scale for attitudes toward war. On the other hand, Campbell (1953) reported that in four of five direct comparisons, the correlations between Remmers and Thurstone scales were as high as the reliability coefficients of the latter themselves.

At any rate, such generalized scales have fallen into disuse. Nevertheless, they have some very definite values which warrant their further development. For one thing, they are *economical*—if their validity can be assumed in new situations, they make unnecessary the development and standardization of specific scales for every attitude object, saving money, time, and effort. For another thing, they are *available at the proverbial moment's notice* —Remmers (1954) cites the case where the master scale for attitude toward any proposed social action was applied immediately following President Roosevelt's announcement of the proposed enlargement of the Supreme Court. But unquestionably, the major scientific value of generalized attitude scales is the matter of *comparability:* When a subject has one attitude score on a Thurstone scale for WAR and another score on a Thurstone scale for CAPITAL PUNISHMENT, we can conclude only in a most tenuous manner, if at all, that he is less favorably disposed toward one than the other. When exactly the same yardstick is used to measure both attitudes, however—again assuming that the generality of the instrument is valid—such direct comparison becomes much more tenable. In later portions of this book, particularly in experiments testing the congruity hypothesis, several examples will be given of studies which would be impossible without the use of generalized, standard measuring instruments, in this case the semantic differential.

When used as a measure of attitude, the semantic differential carries even further the logic used by Remmers in developing his generalized scales. Rather than having different "master" scales for different classes of attitude objects, exactly the same set of evaluative dimensions would be used for all objects of judgment. Rather than using "statements" of any sort with which the subject must agree or disagree, scales defined by pure, abstracted linguistic evaluators would be used. These are at present *ideal* conditions, because we have not as yet done the systematic research necessary to select such scales. From our available factorial data on single concepts we need to select those scales which maintain a high loading on the evaluative factor, regardless of its orientation for judgments of particular concepts; then we need to test the generality of these scales by comparing them with a battery of varied, specific attitude-measuring instruments, demonstrating (a) that these scales maintain high intercorrelation among themselves across the ob-

jects being evaluated and (b) that the summation scores derived from them jointly display high and roughly equal correlations with the various specific attitude-measuring instruments used as criteria. The evidence we have collected so far indicates that this will be a likely conclusion.

Such an instrument, if developed, will still face many of the criticisms aimed at Remmers' scales. Krech and Crutchfield's argument that generalized scales cannot apply with equivalent meaning to varieties of specific objects or concepts would be met by the procedures of developing our evaluative matrix—i.e., by the demonstration that the scales selected do maintain their high and pure evaluative loading despite the nature of the concept being judged. Campbell's argument that generality is achieved at the cost of losing richer information about the structure of the attitude does not seem to us to be a criticism of an instrument *as a measure of attitude*, assumed to be a unidimensional attribute. Other methods can be used to get at the more detailed structure of a concept's meaning; indeed, the semantic differential as a whole (e.g., the profile of the object against the *n*-dimensional differential) is designed to get at just such information, as we suggest in the next section. Finally, there is Newcomb's criticism that in using such scales, subjects react in terms of symbols and not in terms of issue content—he cited the case where people who rate symbols like FASCISM very unfavorably may actually agree with many of the beliefs of Fascists. This is not as much a criticism of generalized attitude scales as it is of *the phrasing of the concept* judged; these subjects did have unfavorable attitudes toward the concept FASCISM and simultaneously favorable attitudes toward statements of authoritarian policies—if subjects are illogical and inconsistent, this is not a fault of the measuring instrument. In fact, comparison of the evaluative locations of concepts like FASCIST and SENATOR MC CARTHY, or even a phrase like CENTRALIZATION OF POWER IN THE HANDS OF A STRONG LEADER, would reveal just such logical inconsistencies.

One of the advantages of the semantic differential in this regard is its flexibility with respect to the nature of the concept judged—ordinary nouns, phrases, pictures, cartoons, and even sonar signals have been used at one time or another.

Meaning vs. Attitude in the Prediction of Behavior

One of the most common criticisms of attitude scales of all types is that they do not allow us to predict actual behavior in real-life situations. Like most such arguments, this one is overdrawn. Most proponents of attitude measurement have agreed that attitude scores indicate only a *disposition* toward certain *classes* of behaviors, broadly defined, and that what overt response actually occurs in a real-life situation depends also upon the context provided by that situation. We may say, for example, that a person with an extremely unfavorable attitude toward NEGRO may be expected to make some negatively evaluating overt response to an object of this attitude if he is in a situation in which he does not anticipate punishment from others about him. As Doob (1947) has put it, "overt behavior can seldom be predicted from knowledge of attitude alone." But there is more involved here than this: It can also be said that the attitudinal disposition itself accounts for only part of the intervening state which mediates between situations and behaviors, albeit perhaps the dominant part. The *meaning* of NEGRO to the individual subject is richer by far than what is revealed by his attitude score. Within the framework of the theoretical model underlying our own research, attitude is one—but only one—of the dimensions of meaning, and hence provides only part of the information necessary for prediction.

By combining judgments derived from scales representing other dimensions with those derived from the evaluative factor alone, additional information can be obtained and prediction presumably improved. Two people may have identical *attitudes* toward a concept (as determined by allocation to the

evaluative dimension alone), and yet have quite different meanings of the concept (as determined by the profiles as wholes). Consider, for example, one of Tannenbaum's observations in the Thurstone comparison study reported above: One subject rated THE NEGRO as *unfavorable, strong,* and *active;* another subject rated THE NEGRO as equally *unfavorable,* but also as *weak* and *passive.* Although no behavioral criteria were available in this study, it seems likely that the former subject would behave differently in a real-life situation (e.g., with fear and avoidance) than the latter. While it is true that different attitudes imply different behaviors toward the objects signified, at least in some contexts, it is not true that the same attitude automatically implies the same behaviors.

A recent pilot study by Tannenbaum demonstrates how increasing the dimensionality of judgment utilized within the differential can increase predictability. This does not, unfortunately, involve direct, overt behavior toward the objects of attitude, but it does approach closer to that real-life situation. Subjects ($N = 40$) were asked to judge three nationality concepts—GERMANS, CHINESE, and HINDUS—against a series of semantic differential scales representative of the three major factors of meaning repeatedly obtained in factor analysis. In addition, these subjects also rated each of the nationalities on a modified Bogardus Social Distance Scale. Separate factor scores were computed for each subject on each concept, and correlation coefficients were then computed both between these scores (e.g., evaluation/potency, potency/activity, etc.) and between them and the Bogardus ratings. While the evaluative factor correlated most highly with the Bogardus ratings—as might be expected—multiple correlation analysis showed that the predictability of the social distance ratings was significantly enhanced by addition of information from the other factors. On the concept GERMANS, for example, evaluative scores correlated only .22 with the Bogardus scale, yet combining all three yielded a multiple correlation of .78. The increases in predictability for the other two concepts were not so great—from .62 to .80 for CHINESE and from .59 to .72 for HINDUS—but support the same conclusion.

REFERENCES

Campbell, D. T.
1953 "Generalized attitude scales." Pp. 90–91 in O. K. Buros (ed.), The Fourth Mental Measurements Yearbook. Highland Park, New Jersey: Gryphen Press.

Cantril, H.
1946 "The intensity of an attitude." Journal of Abnormal and Social Psychology 41:129–136.

Clark, E. K.
1953 "Generalized attitude scales." Pp. 91–92 in O. K. Buros (ed.), The Fourth Mental Measurements Yearbook. Highland Park, New Jersey: Gryphen Press.

Doob, L. W.
1947 "The behavior of attitudes." Psychological Review 54:135–156.

Dunlap, J. W., and A. Kroll.
1939 "Observations on the methodology of attitude scales." Journal of Social Psychology 10:475–487.

Katz, D.
1944 "The measurement of intensity." Pp. 51–65 in H. Cantril (ed.), Gauging Public Opinion. Princeton: Princeton University Press.

Krech, D., and R. S. Crutchfield.
1948 Theory and Problems in Social Psychology. New York: McGraw-Hill.

Newcomb, T. M.
1941 "Attitude scales." Pp. 58–59 in O. K. Buros (ed.), The 1940 Mental Measurement Yearbook. Highland Park, New Jersey: Gryphen Press.

McNemar, Q.
1946 "Opinion-attitude methodology." Psychological Bulletin 43:289–374.

Remmers, H. H.
1934 "Studies in attitudes." Bulletin of the Purdue University Studies of Higher Education, Number 4.
1954 Introduction to Opinion and Attitude Measurement. New York: Harpers.

Remmers, H. H., and E. B. Silance.
1934 "Generalized attitude scales." Journal of Social Psychology 5:298–312.

Suci, G. J.
1952 "A multidimensional analysis of social attitudes with special reference to ethnocentrism." Unpublished doctoral dissertation, University of Illinois.

Tannenbaum, P. H.
1953 "Attitudes toward source and concept as factors in attitude change through communications." Unpublished doctoral dissertation, University of Illinois.

CHAPTER 14 The Semantic Differential and Attitude Research

DAVID R. HEISE

The Semantic Differential (SD) measures people's reactions to stimulus words and concepts in terms of ratings on bipolar scales defined with contrasting adjectives at each end. An example of an SD scale is:

Good __ __ __ __ __ __ __ Bad
       3 2 1 0 1 2 3

Usually, the position marked 0 is labeled "neutral," the 1 positions are labeled "slightly," the 2 positions "quite," and the 3 positions "extremely." A scale like this one measures directionality of a reaction (e.g., good versus bad) and also intensity (slight through extreme). Typically, a person is presented with some concept of interest, e.g., Red China, and asked to rate it on a number of such scales. Ratings are combined in various ways to describe and analyze the person's feelings.

A number of basic considerations are involved in SD methodology:

This review was facilitated greatly by the "Contemporary Bibliography of Research Related to the Semantic Differential Technique," (Urbana, Ill.: January, 1967; mimeographed), made available by Charles E. Osgood. The work was carried out while the author was a staff member in the Methodology in Sociology program at the University of Wisconsin, a project funded by the Institute of General Medical Sciences of NIH. This chapter was prepared especially for this volume.

(1) Bipolar adjective scales are a simple, economical means for obtaining data on people's reactions. With adaptations, such scales can be used with adults or children, persons from all walks of life, and persons from any culture.

(2) Ratings on bipolar adjective scales tend to be correlated, and three basic dimensions of response account for most of the covariation in ratings. The three dimensions, which have been labeled Evaluation, Potency, and Activity (EPA), have been verified and replicated in an impressive variety of studies.

(3) Some adjective scales are almost pure measures of the EPA dimensions; for example, good–bad for Evaluation, powerful–powerless for Potency, and fast–slow for Activity. Using a few pure scales of this sort, one can obtain, with considerable economy, reliable measures of a person's overall response to something. Typically, a concept is rated on several pure scales associated with a single dimension, and the results are averaged to provide a single factor score for each dimension. Measurements of a concept on the EPA dimensions are referred to as the concept's profile.

(4) EPA measurements are appropriate when one is interested in affective responses. The EPA system is notable for being a multi-

variate approach to affect measurement. It is also a generalized approach, applicable to any concept or stimulus, and thus it permits comparisons of affective reactions on widely disparate things. EPA ratings have been obtained for hundreds of word concepts, for stories and poems, for social roles and stereotypes, for colors, sounds, shapes, and for individual persons.

(5) The SD has been used as a measure of attitude in a wide variety of projects. Osgood, et al., (1957) report exploratory studies in which the SD was used to assess attitude change as a result of mass media programs (pp. 305–311) and as a result of messages structured in different ways (pp. 240–241). Their chapter on attitude balance or congruity theory (pp. 189–210) [excerpted in Chapter 13 of this volume] also presents significant applications of the SD to attitude measurement. The SD has been used by other investigators to study attitude formation (e.g., Barclay and Thumin, 1963), attitudes toward organizations (e.g., Rodefeld, 1967), attitudes toward jobs and occupations (e.g., Triandis, 1959; Beardslee and O'Dowd, 1961; Gusfield and Schwartz, 1963), and attitudes toward minorities (e.g., Prothro and Keehn, 1957; Williams, 1964; 1966). The results in these, and many other studies, support the validity of the SD as a technique for attitude measurement. The question of validity, and other issues in assessing attitudes with the SD, will be treated in more detail after a general discussion of SD theory and technique.

THE EPA STRUCTURE

One of the distinctive features of the SD is its reduction of ratings to three basic dimensions of variation. A number of early studies were conducted to determine the dimensions of bipolar adjective ratings (Osgood, et al., pp. 47–66). Of special importance was the thesaurus study in which 76 adjective pairs were chosen from Roget's Thesaurus to represent a great variety of semantic contrasts and the corresponding bipolar scales

were used by one hundred college students to rate 20 different concepts. Correlations between the ratings on different scales were calculated and factored. The EPA structure was clearly evident in the results of this and other early analyses; in the thesaurus study the EPA dimensions accounted for more than two-thirds of the common variance. Some additional dimensions were found in the early studies, and several scales that made distinctions too narrowly descriptive or too highly abstract were found to be unrelated to any of the major dimensions. Yet, for the most part, early work with the SD revealed that ratings on most scales are highly predictable in the three EPA dimensions alone.

The EPA structure holds up with a wide variety of subjects, concepts, and scales. Bopp (reported in Osgood, et al., pp. 223–226) had 40 schizophrenics rate 32 words on a 13 scale form; the usual EPA structure was recognizable. Wright (1958) had 40 concepts rated on a 30 scale SD by a survey sample of 2,000 men and women distributed over the spectrum of socioeconomic status. In this study each concept was rated by a different sample of 50 persons so the mean ratings for different concepts were entirely independent. Wright found four factors in his data, the first three of which clearly were EPA. Heise (1965) had 1,000 concepts rated on eight scales by Navy enlistees; factor analyses of the data based on mean ratings for the 1,000 different words yielded the usual EPA structure. DiVesta (1966) had 100 concepts rated on 27 scales by subjects in grades two through seven (20 subjects for each concept). The usual EPA structure emerged, though there was some tendency for Potency and Activity to merge into a single Dynamism dimension up until the fifth grade. DiVesta also reports another study in which grade school children used 21 scales to rate 100 different concepts (this time with 100 subjects rating each concept) and, combining the data for all grades, the usual EPA structure was found.

Osgood (1962) reports several early studies designed to determine whether the EPA structure is idiosyncratic to English or whether it holds up within other languages and other cultures. G. J. Suci (1960) had illiterate Navajo, Hopi, and Zuni respondents make ratings by pointing; the data obtained revealed Evaluation and Potency factors; Activity did not appear separately, possibly because of the roughness of the data, or perhaps because not enough Activity scales were included. H. Akuto had 100 Japanese subjects rate 90 concepts on 50 scales in Japanese and found that the EPA structure was clearly evident in the factor structure.

More recently, a program of research has been set up to validate the SD in 24 different languages (Osgood, 1964; Jakobovits, 1966). Analyses now have been completed for 15 languages: American, English, Arabic, Cantonese, Dutch, Finnish, Flemish, French, Greek, Hindi, Italian, Japanese, Kannada, Serbo-Croatian, Swedish, and Spanish. In each culture a set of 50 bipolar scales is developed in the native language (rather than by translation) and these are used to rate 100 basic concepts (the concepts are the same for all cultures, having been drawn to be meaningful everywhere and easily translatable). Ratings are made by adolescent males using 20 subjects per concept, and correlations and factor analyses are calculated for the mean ratings on 50 scales over 100 concepts. In these analyses an EPA structure emerges by blind machine analysis in all but two cases, and in these (Hindi and Arabic) the EPA structure can be obtained by appropriate rotation of the factor axes. Of course, the impression of an EPA structure emerging throughout is based on translation of scales back into English, and it could be that translation introduces a cultural bias. To test this possibility, a pan-cultural factor analysis was conducted (Jakobovits) in which the 50 scales from the 15 cultures were entered as variables in one giant factor analysis and correlations were calculated over concepts. In this analysis the first three factors were clearly recognizable as EPA and every culture clearly contributed to the definition of the EPA dimensions. Jakobovits commented, "The fact that each pan-cultural factor is

defined by scale loadings of comparable size across all languages proves the true pan-cultural nature of the semantic space as measured by these procedures" (p. 26).

Characterization of the EPA dimensions —Considering the generality of the EPA dimensions and their importance in research using the SD, it is worth considering in more detail the distinctions that are involved. In the following paragraphs the EPA dimensions are characterized in two ways. First, some of the typical adjective contrasts that define each dimension are presented (taken from Jakobovits). Second, a number of concepts which typically are rated near the extremes of each dimension are given (taken from Jenkins, 1960, and from Heise, 1965).

Evaluation is associated with the adjective contrasts: nice–awful, good–bad, sweet–sour, and helpful–unhelpful. Some concepts which lie on the positive (good) side of this dimension are: DOCTER, FAMILY, GOD, CHURCH, HAPPY, PEACE, SUCCESS, TRUTH, BEAUTY, and MUSIC. Some concepts which lie toward the negative (bad) pole are: ABORTION, DEVIL, DISCORDANT, DIVORCE, FRAUD, HATE, DISEASE, SIN, WAR, ENEMY, and FAILURE.

Some scales which define the Potency dimension are big–little, powerful–powerless, strong–weak, and deep–shallow. Concepts which lie toward the positive (powerful) pole are: WAR, ARMY, BRAVE, COP, MOUNTAIN, ENGINE, BUILDING, DUTY, LAW, STEEL, POWER, and SCIENCE. Concepts which lie toward the negative (powerless) pole are: GIRL, BABY, WIFE, FEATHER, KITTEN, KISS, LOVE, and ART.

Activity scales are fast–slow, alive–dead, noisy–quiet, and young–old. Some concepts high in Activity are: DANGER, ANGER, ATTACK, CITY, ENGINE, FIRE, SWORD, TORNADO, WAR, WIN, CHILD, and PARTY. Among concepts which lie toward the negative pole on the Activity dimension are: CALM, SNAIL, DEATH, EGG, REST, STONE, and SLEEP.

SD space—Sometimes it is convenient to think of the EPA dimensions as forming a three-dimensional space. The SD, or affective, space is illustrated in Figure 1; the origin or center of this space represents neutrality

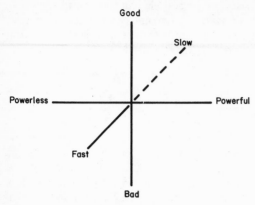

Figure 1. The SD Space.

on all three dimensions. Treating EPA measurements of a stimulus as coordinates allows the stimulus to be positioned as a point in the space, and this point graphically represents the affective response to the stimulus. Some interesting geometric indices can be devised to measure a stimulus' total affectivity and its affective similarity to other stimuli; these indices are presented later.

CONSTRUCTION AND USE OF SD

The following sections discuss how one makes and uses an SD for research purposes, and what kinds of information are provided for analyses. This discussion serves to introduce vocabulary which will be helpful later on.

The primary question in constructing an SD is what scales should be used. Two basic criteria enter into scale selection; relevance and factorial composition.

Scale Relevance

Subjects find it easier to use scales which relate meaningfully to the concepts being judged and which make distinctions that are familiar (Triandis, 1959). For example, in rating persons, sweet–sour is less relevant, and thus harder to use, than helpful–unhelpful; among laymen, talkative–quiet would be

a better scale than manic–depressive. Furthermore (and more important), relevant scales provide more sensitive measurements. More variance is obtained in using relevant scales and the variance of ratings involves less random error (Koltuv, 1962; Mitsos, 1961).

There are two approaches to identifying scales which are relevant for a given class of concepts and a given sample of persons. On the one hand, subjects can be presented with a set of scales and asked to rank them in terms of their meaningfulness in thinking about x, where x is a class of concepts to be rated like People, Newspapers, Organizations, etc. (Mitsos). One then would use the scales ranking highest in meaningfulness for a given population of raters.

A second, more meticulous approach would be to present pairs or triads of concepts from the stimulus concept domain and ask subjects how these concepts differ. One would make up bipolar scales from the distinctions respondents make, omitting any purely denotative distinctions (e.g., blond versus brunette). For example, if subjects frequently drew the distinction of crudeness, an appropriate scale might be crude–gracious. This approach, developed for the study of individuals by Kelly (1955), has been applied successfully in SD studies (e.g., Triandis).

Factorial Composition

The basic goal in an SD study is to get measurements on the EPA dimensions, and since factor analyses show these dimensions to be independent, one seeks measurements that are independent. This means that appropriate scales will measure the dimensions (i.e., scales that have high factor loadings on the EPA dimensions) and will give relatively pure measures of the dimensions (i.e., each scale has a high loading on just one dimension). The only objective way to select factorially pure scales is on the basis of actual factor analyses. Researchers experienced with the SD are aware that intuition is an unreliable guide in selecting factorially pure scales. One can conduct ad hoc factor analyses to learn the factorial composition of new scales, but this is an expensive procedure since studies based on less than 30 concepts and hundreds of subjects are likely to be misleading. The most common procedure is to select scales on the basis of published factor analyses and following are some available reports which indicate the factorial composition of SD scales. The thesaurus study (Osgood *et al.*, pp. 53–61) has been a standard source of factor analytic information on SD scales. Because of the large number of scales considered (76), this is an important source, but the factor loadings should be treated only as rough indicators because of the unusual method of factoring and because only 20 concepts were rated in this study. Wright presents the factorial structure for 30 scales based on data from a survey sample of 2,000 adults rating 40 concepts. DiVesta gives the factor loadings of 27 scales used to rate 100 concepts by a large sample of children. Jakobovits gives the highest loading EPA scales for 15 languages (including English) as derived from the pan-cultural factor analyses.

The published factor analytic studies provide a large fund of scales to draw on and usually one can obtain a subset of scales which are relevant to the concept domain of interest. It should be noted, however, that another problem arises in selecting scales from previous studies—the matter of semantic stability. When applied to a special class of concepts, the words in a scale may take on special meanings and thus the scale is literally a different one than previously studied. For example, the words HOT and COLD are used connotatively in rating many concepts (like PEOPLE) but may be used denotatively in rating physical objects. Since the scale takes on different meanings with different concepts, its factorial composition may be different for the special class of objects. The problem of semantic stability is (along with the problem of relevance) the primary impetus for carrying out special factor analyses for each new content area.

Number of Scales

Assuming that one has a set of relevant scales, each of which loads on one and only one of the EPA factors, the next question is how many scales should be included in the final instrument. More than one scale for each dimension is desirable since this improves the reliability of factor scores. On the other hand, reliability characteristics of SD scales are such that it would rarely be useful to include more than ten scales to measure a dimension, and generally speaking, four scales per dimension can give adequate sensitivity for most purposes.

Contrary to the practice in many published studies, the number of Evaluation scales should not be more than the number of Potency and Activity scales. Evaluation scales always are found to be more reliable than Potency or Activity scales and thus fewer, not more, are needed for a given level of precision.

Equivalent Forms

In research it is often necessary or desirable to do repeated measurement. This introduces the question of equivalent forms. There is evidence that subjects may recall the SD rating they have made previously when the time periods between repeated measurements are short (Miron, 1961). Consequently, such repeated measurements using the same form may not be independent. An example of how this could confound research is given by Coyne and Holzman (1966) who had subjects give SD ratings for their voice at points before and after listening to themselves on a tape recorder. No significant differences were found when the same SD form was used in all ratings, but highly significant changes appeared when subjects used alternate forms of the SD for the different points of time. This experiment suggests that equivalent forms of the SD are necessary in experiments dealing with short range changes in attitudinal reaction.

The primary problem in the development

and use of equivalent forms is the large fund of factor analyzed scales that is required; making up two equivalent forms calls for twice as many scales. Given a fund of scales to draw on, one should try to match factor loadings of scales in different forms. Then an experimental design should be used such that some subjects should use Form A at time 1 and Form B at time 2 while other subjects use Form B at time 1 and Form A at time 2.

Format of SD Test Booklets

There are three possible ways of graphically setting up scales and the concepts to be rated:

(1) Concepts can be presented one at a time, with each concept followed by all of the scales on which it is to be rated; typically, the concept is printed at the top of a page and the scales are arrayed below, one after another, and centered on the page.

(2) A concept and one of the scales on which it is to be rated can be presented as a single item with the various concept-scale combinations arrayed randomly one after another. For example, item 1 might be NEGRO followed by the good–bad scale, item 2 RUS-SIAN followed by the passive–active scale, item 3 JEW followed by helpful–unhelpful, etc. (It is immaterial whether the stimulus word is placed to the left or right of the scale [Osipow and Grooms, 1962].)

(3) A single scale can be presented along with all of the concepts which are to be rated on it; for example, the good–bad scale could be presented at the top of the page and concepts listed down along the side, each followed by scale marking positions.

Studies show that measurements differ very little in going from one format to another (Osgood, et al., pp. 81–82; Wells and Smith, 1960), although format 3 is least desirable since there is some slight tendency for ratings of one concept to affect ratings on another concept. From the standpoint of data handling, format 1 is preferable since it groups the data for a single concept, facilitating key-punching and statistical analyses.

When format 1 is used, the order of concepts in the test booklet is immaterial since anchoring or order effects are not evident using this format. Sommer (1965) made a determined effort to produce anchor effects and found none: for example, POLITICIAN was rated the same whether preceded by JANI-TOR, GARBAGE COLLECTOR, FARMER or whether preceded by STATESMAN, SCHOLAR and SCI-ENTIST. (See also Osgood, et al., pp. 84–85.)

To disguise the nature of an SD test and to prevent subjects from developing response sets which could reduce sensitivity of measurements, it is customary to mix the scales as much as possible. This means alternating Evaluation, Potency and Activity scales rather than presenting them in blocks and alternating directionality so that the scales' good poles, strong poles, or active poles are not always on the same side.

Adverbial quantifiers—To facilitate the rating of intensity, SD scale positions usually are labeled with adverbs like "extremely," "quite," and "slightly." The study by Wells and Smith inquired into whether the adverbs serve any useful function. SD scales with and without adverbial quantifiers were employed with a survey sample of 400 housewives. It was found that the amount of differentiation in SD ratings was substantially greater when adverbial labels were used: no labels led to many more ratings at the end-points of the scales. Furthermore, interviewers reported that the labeled scales were better understood by the respondents and led to greater cooperation in the rating task. Hence, use of adverbial quantifiers is justified.

The metric characteristics of adverbial quantifiers have been investigated in a number of studies (Cliff, 1959; Howe, 1962, 1966a, 1966b). The results indicate that adverbs "extremely," "quite," and "slightly" do define rating positions which are about equidistantly spaced. The results from these studies also suggest some other adverbs which might be used in some SD studies. For example, the adverbs of frequency—"seldom," "often," "always"—might be meaningful in SD studies of roles (i.e., is a LAWYER sometimes powerful, usually powerful, always powerful; is a MOTHER sometimes nice, usually nice, always nice). However, the relationship between such frequency ratings and intensity ratings using the customary adverbs is not known.

Administration of an SD

SDs are easily administered to groups and, when possible, this is certainly the most efficient way to obtain SD data. However, an SD also can be administered successfully on an individual basis by survey interviewers.

Instructions should routinely contain a statement that the purpose of the SD is to find out how people feel about things and so the respondent should rate the way he feels. He should use his first impressions and not try to figure out the "right answer" or the answer that makes most sense. Instructions also should contain an example in which the concept presented would elicit a unanimous response from the subjects, for example, TORNADO. The concept is rated by the test administrator, who explains while making the ratings what the scale positions mean. It has been suggested (Osgood, et al., pp. 82–84) that subjects should be urged to work quickly; however, Miron found that subjects could be urged to work slowly and thoughtfully and the same results were obtained, mainly because after the first few ratings, subjects worked quickly, regardless of what they were instructed to do.

For many subject populations, one can turn to the literature to check the experiences and procedures of others who have worked with similar groups, for example: college students —Osgood, et al.; children—DiVesta (1966), and Kagan, Hosken and Watson (1961); survey respondents—Wright, and Wells and Smith; factory workers—Triandis; juvenile delinquents—Gordon, et al. (1963); illiterates—Suci (1960).

Test length—Osgood, et al. (p. 80) suggested that a subject should be allowed about one hour to make 400 SD judgments (for example, to rate 40 concepts on ten scales). Most college students work faster than this

and the allowance is generous for even the stragglers in a college student population. On the other hand, this timing estimate is a convenient round figure, and it is perhaps minimal for subjects not accustomed to taking tests. In any case, the patience and endurance of unpaid subjects can rarely be strained beyond 400 judgments, and for noncollege subjects (such as survey respondents), the maximum number of ratings undoubtedly is far less—probably more like 50 judgments.

DESCRIPTIVE MEASURES AND PROCEDURES

A typical SD study dealing with a number of concepts, using several scales for each EPA dimension, and employing a sample of respondents, results in thousands of ratings. Various statistics and procedures are available to compress this data to a comprehensible set of measurements.

Factor Scores

The first step in data reduction is to combine ratings on the separate scales into factor scores. This involves first assigning numerical values to the scale positions; for example, $-3, -2, -1, 0, 1, 2, 3$, going from one end of the scale to the other. (To simplify calculations, numerical values should be adjusted for the directionality of scales; for example, the positions numbered 3 through -3 for the scale nice–awful, and -3 through 3 for the scale bad–good.) The responses that were obtained are then coded and a subject's ratings on a concept averaged over all the scales representing a single factor. The product is a single number representing one subject's reaction to one concept on one of the SD dimensions.

Scale weights—Assuming that the factor loadings of the scales for a given dimension are all high and comparable in size, that all the scales load mainly on the one dimension, and that all the scales are of approximate equal relevance so that the rating variances are approximately equal, then it is reasonable to weight the scales equally in calculating the factor scores (i.e., find the simple mean of the ratings). Only if these assumptions are seriously violated, is a more complicated procedure of differential weighting desirable; this could involve weighting each scale by the squared factor loading or the use of multiple regression formulas. Textbooks on factor analysis provide information on the more complicated procedures.

Group means—A frequent second step in data reduction is finding the group means for the factor scores corresponding to different concepts. This simply involves averaging the factor scores over the subjects in the sample. The group means can be viewed as estimates of true factor scores for the particular concept in the particular group or culture—they are the points around which individuals vary. Group means computed from the SD tend to be extremely stable.

Polarization

The factor scores for a concept constitute a complete description of an affective reaction in terms of the EPA dimensions. For some purposes one might not want such detailed information but simply a general measure of the intensity of the affective response independent of its character. This kind of measure, the emotionality of the concept, is given by the polarization measure—the distance between the neutral point or origin of the SD three-dimensional space and the particular concept under consideration. If the neutral point of the scale was assigned a value of zero in the coding process, the factor scores also have their neutral point at zero and polarization is calculated simply by squaring the factor scores, adding, and taking the square root of the sum. That is:

$$P = \sqrt{e^2 + p^2 + a^2}$$

where e, p, and a, are factor-score measurements of a given concept on the three dimensions.

Profile Analyses

The majority of SD studies involve some hypothesis about differences in affective reaction. For example, one might be interested in reactions to NEGROES versus JEWS; the difference in reaction to NEGROES before and after seeing *The Birth of a Nation*, or the difference in reactions to NEGROES among Southerners and Northerners. Various approaches for analyzing differences in affective response have been developed.

Dimensions treated separately—One approach examines the differences on each EPA dimension separately. That is, one would compare the means for concept a versus concept b, for time 1 versus time 2, or for group x versus group y on each of the three dimensions separately. This approach provides the most detailed results, the statistical procedures for comparing means are well-studied and relatively non-problematic, and it is definitely the preferred procedure in most SD studies. In any case, it should accompany other types of profile analysis.

D scores—There are instances in which one would like to have a measure of the combined differences on all three EPA dimensions—a summary measure of the total difference in affective reactions. D scores have come to serve this purpose in SD research. These represent the distance between two sets of SD measurements when both are plotted as points in the three-dimensional SD space. The formula for calculating D scores is as follows: let e_1, p_1, a_1, be the factor score for concept 1 (or time 1 or group 1); e_2, p_2, a_2, the measurements for concept 2 (or time 2 or group 2). Then

$$D = \sqrt{(e_1 - e_2)^2 + (p_1 - p_2)^2 + (a_1 - a_2)^2}.$$

The meaning of D scores can be illustrated by an example. The average EPA factor scores for the concepts HOME, OFFICE, and WORK were drawn from Heise (1965) and entered into the formula for D. It was found that the distance between HOME and WORK is about 3.8 units while the distance between OFFICE and WORK is .8 units. Thus, the affective reaction to WORK is more similar to that for OFFICE than to that for HOME.

Considerations in using D—The reliability of D scores based on group means (where $N = 30$) is adequate; the correlations between test and retest or between alternate groups are above .90 (Norman, 1959). The random distribution of D under various conditions of rating errors has been studied by Cozens and Jacobs (1961).

Despite the simplicity and the reliability of the measure, D scores should be employed conservatively. D scores completely hide the character of a difference, and a large D could be due to a big difference on one dimension or small differences on all three dimensions. When only the D scores are presented, a reader has no way of determining which is the case.

Beyond that, however, they can be misinterpreted and lead to artifactual findings. For example, at one time a popular project was to show that the difference (D) between evaluative ratings of Ideal Self and Actual Self is greater for neurotics than for normals. To simplify matters, suppose that all persons see their ideal selves as quite good (an assumption which is realistic). Now suppose that neurotics have low evaluation of their actual selves, rating their actual selves as slightly bad, whereas normals rate their actual selves as slightly good. Since both groups have the same rating of the ideal self, it inevitably follows that the neurotics are further from their ideal selves. It could be a serious error to say that "what's wrong" with neurotics is the discrepancy between their actual and ideal selves, since perhaps what is really wrong with them is merely their low evaluation of actual self, which produces the discrepancy as an artifact or inevitable side effect. In fact, Bass and Fiedler (1959) did find that D scores added very little to the basic factor scores in predicting maladjustment. Pitfalls involved in D scores are discussed in greater detail in a series of articles by Cronbach (1955, 1958; Cronbach and Gleser, 1953).

EPA Compounds

There are instances in which the EPA dimensions separately are not nearly as interesting as some compound or combination of them. This is true when there is a particular type of affective reaction that is of special interest. Several techniques are available for analyzing compounds of E, P, and A.

Multiple regression—Suppose one wanted to estimate voting behavior from reactions to the concept VOTING, and it was believed that Evaluation, Potency and Activity reactions all are important. An appropriate procedure to find the total relationship between the EPA structure and the behavioral criterion would be to run a multiple regression of voting behavior simultaneously on all three EPA measurements. That is, one would take the observed voting behavior of a subject and relate it, simultaneously, through multiple regression procedures to his observed reactions to the concept VOTING in terms of Evaluation, Potency and Activity. Since the three dimensions are essentially independent, their estimation power will cumulate, and generally speaking, multiple regressions will give significantly better predictions than simple regressions based on each dimension separately.

Characteristic attributes—Different compounds of E, P, and A seem to have special meanings and psychological significances. That is, the shape of an EPA profile can be a fruitful subject for analysis and may itself provide special information for prediction and explanation. Osgood, *et al.* (p. 116–124) developed the idea of characteristic attribute. This is a compounded or complex dimension of reaction involving Evaluation, Potency, and Activity all together in some constant proportions. These proportions are derived by rotating the EPA axis and then recalculating the scores of concepts in terms of the new, compounded dimensions. For example, one could define a dimension of reaction which consists of one part Evaluation, one-half part Potency, and one part Activity —this is the characteristic attribute of suc-

CESSFUL. Any other concept whose EPA measurements are in the same ratio could be compared directly with SUCCESSFUL in the sense that the other concept evokes either more or less of the same complex reaction.

Further, they found (pp. 120–124) that the major reaction to political personages and concepts involved such a compound of feelings—about equal amounts of EPA defining roughly a dimension of progress versus decay. A methodological implication is that in political studies it may be more economical and meaningful to measure candidates and issues directly in terms of the characteristic attribute for politics, using scales like healthy–sick or progressive–degenerative (these are hypothetical scales whose actual properties are not known). Theoretically, the special dimensions suggest that psychological processes involved in politics are of a different nature and character than those involved in family life, for instance; there are habitual modes of response for political objects which do not apply in other domains.

Position indices—Sometimes it is of interest to identify all concepts whose profiles are similar both in terms of shape and elevation; that is, concepts that are at approximately the same place in the SD space. One very rough measure of this type of position is specification of the octant of the SD space in which a concept falls. Jakobovits specified the octant for 100 common concepts as rated in different cultures and showed that there are major differences among cultures in the proportions of concepts lying in each octant.

A more refined procedure is to define a point in the SD space in terms of EPA measurements and then identify all concepts that lie within some distance from this point, calculating the distance by the D score formula. For example, Heise (1965; 1966a) defined the point in the space that corresponds to the affective condition for n affiliation by having a variety of affiliative behaviors rated on the SD. The ratings for all behaviors were averaged on each EPA dimension, giving a single motive profile, which in turn, defined a single motive point in the SD space. The distances between this point and a large number of SD responses to words were calculated, and it was shown that persons aroused in n affiliation tend to use words with affectivity similar to that associated with the motive; that is, they use words that lie close to the motive point.

Jenkins, Russell, and Suci (1959) have prepared tables giving the distances between all 360 concepts in their Semantic Atlas Study (1958).

Visual Presentations

It has been suggested that the EPA relations (Osgood, *et al.*, pp. 93–97) among a set of concepts can be represented visually by making up three dimensional models using wires and small rubber balls. To make a model one calculates the distances between concepts using the D score formula, cuts wires proportional to the distances, and builds the model by inserting the wires in soft rubber balls, each of which represents one concept. One then would have a three-dimensional structure in which the relationships between concepts are visually evident and can be viewed from different perspectives.

Arthur (1965) advocated three-dimensional graphing using perspective charts as a means of reducing EPA measurements to a visual form and claimed that this procedure was substantially easier than model building while giving much the same kind of insight.

Reliability of SD Measurements

A study of the absolute deviations between ratings of a concept in test and retest (with retest up to three months later) was reported in Osgood, *et al.* (p. 127). For evaluation scales it was found that the average difference between ratings on the test and retest was somewhat more than one-half scale units. For Potency and Activity scales the average difference between the test and retest ranged from .7 to 1.0 scale units. The authors concluded from their data that a difference of 3 scale units or more between two ratings on the same scale could be considered statistically significant at the .05 level in a two-tailed test.

DiVesta and Dick (1966) studied the test-retest reliabilities of SD ratings made by grade school children. In their study each subject rated a different concept on a series of scales, and reliabilities were determined by correlating the ratings made on a first test with ratings made one month later on a second test. The correlations for different scales ranged from .27 to .56. DiVesta and Dick found that reliabilities are somewhat higher in the higher grades and also that Evaluation scales tend to be somewhat more reliable at all grade levels.

A reliability study by Norman (1959) gives information on how much shift occurs in ratings, relative to what might be expected if the ratings were purely random. Norman had 30 subjects rate 20 concepts on 20 scales in a test and retest spaced four weeks apart. On the average he found that the amount of shift in ratings was about 50 per cent of what would be expected if the ratings were completely random. More specifically, his results showed that 40 per cent of the scale ratings do not shift at all from test to retest, 35 per cent of the ratings shift by one scale unit, and 25 per cent of the ratings shift two or more scale units. Norman found that ratings are more stable for some concepts than for others, and this seems to be related to the number of meanings for a concept. This may also be a function of how extremely the word is rated. Other studies suggest that concepts whose true values are neutral are rated with less reliability (Peabody, 1962; Luria, 1959). Norman also found that some subjects were more stable than others in making their ratings; in particular, there is a tendency for those who use the end-points of scales more often to have lower test-retest stability. Finally, he found that certain scales are associated with greater stability; in particular, Evaluation scales evoke fewer shifts.

The general impression produced by these test-retest reliability studies is that a person's rating of a single concept on a single scale constitutes a measurement, albeit not an extremely delicate one. Such results may be somewhat misleading, however, because test-retest statistics measure stability as well as reliability. Consequently, low correlations may be due to actual changes in subjects' reactions as well as random errors. In any case, single ratings rarely are used in SD research; instead, factor scores, which should be more reliable because they are the averages of ratings on several scales, are more commonly employed.

Factor score reliability—A study is reported in Osgood, *et al.* (p. 192) in which several controversial topics were rated on six evaluation scales, and factor scores, representing each subject's evaluative reaction to a given topic, were obtained by summing the ratings on the six scales. The correlations between test and retest factor scores ranged from .87 to .97 with a mean of .91. DiVesta and Dick in their study of SD reliability among children made up factor scores by averaging ratings on two scales for a given dimension and correlating the measurements from the first test with those from the second test given one month later. For children in the fourth grade or higher the correlations ranged between .5 and .8 and were highest for Evaluation factor scores; for students in the third grade or lower, test-retest correlations ranged between .4 and .5. (Reduced reliability of factor scores among younger children also was found by Maltz, 1963.) DiVesta and Dick found that test-retest correlations were somewhat higher when the retest followed the first test immediately. In this case the r's ranged between .6 and .8. Norman examined the effect of making up factor scores from various numbers of scales. His results indicate that factor scores are more reliable than single ratings and that most of the gain in precision is accomplished by averaging just three or four scales; going up to an eight-scale factor score seems to add very little additional stability when looking at data from a test and retest spaced one month apart.

The various studies indicate that there is indeed a significant gain in test-retest correlations when factor scores are used rather than individual scale ratings. Furthermore, it appears that most of the possible improvement can be obtained using relatively few scales in making up the factor scores.

Group means—Many SD studies do not focus on an individual's rating of a concept but on a group mean. That is, interest is in the average score in a certain group rather than the score for any one person. In such case, there is averaging both across scales (factor scores) and across persons, and reliabilities should be even higher.

DiVesta and Dick calculated factor score means for groups of three to five children. The immediate test-retest correlations ranged from .73 to .94, figures that are significantly higher than the correlations based on individual subjects. Norman calculated scale means for 20 concepts using groups of 30 raters. The test-retest correlations between means was .96, and the correlations between means produced by two different samples of student respondents was .94. Miron averaged the factor scores for 20 concepts across 112 subjects and obtained test-retest correlations of .98 or more.

These studies reveal that group means on the EPA dimensions are highly reliable and stable even when the samples of subjects involved in calculating the means are as small as 30.

THE SD IN ATTITUDE RESEARCH

Validity

The general validity of the SD for measuring attitudes is supported by the fact that it yields predicted results when it is used for this purpose and also supported by studies which compare SD measurements with attitude measurements on traditional scales. A series of substantive studies was mentioned in the introduction. Now we turn to studies comparing SD measurements with measurements on traditional scales.

Evaluation factor scores for the concepts Negro, Church, and Capital Punishment were found to parallel Thurstone attitude measurements, and correlations between the two types of measurement were in the range of .74 to .82 (Osgood, *et al.*, p. 230 in this book). Evaluation factor scores for Crop Rotation were found highly related to scores on a Guttman scale for the same concept in a sample of farmers; the rank order correlation was .78 between the two sets of measurements (Osgood, *et al.*, p. 231 in this book).

A study by Nickols and Shaw (1964) supported the validity of SD ratings as attitude measurements, but also found that the relationship between SD measurements and Thurstone measurements varies under certain conditions. Attitudes toward College Professors and toward the Church were assessed using Evaluative factor scores and two Thurstone scales. When the attitude object was non-salient for subjects, the relationship between the measurements was high: $r = .71$ for non-college subjects rating Professor and $r = .76$ for college students rating the Church. However, when the attitude object was salient for the subjects, the relationship between the two measures dropped to low values: $r = .29$ for college students rating Professors and $r = .39$ for church attenders rating the Church. Nickols and Shaw noted that while the variations in attitude were less in the high saliency groups, this difference was not enough to explain the drops in correlation. They also presented evidence that the Thurstone scales retained their reliability as measurements of individual differences in the high saliency groups. An ad hoc analysis by this author (using the data summarized by Heise, 1965) indicates that in the case of SD ratings, saliency of attitude objects does not affect their reliability either.

Nickols and Shaw hypothesize that subjects are more sensitive to the social repercussions of their ratings when dealing with salient objects, and that the SD is more transparent as a measure of attitude. Thus, social desirability[1] may enter as a factor in SD ratings of salient objects. This interpretation re-

---

[1] Social desirability is the tendency of subjects to give what they believe are socially acceptable responses.

ceives indirect support from a study by Ford and Meisels (1965) which showed that the social desirability of SD scales corresponded directly to their loading on the Evaluation dimension (the Potency and Activity dimensions are unrelated to social desirability). That being the case, direct SD ratings of objects may not be an efficient approach to attitude measurement when salient or delicate topics are involved. However, before concluding this firmly, one would like to see replications which involve more than two attitude objects. The replications should include: (1) subjects' need for approval as an actual control variable, (2) a third criterion used to show that the SD measurements are the less valid, and (3) SD measurements on all three dimensions.

Tittle and Hill (1967) conducted a study in which various scales designed to measure attitudes toward student political participation were compared with each other and evaluated in terms of their ability to estimate voting behavior [Chapter 30 in this volume]. The SD measurements were obtained by averaging Evaluation factor scores for five concepts (voting, discussing student politics, holding office, assisting in campaigns, and keeping informed). The SD attitude measurement was found to be related to measurements of attitude using other scales. The correlation between the SD measurement and a measurement on a Likert-type scale was .62 (presumably product moment correlation; the type of association measure was not identified by the authors). The SD measure also had some capability for estimating voting behavior. However, the SD measure was less strongly related to behavior than the measurements on other scales, especially the Likert-type scale. The study is an important contribution to the literature on attitude and behavior, but it could have been improved from the standpoint of SD methodology. First, measurements were made only on the Evaluation dimension; past work (Osgood, et al., pp. 120–124) indicates that all three dimensions are important elements in political attitude. Second, the SD scales apparently were all oriented in the same direction (i.e.,

the positive poles of the scales were all presented on the same side) so that response sets could interfere with measurement precision. Finally, it was merely assumed that attitudes toward a variety of concepts would all be equally relevant for predicting voting behavior; actually, this is an empirical question and attitudes toward the five different concepts should not merely have been summed, but entered in a regression analysis.

In summary, most studies provide confirmation that the SD can be used to measure attitudes. Too little methodological research is available to decide whether SD ratings always provide as sensitive a measure of attitude as is given by traditional scales. However, for the present, one perhaps should be cautious in using the SD with highly salient topics since there is some evidence that measures may be confounded by social desirability effects in such instances.

Dimensionality

Measurement on SD scales has been found to have a three-dimensional structure whereas attitude measurements typically are made on a single dimension. What is the relationship between the EPA structure and an attitude measurement?

Osgood, et al. (p. 228 in this book) proposed that in measuring attitudes, just the Evaluation dimension of the SD need be considered. The justification for this suggestion was simply that it seemed reasonable in light of previous writings on attitudes. At one point (p. 233 in this book) they did suggest that considerably more information could be obtained by also measuring Potency and Activity, but they treated Potency and Activity as distinct from attitude. In retrospect, it appears that their identification of the Evaluation dimension with attitude measurement was erroneous, for it seems that the single dimension involved in attitude measurement is only sometimes pure Evaluation, and other times is a compound dimension involving Evaluation, Potency, and Activity.

Taking the extreme empiricist position that attitude is what attitude scales measure, one question that can be asked is, Do traditional attitude scales measure pure Evaluation or do Potency and Activity also get involved? If traditional attitude scales do measure Potency and Activity as well as Evaluation, this should be evident in the content of at least some of the items. The following are a few selected items from scales presented by Shaw and Wright (1967) which suggest that traditional scales in fact do tap Potency and Activity content. *The Anti-Semitism Scale.* (pp. 384–386) "In order to handle the Jewish problem, Gentiles must meet fire with fire and use the same ruthless tactics with the Jews that the Jews use with the Gentiles" (Potency). "Jewish power and control in money matters is far out of proportion to the number of Jews in the total population" (Potency). *Attitude Toward the German People.* (pp. 396–398) "The German soldiers were, almost without exception, cruel and brutal" (Potency). "Germans are slow and unimaginative" (Activity). *Acceptance of Self.* (pp. 432–436) "I am quite shy and self-conscious in social situations" (Activity). "I seem to have a real inner strength in handling things. I'm on a pretty solid foundation and it makes me pretty sure of myself" (Potency).

The Bogardus Social Distance Scale can be taken as a measurement of attitudes toward different nationality groups. Rather low and unstable correlations have been reported between Evaluation ratings of nationality groups and measurements on the Bogardus scale—.22 for Germans, .62 for Chinese, and .59 for Hindus (Osgood, *et al.,* pp. 233–234 in this volume). However, multiple regressions of Bogardus scores on all three EPA dimensions resulted in much higher correlations, and the degree of relationship was about the same for all three nationalities —.78, .80 and .72 for Germans, Chinese, and Hindus respectively. Particularly in the case of the Germans, Evaluation accounted only for about 5 per cent of the variance in Bogardus scores while Potency and Activity accounted for 55 per cent.

In a study by Heise (1966b) EPA ratings

were obtained from subjects in three status groups for a number of concepts specially selected to represent key areas of attitudinal differences. Most of the significant differences between groups appeared on the Potency and Activity dimensions rather than on Evaluation.

Ratings of occupational prestige can be interpreted as measurements of attitudes toward different status positions. It is noteworthy that prestige ratings correlate highest with ratings on the scale successful-unsuccessful (Gusfield and Schwartz, 1963) which loads jointly on Evaluation, Potency, and Activity.

From the above results it appears that what we mean by attitude, both in theory and in measurement, is simply the affective reaction to an object, and this reaction frequently is along a dimension which is a compound of Evaluation, Potency, and Activity. In the vocabulary of SD research, the single dimension represented in an attitude scale corresponds to the characteristic attribute for the attitude object, and this is only sometimes pure Evaluation. Accordingly, studies employing the SD for attitude measurements should make use of all three dimensions to get measurements paralleling those on traditional attitude scales.

Special Features of SD Attitude Measurement

A generalized method—An SD can be used as a generalized technique in the sense that a subject's attitude toward any object might be assessed by having the subject give ratings on the same set of SD scales. The SD offers the usual advantages of generalized attitude scales (Osgood, *et al.,* pp. 231–233 in this volume).

(1) *Economy.* The same bipolar scales can be used to measure attitudes toward any object, so the costs of preparing a different scale for every object are eliminated.

(2) *Instant Readiness.* An SD for measuring attitudes can be made up immediately for crash programs or for topical projects in

social research like studies of disasters, riots or the appearance of new political figures.

(3) *Cross-concept Comparability.* Since attitudes toward various objects are all measured on the same scales, there is the potential for comparing different attitudes.

The major problem in using a single set of SD scales as a generalized attitude scale is the matter of scale relevancy or, more generally, of concept-scale interactions. A single set of scales used for all objects would provide relatively insensitive measurements for some. This may not be objectionable (for example, in exploratory work or in research involving a large number of attitude objects) where a set of scales like those from the pan-cultural factor analyses can be used as a rough and ready instrument for general attitude measurement. Where, however, sensitivity is necessary, it probably is desirable to use the SDs developed for the particular content areas of interest.

Standard metric—One of the unique features of the SD is that attitudes toward a vast array of objects can be measured in terms of basically the same metric on the three EPA dimensions. Thus, all of the objects can be positioned in a single attitudinal space. This feature of the SD has yielded developments and insights that would have been difficult or impossible to obtain using attitude scales in which the metric changes for each object considered.

Congruity theory—Attitude balance theories postulate that when two concepts are associated the attitudes toward the concepts tend to converge, and when two concepts are dissociated (contrasted), the attitudes tend to diverge. While this basic theory has been expressed in a number of ways (see Brown, 1962) a quantitative statement was possible only when attitudes toward different objects could be measured on comparable scales, for only then could attitude convergence or divergence take on a rigorous meaning. The SD provided the required metric and permitted the development of congruity theory, an approach to attitude balance in which predictions about attitude change are made

in terms of formulas (Osgood, *et al.,* 1957, chapter 5). Congruity theory is a topic in itself and is not of central interest here. The interested reader should consult the chapter in Osgood, *et al.* and articles extending and modifying the theory by Fishbein and Hunter (1964), Manis, Gleason, and Davies (1966), and Tannenbaum (1966).[2] What is of immediate interest here is that a mathematical approach to attitude balance required a standardized metric like that provided by the SD.

Homogeneity in attitudes—Differences be-between the average attitudes in various groups are found frequently using both traditional attitude scales and the SD. However, the measurement of many different attitudes on the uniform metric of the SD provides an insight which previously was obscured; attitude differences between groups tend to be smaller than one might expect. This finding develops out of comparing differences between groups with differences between concepts. For example, taking a case where group differences should be extreme—the evaluation of NEGROES by Southern whites and by Negroes—we find a difference of 1.2 evaluation units while the average difference in evaluation between the concepts of FRIEND and ENEMY within the same groups is 3.4 units (Williams, 1966). Similarly, we find that while gang delinquents evaluate FIGHTING more favorably than do middle-class adolescents, the difference between groups on this concept is far less than the differences in attitudes toward the two different concepts of FIGHTING and SCHOLARSHIP within either group. The delinquents do not feel that fighting is really good, it is just somewhat less bad than the middle-class boys view it (Gordon, *et al.,* 1963). When a series of concepts are chosen to tap attitude differences between males and females or between working-class and middle-class subjects, it is found that the differences

---

[2] Recent research by Gollob (1968) and Heise (1969) reveals that the above formulation must be modified, but an attitude-balance formula can be derived that is highly efficient in predicting attitude change.

between groups on the EPA dimensions, while statistically significant, do not approach the maximum possible values (Heise, 1966b).

These results indicate that attitudes toward specific concepts are not as divergent in different sectors of society as one might imagine; thus they imply (assuming an attitude-behavior relationship) that small differences in the distribution of attitudes have a large impact on behavior rates, or that persons in different sectors of society operate in terms of different concepts (Heise, 1966b).

Cross-cultural Comparisons—With cross-cultural validation and extension of SD measurements, the way is opened for cross-cultural comparisons of attitudes. This work has barely begun (Osgood, 1965; Jakobovits, 1966), but already results suggest that while major cultural variations do exist in attitudes toward various objects, there are also some striking uniformities. GIRLS, LOVE, and MARRIAGE, for example, seem to be positively evaluated in several cultures (Osgood, 1965). Much of the variation in attitudes is ecologically determined by the nature of the objects and, even cross-culturally, there is less variation in attitudes than one might expect.

The total image created by this work (admittedly mostly speculation at this point) is that cultural and group differences may amount to shifts and distortions of a basic attitudinal structure rather than complete reformations; while within any culture or group, at the individual level, there is a considerable amount of ongoing attitudinal variation and flux which probably contributes to variations in behavior.

SUMMARY

The SD is a general procedure for assessing affective responses. The technique has three features that distinguish it as an instrument for social psychological research. First, SDs are easy to set up, administer, and code. This, in conjunction with the demonstrated reliability and validity of the procedure, gives it favorable cost-effectiveness. Second, the

EPA structure, which has an unprecedented amount of cross-cultural validation, is interesting theoretically, and measurements on all three dimensions yield a wealth of information about affective responses to a stimulus. The information that the three independent scores give about the character of responses inevitably is lost with alternative measures depending on unidimensionality. Third, since the form of an SD is basically the same whatever the stimulus, research using the SD (and methodological research about the SD) can cumulate.

The SD has been applied frequently as a technique for attitude measurement. Its usefulness in this respect is indicated by the wide variety of meaningful results that have been obtained. Further, SD measurements have been found to correlate highly with measurements on traditional attitude scales. There are, however, a number of questions in the use of SDs for attitude measurement.

When subjects are highly invested in a topic and want to give socially desirable answers, it may be advisable to use an instrument that is less direct than the SD. Social desirability ratings of SD scales correlate very highly with the Evaluation factor loadings of the scales. Thus, if subjects choose to distort their responses toward social desirability, Evaluation scores would be biased upward. If one does use the SD with especially sensitive topics (or respondents) it is worth taking some precaution to guard against social desirability effects (e.g., giving anonymity to respondents). Note, however, that Potency and Activity measurements should be free of this problem since the typical scales for measuring these dimensions are essentially free of social desirability contamination.

Thus far almost all applications of the SD to attitude measurement have relied only on Evaluation measurements. This appears to be an unfortunate tradition. A subjective examination of items in traditional attitude scales suggests that Potency and Activity do get involved in traditional attitude measurements. Furthermore, the multiple correlations of EPA ratings with traditional scales often are much higher than the correlations of Evaluation ratings only with the scales. In the future it would be advisable to obtain ratings on all three dimensions when one is interested in attitudes. Almost certainly the full EPA information will increase the power of analyses.

Perhaps the most important general contribution of the SD is the provision of a single attitude space for all stimuli. This permits analyses, comparisons, and insights that were virtually impossible with traditional instruments.

REFERENCES

Arthur, A. Z.
  1965 "Clinical use of the semantic differential." Journal of Clinical Psychology 21:337–338.
Barclay, A., and F. J. Thumin.
  1963 "A modified semantic differential approach to attitudinal assessment." Journal of Clinical Psychology 19:376–378.
Bass, A. A., and F. E. Fiedler.
  1959 Interpersonal Perception Scores: A Comparison of D Scores And Their Components. 5 Urbana: Group Effectiveness Research Laboratory.
Beardslee, D. C., and D. D. O'Dowd.
  1961 "Students and the occupational world." Chapter 18 in N. Sanford (ed.), The American College. New York: Wiley.
Brown, R.
  1962 "Models of attitude change." Pp. 1–85 in New Directions in Psychology. New York: Holt, Rinehart and Winston.
Cliff, N.
  1959 "Adverbs as multipliers." Psychological Review 66:27–44.
Coyne, L., and P. S. Holzman.
  1966 "Three equivalent forms of a semantic differential inventory." Educational and Psychological Measurement 26: 665–674.
Cozens, W. R., and A. Jacobs.
  1961 "Empirically derived distributions similar to those used in computing the semantic differential." Journal of Psychological Studies 12:143–149.

Cronbach, L. J.
  1955 "Processes affecting scores on 'understanding others' and 'assumed similarity.'" Psychological Bulletin 52:177–194.
  1958 "Proposals leading to analytic treatment of social perception scores." Chapter 23 in R. Tagiuri and L. Petrullo (eds.), Person Perception and Interpersonal Behavior. Stanford: Stanford University Press.
Cronbach, L. J., and Goldine C. Gleser.
  1953 "Assessing similarity between profiles." Psychological Bulletin 50:465–474.
DiVesta, F. J.
  1966 "A developmental study of the semantic structures of children." Journal of Verbal Learning and Verbal Behavior 5:249–259.
DiVesta, F. J., and W. Dick.
  1966 "The test-retest reliability of children's ratings of the semantic differential." Educational and Psychological Measurement 26:605–616.
Fishbein, M., and Ronda Hunter.
  1964 "Summation versus balance in attitude organization and change." Journal of Abnormal and Social Psychology 69: 505–510.
Ford, L. H., Jr., and M. Meisels.
  1965 "Social desirability and the semantic differential." Educational and Psychological Measurement. 25:465–475. (abstract)
Gollob, H. F.
  1968 "Impression formation and word combination in sentences." Journal of Personality and Social Psychology. 10:341–353.
Gordon, R. A., J. F. Short, Jr., D. S. Cartwright, and F. L. Strodtbeck.
  1963 "Values and gang delinquency: a study of street corner groups." American Journal of Sociology 69:109–128.
Gusfield, J. R., and M. Schwartz.
  1963 "The meanings of occupational prestige." American Sociological Review 28:265–271.
Heise, D. R.
  1965 "Semantic differential profiles for 1,000 most frequent English words." Psychological Monographs 70 8:(Whole 601).
  1966a "Sensitization of verbal response-dis-

position by *n* affiliation and *n* achievement." Journal of Verbal Learning and Verbal Behavior 5:522–525.

1966b "Social status, attitudes, and word connotations." Sociological Inquiry 36:227–239.

1969 "Affective dynamics in simple sentences." Journal of Personality and Social Psychology 11:204–213.

Howe, E. S.
1962 "Probabilistic adverbial qualifications of adjectives." Journal of Verbal Learning and Verbal Behavior 1:225–242.

1966a "Verb tense, negatives and other determinants of the intensity of evaluative meaning." Journal of Verbal Learning and Verbal Behavior 5:147–155.

1966b "Associative structure of quantifiers." Journal of Verbal Learning and Verbal Behavior 5:156–162.

Jakobovits, L. A.
1966 "Comparative psycholinguistics in the study of cultures." International Journal of Psychology 1:15–37.

Jenkins, J. J.
1960 "Degree of polarization and scores on the principal factors for concepts in the semantic atlas study." American Journal of Psychology 73:274–279.

Jenkins, J. J., W. A. Russell, and G. J. Suci.
1958 "An atlas of semantic profiles for 360 words." American Journal of Psychology 71:688–699.

1959 "A table of distances for the semantic atlas." American Journal of Psychology 72:623–625.

Kagan, J., B. Hosken and S. Watson.
1961 "Child's symbolic conceptualization of parents." Child Development 32:625–636.

Kelly, G. A.
1955 The Psychology of Personal Constructs. New York: Norton.

Koltuv, Barbara Black
1962 "Some characteristics of intrajudge trait intercorrelations." Psychological Monographs 75:33 (Whole 552).

Luria, Zella
1959 "A semantic analysis of a normal and a neurotic therapy group." Journal of Abnormal and Social Psychology 58:216–220.

Maltz, H. E.
1963 "Ontogenetic change in the meaning

of concepts as measured by the semantic differential." Child Development 34:667–674.

Manis, M., T. C. Gleason, and R. M. Davies.
1966 "The evaluation of complex social stimuli." Journal of Personality and Social Psychology 3:404–419.

Miron, M. S.
1961 "The influence of instruction modification upon test-retest reliabilities of the semantic differential." Educational and Psychological Measurement 21:883–893.

Mitsos, S. B.
1961 "Personal constructs and the semantic differential." Journal of Abnormal and Social Psychology 62:433–434.

Moss, C. S.
1960 "Current and projected status of semantic differential research." The Psychological Record 10:47–54.

Nickols, S. A., and M. E. Shaw.
1964 "Saliency and two measures of attitude." Psychological Reports 14:273–274.

Norman, W. T.
1959 "Stability-characteristics of the semantic differential." American Journal of Psychology 72:581–584.

Osgood, C. E.
1962 "Studies of the generality of affective meaning systems." American Psychologist 17:10–28.

1964 "Semantic differential technique in the comparative study of cultures." American Anthropologist 66(3):171–200 Part 2.

1965 "Cross-cultural comparability in attitude measurement via multilingual semantic differentials." Pp. 95–107 in I. D. Steiner and M. Fishbein (eds.), Current Studies in Social Psychology. New York: Holt, Rinehart and Winston.

Osgood, C. E., P. H. Tannenbaum, and G. J. Suci.
1957 The Measurement of Meaning. Urbana: University of Illinois Press.

Osipow, S. H., and R. R. Grooms.
1962 "On semantic differential resistance to response bias based on stimulus word position." Psychological Reports 10:634.

Peabody, D.
1962 "Two components in psychological scales: direction and extremeness." Psychological Review 69: 65–73.

Prothro, E. T., and J. D. Keehn.
1957 "Stereotypes and semantic space." Journal of Social Psychology 45:197–209.

Rodefeld, R. D.
1967 "The Generalized Attitude of Members Toward their General Farm Organization." Unpublished master's thesis, University of Wisconsin.

Shaw, M. E., and J. M. Wright.
1967 Scales for the Measurement of Attitudes. New York: McGraw-Hill.

Sommer, R.
1965 "Anchor effects and the semantic differential." American Journal of Psychology 78:317–318.

Suci, G. J.
1960 "A comparison of semantic structures in American Southwest culture groups." Journal of Abnormal and Social Psychology 60:25–30.

Tannenbaum, P. H.
1966 "Mediated generalization of attitude change via the principle of congruity."

Journal of Personality and Social Psychology 3:493–499.

Tittle, C. R., and R. H. Hill.
1967 "Attitude measurement and prediction of behavior: an evaluation of conditions and measurement techniques." Sociometry 30:199–213.

Triandis, H. C.
1959 "Differential perception of certain jobs and people by managers, clerks, and workers in industry." Journal of Applied Psychology 43:221–225.

Wells, W. D., and Georgianna Smith.
1960 "Four semantic rating scales compared." Journal of Applied Psychology 44:393–397.

Williams, J. E.
1964 "Connotations of color names among Negroes and Caucasians." Perceptual and Motor Skills 18:721–731.

1966 "Connotations of racial concepts and color names." Journal of Personality and Social Psychology 3:531–540.

Wright, B.
1958 "A semantic differential and how to use it." Chicago: Social Research, Inc. (mimeographed).

CHAPTER **15** **The Construction and Factor Analytic Validation of Scales to Measure Attitudes Toward Education**[1]

FRED N. KERLINGER AND ESIN KAYA

In view of the considerable amount of attention paid to the problem of "Progressivism" and "Traditionalism" in education, it is remarkable that few scientific attempts have been made to explore and measure these dimensions. Nor is it known, assuming they are dimensions, what their nature is. For example, are Progressivism and Traditionalism two ends of one continuum or are they separate and independent dimensions? Naturally, before attempting measurement the dimensions to be measured must be defined. This is, of course, a problem of logical validity. Generally speaking, the logical validity stage of measuring attitudes has usually been an a priori stage. The investigator tries to determine the nature of the variable he seeks to

From Fred N. Kerlinger and Esin Kaya, "The construction and factor analytic validation of scales to measure attitudes toward education," *Educational and Psychological Measurement*, Spring 1959, 13–29. Reproduced by permission of the authors and publisher.

[1] The authors are grateful to the administration of the School of Education, New York University, for its encouragement and financial assistance. They also wish to thank their students of the past year for their enthusiastic and resourceful help in getting subjects and groups outside the university to participate in the study. Finally, thanks are due Dr. Irving Lorge for his skillful programming of the raw data for IBM computation.

measure. In most cases determination boils down to his and other people's judgments. If it is at all possible he will then use empirical or predictive validity to check on his original variable postulation and its measurement. And while he may attain a high degree of predictive validity, he may still know little about the real nature or "reality" of the variable(s) he is measuring. It is true that judges, in the Thurstone manner, and item analysis, in the Likert manner, have been powerful validity tools. But they still lack the intrinsic power to isolate and identify attitudinal factors.

It would seem that the most powerful approach to the construction of a valid attitudinal instrument would be to concentrate strongly on the logical validity stage of measurement. That is to say, it might be better to determine, if possible, the "reality" of postulated dimensions and their nature before going further. If successful, this procedure would probably supply the best information necessary to the definition of the variables to be measured. After this the instrument can be checked against outside criteria—if any can be found. Both of these modes of establishing validity have, of course, been used. Factor analysis is, at least in good part, a logical validity tool. And the usual type of attitude study, where "known" groups are administered the measuring instrument, is associated with predictive validity. If *A* Group which is believed to have a lot of the attitude in question gets a higher mean score on an instrument than does *B* Group, which is believed or known to have little of the attitude, then the validity of the instrument is at least in part established. Unfortunately, it is rare that both methods have been used together. The reasons are obvious. It is extremely difficult and cumbersome to assemble a large number of attitude tests and to give them to a large number of people. And it is needless to mention the difficulty of getting "known" criterion groups against which to check the instrument. Further, to check one instrument against another older instrument, especially when measuring attitudes, can be a dangerous and circular procedure.

The present study is an attempt to solve the above-outlined problem in the field of educational attitudes. Specifically, the study had the following purposes: (a) to test cross-sectionally a theory of educational attitudes proposed in two previous Q studies (1, 2); (b) to test the "reality" of the two factors, Progressivism and Traditionalism, found in the two previous studies; (c) to develop and validate instruments to measure attitudes toward education; and (d) to compare the relative strengths and weaknesses of Likert-type and rank-order forced-choice attitude scales.

In the case of attitudes the most formidable problem is the first step: How is it possible to establish the factors behind the attitudes under study? In short, how can an adequate valid operational definition of the attitude be obtained? Stephenson (4) has made the suggestion which stimulated much of this research. Why not determine the factors through Q methodology and inverse factor analysis and build, say, a forced-choice instrument with the "operational definition" supplied by the inverse factor analysis? Then, after the logical validity problem is

"solved" in this Q fashion, why not administer the resulting instrument to groups of subjects known or believed to possess different quantities of the attitude in question? Such an instrument should have a high degree of validity, if our theoretical and methodological thinking is correct. Concomitantly, the instrument would have the virtue of unidimensionality, often written about but seldom attained. (3, 5.) That is to say, the scale would actually consist of two or more relatively independent unidimensional scales, one for each factor. Moreover, if there is lack of independence or correlation between the factors, this can be readily and empirically determined. This report describes an attempt to follow this reasoning and procedure in the field of educational attitudes. It is particularly concerned with the logical validity stage of the research and the construction and initial validation of the factor instrument.

In the two studies of educational attitudes which preceded the present research two major factors emerged (1, 2). They were very similar in both studies and were labeled: *A:* "Progressivism" and *B:* "Traditionalism."[2] In Q methodology persons are intercorrelated, and the factors are defined by the persons highly loaded on the factors. Actually, however, persons do not define factors, as such; items or statements do. Therefore it is necessary to compute factor arrays. Following Stephenson's suggestion (with some alteration) one selects those persons who are heavily loaded on a factor and not on any other factors, weights their responses to all the items of the Q sort used, and makes up a new factor Q sort which is then conceived

---

[2] In the second of these studies only the two factors emerged; it was not possible to extract any more factors. In the first study, however, four factors emerged. Factor *A* of the second study appeared to be made up of Factors *A* and *C* of the first study. That is, *A* and *C* seemed to be "cooperative" factors, as Cattell calls them. At any rate, Factors *C* and *D* will not be discussed here since they appropriated little of the total common factor variance in the first study and did not emerge at all in the second study, and since Factors *A* and *B* were used to construct the instruments used in the present research.

to be an epitome of the factor in question. By studying the most highly approved and disapproved items of this synthetic Q sort one can get a good idea of the nature of the factor in question. Naturally, any hypotheses as to the nature of the factor are subject to further empirical inquiry before acceptance of the true nature and reality of the factor. In essence, this was the procedure used in this study.

METHODOLOGY

In the first two studies (hereafter called Q-Ed-1 and Q-Ed-2), a theory of educational attitudes was set up and tested. This theory is given in detail in Q-Ed-1 [(1)] and need not be entirely repeated here. However, a paradigm of the theory and of the Q sort used in the two studies will be helpful.

(A) ATTITUDES:
    (1) Restrictive-Traditional
    (2) Permissive-Progressive
(B) AREAS:
    (a) Teaching-Subject
         Matter-Curriculum
    (b) Interpersonal Relations
    (k) Normative-Social
    (m) Authority-Discipline

The paradigm epitomizes the thinking that educational attitudes can be broken down into two broad Attitudes and four content Areas. By combining the two categories we would have in effect two-dimensional statements, an adequate sample of which should represent most statements that can be made on educational matters. For example, almost any statements that could be made about important educational issues can be categorized, say, as *1a, 2a, 1k, 2k*, and the like. (See Table 2.)

The intercorrelation of the Q sorts of the subjects of Q-Ed-1 and Q-Ed-2 were factor analyzed. In both studies, two main factors emerged which provided the basis for item selection for factor instruments. Using the two factors, *A* and *B*, factor arrays were computed for each factor and in both studies, as

outlined above and as described in detail in Q-Ed-2 [(2)]. It is as though we had a Q sort which, in the case of Factor *A*, let's say, was sorted by a "pure" and highly saturated educational "progressive." Proceeding on this reasoning but omitting negatively loaded or disapproved statements, all the statements which had high saturations of "A-ness" and "B-ness" were drawn from both studies. Items highly saturated with a factor were selected by arbitrarily taking the 12 most approved statements of each pure Q sort (*A* and *B*). This yielded about 15 to 18 statements for each factor which was insufficient for the purpose intended. Therefore more high statements were taken from the pure sorts until there was a total of 40; 20 *A* statements and 20 *B* statements.

The 40 statements were put into a seven-point Likert-type scale and administered to two large divisions of individuals: graduate education students in a large Eastern university, and individuals outside the university. About 200 subjects, approximately half students and half people outside the university, responded to the instrument. This stage of the study had two main purposes: to provide a criterion (later to be used in conjunction with the factor-arrays) for judging item adequacy, and generally to try out the scale for unforeseen ambiguities and other deficiencies.

Each individual's scale was scored for *A* and *B* separately. The total group of papers was split at the medians of the *A* and *B* scores, and tetrachoric coefficients of correlation computed between items and total scores. The objective was to find 12 to 15 items for each factor to be combined into a new highly discriminating and valid factor attitude scale. However, when both criteria were used there were too few *A* items. So some compromises had to be made between the factor saturation and item analytic demands: two or three items were included in the final instruments which did not satisfy both criteria.

Twenty items, 10 *A* and 10 *B*, were finally incorporated into two attitude scales, the same items being used in both scales. (The items, with the ES-I item numbers, are given in Table 2.) Education Scale I (ES-I) was a Likert-type scale in the same form as the 40-item scale described above. The order of the A and B items was randomized. Scoring was also the same as with the 40-item scale: each individual had an A score, a B score, and, now, an A-B, or difference, score. The second instrument, Education Scale II (ES-II) was a rank-order forced-choice scale. There was a total of ten items consisting of one tetrad per item. Each tetrad consisted of two A and two B statements, one of which was a highly loaded A statement, and one of which was a highly loaded B statement. The other two statements were merely selected from those statements with no appreciable loadings on A or B. They were, in short, buffer statements surrounding the factor-saturated statements. Subjects were asked to rank-order the four statements in each tetrad according to strength of agreement. It was reasoned that a person with a high degree of A-ness would place a "1" before the highly loaded A item, and that a person with a high degree of B-ness would put a "1" before the highly saturated B item. It was not predicted that the "A person" would systematically put low values on B items, nor that the "B person" would do likewise with A items, since the two factors had been found to be relatively orthogonal to each other. Of course, this ranking procedure unfortunately introduces spurious correlation between items. Despite this, however, it was believed to be important to test the factor theory in two different contexts.

Theoretically, the two scales should measure the same thing. Would they? Would inter-item factor analysis of both scales separately yield the same factors and factor patterns? An important practical question is: Which of the scales would be more valid? We believed, for example, that the forced-choice instrument should be more valid, at least in the sense that the social desirability phenomenon should be less potent, than the "freer" choice situation of the Likert-type

scale. Individuals responding to the tetrads have no idea which are the saturated items and which are not, and only the saturated items are scored. Thus they simply cannot give, say, all high values to A items as they can with the Likert scale.

The two scales were administered to a total of 598 persons consisting broadly of three types: undergraduate education students at a large Eastern university (136), graduate education students at the same institution (157), and people outside the university (305). The scales were administered to the students either by the writers or their assistants. They were administered to the non-university subjects by students in graduate courses in measurement and in social psychology.

Intercorrelations of all the items of ES-I, those of ES-II, and the items of both scales together, were computed.[3] These computations yielded three R matrices consisting of the item intercorrelations of ES-I, those of ES-II, and those of both scales thrown together (i.e., Items 1–20 of ES-I were repeated in the ES-II scale context as Items 21–40).[4] All three matrices were factor analyzed using the Thurstone centroid method and orthogonal rotations. The first of these factor analyses, that of the ES-I items, is the most important and dependable. The factor structure of ES-II was bound to be distorted by the spurious correlation previously mentioned. The factor analyses of this scale alone, and of the two scales together, should show this spuriousness in the form of fairly substantial negative correlations between the factors, in contrast to near zero correlation of the factors

---

[3] All the usual statistics—means, standard deviations, reliability coefficients, etc.—were also computed, but because of space considerations cannot be given in this report. They will be discussed in detail in a future report.

[4] The R matrix of ES-I has been deposited with the American Documentation Institute. Order Document No. 5811 from the ADI Auxiliary Publications Project, Photoduplication Service, Library of Congress, Washington 25, D. C. . . . The R matrices of ES-II and the combined scales were not deposited with the ADI because of the spurious correlation between factors discussed in the text.

of the ES-I analysis—if the theory and its measurement implications are correct.

Finally, product-moment item-total correlations were computed between each item and its total factor score. That is, the responses to each *A* item were correlated with the total *A* scores, and the responses to each *B* item were likewise correlated with the total *B* scores. This was done for both scales. It was not only an item-analysis measure, but another check on the independence of the factors. *A* items should correlate substantially and positively with *A* totals, but should correlate zero with the *B* totals if the two factors are independent, as hypothesized. Naturally, there will be a small amount of negative correlation; but it should not be large, at least in ES-I. With ES-II this will not be the case. Each item should correlate positively with the total scores of its factor and should also correlate negatively and substantially with the other factor. Table 2 gives these correlation coefficients, together with the items themselves and their factor designations, the item-total correlation of each item with its own factor, its item-total correlation with the other factor, and its factor loadings from all three factor analyses.

FINDINGS AND DISCUSSION

Study of the tables shows that almost all expectations were fulfilled. The *R* matrix (deposited with ADI) shows that all the *A* items intercorrelate positively, most of them significantly (*r*'s of approximately .08 and .11 are significant at the .05 and .01 levels, respectively), if at a relatively low level. They range from .058 to .340; their mean, as computed through Fisher's *z*, is .202. The *B* items, too, intercorrelated positively; they range from .087 to .463, and the mean is .258. The difference between these means is not significant (*t* of .97). The correlations between the *A* items and the *B* items (of ES-I) are almost all negative and generally low; they range from —.003 to —.410. Many of them, however, are not significant. Their mean is —.111. Of the 100 correlations of *A*

with *B* items, 32 are not significant at .05, compared to three non-significant correlations of a total of 45 *A* intercorrelations and no non-significant correlations of the total 45 *B* intercorrelations. Thus we would seem to have two clear clusters of correlations, one of the *A* items, positive and significant, one of the *B* items, positive and significant. Two-thirds of the correlations of the *A* with the *B* items are negative and significant, with one-third of them clustering around zero. Evidently we have the two factors originally built into ES-I, and these two factors are negatively correlated, but at a low level.

Table 1 bears out the above analysis. The factor analysis of ES-I yielded three factors, one of which, Factor *C*, seemed not to be too important, and is not discussed in this report. Its variance was used to aid in clarifying the factor structures of *A* and *B*, thus achieving a nice balance between the common factor variances of *A* and *B* (41 per cent and 46 per cent, respectively) and a fair approximation to simple structure. The plot of *A* against *B*, as finally rotated, shows a very clear clustering of *A* items close to the *A* axis and another clear clustering of *B* items close to the *B* axis. There were no items in the space enclosed by the two axes. If they were not on or very near the axes, they were slightly, and in a few cases significantly, negative. As can be seen from the table, the communalities are rather low, ranging from .142 to .433, perhaps indicating a very desirable situation from the measurement point of view. Each item, while clearly belonging to one of the two major factors, is measuring something different from every other item. An interesting, if difficult to interpret, fact is that *A* (Progressivism) seems to be bipolar. *B*, too, may be slightly bipolar, but not as clearly as *A* is. Note that certain *B* items, Numbers 3, 12, and 18, are significantly and negatively loaded on *A*. Two of these three items (12 and 18) are about discipline, and one is on the three R's (Item 3). Another possible clue to some underlying phenomenon is the fact that these three items are also negatively loaded on Factor *C*, i.e., they lie very close

TABLE 1

UNROTATED AND ROTATED FACTOR LOADINGS OF ALL ITEMS, EDUCATION SCALE I*

	F Matrix				V Matrix			
Items	I	II	III	h^2	A	B	C	h^2
(A)								
1	241	314	255	222	440	010	167	222
2	103	373	153	173	386	—136	074	173
5	158	443	—119	236	416	—133	—210	235
7	130	408	—204	225	356	—135	—284	226
8	301	395	—173	277	450	011	—273	277
9	274	455	—025	283	512	—046	—134	282
15	316	479	—067	334	546	—026	—185	333
16	136	338	098	142	366	—089	022	142
17	108	589	234	413	577	—259	117	414
20	211	344	—198	202	352	—032	—277	202
(B)								
3	097	—460	—341	337	—379	349	—268	337
4	229	—329	161	187	—096	379	185	187
6	415	—316	—167	300	—046	522	—161	301
10	327	—393	142	282	—094	496	165	282
11	447	—373	091	347	—019	581	097	347
12	283	—535	—218	414	—305	544	—158	414
13	287	—418	246	318	—114	478	276	318
14	298	—289	213	218	—013	411	221	218
18	252	—542	—221	406	—330	523	—156	407
19	440	—477	109	433	—102	636	133	433

* All decimal points are omitted. Italics indicate significant loadings. Loadings above .30 were considered significant.

together in three-dimensional factor space. They also hang together in their item-total correlations. When they are correlated with the A factor totals, they all show substantial negative correlation. The only fairly safe interpretation that can be made now is that they are apparently an anti-A cluster, perhaps a discipline or "tightening-up-on-our-children" cluster. It should be noted, too, that these items showed the same pattern in the factor analysis of ES-II.

In sum, the factor analysis of ES-I shows that the 20 items belong to two main factors corresponding exactly to the original factor designations of the items in the Q studies, A and B, or Progressivism and Traditionalism. Two totally different procedures, then, produce the same factors. Some readers may say that this is an artifact of using the same

items. But this is the precise point we are trying to make. There is nothing in the present study, except the loaded items, of course, that necessarily dictates the emergence of the same two factors. There might have been four or five factors. Or the items might have emerged in the factor analysis in an entirely different pattern. The conclusion seems unmistakable that we have here two factors which seem to be "real." At least there can be no mistake about the clustering of the items: A items and B items form two almost independent, clear, and unmistakable clusters.

The ES-II item intercorrelations showed very much the same picture as those of ES-I, with one very important exception. As with the ES-I correlations, the A intercorrelations were all positive. The range was from .039 to .346 with a mean of .198. The B

items of ES-II, also like those of ES-I, correlate positively. They range from —.006 to .440; the mean r is .244. Again, we have the tendency for the B items to correlate somewhat higher than the A items, but the difference was not significant (t of .79). The correlations between the A items and the B items are, again as in ES-I, mostly negative (only one was positive) *and significant*. They range from —.517 to .032; the mean is —.220. Only eight of these were not significant at .05 as compared to the non-significance of one-third of the correlations of ES-I. Out of 45 A intercorrelations, four were not significant; and out of 45 B intercorrelations, one was not significant at .05. The parallel here between the ES-I and ES-II results is striking. The big difference between the results from the two scales is, therefore, in the AB correlations. Quite evidently A items are substantially correlated with B items in ES-II and not in ES-I.

These conclusions are confirmed more precisely by the factor analysis. Although efforts were made to rotate the ES-II factors, it was found that no solution was actually feasible without distorting the factor picture. In fact, it seemed that the factors were as much "in place" without rotation as they ever could be. The main reason the factors could not be rotated was the rather strong correlation between Factors A and B. Oblique rotations could have been resorted to, of course, but this would not have helped very much. At any rate, the factor loadings make sense as they stand. (Evidence of this is given by computing rank-order correlations between the item-total correlations of A and the A factor loadings and the item-total correlations of B and the B factor loadings. Both *rho*'s are .91. While this computation is not quite legitimate, since there is a spurious element contributed by the between groups variance of both variables, still it is some evidence that the factors are in place. These *rho*'s drop sharply after rotation.) Assuming, then, the correctness of the factor axes positions, it was clear that there was one rather pronounced bipolar factor, A, and two other

factors, B and C, neither of which seemed clearly interpretable. Factor A was a cross between Factors A and B of ES-I, its positive and negative ends consisting of significantly loaded A and B items, respectively. What were, in ES-I and in Q-Ed-1 and Q-Ed-2, two factors became, in ES-II, one bipolar factor, apparently an artifact of the spurious inter-item correlations of the rank-order forced-choice scale.

When the items of both ES-I and ES-II were intercorrelated and factor analyzed, a picture quite similar to that of the intercorrelations and factor analysis of ES-II appeared. Three factors again emerged. One rotation of Factors II and III sufficed to bring out the factor structure. Clear simple structure was again impossible. And only one factor seemed important, Factor A, which was bipolar, with all A items positively loaded and all B items negatively loaded.[5] Except for further confirmation of the factor structure of the items and some further insight into possible sub-clusters of items, no new information was added.

An interesting question can be asked of the data: How close together in factor space are the identical items of ES-I and ES-II? This question can be answered partially by inspection of the test-item factor plots. If we plot Factor A against Factor B, and A against C, we can determine whether the identical items of ES-I and ES-II lie close together in factor space. The criterion of closeness which was adopted, when the items were plotted on ten to the half-inch graph paper, was whether identical items were within ten of the smallest units of the paper (one-half inch) of each other. This was done for all pairs of items. The items were so numbered that identical items were 20 numbers apart, e.g., 1 and 21, 2 and 22, 14 and 34, and so on. When the distances between these

[5] The table of unrotated and rotated factor loadings resulting from the factor analysis of ES-I and ES-II together has been deposited with the American Documentation Institute. Order Document No. 5812 from the ADI Auxiliary Publications Project, Photoduplication Service, Library of Congress, Washington 25, D. C. . . . .

pairs were measured it was found that, in the A-B plot, only two pairs, 1–21 and 14–34, exceeded one-half inch (.14 and .11). On the A-C plot, only one pair, 14–34, exceeded a half-inch (.12). Two other pairs, 1–21 and 5–25, were exactly a half-inch (.10 and .10). Many of the pairs were practically at the same point in space (seven were .04 or less apart in the A-B plot, and nine were .04 or less apart in the A-C plot). Note that the same pairs, 1–21 and 14–34, exceeded or equaled the criterion on both plots. This agreement seems rather remarkable, especially when we remember that the items of ES-I and those of ES-II were imbedded in different contexts. Evidently the items have "factor space stability."

The final evidence on the validity of the attitude scales and items is summarized in Table 2 where the 10 A items, the 10 B items, the item-total correlations for both scales, and the rotated factor loadings of both factor analyses are given. It can be seen that all the A items of ES-I correlate positively and significantly with the total A scores; the range is .42 to .63. And, while all of the correlations of the A items with the total B scores are significant and negative, only one of them (No. 17) is of much consequence. (Correlations of .08 and .12 are significant at .05 and .01, respectively.) Thus, the A and B items of ES-I are correlated, but at so low a level that they can be considered relatively independent. (The best estimate of this correlation,

TABLE 2

A AND B ITEMS; FACTOR LOADINGS OF ITEMS; ITEM-TOTAL CORRELATIONS

A Items	Item-Total r's*		Factor Loadings†	
	A	B	A	B
1. The goals of education should be dictated by children's interests and needs, as well as by the larger demands of society.	.44 / .49	—.09 / —.35	.44 / —.42	.01
2. No subject is more important than the personalities of the pupils.	.48 / .50	—.21 / —.43	.39 / —.46	—.14
5. Teachers, like university professors, should have academic freedom—freedom to teach what they think is right and best.	.57 / .58	—.23 / —.43	.42 / —.54	—.13
7. Teachers should encourage pupils to study and criticize our own and other economic systems and practices.	.49 / .48	—.22 / —.35	.36 / —.43	—.14
8. The traditional moral standards of our culture should not just be accepted; they should be examined and tested in solving the present problems of students.	.53 / .61	—.12 / —.40	.45 / —.52	.01
9. Learning is experimental; the child should be taught to test alternatives before accepting them.	.59 / .53	—.17 / —.36	.51 / —.48	—.05
15. Education and educational institutions must be sources of new social ideas; education must be a social program undergoing continual reconstruction.	.60 / .56	—.16 / —.41	.55 / —.50	—.03
16. Right from the very first grade, teachers must teach the child at his own level and not at the level of the grade he is in.	.47 / .48	—.17 / —.28	.37 / —.35	—.09
17. Children should be allowed more freedom than they usually get in the execution of learning activities.	.63 / .55	—.36 / —.47	.58 / —.54	—.26
20. In a democracy, teachers should help students understand not only the meaning of democracy but also the meaning of the ideologies of other political systems.	.42 / .41	—.13 / —.25	.35 / —.31	—.03

TABLE 2—(*Continued*)

B Items	Item-Total r's*		Factor Loadings†		
	A	B	A		B
3. Schools of today are neglecting the three R's.	—.32	.47	—.38		.35
	—.46	.51		.52	
4. The pupil-teacher relationship is the relationship between a child who needs direction, guidance, and control and a teacher who is an expert supplying direction, guidance, and control.	—.18	.50	—.10		.38
	—.21	.41		.28	
6. The backbone of the school curriculum is subject matter; activities are useful mainly to facilitate the learning of subject matter.	—.09	.56	—.05		.52
	—.39	.57		.51	
10. The curriculum consists of subject matter to be learned and skills to be acquired.	—.21	.55	—.09		.50
	—.41	.57		.53	
11. The true view of education is so arranging learning that the child gradually builds up a storehouse of knowledge that he can use in the future.	—.13	.61	—.02		.58
	—.44	.59		.54	
12. One of the big difficulties with modern schools is that discipline is often sacrificed to the interests of the children.	—.32	.62	—.31		.54
	—.52	.55		.60	
13. The curriculum should contain an orderly arrangement of subjects that represent the best of our cultural heritage.	—.23	.54	—.11		.48
	—.33	.48		.41	
14. Discipline should be governed by long-range interests and well established standards.	—.13	.46	—.01		.41
	—.34	.50		.42	
18. Children need and should have more supervision and discipline than they usually get.	—.34	.61	—.33		.52
	—.49	.59		.59	
19. Learning is essentially a process of increasing one's store of information about the various fields of knowledge.	—.22	.68	—.10		.64
	—.44	.61		.56	

* The item-total correlations are product-moment *r*'s. The top line given after each item contains the item statistics of ES-I; the bottom line contains the statistics of ES-II. For example, .44 indicates the correlation of Item 1 on ES-I with the *A* total; —.09 indicates the correlation of Item 1 on ES-I with the *B* total. .49 indicates the correlation of Item 1 on ES-II with the *A* total.

† Note that only one factor loading is given for each item of ES-II. This is because the main factor of the factor analysis was bipolar. The signs can also be reversed, providing that, if they are reversed for *A* items, they are also reversed for *B* items.

computed from analysis of covariance, is —.24.)

The picture is similar with the item-total correlations of the *B* items. All are significant and positive; they range from .46 to .68. Again, all the correlations of the *B* items with total *A* scores are significant and negative, with three of them being appreciable (Nos. 3, 12, and 18). The evidence for relative independence is not as good as that for the *A* items, but still for practical purposes the correlation is low enough for the factors to be considered relatively independent. In sum, the item-total correlations of ES-I show that all items, as judged by correlation with

total scores, are valid. And the two factors, while not entirely independent, can be considered relatively independent. This is more true of the *A* items than of the *B* items.

Consideration of the item-total correlations of ES-II shows approximately equal correlations for all the items, both *A* and *B*. None is less than .40. But unlike those of ES-I the correlations of the *A* with the *B* items are negative and substantial. Again this is evidently the result of the rank-order forced-choice procedure discussed earlier, and is further evidence of this point and of the bipolar quality of ES-II.

In order to check on the adequacy of the rotations and on the agreement between the item-total correlations and the factor loadings, rank-order correlation coefficients were computed between the ES-I *A* item-total correlations and the ES-I *A* factor loadings. Similarly, *rho*'s were computed between ES-I *B* item-total correlations and the ES-I factor loadings. These two *rho*'s were .82 and .94, respectively. (*Rho*'s of .56 and .75 are needed for significance at .05 and .01, respectively.) Similar *rho*'s for ES-II were .91 and .91. (But in the latter case the loadings of only one factor, Factor *A*, previously described as bipolar, were used rather than the loadings of two separate factors.) This confirms the correctness of the decision not to rotate the ES-II factors. The correspondence between the rank orders of the factor loadings of ES-I and ES-II, while not as high, are still significant. They are .72 (.05) for ES-I *A* and ES-II *A*, and .78 (.01) for ES-I *B* and ES-II *B*.

CONCLUSIONS

The data seem to confirm the theoretical reasoning outlined earlier. Progressivism and Traditionalism seem to be real attitudinal factors. All the analyses, those of the two Q studies and those of this study, yield two relatively independent and orthogonal factors. The exception to this statement is ES-II which yielded, in place of the two factors, one bipolar factor, a result no doubt due to the forced-choice nature of ES-II. Evidently both ES-I and ES-II are valid measures of educational attitudes, if we examine them from the logical validity point of view. In comparing the Likert-type procedure with a rank-order forced-choice procedure, we find that the results from the Likert scale (ES-I) yielded a clear factor structure of two almost orthogonal factors. Every item in ES-I performed as it should; there were no exceptions. And, while the forced-choice ranking of ES-II may have avoided some of the social desirability phenomenon difficulty that is undoubtedly present in any Likert-type scale, it introduced spurious correlation among the items, and thus is theoretically less satisfying than the Likert-type procedure.

Finally, it would seem that following Stephenson's suggestion for the construction of questionnaires is a fruitful and valuable approach to the construction of attitude scales. If the evidence from this study is representative of other possible attitudinal studies, it would seem that scale construction could be considerably improved and facilitated in this manner. One, Q methodology evidently can, in some cases, be used in place of, or rather, prior to, the usual type of factor analysis (so-called R methodology) and the usual type of item analysis as a potent logical validity tool. Two, Q methodology is a much quicker, simpler, more economical, and perhaps better procedure than the usual intercorrelations of a number of tests using a large number of subjects—at least in situations similar to the one reported here. And it is probably a theoretically sounder procedure than the usual item analytic one. Whether the procedure and the reasoning behind it will hold up in other fields and with other types of scales is, of course, not known. But the present data seem to indicate that items may have intrinsic factor validity which is an absolute sort of thing.

In short, it seems that the very formidable validity problem of attitude scales can be in part conquered by some such procedure as that used in this study. The approach need not, of course, be limited to Q sorts. For example, judges can be used in the Thurstone fashion, and the judges' judgments intercorrelated and factor analyzed. Other possibilities will no doubt occur to the reader. The main point is that some attempt should be made, *before* the usual type of item analysis is used, to solve the logical validity problem in an objective and statistical fashion. Some attempt should be made, in brief, to identify the factors behind the attitudes being measured before constructing and administering attitude scales. Otherwise, psychological and educational measurement falls victim to the "mindless empiricism" criticism of the philosophers. Procedures like Thurstone's,

Likert's, and Guttman's, while effective in identifying "good" items and, in the Guttman case, in attaining unidimensionality, are severely limited. The Thurstone and Likert methods are limited in that, in and of themselves, they give little or no clue to the factors behind the attitudes being measured (unless, naturally, the items are intercorrelated and factor analyzed). Moreover, they are perhaps often multidimensional, and thus conceal the true nature of the variables presumably being measured. The Guttman procedure is limited in that we emerge from it with very short scales of extremely homogeneous items which probably rarely tap much of the richness of any complex attitude structure. The approach is oversimplified, so to speak. It assumes, much as McNemar seems to assume (3), that unidimensional attitudes (factors?) are simple units which, if put together, will form the complex attitudes which people hold toward cognitive objects. This may be fairly true of attitudes toward simple cognitive objects, but it is probably not true of attitudes toward relatively complex cognitive objects like education, social issues, religion, and the like. At the very least, more attempts should be made to solve the validity problem in attitudinal research. Until investigators know what they *are* measuring rather than what they *think* they are measuring, further developments of attitude measurement and the psychology of attitudes can hardly be expected.

REFERENCES

1. Kerlinger, F. N.
   1956 "The attitude structure of the individual: a Q-study of the educational attitudes of professors and laymen." Genetic Psychology Monographs, LIII:283–329.
2. Kerlinger, F. N.
   1958 "Progressivism and traditionalism: basic factors of educational attitudes." Journal of Social Psychology XLVIII:111–135.
3. McNemar, Q.
   1946 "Opinion-attitude methodology." Psychological Bulletin, XLIII:289–374.
4. Stephenson, W.
   1953 The Study of Behavior. Chicago: The University of Chicago Press.
5. Stouffer, S. A., et al.
   1950 Measurement and Prediction. Vol. IV. Princeton: Princeton University Press.

CHAPTER 16

Multiple Scalogram Analysis: A Set-Theoretic Model for Analyzing Dichotomous Items[1]

JAMES C. LINGOES

Among the various criticisms that have been directed against the scaling technique of Guttman (1944), a major one has been in reference to his concept of a "universe of content" (see, for example, Festinger [1947] and Loevinger [1948]). This particular concept lies at the basis for item construction and selection in Guttman's scalogram method. Quite generally what is meant by this phrase is the set of all statements which may be made in reference to a *single* variable or trait, as for example, "love of country," "morale," "motherliness," etc. The crucial part of this broad definition rests in the undefined term "single." The lack of a clear meaning for the important concept of a "universe of content" and the absence of definitive rules for selecting items relevant to the universe have presented both conceptual and practical prob-

From James C. Lingoes, "Multiple scalogram analysis: a set-theoretic model for analyzing dichotomous items," *Educational and Psychological Measurement,* XXIII, Autumn 1963, 501–523. Reproduced by permission of author and publisher.

[1] The author wishes to express his appreciation to Professors C. F. Wrigley, C. H. Coombs, and J. E. Milholland for their helpful comments and criticisms in the preparation of this paper. He would also like to acknowledge the cooperation of Professor R. C. F. Bartels for making the IBM 704/709/7090 computing facilities freely available for the development and testing of the method.

lems standing in the way of a fuller acceptance and a wider application of Guttman's scale analysis.

Another, and equally important, criticism has been directed against the criterion of reproducibility (Festinger, 1947). It would be desirable to have something more than a rule of thumb for guarding against spuriously high reproducibilities as a function of extreme marginal values.

This paper will present a completely objective and empirical procedure for selecting dichotomous items which meet the Guttman scaling criteria. The data are, in effect, permitted to "speak for themselves," without imposing restrictions in advance of our exploring just what, if any, universes or domains are involved. We wish to propose a method of analysis which will extend Guttman's method to the determination of multiple dimensions for dichotomous variables.

The MSA Method

In brief, the Multiple Scalogram Analysis (MSA) method involves selecting an item from the set to be analyzed, finding that item among the remaining items which is most like it and having the fewest errors, determining the number of errors between the candidate item and all of its predecessors, and, finally, applying a statistical test of significance to adjacent item pairs. If both the error and statistical criteria are satisfied, then the item that last entered the scale is used to find an item most like it, etc. Whenever either the error or statistical criterion fails, however, the scale is terminated and another scale is started with a new item chosen from among those that remain, until that point is reached where the item set is exhausted. All items are forced into a positive manifold and monotonicity of item marginals is insisted upon. Once an item enters a scale, it is no longer considered for membership in other scales, i.e., a single classificatory system is employed for items in R-technique and for subjects in Q.

The remainder of this paper will be concerned with definitions of terms, a logical exposition of the objective criteria proposed for linking items and for testing the scale hypothesis, proofs that the method will converge to any level of homogeneity desired, a more detailed presentation of the MSA algorithm, the assumptions underlying the model, examples of analyses, and some critical observations on the advantages and limitations of the proposed method.

The MSA Criteria

If one examines a perfect Guttman scale (see Table 1) and some measures based upon it, several important properties of this matrix of items and subjects are evident. The first class of properties of this matrix will be exploited for bringing items into the scale matrix, i.e., to provide the basis for the *linking criteria,* while the second class will provide us with a statistical concept of reproducibility.

The Linking Criteria

First, the matrix of *phi*-coefficients for the inter-item relationships will form a *positive manifold,* i.e., all of the items will be positively related to each other. Second, the marginal frequencies will be ordered from high to low, i.e., *monotonicity* of item marginals will prevail. Third, the *distance* between adjacent and distinct sets will be *minimal,* as measured by the symmetric set difference (Restle, 1959), i.e., adjacent items will be more like one another than they will be like more remote items. Fourth, *errors* (01s) will be *minimal* for given distances. Although several additional properties of such scales could be listed, e.g., the super-diagonal form of the matrix of *phi*-coefficients or the tri-diagonal form of the inverse of the correlation matrix, these attributes are not directly germane to establishing the criteria used in MSA.

The above four properties of a perfect Guttman scale provide the basis for bringing items together (linking) in the MSA technique. They are intended to substitute for the ranking methods used in scalogram analysis. The symbolic statement of these criteria receive meaning from the cell and marginal designations of Table 2.

(1) $$A \geq \frac{(A+B)(A+D)}{N},$$

or

$$AC \geq BD,$$

the criterion of positive manifold;

(2) $$A + B \geq A + D,$$

or

$$B \geq D,$$

the criterion of monotonicity;

(3) $$(B+D)_{min},$$

the criterion of minimum distances between items or sets; and

TABLE 1

A PERFECT GUTTMAN SCALE

	\multicolumn{5}{c}{Item}					
S	1	2	3	4	5	Score
1	1	1	1	1	1	5
2	1	1	1	1	0	4
3	1	1	1	0	0	3
4	1	1	0	0	0	2
5	1	0	0	0	0	1
6	0	0	0	0	0	0
Sum	5	4	3	2	1	

TABLE 2

A CONTINGENCY TABLE

		j		
		0	1	
i	1	B	A	A+B
	0	C	D	C +D
		B + C	A + D	N

(4) $\qquad D_{min}$,

the criterion of minimum errors within equal distances, i.e., ties in (3) are broken on the basis of the D or error cell. The third and fourth criteria used lexigraphically can be shown to be equivalent to minimizing:

$$[(B + D)^2 + D].$$

The foregoing criteria are necessary but not sufficient conditions for insuring a maximally homogeneous scale. A fifth criterion is required to specify the limits within which one will accept the scale hypothesis and to guard against the possibility of producing a very heterogeneous scale by paying attention to adjacent items only.

The Reproducibility Criterion

In this section we will develop a measure of homogeneity or scalability which will completely specify the bounds of interrelationship existing among all items of a scale. As a background and transition to this development, however, we will first explicate the concept of reproducibility as advanced by Guttman and point out some of its shortcomings.

Guttman has suggested that the *coefficient of reproducibility* (REP) be .90 or above as one of the chief criteria for accepting the scale hypothesis, where REP ". . . is secured by counting up the number of responses which would have been predicted wrongly for each person on the basis of his scale score, dividing these errors by the total number of responses and subtracting the resulting fraction from 1" (in Stouffer, *et al.,* 1950, p. 77), i.e.:

$$(5) \qquad REP = 1 - \frac{\text{Sum of Errors}}{\text{Total Responses}}.$$

The difficulty involved in this formulation is that the manner of counting errors is not made explicit in the measure. Suchman (in Stouffer, *et al.,* 1950), in discussing the scalogram procedure, suggested the use of cut-off points for determining the error count. The method of ranking both respondents and items, however, because of possible tied ranks, may result in varying, albeit small, discrepancies from judge to judge as to the amount of error involved in any given scale.

Goodenough (1944) has recommended a double-counting procedure for errors (counting 1's that should have been 0's and v.v.), which has been re-formulated by Lingoes (1960b) as a set-measure. This conceptualization has the advantage of clearly specifying the error count without relying upon ranked data and, more importantly, it permits a generalization of reproducibility in terms of correlation. The proposed measure is:

$$(6) \qquad REP = 1 - \frac{\sum_i \sum_j |O_{ij} - G_{ij}|}{nm},$$
$$(i = 1, \cdots, n; j = 1, \cdots, m),$$
where:

$n =$ the number of subjects;

$m =$ the number of items;

$O =$ the $n \times m$ *observed* binary matrix of subjects and items;

$G =$ the $n \times m$ error-free Guttman matrix, which has been matched with O on the basis of the n row marginals (subject scores), where "error-free" is defined as a matrix having the following three properties: a) there are never more than two runs or sequences of 1's and 0's in any row; b) if there are two runs in any row, the ordering of 1's and 0's is consistent for all rows with two runs; and c) O and G are monotonically consistent;

$i =$ the rows (subject responses across items) of O and G; and

$j =$ the columns (item responses across subjects) of O and G.

The numerator of (6) is actually the sum of the distances between corresponding rows of O and G over all subjects. This measure of reproducibility is mathematically equivalent to the common elements formula of the product-moment correlation coefficient as applied to two binary matrices (cell-for-cell matching). This equivalence can be easily demonstrated by noting that the number of common elements plus the sum of the distances is equal to the total number of responses.

Rather than use (6) on O directly, since one or more items may have disproportionate amounts of error and yet REP be .90 or more, it is necessary that the fifth criterion be developed on *all* item pairs in the scale matrix. In the special case where $m = 2$, the fourfold table relating any two items of O, say items i and j, as in Table 2, is sufficient to calculate REP, i.e., (6) reduces to:

$$(7) \qquad REP = 1 - \frac{D}{N}.$$

By requiring $D \leq \epsilon N$, i.e., some constant proportion of N, for *every* pair of items, i and j in O, there can be at most $m - 1$ independent sources of error, since the first item of a scale is by definition error-free. We can thus calculate the lower bound of REP, i.e., α, for a matrix of m items by the following formula:

$$(8) \qquad \alpha = 1 - \frac{2\epsilon(m - 1)}{m}.$$

As $m \to \infty$, $\alpha \to 1 - 2\epsilon$, and,therefore, we can specify to whatever degree desired (by making ϵ sufficiently small) the limits within which we will accept the scale hypothesis. For example, setting $\epsilon = .10$ would insure that every pair of items, i and j in O, would be correlated (by common elements) with the corresponding items in G to the extent of at least .90 and, furthermore, the entire matrix O would be correlated with G at a level of .80 or more. To guarantee a REP of .90 for O, it would be necessary to set the upper bound of D at .05N. Empirical evidence would indicate, however, that such a criterion is unnecessarily restrictive and that quite respectable REPs can be obtained with the criterion of .10N. The REP calculated by (6), it might be mentioned, is a more conservative measure, as pointed out by Edwards (1957), than is typically obtained by the ranking method of counting errors.

Although one could use $D \leq .10N$ as the fifth criterion, a more general model is suggested based upon the *phi*-coefficient. Indeed, it will be shown that REP and ϕ are related in a rather simple manner under special conditions. Let us first develop the formula for ϕ on two items from O and the corresponding pair from G, where the pair of items i and j in O are, in effect, treated as one item and the pair from G is treated as the other.

The formula for the product-moment correlation for dichotomous items (following the notation of Table 2) is given by:

$$(9)$$
$$\phi_{ij} = \frac{AC - BD}{\sqrt{(A + B)(C + D)(B + C)(A + D)}}.$$

In the special case where the marginals are equal ($p_i = p_j$), (9) simplifies to:

$$(10) \qquad \phi_{ij} = \frac{AC - D^2}{(A + B)(C + D)},$$

which is the scheme of the formula wanted for pairs of items from both O and G, since they are matched matrices, i.e., the proportions of 1's and 0's in O equal those for G.

The cells and marginals for the fourfold table relating two items from O and two from G by cell-for-cell matching can be calculated from the table relating items i and j in O as follows:

$$(11) \qquad B_{og} = D_{og} = D_{ij},$$

$$(12) \qquad (A + B)_{og} = (A + D)_{og} = (A + B)_{ij} + (A + D)_{ij},$$

$$(13) \qquad (C + D)_{og} = (B + C)_{og} = (C + D)_{ij} + (B + C)_{ij},$$

$$(14) \qquad N_{og} = 2N_{ij},$$

$$(15) \qquad A_{og} = (A + B)_{og} - D_{ij},$$

and

$$(16) \qquad C_{og} = (C + D)_{og} - D_{ij}.$$

Now substituting the known quantities relating items i and j of (11) through (16) into (10) and replacing ϕ_{ij} by ϕ_{og}, we have:

(17)

$$\phi_{og} = \frac{[(A+B)_{ij} + (A+D)_{ij} - D_{ij}]}{[(A+B)_{ij} + (A+D)_{ij}]} \cdot \frac{[(C+D)_{ij} + (B+C)_{ij} - D_{ij}] - D_{ij}^2}{[(C+D)_{ij} + (B+C)_{ij}]}.$$

Dropping the subscripts ij, which are implied in the following equations, and simplifying the bracketed terms, (17) becomes:

(18) $\phi_{og} = \dfrac{(2A+B)(2C+B) - D^2}{(2A+B+D)(2C+B+D)}.$

A little algebra will show that (18) reduces to:

(19)

$$\phi_{og} = 1 - \frac{2ND}{(2A+B+D)(2C+B+D)}.$$

As both of the terms in the denominator of (19) approach N, ϕ_{og} approaches a maximum for a given value of D and as D approaches $N/2$ (its maximum, since $B \geq D$, the criterion of monotonicity), ϕ_{og} approaches zero. Thus, the relationship between pairs of items from O and from G varies between 0 and 1, as does REP. When each of the denominator terms of (19) equals N, i.e., when $A = C$, (19) reduces to:

(20) $\qquad \phi_{og} = 1 - \dfrac{2D}{N}.$

Solving for D in both (7) and (20) we can thus state the relationship between REP and ϕ_{og} in the two item case as:

(21) $\qquad \phi_{og} = 2(REP - .5),$

when the sum of positive endorsements (or negative) for items i and $j = N$.

Formula (19) suggests a more sensitive criterion than $D \leq .10N$, inasmuch that for a given level of ϕ_{og}, the number of errors would approach zero as one of the marginals $(A + D)$ or $(C + D)$ of O approached unity. We could thus take a fixed lower limit of ϕ_{og} as a criterion, which would yield varying values of REP as a function of the item

marginals. Solving for D in (19), we would obtain:

(22)

$$D = \frac{(1 - \phi_{og})(2A + B + D)(2C + B + D)}{2N},$$

for any two items of O. If we set our criterion for $\phi_{og} = .80$, then (22) would become:

(23)

$$D \leq \frac{.1(2A + B + D)(2C + B + D)}{N},$$

for all item pairs in O.

The lower bound of REP, α, now becomes a function of m, D, and the marginals of items $1, \cdots, m$, approaching .80 as a limit as $m \to \infty$, $D \to .10N$, and the item proportions $p_1, \cdots, p_m \to .5$. Equation (23) thus permits one to calculate the lower bound of REP for any given set of marginal values and a fixed N by inserting the proper D values in the following expression:

(24)

$$\alpha = 1 - \frac{2\sum_i (A_i)}{Nm}, (i = 1, \cdots, m - 1),$$

where: $A_i =$ the D value of the ith pair of adjacent items in O.

Thus, for example, if one had nine items with positive response proportions of: .9, .8, .7, .6, .5, .4, .3, .2, and .1 and $N = 100$, the $m - 1 A_i$'s would be: 5.1, 7.5, 9.1, 9.9, 9.9, 9.1, 7.5, and 5.1. These D values when rounded and summed would equal 64, which would have to be doubled since:

(25) $\quad \sum_i (A_i) = .5[\sum_j \sum_k |O_{jk} - G_{jk}|],$
$(i = 1, \cdots, m - 1; j = 1, \cdots, n;$
$k = 1, \cdots, m),$

when errors are independent. Substituting the obtained values of errors in (24) we have:

(26) $\qquad \alpha = 1 - \dfrac{2 \times 64}{100 \times 9} = .858,$

which contrasts with the value obtained by applying the uniform criterion of $D \leq .10N$, i.e., $\alpha = .822$, approximately.

To conclude this topic on the fifth criterion

of reproducibility, we have: a) provided a statistical measure which is sensitive to differences in item marginals, i.e., (19), b) shown the functional relationships between the set-measure implicit in Goodenough's method of counting errors, the common elements correlation coefficient, and the *phi*-coefficient, c) given equations, i.e., (8) and (24), for calculating the lower bound for *REP* for a given set of items and a fixed *N*, and, as a consequence, completely specified the limits of homogeneity for all item pairs in the scale, and finally, d) demonstrated that the systematic application of the here proposed fifth criterion, i.e., (22) will converge to whatever level of homogeneity desired for any set of items by making ϕ_{og} sufficiently large and inserting the calculated *D*'s in (24).

Before detailing the MSA algorithm, a tentative sixth criterion might be added in the nature of a statistical test. Such a test would be desirable as a protection against accepting the scale hypothesis when either *N* is too small or the marginals are too extreme.

The Statistical Criterion

The problem of selecting the most appropriate statistical test is a difficult one and depends to a considerable extent on what assumptions you wish to make and equally importantly on what questions you are asking (Goodman, 1959; Sagi, 1959). The entire question is further complicated by the fact that "the conditions under which tests of significance apply define prior admissible scaling operations. Conversely, different scaling operations usually imply different sampling distributions of the evaluative statistic. The implication is immediately apparent: either scaling operations are restricted to those operations consistent with developed statistical tests, or extensive replication is used as a substitute testing procedure" (Sagi, 1959, p. 26). Integral to the scaling operations proposed, we would like an answer to the following question: Given the observed item marginals of the *m*-1 adjacent item pairs for each MSA

scale, what, under the assumption of independence, are the probabilities of obtaining the observed *D* values?

A special computer program was written to match the item marginals in several empirical matrices, randomly assigning 1's and 0's, and 1,000 samplings were made for each pair of adjacent items. The distribution of errors was found to be hypergeometric for which Fisher's exact test is appropriate. The computation of exact probabilities, even with computers, is a slow process when *N* is large. Consequently, the chi square approximation was settled upon at a level of .001 as the sixth criterion, since this test is sensitive to both sample size and marginal values.

The MSA Algorithm[2]

Although the MSA method is rather simple computationally, a moderately sized sample of subjects and items, say one hundred of each, could be both expensive and time-consuming. Programmed for a high-speed computer, however, time and expense are small indeed (Lingoes, 1962a). The steps outlined below, with their associated comments, constitute the MSA algorithm.

Step 1—Matrix preparation: Having selected the items to be analyzed, set the responses out in matrix form, where the rows represent subjects (1, . . . , *n*) and the columns, items (1, . . . , *m*). There are no restrictions on the specificity or generality of the set of items. They must, however, be in dichoto-

---

[2] The method as reported in this article differs from that of the basic work (Lingoes, 1960b; 1961) in the following fundamental respects: a) (23) was substituted for $D \leq .10N$; b) the criterion of a positive relationship was changed from $A + C \geq N/2$ to $AC \geq BD$; c) previously ties were broken by choosing that item having marginal values closest to preceding items, which stands in contrast with the present fourth criterion; d) the second criterion of monotonicity was not insisted upon in the earlier version; e) unanimous items were excluded in the present model but not in the original; f) three or more items formerly were required to define a scale, which has been changed to two or more; and g) an additional, ancillary statistical test has now been incorporated in the process of scale formation, which was done after the fact in the first version.

mous form. "Trues," "passes," "yeses," etc., are generally denoted by a "1," while their opposites are represented by a "0."

Step 2—Matrix reflection: Calculate the number of positive responses (*Sum*) for each item, eliminating unanimous items and reflecting (ones-complementing) all items whose marginals are less than $n/2$. The marginal sums of all reflected items simply become $n - Sum$.

Step 3—Scale initialization: Choose that item with the largest marginal *Sum*, breaking ties arbitrarily, as the initial item of any scale, by-passing items that have previously entered scales or have remained unclassified by virtue of failing either the reproducibility or statistical criterion. If all items have been scaled or accounted for, the analysis is completed, otherwise proceed.

Given a set of items which form a perfect unidimensional scale, the largest set of items will be included in a scale when the scale is started with items from either of the two extremes (see Table 1). For example, if one started with the $m/2^{th}$ (middle) item, this would bring in the $m/2 + 1^{st}$ item, which would, in turn, link with the $m/2 + 2^{nd}$ item, etc., until the mth item entered the scale. Linking this last item with any of the remaining items would either break the monotonic decreasing series of item marginals or would introduce error. On the other hand, starting with either the first or last item would perfectly reconstruct the scale, one the mirror image of the other. Based on this logic, extreme starting points will yield larger, fewer, and more reproducible scales than any other point. An investigation of several empirical matrices, starting at every possible point (with reflection and without), has confirmed the soundness of this heuristic.

Step 4—Item chaining: After forming the 2×2 tables whose members are the last item that successfully entered the scale and each of the remaining items in turn, calculate: $B + D$ for all pairings where $AC \geq BD$, skipping over any items where $B < D$, or if $AC < BD$, calculate $A + C$ and by-pass pairings where $A < C$. On the basis of these cal-

culations, choose that item as the candidate for the scale which has the smallest distance with its immediate predecessor (breaking ties on the basis of the D or C cell, respectively, for the two cases). If no candidate can be found, return to *Step 3*, otherwise continue.

Step 5—Scale termination: a) If any

$$D < \frac{.1(2A + B + D)(2C + B + D)}{N}$$

for the 2×2 tables formed from the candidate item and all of its predecessors in the scale (making the necessary substitutions in the case of a negative relationship), terminate the scale and return to *Step 3*; otherwise make the following statistical test.

b) If $\chi^2 < 10.83$ (representing a probability at or less than .001), between the candidate item and its immediate predecessor, terminate the scale and go back to *Step 3*; otherwise proceed.

c) If $AC < BD$, reflect the candidate item and return to *Step 4*; otherwise go to *Step 4* directly.

The above five steps represent a complete MSA. If one desires to calculate *REP*s for the matrix of scales, for the individual scales, items, or subjects, one can do so at this point. The logic of the MSA technique, however, in no way depends upon their calculation. The computer program (Lingoes, 1962a) prints out all but the item *REP*s. In addition, the program provides an option for subdividing the sample of subjects on the basis of an error analysis, thus making possible multiple classification as well as single. The intercorrelation of scale scores can be used for testing the independence of the derived MSA scales.

As can be seen from the above description, MSA is a stepwise procedure for obtaining homogeneous classes of variables, which differs in both philosophy and method from either Guttman's scalogram technique or the exhaustive, combinatorial method of Schutz (1961).

Prior to giving some illustrative examples of MSA scales, a brief excursion will be made into some of the underlying assumptions of the model and how it compares with Gutt-man's method.

The MSA Model

The basic approach of MSA can be consid-ered to be *typo-dimensional* (after McQuitty, 1955). Items are analyzed in such a way (di-mensionalized) as to discover the basic align-ments or groupings of subjects (typology) in respect to the items entering a scale. Of course, the converse is true for Q-analysis. The technique was derived in connection with an analysis of senatorial voting behavior (Lingoes, 1960b), but was found to have wider generality. For instance, one could con-sider individuals lying at the extremes of a dimension defined by MMPI items as having the same logical status as oppositely voting senators on a particular set of issues, e.g., farm related. That is to say, in both instances, that involving senators and that of a mixed sample of patients and community subjects, a *latent class* (Lazersfeld, 1950) or a *type* (Mc-Quitty, 1957) is tentatively defined. For sub-sets of items in a unidimensional scale, an hierarchy can be determined, where align-ments change as more and more extreme items or issues are encountered. We thus have, in effect, a dimensionalization of types.

The MSA model is completely determi-nistic like Guttman's (Torgerson, 1958) and assumes that the items to be analyzed are either of the cumulative type or can be made to conform to the characteristics of such monotone items. It is further assumed that the directional nature of the items is a matter for investigation rather than fiat. Like factor analysis, items are brought together regard-less of their direction, the magnitude of the relationship and concordance with the model being the primary considerations. Unlike factor analysis, however, the method is not bound to linear assumptions about the regres-sions involved and does not insist upon mu-tually high or clustered relationships among all the members of the set of variables defin-ing a dimension.

MSA and Scalogram Analysis

Multiple scalogram analysis differs from Guttman's scalogram analysis in several im-portant respects. First, the concept of a "uni-verse of content" is not necessary to MSA, as it is to Guttman's method. This issue is by-passed by allowing the data to form whatever relationships are implicit, consistent with the logical and statistical requirements of the procedure. Although scales are constructed independently of any a priori considerations of meaningfulness, MSA results in scales which have, however, all the statistical prop-erties of unidimensional scales, but obviates the possible criticism of having selected or constructed items which have the greatest probability of fitting the Guttman model. In other words, a model is tested rather than imposed.

Another important difference between the two methods lies in the fact that Guttman uses what might be called a piecemeal ap-proach, i.e., an experimenter selects a set of items as pertinent to some "universe," tests for dimensionality, and if certain criteria are met, accepts the universe as being scalable. If he desires to test another set of items for scal-ability, the above procedure is repeated. MSA, on the other hand, takes a sample of items and attempts to minimize the number of scales for a given set of relationships.

The above differences between MSA and scalogram analysis can be summarized by stating that MSA: a) is *empirical* rather than rational in determining scale membership; b) has the capacity for yielding *multiple* scales when the data demand it, rather than rejecting the scale hypothesis for the set when treated as a whole; and c) has a *statistical* rather than an heuristic decision basis for both grouping items and for testing the scale hypothesis.

MSA Examples

In this section two illustrations of MSAs will be provided covering a hypothetical and an empirical matrix.

A hypothetical two-dimensional case—
The first example is a hypothetical "1,0" data matrix, whose underlying dimensionality is two. The problem posed for the MSA method is to recover these two unidimensional scales such that from a knowledge of the order of the items and the subjects' scores all item responses could be reproduced without error.

Given the data matrix appearing in Table 3, a standard scalogram analysis of these eight

TABLE 3

A Hypothetical Two-space Matrix

S	Item							
	1	2	3	4	5	6	7	8
1	1	0	0	1	0	0	1	1
2	0	0	1	1	0	1	0	0
3	1	0	0	0	1	1	0	0
4	1	0	1	1	0	1	1	0
5	1	1	0	0	1	1	0	1
6	0	0	1	1	0	1	1	0
7	1	0	0	1	0	1	0	0
8	1	0	0	0	1	0	0	1
9	1	0	1	0	1	1	0	0
10	1	0	0	1	1	1	0	1
11	1	0	0	1	1	0	0	1
12	1	0	0	1	1	1	0	0
13	0	1	1	0	1	1	0	0
14	1	0	0	1	0	1	0	1
15	1	1	1	0	1	1	0	0
16	1	0	0	1	0	1	1	0
17	1	1	0	0	1	0	0	1
18	0	0	1	1	1	1	0	0
19	1	0	0	0	1	1	0	1
20	1	0	1	1	0	1	0	0
21	1	0	0	1	0	0	0	1
22	1	0	0	1	0	1	1	1
23	1	1	0	0	1	1	0	0
24	1	0	1	1	1	1	0	0
25	0	0	1	0	1	1	0	0

items and 25 subjects resulted in a *REP* of .70, which was identical to the *minimal marginal reproducibility* (*MMR*) of the matrix, the lower bound for *REP* based upon modal item marginals. This latter coefficient is simply calculated by summing the values appearing in the row *Sum* of the reflected score matrix and dividing by the product *nm* (the

number of subjects times the number of items). *MMR* represents the reproducibility of the matrix using a knowledge of the item proportions only. Thus, for example, one could reproduce at least 80 per cent of the responses to the first item in Table 3 by knowing that this item had an 80/20 split. The verdict of a scalogram analysis in the present instance was that these eight items do not form a scale, i.e., do not represent a single universe of content.

Rather than either discarding these items as nonscalable or manipulating them by combining items, there exist other alternatives, e.g., multiple factor analysis, a nonmetric factor analysis (Coombs & Kao, 1955), Loevinger's method of homogeneous tests (1948), etc. Results and a discussion of these alternatives can be found elsewhere (Lingoes, 1960b; Wilkins and Wrigley, 1961; Wilkins, 1962) and will, therefore, not receive detailed treatment here. Suffice it to say that each of these methods has its own associated problems when presented with a matrix such as that appearing in Table 3, e.g., yielding more complex solutions. A MSA of this matrix, however, recovered the two orthogonal unidimensional scales depicted in Table 4 with a *REP* = 1.00.

Items 3 and 6, in the first scale, and 2 and 5, in the second, were reflected in the process of achieving these scales. Although the scales in the present example were orthogonal, such a result is not in general to be expected. More often than not correlated scales are obtained empirically, requiring other techniques, such as factor analysis, to settle the issue of dimensionality (Lingoes, 1962b; 1962d). Lest it be concluded that in this event the MSA procedure is an unnecessary preliminary, the reader is reminded that a factor analysis at the item level for a set of scalable items will overestimate the true dimensionality by producing "difficulty factors." MSA is a data-reduction method operating on the actual responses (manifest structure) rather than employing some abstraction from the data as represented by correlation coefficients and factor loadings. These are some of the rea-

TABLE 4

Two Orthogonal Guttman Scales

S	1 3 8 6	Item Score	2 4 5 7	Score
1	1 1 1 1	4	1 1 1 1	4
2	0 0 0 0	0	1 1 1 0	3
3	1 1 0 0	2	1 0 0 0	1
4	1 0 0 0	1	1 1 1 1	4
5	1 1 1 0	3	0 0 0 0	0
6	0 0 0 0	0	1 1 1 1	4
7	1 1 0 0	2	1 1 1 0	3
8	1 1 1 1	4	1 0 0 0	1
9	1 0 0 0	1	1 0 0 0	1
10	1 1 1 0	3	1 1 0 0	2
11	1 1 1 1	4	1 1 0 0	2
12	1 1 0 0	2	1 1 0 0	2
13	0 0 0 0	0	0 0 0 0	0
14	1 1 1 0	3	1 1 1 0	3
15	1 0 0 0	1	0 0 0 0	0
16	1 1 0 0	2	1 1 1 1	4
17	1 1 1 1	4	0 0 0 0	0
18	0 0 0 0	0	1 1 0 0	2
19	1 1 1 0	3	1 0 0 0	1
20	1 0 0 0	1	1 1 1 0	3
21	1 1 1 1	4	1 1 1 0	3
22	1 1 1 0	3	1 1 1 1	4
23	1 1 0 0	2	0 0 0 0	0
24	1 0 0 0	1	1 1 0 0	2
25	0 0 0 0	0	1 0 0 0	1

sons why the qualifier "multiple" rather than "multidimensional" was used in the name of the technique. If orthogonal scales exist in the data, the method is adequate to produce them, but an oblique structure for partially-ordered data is the more likely result. The method can be characterized as yielding results which lie somewhere between the raw data (in its fineness of detail) and factor analysis (with its emphasis on the gross outlines of structure).

Voting behavior—As an empirical example, two of six MSA scales will be presented based upon fifty selected voting issues for 88 Senators of the 83rd United States Congress (Lingoes, 1960b). This time, however, the analysis will be done in Q-technique since most of us know more about senators than

TABLE 5

A Guttman Scale of U.S. Senators, No. 1

Senator	Percent-Yes
Humphrey, Hubert H. (D Minn.)	96
Murray, James E. (D Mont.)	96
Jackson, Henry M. (D Wash.)	94
Mansfield, Mike (D Mont.)	92
Kefauver, Estes (D Tenn.)	88
Symington, Stuart (D Mo.)	86
Hennings, Thomas C., Jr. (D Mo.)	86
Kerr, Robert S. (D Okla.)	80
Clements, Earle C. (D Ky.)	72
George, Walter F. (D Ga.)	68
McClellan, John L. (D Ark.)	62
Smathers, George A. (D Fla.)	62
Holland, Spessard L. (D Fla.)	46
Byrd, Harry Flood (D Va.)	36
Bush, Prescott (R Conn.)	30
Flanders, Ralph E. (R Vt.)	30
Knowland, William F. (R Calif.)	30
Bridges, Styles (R N.H.)	30
Hickenlooper, Bourke B. (R Iowa)	30
Dirksen, Everett M. (R Ill.)	28

about the issues on which they vote. The two scales selected for illustration appear in Tables 5 and 6.

The *REP* for the first scale of 20 senators was .959, while that for the second scale of five was .967. The *MMRs* were .761 and .916, respectively. A plausible interpretation of the first scale is that it represents the left-right or liberalism-conservatism dimension of U. S. Senators. The second scale, however, contained members who were at one pole of this dimension only, i.e., liberal Democrats. The ordering in these two scales appeared reason-

TABLE 6

A Guttman Scale of U.S. Senators, No. 2

Senator	Percent-Yes
Magnuson, Warren G. (D Wash.)	94
Morse, Wayne (I Ore.)	92
Monroney, A.S. Mike (D Okla.)	92
Hill, Lister (D Ala.)	92
Sparkman, John J. (D Ala.)	88

able enough, confirming that the MSA method is particularly appropriate in the area of legislative voting (see, for example, Brown, 1962; Brown and Wrigley, 1961; Knudsen, 1962; Lingoes, 1960b; 1962b; 1962d).

Before concluding, it might be noted that the fifty issues forming the basis for the above analysis were selected from a larger set of 128 roll call votes. The means for selecting these 50 items was provided by an error analysis. These 50 items were, as a consequence, those which contained relatively little error, i.e., had $REPs \geq .90$. Such a selection process introduces additional problems of interpretation, e.g., a Q-analysis on all 128 issues would show a negative relationship between the poles of this dimension. What then do the 50 items have in common to produce a completely unreflected scale? Or, why do these same senators scale differently when the remaining 78 items are used? There is not space to discuss this topic here. It is necessary to point out, however, that an R- and a Q-analysis using the MSA method are reciprocal only when the underlying dimensionality of the items and the people is the same. Reciprocity is palpably true for any one unidimensional scale, but not necessarily true for multiple unidimensional scales. A comparison of R- and Q-analysis for senatorial voting issues revealed that the items scale much better than the subjects and that the dimensionality is greater in the former than in the latter. The only justification for selecting these 50 issues as a base in the present illustration was that of not over-burdening the reader with unnecessary complexities.

Discussion

Although the MSA method seems to be quite versatile and meets two of the chief criticisms directed against Guttman's method, i.e., a) the method of selecting items, and b) the quasi-statistical criteria used for scaling, some critical observations are in order.

First, as Restle (1959) has stated elsewhere but is quite appropriate in the present context, it is quite possible for two or more *pure* variables to be related in such a way that they cannot be isolated on the basis of the formal internal evidence of a particular method of analysis. In another article (Lingoes, 1960a), the importance of this sometimes unavoidable limitation had been emphasized relative to the results of factor analyses and was given the label of the *identity error*. The MSA method is not immune from this criticism since it is possible to bring items together from what appear to be conceptually distinct domains. A number of examples come to mind. One could easily find a sample of subjects (e.g., those with low IQ's) in which, for a given set of arithmetic problems and words to be spelled, each subject could spell no better than he could solve problems. In some other sample, however, these two abilities would not correlate very highly. Such arguments as the foregoing may have been instrumental in Guttman's insistence upon a "universe of content" as a major criterion of item selection. In any event, good judgment and external evidence cannot be dispensed with since any empirical or statistical method of analysis, by its very nature, is highly solipsistic.

In the context of MSA one could test the adequacy of one's formulations about domains by including items from what are thought to be different areas. If these items appear in the a priori scales, then we would be in a much stronger position when using such scales in some practical setting, since we had invoked a more rigorous model. The MSA method also could be useful in studying different forms of item construction within the same area of content (see Stouffer, et al., 1950, for other uses of scale analysis).

Second, the fundamental issue regarding the generality of the cumulative model for other kinds of data, e.g., Thurstone scale items, and other models, e.g., Coombs and Kao's (1955) nonmetric disjunctive-conjunctive and compensatory models, needs to be systematically explored. It has been found, for example, that MMPI items do not scale well, probably as a function of the infrequency of endorsement in the pathological direction for a large number of items even in patient samples.

Third, although a large amount of psychological data is binary, much work yet remains to be done in the generalization of the present model to n-chotomous data. A beginning in this direction has already been made by this investigator for resolving a correlation matrix into multiple simplexes. Another approach is afforded by the demonstrated relationship between reproducibility and correlation. It should be quite possible to correlate an observed matrix with more than two categories with a model matrix defined similar to that for binary data. Yet another avenue of approach being tested is use of the MSA method as presently constituted on dichotomized continuous variables. The results of the analysis are then compared with those issuing from analyses using the full range of information, e.g., factor analysis. In the basic study proposing MSA (Lingoes, 1960b), it was found that MSA did slightly, although not significantly, better than multiple factor analysis in predicting voting behavior. This study, however, cannot be considered crucial and additional research is needed.

Fourth, the meager beginnings adumbrated in the present report on subdividing samples of subjects or items on the basis of error analysis require more rigorous treatment. To separate the often confounded sources of error variance is no small task. It might be mentioned here that reliable error can be partialed out by such a strategy. For example, in one study (Lingoes, 1960b) it was found that over independent sets of issues and over a narrow range of REPs for 88 senators the test-retest reliability coefficient for REPs was .63, which, while below acceptable standards, is nonetheless appreciable and suggestive of fruitful results using this approach.

Fifth, and final, some comments should be made on the reliability of the MSA procedure as a function of: a) changes in the scaling criteria and methods; b) changes in the stimuli or items holding subjects constant; and c) changes in the subjects but using the same variables. In discussing these topics it is important to note whether we are talking about error-free data or the more commonly encountered empirical data about which we would like to make some generalizations. Proofs are often possible in the former case but not the latter. For empirical data it is often necessary to offer experimental evidence in the place of proofs. This we shall do.

Same data, different criteria—Evidence based on both error and error-free data is available on this point. Using error-free data it has been found that the minimum criteria of positive relationships, smallest distances, and fewest errors within equal distances for adjacent item pairs, when used in conjunction with *Steps 2* and *3*, will produce the same scales, regardless of the differences between the remaining criteria (excluding the statistical test), if one terminates when any error is introduced.

Error data, however, are much more sensitive to variation in criteria and procedures. The Senate data (Lingoes, 1960b) has been analyzed using the criteria proposed in this paper and the original criteria (see footnote 2). The differences in the two analyses were: a) more scales with the present criteria, with fewer items and higher reproducibilities; and b) very few scales which had perfect overlap. The total number of items which scaled and the over-all reproducibility were, however, quite close. The really important comparison involves the factorial structures of the scales from the two analyses. Here it was found that despite the small item overlap, scale by scale, the same two basic dimensions of domestic and foreign issues were recovered.

A number of analyses, similar in outcome, have led to the conclusion that stability should be sought in the relationships among the scale scores and not in the presence or absence of any particular item or set of items in a given scale when comparing scales using the same data. The most stable factor solutions will be obtained when the average level of difficulty and the average level of reproducibility is preserved for those scales defining any particular factor, even though item overlap differs.

Same subjects, different items—The reader is referred to the cross-validation study by Lingoes (1960b) for detailed evidence on this point. In summary, the findings were that stable results can be achieved using different data (from the same domain in this instance, i.e., voting behavior), both in terms of individual scales defining a set of issues (e.g., farm, foreign aid, etc.) and in terms of the factors issuing from an analysis of scale scores. Here, in contrast to the previous topic, the same method of analysis was employed.

Same items, different subjects—In this section two points will be made. First, even though perfect item overlap might not exist between scales derived on different subjects, it is highly likely, the more homogeneous the scales and the larger the differences between adjacent item marginals, that both scales will cross-validate when used on the sample not used in derivation. Such results are to be expected and are not peculiar to MSA scales, but to Guttman scales in general. Furthermore, the stronger and the more significant are the relationships, the more likely it is that item overlap will exist between scales based upon different samples. To require perfect item overlap in two studies of scale analysis is tantamount to requiring not only the same factors in factor analysis, but identical factor loadings.

Second, although item overlap between scales falls short of perfection, it is still possible to replicate the factor structures based upon the scale scores in different samples. This has been done on an MSA of MMPI items with results that compared favorably to analyses of empirical scales (Lingoes, 1960a).

In conclusion, it seems a fair assessment to say that MSA is at the least more objective than scalogram analysis and can be used wherever the latter is applicable. At the other end of the scale, the present method of analysis is an important extension of Guttman's approach, which may prove helpful in increasing understanding and prediction using

homogeneity principles and an "if . . . then" or contingency model, rather than the conventional "if and only if" model implicit in much of multivariate research.

REFERENCES

Brown, Alicia.
  1962 "A multiple scalogram analysis of the United Nations." Unpublished M. A. thesis, Michigan State University.

Brown, Alicia, and C. F. Wrigley.
  1961 "A multiple scalogram analysis of the United Nations." A paper read at the 1961 Midwestern Psychological Association Convention, Chicago.

Coombs, C. H., and R. C. Kao.
  1955 Nonmetric Factor Analysis. Engineering Research Bulletin, No. 38.

Edwards, A. L.
  1957 Techniques of Attitude Scale Construction. New York: Appleton-Century-Crofts.

Festinger, L.
  1947 "The treatment of qualitative data by 'scale analysis.'" Psychological Bulletin, XLIV 149–161.

Goodenough, W. H.
  1944 "A technique for scale analysis." Educational and Psychological Measurement, IV 179–190.

Goodman, L. A.
  1959 "Simple statistical methods for scalogram analysis." Psychometrika, XXIV 29–43.

Guttman, L.
  1944 "A basis for scaling qualitative data." American Sociological Review, IX 139–150.
  1950 "Relation of scalogram analysis to other techniques." Pp. 172–212 in Stouffer *et al.*, Measurement and Prediction. Princeton, New Jersey: Princeton University Press.

Knudsen, Karel.
  1962 "A comparison of two methods, multiple scalogram analysis and factor analysis for analyzing United Nations voting behavior." Unpublished M. A thesis, Michigan State University.

Lazersfeld, P. F.
  1950 "The logical and mathematical foundation of latent structure analysis." Pp.

362–472 in Stouffer, *et al.*, Measurement and Prediction. Princeton, New Jersey: Princeton University Press.

Lingoes, J. C.
1960a "MMPI factors of the Harris and the Wiener subscales." Journal of Consulting Psychology, XXIV 74–83.
1960b "Multiple scalogram analysis: a generalization of Guttman's scale analysis." Unpublished Ph.D. thesis, Michigan State University.
1961 "Multiple scalogram analysis for MISTIC, ILLIAC, SILLIAC, and CYCLONE." Behavioral Science, VI:97.
1962a "Multiple scalogram analysis; an IBM 704/709/7090 program." Behavioral Science, VII:126.
1962b "A multiple scalogram analysis of three sets of U. S. Senate voting issues." Michigan Psychologist, XXI:6.
1962c "Information processing in psychological research." Behavioral Science, VII: 412–417.
1962d "A multiple scalogram analysis of selected issues of the 83rd U.S. Senate." American Psychologist, XVII:327.

Loevinger, Jane
1948 "The technic of homogeneous tests compared with some aspects of 'scale analysis' and factor analysis." Psychological Bulletin, XLV:507–529.

McQuitty, L. L.
1955 "A method of pattern analysis for isolation typological dimensional constructs." Research Bulletin, Tn-55-62, San Antonio, Texas: Headquarters Air Force Personnel and Training Center.
1957 "Elementary linkage analysis for isolating orthogonal and oblique types and typal relevancies." Educational and Psychological Measurement, XVII:209–229.

Restle, F.
1959 "A metric and an ordering on sets." Psychometrika, XXIV:207–220.

Sagi, P. C.
1959 "A statistical test for the significance of a coefficient of reproducibility." Psychometrika, XXIV 19–27.

Schutz, W. C.
1961 "BC GUTS-GUTTman scaling." Share Distribution No. 1337. Programmed by Eleanor S. Krasnow.

Stouffer, S. A., L. Guttman, E. A. Suchman, P. F. Lazersfeld, Shirley A. Star, and J. A. Clausen.
1950 Measurement and Prediction. Princeton, New Jersey: Princeton University Press.

Torgerson, W. S.
1958 Theory and Methods of Scaling. New York: John Wiley & Sons.

Wilkins, D. M.
1962 "Factor analysis and multiple scalogram analysis: a logical and empirical comparison." Unpublished Ph.D. thesis, Michigan State Unversity.

Wilkins, D. M., and C. F. Wrigley.
1961 "Factors or scales: a logical and empirical analysis." A paper read at the Psychonomic Society Meeting, New York.

CHAPTER 17 Multidimensional Scaling of Attitudes

JOHN ROSS

To define attitudes as those mental structures which organize and evaluate information may be to define them too broadly and in terms none too precise. Nevertheless attitudes will be so defined for the purposes of this chapter. The reason is not so much convenience as aptness. Multidimensional scaling (MDS) provides a picture or map of psychological structures. Its immediate analytic application is to whatever is responsible for the structures it reveals. For the purposes of this chapter attitudes are regarded as the agents responsible for structures within the domain of opinion and belief.. What I mean by an attitude is very like what Harvey, Hunt, and Schroder (1961) mean by a concept. Their book is recommended in elaboration of the idea of an organizing and evaluating mental structure.

THE GENERAL METHOD

Multidimensional scaling was developed by Torgerson (1958) partly from an earlier sketch by Richardson (1938). Torgerson's book remains a fundamental reference. The aim of the method is to construct maps of psychological structures from data on psycho-

logical distances much as a cartographer constructs maps of terrain from distances between fixed points on the terrain. The cartographer makes use of plane geometry and plane trigonometry to construct his map, or, for really precise work, he may employ the geometry and trigonometry of the surface of a sphere. Psychological structures are more complex. MDS, the psychological map-making method, works in the geometry of many dimensions. It normally works in terms of straight line (Euclidean) distances but may be made to work in terms of curved line distances, as the cartographer may work in terms of distances over the curved surface of a sphere.

Cartographers' Map-Making

Imagine five towns: Ayton, Beeton, Ceyton, Diton, and Eaton. A cartographer is supplied with the following table of distances separating the towns.

The only map on a plane surface which is consistent with the distances supplied is the map in Figure 1, or its mirror image. It can be made by setting points representing two of the towns an appropriate distance apart and finding where the others must be with ruler and compass. The reader is invited to

This chapter prepared especially for this volume.

TABLE 1

Distances in Miles Separating Five Towns

	Ayton	Beeton	Ceyton	Diton	Eaton
Ayton	0	1.4	2	1.4	1
Beeton	1.4	0	1.4	2	1
Ceyton	2	1.4	0	1.4	1
Diton	1.4	2	1.4	0	1
Eaton	1	1	1	1	0

try it and see that no other map is possible; that is, the map is fixed by the distances. Note, however, that the directions north, south, east, and west are not determined and cannot be without further information.

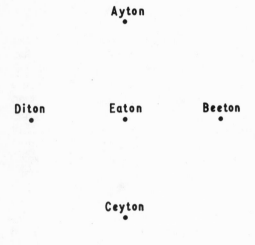

Figure 1. Map of five towns recovered from distances in Table 1.

A Transitional Example

Students at the University of Western Australia were asked to estimate the distances between pairs of cities in Australia. The estimates were averaged to give distances between points on the map of Australia as it was remembered by students. The map reproduced from the averaged distances is shown in Figure 2 superimposed on the real map of Australia. The subjective map might be termed a map of Oz, an unreal land built partly from elements of real Australia and partly from myths that prevail in Western Australia.

Psychologists' Map-Making

The psychologist starts from psychological distance, which can be measured only by inference from responses, since there is no direct access to psychological distance as there is to distances between points in a country.

A first example—The first example comes from outside the domain of attitudes. It is a study by Helm and Tucker (1962) of color perception. They had subjects make direct magnitude estimates of the dissimilarity of pairs of color chips, and took the estimates to provide measures of psychological distance between one color and another. Using methods to be described later, they constructed the maps determined by the distances and found, broadly speaking, two types of maps. Normal subjects yielded maps with the points corresponding to the color chips arranged in a circle, as in Figure 3a. Red-green color deficient subjects yielded maps in which the red-green differences are minimized, as in Figure 3b. Clearly the perceived structure of the colors is different in the two cases, and the difference exposes the deficiency in red-green discrimination for the non-normals. Although Helm and Tucker's work is in the realm of psychophysics rather than attitudes, it illustrates the way MDS works to expose individual differences in psychological structures, and the way it can be used as a basis to infer the agents responsible for the individual differences observed.

A second example—Students at Western Australia were asked to judge dissimilarities between pairs of fingerprints, again by making direct magnitude estimates of dissimilarity. As in Helm and Tucker's study, the estimates were taken to provide measures of distance fairly directly. This map, like Helm and Tucker's, lay in two dimensions—often more are required—and, from the position of the points corresponding to the fingerprints,

Figure 2. A map of Oz, derived from judgments of distances, superimposed on a real map of Australia.

it was clear that only two features contributed to the impression of difference, that is, to psychological distance. One was the extent to which an "arch" pattern was present in the print. The other was the extent to which the print exhibited the symmetrical "whorl" pattern as against the asymmetrical "loop" pattern. All other features like size, number of lines, darkness of the impression, and so on were apparently ignored.

The point the example brings out is the selectivity of the basis for the structure, a point of great importance in the domain of attitudes proper. Psychological structures are not based on all the discernible properties of objects or events but on those properties singled out by the observer as significant. In the domain of attitudes, properties may commonly be attributed to an object or event rather than realistically perceived in it.

STEPS IN MAP-MAKING

There are two methods of map-making. The steps in each will be explained in turn. The "classical" method, announced by Torgerson as long ago as 1952, will be termed MDS (multidimensional scaling). The new method, announced by Shepard in 1962, will be termed PA (proximity analysis). Torger-

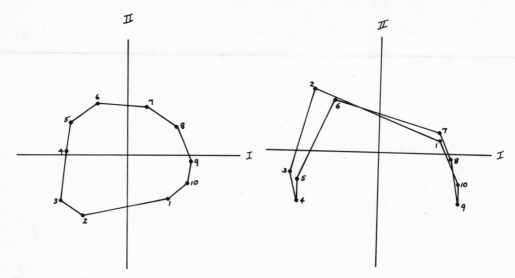

Figure 3a. Map of perceived color structures for normals.

Figure 3b. Map of perceived color structures for color defectives.

son's method has been changed little since its announcement, but Shepard's has been modified in certain technical respects since work by Kruskal in 1964. Guttman and Lingoes have lately developed closely related methods.

Multidimensional Scaling (MDS)

Step 1: Distances—The first problem in MDS is to arrive at estimates of psychological distance between pairs of stimuli. One method is direct magnitude estimation. A subject is presented in turn with all pairs of stimuli. (For n stimuli there will be $n\,(n-1)/2$ pairs. For 10 stimuli there are 45 pairs, for 15 there are 105, for 20 there are 190.) He is required to estimate directly the magnitude of the overall distance between the pairs. He may use numbers or he may move the stimuli (or symbols for them) physically to set them at a distance apart to represent their difference. The latter method has been used by Indow and Uchizono (1960). Helm and Tucker developed an interesting variant in which subjects placed three stimuli (A, B, and C) at once on a grid, setting each so that all three interpoint distances were in the correct proportion to represent the differences

between the three pairs ($A = B$, $A = C$, and $B = C$). Direct estimation methods may employ a fixed standard in the form of a constantly visible pair of stimuli chosen to represent some unit of difference. The subject is then asked to estimate difference between pairs in terms of the standard difference.

The theory of MDS is that the subject is consulting his personal map of the stimuli and estimating distances between stimuli. The point about the Helm-Tucker method using three stimuli at a time is that, no matter how complex the map, any three stimuli selected from it must lie on some plane running through the map and can therefore be properly located on the grid suppled by the experimenter.

Direct estimation methods make the assumption that the subject is capable of giving accurate estimates of stimulus differences, keeping in mind all the properties, real or imagined, that support the mental structure. The assumption may be false, and direct estimation may have to be abandoned as a task too difficult for certain classes of stimuli.

Where direct estimation fails, indirect methods using distance models are normally possible. Torgerson (1958, pp. 259–277) gives a comprehensive review of the main methods. In principle the indirect methods attempt to derive distances from simple responses by using models that connect distances to the simpler responses. All are extensions of methods developed in psychophysics. Pairs of stimuli are compared, one pair with another, the subject nominating the more similar or the more different pair; or pairs may be assigned to categories. Extensions of the laws of comparative and categorical judgment (see Torgerson) are used as the models to derive distances.

The indirect methods normally require more responses than one subject can be asked to give. They require the pooling of data from many subjects and encounter the grave difficulty that different subjects may have different "points of view" about the structure of the stimuli. If so, the results are virtually uninterpretable. Care must be taken to ensure the relative homogeneity of subjects for whom data is pooled, which may be difficult or impossible in the domain of attitude. Tucker and Messick (1963) have attempted to select subjects with similar points of view before pooling them. Their method is discussed later.

Step 2: Maps—With distances in hand, and adjusted if necessary by an "additive constant" (see Torgerson, pp. 268–277) for conversion to "absolute" distances required by the Euclidean "map," the map coordinates may be derived by using computer programs based on a theorem of Young and Householder (1938) and standard matrix algebra routines. The programs have much in common with those for factor analysis.

The process is illustrated in Figure 4. The computer program starts with interpoint distances. It selects an arbitrary point of reference (usually the "centroid" of the configuration of points) and calculates the scalar cross-product for each pair of points with respect to the point of reference. It is instructive to note that factor analysis begins with data in the latter form and that the analysis is virtually identical for MDS and factor analysis

from then on. The program next determines the number of dimensions required to contain the points, simultaneously their "stretch" in each dimension (the latent root-value for each dimension), and, simultaneously again, the reference coordinate for each stimulus on each dimension (the scale value, calculated from latent vectors). The map itself is made by placing points in the positions specified by the reference coordinate values for each dimension.

In practice a set of points produces many dimensions, usually one less than the number of points. In theory only a small number are genuine dimensions, the others being produced by errors in the estimates of distance. The investigator decides (see Hake and Rodwan, 1966) how many dimensions are genuine, and now has a map given by the table of coordinate values for those dimensions he regards as genuine.

The reference point is arbitrary and may be shifted as desired. So too are the directions of the dimensions. Dimensions may be "rotated" as desired. No firm procedures for shifting the reference point (translation) or for rotation exist for MDS as they do for factor analysis. A great deal is left to the discretion of the investigator, from whom good judgment is required.

The final step is to interpret the map. A discussion is postponed until examples are considered.

Proximity Analysis (PA)

Step 1: Distance ordering—Where MDS is a "straight-through" analytic procedure which runs fully determined from the initial distances to the final map, PA is a more approximate recycling procedure, which starts with less information than MDS and ends at the discretion of the user. Technically, PA is termed an *iterative* procedure. It starts with information *about* distances rather than with the distances themselves. At first encounter this sounds hair-raisingly approximate, but surprisingly, it is not.

Normally all that is supplied is the order

Figure 4

THE MAIN STEPS IN MULTIDIMENSIONAL SCALING (MDS)
AND PROXIMITY ANALYSIS (PA)

MULTIDIMENSIONAL SCALING (MDS)

STEP 1: Treatment to obtain distances between pairs of points.

Types of Data	*Treatment*
Magnitude estimates	None. Estimates are treated as distances.
Comparative judgments	Extension of paired comparison model. See Torgerson (1958, pp. 259–277).
Categorical judgments	Extension of comparative judgment model. See Torgerson (loc. cit.). Note: Some studies treat average rating as estimates of distances, but it is not recommended.
Other types of data	Arbitrary distance models. (See person structures: example 2 as an illustration.)

STEP 2: Obtaining maps from distances between pairs of points.

STAGE 1

Each distance, d_{ij}, between a pair of points is converted into a scalar cross-product, b_{ij}^*, between the vectors corresponding for the same pair of points by the formula.

$$b_{ij}^* = \frac{1}{2}\left[\frac{1}{n}\sum_{i=1}^{n} d_{ij}^2 + \frac{1}{n}\sum_{j=1}^{n} d_{ij}^2 - \frac{1}{n^2}\sum_{i=1}^{n}\sum_{j=1}^{n} d_{ij}^2 - d_{ij}^2\right].$$

STAGE 2

From the matrix B^*, containing the b_{ij}^* values, a calculation is performed using matrix methods known as latent root and latent vector analysis (or eigen-root and vector analysis) to arrive at scale or coordinate values for each point on each of the dimensions necessary to make a map of the stimuli.

STAGE 3

The map is drawn and interpretations are made. [See top of page 285.]

PROXIMITY ANALYSIS (PA)

STEP 1: Preliminary treatment of data.
In many cases no preliminary treatment of data is required, since what is observed specifies the rank order of pair dissimilarities. In some cases it is necessary to break ties in the data. In other cases it is necessary to calculate an index of dissimilarity from the data, but the basis of the calculation is typically *ad hoc*.

STEP 2: Obtaining maps from the rank order of pair dissimilarities.

STEP 2 (MDS) IN PICTURES

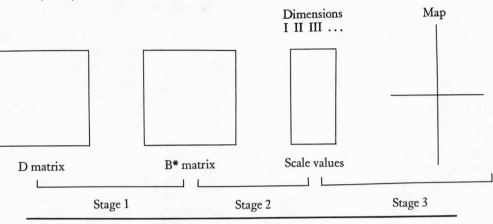

D matrix   B* matrix   Scale values   Map

| Stage 1 | Stage 2 | Stage 3 |

[Proximity Analysis (PA)—*Cont.*]

STAGE 1
Construct a trial map or modify the trial map in a specified number of dimensions.

STAGE 2
Compare the rank order of the separation of pairs of points in the map with the rank order of pair dissimilarities (taken from data). Return to Stage 1 if the correspondence is not good enough, or stop if the correspondence is satisfactory. Correspondence is usually measured by stress, $\left[\sum_{i<j} (d_{ij} - d_{ij})^2 / \sum_{i<j} d_{ij}^2 \right]^{\frac{1}{2}}$, where d_{ij} is a distance in the trial map, and d_{ij} is calculated from the data.

STEP 2 (PA) IN PICTURES

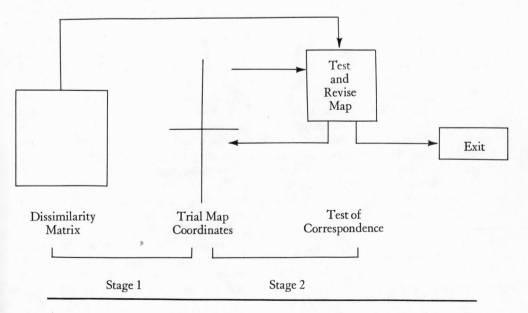

Dissimilarity   Trial Map   Test of
Matrix   Coordinates   Correspondence

| Stage 1 | Stage 2 |

of differences for pairs, from greatest to least—that is, an order from 1 to $n(n-1)/2$ for the pairs from n stimuli (see Figure 4).

It is much simpler to order distances than to find them by direct estimate or model as must be done for MDS. A wide variety of observations can be used to supply an order. For example, the order of similarity of Morse code signal pairs has been determined from the frequency with which they are confused. The higher the frequency of confusion, the more similar a pair is taken to be. In a like manner, pairs of political figures could be ordered in similarity from the number of statements people are prepared to apply in common to both members of the pair. The possibilities are endless, the variety making PA peculiarly apt for studies in the domain of attitudes.

Step 2: Maps—PA methods construct an initial map that is either quite arbitrary or very approximate. The order of distances between pairs of points in the map is compared with the order of distances between pairs of stimuli, and the map is modified to increase the correspondence. Lack of correspondence is measured by "stress" (Shepard, 1962; Kruskal, 1964), and the modification is made to reduce stress. Comparison follows modification and determines a next modification to reduce stress further still. The process, termed an "iterative" procedure, continues until stress is reduced to an acceptable figure. Kruskal's major innovation was to measure stress in a manner theoretically more sound than Shepard's. Guttman and Lingoes propose a novel method, the rank image principle, to make modifications following each measure of stress (Guttman, 1968).

All methods are embodied in computer programs and use computational methods rather than mathematical theorems. Most provide alternative maps in two, three, four, five, and more dimensions. The investigator must choose the best map, often with less to judge by than in MDS methods. The problem of setting a suitable reference origin and of locating dimensions must be faced just as with MDS. The

steps in PA are illustrated in Figure 4.

The comparison phase of the process requires the calculation of distances for pairs of points in the map to place them in order from greatest to least. Distance may be calculated as a Euclidean straight line distance or on some other basis corresponding to distances along paths of varying degrees of curvature. Many programs offer a Minkowski distance function where

$$d_{xy} = \sum_{g=1}^{k} [(x_g - y_g)^r]^{1/r},$$

the exponent value r being set at the user's discretion. Where $r = 2$, distance is Euclidean. Where $r = 1$, distance is "city-block distance" (Attneave, 1950). At other values of r, distance is measured on curved paths between points. (For a general discussion of distance the reader is advised to consult Beckenbach and Bellman, 1961.)

Correspondence of order between map and data might seem a flimsy prop for a map. In a striking demonstration Shepard (1964) has shown that, on the contrary, the test of order is exceedingly strict, guaranteeing a map that reproduces faithfully the structure of an original.

APPLICATIONS TO ATTITUDES

The examples used so far have been of perceptual structures rather than the conceptual structures of opinion and belief. For multidimensional scaling (MDS or PA) to reveal attitudes, subjects must respond because of their attitudes and not just on a perceptual analysis of stimulus object. The problem is partly to select appropriate stimuli and partly to frame instructions that will bring attitudes to bear. Commonly two classes of stimuli are used: objects or events about which attitudes are held (politicians, social actions, social classifications, geopolitical regions, etc.) and statements of belief *or* opinion ("Johnson is a communist," "The Vietnam war is wrong," "The Russians are imperialists," "Negroes are sick," etc.). The subject's task is to make some response from which the psychological distance between the stimuli can be measured (for MDS) or from which distances can be ordered (for PA).

There are two fundamentally different ways to proceed. The first way is to seek conceptual structures. The steps are to calculate distances between stimuli for individual subjects or for groups of subjects and then to find the map of the stimuli for the group of subjects. Differences between subjects or groups in the dimensions of the maps and in the scale values (coordinates) of stimuli can be used to infer differences in attitudes, both with respect to content and to other aspects like complexity (Schroder, Driver, and Streufert, 1967). The second way is to seek person structures. In this case the steps are to calculate distances between subjects and to find a map of the subjects themselves. The map of the persons themselves is used to discover the attitudes on which they differ, and scale values on dimensions provide direct measures of attitudes.

Examples of Attitude Scaling

Conceptual structures: Example 1—Messick (1961) listed the names of all possible pairs of 20 political leaders (190 pairs in all), ranging from Chiang Kai-shek through Hiss and Hitler to Truman and Henry Wallace. Subjects were asked to rate each pair for similarity in political thinking. Psychological distances were calculated from ratings by the indirect means of the successive intervals distance model. MDS showed that a map in two dimensions represented the distances adequately.

Messick's map for two dimensions is partly reproduced in Figure 5. As he points out, the Democrats are clearly separated from the Republicans, and foreign leaders from Americans. The attitudinal considerations at work in the political judgments made appear to be, first, a Democrat versus a Republican dimension and, second, a "foreign ideology" consideration.

Conceptual structures: Example 2—Messick's structure employed MDS with distance estimates based on a successive intervals model. von Wright and Niemelä (1966) report a study on moral attitudes that employs PA and takes the necessary information about distance from a spatial judgment about stimuli. Eight comic strip stories (four frames each) were prepared showing children in culpable behavior. Subjects, young girls (7, 10, and 13 years old) and a group of adult female students, were asked to compare the agents of each pair of stories (28 pairs in all) on the "nice/naughty dimension," putting the stimuli physically close together if the agents were equally naughty or nice, and farther apart the more different they were. It sounds difficult, but even children find the judgment easy with coaching and practice. The order of the stimulus distances was calculated from average settings for each age group. PA was carried out using Kruskal's modification of Shepard's method.

Two-dimensional maps were found for each group. The results suggested that the three younger groups consider first the extent to which the agent shows remorse by apologizing or expressing regret rather than pleasure or spite at the result. Adults seem first to consider the motive. The second consideration is more difficult to discern from the structure and seems to differ even within the younger age groups. The firm conclusions from the study seem to be that moral attitudes change with age, the motive of the agent becoming an increasingly dominant consideration.

Conceptual structures: Example 3—The stimulus objects in example 1 were political figures and, in example 2, social behavior. In both cases stimuli were objects of attitude. Abelson (1954) reports a study in which the stimuli are statements that express attitudes. The statements were about war, armaments, and communism. Some were: "War is the only means of ridding the world of communism," "War is a necessary and useful instrument," "America should increase her present armaments enormously," and "War is tragic and terrible." There were 12 statements in all. Each pair (66 in all) was rated

Figure 5

PARTIAL REPRODUCTION OF MESSICK'S MAP DERIVED
FROM JUDGMENTS OF SIMILARITY OF POLITICAL LEADERS

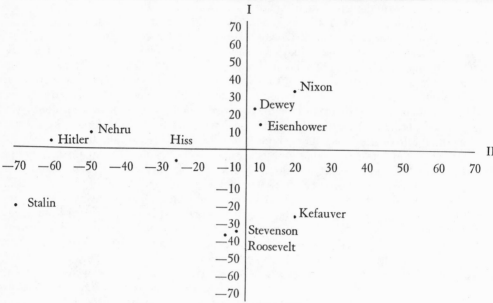

on the extent to which two people stating each were judged to agree in their attitudes. A group of socialists and two groups of conservatives acted as subjects. Median judgments (a crude measure) for each group were used as estimates of the perceived psychological distance between pairs of statements. MDS was used to obtain maps for each of the three groups, two dimensions again sufficing in each case.

The two conservative groups gave virtually identical maps, and it became possible to contrast the conservative map with the socialist map. In both, war and peace sentiments were represented by statements at distant ends of the map, as were hard and soft line sentiments and pro- and anticommunist sentiments. One clear difference is that socialists placed hard line and anticommunist sentiments close together on the map and the hard-soft line and anti-procommunist "dimensions" (directions within the map defined by the location of statements) were

highly intercorrelated. The conservative view virtually identified war-peace with hard-soft line, but distinguished both from attitudes to communism. The Abelson study brings out differences between groups in the relationship between one attitude and another.

Abelson followed his MDS analysis with an attempt to assess the "valence" of each point on the map for each group. The maps became contour maps with high points indicating regions of favor and low points regions of disfavor. Abelson's method is not standard in MDS work. It depends on his own special valence model, which has not had wide application.

Person structures: Example 1—It has been rarer to map subjects than to map their conceptual structures, though the method is simple and general. Distances between pairs of subjects may be calculated from the extent to which they agree in their attitudes. If two subjects both mark a list of statements with "agree" or "disagree," an index of distance can be calculated by counting zero whenever they both mark a statement the same way and counting 1 otherwise. Similarly judges can be compared by comparing their verdicts on the same or similar cases, and politicians or political groups by comparing their voting records. Given distances or enough information about the order of distances, maps may be made of subjects.

Coombs (1964) provides an instructive example. Pairs of psychological journals were compared in terms of the number of cross references each made to the other, and a distance index was calculated. A map of the journals showed that they separated on two dimensions, one a hard-soft, the other an academic-applied distinction. Coombs used a special non-metric multidimensional scaling technique, which will not be discussed here.

Person structures: Example 2—Schubert (1962) carried out an analysis of the 1960 term of the United States Supreme Court "on the premise that a justice reacts in his voting behavior to the stimuli presented by cases before the Court, in accordance with his attitudes toward the issues raised for decision" (p. 107). Schubert used factor analysis, but MDS can be applied to his data. The distance between pairs of judges is calculated by counting 1 whenever the judges agree, and zero otherwise, the total being divided by the number of the cases on which the judges both gave a decision. The index is arbitrary but reasonable, since each disagreement adds to it and each agreement leaves it unaffected.

MDS of the distances produces the two-dimensional map shown in Figure 6. Other information supplied in Schubert's article indicates that two dimensions might reasonably be discerned in the map. One is attitude to cases where civil liberties are at issue and the other is attitudes on both economic liberalism and monetary conflicts of interest between private individuals and government.

It is interesting to note that MDS produces a simpler result—a two-dimensional map—than factor analysis, which yielded six factors, and that the MDS map is consistent

with other evidence reported by Schubert about groupings of the justices in terms of attitude.

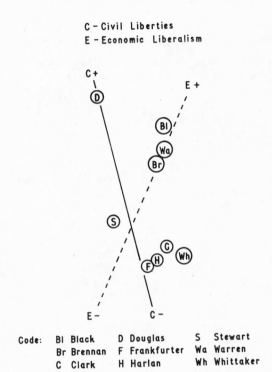

Figure 6.   Map of Supreme Court justices from joint decisions.

Points of View

The answers produced by MDS or PA depend on the distance information used. Where the distances are between objects or statements, the map produced is a map of conceptual structures; where the distances are between subjects, the map is a map of individuals, differentiated in terms of their location on the dimensions of attitude or whatever else is responsible for their behavior. In both cases it is vital that the distances used for analysis can be justified as distances. Two conditions are necessary: (1) that the elements concerned maintain a constant value on each of the properties (real or attributed) that differentiate them, and (2) that every comparison is affected by all the properties that differentiate the pair of elements concerned.

An object or statement that had different meanings in different contexts could not be sensibly treated as a point on a map, any more than could a subject who constantly shifted his attitude. If Russia and China were said to be similar because of their political systems but China and India different because of the color of their people's skins, any distances derived would be pseudo-distances, and any map produced from them would be misleading.

Both difficulties intrude severely whenever data is pooled across subjects, since subjects may differ in point of view, both locating elements differently and differing in the basis of the estimates of distance. Tucker and Messick (1963) have proposed a method to minimize, if not entirely eliminate, the problems created by pooling.

The responses of all subjects to all *pairs* of stimuli are arranged in a matrix or table with rows corresponding to *pairs* of stimuli and columns to subjects. The first level of analysis determines the number of different response types and assigns each subject a set of weights indicating the extent to which his responses reflect each different response type. The analysis provides a subject map, with each point in the map, whether occupied by a subject or not, corresponding to a possible set of responses to all stimulus pairs. This subject map is not readily interpretable in attitudinal terms, though it does function to distinguish subjects and group them into homogeneous clusters.

Points are selected to represent clusters of subjects. A matrix of distances for all stimulus pairs can be calculated for each point selected, and each matrix is analyzed by standard MDS methods. The resulting map is taken to be the conceptual structure for the point chosen and to represent the structure for the group of subjects clustering nearby in the subject map. The map is said to represent a "point of view."

Other methods are currently being developed to handle the problem of individual differences, in a way that meets objections to the method of Tucker and Messick.

Multidimensional Unfolding

In the methods discussed so far the relation between subjects and their conceptual structures is unspecified. There are methods to find maps of conceptual structures and methods to find maps of subjects. The connection between one sort of map and the other is not determinable, even in the Tucker and Messick method, which produces maps of both kinds. Coombs has a model that locates subjects and attitude objects in a joint or common space but until recently his method has been forbidding because of the labor it imposes on the user. Computer programs have now been developed which should make it simple to use.

The Coombs method uses a different form of data than MDS or PA, since it requires a ranking in terms of preference rather than a judgment about pairs of elements. The fact that the data has a different form permits the Coombs model to achieve a joint representation of subjects and objects.

SOME COMMENTS AND CAUTIONS IN INTERPRETING STRUCTURES

The structures mapped by MDS and PA are clues to attitude, with no very clear guidelines to interpretation. It has already been stressed that the user must exercise discretion and judgment in interpretation.

Most multidimensional studies have been exploratory, with interpretation coming at the end and remaining highly speculative. Some studies have been designed to test hypothesis. Guttman (1967) has recently developed a "facet" theory, the express purpose of which is to produce predictions about the outcome of multidimensional analysis from a theoretical analysis of a domain of behavior. The ideal application of MDS and PA is in a rolling sequence of studies from initial exploratory work to final theory-testing, with features of the structural map predicted precisely. Very little work of this ideal kind has been done, and, until it is, results will remain of dubious value.

Dimensions and scale values—The usual interpretation of MDS and PA results is a content interpretation in terms of the dimensions that separate the elements concerned and the scale value of each element on each dimension. In the Messick study of political leaders, two dimensions are identified—Democrat *versus* Republican and American *versus* foreign—and the map in Figure 5 (see p. 288) locates leaders on each dimension. Stalin is highly foreign and slightly Democratic. Nixon is highly Republican and fairly American. The dimensions isolated fill out the content of the attitudes studied.

Recent theoretical work (Beals, Krantz, and Tversky, 1968) has shown that there are conditions under which a dimensional interpretation is illegitimate. The data used to measure psychological distance must have certain formal properties if a dimensional interpretation of any kind is to be made. The possibility of making the necessary formal test for attitudinal data is remote. The user is left with no infallible guide and, once again, is forced to rely on discretion and good judgment about his data even to begin to look for a dimensional interpretation of his results.

Structures and regions—Guttman (1968) has pointed out that MDS and PA maps may be interpreted without resort to dimensions and scale values. It is possible to divide any structure into relatively compact regions that contain sets of elements separated from others. It is further possible to impose some law of formation (central-peripheral, circular, etc.) on the structures on this basis. Interpretations can be tested as readily as can dimensional interpretations. Guttman has suggested that laws of formation such as the simplex, the circumplex, and the radex, as

well as others suggested by facet analysis (e.g., the torex) might replace dimensional analysis as the basis for interpretation of structures. Examples till now are too few to permit proper illustration.

Complexity—Structures can be assessed in terms of complexity without any interpretation in dimensional or other terms. Schroder *et al.* propose measures of differentiation and integration based on MDS and PA structures produced by individual subjects. Briefly, differentiation is determined both by the number of dimensions and the relative size of the dimensions. The more dimensions and the more nearly equal in magnitude (latent root value) all dimensions are, the greater the differentiation. Integration is best determined by repeated studies of the one individual. An attribute such as political belief or personal merit is chosen and a subject is asked to make judgments of similarity with respect to that attribute. The more dimensions that emerge in an analysis (MDS or PA) of the judgments, the greater the prima facie case for higher integration. But since integration is *coherent* complexity, repetition is necessary to ensure that the apparent high dimensionality was not due to error, to inconsistency, or to other sources of perturbation in the judgments. The reader is referred to Schroder *et al.* for details.

CURRENT STATUS

Multidimensional scaling analysis in either of its major forms (MDS or PA) is full of promise as a technique in the field of attitudes, but much has to be learned about applications before it can be considered a routine procedure available to any investigator. Among the problems to be solved are: (1) the best choice of response upon which to base the analysis, (2) the interpretation of maps, and (3) the assessment of the structural characteristics of maps, such as their complexity. It is to be hoped that, as problems like these are solved, multidimensional scaling will become part of the equipment routinely available in the study of attitudes.

Since it is very difficult to obtain satisfactory distance measures in attitudinal work, it is likely that MDS will more and more give way to PA as the standard technique for multidimensional scaling studies of attitude. As the examples have shown, it is relatively easy to obtain a satisfactory index of distance sufficient to make a rank order of distances, which is all PA requires.

Multidimensional scaling holds promise in another direction, which in the long run may overshadow its benefits as a mere computational tool. It should greatly clarify the concept of attitude itself. The effort to arrive at clear interpretations of multidimensional scaling results, and the effort to state in advance what results are expected if a certain hypothesis about attitude is correct, should force conceptual clarity about the complex structures we label as attitudes. Furthermore as social psychologists and sociologists master the formal language in which multidimensional structures are described, they may learn to express what they believe about attitudes in a language more apt than any they possess today.

REFERENCES

Abelson, R. P.
1954   "A technique and a model for multidimensional attitude scaling." Public Opinion Quarterly 18:405–418.
Attneave, F.
1950   "Dimensions of similarity." American Journal of Psychology 63:516–556.
Beals, R., D. H. Krantz, and A. Tversky.
1968   "Foundations of multidimensional scaling." Psychological Review 75: 125–142.
Beckenbach, E., and R. Bellman.
1961   An Introduction to Inequalities. New York: Random House.
Coombs, C. H.
1964   A Theory of Data. New York: Wiley.
Guttman, L.
1967   "The development of nonmetric space analysis: a letter to John Ross." Multivariate Behavioral Research 2:71–82.
1968   "A general nonmetric technique for finding the smallest coordinate space

for a configuration of points." Psychometrika 33:469–506.
Hake, H. W., and A. S. Rodwan.
1966   "Perception and recognition," in J. B. Sidowski (ed.), Experimental Methods and Instrumentation in Psychology. New York: McGraw-Hill.
Harvey, O. J., D. E. Hunt, and H. M. Schroder.
1961   Conceptual Systems and Personality Organization. New York: Wiley.
Helm, C. E., and L. R. Tucker.
1962   "Individual differences in the structure of color perception." American Journal of Psychology 75:437–444.
Indow, T., and T. Uchizono.
1960   "Multidimensional mapping of Munsell colors varying in line and chroma." Journal of Experimental Psychology 59:321–329.
Kruskal, J. B.
1964   "Multidimensional scaling by optimizing goodness of fit to a nonmetric hypothesis." Psychometrika 29:1–27.
Lingoes, J. C.
1965   "An IBM–7090 program for Guttman-Lingoes smallest space analysis—I." Behavioral Science 10:487.
Messick, S.
1961   "The perceived structure of political relationships." Sociometry 24:270–278.
Richardson, M. W.
1938   "Multidimensional   psychophysics." Psychological Bulletin 35:659–660.
Schroder, H. M., M. J. Driver, and S. Streufert.
1967   Human Information Processing. New York: Holt, Rinehart, and Winston.
Schubert, G.
1962   "The 1960 term: a psychological analysis." American Political Science Review 56:90–107.
Shepard, R. N.
1962a   "The analysis of proximities: Multidimensional scaling with an unknown distance function." I. Psychometrika 27:125–140.
1962b   "The analysis of proximities: Multidimensional scaling with an unknown distance function." II. Psychometrika 27:219–246.
1964   "Attention and the metric structure of the stimulus." Journal of Mathematical Psychology 1:54–87.

1966 "Metric structures in ordinal data." Journal of Mathematical Psychology 3: 287–315.

Torgerson, W. S.
1958 Theory and Methods of Scaling. New York: Wiley.

Tucker, L. R., and S. Messick.
1963 "An individual differences model for multidimensional scaling." Psychometrika 28:333–367.

von Wright, J. M., and P. Niemelä.
1966 "On the octogenetic development of moral criteria. A pilot experiment with a multidimensional scaling technique." Scandinavian Journal of Psychology 7:65–75.

Young, F. W., and W. S. Torgerson.
1967 "TORSCA, a FORTRAN-IV program for Shepard-Kruskal multidimensional scaling analysis." Behavioral Science 12:498.

Young, G., and A. S. Householder.
1938 "Discussion of a set of points in terms of their mutual distances." Psychometrika 3:19–22.

CHAPTER **18**   **Attitude as the Individual's Own Categories: The Social Judgment-Involvement Approach to Attitude and Attitude Change**

MUZAFER SHERIF AND CAROLYN W. SHERIF

Problems of attitude and attitude change are urgent and crucial today, perhaps more than in previous periods of human history. Man's mastery of his physical environment—especially his foreshortening of the time required to exchange words, goods, people, and missiles—has created a new world. People differing drastically in attitude find themselves in contact, whether they like it or not and whether for good or ill. At the same time, man's changing environment, both physical and social, demands new modes of adaptation that presume attitude change on a broad scale.

Attitude problems of man's social development and his relations with his fellows have long been recognized as central in social psychology. Research into these problems has flourished for well over three decades. To those familiar with the literature, it is astonishing how little theoretical progress in specifying attitude problems has been made since the formulations of W. I. Thomas, the sociologist, or William McDougall, the psychologist who dealt with attitude problems both in his treatment of social "instincts" and

From Muzafer Sherif and Carolyn W. Sherif, *Attitude, Ego-Involvement and Change*, pages 105–139. Copyright 1967 by John Wiley and Sons, Inc. Reproduced by permission of the authors and publisher.

"sentiments." The now traditional approaches to measurement of attitudes, on the other hand, developed with amazing independence from such theoretical treatments. Therefore, it is not surprising that much of the research literature has little or no bearing on the significant theoretical problems that made attitude a central concept in social psychology.

In this chapter we shall summarize an approach to problems of attitude and attitude change that has developed from concern with the nature of attitudes, with their significance for social-psychological theory, and with measurement techniques veridical to their nature and significance. The label for this approach, the social judgment-involvement approach, reflects the empirical bases for the concept of attitude and for the measurement techniques developed. On the one hand, the approach is based on findings from the experimental study of judgment, both psychophysical and social. Here, we rely heavily on experimental psychology. On the other hand, the approach rests on empirical findings about the involvement of the person's self or ego in an ongoing event or situation. In the latter aspect, we rely on sociologists and the long thin line of psychologists since William James who have stressed that attitudes are not discrete elements in human psychology, but are, on the contrary, constituents of the person's self system.

After discussing briefly the background of the approach, we shall inquire specifically into the nature of attitudes, then present operational measures of attitude, representative findings, and predictions about reactions to communication and attitude change.

BACKGROUND OF THE APPROACH

The social judgment-involvement approach is not presented as a formal model derived logically from a limited set of untested assumptions, although its development follows a logical sequence. This assertion does not reflect disdain for comprehensive theory nor for formal models. On the contrary, the desired goal in the behavioral sciences, as in any science, is theory that is truly comprehensive and models that are *valid*. Our concern is with the means to attain this goal.

Those sciences dealing with human behavior are in their infancy, despite their popularity and despite the pretensions we may maintain with our students, colleagues, or potential buyers of our skills. Man's astonishing mastery of his physical environment in the last two centuries still contains breaks and gaps. His efforts to develop the scientific process for studying his own fate with his fellows cover little more than a century.

There is a fundamental step for the scientific process during the early development of inquiry. The first step in such inquiry is to learn about the phenomena in question. As applied to problems of attitude and attitude change, this step means learning from the actualities of events as persons uphold a position or disdain another, as they react to communication from others with satisfaction or tension, as they categorize that communication as resembling or differing from their position in some degree, and as they change their attitudes and behavior or become more confirmed in their customary grooves, as the case may be.

Of course, the mere description of phenomena is not science in itself. It is, however, a first step, as noted by such diverse authors as the psychologist MacLeod (1951) and the mathematicians Allendoerfer and Oakley (1959), the latter in a college textbook of mathematics.

The next steps involve the laborious specification of the conditions in which the phenomena and their variations are manifested. The aim is to condense these conditions into conceptual terms as variables that can be specified sufficiently to predict the occurrence and the alteration of the phenomena. Without specification of the factors or variables that affect observed phenomena, there may be theory, but it is not scientific. There may be formal logic, but it proceeds from untested premises. In the domain of social behavior, theory then becomes a game. At this stage of development, the behavioral sciences need fewer games and more examination of the assumptions from which their games are played, fewer formal expressions of models limited to an arbitrary set of variables and more empirical specification of the *significant* variables that need to be included in an adequate model.

These are among the reasons that, at this stage of development, the social judgment-involvement approach welcomes the charge of being primitive or even crude. It welcomes the charge because its aim is to examine the nature of the phenomena in question—attitudes and their change—and to specify major variables that are bound to affect these phenomena in all of their variations.

Thus the approach is not merely concerned with how people behave when they experience tension, dissonance, incongruity, or imbalance but in specifying the conditions (variables) that will *produce* such experiences. Its aim is to predict the degree of discrepancy between a communication and the person's attitude that will arouse psychological discomfiture, to predict his reaction to the communication, and to predict how it will or will not affect his attitude. It aims to specify the conditions in which an individual will be susceptible to attempts to change his attitude or be resistant to change even *before* anyone has attempted to alter his view.

These pretensions required a concept of attitude based on assumptions that are empirically valid. They require research into attitude problems that are personally significant and critical. They require a perspective on these problems broader than that provided by an inspection of one or a few samples of persons comfortably situated in an environment that has never challenged their cherished values or has so sheltered them from critical decisions that they see no alternatives but their own limited field. The time has long since passed when the social scientist can generalize about attitude problems on the basis of phenomena observed in a small fraction of a tiny portion of the educated population in one or two of the world's advantaged countries.

Finally, the social judgment-involvement approach has the pretension of developing concepts and operational measures for the *structure* of the person's attitude and his degree of personal involvement in the matter at hand. In these early stages of development, the pretension is to demonstrate the kind of measurement techniques required by an adequate theory. Many technical improvements and elaborations are feasible. . . . Certainly, the use of multidimensional analysis is the obvious next step.

In short, the social judgment-involvement approach has been long in the making, even for a field of inquiry as new as attitude research. Its most recent and complete statement was *Attitude and Attitude Change* (Sherif, Sherif, and Nebergall, 1965). The survey of findings on judgment was presented in *Social Judgment* (Sherif and Hovland, 1961), along with a program of research initiated in 1948. The literature on attitudes and self (ego) involvement was surveyed and summarized in *The Psychology of Ego-involvements* (Sherif and Cantril, 1947).

Because a *valid* model of attitude and attitude change is the ultimate goal, it is all the more important that we proceed from assumptions that are established empirically. Assumptions based on analogy with the more established sciences have not helped but hindered the progress toward this aim.

For example, traditional attitude measurement has been based largely on such models. In research practice the individual's attitude has been represented as a point on a scale derived by analogy from a physical model. Thus, an attitude has been represented as an arithmetic mean of acceptances (positive) and rejections (negative), as a point on an interval scale or a ratio scale with a zero point (as in the measurement of temperature), as a point in two, three, or *n* dimensional space, or as a point on a cumulative scale (as in the measurement of physical distance in Euclidean space). Too often the measurement model and the particular measurement itself have not been referred back to the phenomena they purported to measure.

Although it is true that a two-inch segment of matter is included in a total measurement of ten inches, it is by no means true that a social attitude representing a lesser position will be included in the range of positions acceptable to a person strongly committed to an extreme position. Opposing sides in a conflict, each desiring peace but committed to emerge victorious, need not see a negotiated peace as a position included in their scale. "Desegregation at a reasonable pace" will be jeered by a person committed to "desegregation now" and placed in the detestable category of tokenism.

Therefore, at the outset, the present approach inquires into the nature of the scales to which attitudes are referable. Every attitudinal reaction implies that the person has compared, evaluated, or chosen among alternatives. These are examples of a judgment process. What are the judgment scales that the person uses as his basis for comparison, evaluation or choice? Here it is useful to distinguish between judgment scales that can be assessed relative to physical units—that is, *psychophysical* scales—and those that on the whole cannot be so assessed—that is, *psychosocial* scales.

Psychophysical and Psychosocial Scales

In laboratory research on judgment, the word "psychophysics" is associated with studies assessing judgments relative to the units of a physical continuum or at least to physical gradations. The psychophysical scale is certainly not entirely foreign to the study of social judgment. For example, conceptions of speed and distance can be gauged both against standard measures of these continua and against the distances and speeds that the person has experienced using various social tools. We know that these conceptions differ considerably for a peasant with a donkey and a jet pilot. Thus, while rooted in social experiences, the differences in their conceptions are referable to a scale of physical units.

In social life, however, there are matters of strong concern for which no physical measures are available, such as those for speed and distance. Even the value of a given monetary unit is subject to lengthy and complex decisions, resting ultimately on agreement among those who exchange the money. We are not suggesting that the principles of judgment for psychophysical scales are necessarily invalid for judgments relative to psychosocial scales. On the contrary, we suggest that the way to discover whether these principles are operative is to understand first the nature of psychosocial scales. The same principles may be operative if we take into account both the nature of psychosocial scales and the new factors that enter into the judgment process, factors that may be less important or even absent in psychophysical judgments.

We are not alone in suggesting that psychosocial scales may have properties differing from those of psychophysical scales. Decades ago the sociologist Emile Durkheim (1915) stated forcefully that events of social life are not merely carry-overs of physical events and cannot, therefore, be extrapolated from them on the same continuum.

What are some major properties of psychosocial scales that distinguish them from physical continua? It is not sufficient to point out that psychosocial scales require the consensus of given sets of people, for so do time, weight, distance, and many other physical scales. Two differences between psychophysical and psychosocial scales will suffice to clarify our point in this context.

First, the psychophysical scale based on consensus is, at some point, referable to physical events and can be checked against them. The Indian groups whose calendars were calculated inaccurately soon found the planting season falling in the wrong months. However, psychosocial scales are typically referable only to other social facts: the ways of life, the relationships within and between groups, and their value systems.

Second, psychosocial scales are based on consensus that also establishes limits of acceptability and the limits of what is objectionable. The direct referent for such evaluative boundaries is the consensus itself. The limits not only vary from culture to culture and group to group but in the same groups during different periods of history. For example, a hundred years ago the possibility of a federal graduated income tax in this country was highly objectionable to the great majority; it was supported only by a few radical groups who were thought to be "crackpots." Currently, there is a variety of positions about raising or lowering the tax and about which groups should benefit, but very few persons seriously advocate abolishing it altogether.

What we are saying here is that a psychosocial scale reflects the stands taken by groups, by strata or by an entire society at a given period in their history. They have regularities, and they are patterned, as are the groups that uphold the various stands. In fact the existence of regularities and changes in the patterns is essential if there is to be a social science, for a science cannot be built about a collection of wholly unique events. However, it cannot be assumed that these regularities have the same properties as physical scales.

At any given time, individual differences in attitude can be gauged relative to the regularities and patterns of social organization, the current patterns of acceptability and rejection, and their changes. In fact the individual's attitudes must be gauged relative to the stands taken by others in his own group and in other groups. Thus, the study of attitudes cannot be strictly psychological. The yardsticks that can be developed for valid assessment of individual attitudes are derived from the stuff that should be the domain of study for sociologists, anthropologists, political scientists, and economists.

In order to proceed with an analysis of the judgment process when a person with an attitude on some topic is faced with a communication or other event relevant to it, let us ask some simple questions whose answers will give our direction in research.

WHAT IS AN ATTITUDE?

The present approach starts by asking the following crucial questions: *What is it* that is to be changed when a person is exposed to some attempt to change his attitude? What is it that is resistant to change?

Clearly, the way we answer these questions will affect what and how we study. The need for answers was indicated recently by Allen of the University of Wisconsin (1966) when he wrote: "One of the shortcomings of traditional research in the attitude area is the excessive preoccupation with changing a response on an isolated (and apparently randomly selected) issue in the laboratory at the expense of research on the nature of attitudes" (p. 284).

From studies labeled research on attitude and attitude change, we might conclude that attitude is a blanket term covering any old judgment or opinion that the individual renders. Are we dealing with factors governing the individual's guesses about the number of beans in a jar, or leaves on a tree, or sand pebbles on a square yard of beach? Or are we concerned with his views on his family, on how he sees himself as a person relative to his contemporaries, on the worth of his religion, his politics, his profession, his country,

or his way of life? It is one thing to attempt to change a person who uses a toothbrush to switch from one brand to another. It is quite another thing to persuade someone who has never brushed his teeth that a toothbrush should be used.

In short, when we talk about attitude change are we talking about any change in behavior whatsoever? Or are we talking about changes in the person's stands towards other persons, objects, groups, beliefs, and institutions that he accepts or rejects as related to himself, with all of the commitments, identifications and emotional reverberations associated with such stands?

In order to answer these questions, we need to examine the properties that have made attitude a central problem in social psychology, to characterize the data from which an attitude is inferred, and to formulate a definition of attitude that fits these properties and the data.

Criteria of Attitude

When an attitude is discussed we are not talking about something that can be observed directly. We are speaking of a psychological concept designating something *inside* the individual. Just as we can never directly observe pain, psychological tension, or an unspoken idea, we cannot see an attitude. Nevertheless, the concept of attitude has several characteristics that differentiate it from other concepts referring to internal states of the individual.

Attitudes are not innate—They belong to that domain of human motivation variously studied under the labels of "social drives," "social needs," "social orientations," and the like. It is assumed that the appearance of an attitude is dependent on learning.

Attitudes are not temporary states but are more or less enduring once they are formed —Of course, attitudes do change; but once formed they acquire a regulatory function such that, within limits, they are not subject to change with the ups and downs of homeostatic functioning of the organism or with every just-noticeable variation in the stimulus conditions.

Attitudes always imply a relationship between the person and objects—In other words, attitudes are not self-generated, psychologically. They are formed or learned in relation to identifiable referents, whether these be persons, groups, institutions, objects, values, social issues, or ideologies.

The relationship between person and object is not neutral but has motivational-affective properties—These properties derive from the context of highly significant social interaction in which many attitudes are formed, from the fact that the objects are not neutral for other participants, and from the fact that the self, as it develops, acquires positive value for the person. Therefore, the linkage between self and the social environment is seldom neutral.

The subject-object relationship is accomplished through the formation of categories both differentiating between the objects and between the person's positive or negative relation to objects in the various categories. The referent of an attitude constitutes a set that may range, theoretically, from one to a large number of objects. However, in actuality the formation of a positive or negative stand toward one object usually implies differential attachment to others in the same domain. For example, a singular attraction to one person typically involves a comparison with other persons who are similar and different. The attitude toward the person, therefore, necessarily includes the views toward others with whom he is compared. Needless to say, this process need not be a conscious and deliberate one.

The referents of an attitude, as differentiated from other internal states by the above criteria, may be objects in the person's environment that are nonsocial, in addition to social objects.

As the above criteria imply, the formation of attitudes is integral to the process of form-

ing a self concept. In fact, through the establishment of a constellation of subject-object relationships, the self concept is delineated. Through this process, the groups in which the child is born become not merely external realities to which he must adapt but *reference groups* with which he identifies or strives to identify himself.

Because the criteria for attitude include the person's relatedness to relevant objects on a conceptual level, the present approach is a cognitive approach. However, it is also a motivational-affective approach, for attitudes are not neutral affairs. Finally, it is a behavioral approach because the only possible data from which attitude can be inferred are behaviors, verbal or nonverbal. Attitudes are necessarily cognitive-motivational-behavioral. Any sharp separation of these is bound to be arbitrary and to distort the nature of the phenomena. In actual research practice, treatment of these aspects as "components" typically amounts to using samples of *behavior* in different tasks or situations assigned at different points in time. Although this is legitimate research practice, we should not let our research techniques blind us to the undeniable blending of cognitive-motivational-behavioral in *any* specific situation or task that arouses an attitude.

Defining the Concept

As noted above, attitudes are necessarily inferred from behavior. In defining an attitude, we need to take special note of what *kind* of behavior is evidence for an attitude.

Definitions of attitude have had certain essential features in common. Almost invariably, one of these is that attitudes are acquired or learned. Another is that attitudes are inferred from modes of behavior by the same individual over a time span that are *characteristic, consistent,* and *selective.* Such specification of the data for attitude study was made by the sociologists Thomas and Znaniecki (1918), and included by the psychologists Murphy, Murphy, and Newcomb

(1937); G. W. Allport (1935); Donald Campbell (1950; 1963); Smith, Bruner, and White (1956); and by the authors of the series of volumes from the Yale Communication Research program directed by Carl I. Hovland (e.g., Hovland, Janis, and Kelley, 1953; Rosenberg, Hovland, McGuire, Abelson, and Brehm, 1960).

A definition of attitude should also point to operational tools for assessing attitude and attitude change. It should be formulated in a way that takes into account the nature of psychosocial scales so that the person's attitude can be located relative to a communication intended to change it, beyond the vague statement that it is "similar" or "discrepant."

The definition developed in our approach is based on a body of evidence (*cf.* Sherif and Hovland, 1961; Sherif, Sherif, and Nebergall, 1965). It leads to methods for specifying the structure of an individual's attitude. Briefly it stems from evidence that the characteristic, consistent, and selective modes of behavior from which attitude is inferred are based on characteristic standards and scales for comparison. A judgment process underlies the behavior in which the individual uses a set of categories for *comparing* and *evaluating* items within the stimulus domain in question.

The judgment process in this case is not neutral. In selecting one alternative over others, in seeking some and avoiding other alternatives, in consistently preferring some to others, the individual both discriminates among the alternatives and *evaluates* them. It is as though he were saying "I like and want this one" or "This is the one for me," while avoiding others as objectionable, disgusting, or "definitely not my kind."

Accordingly, the present approach developed the following definition of attitude:

Operationally, an attitude may be defined as the individual's set of categories for evaluating a stimulus domain, which he has established as he learns about that domain in interaction with other persons and which relate him to various subsets within the domain with varying degrees of positive or negative affect.

The data from which attitudes are inferred, therefore, are the person's *consistent* and *characteristic categorizations,* over a time span, of relevant objects, persons, groups, or communications into acceptable and objectionable categories. Change is inferred from the alteration of the individual's acceptance-rejection pattern. A closer understanding of this acceptance-rejection pattern and the analysis of measurable changes has been one of the main tasks in the present approach. From this analysis it has proven possible to make predictions about reaction to communication based on well-known principles governing anchor effects on judgment.

LATITUDES OF ACCEPTANCE, REJECTION, AND NONCOMMITMENT

Proceeding from the definition of attitude, let us specify three concepts for purposes of assessing the structure of an attitude:

Latitude of acceptance—If a person voluntarily states his view on a topic, he usually gives the position most acceptable to him. The latitude of acceptance is simply this most acceptable position *plus* other positions the individual also finds acceptable.

Latitude of rejection—The position most objectionable to the individual, the thing he most detests in a particular domain, *plus* other positions also objectionable to him define the latitude of rejection.

Latitude of noncommitment—While accepting some and rejecting others, the individual may prefer to remain noncommittal in regard to certain positions. Ordinarily, these are the "don't know," "neutral," "undecided," "no opinion," or "no comment" responses in public opinion surveys. In all of our research, the individual has been required *only* to indicate the most acceptable and objectionable positions, being free to accept or reject others but not forced to do so. The positions that he does *not* evaluate as either acceptable or objectionable under these circumstances constitute his *latitude of non-commitment*. As we shall see, some of the most useful predictive indicators discovered in our research are closely related to the size of this latitude of noncommitment, that is, the positions on which the person prefers to remain noncommittal.

What are the advantages of specifying the structure of the person's attitude in terms of latitudes of acceptance, rejection, and non-commitment? *First,* individuals finding the same position as most acceptable *do* differ in their tolerance for other positions and in the range of their rejections. *Second,* the latitudes of acceptance, rejection, and noncommitment differ systematically for persons upholding different positions according to their degree of involvement in the issue at hand.

In translating the concept of attitude into research procedures, we have developed two techniques for assessing latitudes of acceptance, rejection, and noncommitment that differ sufficiently to be spelled out in some detail (*cf.* Sherif, Sherif, and Nebergall, 1965). Although both techniques are closely related to the conception of attitudes, the research procedures, the advantages and disadvantages of each are different, as we shall see. Here, we shall call one procedure the Method of Ordered Alternatives. The second is known as the "Own Categories" Procedure.

Method of Ordered Alternatives for Assessing the Structure of Attitude

Briefly, the Method of Ordered Alternatives (positions) starts with a survey of existing stands upheld by different groups or significant persons on an issue. From the statements obtained through content analysis of the social field, a number are selected to secure latitudes of acceptance, rejection, and non-commitment. Those positions selected represent the entire range of positions sampled, from one extreme to another. The only assumption about their scalar properties is that they do represent the range of the various po-

sitions on the issue and that they can be *ordered* reliably from one extreme to the other by anyone acquainted with the issue in question. No assumptions about the intervals between the available alternatives are made.

The Method of Ordered Alternatives has been used to secure latitudes of acceptance, rejection, and noncommitment on a variety of social issues both in this country and abroad (*cf.* Sherif, Sherif, and Nebergall, 1965; Diab, 1965a, 1965b; Whittaker, 1965; Bieri *et al.,* 1966). In order to obtain measures of the three latitudes, the subject is simply asked to indicate the position most acceptable to him (his own position), any others that are acceptable or not objectionable, the position most objectionable to him, and any others that may be objectionable. Note that he is not asked to respond successively to every statement. In fact many subjects prefer not to do so, and the positions which they *neither* accept nor reject constitute the latitude of noncommitment.

In order to summarize a considerable mass of data briefly here, we utilize findings from a study of the 1960 presidential elections (Sherif, Sherif, and Nebergall, 1965). After presenting illustrative data, we shall draw certain conclusions based on these findings, on a similar study conducted in 1956 (Sherif and Hovland, 1961), on studies of the prohibition issue (Hovland, Harvey, and Sherif, 1957), studies of farm policy by Whittaker (1965), the labor-management issue by Alvar Elbing, the desegregation issue by L. LaFave, and the issue of reapportionment of state legislatures according to population by John Reich (*cf.* Sherif, Sherif, and Nebergall, 1965).

All of the issues mentioned are controversial, and in each case active participants on each side of the controversy have been subjects along with less concerned parties (for example, college students from general classes, school teachers, unselected adult citizens, etc.). Still, for reasons that will become apparent as we continue, certain limitations are imposed upon our generalizations by the subject populations available. For this reason, we take particular note of the work of Diab in circumstances where partisanship is more intense and significant in the lives of individuals....

Figure 1 is a summary of the relative sizes

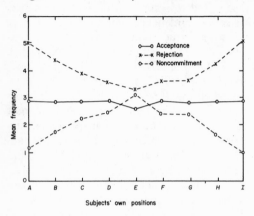

Figure 1. Size of latitudes of acceptance, rejection and noncommitment for persons adopting each of nine positions as most acceptable. The locations represent means for subjects in a study of the 1960 presidential election (from Sherif, Sherif, and Nebergall, 1965, p. 52).

of latitudes of acceptance, rejection, and noncommitment on the 1960 election issue. Although these particular data were obtained in the Pacific Northwest, it should be noted that data obtained in the southwestern region, which has a different population and history, do not differ significantly from these.

The figure presents the mean number of positions in the latitude of acceptance, rejection, and noncommitment for persons adopting each of nine positions as *most acceptable* to them (their own positions). The person's own position is given on the baseline from *A,* the most extreme Republican, to *I,* the most extreme Democratic position. The ordinate represents the mean number of positions responded to in different ways. Solid dots indicate the mean number of acceptances, *X*s the mean number of rejections, and the white circles represent the mean number for noncommitment.

Note that the means for the latitude of acceptance form almost a straight line near three acceptances, regardless of a person's own position. The dip at *E* (the noncommittal position) reflects the heterogeneity of these persons: About 17 per cent of the subjects at *E* (which is nonpartisan) found only the *E* position acceptable, whereas another 40 per cent were "leaners," accepting only one other position on either the Republican or Democratic side. Relationships between the size of the latitude of rejection and the person's own stand and between noncommitment and the person's own stand are both significant.

Certain generalizations are possible from the data in Figure 1 and the other studies mentioned above.

1. The latitude of rejection increases in size as a function of the extremity of the person's position, and the function is curvilinear for bipolar issues such as these.

2. The latitude of noncommitment is inversely related to extremity of commitment, approaching zero for persons with the most extreme commitment.

3. The relative sizes of the latitude of rejection, the latitude of acceptance, and latitude of noncommitment are clearly different for persons upholding the various positions. Relative to the latitude of acceptance, the latitude of rejection is disproportionately greater and the latitude of noncommitment smaller as the person's own position becomes more extreme.

There is considerable evidence from earlier research showing that persons who adopt extreme stands are more likely to be highly involved than those with moderate stands (e.g., Cantril, 1946). Conversely, there is evidence from data on ratings of personality dimensions that the person who is highly involved in a particular personal characteristic is likely to give extreme ratings on that dimension (Tajfel and Wilkes, 1963). In fact a recent review of research on the latter problem concludes that extremity of ratings on personal characteristics varies with the personal importance attached to the characteristic when research procedures do not "impose" the dimension to be rated upon subjects (O'Donovan, 1965, p. 365).

Significant as the association between extremity of position and personal involvement may be, our interest has been in the effects of varying ego-involvement, not in extreme attitudes per se. There are several reasons for this interest. In the first place, extremity of position is frequently identified by psychologists in this country as a sign of pathology. For this reason it is particularly significant that in the review of the literature on extreme ratings of personal attributes, O'Donovan (1965) found evidence that the "pathology-polarization hypotheses are supported by studies in which rating dimensions are imposed upon the subject," and "the meaningfulness-polarization hypotheses are supported by studies in which the subject has the opportunity to provide his own personally meaningful dimensions" or to select dimensions that are more significant to him personally (p. 365). Perhaps our view of persons who take extreme stands has been colored excessively by a norm of "liberal moderation." In other settings extreme stands may be viewed as strong convictions (cf. Diab, 1965a) rather than as symptoms of personal disturbance.

Second, in our research on the 1960 presidential election, *variances* around the mean latitudes for persons upholding different own positions (Figure 1) differed significantly only for those who adopted the E (nonpartisan) position. This finding means that (with the exception of the heterogeneous lot who chose to remain nonpartisan) the distributions around the means in Figure 1 were similar for subjects upholding each position as most acceptable. Thus, there were a number of subjects who chose moderate positions as most acceptable but gave considerable other evidence of being highly involved in the election. These persons also rejected as many as five or six positions out of nine.

Third, although our earlier research had

led us to expect that the size of the latitude of acceptance would decrease with extremity of positions, it is clear from Figure 1 that the mean latitude of acceptance did not vary significantly with own position. There is sufficient evidence from other studies to show that *relative* sizes of the latitudes of acceptance and rejection do differ according to extremity of position and that highly involved subjects do indeed have narrower latitudes of acceptance than uninvolved subjects (*cf.* Whittaker, 1965; LaFave and Sherif, 1962; Reich and Sherif, 1963). However, the size of the latitude of acceptance was not sufficient as an indicator of involvement across varying own positions on the election issue.

The purpose of our concern in securing an indicator of ego-involvement was to make predictions about the placement of five communications on the election issue by subjects upholding different positions. Noting that the size of the latitude of rejection varied systematically with own position and that the variances of subjects upholding different positions did not differ significantly, we adopted size of the latitude of rejection as an operational index of involvement in the issue. As we shall see presently, individuals thus differentiated as to involvement do show systematic differences in their perception of the position presented in communication.

Since noncommitment increases markedly with moderateness of position (Figure 1) and is much more frequent for issues less involving than a national election immediately prior to the event, we have suggested that the relative frequency of noncommitment on several issues may serve as a predictive indicator of the individual's susceptibility to change on these issues. Although research is underway to assess this suggestion, very little has been done to specify all of the conditions associated with high noncommitment. It is an important area of research, since subjects with a large latitude of noncommitment are particularly likely to change their attitudes in response to a communication (Sherif, Sherif, and Nebergall, 1965).

Larimer (1966) has recently shown, with French-speaking and English-speaking Canadians as subjects, that a communication falling within the latitude of noncommitment is evaluated much more favorably than a communication falling within the person's latitude of rejection.

The data obtained by the Method of Ordered Alternatives reveal systematic variations in the structure of an attitude according to extremity of position and according to relative involvement in the issue. The structures revealed are, however, almost starkly geometric. In order to understand the processes underlying the results, we turn now to a consideration of the judgment process when a person appraises stimulus material relevant to his attitude.

In fact, in the present approach, the partitioning of Ordered Alternatives into latitudes of acceptance, rejection, and noncommitment was based on study of the judgment (categorization) process, not on sheerly logical grounds. The judgment process is best revealed through the use of the Own Categories Procedure, to which we now turn.

THE INDIVIDUAL'S OWN CATEGORIES

What psychological processes underlie the differences obtained between latitudes of acceptance, rejection, and noncommitment according to the person's relative involvement? Several psychological theories have proposed that category width (latitude) reflects a personality trait or "style." However, available studies that have correlated the same person's category widths for issues of varying personal involvement have found that personal consistency across issues accounts for no more than 10 to 15 per cent of the total variance (e.g., Sherif, 1961; Glixman, 1965). Therefore we sought a theoretical basis for the phenomena sufficiently broad to incorporate idiosyncratic variables and to account for the fact that an individual may tolerate differences on issues of little concern to him (even to the point of self-contradiction) while see-

ing a matter of high personal concern in terms of "black and white." The theory also had to be sufficiently broad to include the fact that the ranges for tolerance and condemnation vary from one human group to another.

We found such a basis in the psychology of judgment, studied for nearly a century in psychological laboratories in various countries. Our account of the principles essential to the approach is necessarily sketchy here (cf. Sherif, Sherif, and Nebergall, 1965).

Systematic Variations in Judgment

Whether the object of judgment is a weight, the length of a line, the color of a person's skin, or the beauty of a girl, judgment is rendered relative to the immediate stimulus context in which it appears and to preceding contexts. For example, a statement on the issue of segregation in the public schools ("We must keep the future interests of school children in mind") is appraised differently when preceded by other statements opposed to segregation, on the one hand, or by statements favoring segregation, on the other.

However, all stimuli present or just preceding the object of judgment do not have equal weight in affecting the outcome, not even in the psychophysical laboratory where the stimuli are usually neutral. In one of the orthodox psychophysical methods, the standard stimulus that is presented with each new comparison stimulus is more influential than those less frequently presented or not designated as a standard (Helson, 1959, p. 591). Such frequently presented stimuli, or those designated as standards, become anchors for the individual's judgments. Lacking an explicit standard, the individual typically uses the most extreme stimuli presented to him as anchors in sizing up the intermediate values. The end stimuli thus contribute more than others to his judgment of a particular member of a series (Parducci, 1963).

An anchor enhances accuracy of judgment for items coinciding with it in value; but it produces systematic shifts or "displacements" in judgments of objects differing from it in varying degress. An anchor differing slightly from the object of judgment results in displacement *toward* the anchor: this is an *assimilation effect*, well known in studies of perception and now in judgment (*cf*. Sherif, Taub, and Hovland, 1958; Parducci and Marshall, 1962; Helson, 1964). With increasing discrepancies between the anchor and the object of judgment, assimilation ceases, and, after a transition, displacement begins to occur in a direction *away* from the anchor: the difference between the anchor and the object is exaggerated. This is the well-known *contrast effect*. Assimilation and contrast in judgment are complementary phenomena governed by the relationship between anchor and objects of judgment; they are not separate mechanisms, as Helson (1964) has also stressed.

Years ago, Hunt and Volkmann (1937) showed that contrast effects could be produced in the laboratory by instructing the subject to *imagine* the most extreme representative of the dimension being judged. Thus, it is evident that the person's *internal standards* have to be taken into account, as well as the stimulation that he faces within a limited time period.

The foregoing findings provided the basis for the logic in explaining shifts in judgment of attitude statements that occurred according to the person's own attitude in studies of the Thurstone method of equal-appearing intervals (Hovland and Sherif, 1952; Sherif and Hovland, 1953). In these experiments, the subject's task was objective. He was to categorize a series of 114 statements developed by Hinckley according to how favorable or unfavorable they were to the status of Negroes. In one condition, he was to use eleven categories *imposed* upon him by the experimenters' instructions. In the other, he was left free to use any number of categories in any way he chose, in order to differentiate among the statements. In short, the Own Categories Procedure was used. Some of the subjects were highly involved in the issue, either as the first Negro students at a previ-

ously segregated institution or as active white participants in the desegregation movement.

Before presenting illustrative findings from this research, it is important to note that the pool of statements ranged from extremely pro- to extremely anti-Negro statements and also contained a large number of intermediate items having high Q values (high variability). In this and subsequent studies using the Own Categories Procedure, the stimulus materials have contained a large number of items that are categorized by unselected subjects with great variability.

The subject's task is to sort the pool of items into any number of piles or categories that seems necessary so that items within each category seem to him to "belong together." Typically, a category at one extreme is defined by instructions. The person subsequently numbers and labels his own categories relative to that extreme. Upon completion of the task, he may be asked to indicate which categories are acceptable or objectionable to him, if a direct report of latitudes of acceptance, rejection and noncommitment is desired.

Figure 2 presents results with *imposed* categories for moderately favorable subjects (indicated by the arrow at seven on the baseline, with eleven being most favorable). It represents the relative frequencies of judg-

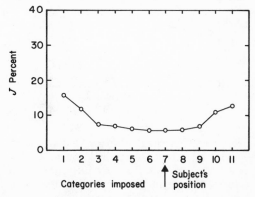

Figure 2.   Percentages of items (J per cent = Judgment per cent) placed in eleven categories imposed by instructions by moderately pro-Negro subjects (data from Sherif and Hovland, 1953).

ment in each of the 11 categories imposed by the instructions. It can be seen that these moderate subjects did a fair job in using the 11 categories about equally, with a slight concentration at each end. They distributed their judgments even more equitably among categories when they sorted the same statement with the Own Categories Procedure, as shown in Figure 3.

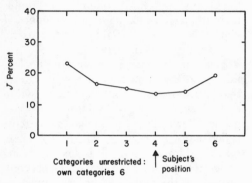

Figure 3. Percentage of items (J per cent = Judgment per cent) placed in own categories by moderately pro-Negro subjects (data from Sherif and Hovland, 1953).

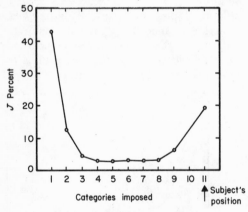

Figure 4. Percentage of items (J per cent = Judgment per cent) placed in 11 categories imposed by instructions by extremely pro-Negro subjects (data from Sherif and Hovland, 1953).

Figures 4 and 5 present comparable data for persons who were highly involved in the Negro issue with own positions at 11, the most favorable extreme. Under the *imposed*

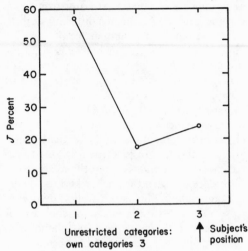

Figure 5. Percentage of items (J per cent = Judgment per cent) placed in own categories by extremely pro-Negro subjects (data from Sherif and Hovland, 1953).

categories condition (Figure 4), these subjects neglected the intermediate categories imposed on them by instructions, producing bimodal distributions of the items with a small mode at the favorable end and a disproportionately high mode at the extreme farthest away from their own stand on the issue.

The bimodal distribution was greatly accentuated under the Own Categories Procedure (Figure 5), owing especially to the tendency for highly involved persons to use fewer categories than less involved subjects. On the average, the most militant Negro subjects used fewer than four categories, placing 65 of the 114 statements in a single objectionable category and 27 in a category acceptable to them. In comparison, unselected white students used more categories, on the average, placing 43 statements in objectionable categories and 38 in categories they later indicated were acceptable.

In that early research, the results for anti-Negro subjects were not a clear reversal of the distributions for pro-Negro subjects. It was suggested that the anti-Negro subjects were less involved in the issue, but it was possible to specify this only by pointing to the striking differences between their activity pertinent to the issue and that of the pro-Negro subjects. Therefore it is particularly interesting that Vaughan (1961) did obtain the reverse of the distributions in Figures 4 and 5 for *anti* subjects, in a situation where the normative trend to appear "liberal" about minority groups was not strong, namely in south Texas. In this case, the *anti* subjects were negative toward Texans of Latin-American origin.

Accounting for the Bipolar Variations in Judgment

Proceeding directly from the findings on assimilation-contrast effects in psychophysical judgments, we can account for both the bimodal distributions in judgments (Figures 4 and 5) and the related finding that the latitude of rejection is disproportionately greater than latitude of acceptance for highly involved subjects. The additional assumptions needed to do so are supported by experimental evidence (Sherif, Sherif, and Nebergall, 1965).

1. If a person has an attitude toward a stimulus domain, his judgments of specific objects in that domain are, to some extent, made relative to his own reference scale, in addition to the context of immediate and preceding stimulation. This reference scale is composed of the individual's own categories. (See the definition of attitude presented earlier.)

2. To the extent that the stimulus domain has high priority in his self system (degree of ego-involvement), the task of categorizing stimuli becomes an *evaluative* task for him, even though he is told to judge according to objective, nonevaluative criteria. Although instructed to heed only the stimulus attributes of the items and to categorize them on an impersonal dimension, the highly involved individual performs the task in terms of his agreements-disagreements with the items. (Vaughan reported that her anti-Latin subjects often objected to the instruction that they sort items only according to how pro- or anti-Latin they were because, in their words, so many of the statements *simply were not true*.) One may *force* the involved person to follow instructions by insisting that he compare one item with another, as in the method of paired-comparisons. He *can* discriminate among the items (*cf.* Kelley *et al.*, 1955); but barring special arrangements forcing him to do so, he does not divorce the task of categorizing items from his evaluations of them. This is the basic reason why the Own Categories Procedure suggests itself as an indirect or disguised method for attitude and personality assessment (Sherif and Sherif, 1964).

3. To the degree that he is ego-involved, the person uses his own position as the main standard for placing items related to it. Since, in our own research, predictions from this postulate have invariably been more accurate when we considered the bounds (limits) of the latitude of acceptance, we are forced to conclude that the involved person also has a clear concept of "how far he will go" and that the latitude of acceptance itself acquires an anchoring function.

The psychological process when the individual is presented with a specific set of stimuli to classify is then analogous to that in the judgment laboratory: Using his own position as an anchor, he is more discriminating about admitting items to acceptable categories than about placing items in objectionable categories. His threshold for acceptance is raised. His latitude of acceptance is comparatively small because he is "choosy" about admitting positions to it. At the same time, however, the use of own position as an anchor results in an assimilation effect. The raised threshold for acceptance is a *relative* matter, for the own position anchor also results in assimilation of positions close to it. This assimilative trend is revealed in the small mode at the acceptable end of Figure 5 and in the tendency for subjects to rate statements more favorably when they are near their own positions (*cf.* Zavalloni and Cook, 1965; Selltiz, Edrich, and Cook, 1965).

Concomitantly, use of own position as an anchor reduces discrimination for positions widely discrepant from it: the threshold for rejection is *lowered* because discrepant items are *contrasted* to the acceptable position and seen as *more* discrepant than they would be by a person who is not involved in the issue. As a result, items that might seem "moderate" to a less involved person are lumped together into one or a few broad categories as *objectionable*. Hence, the highly involved person has a latitude of rejection disproportionately greater than his latitude of acceptance.

4. On a controversial issue (bipolar), the highly involved person uses *fewer* categories than a less committed person, a fact that is probably related to the assimilation-contrast effects relative to his own stand. Logically, at least, these systematic displacements would result in a need for fewer categories.

The twin phenomena, namely a restricted number of categories and unequal use of categories, are intensified by the degree of personal involvement. The evidence stems from two kinds of experiments using the Own Categories Procedure: (*a*) experiments comparing categorizations of the same materials by subjects whose public activities indicate varying involvement (e.g., LaFave and Sherif, 1962; Vaughan, 1961; Reich and Sherif, 1963) and (*b*) experiments varying the stimulus material according to their relative involvement for the same subjects (e.g., Sherif, 1961; Glixman, 1965; Koslin, Waring, and Pargament, 1965).

Using the latter method, Koslin and others had Peace Corps volunteers categorize series of statements on five issues that subjects ranked according to how much time they spent talking on the topic. Using the latter criterion of involvement, the investigators found that latitudes of acceptance decreased and latitudes of rejection increased in width from the least involving issue (housing in India) to the most involving issue (segregation in the United States). The latitude of rejection was greater than the latitude of

acceptance for the latter issue. Furthermore, repetition of the task with items added to each extreme produced significantly *less* shifting of items in the more involving than the less involving issue. In other words, *consistency* in categorizing the items common to the two tasks was greatest for the more involving issue.

More recently, Koslin (1966) had Peace Corps volunteers assess two sets of different statements on motives for joining the Corps, using a modified Own Categories Procedure. The sets of statements were matched by an independent determination of their standard scores derived from paired-comparison judgments. By correlating the mean value of statements the subjects placed into their different categories on the two tasks, Koslin has shown that *consistency* of categorization (reliability) is very high indeed on such an involving topic, even when the specific statements in the two sets differed. The lowest correlation obtained was .95.

Since the systematic displacements and variations in number of categories according to degree of involvement occur even when the person is not instructed to reveal his attitude, we have suggested the Own Categories Procedure as an indirect or disguised test of attitude. For similar reasons, the technique is admirably suited for cross-cultural comparisons and for a nonconfrontive method in locating areas of personal concern in the study of personality. Although the specific content can be adapted to cross-cultural and interpersonal differences, the logic of the method should be invariant since it is based on general principles of human judgment.

PLACEMENT OF COMMUNICATION IS BASIC TO PROBLEMS OF ATTITUDE CHANGE

Attempts at attitude change—whether in interpersonal, group, or mass communication situations—involve some form of communication. The basic information for predicting a person's reaction to a communication is *where* he places its position and the communicator relative to himself. The way that a person appraises a communication and perceives its position relative to his own stand affects his reaction to it and what he will do as a result.

If the foregoing propositions be granted, it becomes apparent that a theory of attitude change has to be capable of predicting the person's judgment of communication. From at least the time of William James, various authors have noted the phenomena of tension, irritation, and discomfiture in response to a situation violating values of some personal importance. The observation is not new. In recent years, a number of theories have developed to predict how the individual will respond to this internal tension, imbalance, incongruence, or dissonance. However, study of the variables affecting whether a communication will or will not arouse such internal tension has not been systematically undertaken within these theoretical frameworks.

By systematic study of the placement and evaluation of communication, the present approach to attitude change has developed a set of generalizations concerning the process of appraising communication. They are basic in predicting whether attitudes change or do not change. As these generalizations indicate, the person's reaction to a communication is predicated upon a patterned psychological process that precludes certain behavioral alternatives and promotes others. Theories that do not take such patterning into account, proceeding instead to predict reaction to communication on the basis of logical alternatives, will necessarily be found to err at some point. The logical alternatives turn out to be related psychologically, such that a person may adopt more than one and in varying degrees. The behavioral outcome is governed by the patterning of a set of variables that are specified in the sections to follow.

Discrepancy between Communication and the Person's Stand

The determination of a discrepancy between a communication and the person's position at the time must be made relative to that person's own categories (his attitude). When groups of individuals are involved, such determination amounts to specifying the position of a communication relative to the psychosocial scale established in the particular group to which the individual belongs (his reference group). On the basis of such specification, the following generalizations were reached about placement and evaluation of communication:

A—To the extent that a communication lies within the latitude of acceptance or nearby in the latitude of noncommitment, it is judged as *closer* to the own position (*assimilated*) and is simultaneously perceived as factual, unbiased, fair, and pleasing (Sherif and Hovland, 1961; Sherif, Sherif, and Nebergall, 1965; Larimer, 1966).

B—As the position of communication becomes more discrepant from the latitude of acceptance and increasingly within the latitude of rejection, it is increasingly judged as *more* discrepant and simultaneously perceived as biased, propagandistic, and false (Sherif and Hovland, 1961; Sherif, Sherif, and Nebergall, 1965; Larimer, 1966; Sherif and Jackman, 1966).

In other words, placement of communication and evaluation of it occur as patterned aspects of the same judgment process governed by the relationship between the communication and the latitudes of acceptance, rejection, and noncommitment.

In studying placements of five communications presenting different positions on the 1960 election campaign, we were able to specify some of the major variables affecting the occurrence of assimilation-contrast effects and the accompanying evaluations of communication. These are presented briefly in terms of the range of positions within which assimilation and positive evaluation will occur.

Degree of involvement—If the person is not involved at all in an issue, discrepancy relative to his own stand becomes a minor issue. The experience of tension, imbalance, or incongruity presumes a discrepancy from a position to which the individual attaches some importance.

In a study of placement of five communications presenting different positions on the 1960 election, ego-involvement was defined operationally in terms of the size of the *latitude of rejection*, with the greater latitude indicating greater involvement in the issue. Discrepancy of the communication was calculated in terms of position steps that it was removed from the limit of the person's latitude of acceptance. The consistent finding was that *less* involved subjects (with smaller latitudes of rejection) assimilated the communication toward their own view over a much wider range of discrepancies than did highly involved persons. Highly involved persons with the same latitude of acceptance as the less involved persons revealed a *narrower* range of assimilation. Conversely, the highly involved person revealed a contrast effect when appraising a communication that a less involved person assimilated. In a recent study, Eagley and Manis (1966) reported a related finding: ego-involved subjects responded more negatively to a discrepant communication than less involved subjects.

We conclude that the range of assimilation is inversely related to the degree of personal involvement.

Structure of the communication—The structure of the communication may be defined operationally in terms of the number of alternative interpretations (placements) it permits. Certain properties of issues (for example, complexity), of statement (for example, ambiguity) and of position (for example, moderate versus extreme) decrease the degree of structure as so defined. Although a great deal remains to be studied about

communication structure, available evidence indicates that the effects of varying involvement cannot be specified without considering this variable.

A—Clear-cut statements of extreme positions are not subject to assimilation-contrast effects to an appreciable degree. It is the somewhat less extreme (Zavalloni and Cook, 1965; Selltiz, Edrich, and Cook, 1965) and especially the intermediate statements (LaFave and Sherif, 1962; Koslin *et al.*, 1965; Sherif, Sherif, and Nebergall, 1965) that are subject to systematic displacement. These findings are probably related, on the one hand, to the fact that extreme positions are frequently stated in unambiguous form and, on the other, to the tendency of advocates of extreme stands to simplify the issue. Definition of the communication variables conducive to lack of structure in the intermediate range will probably require further specification of the nature of verbal ambiguity (*cf.* Zimbardo, 1960; LaFave *et al.*, 1963). Moderate positions are not necessarily ambiguous (*cf.* Sherif and Hovland, 1961; Zavalloni and Cook, 1965), yet the greatest variability in categorizing usually occurs in the intermediate range (*cf.* Edwards, 1946). Further study of the structure variable might well be related to studies of fluid social situations where rumors are rife (e.g., Cantril, 1941). In such situations the individual's use of his own standards in assessing the rumors produces variations that resemble assimilation-contrast effects.

B—The relationship between ego-involvement and communication structure is clear when the communication presents just *two* alternatives, as in the debate format or a systematically counterbalanced statement presenting both sides of an issue with no conclusion (Sherif, Sherif, and Nebergall, 1965). In the 1960 study of election communications, we found that such communications, especially the actual television debates between the two candidates, were highly conducive to assimilation. Proportional to the extremity of their positions, partisans of each side saw their candidate's performance as superior. However, the assimilation trend was much stronger for subjects who were *less* ego-involved. The general trend of assimilation was confirmed more recently in a laboratory study presenting material from the same debates well after the elections, with the interesting difference that some Republican subjects defected toward the then-elected Democratic candidate, Kennedy (Rosnow, 1965).

On the basis of present evidence, we may conclude that the range of assimilation increases as the structure of communication decreases but that high ego-involvement restricts the assimilation range.

Source of the communication—Although little research has been conducted on placement of the position presented in a communication as a function of its source, it is clear that the source is an important variable. When the source is unidentified, the listener typically sizes up his views and, depending upon his placement of the position, attributes the source to an organization friendly or inimical to his reference group, as the case may be (*cf.* Sherif, Sherif, and Nebergall, 1965; Sherif and Jackman, 1966).

Future study of effects of different sources must include more systematic investigation of the person's reference groups and of their friendly or hostile relationship to other groups. Most research in recent years has dealt with the communicator chiefly in terms of his "credibility," a descriptive label that implies a judgment on the part of the subject. The variables affecting judgments of "credibility" are certainly crucial to an adequate theory for reactions to communication. Many years ago, Asch (1940) showed that reaction to communications varied according to whether the communicator was presented as a member of a "congenial" or "antagonistic" group. Subjects went to considerable pains in trying to interpret a communication so that it "fit" the stand of the communicator's group. Such findings would indicate that "credibility" is a complex judgment reflecting both the recipient's reference groups and

the particular attributes prized in its scheme of values.

On the basis of available evidence, the present approach postulates that a source with high status for the individual's reference groups will increase the range of assimilation. The possible interactions between source, the person's involvement in the issue at hand, and his involvement as a group member remain to be explored, insofar as they may affect his placement of communication.

PREDICTIONS ABOUT ATTITUDE CHANGE

The social judgment-involvement approach makes some definite predictions about when attitudes will change, when they will not, and when they will be strengthened in response to communication. These predictions require that the position of communication be specified relative to the person's latitudes of acceptance, rejection, and noncommitment.

The first prediction concerns *susceptibility* to change regardless of the particular communication presented with the intent to change a person's attitude. Susceptibility to change will vary according to the sizes of the person's latitude of noncommitment and latitude of rejection. There is considerable evidence that "moderate" subjects (with large latitudes of noncommitment and small latitudes of rejection) change in laboratory experiments approximately twice as frequently as highly committed subjects with small latitudes of noncommitment and large latitudes of rejection (Sherif, Sherif, and Nebergall, 1965). Therefore, regardless of the discrepancy of the position presented, we predict that the more the person is involved in the issue (the more important it is to him), the *less* susceptible he will be to short-term attempts to change his attitude.

Specification of the structure of a person's attitude in terms of latitudes of acceptance, rejection, and noncommitment permits further predictions about the direction and pat-

tern of change among those who are susceptible. In the study of the 1960 election
campaign, the attitudes of partisans on both
sides and those adopting moderate stands
were assessed twice about a week apart.
Eliminating the most extreme subjects who
could only change by becoming less extreme,
blind predictions of the direction of change
were made based on the pattern of acceptances and rejections during the first session.
Accurate prediction was made for over 70
per cent of the subjects who changed. The
possibility of predicting both susceptibility
and direction of change on such a basis remains to be explored further.

The frequency and the extent of change
as the position presented in communication
differs increasingly from the person's own
stand can be predicted on the basis of the
same variables affecting placement of the
communication. Central to these is the degree of personal involvement. Although the
"balance" and "dissonance" theories have included statements qualifying their predictions according to the "importance" or
"relevance" of the matter at hand, none has
included a theory of self (ego) that leads to
operational measures of this variable. The
typical measure has been self-ratings by the
subjects. The recent emphasis by a number
of researchers within and outside of the "dissonance" movement on the need for specifying the variable of "importance" may hopefully lead to new developments (cf. Walster
and Festinger, 1962; Brock and Becker, 1965;
Zajonc and Burnstein, 1965; O'Donovan,
1965). Meanwhile, the social judgment-involvement approach has suggested a basis for
operationalizing the variable, namely the
process of social judgment as it occurs when
significant constituents (attitudes) of the self
are situationally involved.

Because the theory of cognitive dissonance
has not included a theory of ego-involvements
nor of systematic variations in judgment produced by ego-involved stands, its predictions
about attitude change differ from those of
the present approach in important respects.

Notably, the present approach does not predict a linear increase in frequency or extent
of attitude change as the discrepancy increases between communication and the person's stand. The present approach predicts
increasing frequency and extent of attitude
change with increased discrepancies *only
within the range of assimilation*, which is, we
repeat, affected by the person's involvement
in his stand, the structure of the communication, and the source. Beyond the assimilation
range, the prediction is *decreasing* frequency
and extent of attitude change proportional
to the increasing discrepancy between the
person's stand and the position of communication.

Given some involvement in this issue, we
predict a curvilinear relationship between
attitude change and communication discrepancy. With extreme discrepancies and high
personal commitment, the person will *never*
react to a transitory communication by
changing his attitude. He will feel irritated,
he may derogate the communicator, or speak
to his friends about it; but he will never see
changing his own attitude in the direction of
the communication as a viable alternative.
On the contrary, he is more apt to retrench
in his own stand or to shift *away* from the
communication.

Various writers have pointed to an apparent contradiction in findings on attitude
change as it relates to communication discrepancy. The contradiction *is* apparent, for
it disappears when the conditions of the
various experiments are fully specified. As
the social judgment-involvement approach
predicts, those experiments reporting increased change with increasing discrepancies
have been performed under one or more of
the following conditions:

1. Low ego-involvement or no attitude at
   all at the outset.
2. Ambiguous communications or highly unstructured situations to be judged.
3. Limited ranges of discrepancies.
4. Sources valued highly in terms of the in-

dividual's reference groups (including the experimenter as a source for college students).

Studies reporting a curvilinear relationship between change and discrepancy of communication (e.g., Whittaker, 1965; Aronson *et al.*, 1963; Freedman, 1964; Johnson, 1966) have included involving topics, moderately valued sources, and/or broad ranges of communication discrepancies.

The evidence to date, therefore, falls into a pattern. Low involvement, unstructured stimulus situations, and highly valued sources increase the range of assimilation, within which communication is increasingly effective in producing attitude change. High ego-involvement, structured communications, and less valued sources restrict the range of assimilation, beyond which decreasing frequency and extent of attitude change occurs as the communication becomes more discrepant. Accurate predictions about attitude change can be made only when these variables, at least, are clearly specified.

On our part, we are interested in utilizing the methodological advantages gained from the present approach in further studies of the formation and change of attitudes within the person's reference groups. Attitudes are seldom acquired or changed in lonely situations involving only the individual and a single communicator. The most significant attitudes are acquired with reference to his fellow men with whom he has ties, claims for recognition, and for amounting to something as a person. In previous experiments, interaction among individuals facing common problems or moved by common motives was found to be a potent context for the formation of highly involving attitudes toward other groups and for their change (Sherif, Harvey, White, Hood, and Sherif, 1961). Intensive studies of natural groups (Sherif and Sherif, 1964) have shown that the person's ego-involvements are related to his group membership and that the latitudes of acceptance and rejection differ both for members of different groups and for members of the same group according to their roles and the importance of an issue to that group.

Eventually, accurate prediction of attitude change hinges upon our ability to specify the individual's relative involvement in a variety of value domains, a matter closely related to his roles in various reference groups and to their values. Such specification presumes adequate measurement of his attitudes. The present approach can be extended in these directions to the mutual benefit of research on attitudes and research on group processes, which are undeniably the context for the formation and change of attitudes most significant and consequential for the individual and for his fellow men.

REFERENCES

Allen, Vernon L.
1966   "Review: attitude and attitude change." American Sociological Review 31, No. 2:283–284.

Allendoerfer, C. C., and C. O. Oakley.
1959   Fundamentals of Freshmen Mathematics. New York: McGraw-Hill.

Allport, G. W.
1935   "Attitudes." In C. Murchison (ed.), A Handbook of Social Psychology. Worcester, Massachusetts: Clark University Press.

Aronson, E., Judith A. Turner, and J. M. Carlsmith.
1963   "Communicator credibility and communicator discrepancy as determinants of opinion change." Journal of Abnormal and Social Psychology 67:31–37.

Asch, S. E.
1940   "Studies in the principles of judgments and attitudes: II. Determination of judgments by group and by ego standards." Journal of Social Pychology, SPSSI Bulletin 12:433–465.

Bieri, J., A. L. Atkins, S. Briar, R. L. Leaman, H. Miller, and T. Tripodi.
1966   Clinical and Social Judgment: The Discrimination of Behavioral Information. New York: Wiley.

Brock, T. C., and L. A. Becker.
1965   "Ineffectiveness of 'overheard' counter-

propaganda." Journal of Personal and Social Psychology 2:654–660.

Campbell, D. T.
1950 "The indirect assessment of social attitudes." Psychological Bulletin 47:15–38.
1963 "Social attitudes and other acquired behavioral dispositions." In S. Koch (ed.), Psychology: A Study of a Science. Vol. 6. New York: McGraw-Hill.

Cantril, H.
1941 The Psychology of Social Movements. New York: Wiley.
1946 "The intensity of an attitude." Journal of Abnormal and Social Psychology 41:129–135.

Diab, L. N.
1965a "Studies in social attitudes: I. Variations in latitudes of acceptance and rejection as a function of varying positions on a controversial social issue." Journal of Social Psychology 67:283–295.
1965b "Studies in social attitudes: III. Attitude assessment through the semantic differential." Journal of Social Psychology 67:303–314.

Durkheim, E.
1915 The Elementary Forms of Religious Life. London: Allen and Unwin.
1938 The Rules of the Sociological Method. Chicago: The University of Chicago Press. [1st English translation.]

Eagley, Alice H., and M. Manis.
1966 "Evaluation of message and communicator as a function of involvement." Journal of Personality and Social Psychology 3:483–485.

Edwards, A. L.
1946 "Critique of 'neutral items' in attitude scales constructed by the method of equal-appearing intervals." Psychological Review 53:159–169.

Freedman, J. L.
1964 "Involvement, discrepancy and change." Journal of Abnormal and Social Psychology 69:290–295.

Glixman, A. R.
1965 "Categorizing behavior as a function of meaning domain." Journal of Personality and Social Psychology 2:370–377.

Helson, H.
1959 "Adaptation level theory." In S. Koch (ed.), Psychology: A Study of a Science. Vol. 1. New York: McGraw-Hill.
1964 "Current trends and issues in adaptation-level theory." American Psychologist 19:26–38.

Hovland, C. I., O. J. Harvey, and M. Sherif.
1957 "Assimilation and contrast effects in communication and attitude change." Journal of Abnormal and Social Psychology 55:242–252.

Hovland, C. I., J. L. Janis, and H. H. Kelley.
1953 Communication and Persuasion. New Haven: Yale University Press.

Hovland, C. I., and M. Sherif.
1952 "Judgmental phenomena and scales of attitude measurement: Item displacement in Thurstone scales." Journal of Abnormal and Social Psychology 47:822–832.

Hunt, W. A., and J. Volkmann.
1937 "The anchoring of an affective scale." American Journal of Psychology 49:88–92.

Johnson, H. H.
1966 "Some effects of discrepancy level on responses to negative information about one's self." Sociometry 29:52–66.

Kelley, H. H., C. I. Hovland, M. Schwartz, and R. P. Abelson.
1955 "The influence of judges' attitudes in three methods of scaling." Journal of Social Psychology 42:147–158.

Koslin, B. L.
1966 Personal communication.

Koslin, B. L., P. D. Waring, and R. Pargament.
1965 "Measurement of attitude organization with the 'own category' technique." Prepublication Report, Princeton University.

LaFave, L., and M. Sherif.
1962 "Reference scales and placement of items with the own categories technique." Norman, Oklahoma: Institute of Group Relations (mimeographed).

LaFave, L., R. Szczesiak, J. Yaquinto, and B. Adler.
1963 "Connotation as a supplemental variable in assimilation-contrast principles in psycho-social scales." Fuller report of paper to American Psychological

Association Annual Meetings, Philadelphia (mimeographed).

Larimer, G.
1966 "Social judgment approach to the investigation of French and English Canadian attitudes." Paper presented to annual meetings, Eastern Psychological Association (April), New York City.

MacLeod, R. B.
1951 "The place of phenomenological analysis in social psychology." In J. Rohrer and M. Sherif (eds.), Social Psychology at the Crossroads. New York: Harper.

Murphy, G., Lois B. Murphy, and T. M. Newcomb.
1937 Experimental Social Psychology. New York: Harper.

O'Donovan, D.
1965 "Rating extremity: Pathology or meaningfulness?" Psychological Review 72: 358–372.

Parducci, A.
1963 "Range-frequency compromise in judgment." Psychological Monograph 77, 2: No. 565.

Parducci, A., and L. M. Marshall.
1962 "Assimilation vs. contrast in the anchoring of perceptual judgments of weight." Journal of Experimental Psychology 63:426–437.

Reich, J., and M. Sherif.
1963 "Ego-involvement as a factor in attitude assessment by the own categories technique." Norman, Oklahoma: Institute of Group Relations (mimeographed).

Rosenberg, M. J., C. I. Hovland, W. G. McGuire, R. P. Abelson, and J. W. Brehm.
1960 Attitude Organization and Change. New Haven: Yale University Press.

Rosnow, R. L.
1965 "Bias in evaluating the presidential debates: A 'splinter' effect." Journal of Social Psychology 67:211–219.

Selltiz, Claire, H. Edrich, and S. W. Cook.
1965 "Ratings of favorableness of statements about a social group as an indicator of attitude toward the group." Journal of Personality and Social Psychology 2:408–415.

Sherif, Carolyn W.

1961 "Established reference scales and series effects in social judgment." Doctoral dissertation. The University of Texas.

Sherif, Carolyn W., and N. Jackman.
1966 "Judgments of truth in collective controversy." Public Opinion Quarterly 30:173–186.

Sherif, Carolyn W., M. Sherif, and R. E. Nebergall.
1965 Attitude and Attitude Change. The Social Judgment-Involvement Approach. Philadelphia: W. B. Saunders.

Sherif, M., and H. Cantril.
1947 The Psychology of Ego-Involvements. New York: Wiley. Wiley Science Series (paperback).

Sherif, M., O. J. Harvey, B. J. White, W. R. Hood, and Carolyn W. Sherif.
1961 Intergroup Conflict and Cooperation. The Robbers Cave Experiment. Norman, Oklahoma: University of Oklahoma Book Exchange.

Sherif, M., and C. I. Hovland.
1953 "Judgmental phenomena and scales of attitude measurement: placement of items with individual choice of number of categories." Journal of Abnormal and Social Psychology 48:135–141.
1961 Social Judgment: Assimilation and Contrast Effects in Reaction to Communication and Attitude Change. New Haven: Yale University Press, paperback edition, 1965.

Sherif, M., and Carolyn W. Sherif.
1964 "La méthode des catégories personnelles et les recherche sur les attitudes." Bulletin du C.E.R.P. Centre National de la Recherche Scientifique, Paris, France No. 4, 13:185–197.
1964 Reference Groups: Exploration into Conformity and Deviation of Adolescents. New York: Harper.

Sherif, M., D. Taub, and C. I. Hovland.
1958 "Assimilation and contrast effects of anchoring stimuli on judgments." Journal of Experimental Psychology 55:150–155.

Smith, M. B., J. S. Bruner, and R. W. White.
1956 Opinions and Personality. New York: Wiley.

Tajfel, H., and A. L. Wilkes.
1963 "Salience of attitudes and commitment to extreme judgments in the perception

of people." British Journal of Social and Clinical Psychology 2:40–49.

Thomas, W. I., and F. Znaniecki.
1918   The Polish Peasant in Europe and America. Chicago: The University of Chicago Press.

Vaughan, Kathryn B.
1961   "A disguised instrument for the assessment of intergroup attitudes." Master's thesis, Texas College of Arts and Industries.

Walster, Elaine, and L. Festinger.
1962   "The effectiveness of 'overheard' communications." Journal of Abnormal and Social Psychology 65:395–402.

Whittaker, J. O.
1965   "Attitude change and communication-attitude discrepancy." Journal of Social Psychology 65:141–147.

Zajonc, R. B., and E. Burnstein.
1965   "The learning of balanced and unbalanced social structures." Journal of Personality 33:153–163.

Zavalloni, Marisa, and S. W. Cook.
1965   "Influence of judges' attitudes on ratings of favorableness of statements about a social group." Journal of Personality and Social Psychology 1:43–54.

Zimbardo, P. G.
1960   "Verbal ambiguity and judgmental distortion." Psychological Reports 6:57–58.

CHAPTER 19 Supplementing the Self-Report in Attitude Research

EUGENE J. WEBB AND JERRY R. SALANCIK

On the day of Martin Luther King's funeral, April 9, 1968, many people throughout the country drove with headlights on. The turned-on headlights silently showed the attitudes and mourning of the drivers in an apparently spontaneous display of sorrow. Many states of attitude could yield this same behavior. It might stem as well from a number of situational influences—the model of others, or whites' fear of physical harm in a black community. To study this extraordinary event, Jack Sawyer, a Northwestern University psychologist, chose three racially different locations on Chicago's South Side and observed the proportion of automobiles in each area with headlights lit, the race of the driver and whether he was accompanied or alone. The behavior of whites varied more across the three locations than did the behavior of Negroes. In the dominantly black Woodlawn location, 65 per cent of black drivers and 60 per cent of white drivers drove with headlights on. In the dominantly white South Shore location, 48 per cent of blacks and 14 per cent of whites had lights on (Sawyer, 1968).

Sawyer's study, with its unconventional and innovative method, represents one tech-

nique in breaking the lockstep of the standard data gathering procedures in attitude research. Our knowledge of attitudes is anchored in information collected from a single method in restricted settings—verbal self-reports in the laboratory. Methodologically, this is regrettable. Interviews and questionnaires may intrude as a foreign element into the social setting they would describe; they may create as well as measure attitudes; they may elicit atypical roles and responses; and they are limited to those respondents who are accessible and who will cooperate.

For all these risks, it is understandable why the self-report is the standard procedure. A reasonable concern for controlled measurement, standardized testing, item analysis and easy manipulatable instruments leaves little time or energy for exploring the methodological feasibility of alternative routes to the study of attitudes. The focus of the past has stressed immediate situational control while playing down the question of generalizing to populations and measures beyond those immediately studied. We believe it is appropriate to look now for more complete sets of procedures, for nothing in past technology demands dependence on self-report methods, or on any other single measurement type.

A significant restraint on innovation, how-

This chapter was prepared especially for this volume.

317

ever, has been the intellectual primitivism of the operational definition. Operational definitionalism provided a methodological justification for the scientist not to stray beyond a highly narrow, if reliable, base.[1] One could follow a single method in developing data and be "pure," even if this purity were closer to sterility than virtue.

To define a social attitude, for example, solely by the responses to a list of questionnaire items is eminently legitimate, although only the naive believe that two "strongly agree," one "disagree," and an "I don't know" make an attitude. Actually almost everything we know about attitudes is also suspect because the findings are saturated with the inherent risks of self-report information.

The methodological myopia of operational definitionalism is even less defensible in the light of current thinking about attitudes. An attitude has often been defined as a learned disposition to respond in a consistent manner towards the objects of the attitude (Allport, 1935; McGuire, 1968; Campbell, 1963; Kiesler, Collins and Miller, 1969). Such a conceptualization of attitude should lead one to search for valid relationships among many measurable outcroppings in the realms of

---

[1] It should be noted that social science inherited the lore of the operational definition from the "harder" sciences. It has not always helped them, either. Currently, a significant dispute is under way within cosmology. The so-called naive theory of the expanding universe, the most widely accepted point of view, has been based on specific values of the so-called red shift, a Doppler effect noted on optical spectrographs. The values for this effect have historically employed, via the operational definition route, a constant frequency. But recent work (McCrea, 1968; Burbidge and Burbidge, 1967) suggests that changing the light frequencies analyzed changes the computed velocity of astronomical bodies–an altogether unacceptable finding for the theory. Failure to sample enough values of a critical parameter has often led to elegant laws that do not hold once a broader range of attributes is studied. Examples range from the failure of laws of Newtonian mechanics to work in intermolecular space to the early inability of Manhattan Project scientists to heat uranium and have it remain stable. In the latter case, they simply didn't heat it high enough (Groueff, 1968). The opposite heat situation, working at, say, less than 5 degrees Kelvin, resulted in the failure of old laws to explain new conditions and superconductivity was discovered.

affect, belief, behavioral intention and behavior. The case holds whether one argues for attitude as a unidimensional or multidimensional concept (Fishbein, 1966).

The outcroppings available to the investigator depend on the nature of the setting in which he does his measuring as well as on the measurement he takes. Our purpose here is to suggest some alternative settings for the study of attitudes. Confronted with these alternatives we shall be in a better position to recognize those strong points of the self-report which make it so preponderantly useful, while at the same time so methodologically fallible.

Every data gathering class—interviews, questionnaires, observation, performance records, physical evidence—is potentially biased and has certain validity threats specific to it. Ideally, we should like to converge on knowledge by simultaneously considering information from multiple variants within multiple data classes (Campbell and Fiske, 1959 [Chapter 4 in this volume]). A descriptive list of some strengths and weaknesses of data classes is listed below (from Webb, Campbell, Schwartz, and Sechrest, 1966):

SOURCES OF RESEARCH INVALIDITY

I. *Reactive Measurement Effect*
   1. Awareness of being tested
   2. Role playing
   3. Measurement as change
   4. Response sets
II. *Error from Investigator*
   5. Interviewer effects
   6. Change—fatigue/practice
III. *Varieties of Sampling Error*
   7. Population restriction
   8. Population stability over time
   9. Population stability over areas
IV. *Access to Content*
   10. Restrictions on content
   11. Stability of content over time
   12. Stability of content over areas
V. *Operating Ease and Validity Checks*
   13. Dross rate
   14. Access to descriptive cues
   15. Ability replicate

All classes of measurement are not subject to these potential invalidity threats to the same extent. Self-report measures are more prone to load heavy on the reactive effects and interviewer error side, while observation may or may not. How a student of attitudes may balance validity risks depends both on his strategy of manipulating his subject's world and his choice of data gathering methods.

The researcher himself can change the subject's environment to establish some values of an independent variable or he can take advantage of naturally occurring phenomena. There is the further option of collecting information in a way that avoids the subject's awareness of the manipulation or quite forthrightly lets the subject know what is being investigated.

Much laboratory and field research on attitudes is done with the subject being aware of the content focus of the study. Coupling this awareness with that coming from the use of self-report measures, the potential for error is high. Yet the interview and questionnaire are probably the most flexible and generally useful single devices we have for gathering information. With no other devices can an investigator swing his attention into so many different areas of substantive content, often simultaneously, and also gather intelligence on the extent to which his findings are hampered by population restrictions. Limited only by his ability to ask answerable questions, an investigator can arm a subject with a pencil and piece of paper, pay him a dollar and fifty cents, and be repaid with information on affections, perceptions or depressions.

Flexibility does not come without cost, however. So long as one has only a single class of data collection, and that class is a self-report instrument, one has inadequate knowledge of the rival hypotheses grouped under the term "reactive measurement effects." Control over these potential sources of error, some stemming from an individual's awareness of being tested, others from his selecting one of several roles to play, must be accounted

for by some class of measurement other than the self-report.

In laboratory settings, some attitude change researchers take many precautions to avoid the problem of subject awareness (Aronson and Carlsmith, 1968). Their strategy is to take advantage of the control and flexibility of the laboratory and at the same time to reduce the opportunity for measurement invalidity by constructing elaborate scenarios to lead the subject away from guessing the intent of the study. A common strategy is to remove the dependent measurement from the independent manipulations by using two experimenters; one to do the manipulations and a second, who appears unrelated, to obtain the measurement. Such a strategy, while controlling one major source of error from self-report, still leaves room for criticism on other sources of reactive and interviewer errors. The subject knows he is being tested, and this knowledge alone may be enough to affect attitude measures.

Another source of data using self-report takes advantage of events happening to people without the experimenter's manipulation. A series of studies developed around responses (some self-report, some naturally occurring) to national tragedy after the assassination of President Kennedy (Greenberg and Parker, 1965). Studies such as these are most useful for obtaining information on the effect on attitudes of relatively rare but intensely powerful events not easily reproducible in the laboratory. The excellent review by Fritz (1961) of the effect of natural disasters is an example. This approach, however, has built-in inefficiencies, if one waits for events to occur which in some cases might have been created either in the field or the lab. Some events do occur with great enough frequency to allow reasonably easy assessment of their effects. In a study of the effect of fear, Hillebrandt (1962) observed a short-term decline in the amount of air travel following major airplane crashes.

When naturalistic outcroppings of a non-self-report nature can be opportunistically explored, as in the Hillebrandt study, they are useful sources of data about attitudes. At times, events occur that can help to calibrate conventional experimentation. A Connecticut newspaper recently announced the date on which fluoridation of a city's water supply was to take place. On that date, hospitals reported an increase in complaints of nausea, stomach trouble and dizziness. The chemical, however, was not added to the water until two days after the announced time. Hospitals reported no increase in complaints then (Goldberg, personal communication). The results of this accidental experiment are clear: this evidence of the strength of reaction to fluoridation both confirms and extends the extensive self-report literature on the topic.

For some questions, self-report measures are awkward or impossible and one must turn to less obvious data sources for inferences. Changing attitudes in totalitarian countries are hard to study by asking questions. Resourceful diplomats and reporters estimate attitudes of elites and general populations by watching the outcroppings of shifting power (Webb and Salancik, 1966). At a recent disruptive point in Indonesian politics, for example, President Sukarno's portrait was vanishing from some Djakarta government offices (the military) but not others (some parliamentary offices). As a later, and critical, datum, a monument to Sukarno disappeared from the public square (Friendly, 1967). In like manner, feelings between nations cannot easily be determined directly. Zinnes (1968) tried to make sense of the international tensions surrounding the crisis of 1914. His information came from some three thousand public and private documents created by key decision makers of countries taking part in the drama that led to World War I. Coding each document for perceptions and expressions of hostility from and to others, Zinnes was able to infer that the expression of hostility follows from perceiving the other guy as hostile, confirming other work in ethnocentric attitudes (see Campbell, 1967; Holsti and North, 1966).

Exploitation of natural outcroppings can be cumbersome since the investigator has only limited or post hoc control over the data. One is restricted to content areas and populations that happened to occur. And the dross rate for some content is high; Zinnes had to sift through masses of irrelevant material to test his propositions about international hostility. To reduce these limitations a researcher can manipulate events rather than wait for them to happen. As suggested earlier, the experimenter can intervene so as to limit the subject's knowledge of the testing process. The more unobtrusive the manipulation, the less chance for reactive measurement error.

The most attractive testing strategy is the field experiment in which both the subject matter of the study is disguised and the measurement procedure is unobtrusive. The promise for imaginative research is great with this approach, for the stereotypes of procedure do not apply.

In a study of altruism, Bryan and Test (1966) were interested in determining whether viewing someone else helping a distressed motorist would influence drivers to stop and help a woman repair a flat tire. The scene was a Los Angeles highway. In the model condition a second car with a flat tire was positioned a few blocks before the distressed lady's, and someone was helping the driver fix the flat. The no model condition used only the distressed lady with an unfixed flat. More people stopped when the model was provided. In a less rigorous test, an eighteen-year-old fashion model on a Detroit highway observed that more men stopped to help her fix a flat when she wore an attractive miniskirt and flowing blonde hair than when draped in a long coat with curlers popping from her head (Anonymous, 1967).

Leventhal and Niles (1964) verified laboratory findings on the effects of fear communications on smoking attitudes by going into the field. The authors showed high and low fear films to audiences at the New York Health Exposition. Using a multiple methods approach, they checked the effectiveness of the communications by a standard self-report measure and by the number of viewers who visited a mobile X-ray unit on the fair grounds.

Other investigators have attempted to avoid verbal self-report risks by employing physiological measures. Rankin and Campbell (1955) [Chapter 31 in this volume] studied racial attitudes using galvanic skin resistance as a dependent measure. Their independent variable was subtly introduced while subjects were engrossed in a word association task. The experimenter, who was either Negro or white, simply touched the subject's hand while explaining something. GSR levels, presumably reflecting some affective response tendency, was differential in these conditions. Recently, however, Porier and Lott (1967) [Chapter 32 in this volume] offered explanations other than prejudice which could have accounted for the changes in GSR. Designing a study to control these, the authors failed to replicate Rankin and Campbell.

Gerard (1964) reported an interesting experiment testing the cognitive dissonance prediction that a chosen alternative will increase in value relative to the non-chosen one. Subjects rated paintings for preference, and were told they could have a print of one of the paintings. Two conditions were run in which the individual could choose between either his third or fourth ranked painting and between his third and eighth ranked painting. The finger-pulse amplitude was measured both before and after these choices. Changes in finger pulse immediately after choice were generally in the direction of the dissonance theory prediction.

We may now be on the threshold of significant new applications of physiological measures to attitude research. The promise comes from the extensive technological development in recent years. The impetus of the space program and the flowering of biomedical engineering have produced substantial invention and refinement of hardware. The most significant developments have been with devices which do not restrain the subject. Past demands for fixed body position, bite bars, and direct application of wires or electrodes can now be circumvented, although at a relatively high price. These unattached or remote sensors permit the subject more freedom of movement and the apparatus does not call attention to the "this is an experiment!" condition.

For social research, many unresolved ethical and scientific problems exist (Westin, 1967; Davis et al., 1955). Should one monitor the level of body heat without informing a subject of the measurement? Is thermography related to variables of interest (Stoll, 1964; Skversky et al., 1964; Barnes, 1963)? Can one surreptitiously measure cardiac rate as an index of whether an experimental condition such as fear has been induced in a subject? And how good a measurement of fear is it (Tudge, 1968; Noordergraas and Pollack, 1967; Braunstein, 1953)? Remote heat sensing or measurement of electrical fields (Shafer, 1967) raises many of the questions associated with the so-called lie detector. The ability to hide an electrical monitor in the seat of a chair forces the investigator to ask what he, and his profession, views as appropriate ethical behavior. Debriefing after an experiment may or may not justify the use of hidden sensors. Extensive discourse already exists on the appropriateness of misleading subjects about the purpose of an experiment or their reward for participation. Such discussion should be extended to include the conditions, if any, under which hidden sensing is permissible. If the decision is that no such conditions exist, including ruling out the one-way mirror, then potential value may still reside in the use of such methods when the individual knows and approves of their employment (Thackray and Orne, 1968). Not the least of these problems are scientific, with findings, for example, showing significant differences between Arabs and Israelis on GSR reactivity (Kugelmass and Lieblich, 1968).

Observed social distance is another measure of expanding interest. Fear attitudes toward snakes have been measured by approach distances; subjects will get closer to snakes upon seeing others do so (Geer and

Turteltaub, 1967). In a similar fashion, one could study interpersonal attitudes with seating or standing distance as a dependent measure (Felipe and Sommer, 1966; Sommer, 1967). Both laboratory and recorded natural settings are also amenable to the study of nonverbal aspects of speech behavior as indications of beliefs and feelings (Popov et al., 1966; Webb and Salancik, 1966). Mehrabian and Wiener (1967) have some evidence that tone is more important than content in communicating an attitude. (A more comprehensive review of possible observational measures is compiled in Webb et al., 1966.)

A start in the direction of evaluating alternative data classes is emerging from discussions of differences between verbal and behavioral measures of attitude (Kiesler, Collins and Miller, 1969; Fishbein, 1966; McGuire, 1966; Weick, 1966). We will try to suggest a few general guidelines, but a thorough treatment must await an accumulation of experience with different data classes by investigators using multiple approaches.

The payoff for using supplementary unobtrusive measures is high, but the approach is more demanding of the investigator. Selltiz and her associates (1959) note in their discussion of statistical records:

The use of such data demands a capacity to ask many different questions related to the research problem . . . The guiding principle for the use of available statistics consists in keeping oneself flexible with respect to the form in which research questions are asked (p. 318).

This flexibility of thought is required to handle the reactive measurement effects which are the most systematic weaknesses of all self-report studies. These error threats are also systematically present in observation studies in which the presence of an observer is known to those under study. To varying degrees, measurements conducted in natural settings, without the individual's knowledge, control this type of error possibility. In these studies the individual is not aware of being tested, and there is little danger that the act of measurement will itself serve as a force for change in behavior or elicit role-playing that confounds the data. There is also minimal risk that biases coming from the physical appearance or other cues provided by the investigator will contaminate the results.

Methods not involving self-report also may counter a necessary weakness of the interview and questionnaire—dependence on language. When one is working within a single society, there is always the question of whether the differential verbal skills of various subcultures will mislead the investigator. It is possible, if groups vary in articulateness, to overgeneralize the behavior or attitudes of the group or individuals with the greater verbal fluency. This risk is particularly marked for the interpretation of research reports which liberally employ quotations. The natural tendency of the writer is to choose illustrative quotations which are fluent, dramatic, or engaging. If the pool of good quotations is variable across the subcultures, the reader may mistakenly overvalue the ideas in the quotations. This is a question of presentation, but an important one because of the disproportionate weight that may be placed on population segments.

The differential capacity to use language is one source of error, while the absolute capacity of the language to convey ideas is another. This is an issue strongly present in cross-cultural comparisons where different languages may vary radically as a medium of information transfer. The effect of this is to limit the content possible for study with questionnaires or interviews. If one worked in New Guinea, for example, and had to depend upon the *lingua franca* pidgin widely spoken there, he would find it adequate for answers to "Where do you keep your fishing nets?" but too gross a filter to study the ethnocentricism of a tribe. Pidgin simply does not possess the subtle gradients required to yield textured responses to questions on attitudes toward neighboring tribes or one's own tribe. Although it is theoretically possible to learn all the regional dialects well enough to be competent in a language, in practice this does not occur. A more pragmatic approach is to search for observational or trace evidence which will document aspects of ethnocentricism (e.g., reactions to outsiders, disposition and use of weapons) and then relate it to the verbal responses in the inadequate pidgin.

One more weakness of the dependence on language is that sometimes there is silence. So long as a respondent talks, glibly or not, in a rich language, or not, checks and controls can be worked on the reported content (see Hyman et al., 1954; Kahn and Cannell, 1957). There are, however, situations in which refusals to cooperate preclude any chance of correcting distorted information. This usually results in a biased research population and not a rejection of the findings, because it is almost always possible to find some people who will discuss any topic. But it can also result in a complete stalemate if only the verbal report is considered as the research instrument.

An example of this inability to get data by verbal report, and a nonreactive circumvention, is provided by Shadegg (1964). In his book on political campaign methods, Shadegg writes (page 92) of a campaign manager who used every available means to learn the plans of his opponent, who, reasonably enough, was unwilling to grant a revealing interview. One method arranged for procuring the contents of his opponent's wastebasket: "He came into possession of carbon copies of letters . . . memos in the handwriting of his opponent's manager." Admittedly a less efficient method than the interview, it admirably met the criterion of being workable: "It took a lot of digging through the trash to come up with the nuggets. But . . . daily panning produced some very fine gold." The "investigator" did not limit himself to inferences drawn from observations of his opponent's public acts, but ingeniously was able to develop (although perhaps not ethically) a trace measure to complement the observation. Each aided the other, for the observations give a validity check on the nuggets among the trash, and the nuggets give a more accurate means of interpreting the meaning of the public acts.

The verbal methods are necessarily weak along another dimension, the study of past behavior or of change. For historical studies, there is no alternative but to rely mainly on records of time past. Behavioral research on the distant past is rare, however; more common are studies which center on experiences within the lifetime of respondents. For example, there is a large literature on child rearing practices, in which mothers recollect their behavior of years past. A sole dependence on this type of data gathering is highly suspect. It may be enough to note that Thomas Jefferson, in his later years, observed that winters weren't as cold as they used to be. Available records could be used to check both Mr. Jefferson and other observers of secular changes in winter's fierceness.

For more current evidence on the fallibility of such recall data, see Pyles, Stolz and Macfarlane (1935); McGraw and Molloy (1941); Smith (1958); Weiss and Dawis (1960). Weiss and Dawis wrote: "It is indefensible to assume the validity of purportedly factual data obtained by interview" (p. 384). And the work of Haggard, Brekstad, and Skard (1960) and Robbins (1963) suggests that it is a problem of differentially accurate recall. In Haggard's phrase, the interviews "did not reflect the mothers' earlier experiences and attitudes so much as their current picture of the past" (p. 317).

When, through death or refusal, reports of past behavior are unavailable, a proper contingent strategy is to interview others who have had access to the same information, or who can report it second hand. This is potentially shaky information, but useful if other intelligence is available for a check. For many investigations, of course, the nature of the distortion is itself an important datum and can become a central topic of study when a reliable baseline is possible. If other materials are present, and they usually are in a record-keeping society, the best way to estimate past behavior is to combine methods of study of archival records, available physical traces, and verbal reports, even if second hand.

A final gain from the less reactive methods frequently is the lower cost of data collection. Many scholars know how to conduct massive surveys which effectively control major sources of error; few do so. This knowledge is an underdeveloped resource. With survey interviews often costing ten dollars or more each, the failure is understandable, however regrettable. When the self-report is viewed as the only method, the researcher is doomed either to frustration or a studied avoidance of thoughts on generalizability. Peace of mind will come if the investigator breaks the single-method mold and examines the extent to which other measurement classes can substitute for verbal reports. The cost of collecting each unit of data is low for most other methods. In some cases, the dross rate is high, and it may be necessary to observe a hundred cases before one meets the research specifications. Nonetheless, even under these high dross rate conditions, the cost per usable response is often less expensive than that of a completed interview or returned questionnaire. Note that we add the qualifier "often." The savings are centered in data collection costs, and it may be that all the savings are vitiated by the elaborate corrections or transformations that a particular data series may require. The cost of materials and analysis is an equivocal area indeed.

In the multimethod pattern of testing various outcroppings, the primary gains coming from the less popular methods are protection against reactive measurement threats, auxiliary data in content areas where verbal reports are unreliable, an easier method of determining long-term change, and a potentially lower cost substitute for some standard survey practices. Offsetting these gains, there are associated problems for the less popular measurement classes—indeed, if they were less problematic, we would be writing an argument in favor of an increased use of the self-report.

The most powerful aspect of the verbal methods—their ability to reach into all content areas—is a soft spot in the hidden observation, trace, and archival analysis procedures. We have noted remarkable applications of data from these sources—as in Hillebrandt's study of air crashes, Bryan and Test on altruism, and Zinnes on the perception of hostility—but for some content areas, the most imaginative of investigators will have trouble finding pertinent material. Individually, those methods are simply not as broadly gauged.

Often missing, too, is complete knowledge of the conditions under which the data were collected, the definitions of important terms used in classification, and the control or lack of it over error risks that may be salient. In general, for trace evidence and archival records, a dominant concern is the possibility of selective deposit and selective survival of the research data. Zinnes' study of World War I was fortunate to have fifty years worth of painstaking scholarship available to assess the accuracy and completeness of the documents he used. But this is not the usual case. More often, supportive research must be designed to learn of selective errors and to apply corrections when possible. At other times the researcher must remain in ignorance and make assumptions. If he restricts himself to working with *only* such data, he remains helpless before their vagaries. If he uses other measurement classes, the process of triangulating all the different data may provide a test of his assumptions and reveal the presence or extent of error.

Because of the risks of error and the danger of unknown biases, careful data sampling becomes important. Wherever feasible, locational sampling should be employed, extending over regions as well as areas within a single locality. Similarly, time sampling should be considered not only as a device employed within a single day or week, but applied over months and years. By such effort, we are able to protect against both population and content restrictions, and very often to produce interesting data from comparisons of results from different locations or times. The need for time and location sampling is no less for observational or archival data than it is for interviews or questionnaires, inasmuch as sampling is a problem that transcends the class of measurement.

Another common demand, although not as applicable to the self-report approaches, is for data adjustment and conversion. The need comes from the experimenter's decreased control over the production of his materials. The exception to this is the contrived field experiment, where the investigator can have full control, but the data from archives, trace sources, and observations are frequently too raw to be used as is. We underscore this need because one of the major advantages of the secondary data is their ability to produce fine time-series information. In time series, it is usually necessary to account for extraneous sources of variation, such as secular trends or cyclical patterns. Thus, the "score" which is the basis of comparison is some transformed measure which is a residual of the total score. In other studies, the absolute number of cases varies from unit time to unit time, and the only reasonable comparison score is one which is related in some way, through an average or percentage, for example, to the variable baseline. The investigator may have no control over the flow of an observed population, but he can obtain a count of that flow and use this intelligence as the basis for modifying his comparison score.

The more sophisticated forms of transformation, such as index numbers based on multiple components, demand more information, particularly as one assigns relative weights to components collected into a single score. This is not as awesome as it sounds, and if the investigator is sensitive to the potential usefulness of index numbers, he often finds enough secondary data available for the task, or may obtain new information without extraordinarily high marginal costs. Insofar as these transformations demand time and labor to make the raw data more precise, they are disadvantageous compared with standard self-report procedures.

There are no rewards for ingenuity as such, and the payoff comes only when ingenuity leads to new means of making more valid comparisons. In the available grab bag of imperfect research methods, there is room for new uses of the old. Though our own disposition leans toward non-reactive measures and away from self-report, we do so only in an effort to minimize the investigator's interference in the process of data collection. The goal of all investigation is proper comparison and generalization. For a broader-based and robust knowledge of attitudes, an expansion of our conventional wisdom in research methods is necessary.

REFERENCES

Allport, G. W.
1935   "Attitudes." In C. Murchison (ed.), A Handbook of Social Psychology. Worcester: Clark University Press. 798–844.

Anonymous
1967   "Would you stop for her—or her?" Chicago Daily News, April 10:1.

Aronson, E., and J. M. Carlsmith.
1968   "Experimentation in social psychology," in G. Lindzey and E. Aronson (eds.), Handbook of Social Psychology. Reading: Addison-Wesley.

Barnes, R. B.
1963   "Thermography of the human body." Science 140:870–877.

Braunstein, J. R.
1953   The Ballistocardiogram. Springfield: C. C Thomas.

Bryan, J. H., and Mary Ann Test.
1966   "A lady in distress: the flat tire experiment." Unpublished manuscript: Northwestern University.

Burbidge, G., and M. Burbidge.
1967   Quasi-stellar Objects. San Francisco: Freeman.

Campbell, D. T.
1963   "Social attitudes and other acquired behavioral dispositions." Pp. 94–176 in S. Koch (ed.), Psychology: A Study of a Science. Volume 6 New York: McGraw-Hill.

Campbell, D. T.
1967   "Stereotypes and the perception of group differences." American Psychologist 22:817–829.

Campbell, D. T., and D. W. Fiske.
1959   "Convergent and discriminant validation by the multitrait-multimethod

matrix." Psychological Bulletin 56:81–105.

Davis, R. C., A. M. Buchwald, and R. W. Frankmann.
1955 "Autonomic and muscular responses and their relation to simple stimuli." Psychological Monographs 405:1–71.

Felipe, N., and R. Sommer.
1966 "Invasions of personal space." Social Problems 14:206–214.

Fishbein, M.
1966 "The relationships between beliefs, attitudes and behavior." Pp. 199–223 in S. Feldman (ed.), Cognitive Consistency. New York: Academic Press.

Friendly, A. Jr.
1967 "Sukarno pictures vanish from Djakarta offices." New York Times, March 3:3.

Fritz, C. E.
1961 "Disaster." Pp. 651–694 in R. K. Merton and R. A. Nisbet (eds.), Contemporary Social Problems. New York: Harcourt, Brace & World.

Geer, J. H., and A. Turteltaub.
1967 "Fear reduction following observation of a model." Journal of Personality and Social Psychology 6:327–331.

Gerard, H. B.
1964 "Physiological measurement in social psychological research." Pp. 43–58 in P. H. Leiderman and D. Shapiro (eds.), Psycho-biological Approaches to Social Behavior. Stanford: Stanford University Press.

Goldberg, G.
1967 Personal communication. Yale University, Department of Psychology.

Greenberg, B., and E. Parker (eds.).
1965 The Kennedy Assassination and the American Public: Social Communication in Crises. Stanford: Stanford University Press.

Groueff, S.
1968 Manhattan Project. New York: Bantam.

Haggard, E. A., A. Brekstad, and A. G. Skard.
1960 "On the reliability of the anamnestic interview." Journal of Abnormal and Social Psychology 61:311–318.

Hillebrandt, R. H.
1962 "Panel design and time series analy-

sis." Unpublished master's thesis, Northwestern University.

Holsti, O. R., and R. C. North.
1966 "Comparative data from content analysis: perceptions of hostility and economic variables in the 1914 crisis." In R. L. Merritt and S. Rokkan (eds.), Composing Nations. New Haven: Yale University Press.

Hyman, H. C., J. W. Cobb, J. Feldman, C. W. Hart, and C. H. Stemby.
1954 Interviewing in Social Research. Chicago: University of Chicago Press.

Kahn, R. L., and C. F. Cannell.
1957 The Dynamics of Interviewing: Theory Technique and Cases. New York: Wiley.

Kiesler, C. A., B. Collins, and N. Miller.
1969 Attitude Change: A Critical Analysis of Theoretical Approaches. New York: Wiley.

Kugelmass, S., and I. Lieblich.
1968 "The relation between ethnic origin and GSR reactivity in psychophysiological detection." Journal of Applied Psychology 52:158–162.

Leventhal, H., and P. Niles.
1964 "A field experiment on fear arousal with data on the validity of questionnaire measures." Journal of Personality 32:459–479.

McCrea, W. H.
1968 "Cosmology after half a century." Science 160:1295–1299.

McGraw, M., and L. B. Molloy.
1941 "The pediatric anamnesis: inaccuracies in eliciting developmental data." Child Development 12:255–265.

McGuire, W. J.
1966 "The current status of cognitive consistency theories." Pp. 1–46 in S. Feldman (ed.), Cognitive Consistency. New York: Academic Press.
1968 "Nature of attitudes and attitude change." In G. Lindzey and E. Aronson (eds.), Handbook of Social Psychology. Reading: Addison-Wesley.

Mehrabian, A., and M. Wiener.
1967 "Decoding of inconsistent communications." Journal of Personality and Social Psychology 6:109–114.

Noordergraas, A., and G. Pollack (eds.).
1967 Proceedings of the 1966 Annual Meet-

ing of the Ballistocardiograph Research Society. White Plains: Phiebig.

Popov, V. A., *et al.*
1966 "Analiz intonatsionnoi kharakteristiki rechi kak pokazatelya emotsional'nogo sostoyaniya cheloveka v usloviyakh kosmicheskogo poleta. (Analysis of intonational characteristics of speech as an index of the emotional state of man under conditions of flight in space.) Zhurnal Vysshei Nervnoi Devatel'nosti 16(6):974–983.

Porier, G. W., and A. J. Lott.
1967 "Galvanic skin responses and prejudice." Journal of Personality and Social Psychology 5:253–259.

Pyles, M. K., H. R. Stolz, and J. W. Macfarlane.
1935 "The accuracy of mothers' reports on birth and developmental data." Child Development 6:165–176.

Rankin, R. E., and D. T. Campbell.
1955 "Galvanic skin responses to Negro and white experimenters." Journal of Abnormal and Social Psychology 51:30–33.

Robbins, L. C.
1963 "The accuracy of parental recall of aspects of child development and of child rearing practices." Journal of Abnormal and Social Psychology 66:261–270.

Sawyer, Jack.
1968 "Communication in a tragedy: blacks and whites turn on car lights after King's assassination." Unpublished manuscript. Northwestern University.

Selltiz, C., M. Jahoda, M. Deutsch, and S. W. Cook.
1959 Research Methods in Social Relations. New York: Rinehart & Winston.

Shadegg, S. C.
1964 How To Win An Election. New York: Toplinger.

Shafer, W. A.
1967 "Field effect monitoring systems development." Convair Research Summary (CRS-2) Convair Division of General Dynamics, San Diego.

Skversky, N. J., A. B. Herring, and R. C. Baron.
1964 "Thermography in peripheral vascular diseases." Annals of the New York Academy of Sciences 121:118–134.

Smith, H. T.
1958 "A comparison of interview and observation methods of mother behavior." Journal of Abnormal and Social Psychology 57:278–282.

Sommer, R.
1967 "Sociological space." The American Journal of Sociology 72:654–660.

Stoll, A. M.
1964 "Techniques and uses of skin temperature measurements." Annals of the New York Academy of Sciences 121:49–56.

Thackray, R. I., and M. Orne.
1968 "Effects of the type of stimulus employed and the level of subject awareness on the detection of deception." Journal of Applied Psychology 52:234–239.

Tudge, C.
1968 "Action, reaction and heart disease." New Scientist 38:280.

Webb, E. J., D. T. Campbell, R. D. Schwartz, and J. Sechrest.
1966 Unobtrusive Measures: Nonreactive Research in the Social Sciences. Chicago: Rand McNally.

Webb, E. J., and J. R. Salancik.
1966 "The interview." Journalism Monographs 2. Austin: The Association for Education in Journalism.

Weick, K. E.
1966 "Task acceptance dilemmas: a site for research on cognition." Pp. 225–255 in S. Feldman (ed.), Cognitive Consistency. New York: Academic Press.

Weiss, D. J., and R. V. Dawis.
1960 "An objective validation of factual interview data." Journal of Applied Psychology 44:381–385.

Westin, A. F.
1967 Privacy and Freedom. New York: Atheneum.

Zinnes, G. A.
1968 "The expression and perception of hostility in prewar crisis: 1914." Pp. 85–122 in J. D. Singer (ed.), Quantitative International Politics. New York: Free Press.

SECTION IV   Indirect Tests and Objective Tasks

Overview

Disguised and projective devices have been the most popular alternative to self-report as a means of obtaining behavioral specimens. Among these techniques are doll play, sentence completion, interpretation of ambiguous stimuli, performance of objective tasks and many others. Campbell (1950) referred to this growing collection of ingenious devices as *indirect* assessment techniques. All have in common the attribute that "the investigator interprets the responses in terms of dimensions and categories different from those held in mind by the respondent while answering," (Kidder and Campbell, p. 336). There is an element of deception involved by deliberate action on the part of the investigator in an effort to circumvent the interference of response sets.

The matter of deception raises some ethical issues in the use of indirect measures. There are other shortcomings and limitations as well. Kidder and Campbell in Chapter 20, an extensive revision of Campbell's oft-cited review (1950), deal with four major points: 1) the invasion of privacy issue, 2) the deceptive-deprecatory-exploitative attitudes of psychologists toward "subjects," 3) the failure to do research implied in the introduction of indirect tests, and 4) the disappointing nature of the research results. A revised scheme for classifying indirect tests is presented with an exhaustive review of the literature.

Following are five chapters (21–25) illustrative of this approach to attitude measurement. The first is Proshansky's familiar projective method which requires respondents to write detailed accounts of ambiguous pictures containing social conflict situations.

The use of social schemata devised by Kuethe is not so well-known but has a great deal of promise. The technique is based upon the fact that persons do not arrange human figures randomly in a free-response situation, and upon the hypothesis that the specific social schemata used may be influenced by the respondents' attitudes.

The "error-choice" technique developed by Hammond presents the respondent with what appears to be an information test. The items of the test are constructed so as to force the respondent into a choice of errors; none of the alternative answers provided are factually accurate. Systematic error choices are interpreted as the effect of attitudes.

The techniques of Proshansky, Kuethe and Hammond, and many others, assume that the degree of stimulus structure and/or the psychological "sets" of the respondent affect overt responses. This pair of assumptions is examined experimentally by Thistlethwaite. The evidence is very convincing that both influence reasoning behavior. It is important to note, however, that the greatest degree of relative distortion did not occur on the most ambiguous structures.

Beginning with the assumption "that judgment, being relative to some reference point, varies as a function of anchors established by one's own attitudes" (p. 4–1), Cook and associates undertook a systematic examination of the relation between social attitudes and ratings plausibility of statements about the attitude object (Cook, 1968). Chapter 25 by Selltiz and Cook indicates a strong relationship and the promise of such ratings as a measure of attitude. One should note the similarity of the assumption involved here and the position taken by Sherif and Sherif (see Chapter 18).

REFERENCES

Campbell, D. T.
   1950   "The indirect assessment of social attitudes." Psychological Bulletin 47:15–38.
Cook, S. W.
   1968   "Studies of attitude and attitude measurement: final technical report." Unpublished
          manuscript, Institute of Behavioral Science, University of Colorado.

CHAPTER 20 The Indirect Testing of Social Attitudes

LOUISE H. KIDDER AND DONALD T. CAMPBELL

This is an ambivalent updating of a twenty-year-old review covering *disguised* and *projective* measures of social attitudes (Campbell, 1950). Many of the reasons for positive evaluation of indirect attitude measures still remain. At their best, they are admirably ingenious. They utilize and illustrate psychological laws to a greater degree than direct attitude tests, and are thus more characteristic of measurement in the successful sciences wherein yesterday's crucial experiments are today's routine measurement procedures. And even if not better, they are different, thus fitting in with multiple operationism, which attempts by using multiple methods of, hopefully, independent biases to curb the inevitable biases of single methods (Campbell and Fiske, 1959; Webb, Campbell, Schwartz, and Sechrest, 1966).

Supported in part by National Science Foundation Grant GS 1309. We are grateful to the American Psychological Association for permission to reprint edited fragments of Campbell, D. T., "The indirect assessment of social attitudes," *Psychological Bulletin*, 1950, *47*, 15–38; and Campbell, D. T., "A typology of tests, projective and otherwise," *Journal of Consulting Psychology*, 1957, *11*, 207–210. Our appreciation goes to Stuart W. Cook for providing reports of his extensive research in indirect attitude testing and to Miles L. Patterson and Patricia S. Gilbert for help in locating and abstracting the literature. This manuscript was prepared especially for this volume.

The sources of negative valence do today loom much larger than they did in 1950, and it seems well to review these briefly, raising issues which the reader can keep in mind as we discuss specific problems. Four points can be examined: 1) the invasion of privacy issue, 2) the deceptive-deprecatory-exploitative attitudes of psychologists toward subjects, 3) the failure to do the research implied in the introduction of indirect tests, and 4) the disappointing nature of the research results.

Invasion of privacy—As the atomic scientists discovered, creating tools and placing them in the hands of those apt to use them immorally involves moral problems for the inventor. It is not enough to say that his discovery is neutral, available for good and ill alike—if he can on scientific grounds anticipate the preponderance of likely use, he shares direct responsibility for that likely use. The atomic scientist was therefore responsible for the military use of atomic weapons, since that preponderance of use was clearly anticipatable. It is only the lack of success of the indirect attitude test movement that spared its inventors an analogous problem. If one looks at the applied uses of tests of any kind, the predominant use is supportive of the status quo rather than supportive of change. That is, the tests are used to fit people into the existing institutions. Insofar as tests offer channels of upward social mobility, it is by rewarding those who fit in, or have the potential of fitting in. This is true in a general way of test uses in school and clinic, and is, of course, particularly true of industrial psychology and personnel selection applications —here the uses are entirely on the side of management, never of labor. The indirect test designers should, therefore, have anticipated outcomes like that substantially rumored at the time of the appearance of the 1950 review, to the effect that a well-known applied psychology research institute had designed an attitude test disguised as an information test to weed out applicants with anti-management, pro-union attitudes.

The deceptive-deprecatory-exploitative attitude toward "subjects"—While much of the ingenuity invested in indirect attitude measurement has been the result of competent scientists overcoming genuine obstacles to scientific research, some of it has been the expression of an unworthy attitude toward the subject on the part of the researcher. This excessive and sometimes sadistic glee at deceiving the gullible victim has of course also found expression in the ingenious deceptions and the write-ups of those deceptions in laboratory social psychology. This is not to rule out all deception in research. In all ethical problems, strong principles are in conflict. A most important ethical consideration is our duty to produce a relevant and accurate social science, and this value is frequently sufficient to override our moral aversion to deception, particularly in cases in which no harm or change-of-fate comes to the deceived respondent, and in which he remains essentially anonymous. Even where psychic damage is done, the value of the finding may still justify the study. The present authors would agree that this is so in the Milgram (1963, 1964) studies. But in both experimental artifice and in indirect test invention, sometimes the act of deception becomes an enjoyable end in itself, not only as an intellectual challenge but also from a sense of social superiority

over the subject, the enjoyment of "taking" a gullible sucker. The very use of the term "subject," the reference to both human collaborators and rats as *Ss*, smacks of this implicit social distance and exploitativeness vis-à-vis a subordinate caste. (Much better is the old German *Versuchsperson*, which might best be translated as "researcher." Better, too, the anthropologist's *informant* or the sociologist's *respondent*, which we try to use in this paper.)

How different this deceptive deprecatory approach is from truly levelling with one's volunteer collaborators, sharing with them the research purpose, and trusting them to serve those purposes as best they can. (As implemented through anonymous direct tests, this naive, trusting strategy works better than indirect measures in six out of the eight available validity comparisons which we review below.)[1] Classification of measurement types is discussed in the subsequent section but we can note here that indirect attitude tests face this problem more than do unobtrusive measures (Webb *et al.*, 1966) because, being tests, they demand the cooperation of the respondents and thus involve direct deception and the exploitation of another's good will.

With psychologists and psychological research becoming a standard part of the modal college curriculum, our chronic dishonesty and our subsequent gloating over it contribute to the general degradation of interpersonal trust, even when we are not contributing directly by publishing research on the superior advantages of apparent sincerity in deceiving others. The effects of this are beginning to be felt in the occasional refusal of a subject to participate. The day when student activists take up the cry against involuntary servitude in psychological experiments may not be far off.

Failure to do the implied research—The concept of indirect attitude measurement im-

---

[1] The effectiveness of forthright questioning has also been upheld in the delicate area of studying public housing programs, as reported in private communication from Professor Kiyoshi Ikeda.

plied a criticism of direct attitude measurement which was very much needed at a time when definitional operationism was implicitly claiming perfection for all measuring procedures. As such, the move toward indirect methods was part and parcel of a more general critical approach to research measures which also found expression in such concepts as demand characteristics (Orne, 1962), experimenter effects (Rosenthal, 1966), evaluation apprehension (Rosenberg, 1965; 1969), reactive measures (Campbell, 1957a), guinea-pig effects (Selltiz, Jahoda, Deutsch, and Cook, 1959), "Hawthorne" effects (Roethlisberger and Dickson, 1939), placebo effects, studies of the fakability of tests (Dicken, 1959; 1960), studies of social desirability (Edwards, 1957), studies of the biases introduced when questionnaires are signed, and so forth. All this provides favorable valence toward indirect measures. By and large, however, the designers have been content to assert the advantages of indirect measures and have made few efforts to demonstrate them. Thus after 20 years, this most basic research is still not done.

More specifically, we need research comparing direct and indirect tests in the effort to confirm that the latter are:

a) less affected by experimental manipulation of demand characteristics.

b) less susceptible to manipulation of evaluation apprehension.

c) less likely to be reactive measures as judged by the main and interaction effects of testing as in the Solomon four groups design (Campbell and Stanley, 1966; Solomon, 1949).

d) less susceptible to placebo and Hawthorne effects.

e) less affected by instructions to fake a good impression.

f) less modified by the requirement to sign one's name (Cook, Johnson, and Scott, 1969, report no difference for direct and indirect tests).

g) less affected by the role setting of test administration (e.g. employment applicant, psychotherapy applicant, respondent for the sake of science).

We still need to know whether indirect tests can be evaluated positively to all of these while still demonstrating relevant diagnostic ability.

By and large, there has been no critical literature on indirect tests comparable to that on direct ones. While one might hope that indirect tests would have different method factors (Campbell and Fiske, 1959), there is no reason to expect them to have smaller methods variance. Response sets should be expected in indirect tests wherever there are repetitions of an item format, or where repeated similar guesses are required. Many indirect tests have even more chance of changing attitudes in the process of measuring them than direct tests do.

The disappointing nature of the research results—In the literature we review, the most common evidence of the adequacy of an indirect test is the fact that it correlates positively with a direct test designed for the same purpose. While such evidence provides some minimum comfort, it is hardly any argument for the superiority of the indirect. In those rare cases where there is a third variable or criterion against which both direct and indirect can be compared, the indirect is almost never the better—although it is true that there is a lack of data for settings which would lead to falsification of direct test responses.

The literature here reviewed shows only modest success, and yet considering the dynamics of publishing, this is almost certainly the most promising of the research that has been done. This is a literature to which low budget entrepreneurs can freely contribute. For each, the zest with which he polishes, analyzes, completes manuscripts, endures one editor's contumely to resubmit to another, will all depend upon the exciting nature of the results. Most blah outcomes will go unreported (the elder author of this paper provides noteworthy exceptions). If these published reports represent the best of the disguised testing attempts, we may begin to lose faith in the refinement and reliability of these instruments. Of all our imperfect measures, these are apparently not the least impure.

A TYPOLOGY OF ASSESSMENT PROCEDURES

The title of this chapter identifies our realm as indirect *testing* rather than *assessment. Unobtrusive Measures* (Webb, *et al.*, 1966) deals with assessing attitudes by other than testing and interviewing techniques. In retrospect, all the 1950 survey covered [by Campbell] was testing, requiring the cooperation of the respondents either for the true purpose or for some ulterior reason. It is this reliance on cooperation which makes testing particularly vulnerable to distortion and by the same token makes the deception in indirect testing appear more blatantly exploitative.

In our concern with testing as opposed to assessment in general, we shall elaborate on three dichotomies defining types of tests and refer the reader to Webb *et al.* (1966) for a fuller discussion of the non-test procedures of attitude measurement. The questionable status of some supposedly indirect tests has led us to include them in our discussion, with the observation that they might better be classified as direct. If there is enough disagreement over the indirectness of some of these measures, it might be wiser to consider these classifications also to represent continua rather than dichotomies.

1. *Indirect vs. direct.* In the *direct* test the respondent's understanding of the purpose of the test and the psychologist's understanding are in agreement. Were the respondent to read the psychologist's report of the test results, none of the topics introduced would surprise him. This is obvious in an achievement test given at the end of a course. It is equally evident for the typical public opinion poll. It is probably so for the usual preference tests and adjustment inventories. With some direct attitude questionnaires, it is true, the respondent might be surprised to find him-

self labelled a "segregationist" if he thought of himself as a "moderate." He might not have anticipated the extremity of his score, but he was probably quite aware of the content and direction of scoring.

In the *indirect* test the investigator interprets the responses in terms of dimensions and categories different from those held in mind by the respondent while answering. If a person tells stories to pictures under the belief that his thematic creativity is being measured and the psychologist then interprets the products as depth projections, the test is indirect. If a person judges the logical validity of statements and his responses are scored for race prejudice, the test is indirect. If he thinks his memory powers are being tested while his behavior is interpreted by the investigator in terms of attitudes toward Russia, the test is indirect. In general, whenever responses are taken as symptoms rather than as literal information, the test is indirect.

Characteristic of the indirect test is a *facade.* By this is meant a false assignment to the respondent which distracts him from recognizing the test's true purpose and which provides him with a plausible reason for cooperating. Initially the TAT had such a facade: "This is a test of your creative imagination." The objective test facade is used in an important class of indirect tests of social attitudes, wherein the respondent tries to show his knowledge of current events and is scored for the bias he shows in the directionality of his errors. The expression of aesthetic taste, estimates of public opinion, judgments of moral right and wrong, and judgments of logical consistency all have been used as facades.

2. *Voluntary vs. objective.* In the voluntary test the respondent is given to understand that any answer is acceptable, and that there is no external criterion of correctness against which his answers will be evaluated. He is encouraged in idiosyncrasy and self description. The test assignment may state "this is *not* a test of your ability," or "there are *no* right or wrong answers," or "answer in terms of how *you* really feel." In contrast, in an ob-

jective test the person is told, either explicitly or implicitly, that there is a correct answer external to himself, for which he should search in selecting his answer. The concepts of accuracy and error are in the respondent's mind. Phenomenologically he is describing the external, objective world, although in so doing he is inevitably reflecting his idiosyncratic view of that world, and can be unselfconsciously "projecting" in an important meaning of that word. When the facade succeeds, the respondents believe that they are describing reality, speaking of facts and judgments which are verifiable. They exhibit a phenomenal absolutism, a conviction that what they say reflects the way things are. It does not occur to them that they are projecting instead their view of the world, their hopes and fears, their prejudices and beliefs. This absolutism is a product of the respondent's having taken such so-called objective tests in the past plus his belief in the tester's honesty. If either of these ingredients is lacking, the disguise may be shattered.

3. *Free-response vs. structured*—This dichotomy is already well established in the classification of personality and attitude testing procedures. The free response format has the advantage of not suggesting answers or alternatives to the respondent. It neither limits nor artificially expands his range of possibilities. Projective tests have typically employed free, open-ended formats which enable the respondent to create his own organization and view of the world. Multiple choice TATs or Rorschachs, on the other hand, may impose a set of alternatives which the respondent would never have volunteered if left to his own devices. Structured formats are more frequently found with objective tests and have the advantage of a simple uniform scoring system. They were typical of the personality and attitude measurement devices of the first flowering of such tests in the period from 1920 to 1935 and hence provide the tradition against which both the projective test movement and modern survey research techniques revolted.

The four indirect test types which emerge from the above dichotomies and around which we have organized our survey are as follows:

(i) Voluntary free-response
(ii) Voluntary structured
(iii) Objective free-response
(iv) Objective structured

Voluntary, Free-Response

This category includes the classic projective techniques which capitalize on ambiguous stimuli and require the respondent to employ his own imagination to provide structure. Most of these tests were designed for clinical use but have found extensive application in the testing of social attitudes as well.

Approaches based on the thematic apperception test—Story-telling tasks such as the TAT are particularly useful in studying prejudice among children. For them the assignment is a familiar one and the facade and indirection are easily maintained. Vaughan and Thompson (1961) reported the successful development of a set of matched TAT-type cards to study the attitudes of white New Zealand children toward Maoris. The cards of each pair were identical except for the crucial figure, which was either Maori or white. Stories told by the children revealed a significant rise in unfavorable attitudes between the ages of 8 and 12 years. An earlier investigation (Johnson, 1949) also reports the successful study of Anglo-Spanish attitudes with a specially designed series of pictures. Johnson used six carefully selected conflict situations which were duplicated in three forms: with all Anglo characters (for use with English-American children); with all Spanish characters (for use with Spanish children); and with mixed Anglo-Spanish characters (for use with both groups). Attitudes were assessed by contrasting responses to identical situations when they involved Anglo-Spanish conflict and when depicted by their own group members only. Quantification was achieved by having two judges categorize individual responses on a number of dimensions. Reliability coefficients for six subgroups were over .90.

Rather than compare responses to pictures which were matched for scenes but differed on the race of the crucial figure, Radke, Trager, and Davis (1949) compared the responses of children to Barrier and Non-Barrier pictures in their Social Episodes Test. In the former, one child of a different race watched the others play, and in the latter all of the children were pictured playing together. Stories told in response to the Barrier picture referred to the social disadvantage of being Negro and contained expectations of being rejected. It should be noted that the Barrier pictures emphasized Negro minority group status by depicting one Negro child among many whites and there was no complementary set of pictures in which a white child stood outside the group. The interpretation would be more convincing if there had been this control.

Among projective tests of attitudes of adults, the most widely cited in previous surveys of the literature (Cook and Selltiz, 1964; Deri, Dinnerstein, Harding, and Pepitone, 1948; Krech and Crutchfield, 1948; McNemar, 1946; Williams, 1947) is that of Proshansky (1943) [Chapter 21 in this book]. He intermingled ambiguous pictures of labor situations with the more usual TAT scenes. The pictures were presented to a group by means of slides, with instructions to write for two and one-half minutes on what the slide represented. Each slide was shown for only five seconds. Proshansky found that ratings made from the resulting descriptions correlated .77 and .67 with a direct verbal scale of attitudes toward labor.

Rather than simply instructing their respondents to describe what they saw, several investigators have employed a series of questions around which stories could be organized. Neel and Neel (1953) asked their respondents such questions as "Who are the people in the picture? What has led up to or caused this situation? How do the people in the picture feel about what is happening?" Answers to this projective test failed to correlate significantly with a Likert scale of attitudes toward Negroes. The authors did not consider this an invalidation of the indirect measure, however, since it was able to show significant differences between criterion groups of respondents with known attitudes toward Negroes. Rather they concluded that the two tests were measuring different aspects of prejudice. Adding even more structure to the test, Riddleberger and Motz (1957) asked their subjects a series of questions about eight pictures of Negroes and whites. In addition to the usual assignment to "Describe what you saw," they also asked "How might these people have met?" and "What two words would you use to describe this person?" (sometimes pointing to the Negro and sometimes the white). The respondents were two groups of thirty students selected from a pool of 300 on the basis of extreme scores on the Negro subscale from Adorno *et al.* (1950) *The Authoritarian Personality*. The answers of these criterion groups differed significantly at the .001 level. Prejudiced respondents explained the meeting of the white and Negro in terms of happenstance more often than in terms of intimate arrangements, and the descriptive adjectives which they applied to the Negro were less flattering than those applied to the white.

Specially designed Thematic Apperception pictures were also used by Frenkel-Brunswik, Levinson and Sanford (1947) in their extensive study of the personality correlates of prejudice. In this research the purpose was not so much to measure prejudice as to get a more detailed and qualitative picture of its expression. The complicated interrelationships they found qualify the use of such pictures as attitude measuring instruments. For example, many prejudiced women told warmer and more sympathetic stories to a picture of an elderly black woman than they did to pictures of an elderly white woman (Frenkel-Brunswik and Reichert). While such a finding is consistent with personality theory, it points to the danger of an oversimplified one-to-one interpretation of such material. Problems of interpreting such projective data have been discussed at length by Campbell, Miller, Lubetsky and O'Connell (1964). It is possible that different persons might use different projective mechanisms, and these may be situationally dependent and vary with different traits. In an updating of the 1947 work, Adorno, Frenkel-Brunswik, Levinson and Sanford (1950) report more easily interpretable results using such specially designed TAT-type pictures. When shown a picture of a policeman with a civilian in custody, men who scored high on the F-scale described the civilian as a dangerous criminal, usually Negro or Mexican, and they identified with the police and claimed the arrest was made to protect an imagined white victim. Low F-scale scorers, on the other hand, identified with the prisoner and said he had been arrested for a justified protest for higher wages or for civil rights. Another picture, showing a Negro woman and a young Negro boy, elicited no rejection responses from either the high or low F-scale scorers because both described the characters as "neat" and "clean." High scorers, however, pointed out the uniqueness of these two persons and treated them as exceptions.

Other problems related to the use and interpretation of the TAT have been investigated in a multitrait-multimethod approach to the study of attitudes toward authority (Burwen and Campbell, 1957b). The reliability of the TAT, although low, compared favorably with the reliability coefficients of several other measures. The authority cards of the TAT had a reliability of .55, compared with .46 for a photo judging task, .56 for an autobiographical inventory, .59 for a direct attitude questionnaire, .75 for a sociometric questionnaire and .24 for an adjective checklist. Technically, the study might better be called "multi-target" rather than multitrait. Favorable and unfavorable attitudes were studied toward generalized and specific familial and institutional superiors and subordinates. When "multitarget"-monomethod and monotarget-multimethod comparisons were made, the TAT appeared to be a victim of its own apparatus. Whereas the TAT responses to a symbolic authority correlated .49 with TAT responses to a symbolic peer, the correlation between TAT responses to symbolic authority and responses on other instruments to boss or father ranged from only .03 to .14. This warns that any attempts to use TAT-type tests should include not only other methods in order to establish the validity of a construct but also other attitudes in order to reveal the role of factors which are peculiar to that method. The correlation between two different measures of a single attitude should be not only significantly greater than zero but also significantly greater than the correlation between two different attitudes measured by a single method. In the language of Campbell and Fiske (1959), it is necessary to demonstrate not only the "convergent validity" of a construct but also its "discriminant validity." Before introducing a new concept or construct, in other words, one must demonstrate that it is indeed new and different. If, as in Burwen and Campbell's (1957b) study, the TAT scores for authority and peer figures are more similar than are the scores for authority figures obtained from a TAT and a direct attitude survey, there is no justification for speaking of a generalized attitude toward authority.

The use of matched pairs of TAT cards is one step in the direction of meeting these requirements. If only one set of cards were shown, in which the critical figure was always Negro, for instance, it would be impossible to distinguish between responses which reveal hostility in general and responses which express race prejudice. Direct tests are also susceptible to such confounding (Sullivan and Adelson, 1954). By using matched pairs, it is possible to demonstrate a difference in responses to Maoris and whites, Spanish and Anglo characters, or Negroes and whites. This amounts to the study of two attitudinal objects, or two traits. What remains to be done is the introduction of other methods as well.

Problems of another sort beset the projective tester who tries to use TAT-type materials in cross-cultural research. These problems have been treated extensively by Kaplan (1961a, 1961b), Atkinson (1958), Lindzey (1961), Doob (1965, 1968) and Clignet (in preparation). There are many cross-cultural studies which have attempted to correct the cultural inappropriateness of the standard TAT pictures by using pictures appropriate to the specific culture. However, when these are then used in cross-cultural comparisons, it becomes equivocal whether the differences are due to differences in pictures or to the differences in culture. (Where the studies confirm general psychological laws, this inference is less equivocal.) Beyond problems of custom, Biesheuvel (1958) and Hudson (1967) have warned that the development and interpretation of pictorial materials in an African setting must take into account the pictorial and perceptual habits of the respondents. In an artistic tradition which does not use the rules of perspective drawing or the western conventions of shading, there may be very little relationship between the intended appearance of a picture and its appearance to the receiver. A picture intended to represent cattle grazing in a field, for instance, was drawn in perspective so that those in the background were smaller than those in the foreground. To the African respondents, however, those in the background looked like hyenas or other small animals. Even these nonverbal testing materials are not free from certain culture-bound rules and conventions.

Approaches utilizing doll play techniques —Because of their naturalness and self-sustaining interest, doll play techniques would appear to be a useful method of testing attitudes in children. Arnold Meier (College Study in Intergroup Relations, 1948) developed the "What Would You Do?" test in which cut-outs depicting white and minority group children are manipulated on background scenes of the home, or school. Hartley and Schwartz (1948) manipulated the symbols and characteristics of the background rather than the appearance of the dolls in a study of children's attitudes toward different religious groups. Identical sets of family dolls were employed against backgrounds containing symbols from the Jewish religion, Catholic religion, or no religion. The results indicated that children are able to identify the religious symbols with considerable accuracy and that their play reflects intergroup attitudes in a meaningful way. A similar approach called the "Movie Story Game" (Evans and Chein, 1948) measured not only the spatial patterning of Negro and white dolls but also the child's verbalizations when asked periodically what the identified doll would say. The results indicated effective disguise and general meaningfulness for the test.

Doll play techniques are by no means limited to use with children. As early as 1940 Dubin (1940) utilized toys to assess the attitudes of ten adult respondents. He asked them to "construct on this table a dramatic scene or scenes of the world as you see it today" and later "make a dramatic scene or scenes of the world as you would like it to be." Utilizing these data three judges were able to estimate answers on 21 direct attitude questions dealing with labor, the Negro, internationalism, etc. with an average rank order correlation of .49. There was no evidence presented to support the discriminant validity of these attitudes.

A technique which has more modest aims but perhaps more rigorous measurement possibilities has been developed by Kuethe (1962a, 1962b, 1964). To test the feasibility of the method, Kuethe and Stricker (1963) studied the social schemata of male and female undergraduates by instructing them to place the following sets of figures on a felt field: two men and two women; two men and one woman; one man, one woman, and two rectangles, etc. These sets were given separately in random order and after each was placed on the field, the placement was measured with a ruler, the set removed, and the next set given. Both male and female respondents generally paired the man and woman figures rather than grouping them separately by sex. Ninety per cent of the female and ninety-one per cent of the male respondents placed the man and woman figures side by side and did not allow the rectangles to intervene. The difference between male and female respondents was revealed by the males generally forming one group of alternating man and woman figures and the females forming separate man-woman pairs or subgroups. This was predicted by the authors and presumably reflected the marriage orientation of the female respondents.

Evidence for the validity of the felt board tests comes from a second study by Kuethe (1964) which measured prejudice and aggression [Chapter 22 in this book]. In the first task 74 male undergraduates were given three groups of felt figures consisting of two black and two white men; two black men and one white woman; one white man, one white woman, and one black man. The respondents were instructed to place each set on a blue field in any manner they wished. The resultant organizations were classified in terms of whether black and white were subgrouped apart or grouped together with the figures alternating by color. A comparison of integrated and segregated groupings with the respondents' scores on the Negro subscale of the Ethnocentrism scale yielded a significant chi̧ square. The validity of the test as a measure of aggression was similarly established.

Modifications of the Rosenzweig Picture Frustration Test—Rather than require persons to supply behavioral repertoires for a test character, this test requests them to fill in the dialogue in a series of cartoon drawings involving face-to-face intergroup contacts (Brown, 1947). This technique has been adapted by several investigators for use in studying social attitudes (Reynolds, 1949; Sanford, 1950; Sanford and Rosenstock, 1952). Sanford (1950) presented his respondents with scenes such as an auto accident with one man saying to the other, "It was all your fault." The respondents' replies to the

cartoon character enabled judges to predict their approximate scores on the Authoritarianism-Equalitarianism test. Sanford recommended the use of such projective devices in door-to-door interviewing.

Sommer (1954) tested the susceptibility of the cartoon technique to censorship and distortion by trying to detect deliberate distortions. He employed ten drawings with ambiguous quotations and asked the respondents to fill in the dialogue for the Negro. Following this a Likert-type scale was administered. One group of 18 respondents was given additional instructions—to try to distort their dialogue answers so as to appear very liberal and unprejudiced, but they were asked to answer the Likert scale honestly. Sommer selected the top and bottom quintiles from the Likert scores plus the 18 who distorted their answers and then tried to predict the respondent's Likert scale position by examining his dialogue responses. He was able to detect 12 of the deliberate distortions and among the rest he correctly predicted 85 per cent of the Likert scale positions. These findings suggest that if persons do dissemble on such projective tests, their answers can be detected if the tester so desires.

Another variation on this technique which probably belongs within the limits of this category is the study by Fromme (1941). He presented to the respondents five political cartoons, each with four alternative captions, covering a wide range of pro and con opinion. The respondent was asked to pick the best caption, and this choice, plus the discussion resulting, was utilized in a qualitative analysis of attitude structure.

Sentence completion tests—These are perhaps the least disguised of the indirect measures since little effort is made to deceive in the majority of cases. Most stems make direct reference to the attitudinal object and thus make obvious the tester's intent. Occasionally neutral items may be interspersed among the critical items as in a modification of Rotter's test (1947) used by Shirley Wilcox Brown at the Ohio State University. Examples of

relevant and neutral items are as follows:
1. I feel...
2. Skin color...
3. I hate...
4. Maybe...
5. Some lynchings...
6. The K.K.K....
7. It seems to me that segregation...
15. Negro body odor...
37. Racial intermarriage...

Even in this test, however, no effort at dissembling is made. With instructions which ask the subject to "express your real feelings," without providing any other plausible assignment, he is not likely to miss the purpose of the test even if critical items are embedded among neutral ones.

Another twist to the sentence completion notion avoids all mention of minority groups but provides stereotypic statements which may be completed with names of various minority groups or others (Frenkel-Brunswik, Jones, Rokeach, Jarvik and Campbell, 1946–1947). Examples of items are:

(1) Are there some people who are mean? WHAT PEOPLE?
(2) It would be better if more of a certain type of people were allowed to come into the United States. WHAT PEOPLE?
(3) Some people are poor and it is their own fault. WHAT PEOPLE?

This test elicited mention of foreign and minority groups from about one-third of the children to whom it was administered. From another third or so came one or more anti-prejudice statements. A portion of the students made no responses classifiable in either way and were thus not effectively evaluated. Using a net score (subtracting anti-prejudice responses from the total of prejudiced ones) corrected reliability figures ran around .6 to .8 and correlations with a highly reliable direct test were on the order of .5. The approach is most satisfactory for the comparison of groups of respondents, and for the evaluation of the relative salience and extremeness of attitudes toward different minority groups. In addition unique data on the uniformity of stereotyping were provided.

Also avoiding mention of the attitudinal object in at least some of their sentence stems, Burwen, Campbell and Kidd (1956) tested attitudes toward superiors and subordinates in an Air Force population. Some of their items read as follows, with sample answers given here to indicate the range of responses:

He never felt comfortable in the presence of: (a) his superiors, (b) a general, (c) his men, (d) enlisted men.

Whenever he saw his superior coming he (a) threw up, (b) ducked or lied, (c) saluted, (d) gave him a warm greeting, (e) was very happy.

The test showed acceptable reliability (Kuder-Richardson .69) and correlated .27 with an indirect information test of attitudes and .32 with a direct attitude questionnaire. The case for the construct validity of the sentence completion measure was weakened, however, by a high negative correlation of −.45 with a direct test of alienation and low nonsignificant correlations with 13 reputation criterion measures.

As long as the task is presented in a voluntary framework, it is not too different from any free-response questionnaire on attitudes. Compare, for example, Zeligs' (1937) approach in which school children were asked to "write the most interesting true sentence" they know about each group within a one minute limit. A different set of instructions, however, could perhaps impart a degree of disguise. Getzels and Walsh (1958) used a third-person sentence completion task and presented it as a test of verbal speed. To compare public and private racial attitudes, for instance, they used the following two items: "If Negroes began being admitted to the club, Bill . . ." and "If Negroes began being admitted to the club, I . . .". The latter item conformed more to socially desirable answers. This finding, plus the observation by Hanfmann and Getzels (1953) that in retrospect their subjects admitted that the third person completions referred to themselves, would argue in favor of discarding the first person stems in order to achieve a greater degree of disguise. Cook (1968), however, reports that although answers to first person stems do conform more to socially accepted patterns, the *eta* coefficients for the first person completions were higher than those for the third person stems. Both showed a significant relationship to membership in attitudinal criterion groups. These ranged from groups like CORE on the equalitarian end of the attitude continuum to pro-segregation fraternities on the anti-Negro end. Eta coefficients for the first person completions were .54, .57, and .82 for subjects in three different geographic areas, as compared with .49, .43, and .76 for the third person completions.

In a multitrait-multimethod study of attitudes in a prison population Maher, Watt and Campbell (1960) compared a relatively thinly disguised sentence completion test with a direct structured attitude scale on attitudes toward family and law. The validity coefficients showed the two tests to be mutually validating, with values of .50 and .51 for the two attitudes studied. In terms of discriminant validity, these values were distinctly higher than the heterotrait-heteromethod values of .13 and .12. Methods factors were surprisingly low, with heterotrait-monomethod values of .05 and —.04. Biserial correlations of the test scores with crime committed, however, showed the direct test to be slightly superior, although the difference was not great. The finding that both methods produced the same pattern of correlation with crimes was also regarded as mutually validating.

The virtue of this entire category of voluntary free-response tests lies not so much in their indirection, which is doubtful in many instances, but rather in their freedom. Although the tester does not label the test as an attitude measure, his invitation to the respondent to answer in any way he sees fit the obviously "loaded" questions may be interpreted by the respondent in many ways. While some of the persons may complete their assignments unaware of the experimenter's interest, in a tense situation one could hardly expect to get unconscious or uncensored expressions from unwilling or suspicious respondents. It is, then, the voluntary quality of the responses which leaves open the way for the respondent to question the tester's purpose and to suspect the worst. And it is the freedom of the answers which provides the opportunity for noting novel attitude dimensions unanticipated by the author and justifies the use of these projective techniques.

Voluntary Structured

In light of the evaluation of projective techniques offered in the preceding section, this category would seem to suffer from the faults of voluntary tests without the benefit of free responses. The picture is not entirely bleak, however, for there is considerable leeway for persons to respond voluntarily without their sensing the test as a direct probe, and there are advantages to the unambiguous character of structured responses.

Semantic differential techniques—Perhaps the most frequently used innovation in attitude measurement since the 1950 review has been the "semantic differential." In most cases the semantic differential rating scales are applied directly to the attitude object, and analyzed in terms of total scores on the evaluative component. We shall not review this voluminous literature, classifying it as direct attitude measurement, the modern substitute for Remmers' (1934, 1954; Remmers and Silance, 1934) generalized attitude scales, a set of items ready for use with regard to any attitude topic.

Even in such instances, the semantic differential probably achieves some minimum of indirection. Diab (1965) found that with semantic differential ratings of the concept of "Arab unity" he could differentiate pro- and anti-unity students with more success than could the Hovland-Sherif method of accepting or rejecting a series of statements about Arab unity. He contended that the use of adjectival pairs evoked less conscious censorship than did the use of complete sentences. When the stimuli are presented in such bald terms, however, for most purposes the test could be classified as direct. Persons who rated Nixon and John Kennedy (Stricker, 1963) or "myself" and "my ideal self" (Babbitt, 1962), for instance, were probably very aware of the intent of the investigators. Hicks (1967) also made no attempt to hide the object of investigation from his respondents who rated "Negro," "Peace Corps," and "Journalism" on 14 semantic rating scales. This unmasked form of testing did not suffer from any pressures toward social desirability, however, since the correlation between semantic differential scores for "Negro" and an indirect (Objective Judgments) test of attitudes toward Negroes was equal to the correlation for "Peace Corps" (.47) and was greater than the correlation for "Journalism" (.06). Hicks argued that the testing situation might have seemed sufficiently innocuous to prevent distortion of answers. In the absence of convincing data to show that the indirect "Objective" test was not also susceptible to distortion, however, the interpretation is equivocal.

Perhaps the most indirect of the semantic differential approaches to studying racial attitudes is an investigation of the connotations of color names by Williams (1964). His respondents were asked to rate ten color names on 12 semantic scales with heavy loadings on the evaluation, potency, and activity factors. The experimenter made no reference to race but said instead that he was conducting a research project on colors. After the respondents rated each color, Williams analyzed the data by comparing the ratings given by white and Negro respondents to race-related colors (white, black, brown, yellow, red) and control colors (blue, green, purple, orange, gray). Using those two groups of respondents as criterion groups, he found an interesting interaction—Caucasians gave significantly higher "bad" scores to black and brown than did Negroes.

In another attempt to achieve indirection with the semantic differential, Eisenman,

Bernard and Jannon (1966) had their respondents rank ten Rorschach cards according to the degree to which they symbolized God. Then they rated each card on six benevolence and six potency scales. Just as Williams assumed that in rating the word "black" his respondents were rating something akin to the concept of "Negro," so Eisenman *et al.,* presumed that when respondents rated the cards on the semantic differential they were rating some aspect of "God." The results showed the cards rated most like God were also rated most benevolent and least potent, with a significant negative correlation between the benevolence and potency scores ($rho = -.51$).

Other semantic and word choice techniques—In a modification of the free-association technique, Havron, Nordlie, and Cofer (1957) developed a binary choice test to measure religious and political-economic attitudes and to test radicalism-conservatism and authoritarianism-equalitarianism as well. The respondents were presented triplets of words and told to "Associate the stimulus word with the response word you find easiest to associate with it by drawing a line between the stimulus word and that response word." To maintain a degree of disguise, neutral items were interspersed among the attitudinally relevant triplets. The following are examples of the triplets employed:

(a) Become ethical / forceful

(b) Law understand / obedience

Test-retest reliability was .81 for 57 cases and .87 for 74 cases. Criterial correlations based on the Allport-Vernon study of values and a conservatism-radicalism opinionnaire for the religious-political items and for the radicalism-conservatism items were .81 and .42 respectively (both significant beyond the .01 level). For the authoritarianism-equalitarianism triplets, however, the correlation with the F-scale scores was only .18, which may be the result of a markedly skewed distribution of F-scale scores. There was not enough data reported to assess the discriminant validity of the attitudinal traits.

Another variation on the word association technique was devised by Campbell and Shanan (1958) to study attitudes toward authority. Ostensibly the aim of the task to have Air Force cadets rate 50 photographs on an adjective checklist of 30 items. The variable of interest to the investigators was the coapplication of the word "strict" with two favorable ("loyal" and "intelligent") and two unfavorable ("trouble-making" and "scheming") adjectives. Coapplication was measured by tetrachoric correlations between presence or absence of "strict" and presence or absence of a favorable or unfavorable adjective. Such coapplication was regarded as a functional measure of synonymity. Additional tests and reputational measures relevant to the dimension of authority showed no relationship to the connotative evaluations of the word "strict." The authors concluded that these findings pointed to the invalidity of the construct under examination and did not negate the merit of the semantic analysis.

Tests involving preferences for pictures and objects—These studies, like many already discussed, depend upon the demonstration of a judgment differential of which the respondent is presumably unaware. They are voluntary insofar as judgments are required in situations wherein there is no "objective" right answer. At the same time they retain the advantage of having the respondent (1) work on a task presumably less threatening than the experimenter's primary problem, and (2) report upon external values or realities, rather than upon himself directly.

Murphy and Likert, in *Public Opinion and the Individual* (1937) utilized a wealth of techniques which anticipated the projective testing movement. Among these was the "Ratings from Photographs." Following the general framework of Rice's classic study on stereotypes, they provided labeled pictures of a union president, a railroad magnate, a pacifist, and a Negro civil rights champion. Respondents were asked to judge from these labeled photographs the character of the pic-

tured person, in terms of courage, selfishness, intelligence, conceit, sympathy, practicality, and sentimentality. Contrary to expectation, they found no relationship between attitudes, as measured in a variety of paper-and-pencil tests, and these picture ratings. Such a test could be made "objective" by using a label such as "social intelligence test" or the like.

Hsü (1949) had three female graduate students sort photographs of males for handsomeness, and ten days later for judged membership in the Communist party. The correlations were negative (−.50 and −.21) for the two women who were anti-communist, and positive (.51) for the one woman who was relatively pro-communist. After reading a *Time* report on the blockade of Berlin, the correlations for sorts on a second set of photographs were negative for all three women. A similar technique was employed by Martin (1964). He asked white and Negro respondents to rank ten photographs taken from *Ebony* and *Sepia* according to their beauty. When judges ranked the pictures in terms of their Negroidness, it was found that the ratings of the Negro and white respondents correlated .60 and .55, respectively, with the judges' rankings of Caucasoidness. Martin interpreted this to mean that there was a relative lack of anti-white prejudice among the Negroes in his sample. It is questionable, however, whether the Negroid features were as salient a factor in racial attitudes in 1964 as they might be today. It may be that the test was indeed so indirect that it tapped what might have been a purely aesthetic factor without any attitudinal relevance.

Green and Stacey (1966) used a multiple-choice projective technique to study the self-images of a sample of London voters. They presented eight photographs of men and asked their respondents to indicate which of the men he would most like to be. Later each was asked to indicate which of the photos he thought were Conservative and which were Labor supporters. The judged affiliation of the respondent's most preferred photo was significantly related to the respondent's actual political affiliation. Although Green and Stacey used this technique for measuring the self-images of their respondents, it also offers possibilities for assessing likes and dislikes by comparing the judged affiliation of a photograph with the respondent's own affiliation.

In work now in progress, Cook (1968) has attached a photo of a Negro, a white, or a Japanese-American to one of a trio of personality descriptions. These descriptions had been shown in previous work with persons similar to be equally favorable (or unfavorable) when presented without photos. The personality descriptions were formed by varying the persons' occupation, sociability, dependability and ambitiousness. In order to relieve the respondents of the notion that this was an attitude test, the instructions stressed the relevance of this task to many real-life situations where persons must be evaluated on the basis of such scant information. The subjects were thus motivated to perform well and their attention was focused on the personality descriptions rather than the physical features of the photos. They rated each photo with its accompanying description on semantic differential and social distance scales. Racial attitude scores were derived by taking the difference between ratings of matched white and Negro descriptions. These scores successfully differentiated members of attitudinal criterion groups ranging from strongly equalitarian to anti-Negro. *Eta* coefficients between attitude scores and group membership were .44 and .52 in two different geographic regions. Correlations with attitudes toward occupations, ambitiousness, and the other factors were not given. Triandis, Loh and Levin (1966) employed a similar technique, but in the absence of instructions emphasizing the relevance of the assignment to real-life situations, their test does not meet the requirements for an indirect measure. Their respondents viewed slides of a Negro or white, dressed in a suit or coveralls, accompanied by a tape-recording in which the speaker argued for or against integrated housing and spoke in either excellent or poor English. In rating on semantic

and behavioral differentials, however, the respondents were not motivated to strive for accuracy or to take the role of an interviewer or prospective employer. Although the factorial combination of several variables may have distracted the subjects' attention from the variable of race, there was no real effort made to disguise the purpose of the test.

Tests involving miscellaneous judgments —In Watson's (1925) "Moral Judgments" subtest judgments of approval or disapproval are made about a variety of situations, sets of these situations being identical except for the specific persons or groups involved. For example, unwarranted search is made of a suspected "radical" headquarters on the one hand, while in a parallel item the same type of search is carried out on a business corporation suspected of dishonesty (Watson, 1925). Scoring is done on the basis of discrepancy of judgments between the parallel situations.

Similar in title and in plan to Watson's test was the ingenious approach to Negrowhite attitudes devised by Seeman (1947). While he used equated comparison groups, the technique could be modified for diagnosing bias in individuals. He selected six items from a standard test of moral evaluations on marriage and sexual matters. To one group, the episode items were illustrated by pictures of white couples, to the other with Negro illustrations. Both groups were made up of white college students. Contrary to expectation, the judgments were more lenient— less disapproval—with the Negro illustrations. Furthermore, when the two groups were subclassified according to scores on the Likert scale of attitudes toward the Negro, the major part of the differential was contributed by the more *tolerant* persons rather than the more anti-Negro persons in the two groups. The intolerant extremes in this sample were more consistent, less "biased." These results are important and meaningful, but further indicate the danger of oversimplified interpretations in indirect approaches.

Sherriffs' (1948) Intuition Questionnaire is an example of a test which could be presented with an objective facade but has been used to elicit voluntary judgments instead. His subjects were instructed to "Give a probable explanation for the behavior indicated in each of the following excerpts from life stories taken from a random sample of the population. Include the motivation underlying the behavior and the origins of the motivation." If the subjects could be convinced that the tester had accurate information about the motivations and explanations for the behavior samples, this would qualify as an objective measure. This technique has seen successful application by French (1955) in the measurement of achievement and affiliation motives. Day's (1949) method of asking respondents to explain a sample of daydreams is similar.

A variety of other judgments tests have found disappointingly low or insignificant correlations. The readiness with which judgments of literary merit can be manipulated by the substitution of fictitious authors has been demonstrated by Saadi and Farnsworth (1934) and Sherif (1935). Prestige seems to be one of those forces which can bias the performance on a judgmental task and therefore gives promise as a basis for inferring attitudes. Lewis (1938) seems to have had in mind some such approach. Frenkel-Brunswik, Jones et al. (1946–1947) tried to utilize the prestige effect to measure attitudes toward five minority groups. Instead of literary passages, proverbs or mottoes were used. The adage was attributed to the group as a whole, rather than to individual authors (e.g., "American pioneer saying" or "old Jewish motto"). Eighth and ninth grade students were asked to evaluate the quality of each motto separately—there being ten mottoes attributed to each group. The test yielded a general prejudice score that correlated only .30 with a direct test. Scores on attitudes toward particular out-groups were worthless. It is quite possible that in the form given the task was trivial and the disguise thin.

As Wolff, Smith and Murray (1934) have shown, reactions to group disparagement jokes are correlated with group membership.

Gordon (1947) tried to utilize this phenomenon in the assessment of social attitudes. Twenty-four jokes, both antagonistic and sympathetic, dealing with Negroes and Jews were rated as to their funniness on a 5-point scale. Five groups of college men were used: a Protestant fraternity, a Catholic fraternity, a Negro fraternity, a Jewish fraternity (non-Zionist), and a Zionist club. The groups differed in their responses to these jokes but not as anticipated in all instances. The jokes sympathetic to Jews were rated highest by the two Jewish groups; but the anti-Jewish jokes failed to differentiate the groups. The anti-Negro jokes were rated lowest by the Negro group, but the pro-Negro jokes failed to differentiate. The various groups ranked the individual jokes quite similarly as to popularity, with *rhos* between the orders for the different groups ranging from .71 to .94. With regard to individual differences *within* the various groups, the ratings of the jokes showed no relationship to attitudes toward Negroes or Jews as revealed in a direct attitude test or a test of symbol endorsement.

Employing a battery of materials which are more true to life than many projective tests, Campbell and Mehra (1958) had a group of Air Force cadets observe a sound film of community leaders discussing problems of juvenile delinquency and also had them read a transcript of Air Force officers discussing the reservists' curriculum. The subjects' task was to evaluate specific features of the leader's and group members' performance. The superior-subordinate orientation score looked to whether leaders' actions were evaluated more favorably than group members' reactions, or whether the leaders or group members were blamed for ineffectiveness. This score had a reliability of .45. The test failed to show expected correlations with a wide variety of other efforts to measure "superior-subordinate orientation." For example, it correlated .16 (non-significant) with a reputational measure for leadership, .00 with an indirect objective test of Leadership Knowledge (Campbell and Damarin, 1961) and —.18 (significant at the .02 level) with the F-scale. The negative correlation with the F-scale indicates that the person who is subordinate-oriented and sees the group members as capable of leadership is also more authoritarian. As mentioned before, the general invalidity of measures in this study supports the notion that it may be a case of a nonexistent construct rather than a poor method.

Cook (1968) has reported promising results with a judgments test which involves predicting the relative effectiveness of alternative social policies. He constructed descriptions of alternative remedial programs for minority group progress and varied two factors—the degree of educational opportunity offered and the degree of legislative assurances for equal opportunity. Respondents were asked to predict the effectiveness of the various programs. The expectation was that anti-Negro persons would favor the Negro self-improvement programs and equalitarians would favor programs which stressed legislative controls. His results suggest that this may prove to be the case. Scores on the judgment measure correlated .61 with a previously validated self-report inventory based on preference between the two remedial programs.

A unique measure of social attitudes has been developed by Laughlin and Laughlin (1968) in their study of source effects in the judgment of social argot. Ten expressions were selected from the jargon of pickpockets and Ozark mountaineers, such as "in the gales" and "misbobble." Each item was given one of four different definitions and attributed to either a Nobel prize-winning physicist, a deep sea diver, an organizer for the Black Panthers, or an underworld pickpocket. The following definitions of "misbobble" gave the flavor of the test:

physicist: "failure of an experiment due to a careless oversight."
diver: "unsuccessful dive due to faulty equipment."
organizer: "failure at a rally to sway the audience, use of a poor tactic."
pickpocket: "an unsuccessful attempt to fleece a victim."

The persons rated each item, as attributed to only one of the four sources, for its expressiveness, creativity, acceptability for adoption into the conversation of a learned person, and acceptability for adoption into formal communications such as speeches or journals. Analysis of variance of the ratings showed that for expressiveness there were no differences for the various sources—the pickpocket's use of "misbobble" was considered as expressive as the physicist's. On the other three scales, however, the source to whom the expression was attributed was a significant factor. Ratings for the physicist and diver were all significantly higher than those for the Black Panther and pickpocket, which did not differ from each other. It appears that persons consider the argot of a lower-status individual expressive, but are not willing to use it themselves. The failure to find a difference between ratings for the Black Panther and the pickpocket may have reflected the racial tensions of the period—summer 1967. The authors made no analyses of individual differences in their study but suggest that this may be a potential indirect measure of ethnic attitudes.

The failure of the majority of these tests to demonstrate clear differences between criterion groups of subjects or to correlate significantly with other measures of attitudes may be attributed to many different factors in the various studies. Campbell and Mehra's findings may be the result of testing a homogeneous population where individual differences would not appear. Frenkel-Brunswik et al., (1946–1947) low correlation may have been a function of the task, having little relevance to ethnic attitudes. In general it appears that finding judgment tests which are both indirect and relevant to the attitude under investigation is difficult. The tests requiring character judgments from photographs, for instance, and the "show me the prettiest" approach seem capable of differentiating persons with different attitudes, but they are so thinly disguised that one wonders whether they really qualify as indirect measures. Of the semantic and word choice tests, the semantic differential seems to be open to charges of being either too direct or too bizarre a task to succeed as a disguised test. These negative evaluations are not intended to imply that work with voluntary structured tests is a fruitless endeavor. In general, however, the combination of voluntary judgments and a structured format militates against constructing a test which will be both disguised and relevant to the attitude in question.

The F-scale—The F-scale measure of Authoritarian Personality trends (Adorno, Frenkel-Brunswik, Levinson, Sanford, 1950) was initially intended as an indirect measure of ethnocentrism and anti-minority group attitudes, and for this reason deserves some discussion here. Its initial item pool was made up from personality type content suggested by clinical interviews with prejudiced persons. This item pool was repeatedly refined in terms of item analysis against the Ethnocentrism scale total scores. The item's ability to predict prejudice without obvious minority group content provided the determining grounds for selection. The test itself is voluntary—dealing with matters of opinion and preference and prefaced by affirmations that there are no right or wrong answers. This is indirection by correlated symptom, substituting the direct measurement of a cluster of non-sensitive correlated direct scales for the direct measurement of a sensitive, distortion-prone attitude.

Most of the uses of the F-scale have not been for this purpose, but rather for its own sake as an indicator of a personality syndrome. This enormous literature cannot be covered here. Findings relevant to indirect indications of ethnic prejudice are incidental to this literature. It can be said without claiming to have covered this vast literature (see Christie and Jahoda, 1954; Christie, 1956; Brown, 1965), that usually (although not always, as in the southern United States or in the Middle East) the F-scale correlates substantially with any measure of prejudice, including indicators quite different in questionnaire format (e.g., Campbell and McCandless, 1951). However, in no studies of which we are aware does the F-scale perform better than a direct measure of prejudice. By and large, the purposes for which it was built have not been tested, or where tested, have not been confirmed.

Objective Tests—Free and Structured

The approaches which we will consider below differ from the above mentioned ones perhaps only in degree or in relative emphasis. Yet the distinction involved is important. The characteristics of these disguised, nonvoluntary tests can be stated in a number of different ways.

The respondent participates in an objective task in which he seeks right answers. The voluntarism of the usual projective technique is lacking. To the respondent the situation is similar to that of an achievement or ability test. All respondents have a common motivation in taking the test. All, we may assume, are seeking to perform adequately on the same objective task. Attention is focused on a common goal, oblique to the experimenter's purpose. Rather than capitalizing on freedom and lack of structuring, there is an attempt to diagnose attitudes from systematic bias in the performance of an objective task. The test may be highly structured (directly scorable) and still offer opportunity for the unconcious operation of bias to distort behavior in a systematic and diagnosable manner.

Here is a simple formula for constructing such a test. Find a task which all your respondents will take as objective and in which all will strive to do well. Stress the importance of accuracy and emphasize the fact that there are right and wrong answers. Make the task sufficiently difficult so that answers will not reflect differential knowledge on the part of the respondents. At the same time, tell the subjects that the test is admittedly hard and they may have to guess when they are in doubt. Load the test with content relevant to the attitude under study. Look for systematic error or for persistent selectivity of performance. If such be found, it seems an adequate basis for the inference of an attitude.

Objective Free-Response

These tests employ an objective facade by focusing the respondent's attention on the external world, but they allow him to supply his own answers or perceptions in an unstructured situation.

Auditory and visual interpretation tasks —The oldest and most used of the projective tests in this category is the "Verbal Summator" or "Tautophone" (Grings, 1942). A recording of indistinct vowel sounds is presented with instructions such as "This is a recording of a man talking. He is not speaking very plainly, but if you listen carefully you will be able to tell what he is saying. I'll play it over and over again, so that you can get it, but be sure to tell me as soon as you have an idea of what he is saying." To the authors' knowledge, this technique has been used only for personality assessment. It seems well suited to testing attitudes as well, however, and certainly qualifies as an objective test. The facade is almost always accepted without question and persons manage to produce intelligible verbal content without being aware that it comes entirely from themselves.

A visual variation of the Tautophone is Rechtschaffen and Mednick's (1955) Autokinetic Word Technique. In the normal autokinetic illusion, a single dot of light in an otherwise darkened room appears to move. The subjects were instructed that the light was spelling out words which they were to read and report. All of the respondents "saw" words, and when told about the nature of the experiment were shocked to learn that they themselves had fabricated the content. The test was totally unstructured and the answers were interpreted as personality indicators. The instructions could just as easily limit answers to some particular topic by telling the persons that the words related to communism or religion, and the answers could become diagnostic of attitudes.

A "phony language examination" developed by Nunnally and Husek (1958) offers possibilities for projective testing. Randomly chosen foreign words were scattered throughout English sentences and respondents were instructed to guess the meanings of the words and then decide whether they agreed or disagreed with the sentences. The authors were interested in the influence of sentence structure and the tendency for persons to accept or be suspicious of causal relations. This test could readily be converted into a test of social attitudes by introducing either foreign words or nonsense syllables into sentences which refer to the attitudinal object and asking for a translation of the foreign word. Under the guise of a "test of language ability" this could perhaps pass as an indirect attitude measure.

Tests requiring judgments of behavior and character—The assignment to judge the character of persons presented in photographs can also be presented as an objective task. Common statements in psychology texts as to the impossibility of making valid judgments of this kind may create a problem, although with a properly prepared set of materials (e.g., Campbell and Burwen, 1956) the phenomenological validity of the task is great enough so that even college students will accept it as a legitimate objective task. Campbell and Burwen employed five photographs of men and five of women from each of four age levels in an attempt to investigate trait judgments as a function of age and sex. The respondents, Air Force personnel, were led to believe that information on the personalities of the photographees had been collected prior to the experiment. The task was thus an apparently objective one. The subjects were told to judge the individuals from their pictures and their accuracy would be determined by comparing their judgments with the actual personality information. Responses were obtained on both a free-response format and a structured adjective checklist of 30 traits. Efforts to relate a differential favorableness to older males as opposed to younger males, or a differential favorableness to weak versus strong middle-aged males were so unrewarding as not to have been reported.

Examples of the objective free-response

category are apparently hard to come by not because of the impossibility of devising suitable techniques, but rather because of the rarity with which projective tests are masqueraded as objective tasks with right and wrong answers. All that would be required to turn a TAT question such as "How did the people in this picture meet?" into an objective test would be to inform the respondent that the tester knew how the persons had met. The voluntary character of the test would then vanish. There may, however, be an interaction between structuredness and apparent objectivity.

A conversion of voluntary tests into objective types would seem to be in the spirit of a movement to develop better disguised measures of social attitudes. Since the indirectness of a test is only as good as its facade, the aim must be to develop more convincing facades which focus the respondent's attention elsewhere. The guise of a test of creative imagination has the effect of focusing the respondent's attention upon himself, and in the process of wondering whether he is being sufficiently creative he may also begin to wonder how the tester will interpret his creative endeavors. The practice of "interpreting" a creative work, whether it be a short story, a poem, or a response to an ink-blot is familiar to most persons. Thus, the respondent might not be terribly surprised to learn that the tester was really interested in measuring his attitudes toward minority groups. The objective facade is much less susceptible to such a cracking of the code, since the respondent's attention is focused on the external world and there is no popularized tradition of interpreting motives or prejudices from factual, right and wrong answers.

Objective Structured

While employing many of the same facades as the tests discussed in the previous section, these tests restrict the responses to a set of alternatives specified by the multiple choice format or by the tester's instructions.

Information tests—The reader has probably commented at one time or another upon the inextricable interrelationship between people's attitudes and what they take to be facts. Newcomb (1946) has dramatically portrayed the non-random character of right and wrong answers on an information test in his study of "The Effect of Social Climate upon some Determinants of Information." He comments with regard to the difficult information items, "the direction of guessing is altogether likely to be weighted toward the subject's attitude. If this reasoning is correct, the . . . test tends to become itself an attitude test." Coffin (1941) and Smith (1947) have found beliefs of factual type statements to correlate highly with related attitude tests. This correlation is particularly interesting where the "facts" are difficult to ascertain. The relationship is then a result not only of selective exposure but also of selective "creation." In a study of attitudes toward Russia, M. Brewster Smith (1947) asked his respondents whether Russia had declared war on Japan before or after the atomic bomb was dropped. He reported that in all likelihood, those who answered the question incorrectly had no belief on the matter prior to the asking of the question, and created on the spur of the moment a belief consistent with the direction of their attitudes. Indeed, in looking over the high correlations found in the literature on the relationship between information and attitudes, one is tempted to guess that some reinterpretation of them is in order. If items were slanted so that the correct answers were also the more liberal alternatives, is it not likely that persons of liberal, tolerant attitudes found guessing easier?

Hammond (1948) made perhaps the first deliberate effort to measure attitudes through biased guesses on an information test, measuring attitudes toward labor-management and Russia [Chapter 23 in this book]. His work is worthy of some detailed comment here. We have mentioned that not only guessing behavior but also differential patterns of information may be diagnostic of attitudes. Hammond eliminated the latter by the error-choice technique, in which the respondent was forced to choose between two alternative answers, each of which was, by intent, equally wrong, but in opposite directions from the correct answer. Such items were: "average weekly wage of the war worker in 1945 was (1) $37, (2) $57" and "financial reports show that out of every dollar (1) 16¢, (2) 3¢ is profit." Scoring these information guesses as attitude items gave total scores on 20 such items that differentiated a labor union group from two business clubs with almost no overlap. In spite of the small number of cases (18 union and 42 business) the critical ratios were 11.3 on the labor-management and 12.5 on the Russia questionnaire. Reliabilities on the two scales were roughly estimated at .78 and .87 respectively.

A test very similar to Hammond's was used by Weschler (1950a, 1950b) under the guise of a "Labor Relations Information Inventory." He administered the test to 186 students with known biases. Weschler used some items which permitted correct answers and others which forced the respondent to make an error. He used only the error-choice items in the scoring of the test, determining the weighting of the items by examining how the criterion groups answered them. When weighted in this way, there were 11 significant error-choice items which clearly differentiated the two groups with professed pro- and anti-labor attitudes. Another attempt at using the error-choice technique has been reported by Kubany (1953) who used social work students versus medical students as criterion groups in measuring attitudes toward socialized medicine. (His report on the degree of success in such differentiation is, however, vitiated by the opportunity for capitalizing on chance in the heavy selection of items and the absence of cross-validation samples.)

What we have here is an objective test situation (which could be made more so by using more alternatives and including a correct one) in which people's errors are not random, but systematic. The presence of biased performance clearly necessitates the influence

of some underlying process, which we choose to call attitude. The claim for face validity on such a test might even be judged stronger than the claim that can be made for either the direct or unstructured test. Systematically biased performance in dealing with environmental actualities is an essential practical meaning of attitude.

Cattell et al. (1949, 1950) attempted a large-scale exploration into the "objective" measurement of attitudes using a rationale very similar to the one presented here for non-voluntary attitude tests. Two of the methods may be classified with information test approaches. A sample item from his "False Belief (Delusion)" measure reads: "During the war church attendance increased greatly and since V-J day it has: declined slightly; tended to increase still more; stayed at its high peak; returned to its pre-war level; fallen to its lowest since 1920." Applied to a religious attitude, ten such items gave a Spearman-Brown reliability of .53 and correlated .33 with a paired-comparisons preference test and .10 with records kept of time and money expenditures. Cattell's interest in objective disguised testing continues, as evidenced by his new volume (Hundleby, Pawlik and Cattell, 1965).

In a study of the effects of pro- and anti-Kuomintang propaganda, Parrish (1948, Parrish and Campbell, 1953) used an information test, a public opinion estimate test, and a direct Likert scale. The following item appeared in the information test:

"Chiang Kai-shek and the Kuomintang gained control of China in 1927 by what means: (a) popular election, (b) representative election, (c) replacement of a deceased leader, (d) political party split, (e) armed revolution." The alternatives were weighted in terms of pro-Kuomintang attitudes as: $a = 5, b = 4, c = 3, d = 2, e = 1$. Indicative of the presumptions involved in such tests, and of the differences between 1948 and 1968 in student attitude climates, is the assumption that "armed revolution" was the most unfavorable alternative. The direct test of attitudes demonstrated higher reliability than the other two—it yielded a Kuder-Richardson coefficient of .87 as compared with .57 for the information test and .50 for the public opinion test. Intercorrelations among the three tests averaged .47, .51 and .53, indicating that the two indirect tests shared as much with the direct test as with each other. The information test was superior in the degree to which it reflected propaganda differences, as evidenced by a point-biserial correlation between test scores and the type of propaganda (pro- versus anti-). Corrected for attenuation, this value was .71 for the information test compared with .54 and .59 for the other two. Since, however, the messages were communicated by way of particular information, this is not purely a validity feature.

Some practical applications of the information test format have been reported by Gatty and Hamje (1961) and Westfall, Boyd and Campbell (1957). The latter investigated opinions about hot cereal by asking for estimates of the average cost of a bowl of hot cereal and several cold cereals, or for the estimates of the vitamin, protein, and caloric contents of hot and cold cereals. The heavy users of oatmeal believed it cheaper and more nutritious.

A variety of other attitudes have been tested by means of informational estimates. In an extensive study of superior-subordinate relationships within bomber crews, Campbell and Damarin (1961) employed a Test of Leadership Knowledge along with nine other measures, both direct and projective. The respondents were told that the Leadership Knowledge questions had been taken from ". . . the findings of scientific research on problems of leadership," and they were motivated to perform well by the claim that "Some persons will do much better than others on this test, because of their experience in leadership or because of their better understanding of leadership problems . . ."

The questions dealt with leadership in several situations, one of which was a railroad work gang. To bolster the facade, an elaborate set of instructions preceded the questions:

The following questions are based on a study of some of the differences between railroad section gangs which have records of high and low production. . . . The questions that follow came from the study of 40 of these section gangs. The gangs were divided carefully into matched groups so that differences in the amount of track each gang laid would not be due to differences in the difficulty of their work. You will be asked to make judgments about factors which did make the difference between the high and the low production sections.

1. Foremen of high production sections:
   A. Have been with the railroad for a longer time than foremen of low production sections.
   B. Have been with the railroad a shorter time than foremen of low production sections.
   C. Have been with the railroad about the same length of time as foremen of low production sections.
2. The foremen who spend more time supervising their men than in working alongside the men are:
   A. The high production supervisors.
   B. The low production supervisors.
   C. The two groups are equal on this.

Of all the intercorrelations, only one triad of tests demonstrated any interrelationships or triangulation. The coefficients obtained between these were as follows:

	Uncorrected	Corrected for attenuation
Information test × Direct test	.47	.72
Sentence completion × Direct test	.32	.46
Information test × Sentence completion	.27	.42

The information test produced a respectable reliability of .67 and thus when the correlations were corrected for attenuation, the pattern remained the same. Correlations between the information test and criterial measures were all low and insignificant—e.g., —.01 with total demerits, —.08 with instructors' ratings of military aptitude, and —.10 with a composite reputational score obtained from nominations to questions such as "Who are the men who try harder to be liked by their instructors and superior officers than they do to be liked by their classmates?" In contrast to this, two direct attitude scales correlated significantly with the reputational criteria. Correlations of the Leadership Knowledge test with the F-scale (ranging from .06 to .48) and with a direct attitude test (from .16 to .47) are the only exceptions to the generally negative validation picture. In a non-military setting Burwen and Campbell (1957a) reported that the Leadership Knowledge test failed to correlate with two direct measures. For the college groups tested, however, there was little relationship between any of the measures used, which led the authors to conclude that among those college students no general attitude exists relevant to the superior-subordinate dimension.

In view of the social desirability of appearing unprejudiced, an "objective" test of information about minority groups would appear particularly appropriate in place of direct questioning. An early form of such a test is reported in Rankin (1951) and Rankin and Campbell (1959) and was used in the unpublished Master's thesis of Kremen (1949). These appeared to be bona fide information tests, but in fact the authors had not done the research to determine the right answer. With the assistance of Miss Florence Simon these beginnings were revised and expanded into a 50-item test with a specific right answer and a bibliographical source for each item. This was done both in order to backstop the facade and to make available actual data on the state of the respondents' information. Considerable unpublished research has been done with this test. Campbell, in 1951, collected data from 500 respondents at four universities, Negro and white, Northern and Southern.[2]

In examining the "definition of the situation" or the stereotype of the person hostile to Negroes, and the views held by those who are favorably disposed, it was felt that these eight paradigms, among others, are to be found:

1. Negroes are (are not) inferior, different, in a. intelligence, b. culture, c. physical traits, d. morality
2. Negroes do (do not) get a fair chance in America. a. restriction of social freedom, b. income differential, c. education, d. housing
3. Majority persons like myself are (are not) hostile toward Negroes.
4. Removal of segregation does not (does) improve the situation.
5. Negroes are (are not) threatening, dangerous, powerful.
6. Prejudice is (is not) universal and has (has not) always been with us.
7. Negroes do (do not) prefer segregation.
8. Miscegenation is (is not) bad.

All of these are essentially factual, or are "beliefs" rather than "valuations" in Myrdal's (1944) terms. In designing test items we were essentially spelling out these paradigms in more detailed form. Some items of fact may imply more than one paradigm. Where these are conflicting in implication, the item probably lacks diagnostic value. For example, an item on tuberculosis rates among Negroes is appropriate to both 1c and 2d, and hence would not be expected to be attitude diagnostic. Such was the case with some items.

The items were presented in both multiple-choice and free-response forms. The multiple-choice form of the test has a number of obvious advantages over the free-response form. Foremost among these is the ease of answering on the part of the test taker and

---

[2] Professor Warner Wilson of the University of Alabama is attempting to collect 1968-1969 testings of the same schools with a modified version of the test and it is hoped as a part of this larger comparison the data will eventually be published.

the ease of scoring on the part of the research person. The disadvantages are in part peculiar to the purposes and content area of this particular study. First there is difficulty in selection of alternatives. If improperly selected, a large proportion of the respondents will concentrate their choices on some single alternative while some will receive no use. A correlated disadvantage of the fixed alternatives is that they provide a perspective for the person taking the test or give him some minimal information if, in fact, they do center around the correct answer and restrict themselves to popularly used items. The perspective or frame of reference thus provided could, in a test like this, have a propagandizing or educative effect upon some of the persons taking the test. Inasmuch as the popular range of expectation on many of the items will tend to be unfavorable to the Negro, however, a test based upon fixed alternatives might have an undesirable effect upon the attitudes of the test taker. It is for these reasons that items requiring answers in percentage terms were given in free-response form.

Examples of some of the free-response and multiple-choice items are as follows:

In 1948 what percentage of all persons arrested for drug violations were colored?

Intelligence tests given to the soldiers during World War I indicated that the Negroes of Ohio as compared to the whites of Kentucky tested on an average: 1) much lower 2) slightly lower 3) the same 4) slightly higher 5) much higher

Since the correct answers were included among the alternatives and were obtainable in the percentage estimates, two methods of weighting the answers were possible. A uniform weighting approach included the correct answers and gave them a weighting of zero, and the wrong answers on either side were given plus and minus weights in accordance with their distance and direction from the right answer. In the second item above, for instance, number four was the cor-

rect answer. Numbers one, two and three would thus be weighted minus 3, minus 2 and minus 1, and answer number five would be weighted plus 1. For all practical purposes the correctness of the answer has been disregarded and it has been used just as the other alternatives. This would be a small matter if it were certain that everyone was guessing and that no one came into the test-taking situation sufficiently well-informed to be able to pick out the correct answer on the basis of neutral objective information. It could also be justified, particularly for those items in which the correct answer is at one or another extreme, by the argument noted above that a person's attitudes may be diagnosed by the kinds of correct facts which he accumulates.

The alternative approach to scoring has been called the preponderance score. In this computation the items which a person scores correctly are disregarded for attitude diagnosis. Instead, the percentage of his error points in a pro-Negro or anti-Negro direction is computed. If we were to meet a test taker who was very well informed, we would have relatively few items on which to diagnose his attitudes. Nonetheless, we would use the few items on which he had made errors and study the preponderant direction of errors in this small sample. In the research done by Campbell these two scoring methods were compared by correlating the indirect test scores with a direct test. The correlations showed no consistent superiority of either method. The trend, however, was most strongly in favor of the uniform weighting approach. Of 28 comparisons available, the uniform approach was superior in 23. Thus, while the logical purist may very well continue to favor the preponderance method, and while it would be definitely preferable for studies based upon populations that had special training in this area, the statistical analysis would seem to favor the employment of the uniform method of scoring. The two methods of scoring correlated.

Several sets of data comparing the indirect

information test with a direct test of racial attitudes seem to indicate that the direct test has higher validity as well as reliability. Kremen (1949) used an early version of the information test along with a direct test in an attempt to evaluate the effect of student role-playing of a discrimination episode upon attitudes toward the Negro, using a multiple-choice information-type indirect test and a direct test. While neither test reflected the role-playing in mean scores, her findings have importance for attitude measurement, inasmuch as role-playing lowered the relationship between the direct and indirect test. The results from ten sociology classes (five pairs in which the instructor and subject were the same) are presented below:

Correlation between
Direct and Indirect
Tests
Role-playing Classes: .39 .36 .20 .53 .38
Paired Control Classes: .54 .70 .35 .58 .60

For all classes combined, the direct test had a reliability of .89, the indirect test .42 (Kuder-Richardson, Formula 14). The explanation of this phenomenon is not obvious from her data insofar as analyzed. She does not report reliability values separately for the ten classes.

In yet another attempt to use the information test to measure attitudes toward Negroes, Rankin (1951; Rankin and Campbell, 1959) also obtained GSR measures and direct test scores from 26 white male respondents. The GSR measures were obtained by telling the persons that their reactions to emotional words would be measured by the apparatus. During this supposed word-reaction test, the left hand GSR apparatus (actually a dummy) was adjusted four times, twice by a Negro experimenter and twice by a white. Each person's GSR score was computed by subtracting the sum of his responses to the white from the sum of his responses to the Negro. The direct attitude questionnaire and information test were both answered anonymously. Intercorrelations among the tests were as follows:

GSR × Direct   .40
GSR × Indirect   .20
Direct × Indirect   .70

Although the number of observations was too small to demonstrate significant differences, these values provide further evidence of the superiority of the direct test.

In an attempt to understand these results, one could surmise that the direct and indirect tests are measuring different aspects of an attitude—direct tests measured the valuations and indirect the cognitive or belief structure. A GSR would seem intuitively to have very little in common with a test of beliefs and stereotypes, but may share more with an instrument which taps evaluative tendencies.

Some of Campbell's (1951) unpublished data yielded rather high reliability coefficients for the information test (ranging from .66 to .79). Correlations of the information test with a direct scale ranged from .45 to .57 and with the F-scale ranged from .37 to .45. Several other "validity" coefficients, using a priori criterion groups, showed the direct test to be superior. Assuming that Negroes would be more pro-Negro than whites, the two tests were correlated with ethnicity for the following subject groups (biserial correlations).

	Direct test	Indirect test
Southern U. whites vs.		
Black U. Negroes	.54	.22
Normal U. whites vs.		
Normal U. Negroes	.61	.46
Downtown U. whites vs.		
Downtown U. Negroes	.18	.12

Assuming that Southern whites should be more anti-Negro than Northern whites, the following biserial correlations were obtained:

	Direct test	Indirect test
Northern U. whites vs.		
Southern U. whites	.34	.16

And assuming that white liberal-radical students should be more pro-Negro than a group of traditional non-intellectual whites, the following values were obtained:

	Direct test	Indirect test
Normal U. whites vs. Downtown U. whites	.50	.73

Only in the last comparison did the indirect test fare better, due to the surprising anti-Negro attitudes of the Normal U. whites and the surprising pro-Negro attitudes of Downtown U. whites on this test. The Downtown U. whites were even more pro-Negro than the Normal U. Negroes on the information test.

The discrepancy in information test scores between students at these two universities might be explained in terms of the locations as well as the composition of the student bodies of the two schools. Both were situated in a large northern metropolis, but Normal U. was a teacher training college located about one mile from the Negro ghetto. The whites attending came largely from uneducated families in another part of the city and traveled through the ghetto each day while commuting. Their perceptions of the Negro attributes and environment probably were heavily influenced by their daily commuting experiences. The white students attending Downtown U., on the other hand, did not travel through the ghetto each day and had the majority of their contacts with Negroes limited to the Negro students attending their college.

Such daily contacts and commuting experiences are perhaps only a small part of a longer history and socialization process which have produced the beliefs and stereotypes revealed by the information test. The Normal U. whites came from lower-middle class homes which probably taught a strong version of the doctrine of individualism and self-reliance. The parents of these students have made it far enough to send a child to college and they have only themselves to thank for it. Anyone who has not "made it" has, by the same token, only himself to blame. Attributing success and failure to individual effort or laziness not only provides a simple explanation and rationalization for the rela-

tive social positions of Negroes and whites but also provides a large increment of self-esteem for the Normal U. white who is experiencing mobility. The same holds true for the Normal U. Negro, who can attribute his college enrollment to his own hard work and perseverance, and must attribute the failure of fellow ghetto residents to weaknesses in their character and intelligence. The information scores of the Normal U. Negroes showed that they accepted and internalized those derogatory beliefs and stereotypes which their white classmates held. Such beliefs would be functional not only in providing explanations for the success and failure of various groups or persons but also for socializing the Normal U. Negro into his new career pattern—a teacher in the white middle class school system. The Downtown U. students, on the other hand, have probably developed much more complex notions of the factors contributing to social status and are less likely to seek causes and rationalizations in terms of ethnic weaknesses. The whites and Negroes of Downtown U. both scored more pro-Negro than any of the other groups, white or Negro, on the information test.

With criterion groups such as these the information test can provide valuable insights into the belief structures and cognitive maps of individual and groups. Item analyses may reveal the particular areas of belief which contribute to the negative valuations of a social object and provide an understanding of the past history which may have led to those views. Although it fails to match the "validity" values of a direct test, the information test seems to be providing valid information of a different type, which may contribute to what has been called the "sociology of knowledge of the man-on-the-street" (Campbell, 1953a).

Green (1954) used the same test with Northern Negro, Southern white and Southern Negro college students as criterion groups. Split-half reliability coefficients ranged from .33 for the Southern whites to .82 for the Southern Negro samples. Correlations between the indirect test and a direct questionnaire reached .64. In accord with the validity data reported by Campbell (1951), the information test again appeared to be less sensitive than the direct. The writers computed the following point-biserial correlation coefficients from Green's data:

On the assumption that Negroes are more pro-Negro than whites—

	Direct	Indirect
Northern Negro versus Southern white sample	.86	.78

Where lie the faults and weaknesses of information tests as attitude measures? Are facts and attitudes indeed as unrelated as rational man would like to believe? The consistently lower reliabilities and validities of the information test when compared with direct tests might be taken as evidence of man's ability to maintain unbiased views of "reality" in spite of his personal prejudices and values. Or, they may reflect instead some confounding of the test scores with other irrelevancies and errors. One possible source of error lies in the seemingly non-monotonic functions to which some items might give rise. The same answer to a given question might mean two different things to two different respondents. Underestimating the number of Negro students in American colleges, for instance, might mean that "black people don't have the ability to become doctors" or that "white society continually refuses to provide equal opportunity." By the same token, overestimating the proportion of Negro students receiving national awards could be the response of a poor white who feels threatened and feels that more than enough has been done in the way of programs for minority group progress, or could be the response of a middle class "liberal" and sponsor of civil rights legislation who believes that the programs must have accomplished something. Even if the full content of a respondent's thought could be ascertained, it is not clear that one view is pro-Negro and the other anti-Negro, one favorable and the other unfavorable. The view that "white society continually refuses to provide equal opportunity," for instance, could reflect condescension as well as a pro-Negro or favorable attitude. Thus, not only are the items likely to be non-monotonic, but the dimensions along which the responses fall may be multiple.

Tests of ability to do critical thinking— The syllogism approach was anticipated by Goodwin Watson's *Measurement of Fair Mindedness* published in 1925. By fair-mindedness, Watson seems to have meant something roughly equivalent to tolerance, critical thinking, or open-mindedness. His tests were designed to measure this trait, but in the process Watson recognized that the "errors" or lapses from fair-mindedness contained clues as to the biases or attitudes of the respondents, and a secondary "analytic" scoring was made in those terms. The *Inference Test* provided statements of fact followed by several conclusions that might be drawn, only one of which was logically justified, the others offering opportunities for the intrusion of personal biases in various directions. This test has been expanded in the Watson-Glazer Tests of Critical Thinking (Glazer, 1941) which could be scored for various prejudices although they have not been so used as far as the authors are aware. Gilbert (1941) also made use of the same technique in a study in which high school children were given hypothetical racial problems for which they could choose strictly logical conclusions or conclusions showing bias. Work in progress by Cook (1968) represents an extension of this method. The task is presented as a test of ability to make correct interpretations of scientific facts. Preliminary results show that prejudiced and unprejudiced persons make different systematic errors in their choice of answers.

Morgan (1943, 1945; with Morton, 1944) developed an objective test which presented the same syllogisms in two forms—impersonal or abstract (e.g.,"No *A*'s are *B*'s. Some *C*'s are *B*'s. From these statements it is logical to conclude: No *C*'s are *A*'s . . .") and with content ("A trustworthy man does not engage in deceitful acts. The bombing of Pearl

Harbor by the Japanese was a deceitful act. From these statements it is logical to conclude: No Japanese are trustworthy....") By studying the shift in the popular response from the nonsense to the meaningful form, Morgan attempted to diagnose group attitudes.

Morton (1942), a student of Morgan, also compared the distortion of reasoning on abstract and concrete emotional materials. He varied not only the content of the syllogisms but also their form, paying particular attention to atmosphere effects. A concrete item with a particular-negative atmosphere is as follows:

Some large empires do not exploit the people under their control; since Japan is not a large empire:
1. Japan will exploit the people under her control
2. Japan may exploit the people under her control
3. Japan will not exploit the people under her control
4. Japan may not exploit the people under her control
5. None of the given conclusions seems to follow logically.

This is an invalid syllogism, and its particular-negative atmosphere would lead a person to accept conclusion number 4. Most persons tended to answer, however, with number 1 or 2, and only one person said Japan would not exploit persons under her control. Morton concluded that persons reason differently when confronted with syllogisms phrased in abstract and concrete terms, and the direction of change is generally in accord with the popular opinion publicized by the press and radio. Lansdell (1946) utilized the same technique for studying covert attitudes toward marriage, attempting to apply it for the diagnosis of the attitudes of a single individual.

Several investigators have devised syllogisms tests in which no choice of conclusions is offered but rather the persons are required to judge the validity of the complete syllogism as stated (e.g. Feather, 1964; Janis and Frick, 1943; Thistlethwaite, 1950; Thouless,

1959). Thistlethwaite (1950) investigated a variety of attitudes in a test which contained syllogisms dealing with Negroes, Jews, women, and various nationalistic themes [Chapter 24 in this book]. Embedding the critical items in a nest of neutral items probably facilitated the guise as a test of reasoning ability. His results supported the hypothesis that attitudes distort logical performance since he found that criterion groups of students from the North and South differed significantly in their performance. A weakness in his method, however, lay in the fact that all items were designed so that prejudiced persons would make more errors than the non-prejudiced. It would seem advisable to design items such that persons with pro and con attitudes would both make errors, though in opposite directions or on different items.

This rule was followed by Thouless (1959). He used items such as the following: "Slave labor was inefficient because of the lack of incentive to individual effort. Competitive civilizations have prospered because they have provided incentive to individual effort but under socialism such incentives would disappear. We see, therefore, that *socialism is a form of slavery*." His subjects were instructed first to read only the underlined conclusion, ignoring the rest, and indicate whether they thought the conclusion alone was true or false. After this they read the entire argument for each and decided whether it was "sound" or "unsound," logical or not. Using both sound and unsound syllogisms for both pro- and anti-socialism statements, Thouless computed each person's score by obtaining the difference between the number of times he made an error in the direction of his prejudice and the number of times he erred in the opposite direction. With a sample of adult students, ranging in age from 23 to 58, he found 40 per cent erroneous judgments, and of these 78 per cent were in the predicted direction, yielding a chi square of 24 which was significant beyond the .000001 level. With a sample of university students, however, there were only 10 per cent erroneous judgments and the direction of those errors did not conform to the subjects' attitudinal biases. The failure of the syllogisms test to measure attitudes with this sample could perhaps be attributed to the higher education and intelligence of the university students, making them less susceptible to distortions in reasoning; or, as suggested by Thouless, they may have approached the test with greater suspicion and thus made conscious efforts to hide their views. These problems encountered by syllogisms tests will be discussed in greater detail below.

Feather (1964) also employed both valid and invalid pro- and anti-religion syllogisms and predicted that pro-religion persons would err more often in the direction of accepting invalid pro-religion statements and rejecting valid anti-religion statements, and that anti-religion respondents would err likewise on the two other types of items. Examples of his syllogisms are as follows:

Pro-religious valid: People who are without religion are spiritually devoid and need the Christian teachings to show them the true way of life. Atheists and agnostics are people without religion and devoid of spiritual life. Therefore, atheists and agnostics need Christian teachings to show them the true way of life.
Pro-religious invalid: A charitable and tolerant attitude towards mankind helps to bring people together in love and harmony. Christianity always helps to bring people together in love and harmony. Therefore, a consequence of Christianity is a charitable and tolerant attitude towards mankind.

His hypothesis was confirmed by his pro-religion respondents, who made significantly more pro- than anti-religion errors (p < .001). But for the anti-religion subjects there was no significant difference in the direction of their errors. Furthermore, whereas persons with strong pro-religion attitudes made more pro-religion errors than did persons with weak attitudes, the opposite was found for anti-religion respondents—the stronger their attitudes, the fewer their errors. These contradictions can be resolved by

taking into account the critical abilities scores of both sets of subjects, as measured by their performance on neutral syllogisms. The anti-religion subjects had significantly higher critical ability scores than the pro-religion respondents, and the stronger their opinions against religion, the higher their critical abilities.

These findings suggest that the usefulness of the syllogisms test as an indirect attitude test may be limited by such factors as education, training in logic, and general critical abilities. At one extreme, it is likely that an uneducated person might not even grasp the distinction between the logical soundness of an argument and its empirical validity. For him, the instructions to judge the soundness of an argument may be no different from asking him whether he agrees or disagrees with the conclusion. Under such conditions the test loses all disguise. If, on the other hand, the subjects possess a high degree of education and training, and can easily distinguish between the logical and descriptive truth of an argument, the test may again fail not because it lacks disguise but because it does not tap attitudes at all. In addition to the evidence from Thouless and Feather, Shelley and Davis (1957) report that a class of logic students made fewer errors in judging the validity of syllogisms than did a control class.

If this analysis is correct it suggests an inverted U-shaped function relating the usefulness of the syllogisms test as an indirect attitude measure to the level of education of the respondents. For persons with very little training, the test measures attitudes, but it is hardly disguised; for persons with a great deal of education and training in logic the test is neither a direct nor an indirect measure of attitudes because they make almost no errors. Only for the middle range of respondents, who know enough about the distinction between logical and descriptive truth to follow the instructions but who still make errors, is the test both an attitude measure and a disguised one at that.

Tests employing bias in learning and

memory—The use of learning and recall errors in the diagnosis of individual attitudes epitomizes the disguised, structured, and non-voluntary approach. Pioneers in the use of this technique are Horowitz and Horowitz (1938). In their study of the development of social attitudes among the children of a Southern community they invented a number of techniques. While designed to portray group differences, many of them should be appropriate to individual testing. Their Aussage Test involved exposing a complicated picture for two or three seconds, following which they tested for recall through a series of standardized deliberately leading questions. For example, the question "who is cleaning up the grounds" to Picture 10 brought answers referring to a non-existent Negro in some 70 per cent of the cases. To Picture 4 the misleading question "what is the colored man in the corner doing" brought a steadily increasing proportion (in reports from higher age groups) of menial activities for the non-existent character.

Their Perception-Span Test involved a series of posters each having pictures of 10 items mounted upon it. These were exposed for ten seconds and the children asked to "tell all the pictures you can remember." While there were difficulties with perseveration and blocking, some age group differences were noted, with the younger children failing to note Negroes and the older ones showing a selective awareness for them. A Recall Test asking for the reproduction of ten words used earlier in a word association test seemed also to indicate that in the younger years the word "Negro" was less well remembered than would be expected. The Pictorial Recognition Test, involving the recognition of faces previously viewed, finds the faces of whites more frequently recognized than the faces of Negroes.

Seeleman (1940–1941) confirmed this finding with respect to individual differences within the group. Presenting sets of Negro and white photographs, she tested for later recognition by asking that the previously exposed pictures be picked from a larger group.

The discrepancy between memory for white and Negro faces was checked against attitudes on a direct test. Using people in the extreme quartiles on the direct test only, the test and memory-bias scores correlated .64 and .71 with different populations. A similar test conducted by Rokeach (1952) obtained somewhat different results. He found that although prejudiced persons distort the recall of Negro names, they also distort the recall of white names more than unprejudiced persons do.

In a preliminary investigation Murray Jarvik (Frenkel-Brunswik *et al.*, 1946–1947) attempted to utilize memory distortion as an indicator of attitudes. Sixth, seventh and eighth grade students were read five-minute stories and then were asked to write down all they could remember of the story. The stories had simple dramatic plots but were full of confusing detail and lacunae with regard to specific names, characteristics, and ethnic identities. Opportunity was given for memory distortion in the direction of common stereotypes. The results were essentially negative. However, motivation and literacy were both low in this sample of respondents. Using a similar method with a sample of college students, Alper and Korchin (1952) tested for recall of a letter about coeducation which was generally unflattering to women. Their male subjects recalled significantly more than the females did, and the females made more distortions in recall.

Cattell *et al.* (1949, 1950) utilized three techniques involving memory and learning biases. His test of "Immediate Memory" was based upon selective recall for attitude-relevant statements from sets of 12 presented at one-second intervals. In the total there were over 500 statements. Spearman-Brown reliability figures for eleven attitudes ranged from .13 to .86, averaging .50. Correlations with other measures were essentially zero. In the scoring both "facilitating" and "frustrating" statements relative to the attitude were pooled. Cattell recommended that in future research these be separated. Taft (1954) did note the differential recall of favorable items from a passage about "One of the greatest Negro baseball pitchers in America . . ." He read the story aloud to two groups of Negro and white boys and tested for immediate and delayed recall. On delayed recall, three days after the story, the Negroes recalled favorable items best and the whites recalled unfavorable items best.

Cattell's "Distraction" method involved the exposure for ten seconds of statements related to attitudes. Around the statement were scattered 12 or 13 nonsense syllables. Subjects were held responsible for recalling the statement and nonsense syllables. The original hypothesis was that the stronger the attitude the poorer the nonsense syllable learning because of distraction. Actually, the opposite effect was found. With a Spearman-Brown reliability of .64 for one attitude (being smartly dressed), the correlation with the paired comparison preference measure was —.29, with time expenditure —.10, with money expenditure —.08, and with an information test —.35. Contrary to these findings, however, Burtt (1942) found that greater distractability was associated with stronger interest.

Another demonstration of the effect of attitude strength on memory has been reported by Doob (1953). On the first day of testing his subjects were given a questionnaire in which five paragraphs dealt with controversial subjects—advertising, religion, the Tennessee Valley Authority, the function of a liberal arts education, and war between the United States and Russia. Their task was merely to read the items and indicate their agreement or disagreement with the paragraph on a five-point scale. Two days later the memory test was administered by reminding the respondents that "The day before yesterday you read through some statements on various topics. In the space below, please LIST the topics you remember at this time." In addition, they were told "for each topic you have listed above, please recall as many of the arguments and ideas as you can which were advanced in the original state-

ments." The results suggest that the quantity and quality of recall are determined by different factors. Quantity of recall was associated with attitude intensity: items with which persons fully agreed were recalled more than items with which they merely agreed, and a similar pattern appeared for disagreement. Quality of recall, on the other hand, was associated with congruence of attitudes and items: paragraphs with which the respondents agreed were recalled more accurately.

In addition to attitude intensity, the incentive provided for memory is another factor which must be considered in interpreting the results of tests of memory. Jones and Aneshansel (1956) instructed their pro-segregation subjects that they would be asked to provide counter-arguments to pro-segregation statements later in the experiment. Under these conditions pro-segregation subjects learned the *anti*-segregation items better than anti-segregation subjects did. These results warn against applying a uniform rule of interpretation to such indirect attitude tests.

A third variable, the plausibility of the statements, also has complex effects upon learning and recall. Jones and Kohler (1958) report that persons learn plausible statements supporting their beliefs and implausible statements opposing their beliefs better than they learn implausible-favoring or plausible-opposing items. Attempts to use this as an indirect test of attitudes should perhaps await further confirmation, however.

It often happens that disconfirmation of a widely accepted hypothesis is regarded as failure rather than success. Witness the title used by Waly and Cook (1966), "Attitude as a determinant of learning and memory: A failure to confirm." Since that "failure," there have been others (Greenwald and Sakumura, 1967; Brigham and Cook, 1969). These more recent experiments, which have both replicated the conditions used by Jones and Kohler (1958) and elaborated the design and number of conditions, report no relationship between attitude, plausibility, and memory. Greenwald and Sakumura (1967) suggest that another variable—information novelty—might be more facilitative than is covaluant information. An ironical extension of this suggestion, noted by Brigham and Cook (1969), predicts the opposite of the Jones-Kohler work—namely, that plausible-contravaluant or implausible-covaluant information may be more novel and thus more easily remembered. No explicit tests of this new hypothesis have been made, but the contradictory and sometimes confusing outcomes of experiments in this area present a strong case for further testing.

Tests employing bias in perception—Distortion in accordance with beliefs and attitudes has been demonstrated not only in memory but also in immediate visual perception. Binocular rivalry tests are an innovation in attitude testing which have found successful application in some settings. Bagby (1957) used a series of ten stereogram slide pairs of similar scenes in Mexico and the United States. With both Mexican and American respondents he found that the person's own cultural content predominated in reports of what was seen. Pettigrew, Allport, and Barnett (1958) turned this into an index of racial attitudes. In a test which could be subtitled, "nothing's either black or white but thinking makes it so," they presented pictures of four racial groups to respondents in South Africa. The four groups were African, Colored, Indian and European. Because of the greater apprehensiveness of the Afrikaaner population, it was predicted that they would show either excessive vigilance or defense and report "white" or "black" more often than "colored" or "Indian." Their results confirmed this prediction—Afrikaaners reported seeing significantly more European and African faces whereas the English, Colored, Indian and African respondents gave more "fusion" reports such as "Indian" and "Colored." This finding was "in line with the bifurcation hypothesis, i.e., highly involved subjects generally require a minimum number

of categories and ignore small differences between stimuli." (p. 276)

Reynolds and Toch (1965) attempted to use similar binocular rivalry techniques by presenting biracial stereograms to an American sample. They expected unprejudiced persons to report more black-white fusions and prejudiced persons to experience more rivalry. In their first study they found no significant differences in the number of fusion and rivalry reports by high and low prejudice subjects. In a second study, using a liberal criterion of fusion, the results reached significance. Because of the strong constancy effects the authors felt the stereogram method was weak and inappropriate for demonstrating the effects of prejudice. It may be that tests of binocular fusion are particularly suited to a setting where "fusion" reports such as "Indian" or "Colored" are part of the vocabulary, as in South Africa. Doob (1968) reports that attempts to use binocular rivalry techniques in Jamaica were singularly unsuccessful, though the failure appeared to be due to faulty equipment.

Several other binocular rivalry and misperception tests have also produced negative results. Cook (1968) developed several types of materials suitable for binocular viewing. One test presented pairs of faces—half the pairs had Negro faces and half had white faces—with words written across the foreheads. The words differed in only one letter, such as "bad" and "bag." Cook predicted that prejudiced persons would be more likely to report seeing the negative words when presented against a background of Negro faces and the positive or neutral words against white faces. Instead he found no differences between anti-Negro and equalitarian groups of subjects. Both saw significantly more positive words against the background of Negro faces than against white photos. Another test used pairs of scenes, half involving Negroes and half whites. The activity in one slide of each pair was derogatory (e.g., pointing a gun) and in the other was neutral (e.g., pointing a finger). Cook reasoned that anti-Negro subjects might associate threat or danger with Negroes more than with whites, or might be more likely to perceive uncontrolled or irresponsible behavior associated with Negroes. Contrary to prediction, there was no difference between the two subject groups on their perception of the Negro slides. There was some indication, however, that equalitarian persons saw more activities with a positive connotation regardless of the race of the stimulus person, which is consistent with other reports that certain personality types tend to perceive positive or negative aspects of interpersonal relations.

Failure to find perceptual correlates of attitudes with a different method was also reported by Cattell *et al.*, much earlier (1949, 1950). They employed a misperception test which required subjects to note the misspellings of tachistoscopically presented attitude statements. The overlooking of mispellings was regarded as a sign of strong attitude, but it correlated negatively with other attitude indices.

A unique demonstration of errors in the perception of social objects is that of Kuethe (1962). He presented a pair of male and female figures placed thirty inches apart. After five seconds he removed the figures and instructed the respondents to replace them in the same locations. The next respondent viewed the figures as they had been placed by the previous person, and the procedure was repeated. The serial reproduction by thirty respondents showed a significant tendency for the male and female figures to be placed closer and closer, whereas a pair of rectangles was maintained at the original separation of thirty inches, without any systematic distortion. In the elaboration of this technique, Kuethe (1962) concluded that it was the specific content of the figures which determined both the direction and magnitude of the distortion. Two men facing away from each other were replaced with greater distance between them while two figures facing each other were replaced closer together. The distortion apparently occurs at the time of re-

construction rather than during the original perception or during retention, for when subjects viewed two rectangles and were then instructed to place male and female figures in the places where the rectangles had been, they showed the systematic errors associated with the man-woman schemata.

In contrast to the traditional social distance tests, this method approximates what could be called a "Social Distances of Third Persons" test. Like Getzels' third-person sentence completion stems, this task requires the respondent to guess or reconstruct the distance between two others, without being aware of his own contribution or intervention in the process. This method could be expanded to test other social schemata, by varying the racial, religious or other characteristics of the figures.

Estimation of group opinion and social norms—As Travers (1941) and Wallen (1943) and others have demonstrated, there is a persistent correlation between a person's own attitude and his estimate of group opinion. While a few persons may perceive themselves as unrepresentative of the population and chronically underestimate the popularity of their own views, as in the sample of college professors studied by Lana (1964), the prevailing tendency is to overestimate the size of the group agreeing with oneself.

The technique is by no means entirely new. In 1929 Sweet, using a test designed by Goodwin Watson, found boys' estimates of group opinions valuable in diagnosing adjustment problems. Katz (1947), Murray and Morgan (1945), and Newcomb (1943) all used percentage estimates of group opinion, although some of their data are not reported in terms of the responses of individuals. It might be pointed out that the correlation involved in these studies is not necessarily to be interpreted as projection. In a group of any size, the respondent has an uneven acquaintanceship, and probably associates more with those having tastes like his own. Basing his estimates of group opinion upon his own experience in the group, his error may be in part a sampling bias as well as biased perception. Furthermore, the causal relation may be from belief about group opinion to formation of own attitude, as seen in bandwagon effects (see Lipset, Lazarsfeld, Barton and Linz, 1954).

Parrish (1948, and Parrish and Campbell, 1953) used a public opinion estimate test with items dealing with United States opinion on China, the opinion of Americans with experience in China, and the opinions of the Chinese. Only the first type are directly comparable to the Travers and Wallen situation, and these did not fare very well in item analysis. An item from the public opinion test reads as follows: "In April, 1948, the Gallup Poll asked the American public the following question: 'Do you approve or disapprove of the U. S. giving the Chiang Kai-shek (Nationalist) government more military supplies, goods, and money?' What per cent answered 'approve'? (a) 13 per cent, (b) 28 per cent, (c) 40 per cent, (d) 56 per cent, (e) 71 per cent." The public opinion test had an average reliability of .50, compared with .87 for a Likert scale of attitudes toward the Kuomintang. The public opinion test correlated .51 with an information test of attitudes and .53 with the Likert scale.

A test of group opinion was used in a study of morale among submarine officers conducted by Campbell (1953b, 1956). The respondents first completed an anonymous direct "Secret Ballot" test of ship morale. This was followed by an indirect test of group opinion with instructions which read "You and the other members of the ship's company have voted on the 'Secret Ballot.' Your job on this test is to guess the results on that ballot. We want your judgment or guess as to *how your own ship* voted and your guess as to *how the whole squadron* voted. . . . Some people are much better at this sort of thing than are others. It has been said that good leaders are better at knowing what the group thinks. This is one of the problems we are trying to study." The results which follow compare the direct questionnaire and

the estimates of own ship since estimates of squadron opinion correlated negatively with almost all critical measures.

	Direct	Indirect
Reputation for morale with other ships	.75	.49
Reputation for morale with squadron headquarters (officers)	.70	.37
Reputation for morale with squadron headquarters (enlisted)	.93	.71
Reenlistment rate	.26	.15
Total offenses	.39	.18
Strictness	.55	.44
Requests for transfer	−.19	−.56
Reputation for efficiency	.62	.45

Although the differences between the direct and indirect tests are not significant since the values are based on an N of ten ships, the consistent superiority of the direct test leaves little room for doubting its relative strength over the public opinion test.

Moving the social psychology laboratory into the field, Breed and Ktsanes (1961) examined the correlation between "pluralistic ignorance" and attitudinal bias. They first asked a sample of church members and a sample of city residents what they would do if their church or schools were desegregated. After this the respondents were asked how they thought others in the study (other church members or other townspeople) would respond. Dividing the respondents into "segregators" and "integrators" on the basis of how they said they would respond, the authors found the segregators clearly denied the existence of an anti-segregation public. Not a single segregator said that any of his fellow church members or townspeople would take a tolerant position, whereas in actual fact 27 per cent of the sample did take a liberal stance.

Test involving miscellaneous abilities— Another of the tests in the Horowitzes' study (1938) was labeled the Categories Test. This test was modeled directly upon a typical intelligence test item. Five pictures were presented and the question was asked, "Which one does not belong?" As they adapted it, the item could be answered in more than one way, the choice presumably showing something about those social categories important for the child. For example, a page might contain pictures of three white boys, one white girl, and one Negro boy. In this instance, the child could use either sex or race as the dominant category. Other items provided opportunities to categorize by age and socioeconomic status as well. Hartley (1946) also used the categorization of photographs as a measure of ethnic salience. The task was presented in a voluntary framework, however, with instructions reading, "You can classify them on any basis you want to!" and as such could not qualify as a test of "abilities."

In the Murray and Morgan (1945) "Study of Sentiments" several of the indirect methods employ an ability test facade. The "Sentiments Examination" Section A, Part 1, asks for the "most descriptive adjectives" for 48 stimulus words, "the S being led to believe that the examiner is interested in testing the range of his vocabulary." In Part 3 "the S is led to believe his verbal ability is being tested with a simile completion test" (e.g., "As pathetic as a . . ."). In the "Arguments Completion Test" the respondent is asked to continue and finish an argument, the beginning of which has been described. "Being led to believe his powers of argumentation are being tested, the subject quickly becomes involved in the controversy he or she is inventing, and ends by exposing more of his own sentiments than he might otherwise have done." (pp. 58–60).

Cook (1968) has proposed several tests of classification and clustering which are analogous to the categories test though in different sensory modes. A verbal free recall test of a list of names of well-known persons could be presented as a test of memory. He suggests as an example a list containing the names of four baseball players, four musicians, four political figures and four actors, with one name in each category referring to a Negro. The clustering in free recall would indicate which categories the respondent employs. And a test of auditory clustering could be devised using methods of dichotic listening.

A multiple choice TAT test disguised with a facade which claims it is a test of detective abilities has also been used by Cook (1968). Each picture used in the test is presented in five stages, ranging from very little information in the initial stage to a complete (though still ambiguous) picture in the final stage. Respondents are told that detective skill is reflected in correctly diagnosing the situation as early as possible in the series of pictures. To reinforce this idea the test is speeded. Half of the pictures have white characters only; half contain Negroes and whites. This permits the use of a difference score.

Each stage of each picture is accompanied by questions such as:

1. Are A and B friends? a) Yes b) No
2. a) A and B planned to meet
   b) A and B preferred not to meet

Cook's failure to obtain significant results with this test may be a function of insufficient disguise. With pictures of persons who differ only in racial features and with questions dealing exclusively with A and B's reactions to one another, the supposed detective nature of the task may not have been convincing.

A more successful demonstration of systematic bias in "abilities" has been reported by Clarke and Campbell (1955). The study dealt with the effect of the common stereotype of Negro intellectual inferiority on judgments of the academic achievements of specific Negroes. In several integrated seventh and eighth grade classes, the students were asked to predict one another's test scores prior to objective examinations. Comparisons of predicted and obtained scores revealed a tendency for the white students to underestimate the scores of their Negro classmates. The mean standard score of the Negro students was $-.78$ while the mean standard score as estimated by the whites was $-.97$. This discrepancy in the predicted direction was significant at the .01 level.

Another task presented as a problem of making "estimates" has been used to test attitudes toward various consumer products. Westfall, Boyd and Campbell (1957) instructed over 1,200 respondents: "Now we'd like to find out what kind of people you think eat hot cereal the most. For each of the following groups indicate whether you think they eat a lot of hot cereal, a little hot cereal, or practically no hot cereal." The target persons were farmers, teen-age girls, doctors, lawyers, elderly people, and several others. They found that over half the respondents thought movie stars ate none, while farmers, athletes and poor people were believed to eat a lot of hot cereal.

Tests involving ability to judge character —As mentioned earlier in relation to free-response tests, the assignment to judge character can be given as an objective task. Such objectivity was approached in the "Faces Game," originally developed by Radke (Rose, 1948, pp. 50–51) and modified by Chein and Schreiber (American Jewish Congress, 1947). In this test children were told "Let's see how good you are at telling what people are like just by looking at their faces." Thirty-four sets of four pictures (two white and two Negro for all but four sets) were presented, each with questions such as "one of the girls in this row is very lazy and never bothers to do anything" or "one of the boys in this row is the best sport in his class; which one?" Two scores were provided: one the *white salience* score (the total mentions of white children for items either good or bad), and the other the *prejudice score* (the ratio of unfavorable choices of faces of the other group to total choices). The test produced significant individual and group differences, and showed retest reliabilities over a six-month period of .50 and .36 for white and Negro children, respectively, on the prejudice score. For the white salience score the values were .32 and .16.

In another study (Radke and Trager, 1950) grade school children were asked to identify which of two houses the Negro and white dolls lived in, which houses the dolls

preferred, and which set of clothing belonged to each doll. The choices were between a lower class and middle class house, and between servant's dress and street clothes. In another instance (Radke, Sutherland, and Rosenberg, 1950), they were asked to choose from a series of pictures to show which "is the smartest in the school," "which is very mean," etc. In both cases their choices reflected a comprehension of social differentiation and revealed prejudices and stereotypes with regard to Negroes.

Tests involving miscellaneous judgments —There is a fairly extensive literature on the effects of attitudes on ratings of the favorability of statements. Although most of these studies have not employed instructions which would encourage the subjects to believe that the test was tapping their attitudes, the testers have not taken care to put up an objective facade, either. In an exploration of a multitrait-multimethod matrix, Hicks (1967) did try to create an indirect test by asking subjects to rate the favorability or unfavorability of statements, with instructions reading, "Remember, we want your OBJECTIVE JUDGMENT about each statement *as it stands*." Three methods—a Likert scale, semantic differential, and the "objective" judgments— were used to measure three attitudes— toward Negroes, the Peace Corps, and journalism. Corrected Spearman-Brown reliability coefficients were high for all three methods and three attitudes, ranging from .82 to .95, with no obvious differences for the different methods. In this case, then, the reliability of the indirect measure matched that of a direct test. The validity coefficients showed the semantic differential correlating higher with the Likert than with the indirect test, ranging from .53 to .69 in the former and .06 and .47 in the latter case. Hicks accounts for this difference by noting that the objective judgment instructions are incompatible with evaluative attitudinal responses, and to the extent that the objective judgments prevail, one would expect the correlation with another attitude measure to decline. A comparison of monomethod and monoattitude value also showed the Likert scale to be superior, yielding slightly less methods variance than the "objective" judgments. Hicks does not rule out the usefulness of this indirect test, however, since problems of social desirability might not have been operating strongly enough to make an indirect test particularly valuable.

There is a variation on the theme of making objective judgments of statements which Waly and Cook (1965) have found useful as an indirect attitude test. They had their respondents rate the plausibility of statements by instructing them as follows: "We are interested in arguments for segregation and for integration to be used in the construction of a psychological test . . . Imagine that you are judging a debate between two teams on the topic of segregation vs. integration. Acting as an impartial judge, you are to rate each argument presented by either side in terms of its effectiveness." The subjects were presented with statements which prior ratings had shown were judged to range from clearly effective to clearly ineffective on both sides of the argument. Examples of the four types are as follows:

Ineffective pro-segregation: Among the unfortunate consequences of racial integration is the mental deficiency which is often found in children of mixed marriages.
Effective pro-segregation: Immediate desegregation damages the Negro by giving him responsibilities for which he does not have the necessary background and preparation.
Ineffective pro-integration: If integration is adopted race hatred will quickly disappear in Southern communities which are now torn apart by the issue.
Effective pro-integration: Segregation leads to a waste of our human resources by decreasing the scientific and professional training given to capable Negroes.

The respondents also answered a self-report questionnaire which correlated significantly ($r = .84$) with the plausibility ratings. This approach was first used by Watson in his Arguments Test in 1925.

As with the syllogisms tests, it might be helpful to analyze the various interpretations which the subjects might make of the instructions. In a task which merely instructs persons to judge the "strength" of an argument, without specifying whether it is the logical or empirical truth or the linguistic eloquence which they are to judge, the results may be difficult to interpret since different subjects may perceive the assignment in different ways. Some might try to judge the elegance of the statements, or the descriptive truth of the premise, or the internal consistency of the argument, or the empirical truth of the intervening arguments. If they interpret the instructions to mean "tell me whether you agree or disagree with the conclusion" this amounts to no more than a direct attitude test. If, on the other hand, the subjects accept the assignment to rate the "effectiveness" of the statements much as a debate judge would do, then the various items must be matched for elegance and consistency so that the only variable which could determine the subject's answer would be the extent to which his views agreed with the content of the argument.

Less objective in appearance and more in the tradition of the studies of attitudes as anchors, Ager and Dawes (1965) had their subjects perform a paired-comparisons task in which the pairs were statements about science which came from six categories of favorability in a previous ranking by other respondents. Instead of recording the relative ratings of favorability, however, the authors were interested in the error patterns (errors being defined as discrepancies from a consensus ordering of the statements obtained in a previous study). In line with the findings of Hovland and Sherif (1952; Sherif and Hovland, 1953), they predicted that persons would not only lump together the statements which were at the opposite pole from their own attitudes but would also be unable to discriminate among them. Thus, the number of errors should be a positive function of the distance of the judged categories from the subject's own position. A significant interaction of criterion groups by pairs of statements confirmed this prediction.

GENERAL CONSIDERATIONS
AND CONCLUSIONS

The reliability coefficients reported for the indirect attitude tests reviewed here are probably among the highest of their kind, since they have passed through the selection processes of publication procedures. Still, they generally fall below the levels considered respectable, and where comparisons between direct and indirect tests are available, the latter clearly come out in second place. A comparison with direct tests might not be entirely appropriate, however, in light of what consistency on the two different measures signifies. It is highly probable that the desire to appear consistent, even on anonymous questionnaires, may inflate the reliability ratings for direct tests. Such self-conscious and possibly superficial consistency is hardly comparable with the unplanned systematic biases revealed in errors on an information test or in judgments of logical validity. It is, moreover, this unself-conscious consistency which is more in keeping with the notion of attitude and which gives vitality to current usage of the concept.

Validity of indirect tests—Indications of the validity of an instrument come in at least two general forms. One form consists of "validity correlations" of the instrument with criterial measures. The other—trans-situational validity—consists of evidence that the test produces the same results in a variety of circumstances and is not buffeted about by various irrelevant demands. The validity evidence of either form which is available for indirect tests is no more flattering than the evidence for direct attitude tests.

During the writing of this chapter, two studies were conducted to compare the trans-situational validity of direct and indirect tests by subjecting them to anonymous or signed conditions. Kidder (1969) found that responses on a direct test of opinions about military training on campuses were unmoved by the normative demands of signing one's name or the informational demands of seeing how "other students" answered. An indirect test of "Knowledge about ROTC," on the other hand, was significantly influenced both by seeing how "others" answered and by an interaction of that variable with the demand of signing. The author concluded that persons were willing to present the same "self" under private and public conditions when the direct test asked for such presentations and the items were unambiguous and almost stereotypic. On a more ambiguous task, however, which required difficult estimations and reports about external facts, answers were skewed to conform to "others" answers and signing increased the distortion.

Cook, Johnson and Scott (1969) also found that of three instruments covering 14 attitude topics, the direct test and one of the indirect tests were not significantly affected by identified and anonymous conditions, while a second indirect test showed more counternorm responses under anonymous than under identified answering. These results can be interpreted in two opposite fashions: 1) the counternorm responses represent the superior validity of the anonymous indirect test (as suggested by Cook, Johnson and Scott), or 2) the robustness of the direct test and the first indirect test reflects *their* superior trans-situational validity. This tie is broken at least partially by the criterial correlations of each test with friends' ratings of the respondents. The mean correlation of the direct self-report instrument was significantly greater than that of the two indirect tests. Validating tests by examining criterial correlations is often a delicate operation, however, as is described in the following sections.

Where comparisons of the criterial correlations of direct and disguised measures are available (e.g., Campbell, 1953, 1955; Campbell and Damarin, 1961; Green, 1954; Rankin and Campbell, 1959), the indirect test fails to reach the levels of the direct tests. In order to evaluate these findings, it might be helpful to delineate some of the factors involved in such criterial correlations to determine whether the direct and indirect tests are tapping different attitude universes or just different levels of the same universe.

The most obvious distinction between the direct and disguised measures is the extent to which they are sensitive to the operation of social norms. This distinction indeed provides the rationale for developing and using indirect measures. Indirect tests, it was hoped, would elude the respondent's censorial eye and be free from normative pressures. They were intended to reflect underlying *processes* which represent a person's "true" feelings, not distorted by concerns with social appearances. The notion that attitudes are found and expressed in misperception, in memory biases, in selective learning, in faulty logic, and in many other cognitive and behavioral processes is consistent with a theory of social attitudes developed by Campbell (1963). That theory contends that a host of seemingly unrelated terms such as acquired drive, belief, conditioned reflex, fixation, judgment, stereotype, and valence, to mention only a few, are all functionally synonymous with the concept of attitude. All describe the residues of past experience which are the stuff of which attitudes are made. They are the underlying processes, or the behavioral manifestations of underlying processes, which are products of learning. In contrast to such "natural" manifestations of attitudes, the verbal reports obtained by direct attitude questionnaires may seem artificial and molded by social considerations. Rather than say what he honestly thinks and feels, a person may say what he thinks he ought to say or what he thinks the tester would like to hear. If these two types of measures are tapping different realms of attitudes, one characterized by norms and the other by processes, it might be reasonable to expect the validity criteria of the two to be drawn from similarly diverse realms. Reputational measures, then, would be classified in the "normative" category since they are also derived from behavior in social situations, and as such would be expected to correlate more highly with the direct tests. Similarly, the distinction between Northern and Southern whites might involve a large "normative" component insofar as open expression of race prejudice is less sanctioned by the norms of colleges in the North than in the South.

If one were to search for suitable criterial measures for indirect tests, one might look for other measures which tap "processes," unencumbered by normative influences. Two indirect tests, in other words, should correlate more highly with each other than with a direct test. The few studies which have employed multiple indirect and direct methods have not substantiated this (e.g., Hicks, 1967; Campbell, 1955; Parrish and Campbell, 1953). Reasons for this failure may lie in the contamination of the indirect tests by other factors, not normative factors but irrelevant abilities or judgments. The syllogisms test, for instance, is influenced by education and training in logic; binocular rivalry tests contain constancy factors; and TAT measures have their own peculiar methods variance.

Perhaps this distinction between the operation of norms and processes, while useful, should not be so overdrawn. Rather than try to distinguish between two attitude realms— one overt and the other covert, one public and one private, one socially acceptable and the other taboo—it might be more useful to try to scale the various expressions of attitudes in terms of their different thresholds.

The notion of a hierarchy of responses with successively higher thresholds is familiar in the verbal learning tradition. If one considers the learning of paired associates, for instance, it is apparent that different tests will reveal different degrees of learning, depending upon the thresholds for the responses required by each. A hierarchy of tests with progressively lower thresholds is as follows (Campbell, 1963):

Recall
Recognition
Savings in relearning

Similarly, in diagnosing social attitudes, each test involves responses with different thresholds, such that one measure indicates the existence of an attitude under study while another seemingly denies it. A hierarchy of attitude tests might be as follows (Campbell, 1963):

(1) Autonomic response
(2) Verbal report on perceived character of the stimulus
  e.g., "The average I.Q. of Negroes is lower than that of whites."
(3) Verbal report on own response tendency
  e.g., "I would not let a Negro move onto my block."
(4) Overt locomotor response
  e.g., refusing to serve Negro patrons

One could imagine situations in which some of the relations would be reversed. For instance, a person might refrain from verbal expressions of prejudice but his overt behavior may go so far as refusing to rent his house to Negroes, or organizing a parents' group to protest school desegregation. Whereas the hierarchy of tests for non-social behavior, such as paired-associate learning, is relatively stable, the ordering of thresholds for social behavior varies with the incentives and prohibitions of the moment.

If the concept of a hierarchy of tests with different thresholds is accurate, one would expect tests with similar thresholds to correlate more highly than those with different thresholds. In choosing criterial measures for validation, in other words, it is meaningless to say that one test has higher "validity" coefficients without considering the positions of the tests and criterial measures in such a hierarchy. A look at the various criterial measures which have been used in the literature reviewed here suggests that many of them occupy positions in the hierarchy which are closer to the direct than to the indirect measures. Reputational measures, for instance, are derived from social interaction and are more likely to share the thresholds of overt locomotor responses and verbal expressions of response tendencies than the thresholds of statements of belief.

The issue of comparative validity is not easily resolved. One might speak of a test as being a valid measure of something, but a reasonable question might be "valid for

what?" The answer "for prediction" is a non-answer unless one specifies what it is that the test is supposed to predict. Since we are considering social attitudes, it seems intuitively reasonable that the test would be used to predict social behavior. If this is the case, then the direct tests, which are influenced by normative factors and considerations of social desirability, are probably the more valid predictors. If, however, one were interested in studying stereotypes and ethnocentric belief systems, the indirect information tests may well be the more valid instruments.

From a less practical, more theoretical point of view, the concept of construct validity calls for correlation with as many dissimilar methods as possible rather than with one other related measure. Every measurement technique, be it direct or disguised, involves certain irrelevant factors which do not properly belong to the construct under consideration. Likert scales contain response biases, syllogisms tests tap logical abilities, and estimates of public opinion depend upon the respondent's perception of himself as belonging to the majority. The demonstration of construct validity requires that the correlation between two such different methods measuring the same trait be significantly greater than zero and also greater than the correlation between two different traits measured by the two different methods. The more dissimilar the different methods, the more impressive and convincing the validity coefficients are. Any construct which survives the triangulation of various irrelevancies of different tests has earned the name by which it goes. Indirect tests thus have an important role in such triangulation processes, since they involve different methods and irrelevancies.

Relation of attitude testing to attitude theory—The operational definition of an attitude, as evidenced by the requirements of reliability and reproducibility coefficients, is *consistency of response to social objects*. Spearman-Brown reliabilities, Kuder-Richardson coefficients, and Guttman's Reproducibility coefficient all demand such consistency of response, and in order to qualify as an attitude scale, a test must meet this minimal requirement. Such consistency at a molecular level, among responses on a single instrument, finds a parallel at a molar level. Validity coefficients require consistency across measuring instruments and across modes of responding. This means that different modes of expression are intersubstitutable, as co-symptoms of the same underlying disposition to respond.

Evidence of response consistency is a requirement which is not peculiar to the study of social attitudes. It is the sine qua non of all studies of learning, the most elementary datum of psychology. Any test of a habit, a set, a preference, a cognitive map, or a motive requires evidence of a consistent tendency to respond. It is by no means coincidental that the experimental psychologist studying rat learning and the social psychologist studying attitudes should use similar criteria. They are both engaged in a diagnostic venture, trying to identify what has been learned.

Most contemporary attitude theorists would say that attitudes are learned, whether they conceive of them as dispositions to respond or to perceive or feel, or think. Operationally, in fact, it is impossible to distinguish between an attitude and a habit. This does not imply a narrowness of definition, however, but rather a breadth and scope which some readers might find unimaginable. Campbell (1963) has sought to demonstrate the functional synonymity of terms as diverse-sounding as "anticipation," "cognitive structure," "life space," and "attitude." All of these terms refer to the fact that something has changed, some residue has been left, as a function of past experience. They all represent attempts to identify some underlying process, though with slightly different connotations and concomitant slightly different methods of approach. A psychologist interested in life space may record the gross locomotor activity; another, interested in motives and intentions, may ask his respondents directly what they would do in certain situations; one interested in beliefs and stereotypes might pose direct questions or use indirect tests of "information," and so on. None of these methods is clearly superior to the others in tapping the true processes. No one of them is free of systematic irrelevancies which are of little interest to the student of social attitudes. It is rather their use in combination, in a triangulation of knowledge processes, that contributes most to the understanding of acquisition and expression of attitudes.

Recommendations for the Use of Indirect Tests

Suggestions for the use of indirect tests must be tempered by considerations of their efficacy as well as their ethical status. The ethical problems surrounding the application of disguised tests in administrative settings (see Weschler, 1951) may serve to inhibit the use of methods designed to probe those levels of feeling and belief which a person considers private. At the same time, the benefits obtained from the judicious use of these ingenious instruments encourage their further use and development in certain prescribed manners and areas.

Cautions concerning indirect testing— There was a rumor circulating among labor leaders in the 1950s which came to the attention of one of the authors and which deserves mention here. The rumor had it that certain personnel managers were employing indirect tests of labor-management attitudes in order to identify persons with strong pro-labor sentiments and prevent them from entering the firm. A "Test of Your Information about Industry" might well seem like a reasonable entrance exam and could, if well written, deceive many an eager applicant. Feeling practically defenseless in the face of hidden weapons such as these, it is not surprising that union leaders should have protested. The potential power of such instruments threatens not only the privacy of a person's mind but also the security of his job. If there is resistance and resentment against the direct questions of census takers (e.g., do you have a flush toilet in your house?), it should come as no shock to an industrial psychologist or personnel manager that disguised tests would infuriate the unsuspecting job applicant or employee. Census data, at least until now, have not been used to discriminate against anyone in matters of hiring or promotion. And if employers began to use such direct data there would be little to prevent a person from answering in ways which would not jeopardize his chances. The plausible facades of indirect attitude tests effectively prohibit self-defense and permit testing in many administrative settings where attitude scores might otherwise be unobtainable.

If a psychologist has devised an instrument which permits such invasions of privacy to occur, does he not also share in the responsibility for its use? The authors venture to argue that he does, and that he might consider it part of his ongoing research to investigate the applications of his instruments.

The ethical problems which arise from administrative applications of indirect attitude tests do not disappear entirely in the pure research laboratory. Although no crucial decisions hinge upon a person's systematic errors on an information test or his stories told to TAT cards, the invasion of privacy and the use of deception may well arouse the anger of the respondent and raise ethical questions for the tester. Perhaps the only means of avoiding these problems while still obtaining the desired information is to guarantee absolute anonymity to the subjects.

Anonymity, although sounding like a well-defined condition in itself, comes in varying forms and degrees. Sampling the studies reviewed in this chapter reveals that most investigators made no reference to assuring their respondents of anonymity (e.g., Ager and Dawes, 1965; Alper and Korchin, 1952; Burwen, Campbell and Kidd, 1956; Campbell and Damarin, 1961; Campbell and Shanan, 1958; Doob, 1953; Feather, 1964; Getzels and Walsh, 1958; Hammond, 1948; Hsü, 1949; Janis and Frick, 1943; Jones and

Kohler, 1958; Kuethe, 1964; Newcomb, 1943; Proshansky, 1943; Rokeach, 1948; Shelley and Davis, 1957; Sherriffs, 1948; Sommer, 1954; Thistlethwaite, 1950; Waly and Cook, 1965). One pair of investigators tried to assure the participants of "practical" anonymity by telling them that even though they signed their names the information would not become part of their permanent records (Burwen and Campbell, 1957); and some guaranteed absolute anonymity by using unsigned tests (e.g., Himmelfarb, 1966; Jones and Aneshansel, 1956; Parrish and Campbell, 1953; Rankin and Campbell, 1959; Weschler, 1950b; Williams, 1964).

We advocate using anonymous forms wherever possible. Some indirect tests might admittedly benefit from having subjects sign their names in the belief that their "information" scores will be taken seriously as measures of knowledge or ability. Some criterial correlations, as with reputational measures, might also require identifiable papers. Whenever the facade will not suffer from anonymity, however, and criterial measures can also be obtained, it would seem advisable to avoid identifying respondents and the concomitant criticism which indirect testing bears.

It might be pointed out that indirect *assessment* (e.g., Webb *et al.*, 1966), unlike testing, does not encounter the same problems of deception and personal prying when it relies on group data, physical traces, and simple observation of public behavior. Many of these measures are anonymous of necessity, and others are part of the public domain of observable behavior and constitute no more an invasion of privacy than does one person's watching another (although even this may be considered a breach of good faith by some, e.g., Webb *et al.*, 1966, p. vi).

Contributions of Indirect Testing

If we find that anonymous data from indirect attitude tests suffice, may we not also be satisfied with unsigned direct attitude questionnaires? Moreover, if guaranteed anonymity reduces or eliminates distortion on direct tests, why bother with the oddball measures and uncertain gimmicks at all? Quite aside from the intrinsic rewards of creating and using an ingenious instrument, there are at least two benefits from indirect tests which, in the minds of the authors, justify their use.

Multitrait-multimethod matrices — This procedure for establishing construct validity by using at least two traits and two methods has been advocated elsewhere by Campbell and Fiske (1959). Briefly, the design requires that the correlation between two measures of a single trait be not only greater than zero but also greater than the correlation of two different traits measured by two different methods. In addition, it is desirable for that validity coefficient to be greater than the correlation between two different traits measured by a single method. The necessity for at least two traits and two methods derives from the imperfections and irrelevancies that inevitably adhere in any measurement effort. Single operations are thus better construed as approximations to knowledge rather than as definitions, and multiple operations are advocated in their stead. The interpretation of results obtained from any single measure is equivocal, for there is no way of distinguishing between variance contributed by the trait and variance attributable to the method. "Halo effects" and response sets are examples of methods factors which contaminate data and make interpretation problematic. They must be extracted as completely as possible in order to demonstrate the validity of the trait under study. Elimination of methods factors cannot be achieved by looking for a "pure" instrument, however, since none is perfect. Rather, we may take account of the imperfections and employ multiple measures with heterogeneous irrelevancies so that what is shared is not methods variance but the trait.

It is in this context that indirect tests, with their novel methods and heterogeneous irrelevancies, can contribute to the discovery of constructs. High correlations between widely different methods provide convincing evidence of the existence of a trait. Low correlations, however, may suggest one of several other alternatives. Neither method may measure the trait with any degree of precision. One method may fail to measure a particular trait but succeed in measuring another. Or both may be tapping different aspects of a trait, leading to theoretical developments which would not have occurred had the trait been assumed to exist as a unified element (Campbell and Fiske, 1959).

Some of the studies reviewed here do suggest that direct and indirect tests are tapping different aspects of attitudes. The distinction lies not only in the dimensions of public versus private or overt versus covert processes, but might be expressed in terms of the difference between beliefs and valuations. Tests of information, or public opinion, or syllogistic reasoning all seem to be measuring what Myrdal (1944) has called the "belief" component of attitudes. This aspect of indirect methods relates to the second justification for using these tests.

A sociology of knowledge of the man-on-the-street—The information test format is perhaps best suited for studying what men believe, what they take to be truth, about other men. Direct tests containing items such as "I believe all Englishmen are snobs: fully agree, agree, don't know, disagree, fully disagree," may also tap the belief system of the respondent but they do not play upon the phenomenal absolutism of men's beliefs and perceptions. An objective facade and a stress upon facts and accuracy are better able to explore the relationship between men's hopes and fears and their perceptions of reality.

The interplay between facts and attitudes is a topic of profound theoretical and practical significance. In the words of Solomon Asch (1952), "That there can be disagreement about facts is a matter of the greatest consequence. For facts have a special status; the world is built on them. It is therefore pertinent to ask: What forms of interaction take place between an existing attitude and a fact relevant to it?"

The interaction seems to work in complex ways. Beliefs are undoubtedly products of experience—results of contiguity between stimuli or between stimuli and responses—and these experiences evoke certain evaluations of the attitudinal objects. If a child, for instance, is exposed only to minority group children who rank at the bottom of his class, his beliefs about those children are likely to be tinged by negative evaluations. However, negative and positive evaluations predispose a person to seek particular kinds of verifying information in order to justify his judgments. His beliefs then become convenient rationalizations for his feelings; and beliefs which justify deeply felt prejudices are no less real or true for the beholder than are the more neutral beliefs about the weather or the shape of the earth.

Studying the beliefs and knowledge systems of social groups serves at least two functions. First, a revelation of a man's beliefs is a revelation not only of his thoughts but also of his feelings about and response tendencies toward others. An enlightened student of social science might argue that negative valuations do not follow logically from a belief that Negroes receive lower grades than whites. And he may be right. But in fact our beliefs are accompanied by judgments of right and wrong, good and bad, and only the blandest observations pass through our perceptual filters without positive and negative tags. By studying these beliefs which rationalize men's biases and prejudices, we may come to understand, predict, and perhaps control some of the bigotry which now prevails.

The second function of a sociology of knowledge of the man-on-the-street is closely related to the first. As suggested by Myrdal (1944), a study of misinformation and selective ignorance has educational implications. Admittedly, filling in blind spots or correcting errors in belief is more difficult with attitudinally relevant topics than it is with spelling and simple arithmetic. The same skills and processes which created the distortions in original learning can create interference for educationally corrective programs. Nonetheless, new experiences may be provided, new contiguities established, and new belief systems may begin to emerge.

Neither of these functions violates the code of anonymity which is advocated here. Rather than a study of individual differences, a study of group beliefs and attitudes is in order. Item analysis should reveal the particular areas of information which are distorted and in need of change. And group data on shared backgrounds and experiences may suggest which variables are important in the creation of the beliefs and which may be manipulated in the educational venture.

Conclusions

If we use our indirect tests in the manner suggested above, as a means of achieving a triangulation of knowledge processes and as instruments for studying shared beliefs, we may diminish some of the objectionable aspects of these hidden measures. Rather than focus upon the idiosyncracies of individuals we might turn to a study of groups. Rather than speak of "subjects" who must be coerced or cajoled into cooperating and whose defenses must be overcome, we might return to the view of the German psychologists who treated their respondents as *Versuchspersonen*, or fellows in research. And rather than regard our indirect measures as access routes to areas which are taboo, we might think of them as just another imperfect measure of the traits which are also assessed by direct tests.

Our disappointment with the statistical credentials of indirect attitude tests may be a function of our hopes and expectations for these methods. By disguising our intents we had hoped to break through barriers. By evading conscious censorship we hoped to arrive at the "truth." In retrospect, we might be advised to relinquish these notions and to recognize the tests for what they are—novel and creative—but still fallible measures of the multifaceted processes we call attitudes.

REFERENCES

Adorno, T. W., E. Frenkel-Brunswik, D. J. Levinson, and R. N. Sanford.
1950   The Authoritarian Personality. New York: Harper.

Ager, J. W., and R. M. Dawes.
1965   "Effect of judge's attitudes on judgment." Journal of Personality and Social Psychology 1(5):533–538.

Allport, G. W.
1935   "Attitudes." Chapter 17 in C. Murchison (ed.), A Handbook of Social Psychology. Worcester: Clark University Press.

Alper, T., and S. J. Korchin.
1952   "Memory for socially relevant material." Journal of Abnormal and Social Psychology 47:25–37.

Asch, S. E.
1952   Social Psychology. Englewood Cliffs: Prentice-Hall.

Atkinson, J. W. (ed.).
1958   Motives in Fantasy, Action, and Society. Princeton: Von Nostrand.

Babbitt, H. G.
1962   "An attempt to produce changes in attitudes toward the self by means of verbal conditioning." Journal of Verbal Learning and Verbal Behavior. 1(3): 168–172.

Bagby, J. W.
1957   "A cross-cultural study of perceptual predominance in binocular rivalry." Journal of Abnormal and Social Psychology 54:331–334.

Bain, R.
1928   "An attitude on attitude research." American Journal of Sociology 33: 940–957.

Bartlett, F. C.
1938   "The cooperation of social groups: A preliminary report and suggestions." Occupational Psychology 12:30–42.
1939   The Study of Society. London: Kegan Paul.

Berg, K. R.
1962   "Ethnic attitudes and agreement of white persons with a Negro person in the autokinetic situation." Dissertation Abstracts 23(1):334.
1966   "Ethnic attitudes and agreement with a Negro person." Journal of Personality and Social Psychology 4(2):215–220.

Bernberg, R. E.
1951   "The direction of perception technique of attitude measurement." International Journal of Opinion and Attitude Research 5:397–406.

Biesheuvel, S.
1958   "Methodology in the study of attitudes of Africans." Journal of Social Psychology 47:169–184.

Bray, D.
1950   "The prediction of behavior from two attitude scales." Journal of Abnormal and Social Psychology 45:64–84.

Breed, W., and T. Ktsanes.
1961   "Pluralistic ignorance in the process of opinion formation." Public Opinion Quarterly 25(3):382–392.

Brigham, J. C., and S. W. Cook.
1969   "The influence of attitude on the recall of controversial material: A failure to conform." Journal of Experimental Social Psychology 5:240–243.

Brinton, J. E.
1961   "Deriving an attitude scale from semantic differential data." Public Opinion Quarterly 25(2):289–295.

Brown, J. F.
1947   "Modification of the Rosenzweig picture frustration test to study hostile interracial attitudes." Journal of Psychology 24:247–272.

Brown, R. S.
1965   Social Psychology. New York: The Free Press.

Burtt, H. E.
1923   "Measuring interests objectively." School and Society 17:444–448.
1942   Principles of Employment Psychology (revised edition). New York: Harper.

Burwen, L. S., and D. T. Campbell.
1957a "A comparison of test scores and role playing behavior in assessing superior vs. subordinate orientation." Journal of Social Psychology 46:49–56.
1957b "The generality of attitudes toward authority and nonauthority figures." Journal of Abnormal and Social Psychology 54:24–31.

Burwen, L. S., D. T. Campbell, and J. Kidd.
1956 "The use of a sentence completion test in measuring attitudes toward superiors and subordinates." Journal of Applied Psychology 40:248–250.

Campbell, D. T.
1950 "The indirect assessment of social attitudes." Psychological Bulletin 47:15–38.
1951 Miscellaneous data on the attitude-diagnostic information test regarding the American Negro. Unpublished data.
1953a "Systematic misinformation about the American Negro as studied through an attitude-diagnostic information test." Unpublished manuscript.
1953b "A study of leadership among submarine officers." Studies of Naval Leadership. Duplicated Research Report, The Ohio State University Research Foundation. 210 pages.
1955 "The prediction of superior-subordinate relationships within bomber crews." Final Report to the Air Research and Development Command. Mimeograph: University of Chicago. 15 pages.
1956 Leadership and its Effects upon the Group. Bureau of Business Research Monograph 83: The Ohio State University.
1957a "Factors relevant to the validity of experiments in social settings." Psychological Bulletin 54:297–312.
1957b "A typology of tests, projective and otherwise." Journal of Consulting Psychology 21:207–210.
1963 "Social attitudes and other acquired behavioral dispositions." Pp. 94–176 in S. Koch (ed.), Psychology: A Study of a Science. New York: McGraw-Hill.

Campbell, D. T., and L. S. Burwen.
1956 "Trait judgments from photographs as a projective device." Journal of Clinical Psychology 12:215–221.

Campbell, D. T., and F. L. Damarin.
1961 "Measuring leadership attitudes through an information test." Journal of Social Psychology 55:159–176.

Campbell, D. T., and D. W. Fiske.
1959 "Convergent and discriminant validation by the multitrait-multimethod matrix." Psychological Bulletin 56:81–105.

Campbell, D. T., W. H. Kruskal, and W. P. Wallace.
1966 "Seating aggregation as an index of attitude." Sociometry 29:1–15.

Campbell, D. T., and B. R. McCandless.
1951 "Ethnocentrism, xenophobia and personality." Human Relations 4:185–192.

Campbell, D. T., and T. H. McCormach.
1957 "Military experience and attitudes toward authority." American Journal of Sociology 52:482–490.

Campbell, D. T., and K. Mehra.
1958 "Individual differences in evaluations of group discussions as a projective measure of attitude toward leadership." Journal of Social Psychology 47:101–106.

Campbell, D. T., N. Miller, J. Lubetsky, and E. J. O'Connell.
1964 "Varieties of projection in trait attribution." Psychological Monographs 78:15(whole 592).

Campbell, D. T., and J. Shanan.
1958 "Semantic idiosyncrasy as a method in the study of attitudes." Journal of Social Psychology 47:107–110.

Campbell, D. T., and J. C. Stanley.
1966 Experimental and Quasi-experimental Design for Research. Chicago: Rand McNally.

Carmichael, D. M.
1938 "The cooperation of social groups." British Journal of Psychology 29:206–231; 329–344.

Cattell, R. B.
1936 A Guide to Mental Testing. London: University of London Press.
1944 "Projection and the design of projective tests of personality." Character and Personality 12:177–194.

Cattell, R. B., A. B. Heist, P. A. Heist, and R. G. Stewart.
1950 "The objective measurement of dynamic traits." Educational and Psychological Measurement 10:224–248.

Cattell, R. B., E. F. Maxwell, B. H. Light, and M. P. Unger.
1949 "The objective measurement of attitudes." British Journal of Psychology 40:81–90.

Christie, R.
1956 "Some abuses of psychology." Psychological Bulletin 53:439–451.
Christie, R., and M. Jahoda (eds.).
1954 Studies in the Scope and Method of "The Authoritarian Personality." New York: Free Press.
Clarke, R. B., and D. T. Campbell.
1955 "A demonstration of bias in estimates of Negro ability." Journal of Abnormal and Social Psychology 51:585–588.
Clignet, R.
"Psychological research in Africa: significance and method. In preparation for a volume on social sciences in Africa, edited by W. Schwab.
Coffin, T. E.
1941 "Some conditions of suggestion and suggestibility: a study of certain attitudinal and situational factors influencing the process of suggestion." Psychological Monographs 4:(whole 241).
College Study in Intergroup Relations (Lloyd Allen Cook, director).
1948 "Study forms and technics in intergroup relations." Supplementary Sheet 5 (Mimeographed). Detroit: Wayne University.
Commission on Community Interrelations of the American Jewish Congress (Stuart Cook, research director).
1947– "The face game." Unpublished re-
1948 search on a modified version (by Chein and Schreiber) of a test originally developed by Marian Radke.
Cook, S. W.
1960 "The conceptualization and measurement of attitude." Duplicated Research Report. New York University.
1968 "Studies of attitude and attitude measurement." Mimeograph, AFOSR Technical Report, Institute of Behavioral Science, University of Colorado: 130 pages.
Cook, S. W., R. C. Johnson, and W. A. Scott.
1969 "Comparative validities of direct and indirect attitude measures." Unpublished manuscript, University of Colorado.
Cook, S. W., and C. A. Selltiz.
1964 "A multiple-indicator approach to attitude measurement." Psychological Bulletin 62:36–55.
Davis, T. E.

1937 "Some racial attitudes of Negro college and grade school students." Journal of Negro Education 6:157–165.
Day, D.
1949 "Dream interpretation as a projective technique." Journal of Consulting Psychology 13:416–420.
DeFleur, M. L., and F. R. Westie.
1958 "Verbal attitudes and overt acts: An experiment on the salience of attitudes." American Sociological Review 23:667–673.
Deri, S., D. Dinnerstein, J. Harding, and A. D. Pepitone.
1948 "Techniques for the diagnosis and measurement of intergroup attitudes and behavior." Psychological Bulletin 45:248–271.
Diab, L. M.
1965 "Studies in social attitudes: III. Attitude assessment through the semantic differential technique." Journal of Social Psychology 67(2):303–314.
Dicken, C. F.
1959 "Simulated patterns on the Edwards Personnel Preference Schedule." Journal of Applied Psychology 43:372–378.
1960 "Simulated patterns of the California Psychological Inventory." Journal of Counseling Psychology 7:24–31.
Doob, L. W.
1953 "Effects of initial serial position and attitude upon recall under conditions of low motivation." Journal of Abnormal and Social Psychology 48:199–205.
1965 "Psychology." Pp. 373–416 in R. A. Lystad (ed.), The African World. New York: Praeger.
1968 Personal communication.
Dubin, S. S.
1940 "Verbal attitude scores predicted from responses in a projective technique." Sociometry 3:24–28.
Edwards, A. L.
1948 "Political frames of references as a factor influencing recognition." Journal of Abnormal and Social Psychology 36:34–61.
1957 "The Social Desirability Variable in Personality Assessment and Research. New York: Dryden.
Eisenman, R., J. L. Bernard, and J. E. Jannon.
1966 "Benevolence, potency, and God: A semantic differential study of the

Rorschach." Perceptual and Motor Skills 22(1):75–78.

Evans, M. C., and I. Chein.
1948 "The movie story game: A projective test of interracial attitudes for use with Negro and white children." Paper read at the 56th annual meeting of the American Psychological Association, Boston (September).

Feather, N. T.
1964 "Acceptance and rejection of arguments in relation to attitude strength, critical ability, and intolerance of inconsistency." Journal of Abnormal and Social Psychology 69(2):127–136.

French, E. G.
1955 "Some characteristics of achievement motivation." Journal of Experimental Psychology 50:232–236.

Frenkel-Brunswik, E., H. E. Jones (directors), and M. Rokeach, M. Jarvik, and D. T. Campbell (staff).
1946– Unpublished research on the personal-
1947 ity correlates of antiminority attitudes among grade school children. University of California Institute of Child Welfare, financed by a grant from the American Jewish Committee.

Frenkel-Brunswik, E., and S. Reichert.
"Personality and prejudice in women." Unpublished manuscript.

Frenkel-Brunswik, E., D. Levinson, and R. N. Sanford.
1947 "The anti-democratic personality." In T. M. Newcomb and E. L. Hartley (eds.), Readings in Social Psychology. New York: Holt.

Fromme, A.
1941 "On use of qualitative methods of attitude research." Journal of Social Psychology 13:429–460.

Fryer, D.
1931 The Measurement of Interests. New York: Holt.

Gatty, R., and K. H. Hamje.
1961 "The error-choice technique in image research." Unpublished manuscript: Rutgers State University.

Getzels, J. W., and J. J. Walsh
1958 "The method of paired direct and projective questionnaires in the study of attitude structure and socialization." Psychological Monographs 72:(whole 454.

Gilbert, H. H.
1941 "Secondary science and pupil prejudice." Journal of Educational Research 35:294–299.

Glazer, E. M.
1941 "An experiment in the development of critical thinking." Teachers College Contributions to Education, 843. New York: Bureau of Publications, Teachers College, Columbia University.

Golightly, C., and D. Byrne.
1964 "Attitude statements as positive and negative reinforcers." Science 146:798–799.

Gordon, R. L.
1953 "The effect of attitude toward Russia on logical reasoning." Journal of Social Psychology 37:103–111.

Gordon, S.
1947 "Exploration of social attitudes through humor." Master's thesis, University of Illinois.

Gore, P. M., and J. B. Rotter.
1963 "A personality correlate of social action." Journal of Personality 31:58–64.

Green, J.
1954 "The use of an information test about the Negro as an indirect technique for measuring attitudes, beliefs, and self-perceptions." Unpublished doctoral dissertation, University of Southern California.

Green, R. T., and B. G. Stacey.
1966 "A flexible projective technique applied to the measurement of the self-images of voters." Journal of Projective Techniques and Personality Assessment 30(1):12–15.

Greenwald, A. B., and J. S. Sakumura.
1967 "Attitude and selective learning: Where are the phenomena of yesteryear?" Journal of Personality and Social Psychology 7:387–397.

Gregor, J. A., and D. A. McPherson.
1966 "Racial attitudes among white and Negro children in a deep-South standard metropolitan area." Journal of Social Psychology 68(1):95–106.

1966 "Racial preference and ego identity among white and Bantu children in the Republic of South Africa." Genetic Psychological Monographs 73(2):217–253.

Grings, W. W.
1942 "The verbal summator technique and abnormal mental states." Journal of Abnormal and Social Psychology 37: 529–545.

Guttman, L.
1944 "A basis for scaling qualitative data." American Sociological Review 9:130–150.

Hammond, K. R.
1948 "Measuring attitudes by error-choice; an indirect method." Journal of Abnormal and Social Psychology 43:38–48.

Hanfman, E., and J. W. Getzels.
1953 "Studies of the sentence-completion test." Journal of Projective Techniques 17:280–294.

Hartley, E. L.
1946 Problems in Prejudice. New York: Kings Crown Press.

Hartley, E. L., and S. Schwartz.
1948 "A pictorial doll-play approach for the study of children's intergroup attitudes." Mimeographed preliminary draft. Research Institute in American Jewish Education, American Jewish Committee.

Havron, M. D., and C. N. Cofer.
1957 "On the learning of material congruent and incongruent with attitudes." Journal of Social Psychology 46:91–98.

Havron, M. D., P. G. Nordlie, and C. N. Cofer.
1957 "Measurement of attitudes by a simple word association technique." Journal of Social Psychology 46:81–89.

Hermann, M. G.
1968 Indirect Methods of Assessing Personality. Research Bulletin, Educational Testing Service, Princeton, New Jersey.

Hicks, J. M.
1967 "Comparative validation of attitude measures by the multitrait-multimethod matrix." Educational and Psychological Measurement 27:985–995.

Himelstein, P., and J. C. Moore.
1963 "Racial attitudes and the action of Negro and white background figures as factors in petition-signing." Journal of Social Psychology 61(2):267–272.

Himmelfarb, S.
1966 "Studies in the perception of ethnic group members: I. Accuracy, response bias, and anti-Semitism." Journal of Personality and Social Psychology 4 (3):347–355.

Horowitz, E. L.
1936 "The development of attitude toward the Negro." Archives of Psychology 28:number 194.
1940 "Some aspects of the development of patriotism in children." Sociometry 3: 329–341.
1944 "'Race' attitudes." In O. Klineberg (ed.), Characteristics of the American Negro. New York: Harper.

Horowitz, E. L., and Ruth E. Horowitz.
1938 "Development of social attitudes in children." Sociometry 1:301–338.

Hovland, C. I., and M. Sherif.
1952 "Judgmental phenomena and scales of attitude measurement: Item displacement in Thurstone scales." Journal of Abnormal and Social Psychology 47: 822–833.

Hsü, E. H.
1949 "An experimental study of rationalization." Journal of Abnormal and Social Psychology 44:277–278.

Hudson, W.
1967 "The study of the problem of pictorial perception among unacculturated groups." International Journal of Psychology 2:89–109.

Hundleby, J. D., K. Paulik, and R. B. Cattell.
1965 Personality Factors in Objective Test Devices: A Critical Integration of a Quarter of a Century's Research. San Diego: Knapp.

Janis, I. L., and F. Frick.
1943 "The relationship between attitudes toward conclusions and errors in judging logical validity of syllogisms." Journal of Experimental Psychology 33:73–77.

Johnson, C. G.
1949 "An experimental analysis of the origin and development of racial attitudes with special emphasis on the role of bilingualism." Doctoral thesis, University of Colorado.

Jones, E. E., and J. Aneshansel.
1956 "The learning and utilization of contravaluant material." Journal of Abnormal and Social Psychology 53:27–33.

Jones, E. E., and R. Kohler.
1958 "The effects of plausibility on the learning of controversial statements." Journal of Abnormal and Social Psychology 57:315–320.

Kalpakian, E. Y.
1947 "The construction of a disguised test by use of photographs for the study of attitudes toward Negroes." Master's thesis, Clark University. Clark University Bulletin Abstracts of dissertations and theses. Worcester, Mass.

Kaplan, B. (ed.).
1961a Studying Personality Cross-culturally. New York: Harper.

Kaplan, B.
1961b "Cross-cultural use of projective techniques." In F. L. K. Hsü (ed.), Psychological Anthropology. Homewood, Illinois: The Dorsey Press.

Katz, Martin R.
1947 "A hypothesis on anti-Negro prejudice." American Journal of Sociology 53:100–104.

Kidder, L. H.
1969 "Comparisons of a direct and an indirect attitude test: Their relative susceptibility to distortion." Unpublished Master's thesis. Northwestern University.

Krech, D., and R. S. Crutchfield.
1948 Theory and Problems of Social Psychology. New York: McGraw-Hill.

Kremen, E. O.
1949 "An attempt to ameliorate hostility toward the Negro through role playing." Master's Thesis, The Ohio State University.

Kubany, A. J.
1953 "A validation of the error-choice technique using attitudes on National Health Insurance." Educational and Psychological Measurement 13:157–163.

Kuder, G. F., and M. W. Richardson.
1937 "The theory of the estimation of test reliability." Psychometrika 2:151–160.

Kuethe, J. L.
1962a "Social schemas." Journal of Abnormal and Social Psychology 64:31–38.
1962b "Social schemas and the reconstruction of social object displays from memory." Journal of Abnormal and Social Psychology 65:71–74.

1964 "Prejudice and aggression: A study of specific social schemata." Perceptual and Motor Skills 18 (1):107–115.

Kuethe, J. L., and G. Stricker.
1963 "Man and woman: Social schemata of males and females." Psychological Reports 13:655–661.

Lana, R. E.
1964 "Perceptions of social controversy in professors and college students." Journal of Psychology 57(1):213–218.

Lansdell, H.
1946 "A study of distorted syllogistic reasoning as a means of discovering covert attitudes toward marriage." Bulletin of Canadian Psychological Association 6:98 (Abstract).

LaPiere, R. T.
1934 "Attitudes vs. actions." Social Forces 13:230–237.

Laughlin, P. R., and R. M. Laughlin.
1968 "Source effects in the judgment of social argot." Journal of Social Psychology 78:249–254.

Leblanc, M.
1958 "Acculturation of attitude and personality among Katangese women." Journal of Social Psychology 47:257–264.

Lefford, A.
1946 "The influence of emotional subject matter on logical reasoning." Journal of General Psychology 34:127–151.

Lewis, H. B.
1938 "An approach to attitude measurement." Psychological League Journal 2:64–67.

Levine, J. M., and G. Murphy.
1943 "The learning and forgetting of controversial material." Journal of Abnormal and Social Psychology 38:507–517.

Likert, R.
1932 "A technique for the measurement of attitudes." Archives of Psychology. New York No. 140.

Lindgren, H. C.
1954 "The use of a sentence completion test in measuring attitude changes among college freshmen." Journal of Social Psychology 40:79–92.

Lindzey, G.
1961 Projective Techniques and Cross-cultural Research. New York: Appleton-Century-Crofts.

Lipset, S. M., P. F. Lazarsfeld, A. H. Barton, and J. Linz.
  1954 "The psychology of voting: an analysis of political behavior." In Lindzey, G. (ed.), Handbook of Social Psychology, Vol. II, Cambridge, Massachusetts: Addison-Wesley.

Loeblowitz-Lennard, H., and F. Riessman, Jr.
  1946 "A proposed projective attitude test." Psychiatry 9:67–68.
  1946 "A preliminary report on social perception test—a new approach to attitude research." Social Forces 24:423–427.

Loevinger, J.
  1948 "The technic of homogeneous tests compared with some aspects of 'scale analysis' and factor analysis." Psychological Bulletin 45:507–529.

Lubetsky, J., and D. T. Campbell.
  1963 "Age and sex as sources of stimulus equivalence in judgments of photos and peers." Journal of Clinical Psychology 19:502–505.

Maher, B. A., N. Watt, and D. T. Campbell.
  1960 "Comparative validity of two projective and two structured attitude tests in a prison population." Journal of Applied Psychology 44:284–288.

Malof, M., and A. J. Lott.
  1962 "Ethnocentrism and the acceptance of Negro support in a group pressure situation." Journal of Abnormal and Social Psychology 65:254–258.

Martin, J. G.
  1964 "Racial ethnocentrism and judgment of beauty." Journal of Social Psychology 63(1):59–63.

McGregor, D.
  1938 "The major determinants of the prediction of social events." Journal of Abnormal and Social Psychology 33:179–204.

McNemar, Q.
  1946 "Opinion-attitude methodology." Psychological Bulletin 43:289–374.

Milgram, S.
  1963 "Behavioral study of obedience." Journal of Abnormal and Social Psychology 67:371–378.
  1964 "Group pressure and action against a person." Journal of Abnormal and Social Psychology 69:137–143.

Miner, J. B.
  1963 "Occupational differences in the desire to exercise power." Psychological Reports 13(1):18.

Morgan, J. J. B.
  1943 "Distorted reasoning as an index of public opinion." School and Society 57:333–335.
  1945 "Attitudes of students toward the Japanese." Journal of Social Psychology 21:219–246.

Morgan, J. J. B., and J. T. Morton.
  1944 "The distortion of syllogistic reasoning produced by personal convictions." Journal of Social Psychology 20:39–59.

Morton, J. T.
  1942 "The distortion of syllogistic reasoning produced by personal convictions." Unpublished doctoral dissertation, Northwestern University.

Murray, H. A.
  1938 "Explorations in Personality. New York: Oxford University Press.

Murray, H. A., and C. D. Morgan.
  1945 "A clinical study of sentiments." I and II. Genetic Psychological Monographs 32:3–311.

Murphy, G., and R. Likert.
  1937 Public Opinion and the Individual. New York: Harper.

Myrdal, G.
  1944 An American Dilemma, Vol. II, New York: Harper.

Neel, R. G., and A. F. Neel.
  1953 "A demonstration of the validity of a picture technique for measuring attitude." Paper presented at Midwest Psychology Association, Columbus.

Newcomb, T. M.
  1943 Personality and Social Change. New York: Dryden Press.
  1946 "The influence of attitude climate upon some determinants of information." Journal of Abnormal and Social Psychology 41:291–302.

Noland, E. W.
  1944 "Factors associated with absenteeism in a south central New York State industry." Ph.D. thesis on file in the Cornell University Library.

Nunnally, J., and T. R. Husek.
  1958 "The phony language examination: An approach to the measurement of re-

sponse bias." Educational and Psychological Measurement 18:275–282.

Orne, M. T.
1962 "On the social psychology of the psychological experiment: with particular reference to demand characteristics and their implications." American Psychologist 17:776–783.

Parrish, J. A.
1948 "The direct and indirect assessment of attitudes as influenced by propagandized radio transcriptions." Master's thesis, The Ohio State University.

Parrish, J. A., and D. T. Campbell.
1953 "Measuring propaganda effects with direct and indirect attitude tests." Journal of Abnormal and Social Psychology 48:(1)3–9.

Pettigrew, T. F., G. W. Allport, and E. O. Barnett.
1958 "Binocular resolution and perception of race in South Africa." British Journal of Psychology 49:265–278.

Proshansky, H.
1943 "A projective method for the study of attitudes." Journal of Abnormal and Social Psychology 38:393–395.

Radke, M., J. Sutherland, and P. Rosenberg.
1950 "Racial attitudes of children." Sociometry 13:154–171.

Radke, M., and H. G. Trager.
1950 "Children's perceptions of the social roles of Negroes and whites." Journal of Psychology 29:3–33.

Radke, M., H. G. Trager, and H. Davis.
1949 "Social perceptions and attitudes of children." Genetic Psychological Monographs 40:327–447.

Rankin, R. E.
1951 "The galvanic skin response as a physiological measure of social attitudes." Unpublished Master's thesis, The Ohio State University.

Rankin, R. E., and D. T. Campbell.
1959 "Galvanic skin response to Negro and white experimenters." Journal of Abnormal and Social Psychology 51:30–33.

Rechtschaffen, A., and S. A. Mednick.
1955 "The autokinetic word technique." Journal of Abnormal and Social Psychology 51:346.

Remmers, H. H.
1934 "Generalized attitude scales—studies in social-psychological measurements." Purdue University Studies in Higher Education: Studies in Attitudes—A Contribution to Social Psychological Research Methods no. 26:7–17.
1954 Introduction to Opinion and Attitude Measurement. New York: Harper.

Remmers, H. H., and E. B. Silance.
1934 "Generalized attitude scales." Journal of Social Psychology 5:298–312.

Reynolds, R. T.
1949 "Racial attitudes revealed by a projective technique." Journal of Consulting Psychology 13:396–399.

Reynolds, D., and H. H. Toch.
1965 "Perceptual correlates of prejudice: Stereoscopic constancy using biracial stereograms." Journal of Social Psychology 66(1):127–133.

Riddleberger, A. B., and A. B. Motz.
1957 "Prejudice and perception." American Journal of Sociology 62:498–503.

Robbins, I.
1948 "Point of view and quality of thought in attitude measurement." Improving Educational Research. Pp. 52–56. American Educational Research Association 1948 Official Report, Washington, D.C.

Roethlisberger, F. J., and W. J. Dickson.
1939 Management and the Worker. Cambridge, Mass.: Harvard University Press.

Rokeach, M.
1952 "Attitude as a determinant of distortions in recall." Journal of Abnormal and Social Psychology 47:482–488.

Rose, A.
1948 Studies in Reduction of Prejudice. Chicago: American Council on Race Relations.

Rosenberg, M. J.
1965 "When dissonance fails: On eliminating evaluation apprehension from attitude measurement." Journal of Personality and Social Psychology 1:28–42.
1969 "The conditions and consequences of evaluation apprehension." In R. Rosenthal and R. Rosnow (eds.), Artifact in Social Research, New York: Academic Press.

Rosenthal, R.

1966   Experimenter Effects in Behavioral Research. New York: Appleton-Century-Crofts.

Rotter, J. B., and B. Willerman.
1947   "The incomplete sentences tests as a method of studying personality." Journal of Consulting Psychology 11:43–48.

Ruch, F. L.
1937   Psychology and Life. (1st ed.), Chicago: Scott Foresman and Company.

Saadi, M., and P. R. Farnsworth.
1934   "The degrees of acceptance of dogmatic statements and preferences for their supposed makers." Journal of Abnormal and Social Psychology 29:143–150.

Sallery, R. D., and H. C. Lindgren.
1966   "Arab attitudes toward authority: A cross-cultural study." Journal of Social Psychology 69(1):27–31.

Sanford, F. H.
1950   "The use of a projective device in attitude surveying." Public Opinion Quarterly 14:697–709.

Sanford, F. H., and I. M. Rosenstock.
1952   "Project techniques on the doorstep." Journal of Abnormal and Social Psychology 47:3–16.

Seeleman, V.
1940–   "The influence of attitude upon the
1941   remembering of pictorial material." Archives of Psychology, New York 36: no. 258.

Seeman, M.
1947   "Moral judgments: A study in racial frames of references." American Sociological Review 12:404–411.

Selltiz, C., and S. W. Cook.
1966   "Racial attitude as a determinant of judgments of plausibility." Journal of Social Psychology 70:139–147.

Selltiz, C., M. Jahoda, M. Deutsch, and S. W. Cook.
1959   Research Methods in Social Relations. New York: Holt, Rinehart, and Winston.

Shakow, D., and S. Rosenzweig.
1940   "The use of the Tautophone as an auditory apperceptive test for the study of personality." Character and Personality 3:216–266.

Shelley, H. P., and R. E. Davis.
1957   "Relationship of attitude to logical problem-solving." Psychological Reports 3:525–530.

Sherif, M.
1935   "A study of some social factors in perception." Archives of Psychology, New York, no. 187.

Sherif, M., and H. Cantril.
1947   The Psychology of Ego-involvements. New York: Wiley.

Sherif, M., and C. I. Hovland.
1953   "Judgmental phenomena and scales of attitude measurement: Placement of items with individual choice of number of categories." Journal of Abnormal and Social Psychology 48:135–141.

Sherriffs, A. C.
1948   "The 'intuition questionnaire': A new projective test." Journal of Abnormal and Social Psychology 43:326–337.

Sletto, R. F.
1937   Construction of Personality Scales by the Criterion of Internal Consistency. Hanover: The Sociological Press.

Smith, G. H.
1947   "Beliefs in statements labeled fact and rumor." Journal of Abnormal and Social Psychology 42:80–90.

Smith, M.
1947   "The personal setting of public opinions: A study of attitudes toward Russia." Public Opinion Quarterly 11:507–523.

Solomon, R. L.
1949   "An extension of control group design." Psychological Bulletin 46:137–150.

Sommer, R.
1954   "On the Brown adaptation of the Rosenzweig P-F assessing social attitudes." Journal of Abnormal and Social Psychology 49:125–128.

Springer, D. V.
1950   "Awareness of racial differences by preschool children in Hawaii." Genetic Psychological Monographs 41:215–270.

Stricker, G.
1963   "The use of the semantic differential to predict voting behavior." Journal of Social Psychology 59(1):159–167.

Sullivan, P. L., and J. Adelson.
1954   "Ethnocentrism and misanthropy." Journal of Abnormal and Social Psychology 49:246–250.

Sweet, L.
1929 The Measurement of Personal Attitudes in Younger Boys. New York: The Association Press.

Taft, R.
1954 "Selective recall and memory distortion of favorable and unfavorable material." Journal of Abnormal and Social Psychology 49:23–28.

Taylor, R. G.
1966 "Racial stereotypes in young children." Journal of Psychology 64:137–142.

Thistlethwaite, D.
1950 "Attitude and structure as factors in the distortion of reasoning." Journal of Abnormal and Social Psychology 45: 442–458.

Thouless, R. H.
1959 "Effect of prejudice on reasoning." British Journal of Psychology 50:289–293.

Thurstone, L. L., and E. J. Chave.
1929 The Measurement of Attitude. Chicago: University of Chicago Press.

Travers, R. M. W.
1941 "A study in judging the opinions of groups." Archives of Psychology, New York, no. 266.

Triandis, H. C., W. D. Loh, and L. A. Levin.
1966 "Race status, quality of spoken English, and opinions about civil rights as determinants of interpersonal attitudes." Journal of Personality and Social Psychology 3:468–472.

Vaughan, G. M., and R. H. T. Thompson.
1961 "New Zealand children's attitudes toward Maoris." Journal of Abnormal and Social Psychology 62:701–704.

Wallen, R.
1943 "Individuals' estimates of group opinion." Journal of Social Psychology 17: 269–274.

Waly, P., and S. W. Cook.
1965 "Effect of attitude on judgments of plausibility." Journal of Personality and Social Psychology 2:745–749.
1966 "Attitude as a determinant of learning and memory: A failure to confirm." Journal of Personality and Social Psychology 4:280–288.

Watson, G. B.
1925 "The measurement of fair-mindedness." Teachers College Contribution to Education no. 176. New York: Teachers College, Columbia University.

Webb, E. J., D. T. Campbell, R. D. Schwartz, and L. Sechrest.
1966 Unobtrusive Measures : Nonreactive Research in the Social Sciences. Chicago: Rand McNally.

Weschler, I. R.
1950a "An investigation of attitudes toward labor and management by means of the error-choice method." Journal of Social Psychology 32:51–62.
1950b "A follow-up study on the measurement of attitudes toward labor and management by means of the error-choice method." Journal of Social Psychology 32:63–69.
1951 "Problems in the use of indirect methods of attitude measurements." Public Opinion Quarterly 15:133–138.

Weschler, I. R., and R. Bernberg.
1950 "Indirect methods of attitude measurement." International Journal of Opinion and Attitude Research 4:209–229.

Westfall, R. L., H. W. Boyd, and D. T. Campbell.
1957 "The use of structured techniques in motivation research." Journal of Marketing 22:134–139.

Williams, J. E.
1964 "Connotations of color names among Negroes and Caucasians." Perceptual and Motor Skills 18:721–731.

Williams, R. M. Jr.
1947 The Reduction of Intergroup Tensions. New York: Social Science Research Council Bulletin no. 57.

Wolff, H. A., C. E. Smith, and H. A. Murray.
1934 "The psychology of humor; 1. a study of race disparagement jokes." Journal of Abnormal and Social Psychology 28:341–365.

Zeligs, R.
1937 "Racial attitudes of children." Sociological and Social Research 21:361–371.

CHAPTER 21

A Projective Method for the Study of Attitudes*

HAROLD M. PROSHANSKY

There is an abundance of information at hand regarding social attitudes, their intensities, their interrelations, and their dependence upon background factors (1; 2). On the other hand, there is a dearth of information as to their relation to character structure, e.g., their reciprocal relation with perceptual and with motor habits. In particular, there is very little clear information as to the relation between verbally expressed attitudes on social issues and the underlying dynamics of individual personality. Since the projective methods have been developed chiefly for the purpose of defining unconscious dynamics as related to immediate attitude and conduct, it may appear reasonable to develop a projective procedure for this express purpose. To do so would necessitate the utilization, on the one hand, of a reliable and valid indicator of attitude of the type familiar to us through

attitude scales and, on the other hand, to press into service a projective technique suitable for those subjects whose attitudes are in question. This would be a continuation of our earlier study demonstrating the influence of affective experience upon perception (6); individual affective organization would be expected to influence both perceived and verbally experienced attitudes.

Accordingly, we made use of an attitude scale devised by T. M. Newcomb (5) to investigate attitudes towards organized labor, and of a method derived from the Murray Thematic Apperception Test (3; 4). Our hypothesis was that extreme groups, i.e., those inclining towards strongly pro-labor or anti-labor attitudes, would reveal their social orientation through their manner of report upon pictures of social conflict situations. Since the Murray cards were not primarily designed for the study of controversial social issues as such, we culled through magazines and newspapers to make up our own list of standard pictures. A group of subjects sorted the pictures into various categories, those being selected which in the judgment of three judges were ambiguous with respect to outcome as far as labor was concerned, i.e., indicating neither victory nor defeat for the labor

From Harold M. Proshansky, "A projective method for the study of attitudes," *Journal of Abnormal and Social Psychology*, 1943, *38*, 393–395. Copyright 1943 by the American Psychological Association, and reproduced by permission of the author and publisher.

* The assistance of Otto Klineberg and Gardner Murphy is gratefully acknowledged; our thanks are due also to Sherman Ross, Stanley Seeman, Edward Jerome, and Etta Proshansky for their assistance in the conduct of the experiment.

cause. A few other pictures having nothing to do with labor were added to disguise our purpose.

The subjects of our study were male college students selected from two institutions, the one group known to be markedly pro-labor, the other markedly anti-labor in general orientation. There were 17 subjects from College A, anti-labor, and 18 from College B, pro-labor. The age range was 20–23. We secured from each individual in each group a response to the items of the Newcomb scale. The scale brought out sharply the attitude trends of which we were already aware, but served also to indicate individual differences. The two groups are significantly distinct by the conventional criteria.

At a later date the pictures were presented one at a time by means of slides before each of the groups. Upon the completion of each five-second exposure, the subjects were instructed to write two and a half minutes. The instructions were as follows:

You will be shown a number of slides exposed for a short period of time. Examine each one carefully, and then give a detailed account of what you think the picture represents. If you wish, make up a story about each picture. You will be allowed only 2½ minutes to write your response, so answer as fast as you can. Although the exposure of each picture will be short, do your best and try to remember as much of the picture as you can. In any event, whether you give your impression or tell a story, be brief, be accurate, and don't lag.

The method clearly permitted autistic distortion at the time of the original perception, or retrospective falsification as attitude got in its work upon memory, or sheer elaboration of the meaning of the picture, consciously going beyond anything that the picture offered.

The quantitative results indicate very considerable agreement of the attitude scale and the picture responses as evaluated by three judges, all of whom were professional personnel workers. In group A the correlation of the two methods is .87; in group B, .67. (The

CR of the difference between the two r's as determined by Fisher's z is not significant.) We have then preliminary evidence that the perception and interpretation of the pictures serves adequately for group purposes as an indicator of the attitudes which appear in the Newcomb scale.

The present data do not indicate to what degree the attitudinal factors dominate the original *perception* of the picture during the exposure. Rather, they throw light upon that type of life situation in which all three of the distorting factors mentioned above are manifest, the conflict item being perceived with a bias in the first place, but the bias leading to conscious and unconscious elaborations in which memory and report are involved. Two examples will serve to show this intermixture.

Home of a man on relief—shabby—dresses poorly. Scene is probably in a shack down south. Also might be the home of some unemployed laborer. Horrible housing conditions. Why don't the government provide for these people. The ordinary worker is always forgotten and allowed to rot.

Picture of one room, very messy, stove in the center, woman on the left, man standing next to stove, couple of children near them. This is a room of what we call "poor people." They seem to be messy, sloppy people, who seem to enjoy dwelling in their own trash.

Subsequent research may proceed in either of two directions: (1) the development of the method in the direction of naturalness, approximating more and more the life situations under which cognitive functions are distorted by affect in a complex multi-functional form; (2) greater restriction of the problem, i.e., "artificial" simplification of the processes. An example of the former would be the use of motion pictures of street scenes which are to be explained to someone else 24 hours later; an example of the latter would be the present procedure but with limitation to two seconds' exposure, the report being made by a check or one-word response while the picture is still on the screen, the aim being to get perceptual distortion with as little opportunity for memory distortion as possible.

It should be added that the method as described proved rich indeed in material for clinical insights and interpretation. Both the content of the individual's bias and its relation to the total personality should be discernible in the analysis of a variety of attitude reports as gleaned by a picture method of this general type.

REFERENCES

1. Allport, G. W.
   1935 "Attitudes." Pp. 798–845 in C. Murchison (ed.), Handbook of Social Psychology. Worcester: Clark University Press.
2. Fromme, A.
   1941 "On the use of certain qualitative methods of attitude research: a study of opinion on the methods of preventing war." Journal of Social Psychology 13:429–439.
3. Morgan, C. D., and H. A. Murray.
   1935 "A method of investigating fantasies." Archives of Neurology and Psychiatry 34:289–306.
4. Murray, H. A.
   1938 Explorations in Personality. New York: Oxford University Press. Pp. 530–545.
5. Newcomb, T. M.
   1939 "Labor unions as seen by their members: an attempt to measure attitudes." Pp. 313–338 in G. W. Hartmann and T. M. Newcomb (eds.), Industrial Conflict. New York: Cordon.
6. Proshansky, H., and G. Murphy.
   1942 "The effects of reward and punishment on perception." Journal of Psychology 13:295–305.

CHAPTER 22 Prejudice and Aggression: A Study of Specific Social Schemata[1,2]

JAMES L. KUETHE

In recent investigations Kuethe (1962a, 1962b; Kuethe and Stricker, 1963) showed that Ss use specific social schemata to organize human figures in a free response situation. These schemata have high commonality and are determined by the content of a given group of figures. One of the most basic schemata places human figures together and does not allow non-human figures to intervene. When Ss reconstruct a social configuration they err in placing human figures too close together. The reconstruction of non-social displays is relatively accurate.

When a person is prejudiced against a particular group, he may employ schemata that a person who was not prejudiced would not use. Specifically, it is predicted that the popular schema that groups *all* people together will not be employed by a given individual if some of the people form a sub-group toward which the individual is prejudiced. When a

prejudiced individual is free to organize a group of human figures, he may employ schemata that subgroup in a manner consistent with his prejudice. One aim of the present series of investigations was to use the technique for the study of social schemata developed by Kuethe (1962a) to examine the schemata used by individuals differing in prejudice toward Negroes.

A second objective was to study the arousal of aggressive schemata and the relationship between the ease of arousal of schemata of prejudice and schemata of aggression. Some theorists have regarded prejudice as a function of variations in aggressive tendency. One view is that an individual reduces his hostility by displacing it, in the form of prejudice, upon some minority group which is helpless.

Lindzey (1950a, 1950b) tested the proposition that "Individuals high in minority group prejudice will show more evidence of outwardly directed aggressive tendency than those low in minority group prejudice." The measures of aggressive tendency and prejudice were based on verbal responses to various tests and scales. The experimental test of this proposition did not reach statistical significance.

The felt figure technique provides a non-verbal measure of social schemata. A major

Reprinted with permission of author and publisher: James L. Kuethe, Prejudice and aggression: a study of specific social schemata. *Perceptual and Motor Skills,* 1964, *18,* 107–115.

[1] The author wishes to express his appreciation to Richard J. Coleman, Michael J. Golden, and Daniel R. Solin for their assistance.

[2] This investigation represents one part of a project supported by the Carnegie Corporation of New York.

aim of the present investigation was to relate schemata of prejudice and aggression expressed with the felt figure technique to traditional verbal measures of prejudice and aggression schemata.

EXPERIMENT I

Method

Ss were 74 male undergraduates who performed the required tasks individually.

A piece of blue felt, 2 yards by 1½ yards, was stretched on a wall of the experimental room. On each trial S was given a group of human figures cut from felt and was told to place them on the blue felt field in any man-

ner he wished. The nap of the felt permitted the figures to cling wherever they were placed. The main advantage of the technique is that the figures may be placed anywhere on the field and in any orientation. When the figures are removed, no mark is left on the field that could influence future trials.

The complete lack of restraint on the nature of the response, permits the full operation of whatever schema is prepotent. S can either place the figures at random on the field or he can organize his response on the basis of some schema. Response sets of all varieties are permitted expression when people must perform in an ambiguous situation.

Each S placed three groups of figures on the field. The three groups are shown in Figures 1 and 2; they were (1) two men cut from black felt and two men cut from white felt; (2) two men cut from black felt and a

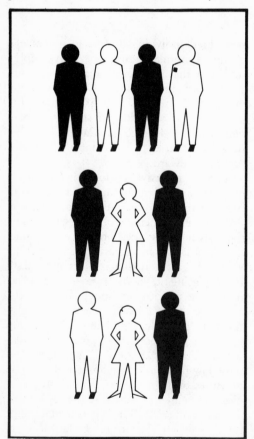

Figure 1. Typical organizations of the sets of the white and black figures that did not segregate the figures by color.

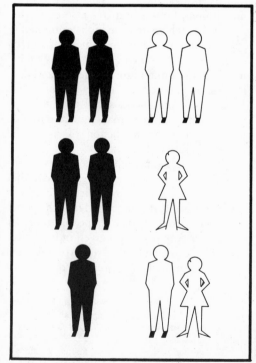

Figure 2. Typical organizations of the white and black figures that segregated the figures by color.

woman cut from white felt; (3) a man and a woman cut from white felt and a man cut from black felt. The figures were between 7 and 10 inches tall.

The order in which the sets of objects were placed on the field was randomized for each S to control for any influence that one set of objects might have on the reaction to another set. After S had placed the objects on the field, E recorded the relative placement of the objects. E then removed the objects from the field and gave S the next set of objects.

The Negro sub-scale of the Ethnocentrism Scale (Adorno, *et al.*, 1950) was administered to each S at the end of the experiment.

Results

The organizations of the human figures could be classified as to whether the black and white human figures were sub-grouped apart by color or grouped together with the figures alternated by color. Figure 1 shows organizations of the sets of black and white figures that did not segregate the black figures away from the white figures. Typical organizations that segregated the black figures away from the white figures are shown in Figure 2.

The number of organizations that grouped the figures apart by color was determined for each S which yielded a score of 0, 1, 2, or 3. Each S was also classified as to whether his score was above or below the group median score on the Negro sub-scale of the Ethnocentrism Scale.

Table 1 shows the classification of Ss on the basis of whether they gave 0 or 1 vs 2 or 3

TABLE 1

FREQUENCY OF USE OF 0 OR 1 VS 2 OR 3 SUB-GROUPING BY COLOR SCHEMATA AND SCORING ABOVE OR BELOW MEDIAN ON THE NEGRO SUB-SCALE

Sub-grouping by Color Schemata	Negro Sub-scale	
	Below Median	Above Median
(0,1)	32	9
(2,3)	5	28

"segregated" organizations and whether they scored above or below the group median on the Negro sub-scale of the Ethnocentrism Scale. The relation between using sub-grouping by color schemata and the ethnocentrism sub-scale score was significant ($\chi^2 = 26.4$, $p < .001$).

EXPERIMENT II

Method

The method in Exp. II was the same as that in Exp. I except that the groups of figures placed by Ss were different. In this experiment all of the figures were cut from yellow felt.

Each S placed three groups of figures on the felt. The three groups are shown in Fig-

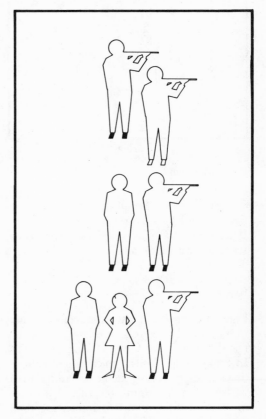

Figure 3. Typical organizations that minimized the aggressive theme.

ures 3 and 4; they were (1) two men with rifles; (2) a man with a rifle and a man without a rifle; (3) a man with a rifle, a man without a rifle, and a woman.

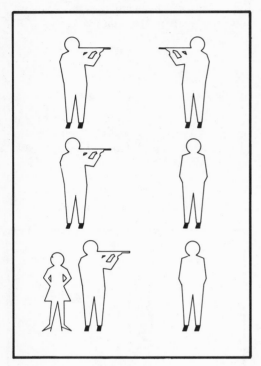

Figure 4.   Typical organizations that used an aggressive theme.

There were 50 Ss, all of whom had participated in Exp. I. At the conclusion of Exp. II the Rosenzweig Picture-Frustration Study was administered to all Ss.

Results

Figure 3 shows typical organizations that minimized the aggressive theme, given the fact that at least one figure was aiming a rifle. In Figure 4 are shown typical organizations that use an aggressive theme where the man with the rifle is aiming the rifle at another member of the group. It is interesting that, while many Ss employed schemata where the man was aiming the rifle at both the other

man and the woman or at the other man alone, no S allowed the man with the rifle to aim at the woman alone.

Each S was given a score of 0, 1, 2, or 3 depending upon how many aggressive schemata he employed in the free placement of the figures.

The Ss' Rosenzweig Picture-Frustration Study responses were scored by two independent judges for number of extrapunitive responses. Ss were classified as above or below the median in number of aggressive responses.

Table 2 shows the relationship between

TABLE 2

FREQUENCY OF USE 0 OR OF 1 VS 2 OR 3 AGGRESSION SCHEMATA AND SCORING ABOVE OR BELOW MEDIAN IN EXTRAPUNITIVE RESPONSES ON ROSENZWEIG P-F STUDY

Aggression Schema	Rosenzweig P-F Study Extrapunitive Responses	
	Below Median	Above Median
(0,1)	19	7
(2,3)	6	18

extrapunitive aggressive verbalizations on the Rosenzweig test and 0 or 1 vs. 2 or 3 aggressive schemata in the figure organizations. The relationship was significant ($\chi^2 = 9.7$, $p < .01$). The use of 0 or 1 vs. 2 or 3 aggressive schemata was not significantly different from the use of 0 or 1 vs. 2 or 3 prejudice schemata ($\chi^2 = 0.24$, $p > .05$).

The relationship between scores on the Ethnocentrism sub-scale and scores on the Rosenzweig test was not significant by a median test ($\chi^2 = 1.11$, $p > .05$).

EXPERIMENT III

Method

Exp. III was designed to explore the application of aggression schemata in two extreme situations; a situation where aggression would be highly appropriate and a situation where aggression would be highly inappropriate. Using the free placement procedure as in Exps. I and II, one hundred Ss placed two groups of figures; they were (1) a man with rifle, woman, and bear and (2) a man with rifle, and child.

Results

The placements of the set containing man with rifle, woman, and bear are shown in Figure 5. The "conventional" schema of

Figure 5. Organizations of the man, woman, and bear set of figures. At the top, the popular organization (89 Ss); in the middle, an "imaginative" organization (8Ss); at the bottom, a bizzare organization (3 Ss).

woman behind man who is shooting at bear was employed by 89 Ss. The much more "imaginative" schema that has the man saving the woman who is at the mercy of the bear was used by 8 Ss. Three Ss gave bizarre re-

sponses (i.e., man aiming his rifle at the woman).

The set containing the man with rifle and the child was usually organized with the child standing behind the man (93 Ss) or under the rifle in front of the man (5 Ss). Only 2 Ss placed the figures with the man aiming the rifle at the child.

Of the one hundred Ss, only three failed to employ a schema that had the man aiming his rifle at the bear and only two Ss allowed the man to aim his rifle at the child.

DISCUSSION

Prejudice

Racial or religious prejudice is based on the application of specific subgrouping schemata. When individuals are thought of as "set apart" in a group, it is very difficult to apply other schemata when thinking about them. If, for example, a person thinks of a racial group as a group separate from his own, he is unlikely to inter-rank persons from that group with those from his own group on any one dimension, e.g., intelligence. He is more likely to consider the entire "other group" less intelligent than his own.

Those Ss with high scores on the Negro sub-scale of the Ethnocentrism Scale employed sub-grouping schemata when organizing the groups of white and black figures. Ss that grouped all of the figures together had low scores on the attitude scale. It may not be that Ss who group the black figures separate from the white figures are prejudiced per se against the black figures. An alternate hypothesis is that the prejudiced individual tends to employ grouping schemata in general; that is, he is more categorical in his thinking.

Those organizations where the figures are segregated by color involve the application of specific schemata. Pilot studies have shown that a woman figure is placed between two men figures by almost all Ss when the figures are cut from the same color felt. In the present study those Ss with low scores on the prejudice scales reacted to the black and white figures by applying the same schemata that Ss use when the figures are all the same color. The low prejudice Ss treated the figures as though color was unimportant as a basis for organization.

The tendency to group people together permits them to be considered together and inter-ranked on many dimensions. The tendency to sub-group people on any basis, including race and religion, prevents them from being brought together and compared individually. When different groups are brought together, e.g., in the army, prejudices are often weakened as the artificial creation of one group allows the prejudiced person to make individual comparisons.

A person may be identified as prejudiced toward a specific group when he possesses specific schemata revealed by both verbalizations and non-verbal organizations which become aroused when he thinks about that group.

Aggression

The present investigations support Lindzey's finding (1950a) of no significant relationship between general aggressive tendencies and minority group prejudice. As Lindzey has pointed out, there is always the possibility that being prejudiced reduces hostility so that prejudiced individuals have no more aggressiveness left over that can be measured than do non-prejudiced individuals. However, this is a matter of speculation.

A central result of this series of studies was the finding of general aggressive tendencies that are revealed by both verbalizations (extrapunitive responses on the Rosenzweig test) and non-verbal organizations (the felt figure technique). The results suggest that, since the felt figure technique does not require a reaction to frustration, a general readiness to employ aggressive schemata was being measured.

The correlation with extrapunitive verbalization seems to indicate that extrapunitive verbalizations reflect a general trait of the individual and are not necessarily a specific reaction to frustration. This is not to deny that frustration probably helps arouse the aggressive pattern.

Some aggression schemata were acceptable while others were not. It was not acceptable for the man to aim his rifle at the woman unless the other man was placed with her nor was it acceptable for the man to aim his rifle at the child. The effect of the culture is apparent in these taboos. It was highly acceptable for the man to aim his rifle at the bear; this schema had almost complete commonality.

While most Ss placed the woman in back of the man who was aiming at the bear, a few Ss had the man saving the woman who was at the mercy of the bear. This latter organization employs the same generic schema but in a much more creative way. It may be that people appreciate some organizations, for example, in art, because they possess and as a result can relate to the generic schema. At the same time they may be intrigued by the specific creative way in which the generic schema is presented.

In general, it was found that prejudice and aggression are revealed by both the verbal behavior of Ss and by the free organizations they produce with social objects. The social schema aroused by specific social stimuli determines both an individual's verbal and non-verbal behavior. The fundamental social schema causes social verbal units relevant to the schema to be encoded in relationships consistent with the schema. Once a verbal element is encoded, the schema provides its associative relation to other elements, both verbal and non-verbal, within the schema.

REFERENCES

Adorno, T. W., E. Frenkel-Brunswik, D. J. Levinson, and R. N. Sanford.
   1950 The Authoritarian Personality. New York: Harper.
Kuethe, J. L.
   1962a "Social schemas." Journal of Abnormal and Social Psychology 64:31–38.
   1962b "Social schemas and the reconstruction

of social object displays from memory."
Journal of Abnormal and Social Psy-
chology 65:71–74.
Kuethe, J. L., and G. Stricker.
  1963   "Man and woman: social schemata of
         males and females." Psychological Re-
         ports 13:655–661.
Lindzey, G.

1950a "Differences between the high and
       low in prejudice and their implications
       for a theory of prejudice." Journal of
       Personality 19:16–40.
1950b "An experimental examination of the
       scapegoat theory of prejudice." Journal
       of Abnormal and Social Psychology
       45:296–309.

CHAPTER 23   Measuring Attitudes by Error-Choice: An Indirect Method

KENNETH R. HAMMOND*

INTRODUCTION

There can be little dispute with the growing restlessness over present methods of attitude measurement (4). Impressed with the results of *projective techniques* used in personality diagnosis, social psychologists show signs of seeing possibilities in this method, or at least, in approaches to it. This paper will be concerned with the exploratory development and application of a method which, while not deserving the term projective, might at least be termed "indirect."

Since much of the difficulty with present methods of attitude measurement lies in the trouble authors have in deciding just what it is they are trying to measure, the writer suggests we put to use experimentally derived, rather than logically derived, concepts concerning attitudes and consider an attitude as a (nonprimary) *source of energy, or an affective state, capable of producing error in perception and recall,* recognizing that the

From Kenneth R. Hammond, "Measuring attitudes by error-choice: an indirect method." *Journal of Abnormal and Social Psychology,* 1948, *43,* 38–48. Copyright 1948 by the American Psychological Association, and reproduced by permission of the author and publisher.

* From the Psychological Laboratory of the University of California. This study was carried out under the supervision of Professor R. C. Tryon.

nature of this source of energy or affective state is still only roughly delineated.

The trap of definition will be avoided, then, by being concerned only with the *effect* of attitude, and we shall leave the problem of definition to those who are willing to be concerned with it. The particular effect with which we shall be concerned here will be the systematic *error in perception and recall.* The technique to be developed here strives to leave the subject no alternative save error, eliminating reality as a factor, thereby affording a measure of the constancy and direction of the error.

EXPERIMENTAL BACKGROUND

The fact that perception may be influenced or that systematic errors may be induced has long been established. Sherif (8, 9, 10) has surveyed the literature and noted the evidence concerning the constancy of the direction of error in experimental situations. I quote:

The literature is rife with data which support the formulations reached from our survey of general psychology; that perception and judgment are selective and operate within a referential framework, ... once established these frames and points of reference serve as anchorages for perception and judgment.

Sherif has concerned himself with this problem in connection with the autokinetic effect produced by a stationary pin point of light in a dark room (8). His experience with this phenomenon leads him to this point of view:

The first stage of attitude formation—in the most complicated social situations as well as in a restricted laboratory experiment—is a perceptual stage.

Moreover,

in many cases the objective set is dominant in the situation. There are cases, however, in which this objective determination is lacking, thus allowing internal factors such as attitudes, subjective norms, and values to play the dominant role in organization of the perceptual field. (9)

The "cases in which this objective determination is lacking" certainly occur in the field of social psychology.

Sherif's work is important not only because of his own experiments but because he has brought to focus a great portion of data from experimental psychology in such a manner as to provide a valuable tool for social psychology.[1]

For our purposes the importance of the many previous laboratory experiments is this: The field of social events and personalities presents complex and confusing stimuli to the observer. If we know that the perception of such stimuli may be distorted by social factors, we then have the possibility of utilizing this phenomenon.

As for selective forgetting, Edwards has surveyed the literature and concludes that experiences which harmonize with an existing frame of reference will not only be learned and remembered better than conflicting experiences but that experiences that are in opposition will be recast and thus assimilated more rapidly, and the chances are slight that conflicting experiences will cause serious

reorganization. Edwards' own experiments support these conclusions (1, 2).[2]

The significance of these prior experiments for our purpose is this: The error-choice method used here provokes the subject to draw upon his memory of events in order to decide which answer is "correct." Since the field from which he does draw is ambiguous and confused at best, we know from the above evidence that the subject will select those pseudo-facts from memory which fit his frame of reference or support his established premise. Recall under these circumstances can be demonstrated to be selective, i.e., nonrepresentational, therefore erroneous.

The instrument for measuring the effect of attitude, then, will make use of these two dynamics: (1) the distortion of perception and (2) the selective recall of the previous perceptual experience.

A general statement of the problem can now be made as follows: We are attempting to measure the effect of attitude, herein considered to be a (nonprimary) source of energy, or affective state, capable of distorting perception and recall with reference to an unstructured, ambiguous world of social events, by measuring the constancy of the direction of the error into which the respondent will be forced.

Questionnaire Development

Three series of items were presented under the guise of an "information test."[3] One se-

---

[1] Proshansky and Murphy (7), Wallen (13), Zillig (16), and Thorndike (11) have also contributed positive and interesting results which bear on the problems of social dynamics affecting perception.

[2] Further studies may be found in articles by Levine and Murphy (3), Watson and Hartmann (14), and Wallen (12). See Cantril and Sherif (10) for an extensive survey and bibliography.

[3] See Newcomb (6), who discovers the relationship of an information test to attitudes. He notes that a certain information test was difficult, thus more guessing was to be expected and "the direction of the guessing is altogether likely to be weighted toward the subject's attitude. If this reasoning is correct, the . . . test tends to become itself an attitude test."

See also Myrdal (5): "In most cases, the indirect analysis of the valuation sphere, through the study of the deviations of beliefs from true knowledge, is likely to reach deeper than does the direct analysis. An individual continually tends to arrange his valuations so that

ries of eight questions was made up with alternate answers equidistant from the truth in opposite directions [Example: "Average weekly wage of the war worker in 1945 was (1) $37, (2) $57"]. In this case the facts were determinable. The second series of 12 questions also offered alternative opposing answers [Example: "Russia's removal of heavy industry from Austria was (1) legal, (2) illegal"]. In this case, the facts were indeterminable. There was, then, a total of 20 of these two types of questions in each test. It was the responses to these items, hereafter referred to as "nonfactual" items, that were scored. The third series of questions consisted of 20 straight information items, which were interspersed among the 20 items mentioned above. These will be referred to as "factual" items and were introduced in order to aid in disguising the test.

One test concerned Russia and consisted of 20 factual and 20 nonfactual questions. A second test concerned Labor-Management and also consisted of 20 factual and 20 nonfactual questions.

The subjects were told that these were information tests, that they would probably not know the answers to all the questions, that when they were in doubt they should guess, and emphasis was placed on working as rapidly as possible.

In constructing an item the principal requirement was to eliminate reality, the truth of the matter, as a factor and thus *force the respondent into a choice of errors* and still make the item sound like an information item. Reality was eliminated (1) by putting the answers equidistant from the truth in opposite directions and (2) by using questions where the truth is indeterminable and putting the answers to opposite extremes.

The original selection of the items was based principally on "hunch." Since these two controversial subjects, Russia and Labor-Management, have given rise to a maze of

contradictory and confusing "fact" the writer could only guess *which* "facts" would provide items that would sound like information items and at the same time afford logical justifications for a pro- or anti-premise. The check on the writer's selection of items was afforded by the following validation procedure.

For example, if a group of people whose ways of life are such that one would expect a bias *in favor* of Labor and Russia makes constant errors in a *pro-* direction on the items, we then have a certain substantiation of the "hunch" that these items would provoke positive errors. If we go further, and find that a group of people whose ways of life are such that one would expect a bias *against* Russia and Labor makes constant errors in an *anti-*direction, then we have a double substantiation of the "hunch" concerning the items—they provoke constant errors in opposite directions for groups with opposing bias. This was chosen as the criterion for an item: Does it or does it not discriminate between groups with opposing bias, i.e., does the item discriminate between "known groups"?

The writer's hypothesis in connection with the instrument developed, then, was this: Given two groups of individuals whose ways of life indicate beyond all reasonable doubt that they have opposing frames of reference concerning Labor and Russia, the members of these groups will err systematically in opposite directions. In statistical terms this means that the means of these groups will be significantly different in the direction predicted, that is, the pro-Labor group will have a high mean score, the anti-Labor group will have a low mean score, and the same in connection with the Russia form.

Validation Groups

The experimental validation groups consisted of the following: (1) a group whose ways of life were such that one would expect a bias in favor of Labor and Russia, consisting of 18 adults who are employed by a major labor organization in clerical and semi-pro-

they may be presented in an acceptable form. But in his beliefs concerning social reality—which are shaped to give the appearance of rational organization to his morals—he reveals himself."

fessional positions (hereafter referred to as *Union*), (2) a group whose ways of life were such that one would expect a bias against Labor and Russia. This latter group was made up of two businessmen's luncheon clubs. One club, hereafter referred to as *Bus 1*, was made up of 23 middle-aged businessmen whose income varied from $10,000 a year up. They were, in general, employers. The second club, hereafter referred to as *Bus 2*, was fostered by *Bus 1* and was composed of 19 younger businessmen in their thirties.

To sum up, the subjects consisted of a group of people who work for a labor organization and two groups of people gathered together on the basis of having common business interests.

Results

The two filled-out questionnaires, Labor and Russia, each include 20 non-factual items to be scored. A priori determined positive (or pro-) systematic errors were given a score value of one on each item; negative errors, no value. Thus, a high score indicates a pro- bias, or positive systematic error. A low score indicates the reverse.

The Labor questionnaire means and *sigmas* are presented in Table 1.

TABLE 1

LABOR QUESTIONNAIRE

Group	Mean	SD	N
Bus 1	8.21	3.45	23
Bus 2	9.93	3.00	19
Union	18.1	.84	18

The Russia questionnaire means and *sigmas* are presented in Table 2.

Fisher's test for significance of differences of means between small samples shows no significant difference between groups *Bus 1* and *Bus 2*. However, it is interesting that the questionnaire was able to elicit a difference in means in the direction anticipated between a more structured, older, business group and

TABLE 2

RUSSIA QUESTIONNAIRE

Group	Mean	SD	N
Bus 1	6.52	4.47	23
Bus 2	7.26	3.89	19
Union	16.5	1.96	18

a less homogeneous, younger group. On the basis of no significant difference between these two groups, however, they were combined and compared with the labor group.

The means and *sigmas*, as well as the critical ratios for these two groups (Bus_{com} and Union) are seen in Tables 3 and 4.

TABLE 3

LABOR QUESTIONNAIRE

Group	M	SD	N	CR
Union	18.1	.84	18	11.3
Bus_{com}*	8.9	3.30	42	

* Bus 1 and 2 combined.

TABLE 4

RUSSIA QUESTIONNAIRE

Group	M	SD	N	CR
Union	16.5	1.96	18	12.5
Bus_{com}	6.78	4.06	42	

Concerning validation of items see Figure 1 for a statistical and graphical presentation. Each item is plotted for the percentage of labor and business group subjects answering the item in the same way, i.e., making an error in the same direction. For example, on Item 33 on the Labor questionnaire, *100 per cent* of the Union group answered in a pro-labor manner while only *23 per cent* of Bus_{com} answered it in a pro-labor manner. On Item 43 on the Russia questionnaire *83 per cent* of the Bus_{com} group answered in an anti-Russian manner while only *21 per cent* of the Union group answered in an anti-Russian manner. Those items falling outside the dot-

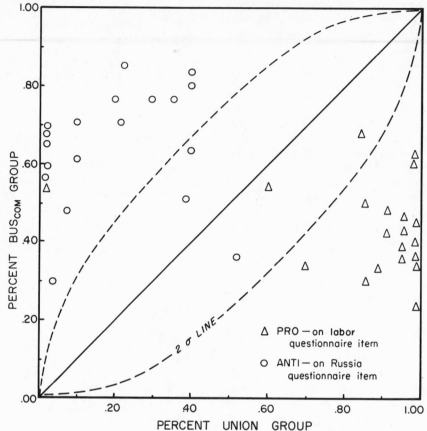

Figure 1. Item Validity: Percentage of Criterion Groups Answering "Nonfactual" Items the Same Way [Redrawn by K. R. Hammond, 1969].

ted line show a difference in error-choice significant at the 5-per-cent level.[4]

[4] The locus of the dotted 2-*sigma* line is plotted from points derived from a formula developed by George Kuznets and R. C. Tryon of the University of California. The formula for the case sigma equals 2 is

$$P_2 = \frac{(N_2 p_1 + 2) \pm 2\sqrt{1 + p_1 q_1 \left(\dfrac{N_2}{N_1}\right)(N_1 + N_2 + 4)}}{N + 4}$$

where P_2 = point to be plotted an ordinate
P_1 = given point on abscissa
$q_1 = (1 - p_1)$
N_1 = No. of cases in group plotted on X axis.
N_2 = No. of cases in group plotted on Y axis.
This graphic method of determining significant differences is an analogue of that proposed by J. Zubin in "Note on a graphic method for determining the significant difference between group frequency," *J. educ. Psychol.*, 1936, p. 431–444, in which the procedure is a development of Zubin's C_1 equation (2, p. 432).

The ease with which high discriminatory values for items may be secured by this technique is impressive when one considers that selection of items was based principally on the writer's hunch. It should be noted that this summary treatment produced only 5 poor items out of 40.

Reliability coefficients were obtained by the split-half method from a sample made up of 10 cases from the Union group, 40 cases from the Bus$_{com}$ group, and 10 college students chosen at random from a large sample used as an experimental group under circumstances to be discussed later. These cases were used in an effort to obtain a heterogeneous sample somewhat representative of the population. The reliability coefficient obtained on the Labor questionnaire, corrected by the Spearman-Brown formula, was .78. On the Russia questionnaire the corrected reliability coefficient was .87.

SUMMARY

To summarize up to this point, an approach to attitude measurement was attempted by considering an attitude as a (nonprimary) source of energy, or an affective state, capable of producing error in perception and recall. We then dealt with this *effect* of attitude and ignored its ultimate nature.

Under the guise of an "information test" items were presented with alternate choices for answers, both choices being incorrect, either equidistant from the truth or truth being indeterminable. The subject was forced into error. This method is termed the "error-choice technique."

The question was then raised in the form of an hypothesis that the error-choice technique would elicit from "known groups" constant errors opposite in direction. The hypothesis was sustained to the extent that the mean errors in each group were found to be significantly different in the direction predicted. The difference was sufficiently great to justify our speaking of a positive systematic error for one group as against a negative systematic error for the other.

High reliability coefficients were obtained from a heterogeneous sample.

Suggestions for improving the technique are as follows:

1. The original selection of items should be based on a definite objective. Validation is not the only goal in connection with this technique. It should also provide a definite clue as to the prevailing set of "factual" justifications which a sample is using. The suggestion is made that, rather than selecting items by "hunch," one should make use of some type of content, or symbol analysis, such as White's "value-analysis" in selecting items (15.)

2. The test should be carefully disguised. Present experience indicates that perhaps two neutral items to one "nonfactual" item is necessary.

3. It is possible to offer more than two answers. It seems probable that tests constructed with four error-choices to provide for "intensity" of error would prove useful for scaling items.

4. Not mentioned above was the fact that, for purposes to be developed later, each factual item was paired with a "nonfactual" item, thus affording a bona fide information test on precisely the same material on which error-choices were based. It is thus possible with this technique to correlate the information level of a group with their systematic error-choices. The factual items used to disguise the test therefore need not be dead weight; rather, they make the instrument more productive.

This Technique in Relation to Test "Set"

Interest is increasingly becoming focused upon the problem of attitude test "set." It is the same problem that turned clinical psychologists from personality questionnaires to the use of projective techniques. The question is whether or not the subject is responding to the test items in terms of the test situation. Clinicians have learned that projective techniques have more often than not turned up dynamics that were rejected or denied by the subject in answer to direct questions. With this in mind, the question of whether or not the error-choice technique would evoke responses different from those evoked by a direct method was raised.

The problem was stated as follows: Will the error-choice technique evoke a different sort of response to the same item depending upon whether the items are presented as "information test" items or as "attitude test" items? Will the response be different under conditions of awareness from that under conditions of unawareness? That is, holding the item constant, will responses vary with a change in the respondent's "set" toward the test?

This problem was made subject to experiment in the following manner. The "information test" given to the validation groups was split into two forms. One form was that originally given to the validation groups, and was labeled "INFO." Form INFO again was given as an "information test." The other form contained the nonfactual items *separated* from and preceding the factual items, and was labeled "ATT-INFO."[5] The first part of ATT-INFO, containing the nonfactual items, was preceded by instructions to the effect that this was an "attitude test," that neither of the answers were correct, and that one should indicate his "attitude, his feeling" about the question, and instructions were given how to mark a pro- or anti- answer. The part containing the straight information items was preceded by instructions to the effect that this was an information test.[6]

These two forms were administered to a sample consisting of students in an elementary psychology class. Ninety-seven subjects received form INFO, 47 received form ATT-INFO.

Results—The response on each item under both forms is expressed graphically and statistically in Figure 2. By plotting the percentage of the subjects who answered a given item in the *same way* on both INFO and ATT-INFO, as in Figure 2, we can discover whether subjects responded to the error-choice technique (INFO) in the same manner in which they responded to the questionnaire which expressly calls for attitudes (ATT-INFO).

On the Labor questionnaire we find that the items tend to fall along the equal percent-

age line, and few fall outside the dotted (2-*sigma*) line. In other words, about the same percentage in each group answered *the same item in the same way*. The items are obviously positively correlated. It should be noted, however, that about one-third of the items do fall outside the 2-*sigma* line; that is, a change did occur in about one-third of the items significant at the 5-per-cent level.

On the Russia questionnaire, Figure 3, we find that more items are scattered away from the equal percentage line and that more of them show significant differences. In this case, the items appear somewhat negatively correlated. Responses to the same item tended to be different depending upon whether they were presented as part of an "attitude test" or as part of an "information test." In this instance, then, responses varied with awareness, with the "set" the respondents took toward the test situation.

Other concomitant effects of presenting the same item under a different test situation may be briefly stated: (1) The mean scores did not vary significantly. (2) Variability tends to increase on that error-choice form which produces the greater shift in responses. (3) Reliability, although low (.33 on the Labor form, .51 on the Russia form, both corrected by the Spearman-Brown formula), also tends to increase on the form which produces the greater shift in responses.

These low reliability coefficients, obtained under circumstances which ordinarily provide very high reliability coefficients, are provocative and lead the writer to offer his resultant hypothesis. *Reliability is a function of the control the subjects have over reproducing attitudes which they deem proper for a given test situation.* For example, if we handed our sample a slip of paper and asked the subjects to indicate whether they were pro- or anti- labor, would we not get a high reliability coefficient if we did the same thing a week later? Orthodox questionnaires resemble this situation insofar as they make the implication of each item clear to the subject. The error-choice technique, on the other hand, prevents control because the implica-

---

[5] Nonfactual items are the items upon which the error-choice scores were computed in connection with the validation groups. Factual items are the straight information items interspersed among the nonfactual items in order to aid in disguising the test.

[6] The order of the information questions and attitude questions was reversed on a third form given to the subjects for control purposes (INFO-ATT). No significant difference occurred between these forms, i.e., it made no difference in the mean score whether attitude items came first or last. However, the ATT-INFO form was used for comparative purposes since it is not preceded by a test, even though this does not appear to be a disturbing factor.

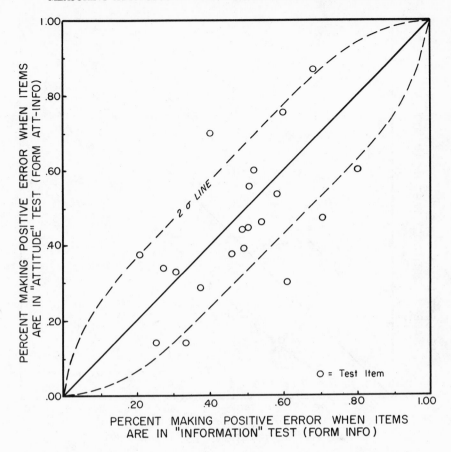

Figure 2.   Relationship between "Nonfactual" Items Given as Attitude Questions (Form ATT-INFO) and Given as Information Questions (Form INFO)—Labor Questionnaire [Redrawn by K. R. Hammond, 1969].

tions of the items are not clear. For a subject attempting control, this produces affect—and affect reduces reliability because it introduces an unstable variable.

Lest it be assumed that low reliability is a function of the items' subject matter, it should be reported that these same items presented in orthodox agree-disagree form produced reliability coefficients of .66 on the Labor questionnaire and .79 on the Russia questionnaire, corrected by the Spearman-Brown formula.

Since the error-choice form which elicited a shift in response produced the higher coefficient, it is suggested that greater disguise,

greater departure from orthodox methods, is the road to more *meaningful* high reliability coefficients.

Summary—To summarize the latter section, evidence was presented to the effect that (1) responses may differ for an item depending on whether that item is presented as an "attitude test" item or an "information test" item, (2) when this difference in response occurs, variability and reliability tend to increase on the error-choice form which evokes the difference, (3) reliability is low for error-choice forms given to a homogeneous college-student sample.

Since the error-choice technique is able to

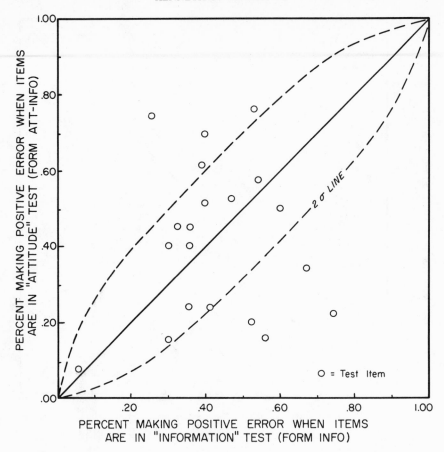

Figure 3. Relationship between "Nonfactual" Items Given as Attitude Questions (Form ATT-INFO) and Given as Information Questions (Form INFO)—Russia Questionnaire [Redrawn by K. R. Hammond, 1969].

shift responses, the author suggests that it is a technique adapted to the purpose of eliminating the factor of "attitude test set," inasmuch as the respondents are unaware of the implication of their error-choices. The implication of which they are unaware is that they are making the same error-choice that was demonstrated to be part of the systematic error-choice made by "known groups." The reader should not lose sight of the relationship this procedure bears to that of the projective techniques used in clinical psychology.

In conclusion, the writer hopes that the above material offers a technique which, given a portion of the time and consideration previous methods have received, should prove useful.

REFERENCES

1. Edwards, A. L.
   1942 "The retention of affective experiences: a criticism and restatement of the problem." Psychological Review 49:43–53.
2. Edwards, A. L.
   1941 "Political frames of reference as a factor influencing recognition." Journal of Abnormal and Social Psychology 36:34–64.
3. Levine, J. M., and G. Murphy.

1943   "Learning and forgetting controversial material." Journal of Abnormal and Social Psychology 38:
507–517.
4. McNemar, Q.
1946   "General review and summary:
opinion-attitude methodology."
Psychological Bulletin 43:289–369.
5. Myrdal, G.
1944   An American Dilemma. New
York: Harper.
6. Newcomb, T.
1946   "The influence of attitude climate
upon some determinants of information." Journal of Abnormal and
Social Psychology 41:291–303.
7. Proshansky, H., and G. Murphy.
1942   "Effect of reward and punishment
on perception." Journal of Psychology 13:295–305.
8. Sherif, M.
1936   Psychology of Social Norms. New
York: Harper.
9. Sherif, M.
1935   "A study of some social factors in
perception." Archives of Psychology No. 187.
10. Sherif, M., and H. Cantril.
1946   "Psychology of 'attitudes'." Part II
Psychological Review 53:1–24.
11. Thorndike, E. L.
1920   "A constant error in psychological
ratings." Journal of Applied Psychology 4:25–29.
12. Wallen, R.
1942   "Ego-involvement and selective
forgetting." Journal of Abnormal
and Social Psychology 37:20–39.
13. Wallen, R.

1940   "Individual estimates of group
opinion." Journal of Social Psychology 4:25–29.
14. Watson, W. S., and G. W. Hartmann.
1939   "The rigidity of a basic attitudinal
frame." Journal of Abnormal and
Social Psychology 34:314–335.
15. White, R. K.
1944   "Value analysis." Journal of Social
Psychology 19:351–358.
16. Zilling, M.
1928   Einstellung und Aussage. Zeit-
schrift für Psychologie 106:58–106.

APPENDIX

SAMPLE "NONFACTUAL" QUESTIONS FROM
"INFORMATION" TEST

(6) Financial reports show that out of every
dollar $\begin{Bmatrix} (1) & 16¢ \\ (2) & 3¢ \end{Bmatrix}$ is profit.

(17) Man-days lost because of strikes from
January to June, 1946, were
$\begin{matrix} (1) & 34.5 \\ (2) & 98.6 \end{matrix}$ million.

(20) Most unions have initiation fees
$\begin{matrix} (1) & \text{over} \\ (2) & \text{under} \end{matrix}$ $35.

(44) Molotov is known in diplomatic circles for
his $\begin{matrix} (1) & \text{excellent} \\ (2) & \text{poor} \end{matrix}$ manners.

(54) There $\begin{matrix} (1) & \text{is} \\ (2) & \text{is not} \end{matrix}$ freedom of religion in
Russia.

(66) In most countries surrounding Russia
where Communists are now in the govern-
ment they have been $\begin{matrix} (1) & \text{duly elected.} \\ (2) & \text{appointed by} \\ & \text{Moscow.} \end{matrix}$

CHAPTER 24

Attitude and Structure as Factors in the Distortion of Reasoning[1]

DONALD THISTLETHWAITE

INTRODUCTION

Some progress has been made recently toward showing the effects of a variety of "sets" upon reasoning, but very little has been done which bears upon the questions, "Why does some reasoning differ greatly from reality while other reasoning does not?" "Why does an appropriate isolation of thought from wishes and desires occur in some individuals but not in others" (4, p. 288)? "What are the determinants in the psychological field for these differences?" The writer is aware of no systematic attempt to answer these questions, despite the fact that their solution is not only of considerable practical, but also of general theoretical, significance. One of the objects of this investigation is to obtain data bearing upon these questions.

From Donald Thistlethwaite, "Attitude and structure as factors in the distortion of reasoning," *Journal of Abnormal and Social Psychology*, 1950, *45*, 442–458. Copyright 1950 by the American Psychological Association, and reproduced by permission of the author and publisher.

[1] This study was done at the University of California in 1948 in partial fulfillment of requirements for the M.A. degree. The writer wishes to acknowledge his debt to Professor David Krech and to Dr. Else Frenkel-Brunswik for guidance and suggestions, and to Professors D. K. Adams, H. G. Canady, S. C. Eriksen, E. L. Hartley, R. H. Waters, and G. B. Vetter for assistance in obtaining samples.

Previous studies on the effect of attitude upon reasoning have either relied upon questionnaire material used in conjunction with syllogistic tests (7, 9) or have failed to include control groups with which the experimental subjects could be compared (11, 12). The experiment to be reported includes a number of control groups, and unlike previous studies utilizes logical material other than syllogisms. Non-syllogistic forms of inference were employed because it was felt (1) that the latter may be made more representative of the varied forms which inference commonly assumes, and (2) that propositions of the A, E, I, or O type (to which the syllogism is limited) are peculiarly conducive to "atmosphere effects." Such effects operate concomitantly with those arising from the attitudes and beliefs of the respondents hence some masking or opposition of competing response tendencies is involved. This difficulty is avoided somewhat with the material used here, since many of the propositions do not contain the quantification symbols "all", "some", or "no". To be sure some degree of quantification is always implied in any given statement; however, if left implicit it is much less likely to create an atmospheric set. With this material and with a more liberal sampling of students with differing attitudes and beliefs it was hoped that the hypothesis that attitude is a determinant of reasoning could be subjected to more conclusive tests.

Ambiguity in the perceptual field has been the object of investigation; see for example Bruner and Goodman (1) and Levine, Chein, and Murphy (10). However, no attempt has previously been made to consider the effect of defined degrees of "structure" upon reasoning. The usual practice in such perceptual experiments is for the experimenter arbitrarily to designate one set of materials as the more ambiguous or less highly structured, assuming that the assigned values do in fact enter into his subject's psychological field without inversion or distortion. The assumption is that what is well-structured for the experimenter is well-structured for the subject, or that a stimulus having a particular value of structure for one observer has a similar value for other observers. The difficulty with this approach is that we can never be sure that the results reflect the determinants operating in the subject's psychological field. Assimilation of certain effects under the operation of structural factors adds little to our understanding if we are not sure of the identity and reference of these factors.

Although the *degree* of structure a stimulus may have for a percipient has generally been recognized as an important variable in perception, there has been little, if any, explicit recognition of the possibility that structures may also vary in *direction*. For example, the fact that a given form of inference possesses a high degree of structure for a subject may be inferred from consistency of interpretation of the form upon repeated presentations. The fact that a form of inference possesses a certain direction of structure for a subject may be inferred from the predominance of one interpretation over others upon repeated presentation of the form in question. If the form is more frequently judged to be valid than invalid then the structure in the subject's psychological field is said to possess the direction of "leading to judgments of validity."

Since the object of experiment in this instance is to generalize to structures as operative in the subjects' psychological fields, designations of particular degrees and directions of structure have been made in terms of behavioral criteria. Very few investigators would be interested in limiting the generality of their findings to the class of structures "as perceived by experimenter X." Yet this is precisely the limitation imposed upon many findings by the procedure of arbitrarily assigning structural values to particular geographical stimuli.

METHOD

The Test Material

On the basis of several pre-tests administered to students at theUniversity of California, six forms of inference[2] ranging from easy to relatively hard levels of difficulty were selected. A preliminary test was constructed containing arguments the contents of which on a priori grounds were either high in emotional value (emotive items) or of low emotional value (neutral items). This was administered to a new sample of 121 students, and the results formed the basis upon which the final test was constructed. A measure of the "distortion" produced by attitudes and beliefs was available from differential responses to emotional and neutral items embodied in identical forms of inference. The distribution of differences between numbers of emotional and neutral errors for each subject thus was in effect a distribution of distortion scores. Those arguments intended to be highly emotive and found to be significantly discriminatory between the upper and lower quartiles of this distortion score distribution were re-

---

[2] A "form of inference," as used here, refers to a series of skeletal statement-forms composed of variables which becomes an argument when suitable substitutions are made for all the variables involved. For example, when substitutions are made for the variables p and q in the form of inference "If p then q, and not p; therefore not q" the following statement, or argument, may be obtained: "If this is a desirable neighborhood, then it is close to transportation services. This is not a desirable neighborhood. Therefore it is not close to transportation services."

tained. Of the items intended to be of neutral emotional value only those were retained which were in fact responded to similarly by both extremes of the above distribution. Additional emotional and neutral items were added, patterning them closely after those which already satisfied the above criteria.

The test material thus selected consisted of 72 arguments, 36 presumably of relatively neutral content, and 36 presumably containing statements and especially conclusions about which highly ethnocentric[3] respondents have strong attitudes and beliefs. Of these latter items, 12 deal with Negroes, 12 with Jews, 6 with the "proper role" of women, and 6 with various nationalistic themes. These contents were so distributed that there was an equal number of Negro, Jew, women, and "patriotic" arguments built about each of the six forms of inference.

Subjects were told that the series of items was designed to test reasoning ability; this belief was fostered by seemingly timing the performance of each individual. They were instructed to "determine whether the conclusion follows from the given statement or statements," and to indicate their judgments of validity by circling a "T" or "F" opposite each conclusion. The conclusions of the emotional items were designed so that ethnocentric subjects would judge them incorrectly thus getting a large number of errors on the 36 emotional items of the test. On the other hand, it was anticipated that anti-ethnocentric subjects, or those intolerant of prejudice, would judge these conclusions correctly, thus getting a small number of errors on this half of the test. For example, one argument dealing with Negroes was as follows:

---

[3] Ethnocentrism is indicated in the test by responses consistent with anti-Semitic and anti-Negro attitudes and beliefs, with a hierarchical conception of the relation between sexes which alleges that women ought not to encroach upon masculine prerogatives, and with certain invidious patriotic and nationalistic attitudes and beliefs. Evidence suggesting that these attitudes and beliefs tend to cluster together and constitute a type of personality pattern has been reported by Frenkel-Brunswik and Sanford (5) and Frenkel-Brunswik, Levinson, and Sanford (6).

Given: If production is important, then peaceful industrial relations are desirable. If production is important then it is a mistake to have Negroes for foremen and leaders over Whites.

Therefore: If peaceful industrial relations are desirable, then it is a mistake to have Negroes for foremen and leaders over Whites.

This argument is invalid and a subject who accepts the conclusion as following from the premises commits an error.

The neutral item which was approximately matched with the above argument with regard to sentence length, comprehensibility, and formal pattern was as follows:

Given: If the game is crucial then a large attendance is desirable. If the game is crucial then it is a mistake for the team members not to practice today.

Therefore: If a large attendance is desirable then it is a mistake for the team members not not practice today.

Neutral arguments like the foregoing whose contents refer to matters so prosaic as to seem trivial (or to unfamiliar and remote groups as in some of the other neutral arguments) are assumed to be judged almost entirely upon the basis of structural properties, and very little if at all on the basis of attitudes and beliefs. The test[4] thus consisted of 36 pairs of items matched so that they were formally identical and linguistically similar, but constructed so that they presumably differed in degree of emotive content. Subjects from a region in which ethnocentric attitudes and beliefs are common would then be expected to make a greater number of errors on the emotional items than on the matched neutral items. Similarly, subjects recruited from a social atmosphere in which prejudice is not sanctioned would then be expected to make a smaller number of errors on the emotional than on the neutral items.

By obtaining samples from several northern (or western), as well as southern uni-

---

[4] Unfortunately the length of the test precludes its full presentation here. . . .

TABLE 1

DESCRIPTION OF SUBJECTS

Group	N	Number of Men	Number of Women	University and State
1	101	60	41	New York University, New York
2	59	53	6	College of City of New York, New York
3	65	45	20	University of California, Berkeley, Calif.
4	84	39	45	Duke University, North Carolina
5	89	67	22	Vanderbilt University, Tennessee
6	87	58	29	West Virginia State College, West Virginia (all Negroes)
7	74	53	21	University of Arkansas, Arkansas
Totals	559	375	184	

versities, it was hoped to obtain groups from both types of social atmosphere. Table 1 shows how the 559 subjects were distributed among the 7 groups.

A Scale of Orders of Structure

I previously spoke of judgments of neutral arguments being made on the basis of structural properties. How is the structure of logical material to be described and measured? "Structure" as used here is a construct referring to an assumed entity operating in the psychological field at the time of the judgment or perception. Its attributes are measured by overt responses of the subject. Just as the structure of a stimulus figure may be inferred from the *perceived* patterning of the sense qualities of that figure, so the structure of a class of syllogisms may similarly be inferred from the *perceived* truth-value of that class when its members are expressed in non-emotive language. Arguments in markedly different formal patterns and contents may, being perceived similarly, give rise to similar structures. And conversely, the same form of inference may possess different structures for different observers. At the risk of repetition it is to be stressed that structure, as described here, is not to be identified with formal pattern, but is determined by behavioral criteria. The perceived truth-value of a form of inference, of course, refers to the subject's judg-

ments of the validity of that form, or to his judgments as to whether the conclusion follows from the premises, and does not involve the question of the truth or falsity of the particular statements comprising the premises and conclusion. For this reason it is important to specify that structure is to be measured solely by means of performance on neutral arguments, since it is only here that we can assume that judgments are relatively uncontaminated by attitudes and beliefs.

Just as the perception of a figure may deviate from the actual physical properties of the figure, similarly the perceived truth-value of an argument is not necessarily identical with the value which would be assigned by the logician. The person without logical training commonly manifests equivocality in his judgments of formal arguments by assigning contradictory judgments to the same form of inference presented at different times or in slightly different language (13). A single valid statement-form presented in six neutral arguments, as in the test material already described, may be judged valid on half the arguments and invalid on the other half. In such a case the perceived truth-value or structure would be considered ambiguous, or in the terminology to be used herein to have a structure of the third order. We may reformulate the foregoing by stating that the degree and direction of structure of a form of inference for any given individual is measured by his performance on that form when a variety of substitutions of non-emotive character are made for the variables involved.

The following forms of inference were represented in the test items:

1. If p then q, and not p; therefore not q. (invalid)
2. If p then q, and if p then r; therefore if q then r. (invalid)
3. If not p then q, and if not r then s, and if p then not s; therefore q or r. (valid)
4. If p or q then r, and if not q then s, and not r; therefore s. (valid)
5. If p then q, and q; therefore p. (invalid)
6. If p then q, and if q then r; therefore if p then r. (valid)

When proper substitutions are made for each of the variables in a given form of inference a number of arguments may be obtained. For each of the above forms, six arguments of supposed neutral content were derived by appropriate substitutions. Performance on the six neutral items representing a given form of inference yielded an empirical measure of the degree and direction of structure of that particular formal pattern for each respondent. By this method the seven classes of structure shown in Table 2 were obtained. They range from those of zero order (none of the six items judged "valid") to those of the sixth order (all six items judged "valid"). The direction of structures at the extremes is fairly clear: structures of zero order have the direction of leading to judgments of invalidity while those of the sixth order have the direction of leading to judgments of validity. What shall we say,

however, of those forms of inference judged "invalid" twice and "valid" four times on neutral items? If we consider the responses to these forms statistically we may say that these forms of inference have an overall direction of structure for the subject in question, i.e., they lead to responses of "valid" most of the time, although their degree of structure must be less than forms of the sixth order since the latter lead to judgments of validity consistently. Similarly, forms of inference which are judged "valid" on five of six items may be said to possess the same direction of structure but to be intermediate in degree of structure between forms whose structures are of the fourth and sixth orders respectively. Forms of inference which are judged valid just as often as invalid are said to possess structures of the third order, and in a statistical sense these structures possess neither direction nor degree. Yet it seems clear that they belong on the same continuum of structures as those of more pronounced degree and direction. To summarize, a scale of structures was defined consisting at one end of those forms of inference consistently judged invalid and at the other end of those consistently judged valid. The intermediate scale positions represent structures of lesser degree than those found at either end, while at the midpoint of the scale are found ambiguous structures which lead to judgments of validity and invalidity equally often. By comparing scores on emotional arguments of different degrees and directions of structure it is possible to determine how distortion of reasoning varies with structural properties.

TABLE 2

DESCRIPTION OF SCALE OF STRUCTURAL ORDERS

	Order of Structure						
	0	1	2	3	4	5	6
Number of neutral items judged to be invalid	6	5	4	3	2	1	0
Number of neutral items judged to be valid	0	1	2	3	4	5	6

RESULTS AND DISCUSSION

Distortion Scores as a Function of Attitude

Reliabilities of the two halves of the reasoning test calculated by the split-half method and corrected by the Spearman-Brown formula ranged from .57 to .91 on the neutral part of the test, and from .61 to .92 on the emotional part. When all seven groups are combined reliabilities on the neutral and emotional subscales are .77 and .80 respectively. These coefficients indicate a sufficiently high degree of consistency in responses to justify group comparisons. When a third of the neutral subscale is considered, as is done in the analysis of responses to the arguments matched with Negro themes, the lowest of the above coefficients (.77) drops to .53, a rather low but nonetheless significant value.

It has already been suggested that the number of errors on neutral items may be taken as a measure of the cues derived by the subject from the formal patterns and grammatical properties of the arguments. Judgments on the emotional arguments will presumably be based on these same cues and *in addition* on attitudes evoked by the content of these items. A convenient measure of the effect of attitudes upon judgments of emotional arguments would be the difference between emotional and neutral scores, which will be called the "absolute distortion," or simply "distortion." For example, Group 1 (New York) had means of 16.2 and 17.2 on the neutral and emotional subscales respectively. The mean distortion for this group is 1.0 errors. On the other hand, Group 4 (North Carolina) had means of 18.5 and 21.7 on the subscales, or a mean distortion of 3.2 errors.

In order to determine whether the mean distortions for the several groups differ significantly it is necessary to make adjustments for differences in neutral scores. This can be done by means of analysis of covariance. The F-test will tell us whether the neutral scores are sufficient to explain the group distortions, or whether after these distortions are adjusted to a common neutral score basis they still differ significantly.

Since the covariance method, as applied to our problem, is based upon adjustments made on the basis of deviations from an average regression of distortions on neutral scores, it is first necessary to determine whether the separate group regression coefficients do in fact belong to a common population. In Table 3, these coefficients are

TABLE 3

REGRESSIONS OF DISTORTIONS ON NEUTRAL SCORES FOR SEVEN GROUPS OF STUDENTS

Group	Regression Coefficient
1 New York	—.245
2 New York	—.208
3 California	—.047
4 North Carolina	—.595
5 Tennessee	—.254
6 West Virginia	—.371
7 Arkansas	—.272

summarized. When the F-test was applied it was found that the group regression coefficients differed significantly at the .01 level. We are therefore not justified in assuming that they belong to a common population. A glance at Table 3 shows that the coefficients for Groups 3 and 4 differ most widely. If Group 3 is eliminated then all of the coefficients exceed .20 in absolute magnitude. Since Group 3, the California sample, was recruited from philosophy classes, whereas all other samples were drawn from psychology classes, it was decided to drop this group from further covariance analysis. When the above test was repeated using only six groups the F-value was 2.0 and not significant.[5] We thus have left only those groups in which the regressions of distortion on neutral scores are such that they may be considered to belong to a common population. We may therefore properly regard the average regression as the best available estimate of the population re-

___

[5] The degrees of freedom for the greater mean square in this latter test were 5, and for the smaller, 482.

gression, and may legitimately adjust the group distortions in terms of their deviations from this average regression. The regression of distortions on neutral scores does not depart significantly from linearity either for scores on the ethnocentrism scale as a whole or for scores on the anti-Negro subscale, hence we may properly use deviations from the average linear regression in making adjustments.

Use of the covariance method also assumes that the variances of adjusted distortions do not differ significantly among the groups. Unfortunately this condition is not met by the data even when Group 3 is excluded. Heterogeneity in the residual variances from group to group means that we cannot be sure that the within (error) variance represents each group variance with its proper weighting. The probable effect of this heterogeneity is to render the F-test less sensitive, although we may be reasonably sure that it will indicate the approximate probability of the obtained differences occurring if the null hypothesis were correct.[6]

The results of the comparison of adjusted group distortions, shown in Table 4, indicate that there are differences in distortions which

[6] For a more complete discussion of the accuracy of such an estimate see Cochran (3).

cannot be accounted for on the basis of differences in general reasoning ability. The F-value for the test of the significance of differences in distortions between groups is convertible to a P-value less than .01. That these differences in mean distortions are to be interpreted as arising from the differential attitudes and beliefs common to the "northern" as contrasted with the "southern" groups is shown by a further comparison of the mean distortions of each section. It is important to recall that the West Virginia sample consisted entirely of Negro students. Since one-third of the emotional arguments of the test had as their content statements evocative of prejudice against Negroes, we may assume that members of this group will reject conclusions impugning them and accept those which are more complimentary. That this assumption is amply justified will be indicated below in a separate analysis of responses to the Negro subscale. It seems reasonable in view of this to combine the West Virginia sample with those from New York in a "northern" group. Samples from Arkansas, North Carolina, and Tennessee would then constitute the "southern" group. When these sections were compared it was found that the adjusted mean distortion in the southern group was 2.92 errors, while that for the

TABLE 4

MEAN NEUTRAL SCORES AND ADJUSTED DISTORTIONS FOR GROUPS AND SECTIONS
SCORES ON ETHNOCENTRISM SCALE

Group or Section	N	Mean Neutral Score (Errors)	Adjusted Mean Distortion (Errors)	Level of Significance of Differences in Distortions
New York (2)	59	16.17	.50	
West Virginia	87	18.75	1.94	
New York (1)	101	18.68	1.96	$P < .01$
Arkansas	74	18.03	2.34	
Tennessee	89	17.10	2.98	
North Carolina	84	18.46	3.40	
Northern	247	18.10	1.59	$P < .01$
Southern	247	17.84	2.92	

northern group was 1.59 errors. The obtained F-value shows that this difference is significant beyond the .01 level. It has been shown therefore that distortions, determined on the basis of the total ethnocentrism scale, differ markedly between southern and northern samples even after the comparison is made on a common neutral score basis.

Scores on anti-Negro subscale—The preceding data show the influence of a complex of attitudes and beliefs, which may be called ethnocentrism, upon reasoning; the present section shows the effect of anti-Negro attitudes and beliefs upon reasoning. Table 5 shows the results of the covariance analysis of scores on the 12 Negro items and their neutral counterparts. Approximately the same rank order of group distortions holds for this subscale as for the larger ethnocentrism scale. The Negro group from West Virginia exhibits one of the smallest distortions, as would be expected on the basis of the content of this subscale. It has accordingly been grouped with the New York groups to form a northern section. As in the analysis above, both differences in distortion between groups, and those between "north" and "south" sections proved to be highly significant.

Average distortions on the Anti-Semitic, Women and Patriotic subscales did not differ

significantly between the groups, hence no detailed examination of them is necessary.

Distortion as a Function of Structure

It will be recalled that the structure of a form of inference for any given subject is inferable from its perceived truth-value, when the latter is measured by performance on non-emotional arguments representative of the form in question. From this method of determination it follows that a given form of inference may possess different structures for different individuals. The six neutral arguments representing a given form of inference in the present test material may all be judged valid by some subjects, while others may evaluate most or all of them invalid. It is advantageous therefore to segregate all responses to groups of formally identical arguments into the seven possible structures, grouping them into the classes zero order, first order, etc., to sixth order. This means that different forms of inference, when perceived similarly, will be grouped together in the same structural class.

Now as long as we consider test items which are homogeneous with respect to validity, the number of neutral arguments judged valid will be perfectly correlated with

TABLE 5

MEAN NEUTRAL SCORES AND ADJUSTED DISTORTIONS FOR GROUPS AND SECTIONS
SCORES ON ANTI-NEGRO SUBSCALE

Group or Section	Mean Neutral Score (Errors)	Adjusted Mean Distortion (Errors)	Level of Significance of Differences in Distortions
New York (2)*	5.29	−.40	
West Virginia (Negro)	6.12	.57	
New York (1)	6.16	.66	$P < .01$
Tennessee	5.96	1.00	
Arkansas	5.97	1.15	
North Carolina	6.17	1.39	
Northern	5.94	.41	$P < .01$
Southern	6.04	1.18	

* N's are the same as in Table 4.

the number of neutral errors. For assuming that the test contained only invalid arguments (by the logician's rules) the number of items judged valid is equivalent to the number of errors. Similarly, with a test containing only valid arguments the number of items judged valid would correlate perfectly (although negatively) with the number of errors. Therefore if we consider the valid and invalid forms of inference *separately*, then numbers of neutral errors for each form may be taken as convenient indices of the various structural orders discussed above.

Let us confine attention for the moment to responses to arguments constructed in the fashion of the three *invalid* forms of inference. The method of segregating responses in the different structural orders is illustrated in Tables 6 and 7. Responses to invalid arguments from three subjects selected from Group 1 are shown. Since there were 12 items of each of the three forms, 6 of which had neutral and 6 had emotive content, we can obtain 3 pairs of performance values for each subject. The first members of the pairs indicate the subtotals of neutral errors on the forms and consequently the structures of these forms for that subject. These values, or structural orders, are recorded in the column labeled "neutral errors" in Table 6. The second members of the pairs represent the subtotals of emotional errors. These latter values are recorded under the column labeled "emotional errors." In Table 7, the subtotals of emotional errors have been segregated according to the structure of the form from

TABLE 6

ERRORS SEGREGATED BY FORMS OF INFERENCE

Subject	Invalid Forms of Inference	Neutral Errors (Order of Structure)	Emotional Errors
John F.	1	6	5
	2	4	5
	5	5	5
Ruth H.	1	3	1
	2	3	5
	5	2	3
Robert M.	1	4	5
	2	1	3
	5	0	0

TABLE 7

EMOTIONAL ERRORS SEGREGATED ACCORDING TO ORDER OF STRUCTURE

Subject	Order of Structure						
	0	1	2	3	4	5	6
John F.					5	5	5
Ruth H.			3	5			
Robert M.	0	3			5		
Average number emotional errors	0	3.0	3.0	3.0	5.0	5.0	5.0

which each subtotal was obtained. For example, we may consider the performance of John F. whose errors are shown in Table 6. Form 1 was missed six times on the neutral items and therefore has a structure of the sixth order (i.e., was judged valid six times). Hence we locate the proper structural category in Table 7 and enter the number of errors on the emotional items of this form—in this case five. On form 2 this same subject made four errors on neutral items and five errors on emotional items. This performance is therefore recorded in Table 7 by entering a 5 under fourth order structures. Performances on each of the three forms of inference for each subject can thus be classified so that arrays of emotional scores are obtained for each order of structure The average number of emotional errors occurring for each structural order can then be determined, as has been done for the three illustrative cases in Table 7.

The foregoing method of segregation can similarly be applied to valid arguments. The chief difference is that the maximum number of neutral errors occurs at, and defines, zero order structures (i.e., those judged valid zero times). The relationship between order of structure and number of neutral errors is just opposite to that described above for invalid arguments. For this reason it is necessary to report the results of the analysis of responses to valid and invalid arguments separately.

Unfortunately the convenient measure of absolute distortion used previously, i.e., the difference between mean neutral and emotional scores, is not suitable for comparing distortions at various degrees of structure. On this basis it would be expected purely on psychometric grounds that the greatest absolute distortion would occur on those structural orders in which neutral errors are minimal. The covariance method which is appropriate for partialing out differences in neutral scores could not be used here because the assumptions underlying its use were not fulfilled. A crude index was therefore adopted which shows the amount of distor-

tion as a fraction of the amount that could have occurred. We may define this "index of distortion" as a ratio between the amount emotional errors exceeded neutral errors and the total amount by which emotional errors could have exceeded neutral errors.[7] If we let p represent the index of distortion, then

$$p = \frac{E - N}{6 - N}$$

where E is the number of emotional errors, N the number of neutral errors, and $6 - N$ the amount by which E could have exceeded N. For example, the p-value for structures of the fourth order, determined on the basis of the three subjects' performances shown in Table 7 may be calculated by substituting 5.0 for E and 4 for N:

$$p = \frac{5.0 - 4}{6 - 4} = .50$$

Use of this index assumes that it is possible for emotional errors to exceed neutral errors. Unfortunately this is not the case when the number of neutral errors is six. Hence at sixth order structures for invalid arguments and at zero order structures for valid arguments the above ratio has little meaning, and index values for these structures cannot properly be computed.

Furthermore by thus expressing the index, we are confining our attention to that part of the sample which tends to exhibit ethnocentric attitudes and beliefs, for the ratio assumes that distortions are occurring in the direction in which emotional scores exceed neutral scores. This is not a serious limitation since for approximately two-thirds of the total sample emotional errors exceeded neutral errors.

A further difficulty arises in considering the probable effect of variable errors of measurement at each of the defined levels of

---

[7] The ratio between observed deviations and maximum deviations possible is commonly used in psychological evaluations. Brunswik's constancy ratio introduced in the study of perceptual size constancy is one example of its use. See Brunswik (2, p. 19) and Woodworth (14, p. 605).

structure. In lieu of any better method of estimating the degrees of regressions of emotional errors at the extremes of the scale of structures, where for zero-order structures E-values on invalid arguments tend to be inflated while for high order structures E-values on invalid arguments are depressed, it was decided to approximate the neutral values in the equation for p in a crude experimental fashion, i.e., on the basis of the performance of a "neutral-scoring" group selected from the total sample. The "neutral-scoring" group consisted of a sample of those subjects exhibiting no difference, or at most a negligible difference of one error, between total emotional and neutral scores. There is no basis for supposing that *for these subjects* attitudes and beliefs had any appreciable effect upon responses to emotional items. It is as if the numbers of emotional errors of such "neutral" subjects were determined solely by (a) the way in which the arguments were structured for each percipient and (b) chance errors of measurement. If we segregate the errors of this neutral group as in Tables 6 and 7, the average number of emotional errors under each structural order will represent the values which would be obtained simply on the basis of the joint operation of these factors. The "ethnocentric" subjects, on the other hand, whose emotional scores were to be evaluated, consisted of a sample of those subjects whose total emotional scores exceeded their total neutral scores by four or more errors. The distributions of neutral scores of these "neutral" and "ethnocentric" samples were identical, since members of the samples were matched in neutral scores. Whenever more than one subject could be matched with a given neutral-scoring subject selection was made randomly. There were 108 subjects in each sample.

In Table 8 the average emotional scores for the neutral and ethnocentric groups are shown for each value of structure.[8] As has been pointed out above the scores for the neutral group may be taken as values for N in the formula for p. The values for E are of course the average emotional scores for each structural order obtained from performances of the ethnocentric group. Indices of distortion have been calculated separately for invalid and valid arguments for each structural order and plotted in Figures 1 and 2.

Measures of distortion appear to vary in an approximately linear fashion with order of structure. For *invalid* arguments high order structures include those forms of inference judged valid (and therefore incorrectly) on most of the neutral arguments of these forms. For ethnocentric subjects this means that the material comprising the emotional items of

_____

[8] No attempt was made to calculate p values for sixth-order structures arising from invalid arguments and zero-order structures from valid arguments for reasons already discussed.

TABLE 8

COMPUTATION OF INDICES OF DISTORTION

Structure	Av. No. Emotional Errors of Neutral Group (N)		Av. No. Emotional Errors of Ethno-centric Group (E)		Index of Distortion (p)	
	Invalid	Valid	Invalid	Valid	Invalid	Valid
0	.38	—	1.57	—	.21	—
1	1.11	4.00	2.91	5.00	.37	.50
2	2.35	3.85	3.16	4.90	.22	.49
3	3.24	3.19	4.72	4.31	.53	.40
4	3.58	2.11	4.67	3.61	.45	.39
5	4.76	1.29	5.49	2.06	.59	.16
6	—	1.43	—	1.59	—	.03

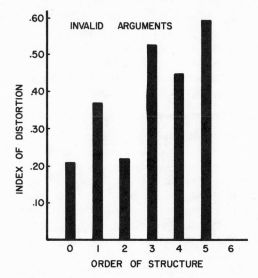

Figure 1. Distortion of Reasoning with Changes in Degree and Direction of Structure.

these forms is structured in a way which facilitates the *same* organization that is promoted by the subjects' attitudes.[9] Hence the degree of distortion should be greatest at this

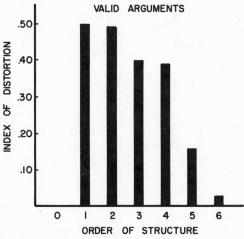

Figure 2. Distortion of Reasoning with Changes in Degree and Direction of Structure.

[9] The reader will recall that emotive arguments whether valid or invalid were designed so that ethnocentric respondents would judge them incorrectly. That is, such respondents should tend to judge valid items invalid, and invalid items valid.

extreme of the structural scale. On the other hand, zero order structures consist of forms of inference judged invalid (and therefore correctly) on all six of the neutral arguments of these forms. Since the conclusions of the matched emotional arguments are so phrased that the ethnocentric respondent who evaluates arguments in accordance with his attitudes and beliefs will judge them incorrectly, there should be an opposition between structural and affective elements at this end of the structural scale. Hence the degree of relative distortion should be smaller as the order of structure becomes lower. This hypothetical relationship appears to be confirmed by the general trend of the *p*-values shown in Figure 1.

On the other hand, the functional relationship between order of structure and degree of distortion should be just the reverse for *valid* arguments. For such arguments zero order structures include those forms of inference consistently judged invalid (and therefore incorrectly). Thus the material of low order emotional arguments is structured in a way which facilitates the same organization promoted by ethnocentric attitudes and beliefs. Hence the greatest degree of distortion should occur at low order structures. On the other hand conflict, or opposition between structural and affective forces, should occur at sixth order structures, for responses to neutral arguments indicate that this class of valid forms of inference is structured in the direction of judgments of validity. Yet ethnocentric subjects in order to make evaluations consistent with their attitudes must judge them invalid. Hence the degree of relative distortion should be smallest at this end of the structural scale. It can be seen in Figure 2 that this hypothetical relationship is clearly indicated by the negative slope of the curve.

INTERPRETATION

One of the central factors operating in perceptual and cognitive processes is presumably a desire, or tendency, to "objectify" the organism's interpretation of its environment.

Such an orientation is favored by the exigencies of life and daily adaptive requirements. There is therefore a tendency for the normal and efficiently functioning organism to isolate certain interpretations of its environment from other intrapersonal wishes, needs, and motives which block correct perception and judgment. Such isolation regularly occurs whenever we attempt to think objectively or to keep our observations independent of our wishes. These attempts at isolation will be more or less successful depending upon the proximity of the material to be judged, perceived, or interpreted, to other strong attitudes and beliefs of the organism. If, as in the present experiment, we present the organism with two samples of material, one neutral and the other emotive, isolation will occur less readily with the emotive material than in the case of the neutral material. Organization in an objective, part-isolating direction occurs when it is not blocked or overcome by other competing organizing tendencies. We would expect on such a basis that emotive material would be judged less objectively than neutral material, that southern groups would show more distortion of reasoning than northern groups on emotive content dealing with Negroes, and that Negroes would show less distortion than southern Whites on the same items. These expectations are confirmed by the results.

One hypothesis which has been advanced (1), attempting to specify the functional relationship between the degree of structure of a stimulus and the perceptual distortion produced by organizing factors might be called the "ambiguity hypothesis." According to this view the greater the equivocality of a stimulus situation (presumably the "outer" factors) the greater the chance for behavioral factors (presumably "inner" determinants) to operate in the determination of perception. However, once it is asked *whether "structure" is a determinant within the subject's psychological field* such a formulation appears less plausible. For if it is not in the field then structures per se have nothing to do with perception; but if it is, then the dichot-

omy between behavioral and structural factors no longer differentiates between the "inner" and the "outer." The neglected alternative of defining structure so that it is clearly inside the organism, giving it the same status as any other set of determinants in the psychological field, suggests that "structural" factors have "direction" attributes just as behavioral determinants.[10] We can, of course, create stimulus material which is structured in a direction similar to that of other determinants. The "ambiguity hypothesis" appears to be based upon the tacit assumption that the stimulus material is never structured in a direction which facilitates the same organization as that promoted by the dominant "behavioral" factors. When "structure" is defined so that it can meaningfully be said to be a determinant in the psychological field, it is evident that this assumption is untenable. The present study specifically illustrates the possibility that stimulus material may under certain conditions facilitate the *same* organization as that promoted by dominant attitudinal factors. For example fourth and fifth order structures observed in the ethnocentric subject's judgments of invalid arguments, or first and second order structures observed in his judgments of valid arguments, all appear to be members of the class in question.

One consequence which follows from the procedure and analysis adopted herein is that attitudes and beliefs may be revealed on material of high degrees of structure just as effectively as on that of low structures. It is only necessary to take into account, by some behavioral criteria independent of attitude, the probable degree and direction of structure of the material for each percipient. The unique status which has been accorded to ambiguous structures would therefore seem to be based not upon a psychological law but rather upon convenience.

---

[10] A point of view similar to that expressed here is that of Krech (8), who proposes replacing dichotomized categories of separate, non-interacting "factors" by a single construct, to be called "Dynamic Systems," which varies along several different dimensions.

In the absence of a control group with which the relative distortions of the ethnocentric sample might be compared, the results shown in Figures 1 and 2 must be interpreted with caution. Let us assume, however, that the trends shown are statistically significant and that they are specific to ethnocentric samples. How might we interpret them rationally? The increase in relative distortion with increases in the degree to which material is structured in directions consonant with ethnocentric attitudes might be interpreted as the resultant of interactions between forces or tensions in the psychological field. Thus, considering invalid arguments at the zero order end of the structural scale, tensions induced by structural properties promote an organization which is contradictory to that promoted by tensions arising from attitudes and beliefs. In the case of judgments of material of first and second order structures, the opposition between structural and attitudinal force is lessened, due to the fact that the *degree* of structure decreases as we ascend from zero to third order structures. At the midpoint of the structural scale structural forces are minimal, for in a statistical sense they lack both magnitude and direction. Such third order structures are ambiguous in the sense that they are equally susceptible of two different interpretations.[11] Beyond this midpoint, in the case of fourth and fifth order structures, both structural and attitudinal tensions promote the same organization. The degree of structure increases as the order increases, hence structural tensions will be greatest in magnitude for high order structures approaching the upper limit of the structural scale. Thus there occurs an interaction between structural and attitudinal tensions such that the operation of attitudinal tensions is inhibited by low order classes of structure while it is enhanced and facilitated by high order classes of structure. On such a basis the results summarized in Figure 1, namely, the least relative distortion on low order structures, medium on those which are ambiguous, and the greatest on high order structures, would of course be expected. Similarly, an exactly analogous interpretation could be made for the decrease in relative distortion on valid arguments with increase in order of structure.

SUMMARY

Judgments of the validity of neutral and emotional arguments were obtained from 559 college students from seven universities in the North, South, and West. Reliabilities on the neutral part of the test range from .57 to .91, and on the emotional part from .61 to .92. Analysis of the covariance of errors on neutral items and of distortion scores indicates that the hypothesis that attitudes and beliefs are a determinant of reasoning cannot be rejected: groups from southern states differ significantly from northern groups in distortions of reasoning, both on the ethnocentrism scale as a whole and on the anti-Negro subscale considered by itself.

There appears to be a linear relationship between the degree of relative distortion and changes in the degree and direction of the structure of the forms of inference, i.e., as the structure of the form becomes increasingly compatible with prejudiced responses the degree of relative distortion increases. The greatest degree of relative distortion did not occur on the most ambiguous structures, but rather on those structures most consonant with the relevant attitudes and beliefs of the subjects.

A method of measuring "structure" is suggested which is based upon certain behavioral criteria so that attributes of direction as well as of degree can be inferred. The empirical results of the present experiment and the analysis of structure as an entity which may possess direction, taken together, strongly suggest that the unique status accorded ambiguous structures as means of evoking atti-

---

[11] The question of whether this behaviorally defined class of structures is equivalent to what clinicians mean when they speak of "ambiguous structures" need not be raised. All that is claimed here is that third-order structures are *more ambiguous* than any of the other defined orders of structure.

tude is based upon convenience rather than upon empirical and rational grounds.

REFERENCES

1. Bruner, J. S., and C. C. Goodman.
   1947   "Value and need as organizing factors in perception." Journal of Abnormal and Social Psychology 42: 33–44.
2. Brunswik, E.
   1947   Systematic and Representative Design of Psychological Experiments. Berkeley and Los Angeles: University of California Press.
3. Cochran, W. G.
   1947   "Some consequences when the assumptions for the analysis of variance are not satisfied." Biometrics Bulletin 3:28–32.
4. Fenichel, O.
   1945   The Psychoanalytic Theory of Neurosis. New York: Norton.
5. Frenkel-Brunswik, E., and R. N. Sanford.
   1945   "Some personality factors in anti-Semitism." Journal of Psychology 20:271–291.
6. Frenkel-Brunswik, E., D. J. Levinson, and R. N. Sanford.
   1947   "The antidemocratic personality." In T. M. Newcomb and E. L. Hartley (eds.), Readings in Social Psychology. New York: Holt.
7. Janis, I. L., and F. Frick.
   1943   "The relationship between attitudes toward conclusions and errors in judging logical validity of syllogisms." Journal of Experimental Psychology 33:73–77.
8. Krech, D.
   1949   "Notes toward a psychological theory." Journal of Personality 18:66–87.
9. Lefford, A.
   1946   "The influence of emotional subject matter on logical reasoning." Journal of General Psychology 34: 127–151.
10. Levine, R., I. Chein, and G. Murphy.
    1942   "The relation of the intensity of a need to the amount of perceptual distortion; a preliminary report." Journal of Psychology 13:283–293.
11. Morgan, J. J. B., and J. T. Morton.
    1943   "Distortion of reasoning as an index of public opinion." School and Society 57:333–335.
12. Morgan, J. J. B., and J. T. Morton.
    1944   "The distortion of syllogistic reasoning produced by personal conviction." Journal of Social Psychology 20:39–59.
13. Winthrop, H.
    1946   "Semantic factors in the measurement of personality integration." Journal of Social Psychology 24: 149–175.
14. Woodworth, R. S.
    1938   Experimental Psychology. New York: Holt.

CHAPTER 25

Racial Attitude as a Determinant of Judgments of Plausibility[1]

CLAIRE SELLTIZ AND STUART W. COOK

INTRODUCTION

Waly and Cook (5) have reported high correlations between ratings of the plausibility of statements about segregation and raters' racial attitudes as indicated by a self-report inventory. In discussing this finding they suggested that ratings of plausibility might serve as an indirect indicator of attitude. The purpose of the present study was to explore this suggestion by having criterion groups of Ss with known positions on race relations rate the plausibility of arguments for and against segregation.

METHOD

Materials

The materials were the same as those used by Waly and Cook: 20 statements supporting segregation and 20 supporting integration,

with half of the statements in each set being intended as poor or ineffective arguments and half being intended as good or more effective arguments. The 40 items were arranged in random order, and each one was labeled "pro-segregation" or "pro-integration." Under each statement was an 11-point graphic rating scale ranging from *very ineffective* (−5) to *very effective* (+5). An example of a statement intended as a relatively effective argument for integration is as follows:

"Requiring the Negro to attend separate schools carries the implication of inferiority even if equally adequate facilities are provided."

The instructions were the same as those used by Waly and Cook. Briefly, the rationale given was that the arguments were to be used "in the construction of a psychological test," and that in order to find out which would be the best ones to include, it was important to

−5	−4	−3	−2	−1	0	+1	+2	+3	+4	+5
very ineffective		moderately ineffective		slightly ineffective		slightly effective		moderately effective		very effective

From Claire Selltiz and Stuart W. Cook, "Racial attitude as a determinant of judgments of plausibility." *Journal of Social Psychology*, 1966, 70, 139–147. Copyright 1966 by the Journal Press, and reproduced by permission of the authors and publisher.

[1] This study was part of a program of research on the measurement of social attitudes supported by grants from the National Science Foundation and the Air Force Office of Scientific Research. The point of view and goals of the total program are described in Cook and Selltiz (1).

know how a large number of people, "looking at them independently and objectively," viewed the statements. Ss were asked to imagine that they were judging a debate between two teams on the topic of segregation *vs.* integration, and, acting as impartial judges, to rate each argument presented by either side in terms of its effectiveness. They were instructed to rate a statement —5 if they considered it "a very poor argument *for the side that it supports* and [one that] could easily be torn down by the opposition," to rate a statement +5 if they considered it "one of the best arguments that could possibly be advanced," and to use one of the numbers from —4 to +4 for statements that they felt were somewhere between these extremes.

Procedure

This was one of a battery of measures in a program concerned with evaluating the effectiveness of various techniques for measuring attitudes toward social groups and with interrelations among different aspects of attitude as tapped by different measures. The tests in the battery were administered in two sessions of about one hour each, two weeks apart.

At the first session, four instruments were administered in the following order: (*a*) a "Test of Logical Reasoning," consisting of ten syllogisms with varied content, given simply to fill in time while waiting for late Ss; (*b*) a sentence-completion test with sentence stubs worded in the third person, modeled on the Paired Direct and Projective Questions technique developed by Getzels (2, 3)—15 sentence stubs about situations involving Negroes were embedded in a total of 75 stubs, the others having to do with general ideology, relations with parents, various kinds of nonconforming behavior, reactions to stress, etc.; (*c*) the ratings of plausibility; and (*d*) a questionnaire asking S to indicate his *family's* opinions on several items having to do with race relations.

In the second session, Ss filled out five questionnaires, four of them essentially undisguised measures of attitude toward Negroes and various aspects of race relations.

Scoring

The plausibility ratings were scored by the system developed by Waly and Cook. Ss' ratings of the pro-segregation items were assigned scores from +5 = 0 to —5 = 10: that is, the more *ineffective* a pro-segregation argument was considered to be by the S, the higher his score. This was reversed for the pro-integration arguments. Thus, a high score for the total set of 40 items resulted from judging integration items as effective and segregation items as ineffective. An individual score could range from zero at the anti-Negro end of the scale to four hundred at the equalitarian end. In terms of the basic hypothesis, a high score on the plausibility measure should be associated with an equalitarian attitude, or lack of prejudice.

Subjects

Subjects were white American college students. (Some foreign students and some Negroes were included in the groups taking the tests, but their responses were not included in the analysis.) For reasons having to do with the overall design of the study, only those Ss who attended both testing sessions (i.e., for whom there were complete or almost-complete data) were included in the analysis. A total of 540 Ss were included in the analysis of the plausibility ratings.

All Ss were members of organizations, or participants in activities, that could be thought of as constituting criterion groups. That is, the organizations or activities were such that it seemed reasonable to believe that many, if not all, of their members would hold specified attitudes about race relations. The kinds of groups, and the assumptions about the attitudes of their members, are listed below:

Group I—Ss with strongly equalitarian attitudes and active concern with race relations. The authors assumed that white students active in civil rights organizations or having participated in pro-integration activities were likely to meet this description.

Group II—Ss with equalitarian attitudes but not active concern. The authors assumed that white students taking *elective* courses in intergroup relations or minority group problems were likely to fit this criterion, since they voluntarily expose themselves to information about minority groups which is typically presented with an equalitarian view, but are not participating actively in efforts to change race relations. (All Ss were asked to list the organizations to which they belonged, and Ss in these classes who reported membership in pro-integration groups were transferred to Group I.)

Group III—Ss with anti-Negro attitudes. It is difficult to find student organizations of which most or all members can be assumed to fit this description. However, other studies in the present program [Zavalloni and Cook (6); Selltiz, Edrich, and Cook (4)] had found relatively high proportions of such Ss in right-wing political organizations and in selected fraternities and sororities. In the present study, both these kinds of groups were used as sources of Ss in this category. In selecting the fraternities and sororities, the authors used as informants students in strategic positions in the campus social structure and representing different points of view; only those fraternities or sororities mentioned by a number of informants as being generally believed to have strong, though not necessarily official or explicit, policies against admitting Negroes were used as sources of Ss.

Ss from each of these three types of groups were recruited in each of three geographical regions—Northeast, Rocky Mountain, and Border South—and the data from each region were analyzed separately, thus providing three replications of the study.

Ss in organizations were approached, through the local chapters of their organizations, as "informed students with points of view on public issues." Three dollars were paid for each such S who attended both testing sessions, the payment being made either

to the organization's treasury or to the individual Ss, as the organization chose. The tests were administered at the regular meeting time of the group and usually in its regular meeting place. Ss in race relations classes were recruited through announcements in class and were paid three dollars each for participation in the two sessions. The number of Ss at a testing session ranged from five to 60.

FINDINGS

Self-Description of Attitude by Members of Criterion Groups

As noted in the Procedure section, four undisguised measures of racial attitude were among the questionnaires administered to Ss. The intercorrelations of these four measures were high; the median r between the measures for the Ss in the Northeast was .80, for those in the Rocky Mountain region, .72, and for those in the Border South, .87.

Within each of the three regions, the three types of groups differed significantly in the predicted order on all of the undisguised attitude measures: that is, Ss in militant civil rights organizations scored most unprejudiced, those in race relations classes next most unprejudiced, and those in conservative organizations and in selected fraternities and sororities most prejudiced. As an example, the scores on a self-report Opinion Inventory[2] are shown in Table 1. The upper part of the table shows Ns, mean scores, and SDs; the lower part shows relevant data from the analyses of variance, F ratios, and η's (eta's) between scores and group membership. Within each region, as predicted, Ss in Group I have the highest (least prejudiced) scores and those in Group III the lowest (most prejudiced). Moreover, as expected, the standard deviation was highest in Group III, reflecting the greater heterogeneity of the conservative organizations, fraternities, and sororities with respect to racial attitudes. In terms of scores on this measure, it is apparent

---

[2] This is a revised version of a questionnaire originally developed by Mary Evans Collins.

TABLE 1

SCORES ON SELF-REPORT OPINION INVENTORY[a]

Group	Northeast	Rocky Mountains	Border South
Group I			
(Civil rights groups)			
N	97	95	33
Mean	57.19	56.47	56.70
SD	2.91	3.21	2.30
Group II			
(Race relations classes)			
N	65	50	6
Mean	55.32	52.08	48.67
SD	7.53	8.07	9.54
Group III			
(Conservatives and exclusionists)			
N	79	54	55
Mean	43.25	46.57	24.64
SD	14.21	10.63	12.89
Analyses of Variance			
Between groups			
MS	4683.47	1699.24	11004.97
df	2	2	2
Within groups			
MS	84.79	51.80	105.44
df	238	196	91
F ratio	55.24*	32.81*	104.37*
η	.56	.50	.83

[a] Possible range of scores: 0 to 62.
* $p < .001$.

that, on the whole, Ss in Group III are not strongly anti-Negro; their absolute scores suggest that in the Northeast and the Rocky Mountain area the average S in Group III is, in fact, moderately unprejudiced, while in the Border South the average S in Group III is moderately prejudiced. These findings are consistent with those of earlier studies in this series (4).

Plausibility Scores of Members of Criterion Groups

Table 2 shows, for the three criterion groups in each of the three regions, the scores derived from the plausibility ratings. Again, the upper part of the table shows Ns, means, and SDs; the lower part shows data from the analyses of variance, the F ratios, and ηs. Within each region, as predicted, the criterion groups differ significantly ($p < .001$) in their ratings of the plausibility of the arguments, with actively pro-integration Ss scoring highest (i.e., seeing pro-integration arguments as most plausible, pro-segregation arguments as least plausible) and members of conservative political organizations and of exclusionist fraternities and sororities scoring lowest. The ηs between plausibility scores and group membership are .63, .33, and .72 in the Northeast, Rocky Mountain, and Border South regions, respectively. Table 3 shows the cumulative percentage of subjects in each criterion group who achieved pro-

TABLE 2

SCORES BASED ON PLAUSIBILITY RATINGS[a]

Group	Northeast	Rocky Mountains	Border South
Group I			
(Civil rights groups)			
N[b]	101	95	33
Mean	295.95	275.57	275.18
SD	36.80	31.47	29.36
Group II			
(Race relations classes)			
N	68	49	6
Mean	281.00	268.29	259.00
SD	40.14	43.35	39.43
Group III			
(Conservatives and exclusionists)			
N	78	54	56
Mean	209.85	243.43	179.02
SD	61.24	45.19	52.89
Analyses of Variance			
Between groups			
MS	175699.86	18136.75	101529.89
df	2	2	2
Within groups			
MS	2181.30	1495.02	2057.00
df	244	195	92
F ratio	80.55*	12.13*	49.36*
η	.63	.33	.72

[a] Possible range of scores: 0 to 400.
[b] Ns differ slightly from those in Table 1 because some Ss did not complete both questionnaires.
* $p < .001$.

integration scores of designated levels on ratings of the plausibility of arguments.

Correlation between Self-Report and Plausibility Scores

Waly and Cook reported correlations of .64 and .88 in a Midwestern university and a Border-South college, respectively, between plausibility scores and scores on an earlier version of the self-report Opinion Inventory. In the present study, too, the plausibility scores correlated substantially with scores on the undisguised attitude measures. Correlations with the revised version of the Opinion Inventory used in the present study were .76 in the Northeast, .54 in the Rocky Mountain area, and .78 in the Border South.

DISCUSSION

In both the Northeast and the Border South, the size of the correlations between the plausibility ratings and both the self-report measures and criterion-group membership suggests that plausibility ratings may be a useful indicator of attitude. However, the correlations in the Rocky Mountain region, although highly significant statistically, indicate that only 29 per cent of the variance on the self-report measure, and only 11 per cent of the variance in group membership, can

TABLE 3

PERCENTAGE OF SUBJECTS ACHIEVING SCORES OF A DESIGNATED LEVEL OR LOWER ON RATINGS OF THE PLAUSIBILITY OF ARGUMENTS

Pro-integration score	Criterion groups by region								
	Northeast			Rocky Mountain			Border South		
	I	II	III*	I	II	III	I	II	III
400									
350	95	97		99	98				
300	53	65	99	81	84	94	88	83	
250	13	19	73	21	22	50	21	50	89
200	1	3	37		14	15			64
150		1	17		2	2			29
100			5			2			11
50			3						4
0									

* Group I = Civil rights groups, Group II = Race relations classes, and Group III = Conservatives and racial exclusionists.

be accounted for by the plausibility measure. Why this should be so is not entirely clear. One possible reason may be that the entire Rocky Mountain sample is more homogeneous than are the other samples, and the criterion groups not as different from each other as in the other two regions. This possibility is supported by the facts that almost all the measures in the battery show lower intercorrelations, and discriminate less well between criterion groups (yield lower ηs), in the Rocky Mountain area than in the other two regions. However, for most of the other measures the correlations are only slightly lower in the Rocky Mountain region than in the Northeast, whereas in the case of the plausibility measure the differences are substantial.

Despite its relatively poor discriminatory power in this one region, the results do confirm the Waly-Cook conclusion that attitude influences ratings of plausibility, and support the view that ratings of plausibility may be a useful indicator of attitude. For the criterion groups used in this study, such ratings show no advantage over direct self-report measures. However, there are situations where it is desirable to use an indirect rather than a direct measure. This is true, for example, in situations where Ss may be strongly motivated to "make a good impression" or to give socially approved responses. There was no great pressure in this direction in the present study. Ss were not known to the testers; in fact, for the great majority of Ss, the testers were from a different institution, and so there was little reason for Ss to be concerned with making a good impression on them. In addition, the very fact that these Ss were in organizations with more or less clear positions on issues of race relations suggests that these were individuals who were, on the whole, willing to avow their true views, even though these might not be approved by the tester. In situations with increased pressure toward giving socially approved responses, indirect measures, such as ratings of plausibility, may be more useful than direct self-report measures.

Another situation in which an indirect attitude measure may be preferable to a direct one is in experiments designed to bring about change in attitudes. Such experiments often require repeated measurement of the same Ss. This involves the danger that Ss will realize the connection between the experimental manipulation and the attitude measure and may try to cooperate with the experimenter by giving the responses they believe he wants on the post-experimental measure (or, occasionally, to thwart him by not giving the responses they believe he wants). An indirect indicator would, of course, minimize if not eliminate this danger.

REFERENCES

1. Cook, S. W., and C. A. Selltiz.
   1964 "A multiple-indicator approach to attitude measurement." Psychological Bulletin 62:36–55.
2. Getzels, J. W.
   1951 "The assessment of personality and prejudice by the method of paired direct and projective questions." Unpublished Doctoral dissertation, Harvard University, Cambridge, Massachusetts.
3. Getzels, J. W., and J. Walsh.
   1958 "The method of paired direct and projective questionnaires in the study of attitude structure and socialization." Psychological Monographs 72:No. 454.
4. Selltiz, C., H. Edrich, and S. W. Cook.
   1965 "Ratings of favorableness of statements about a social group as an indicator of attitude toward the group." Journal of Personality and Social Psychology 2:408–415.
5. Waly, P., and S. W. Cook.
   1965 "The effect of attitude on judgments of plausibility." Journal of Personality and Social Psychology 2:745–749.
6. Zavalloni, M., and S. W. Cook.
   1965 "Influence of judges' attitudes on ratings of favorableness of statements about a social group." Journal of Personality and Social Psychology 1:43–54.

SECTION **V**   **Direct Observation Techniques**

Overview

Behavioral specimens obtained by direct observation of responses to an attitude object would be preferable to specimens obtained by other means. Many of the weaknesses of verbal self-description are thereby avoided, such as voluntary distortion, self-consciousness, reactive effects upon the attitude being measured, and awkwardness of administration. Direct observation specimens have a compelling authenticity and one would expect to find a massive collection of techniques available for making such observations. The facts of the matter are quite to the contrary. There are relatively few techniques available to attitude researchers for collecting behavioral specimens by direct observation.

Until recently, the compelling qualities of direct observation were considerably counterbalanced by problems of 1) standardization and 2) difficulty of accumulating large numbers of observations quickly. For example, LaPiere (1934) traveled about the country with an Oriental couple and noted their reception by hotel personnel. The situations in which observations were made varied in unknown ways and several weeks were required to obtain a relatively small set of observations. The Kutner, Wilkins and Yarrow procedure described in Chapter 26 reduced these limitations somewhat by limiting observation situations to one community. The strategy seems to have involved making the direct observations in the respondents' "natural habitat." Thus, the researcher had to travel about and use ingenious and clever tactics to present the attitude object unobtrusively and collect the specimen of behavioral response without detection.

More recently techniques have been devised which permit greater standardization and greater yields in observations. The shift in approach rests upon the assumption that contrived situations are as satisfactory as natural ones, provided the respondent accepts the situation as one in which his actions will have real consequences. The contrived situation and experimental procedure used by Linn in Chapter 27 is quite representative of the newer approach. Still, there is the problem of obtaining large numbers of observations quickly; respondents are interviewed individually. The obvious next step in this approach is to develop contrived situations which permit individual observation of respondents in groups. One wonders whether Linn's photographic releases could be successfully presented to groups with individual responses recorded privately to prevent group interaction effects.

The approach used by Gage and Shimberg (Chapter 28) exposes another facet of direct observation techniques. Rather than observing the respondent during an act, they recover evidence of his action object *after* the act. The utility and potential of this tactic—use of archival records—is discussed and illustrated convincingly by Webb *et al.* (1966). Another noteworthy aspect of Gage and Shimberg's technique is the use of Guttman scale analysis with direct observation specimens, rather than self-report specimens. The implications of treating different types of specimens with the same analysis procedures and using a variety of analysis procedures on the same type of specimen need much more attention.

A final facet of direct observation to be recognized is the matter of collecting group, or aggregate, specimens rather than individual specimens of behavior. For most research purposes the individual records are preferred. However, there may be occasions when group, or aggregate, data are satisfactory. The choice depends, first, upon the research purposes and, second, upon the feasibility of specimen collection. The technique for using seating aggregation as an index of racial attitudes, developed by Campbell, Kruskal and Wallace (Chapter 29) is an excellent illustration of this facet of direct observation. And its potential application in other than classroom situations is clear and promising.

This introductory statement began on the note that direct observation specimens are very compelling as a basis for inferring attitudes. The accuracy of this assertion is nowhere more apparent than in the continued use of "behavior" as a criterion for validating other types of specimens; especially those obtained through self-report. It is helpful to notice that the behavior referred to is actually a specimen of the respondent's behavior toward the attitude object obtained by direct observation of the respondent. The "behavior" is therefore properly interpreted as another basis for inferring the respondent's attitude. Rather than speaking of validating a self-report measure or indirect test by comparing its results with behavior, it is more accurate to speak of *convergence* of measures based upon different types of specimens. To a considerable extent the continuing discussion of "attitudes vs. actions" is misguided and would be more profitably understood as an issue of *convergent validation*. It is in this light that the Tittle and Hill investigation (Chapter 30) is presented as the final selection on direct observation techniques. The reader is invited to alter the rhetoric of their report from that of predictive validity, with the direct observation specimen used as the criterion variable, to that of convergent validity, with the direct observation viewed as merely another basis for inferring attitudes.

REFERENCES

LaPiere, R. T.
   1934   "Attitudes vs. actions." Social Forces 13:230–237.
Webb, E. J., D. T. Campbell, R. D. Schwartz, and L. Sechrest.
   1966   Unobtrusive Measures: Nonreactive Research in the Social Sciences. Chicago: Rand McNally.

CHAPTER 26   Verbal Attitudes and Overt Behavior Involving Racial Prejudice[1]

BERNARD KUTNER, CAROL WILKINS AND PENNY RECHTMAN YARROW

The problem of explaining discrepancies between verbal attitudes and actual behavior relevant to these attitudes has been the subject of considerable theoretical thought (1). Empirical investigations of this problem have been exceptionally sparse. The classic study of LaPiere (2) demonstrated that when an innkeeper was confronted with a white person and a Chinese couple "in the flesh," requesting lodging, the trio were almost never denied it. Yet when a mailed request was sent to the same innkeeper requesting lodging for himself and his Chinese companions there was an almost universal rejection of the request. What is the nature of the situation in each case that leads to such diametrically opposed behaviors? Put in another way our question is: Why is there a discrepancy between behaviors supposedly dependent upon the same constellation of attitudes?

From Bernard Kutner, Carol Wilkins [Giniger] and Penny Rechtman Yarrow, "Verbal attitudes and overt behavior involving racial prejudice," *Journal of Abnormal and Social Psychology*, 1952, 47, 649–652. Copyright 1952 by the American Psychological Association, and reproduced by permission of the authors and publisher.

[1] The authors feel greatly indebted to Dr. Isidor Chein and Dr. Harold Proshansky for reading and criticizing the manuscript.

Our procedure was as follows:

Three young women, 2 white and 1 Negro, all well dressed and well-mannered, entered 11 individual restaurants in a fashionable Northeastern suburban community, Subtown. In each case, the white women entered first, asked for a table for three and were seated. The Negro woman entered a short while later, informed the hostess or headwaiter that she was with a party already seated, found her table and sat down. This procedure was repeated in each of the 11 restaurants and taverns.

In each case all three women were served in a manner in no wise different from the usual service accorded patrons at each establishment. At two places the group was taken unusual notice of by other patrons but in no instance was anything but exemplary service accorded them by the management, waiter, etc.

Two weeks following each visit, a letter signed with an assumed name was sent to each establishment. The return address was that of a cooperating resident of Subtown. The letter read as follows:

Dear Sir:

A group of friends and I are planning a social affair to be held in Subtown in the near future.

TABLE 1

SUMMARY OF RESPONSES TO LETTER AND PHONE CALLS

Restaurant	Response to Letter	Telephone Call	Control Call
A	No reply	Didn't get any letter. We don't take large parties. We've got dancing after 6 P.M. [They actually don't.] Are you colored? [Yes.] I like everyone. My kitchen help are colored and they are wonderful people. But we have a certain clientele here . . . This place is my bread and butter. Frankly I'd rather you not come. Try in T——— [next town].	Took reservation.
B	No reply	I didn't get your letter. We can't have you. It's against the law.	Took reservation.
C	No reply	I got the letter. How many? [Negroes] I don't mind but customers might. In fact some of my help are colored. I had trouble about this before. Frankly I prefer you don't come but if you can't find another place we won't embarrass you here.	Took reservation.
D	No reply	We didn't get a letter. We don't take reservations. We take care of our regulars. A few Negroes come in just to eat. I *would* mind you coming.	Said they didn't take reservations but we should come in any time about them.
E	No reply	I didn't get any letter. Call any time to make reservation. [Hung up before reservation could be made.]	Took reservation.
F	No reply	Yes, I got your letter. I refuse to discuss it on the phone. What is the purpose of your party? What school did you attend? Why are you never home when I call? How	Took reservation.

I should like to make reservations to have them for dinner at your restaurant. Since some of them are colored, I wondered whether you would object to their coming.

Could you let me know if the reservations may be made so that I may complete the arrangements as soon as possible?

Yours truly,

M. . . . . . B. . . . . .

Where appropriate, the term "beer party" was substituted for "social affair" and "tavern" for "restaurant."

Since no letters were returned by the Post Office,[2] it may be assumed that all were delivered. Seventeen days after the letters were sent out, no replies of any kind had been received. At this point each establishment was called by phone by one of the white women and essential parts of the letter repeated. In each instance the manager or his representative answered the phone and he was asked for reservations for the party. One day later "control calls" were made by the same per-

[2] As an added precaution, the local postman was requested to deliver to the address used any returned letters or regular mail bearing the fictitious name on the envelope.

TABLE 1—(*Continued*)

SUMMARY OF RESPONSES TO LETTER AND PHONE CALLS

Restaurant	Response to Letter	Telephone Call	Control Call
		many Negroes are in the party? [5 out of 10] That's a large percentage isn't it? [Insisted he call us, instead of vice-versa.]	
G	Reply received 19 days after our letter was mailed.	A letter to you is in the mail. Reservations are available if you come in and make them.	Took reservation.
H	No reply	Didn't get letter. We have limited space. No reservations are taken. It's hard to answer you. You know Subtown. . . . We don't object but our patrons would. I won't answer on the phone. Come in about it.	Took reservation.
I	Reply sent as result of phone call.	Didn't get letter. [Hostess] We don't like that. Is it absolutely necessary to have them? [Manager]: if it's okay with you I guess it's okay with us.	Took reservation.
J	No reply	Didn't get letter. How many? [10] No reservations for more than 8 on weekends. I will mail you our menu for the following weekend. [Never received.] I'm too busy to look up reservation availability. [Asked on two occasions that we call back.]	Took reservation.
K	No reply	Didn't get letter. I'd think you'd want to come in to discuss something like that. Mixed group? How many people? We can't turn anyone away but never take reservations. You can have a separate room if you come in about it.	Took reservation.

son. She merely requested reservations for a party of friends to be held in the near future. Table 1 summarizes the nature of the responses to the letter, and to each phone call.

It will be noted that no spontaneous replies to the letter were received although two letters were received as a consequence of the first phone call. Three of the 11 managers admitted having received the letter, eight denied having received it.

With regard to reservations, except for Restaurant D (which has a "no reservation needed" policy), every control call terminated with a specific reservation. Ignoring Restau-

rant D, no manager accepted the phoned request for reservations when told that Negroes would be in the party. Three managers claimed that they do not take reservations; another said that he would accept a phoned reservation, but hung up before it could be made. Three maintained that they could make "arrangements" only if someone came in to the restaurant about it. One of the latter group suggested the possibility of a separate, private room for the dinner. Two managers suggested that we call back at another time. One of these managers went as far as to visit the address on our letter and demanded to know who the writer was and why she was causing a disturbance. During this visit he obtained the phone number and subsequently phoned back three times asking to speak to our fictitious writer.

Finally, one manager turned down the phoned request on the grounds that it was against the law to admit Negroes to his tavern.[3]

It is obvious from Table 1 that the managers were disturbed by both the letter and the first call—they wished to avoid, if possible, having any Negro patrons but they also did not (for whatever reason) wish to give a categorical "No" to the request. To avoid the possibility of a charge of discrimination, they tried to dissuade the caller from coming to their restaurant, denied that they took reservations, requested a personal interview to discuss the matter, etc.

Nevertheless, five managers finally gave tentative approval for the party, two confirming the conversation with a letter. While none of these agreements was made unconditionally, tacit agreement was implied. Three others indicated that while they are unprejudiced themselves (Negro help in kitchen, some Negroes eat there, etc.) they felt that it would be better if our assistant "listened to reason" and went elsewhere.

To call the behavior of the managers inconsistent with either their attitudes or their alleged previous behavior seems trite. The manager or owner of a business that depends on majority group patronage (which he may perceive, rightly or wrongly, as hostile to minority group "intruders") may nevertheless not object when a minority group member appears on the premises. Several hypotheses suggest themselves as possible explanations of his behavior:

1. He fears the consequences of violating the law forbidding discriminatory practices.

2. He may wish to avoid a scene that might not only be a disturbance of the peace but might also call particular attention to the presence of the unwanted guest.

3. Without consciously realizing what the rationale of his behavior may be, the reality situation moves him to adopt one of two competing motives: (a) to do nothing, thus preserving peace and order, or (b) to refuse admission or service because he or his white patrons are offended by Negroes.

Whatever the underlying explanation may be, three levels of response have been found in the present study. These are reactions to each of the three situations with which each manager was confronted. The letter, which may be described as a relatively impersonal contact, produced uniform results: no reply, or at most, one very belated reply. The phone call, which may be described as a partial personal contact, produced a variety of responses ranging from implied acceptance to attempts to rationalize or justify outright rejection of the requests with numerous intermediary responses ("call back," "come in and see us," "couldn't you go to another place?", etc.). The direct contact, which may be described as fully personal in nature, also produced uniform results: admission of the Negro and excellent service in each establishment.

Thus, in addition to the contradictory behaviors found by LaPiere, the managers in the present study exhibited relatively consistent techniques designed to dissuade or discourage our requests for reservations when such requests were made by phone.

Taking the three situations into consideration it would appear, at least for our sample, that the mode of dealing with a minority group member whose presence "violates" culturally established norms varies widely. Discriminatory treatment is minimized when challenged in a direct face-to-face situation,[4]

---

[3] A state law on discrimination does exist, but it *forbids* denial of service to a person in a public place on the grounds of race, religion, or creed.

[4] This hypothesis is supported by a finding of Saenger and Gilbert (3) that a discrepancy between attitudes and behavior occurs where the individual is under high motivation to purchase an article and ignore the fact that the clerk may be a Negro or that the *fait accompli* of a Negro salesclerk makes his presence acceptable. In either case the reality situation appears to act to reduce overt discrimination.

but is maximized when proposals to "violate" group norms are *suggested*. Indirect evidences of discriminatory behavior (subterfuges of various sorts) appear when a direct non-face-to-face challenge is made. At least in the cultural climate of a suburban Northeastern community, the hypothetical Negro is more easily discriminated against than is the Negro-on-the-spot. Certainly we do not expect identical results in different cultural climates (e.g., in the South, or to take a less extreme illustration, the East Side Restaurant Survey of New York City which has shown that Negroes are accorded inferior treatment —poor service, undesirable seating locations, etc.—in many New York restaurants). It may, however, be presumed that the same or related dynamic factors are operating in all three instances.

REFERENCES

1. Chein, I., M. Deutsch, H. Hyman, and Marie Jahoda (eds.).
    1949   "Consistency and inconsistency in intergroup relations." Journal of Social Issues 5:No. 3, entire number.
2. LaPiere, R. T.
    1934   "Attitudes vs. actions." Social Forces 13:230–237.
3. Saenger, G., and E. Gilbert.
    1950   "Customer reactions to the integration of Negro sales personnel." International Journal of Opinion and Attitude Research 4:57–76.

CHAPTER 27   Verbal Attitudes and Overt Behavior: A Study of Racial Discrimination*

LAWRENCE S. LINN

The present study is concerned with the relationship between verbal attitudes as expressed through response items on an attitude questionnaire and subsequent overt behavior.[1] It is incorrect to assume that the response to a verbal question (printed or oral) necessarily reveals an attitude which would become operative in the situation depicted in the question. This study will examine the utility of attitude measurements as a means for predicting future behavior. Since considerable funds are expended on attitude research each year and since such research constitutes a large bulk of the social science enterprise, it is essential to make clear what relevance such data have and what kind of restrictions must be placed on their application. This is not to say that there are no verbal attitudes which correlate highly with behavior. But, if the goal of a research project is to predict behavior on the basis of verbal attitudes, evidence must be cited showing the probability of accurate prediction and the degree of validity in generalizing from an attitude to behavior.[2]

The present study will examine the relationship between expressed racial attitudes and overt behavior, looking at the level of

From Lawrence S. Linn, "Verbal attitudes and overt behavior: a study of racial discrimination," *Social Forces*, 1965, *43*, 353–364. Copyright 1965 by the University of North Carolina Press, and reproduced by permission of the author and publisher.

* The author is indebted to David Mechanic for his valuable advice and criticism in the designing and carrying out of this study and to Michael Hakeem, Gerald Marwell, and William H. Sewell for their criticisms of the text. The work reported here was supported by a NIMH training program in social psychology (Grant #2N–7413).

[1] One of the most diversely defined concepts in social psychology is attitude. Not only are there vast differences concerning what properly constitutes an attitude, but there has been developing a large literature debating how attitudes should be measured. Both of these topics have been thoroughly discussed in a recent article by Melvin DeFleur and Frank Westie, "Attitude as a Scientific Concept," *Social Forces*, 42 (October 1963), pp. 17–31, so that a long theoretical analysis of the problems of defining and measuring attitudes will not be dealt with in this paper. This is not to say that they will be ignored; they will be discussed, but relevant only to issues that are raised in this research.

[2] Robert K. Merton has pointed out that it should not be assumed that overt behavior is intrinsically any "more real" than verbal behavior nor should it be considered as more "truthful." Overt actions do not necessarily reflect verbal attitudes and may deliberately conceal or disguise them. In fact, there are times when it may be valuable to know a person's verbal opinion even if it is not directly related to his behavior. . . . See Merton, "Fact and Factitiousness in Ethnic Opinionaires," *American Sociological Review*, 5, (1940).

precision and accuracy that can be obtained in predicting behavior from attitude scores based on written verbal responses. It will also be of interest to examine how people will account for discrepancies between their expressed attitudes and their behavior if and when discrepancies exist. But, before turning to a discussion of the empirical findings of this study, it would be beneficial to review the studies done in the past on the relationship between attitudes and action, paying particular attention to the following three variables: (1) the *method* of attitude and behavior measurement, (2) the *prevalence* of discrepant behavior between attitude and action, and (3) the *direction* of the discrepant behavior.

The first study which examined the relationship between human behavior and expressed attitudes was the classical study by LaPiere.[3] LaPiere traveled through the United States with a Chinese couple, stopping at many hotels, motels, and restaurants, but they were refused service only once. In a follow-up study, he mailed questionnaires to the proprietors of the establishments visited in order to find out if members of the Chinese race would be accepted as guests. Approximately 93 per cent of the restaurants and 92 per cent of the sleeping places indicated that they would not accept or accommodate Chinese people. A control group of other restaurants and hotels were also sent questionnaires, and almost identical results were obtained. This study clearly shows a large discrepancy between expressed attitudes and overt behavior but in a *positive* direction. In other words, although the hotel and restaurant owners expressed a verbal policy of discrimination, when confronted face-to-face with the situation, they did not discriminate. However, it must be pointed out that the LaPiere study has certain methodological problems which reduce the validity of the results and which make a comparison of attitudes and action less credible. First, the questionnaire which

he used to measure attitudes toward the Chinese dealt with general prejudice indices and was *not* necessarily comparable to the behavioral situation in the study. Secondly, LaPiere's presence with the couple probably had a considerable biasing effect. Much different results would have been obtained had the couple gone across the country alone. Nevertheless, the study, even with its problems, does demonstrate a considerable discrepancy between expressed attitudes and overt behavior.

A more recent study by Kutner, Wilkins, and Yarrow[4] [Chapter 26 in this volume] seems to substantiate LaPiere's findings that attitude scores alone are not sufficient predictors of behavior and that racially discriminatory behavior may be less likely to occur in a face-to-face situation. In their study, two white women and one Negro woman entered 11 restaurants in a fashionable community and were served in a normal manner. Two weeks later, letters were sent to each establishment inquiring about reservations for a social affair. Included in the letter was the sentence, "Since some of them are colored, I wondered whether you would object to their coming?" Seventeen days after the letters were sent out, no replies had been received, and thus telephone calls were made repeating parts of the letters. In eight of the 11 cases, the managers denied receiving the letters. In a control phone call made a day later, no reference to the racial character of the group was made, and all but one restaurant accepted the reservation of the party. Thus, this study, like the LaPiere study, demonstrates a substantial discrepancy between verbal attitudes and subsequent overt behavior involving racial prejudice. Again, it should be noted that the discrepancy is in the *positive* direction, moving from a conservative, prejudicial attitude position to a more liberal, behavioral one.

---

[3] Richard LaPiere, "Attitude vs. Action," *Social Forces*, 13 (December 1934), pp. 230–37.

[4] Bernard Kutner, Carol Wilkins, and Penny Yarrow. "Verbal Attitudes and Overt Behavior Involving Racial Prejudice," *Journal of Abnormal and Social Psychology*, 47 (1952), pp. 649–52.

There are further lines of evidence which demonstrate the discrepancy between verbal attitudes and overt behavior. Saenger and Gilbert,[5] when testing the hypothesis that anti-Negro prejudice in white department store customers would not lead to discrimination against Negro sales personnel or the stores employing them, found that there was no tendency in prejudiced individuals to avoid dealing with Negro clerks. Minard,[6] in examining the attitudes and behavior of white coal miners toward Negroes within the same mine and outside it, found that racial integration and equality only existed within the work roles of the mine. Outside the job, the two races occupied different status levels in almost every situation. In the Saenger and Gilbert study, the discrepant behavior was again in the positive direction. In the Minard study the direction is less clear, but it appears that the discrepancies in behavior ran in both directions.

Fishman,[7] in his introduction to a study of the Negro's entrance into Bridgeview, a New Jersey suburb near New York City, found a clear discrepancy between expressed attitudes and actual behavior that ran in both the positive and negative directions. He found that many people who, for the most part, had negative attitudes toward the Negro nevertheless remained in an interracial community which was progressively becoming more Negro. Yet, others who had positive attitudes toward Negroes moved away.

DeFleur and Westie[8] have also studied the relationship between attitude and action.

[5] Gerhart Saenger, and Emily Gilbert. "Customer Reactions to the Integration of Negro Sales Personnel," *International Journal of Opinion Attitude Research*, 4 (1950), pp. 57–76.

[6] R. D. Minard. "Race Relationships in the Pocahontas Coal Field," *Journal of Social Issues*, 8 (1952), pp. 29–44.

[7] J. Fishman, "Some Social and Psychological Determinants of Inter-Group Relations in Changing Neighborhoods: An Introduction to the Bridgeview Study," *Social Forces*, 40 (October 1961), pp. 42–51.

[8] Melvin DeFleur, and Frank Westie, "Verbal Attitudes and Overt Acts: An Experiment on the Salience of Attitudes," *American Sociological Review*, 23 (1958), pp. 667–673.

After the administration of a prejudice scale to a group of college students, those scoring high and low were recalled as subjects and given a projective test in which each was shown slides of pairs of Negro and white men and women in various social situations. At the end of the projective test session, each S was asked to pose with a Negro person of the opposite sex. The Ss were then given a standard photographic release agreement which consisted of a graded series of situations in which the photograph might be used. The S was asked to sign his name to each release. The relationship between the amount of prejudice expressed on the questionnaire and the level of signed agreement to be photographed with a Negro is shown below.

signed level of agreement	prejudiced	non-prejudiced
Below mean	18	9
Above mean	5	14

$$x^2 = 7.264$$
$$p = .01$$

Although DeFleur and Westie found the relationship between attitude and action statistically significant, it was not found to be a linear relationship. Fourteen students, about 30 per cent of the sample, showed discrepant behavior. DeFleur and Westie considered these 14 cases to be too many to be attributed to measurement error and therefore suggest that the lack of a linear relationship may be explained by an intervening variable related to social involvement.

Even though the DeFleur and Westie study is methodologically superior to its predecessors, there are still problems of the reliability and validity of attitude measurement. For example, Ss in their study were chosen on the basis of high and low prejudice scores on Summated Difference Scales. In this technique the S is asked many questions which involve him in a hypothetical relationship with both a Negro and a white of the same occupation. The Ss are scored according to the total number of racial discrepancies for each occupational category. This method of attitude assessment actually may not measure the same attitude objects or situational variables involved in the willingness to pose for a picture with a Negro in various social situations. Therefore, in attempting to improve attitude measurement, the present study will use attitude objects (items on the questionnaire) identical to the behavior observed (the signing of photographic releases). Since all the past studies have lacked a reliable or precise attitude measurement that validly could be related to the observed behavior, it is important to see if a linear relationship might exist when direct comparisons between attitude and behavior can be made in a more credible manner. If discrepant behavior continues to exist even after refinements have been made, then, as has been suggested, it might be beneficial to look for intervening variables which would account for the Ss' discrepancies.

A second improvement built into the design of the present study involves making the experimental situations more credible. This was, in part, accomplished by the fact that the Ss did *not* know that they were subjects in a psychological experiment and also by the use of Negro experimenters. The effect of their presence will be discussed later in the paper, but here it might be pointed out that besides making the situation more real, their presence should also serve to intensify the Ss' attitudes towards Negroes.

A final advantage of the present study is the use of a post-test interview. This interview session will serve as a check on the validity of the behavior-measuring instrument (the photographic releases) and hopefully will give insight into some of the social-psychological aspects of the Ss' behavior.

Thus, the concern of the present study is to examine the relationship between racial attitudes and overt behavior looking at (1) the level of consistency between the two phenomena, which implies (2) the ability to predict behavior accurately on the basis of attitude

scores, and (3) the existence of intervening variables such as peer or family reference groups which would account for any discrepant behavior.

Therefore, the present study will examine and test the following hypothesis:

Individuals with either positive or negative verbal attitudes do not necessarily act in accord with those attitudes in an overt situation, even when the measuring instrument apparently taps the same attitude objects that are involved in the behavior.
A. This implies that attitudes may often be poor indicators of behavior and that their use in this direction must be carefully restricted.
B. The accuracy of an attitude scale as an indicator of behavior can be determined by empirical research and is necessary in determining the validity of the instrument.

METHOD

Subjects

All of the Ss in the present study were females enrolled in introductory courses in sociology at the University of Wisconsin. An attitude questionnaire was administered to ten discussion sections and scattered among the total number of questions were 14 items concerning attitudes toward Negroes. The 14 questions were used by the present study to construct the following two attitude scales:

Scale I

1. I would be willing to pose with a Negro of the opposite sex if the picture were to be used in laboratory experiment work where it would be seen only by professional sociologists and psychologists.
2. I would be willing to pose with a Negro of the opposite sex if the picture were to be published in a professional journal and read only by professional sociologists and psychologists.
3. I would be willing to pose with a Negro of the opposite sex if the picture would be shown to a few dozen university students in a laboratory situation.
4. I would be willing to pose with a Negro of the opposite sex if the picture were to be used as part of a projective personality test to be used

widely by psychologists and sociologists to measure people's attitudes.

5. I would be willing to pose with a Negro of the opposite sex if the picture were to be published in the student newspaper in my own university as part of a campus-wide campaign for racial integration by an organization like the NAACP.

6. I would be willing to pose with a Negro of the opposite sex if the picture were to be published in my hometown newspaper as part of a publicity campaign by an organization like the NAACP for racial integration.

7. I would be willing to pose with a Negro of the opposite sex if the picture were to be used in a brochure of an organization like the NAACP and circulated in a nationwide campaign for racial integration.

Scale II

8. I don't mind going to a racially integrated school, Negroes and whites mixed together.

9. I wouldn't mind living in a neighborhood where there were some Negroes integrated into the community.

10. I wouldn't mind if a Negro lived next door to me in my home community.

11. I wouldn't mind if a Negro family lived in the same building in which I lived.

12. I wouldn't mind attending a party in which there were both Negro and white couples.

13. If I were unattached, I would have no objection to dating a Negro person of the opposite sex.

14. If I were in love, I would have no objections to marrying a Negro of the opposite sex.

Design and procedure

Four weeks after the administration of the attitude questionnaire, it was announced to each of the classes sampled that:

Two student representatives of the Psychological Testing Company, Boston, Mass., will be interviewing students on campus during the next ten days. They are interviewing Wisconsin students who may be interested in helping to develop a new semi-projective personality test. Participation is completely voluntary, and not all of you will be asked to take part at the same time. ... The interview session will take about 15 min-

utes. The names of those who are asked to help construct the test have been given to your teacher along with an appointment sign-up schedule. If your name is on the list, and, if you desire to participate, sign up now or after class for a time that is convenient to you.

The students who were asked to volunteer were all of the 18- and 19-year-old girls who had previously responded to the attitude questionnaire. The girls who signed up for interview appointments were told to wait in chairs outside the Psychological Testing Company office until called. The white E greeted the S and ushered her into the office, introducing himself and E' (a light-skinned Negro) as representatives of the Psychological Testing Company. The S was seated directly opposite the two Es. In the first part of the interview, the Es discussed the general plans of the "Test Construction Program." The Ss were shown the TAT test as a model for construction and given a short lecture on the construction, purpose, and use of projective personality tests. The second phase of the interview became more specific:

(Dialogue—E', light-skinned Negro). What the company is interested in developing is a set of cards which will be used similarly to the TAT that you have just seen, but with pictures of people of different races who will portray various social situations. The number of people in each picture will vary, but the focus of attention of each one will be on a racially integrated couple, a Negro and a white. The subject matter of the pictures will be typical social scenes like playing cards or chess, studying together, dancing, or sipping a coke. . . .

(Dialogue—E, white). More specifically, we have asked you here today to see if you would be willing to help us with our test construction program and if you would therefore be willing to pose for a photograph with a Negro of the opposite sex of the type that has just been described to you. If you are interested in helping us construct the test, we would like you to indicate the conditions under which you will allow the pictures to be used. This is formally done by the signing of these photographic releases. The signing of a photographic release agreement is standard procedure and is necessary in any situation in which a photograph of an individual is used in any professional way. You may sign some of them, all of them, or none of them as you see fit. . . .

If the S signed any of the releases, E' set up an appointment on a future date for taking the photograph. The S was told that the photo appointment would take only 15 minutes and that she should wear neatly-appearing school clothes.

For the final phase of the interview, the Ss were asked to talk to a representative of the National Association for the Advancement of Negro Right[s] (NAANR), a dark-skinned Negro (E''). After introductions were made, E'' explained to the S what the NAANR was and why they were interested in the photographs, explaining that they would be interested in them for various campaigns and publicity programs for racial integration. The S was then asked to sign three more photographic release agreements. The four photographic release agreements which E' presented to the S were identical to the first four items in Scale I which the S had previously completed four weeks ago. The three releases which E'' presented to the S were identical to the remaining three items in Scale I.

The Ss who were supposedly to have their pictures taken returned individually several days later for their appointments. They were met by the white E at the Psychological Testing Company office and were asked to come and sit down for a minute so that some details could be ironed out before posing for the pictures. The S was seated and asked if she had changed her mind about participating in the program. After answering the question, the S was then told that the "construction program" was an experiment, was given some explanation, and finally interviewed about the entire situation. The content of the interview and the results of the information gained from it will be reported in another section of the paper. Also, Ss who refused to sign any of the releases were contacted by

telephone, told that the "construction program" was an experiment, and asked to return for an interview.

RESULTS AND DISCUSSION

Relationship between Attitude and Action

Degree of relationship—As has been discussed, past studies examining racial attitudes and overt behavior have found varying relationships between the two variables. For example, the studies by LaPiere, Kutner, and others have shown that, when people who have racially prejudiced attitudes are placed in a situation calling for overt action, they fail to behave in a discriminatory fashion. Although the magnitude of the results of these studies was impressive, the methodological problems inherent in each study were so large that a more careful analysis of the problem was necessary. DeFleur and Westie attempted such a study using an experimental laboratory approach in examing the problem. They found that racial attitudes were *positively* related to behavior at the .01 level of confidence. Yet, in spite of the statistical significance, almost one-third of the cases were clear instances of discrepant behavior. The present study devised a means of measuring racial attitudes (Attitude Scale I) in which direct comparison can be made from the attitude scores to the overt behavior observed. An attitude score ranging from 0–7 was compiled for each S, showing the degree of willingness to pose for a photograph with a Negro in a social situation. Similarly, a comparable behavior score was compiled for each person, indicating the *signed* level of agreement to pose for a photograph with the Negro. Mean and median scores were compiled for both attitude scales (I and II) and the scale of overt behavior. (See Table 1.) Notice that for both attitude scales, the mean and the median are considerably higher than for the behavioral scale, showing a marked difference between attitude and overt behavior. Focusing more closely on discrepant behavior, 59 per cent of the total sample ($N = 34$)

TABLE 1

The Mean and Median Scores for the 34 Subjects on Two Attitude Scales and a Behavior Scale

Scale	Mean	Median	N
Attitude Scale I	4.9	5.5	34
Behavior Scale	2.8	2.5	34
Attitude Scale II	4.3	5.0	34

was found to have discrepant scores of *two* or more (out of a possible 7), and 65 per cent of this group had scores showing *three* or more discrepancies. More significant relationships can be seen in Table 2, where the responses have been divided into three categories for each variable—low (score of 0–2), medium (score of 3–5), and high (score of 6–7) willingness to pose for a photograph with a Negro for the attitude variable; and low (score of 0–2), medium (score of 3–5), and high (score of 6–7) level of signed agreement to pose for such a photograph. A chi-square test was run on Table 2, and an *r* correlation was run on the two variables. Neither test showed the variables to be significantly related, thus confirming the hypothesis that individuals with either positive or negative verbal attitudes do not necessarily

act in accord with those attitudes in an overt situation even when the measuring instrument apparently taps the same attitude objects involved in the observed behavior.[9]

Direction of discrepant behavior—Thus far, the present study has shown that there is no linear relationship between expressed attitudes and overt behavior and that, in fact, 52 per cent of the Ss in the sample showed behavior which was inconsistent with previously expressed attitudes. The purpose of this section is to analyze and discuss the direction of these discrepant cases. In Table 2, the marginal totals clearly show that, whereas 50 per cent of the respondents verbally expressed a high willingness to pose for a photograph with a Negro, only 24 per cent of the respondents showed a high level of signed agreement to pose for such a photograph. By the same token, whereas only 18 per cent of the respondents verbally expressed a low willingness to pose with a Negro, 52 per cent of the respondents, when confronted with the ac-

[9] It should be pointed out that the Chi-square test and *r* correlations are both very sensitive to sample size. The relatively small sample size in the present study probably accounts for the lack of statistical significance. Regardless, the major concern here is to point out that more than 50 per cent of the Ss of the study showed behavior which was discrepant with their previously expressed attitudes.

TABLE 2

The Relationship Between the Scores on Attitude Scale I, Showing the Level of Willingness to Pose for a Photograph with a Negro of the Opposite Sex and the Signed Level of Agreement to Pose for Such a Photograph (N = 34)

Verbal Attitude	Overt Behavior				
	High level of signed agreement (6–7)	Medium level of signed agreement (3–5)	Low level of signed agreement (0–2)	Percent of Total	N
High level of willingness (6–7)	7 (41%)	3 (18%)	7 (41%)	17	(50%)
Medium level of willingness (3–5)	1 (9%)	4 (36%)	6 (55%)	11	(32%)
Low level of willingness (0–2)	0	1 (17%)	5 (83%)	6	(18%)
Totals	8 (24%)	8 (24%)	18 (52%)	34	(100%)

$x^2 = 7.26$ with 4 degrees of freedom; not significant.

tual situation, expressed a low level of signed agreement. Of the 18 cases showing discrepant behavior in Table 2, 89 per cent (16 cases) were discrepant in a "negative" direction. By negative it is meant that more liberal, less prejudiced attitudes were originally expressed, but, when the individual was confronted with the real situation, his behavior became more discriminatory than his attitudes had formerly indicated. Only *two Ss* in the present study deviated from their expressed attitudes in a "positive" direction. How can the negative direction of the discrepant behavior be accounted for in the present study? What factors might be attributed to its cause?

Some of the directional disparity—but certainly not all of it—might be due to more valid, reliable, and precise measurement of variables. Of more importance, however, in the present study is the cultural milieu of the S. That is, the Ss were college students attending a large midwestern university which has a reputation for being politically and racially liberal. Within this climate of university liberalism, it is a social and cultural norm held by most faculty and students to take a liberal position on racial integration. Liberal attitudes toward the Negro are, in most circles, not only criteria for social approval but a sign of intellectual maturity— a sign of a "liberal education." It is therefore not surprising that 50 per cent (17) of the Ss expressed highly liberal racial attitudes and 32 per cent (11) expressed attitudes that fell within the middle range. In other words, the skewed distribution of attitude scores toward the liberal direction is at least in part due to the students' playing, or attempting to play, their social role of the liberal college student. However, this role of "racial liberalism" with its associated constellation of attitudes is quite contradictory to the way in which most people have been socialized into our society. Contrary to the university atmosphere, most segments of American society and the norms associated with them do *not* see racial integration as being socially acceptable; in fact, integration is probably more

often viewed as something either to fear or to avoid on a personal level. The present study therefore suggests that discrepant behavior in a negative direction is partially due to a breakdown of *unstable* attitudes which are part of a social role that has never been behaviorally put to test. Further evidence for and development of this position will be presented later in the paper.

The salient effect of Negro experimenters and its effect on action—Both of the Negroes used in the present study were intelligent and impressive college graduates. However, in spite of their attractiveness, the Ss were very conscious of their race. For many of them, the experimental situation provided the first actual face-to-face contact with a Negro. This situation became very stressful for some, producing strong feelings of uncertainty. Three of the Ss never kept their appointments to have their pictures taken even though they had signed photographic releases. These three Ss could not be recontacted, and they refused to respond to several telephone messages. Three other girls who signed release agreements refused to have their pictures taken, saying that they had changed their minds and did not want to participate.

It is interesting that on the attitude questionnaire only *two Ss* were not willing to pose for a photograph with a Negro no matter how the picture would be used, but, when confronted with the actual situation, *twelve Ss* refused to sign any of the releases. The act of refusing to sign any of the photographic releases in the presence of a Negro, while at the same time holding more liberal attitudes, appeared to be a confusing and stressful situation for the S. Several girls, at the time they were asked to sign the releases, explained in an almost remorseful tone, "I want to . . . but I can't!"

Of course, the Ss level of involvement with a Negro in the present study is much different than allowing a Negro to take a room in a motel, allowing him to eat in a restaurant, working with him in a coal mine, or buying merchandise from him in a department store. Posing for a photograph with a Negro of the

TABLE 3

THE RELATIONSHIP BETWEEN PREJUDICE SCORES ON ATTITUDE SCALE II AND THE LEVEL
OF SIGNED AGREEMENT TO POSE FOR A PHOTOGRAPH WITH A NEGRO (N = 34)

| | Overt Behavior | | | | |
Verbal Attitude	High level of signed agreement (6–7)	Medium level of signed agreement (3–5)	Low level of signed agreement (0–2)	Total	Percent of N
Low prejudice (5–7)	7 (30%)	6 (27%)	10 (43%)	23	(68%)
High prejudice (1–4)	1 (10%)	2 (18%)	8 (72%)	11	(32%)
Totals	8 (24%)	8 (24%)	18 (52%)	34	(100%)

x^2 = 3.79 with 2 degrees of freedom; not significant.

opposite sex, in which the photograph would be used in the situations depicted in the present study, involves an extremely high degree of personal social involvement, much greater than that required in the situations depicted in other studies. In summary, however, it can be said that the use of Negro experimenters in the present study seems to have served its purpose. It heightened the Ss' attitudes toward the Negro in general and made the situation more credible and immediate.

Attitudes as predictors of behavior—This final section discussing the relationship between attitude and action will examine the reliability and validity of the racial attitude as a predictor of behavior as found in the present study. Again looking at Table 2, which shows the relationship between scores from Attitude Scale I and the subsequently observed overt behavior, it can be said that imprecise and unreliable prediction occurs only for Ss who hold more liberal attitudes (high and medium willingness to pose). For those Ss who expressed prejudiced attitudes (low willingness to pose), their behavior in all but one case was consistent. The same trend was found when Attitude Scale II was used as a predictor of overt behavior. As shown in Table 3, a total of 70 per cent of the predictions made for Ss with *low* prejudice attitudes were inaccurate. However, for Ss with *high* prejudice attitudes, 72 per cent be-

haved consistently with their attitudes, making prediction of behavior for this group reasonably accurate.

Therefore, it is apparent from the findings shown in Tables 2 and 3 that Ss with racially prejudiced attitudes can be expected to behave in accord with those attitudes; prediction of overt behavior for Ss with liberal racial attitudes can be made no better than by chance; and, finally, that Ss who exhibit racially discriminatory behavior may actually hold to liberal attitudes as often as not.

Post-Test Interview

There were two major functions which the post-test interview session was to serve in the present study: (1) as a validity-check on the measurement of behavior and (2) as a means of gaining insight into the Ss perceptions and feelings about the experimental situation.

Validity check—In the present study, appearance or non-appearance for the "picture taking" session was a means of checking the precision, reliability, and validity of the photographic release agreement as a measure of behavior. That is, it is possible that, even though an S has signed an agreement to have her photograph released, she may refuse to have her picture taken(not keeping her appointment) or she may change her mind on how the pictures are to be used. Thus, one of the reasons for having Ss return for a picture posing session rather than ending the experiment immediately after signing the releases was to correct for measurement error. In fact, it was found that corrections had to be made for six cases, 18 per cent of the total sample. Of these six cases, three never showed up for their appointments or responded to any subsequent phone messages. The other three changed their minds about participating.

A second means for checking the validity of the study was to ask the Ss if they had any knowledge that they were participating in a psychological experiment, and secondly, if the experimental situation seemed credible. Of the 29 Ss interviewed, only one thought that the present study was an experiment. *All 29 Ss felt that the situation was credible.*

Persuasion, salience, and the effect of Negro experimenters—One of the goals of the research design was to make the situation as credible and realistic as possible without persuading or forcing the Ss into behavior which was against their wishes. As has already been pointed out, all Ss indicated that the situation was credible, but the question still remains, had they been persuaded into making a decision to sign (or not sign) the photographic releases? Out of the 29 Ss interviewed, only four indicated that they had felt persuaded and not in full control over the decision to sign or not to sign the release agreements.

Yet, although most of the Ss did not feel that they had been persuaded, it was interesting that 38 per cent of the sample (11 cases) felt that the presence of a Negro had "bothered" them. Some students indicated that the presence of the Negro had an effect on their action; others found his presence made the decision to sign the releases more "uncomfortable." For example:

I didn't know if I should sign or not. I really couldn't visualize the consequences. Yes, I was aware of the fact that there was a Negro present. I couldn't look at him but only at you (white E) when I told you I wouldn't sign the releases.

It was really a very embarrassing type of situation. What could he (the Negro E) be thinking of me?

I felt a little pressured. The presence of a Negro made it a little uncomfortable. If I didn't sign, it made me not look like a good American. I thought the pictures were too much like dating, and I don't like that. I really felt guilty for not doing my part.

You *want* to say yes, but because he is a Negro there are strong social pressures. It was like I was discriminating against him to his face.

The majority (62 per cent) of the Ss reported that they were not bothered or influenced in a negative way. In fact, some Ss commented that the presence of a Negro made the situation more real. For example:

The presence of a Negro really had no effect in my signing the releases, but he made the situation seem more important, just his being there. The Negro being right there showed that he felt it was important and thus you wanted to help him.

Discrepant behavior: how the Ss explain it—As has been pointed out earlier, 59 per cent of the sample were found to have two or more discrepant responses between their verbal attitudes and overt behavior. In the process of interviewing, these Ss were confronted with their differing attitudes and action scores and asked, "How would you account for your discrepant behavior?" Most of the responses could be classified into a single category. Essentially, this group of Ss saw the signing of the photographic releases as being a different, more "real" situation than answering questions on a questionnaire. Yet, the questionnaire response was also seen as representing "what I *should* or *would like* to do" and the signing of releases as being "what I *could* or *had* to do." For example:

I don't really know how I feel until I'm actually confronted with the situation. You *think* you should act one way, but you're not sure and probably won't.

In the questionnaire I wasn't faced with the real thing. It (the signing of the releases) *should* be done, but I can't. Those were my desires, but I couldn't do them. I had to think of my parents and of my hometown.

When it comes down to it, I guess I back down. I hadn't given another thought to the questionnaire, but the face-to-face situation made be back down. It was nice to think I'd be willing!

At that time (time of the questionnaire) I was thinking of what I *should* do, but when confronted with the situation, I thought more deeply about participating. I was worried about other people and what they would think. I was not worried for myself.

On the questionnaire it seemed all right but when it came to the *real* thing, it seemed "scary." It wouldn't have been so bad for a large group picture. Did anybody else do what I did?

Discrepant behavior: an analysis and its relationship to reference group theory—De-Fleur and Westie in trying to explain the lack of a straight-line relationship between attitudes and action suggest that a conscious consideration of reference groups intervenes and is responsible for making the decision to act or not to act consistently with one's attitudes. They therefore conclude that the decision to pose or not to pose for a photograph with a Negro was a peer-directed one. The present study recognizes the importance of reference groups in the decision-making process but believes that they are more inclusive than peers alone and furthermore should be seen as antecedent rather than intervening variables. In other words, reference groups influence the individual by being part of his normative system which reflects the attitudes and norms of the society in which he lives, as well as his community, family, friends, and school. Prejudice and discrimination are the products of learning the customs, beliefs, values, and norms of these various social groups and institutions. Thus, the group, whether community, family, or friendship, becomes the agent of attitude formation for

the individual through the processes of interaction, identification, or association. The forces which account for an individual's behavior are far greater than just his immediate referents. In fact, quite often people will behave in ways contrary to their peers. Therefore, prejudice and discrimination as conceived by the present study are products of experience and learning which have occurred throughout one's life-time. Several sociologists have described the process as follows:

Prejudices are generally acquired slowly and over a period of time. The child acquires his ethnic and racial attitudes as he learns other social lessons, from adults, from his peers, and from his life experiences. . . .[10]

Few parents actually teach their children to be prejudiced; however, their own attitudes and behavior, their restrictions on the playmates of their children, and the tendency to stereotype all individuals of a given racial or religious group with certain physical, behavioral, and mental characteristics results in a pattern of prejudice which their children imitate. It is not the parents' attitudes alone, but the whole home influence that is responsible for the development of prejudice.[11]

Thus, for the most part, the values and norms of the general society do *not* foster the nature and degree of integration as depicted in the present study. These values, which often characterize the Negro as being dirty, dangerous, and dumb, may be learned, overtly or covertly, within the context of the family, the community or the school. These values of racial prejudice and the associated norms of segregation and discrimination are part of what is taught and what is learned in our society.

On the other hand, within the university community there exists a "subculture" in which the prevailing values and norms ap-

---

[10] M. Vosk, "Correlates of Prejudice," *Review of Educational Research,* 23 (1953), pp. 353–361.

[11] Elizabeth Hurlock, *Child Development* (3d ed.; New York: McGraw-Hill Book Co., 1956), p. 290.

pear to be quite opposite of those of the general society. As has already been mentioned, in this "subculture" it is the social norm to take a liberal position on racial integration. Figure 1 shows this skewed distribution of at-

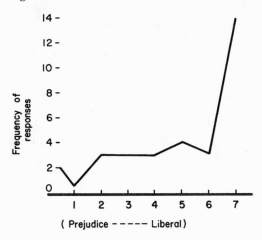

Figure 1.   Frequency of responses to Attitude Scale I.

titude scores toward the liberal direction, quite contrary to what might be expected from society in general.

Thus far, two antecedent variables have been introduced which are thought to explain the lack of a straight-line relationship between verbal attitudes and overt actions: (1) that racial prejudice and/or racial discrimination have been either overtly or covertly the prevailing norm in the general society and (2) that the social norm in the "university subculture" is one advocating racial liberalism, a norm which conflicts with the norms of the general society. But a third and most crucial variable which must be added in order to account for the behavior in the present study as well as in the past ones is the concept of social involvement. The level of social involvement is determined by the amount of interaction with the attitude object, the degree of visibility of this interaction, who views it, and what consequences, positive or negative, might arise.

Hopefully, by relating these three variables together, it will be possible to arrive at one possible explanation for discrepant behavior in both a positive and negative direction.

The Ss in the present study as well as in the DeFleur and Westie study were young college girls who had only recently been exposed to the norms and values of the liberal university subculture. As has been shown, a large number of them, when asked to indicate their attitudes toward Negroes in a questionnaire, had already begun to play their university social role as a racial liberal. The questions asked the Ss if they would be willing to pose for a photograph with a Negro of the opposite sex which would be used in situations with varying degrees of visibility, seen by various kinds of audiences, and having different kinds of potential consequences. Posing for a picture with a Negro which eventually will be published is a situation with a high degree of social involvement, especially when compared with the situations depicted in other studies, such as serving a Negro in northern restaurants or working with Negroes in a coal mine.

However, for many of the Ss, the role of a racial liberal had been discussed or thought about only on a symbolic or hypothetical level and had rarely, if ever, been put to empirical test. Most of the Ss had no chance to test their attitudes with overt action in real situations. Thus, they had no way of reinforcing, modifying, or possibly even rejecting the validity or stability of their attitudinal position. The present study provided a very clear opportunity for Ss with racially liberal attitudes to act overtly in the direction of their convictions, but it was interesting, yet not unusual, to find that a large number of girls were unable to act in this way. The explanation offered by the present study suggests that the Ss were confronted with two sets of conflicting roles; that the overt behavior which resulted (various degrees of discrimination) was due to the stronger role, the more stable and comfortable role, the more imprinted, tested, and experienced role becoming operative and dominant over the weaker one. But, this process of the "differential association" between two opposing sets of norms and associated roles was dependent upon the required level of social involvement with the attitude object. Therefore, the following hypothetical statement can be made in explaining when and why discrepant behavior occurs: The level of consistency between racial attitudes and racial behavior is a function of the stability of the attitude position and of the degree of social involvement required between the individual and the attitude object. Therefore, the following types of propositions can be made:

1. Discrepant behavior in a negative direc-

tion (racially liberal attitudes which are inconsistent with subsequent discriminatory behavior) will increase if the liberal attitudes represent an *un*stable position (the lacking of actual experience and reality-testing) and if the level of social involvement with the attitude object is high.

2. Discrepant behavior in a positive direction (racially prejudiced attitudes which are inconsistent with subsequent behavior which is non-discriminatory) will increase if the level of social involvement is low and if the prejudiced attitudes have not been overtly tested. Both of these propositions assume that the measurements of attitude and behavior can be validly compared.

CHAPTER 28

Measuring Senatorial
"Progressivism"

N. L. GAGE AND BEN SHIMBERG

ANALYSIS OF POLITICAL BEHAVIOR

If such constructs of political discourse as "progressivism" are actually descriptive of legislative behavior, then it should be demonstrable that (1) a sample of legislative acts can be selected from the universe of bills[1] in any legislative session so as to represent the political dimension being considered and (2) the votes of legislators on the sample of bills can be summarized in a single index that univocally describes their voting behavior along that dimension.

It often falls upon political analysts and editorial writers to interpret for the electorate the voting records of their representatives. When a legislator stands for re-election, such commentators point to votes on single bills or groups of bills as a basis for overall judgment regarding the candidate's merit, say his "conservatism" or "liberalism." One plausible assumption in such evaluation is that past vot-

From N. L. Gage and Ben Shimberg, "Measuring senatorial 'progressivism.'" *Journal of Abnormal and Social Psychology*, 1949, *44*, 112–117. Copyright 1949 by the American Psychological Association, and reproduced by permission of the authors and publisher.

[1] The term "bills" is here used to designate any proposition, motion, resolution, etc., on which a record vote is taken.

ing is indicative of the legislator's future political orientation. Frequently, a second assumption is that the bills singled out for attention are "all of a piece" so that voters can consider them collectively in reaching an overall judgment concerning the candidate's record and potentialities. An implication of this assumption is that votes on these bills form a meaningful pattern in which a single index will specify the legislator's position on any single bill.

THE UNIDIMENSIONALITY OF BILLS

An instance of this type of political analysis is the tabulation of voting records published by the *New Republic* after each session of Congress. The editors select a sample of about a dozen bills or propositions voted on during the session. For each bill, the editors tabulate the votes of all Senators and Representatives as "plus" or "minus" to designate "progressive" or "anti-progressive" votes, respectively. The recording of votes in this manner implies, of course, that a "plus" on one bill stands for the same political orientation as a "plus" on any of the other bills in the sample. In other words, it is implied that the bills constitute a homogeneous set of questions, each testing the same political characteristic.

If these implications are valid, the bills should constitute a unidimensional scale in the sense set forth by Guttman (2). Thus a total score based on the number of "plus" votes of each legislator should enable the reproduction of his votes on each of the selected bills. The coefficient of reproducibility, that is, the percentage of correct predictions of specific votes from the total scores, should be 90 per cent or higher.

The application of the technique to test for unidimensionality is general. Any interested group may determine, according to its own standards and its own frame of reference, whether a bill is "progressive" or "anti-progressive," "pro-labor" or "anti-labor," "good" or "bad." Thus one group might call a bill "progressive" while another might call it the opposite. This will make no difference in the scalability of the bills as long as each group is consistent in its judgments. The unidimensionality of the bills finally selected is an indication of how consistently the group was able to isolate bills that tested the characteristic in which they were interested.

To determine the unidimensionality of two sets of bills selected by the editors of the *New Republic*, we have applied the Cornell technique of scale analysis (3). The voting records subjected to scale analysis were those of 89 senators in the second session of the Seventy-ninth Congress and of 95 senators in the first session of the Eightieth Congress (7, 8). (Only senators for whom records were available on all bills in the sample were considered.)

RESULTS OF SCALE ANALYSIS

For the Seventy-ninth Congress, the voting records of senators on 14 bills were tabulated by the *New Republic*. Scale analysis of all 14 bills yielded a coefficient of reproducibility of 84 per cent. On four of these bills the error in reproducibility was substantially higher (mean error, 27 per cent) than that for the other ten (mean error, 13 per cent). New

total scores were then obtained with these four bills disregarded. The scale analysis was repeated and now yielded a reproducibility coefficient of 88 per cent. Other requirements of scalability, concerning range of marginals, random scatter of errors, and number of items in the sample (4) were also met. It was concluded that the ten remaining bills constituted a scale sufficiently unidimensional to justify the use of the single total score as an index of "progressivism."

While the immediate purpose of the scale analysis was to determine unidimensionality, the identification of bills that did not belong on the major continuum may be equally significant. We can say that considerations other than "progressivism," as operationally defined by the ten unidimensional bills, were operative in the voting on the four eliminated bills. For example, two of these four bills were motions to invoke the cloture rule in the debates on Fair Employment Practices and Anti-Poll Tax legislation. As we might expect, many of the conservative, "anti-progressive" Republican senators voted "progressively" on these bills. Progressive votes here were probably reflections of impatience with filibuster tactics as much as of a desire to promote the legislation in question. Similarly, the other two eliminated bills, concerned with the presidential power to reduce tariffs and with the Bretton Woods monetary agreement, found "progressives" and "anti-progressives" voting in the same way. Again we must infer that different motives operated to make "strange bedfellows."

Ten bills were included in the *New Republic's* tabulation of senatorial voting records in the Eightieth Congress. Scale analysis of all ten bills yielded 88-per-cent reproducibility. On two of the bills the errors of reproducibility were disproportionately high, both being 23 per cent, as against an average of 8.5 per cent for the other eight bills. Repetition of the scale analysis with these two bills omitted raised the reproducibility to 91 per cent and the other requirements of scalability were also met. Again the scale analysis identified bills (dealing with Greek-Turkish aid and wool tariff) that did not cohere with "progressivism" as conceived by the editors of the *New Republic*.

CORRELATES OF VOTING BEHAVIOR

Having established the existence of unidimensional scales, we could assign to each senator a total "progressivism" score based on his voting record in a given session. Each "plus," or "progressive," vote was assigned a value of one; each "minus" vote, a value of zero. The quantitative measures thus obtained make possible statistical investigations of the correlates of legislative behavior.

Session-to-Session Consistency—To test the popular assumption that voting behavior in one session of Congress can be predicted from that in a preceding one, we correlated the two "progressivism" scores of the 72 senators who were present in both the Seventy-ninth and the Eightieth sessions of Congress. The *r* of .82, whose supporting data are given in Table 1, bears out this assumption. These results agree closely with those reported by Brimhall and Otis (1).

Age vs. "Progressivism"—Another popular stereotype is that younger senators are

more "progressive." The correlation coefficients between age and "progressivism" scores do not support this view. As is shown in Table 2, the *r*'s in the Seventy-ninth and Eightieth Congresses were .19 and .05, respectively.

Junior vs. Senior Senators—How closely do the views of senators from the same states correlate?[2] This question can be answered from the data in Table 3. Here we see that the tendency for junior and senior senators from the same state to vote in the same way is negligible, the *r*'s being .31 and .10 in the Seventy-ninth and Eightieth Congresses, respectively.

How do the mean "progressivism" scores of junior and senior senators compare? We find that the data for the Seventy-ninth Congress show practically no difference between junior and senior senators. In the Eightieth Congress, however, we find the difference between junior and senior senators significant beyond the .01 level ($t = 3.64$).

The insignificant difference between the means of junior and senior senators in the Seventy-ninth Congress and the highly sig-

---

[2] The senator who has represented a state for the longer time in the Senate is considered the senior senator from that state.

TABLE 1

SESSION-TO-SESSION CORRELATION OF "PROGRESSIVISM" SCORES

	No. of Bills	No. of Senators	Mean	SD	r
79th Congress	10	72	3.64	2.76	.82
80th Congress	8	72	3.32	3.37	

TABLE 2

CORRELATIONS BETWEEN AGE AND "PROGRESSIVISM"

	Progressivism			Age		r
	N	Mean	SD	Mean	SD	
79th Congress	89	3.60	3.51	58.93	9.99	.19
80th Congress	95	3.28	2.64	57.03	10.11	.05

TABLE 3

COMPARISON OF "PROGRESSIVISM" SCORES OF JUNIOR AND SENIOR SENATORS PAIRED BY STATES

	Jr. Senators			Sr. Senators		r	t
	N	Mean	SD	Mean	SD		
79th Congress	41	3.26	3.46	3.53	3.48	.31	.42
80th Congress	47	2.38	2.27	4.17	2.70	.10	3.64

nificant one in the Eightieth Congress reflect recent political trends. Senators of the Seventy-ninth Congress were elected during the war years when "progressive" and "anti-progressive" political tendencies were not strong factors in senatorial elections. The expectation that junior and senior senators in the Seventy-ninth Congress would not differ in "progressivism" is thus borne out. The election in the fall of 1946, however, showed a strong post-war swing toward conservatism. This would lead us to expect a greater difference between junior and senior senators in the Eightieth Congress; this difference did, in fact, materialize. The validity of the two progressivism scales is thus, to some extent, supported.

Regional differences—We can test popular stereotypes concerning the relative "progressivism" of senators from the various regions of the nation by comparing the mean "progressivism" scores of senators grouped according to the regions that they represent. The 48 states were grouped into the follow-

ing four regions: Northeast, Midwest, South, and Mountain-Pacific. Table 4 shows the mean raw scores, mean T-scores, standard deviation, and number of senators in each of the four regions for the Seventy-ninth Congress.

An analysis of variance shows that the differences among the senators for the four regions were highly significant. The senators from the Mountain-Pacific region were most "progressive" and those from the Midwest were least "progressive." Southern senators were only slightly more "progressive" than those from the Midwest.

The election of November 1946 resulted in Republican control of the Senate. This meant that the Southern (almost entirely Democratic) senators no longer shared responsibility with their Northern colleagues for control of the Senate. The split between Northern and Southern Democratic senators that had been so wide when the Democrats were in control seemed to be narrowed substantially under these circumstances. This leads us to

TABLE 4

REGIONAL DIFFERENCES AMONG SENATORS, SEVENTY-NINTH CONGRESS

	N	Mean Raw Score	Mean T-Score	SD
Northeast	18	4.72	53.19	3.96
Midwest	23	1.91	45.18	2.60
South	29	2.45	46.72	2.75
Mt.-Pacific	19	6.32	57.75	2.99
Total	89	3.60	50.00	3.51

F = 9.14, $p < .01$

TABLE 5

REGIONAL DIFFERENCES AMONG SENATORS, EIGHTIETH CONGRESS

	N	Mean Raw Score	Mean T-Score	SD
Northeast	18	3.33	51.13	2.69
Midwest	24	1.67	44.83	1.60
South	31	3.68	52.45	2.61
Mt.-Pacific	22	4.45	55.37	2.74
Total	95	3.28	50.00	2.64

F = 5.22, $p < .01$

expect that Southern senators will become relatively more "progressive" in the Eightieth Congress. We find that this is the major shift in regional standing that occurs in this Congress as compared with the Seventy-ninth Congress. We see in Table 5 that senators from the Mountain-Pacific states are still the most "progressive," senators from the Midwest are still the least "progressive," and senators from the Northeast still occupy an intermediate position. But the Southern senators, rather than resembling the Midwestern (primarily Republican) senators most closely, are now much higher in their relative "progressivism" standing.

The analysis of voting by political party affiliation, given below, throws further light on this shift. We have here evidence that the "out-party" huddles together in its minority status and seeks to bolster itself through a solidarity that submerges ideological differences beneath stern political considerations.

Party differences—Until 1933, many political scientists pointed to an absence of fundamental difference between the two major American political parties. The parties have usually differed; that is, unity has not characterized Congress except in times of crisis. But have these party differences on individual bills been solely a matter of jockeying for political advantage or has there been a general pattern underlying each party's position?

The unidimensional "progressivism" scores reveal a "method" not only in the voting of individual senators, but in that of their parties. Table 6 shows the means and standard deviations of the "progressivism" scores of various political party groupings in the Seventy-ninth Congress.

The Democrats were significantly more "progressive" than the Republicans. When the Democratic senators are divided into Southern and non-Southern groups, even greater differences appear. Similarly, the non-Southern Democrats are much more "progressive" than the Republican senators; but the difference between the Southern Democrats and Republicans is barely significant. In the Seventy-ninth Congress, when the Democratic Party was in the majority, "conservative" Southern senators frequently had to vote against their more "progressive" colleagues to prevent the passage of "progressive" legislation. But in the Eightieth Congress, the Republican Party had control, carried out the conservative functions desired by the Southern senators, and freed the latter to cultivate party solidarity.

This explanation of the apparent connection between majority-minority status and the "progressivism" of the Southern senators is supported by the data on party differences in the Eightieth Congress when the Democratic Party was no longer in control. Table 7 shows that Republicans and Democrats dif-

TABLE 6

"PROGRESSIVISM" SCORES BY PARTY GROUPINGS, SEVENTY-NINTH CONGRESS

	N	Mean Raw Score	Mean T-Score	SD	t
All Senators*	89	3.60	50.00	3.51	. . . .
All Democrats	51	5.10	54.28	3.49	6.30
All Republicans	37	1.38	43.67	1.98	
Southern Democrats	26	2.69	47.41	2.80	56.9
Non-Southern Democrats	25	7.60	61.40	2.12	

t (Republicans vs. Southern Democrats) = 2.01

t (Republicans vs. Non-Southern Democrats) = 11.47

* Includes one senator from the Progressive Party.

TABLE 7

"PROGRESSIVISM" SCORES BY PARTY GROUPINGS, EIGHTIETH CONGRESS

	N	Mean Raw Score	Mean T-Score	SD	t
All Senators	95	3.28	50.00	2.64	
All Democrats	44	5.27	58.48	2.24	9.11
All Republicans	51	1.59	44.53	1.54	
Southern Democrats	26	4.35	55.00	2.30	4.09
Non-Southern Democrats	18	6.61	63.56	1.25	

t (Republicans vs. Southern Democrats) = 5.41

t (Republicans vs. Non-Southern Democrats) = 13.42

fer in the same direction and just as significantly as in the Seventy-ninth Congress. But the difference between Southern and non-Southern Democrats, while still large, has greatly diminished. In terms of T-scores (whose standard deviation is 10 by definition) the difference between Southern and non-Southern Democrats has changed from about 14 T-score units in the Seventy-ninth Congress to only 8.5 T-score units in the Eightieth Congress.

The difference between the Republicans and the non-Southern Democrats remains very large. Republicans and Southern Democrats who did not differ strikingly in the Seventy-ninth Congress, now differ widely; the difference increased from about 3.5 T-score units in the Seventy-ninth Congress to about 10.5 T-score units in the Eightieth Congress.

SUMMARY AND CONCLUSIONS

A technique has been formulated and applied for quantifying legislative behavior. It provides a method for identifying bills that cohere in a unidimensional scale, making possible the ranking of legislators on a single political continuum.

1. Scale analysis was employed to test the scalability of senatorial votes on bills considered indicative of the "progressivism" of senators in the Seventy-ninth and Eightieth Congresses. Ten bills in the Seventy-ninth

Congress and eight in the Eightieth Congress proved to be unidimensional.

2. The session-to-session consistency of the progressivism scores was .82.

3. Correlations between age and "progressivism" scores were .19 and .05 in the Seventy-ninth and Eightieth Congresses, respectively.

4. Correlations between progressivism scores of senators from the same state were .31 and .10 in these two Congresses, respectively.

5. Differences between junior and senior senators were not significant in the Seventy-ninth Congress; in the Eightieth Congress the senior senators were significantly more "progressive."

6. Regional differences in "progressivism" among senators were highly significant in both Congresses.

7. Differences in "progressivism" between Republican and Democratic senators were significant in both Congresses. Differences between Southern and non-Southern Democrats decreased sharply in the Eightieth Congress as compared with the Seventy-ninth. This shift is attributed to the change of the Democratic senators from majority to minority status.

8. The internal consistency (unidimensionality) of the votes within a single session and the session-to-session correlation of the total scores justify the hypothesization of "progressivism" as a common trait (in G. W. Allport's sense) of senators. This does

not, of course, mean necessarily that "progressivism" is primary in the parsimonious, or simple structure, sense of factor analysis. It does mean that "progressivism" scores could be used in a correlation matrix with other data on senators to arrive through factor analysis at a set of primary common traits. Individual traits may perhaps be indicated by those senators who are non-scale types, that is, whose voting patterns do not conform to those inherent in the demonstration of unidimensionality.

BIBLIOGRAPHY

1. Brimhall, D. R., and A. S. Otis.
   1948 "Consistency of voting by our Congressmen." Journal of Applied Psychology 32:1–14.
2. Guttman, L.
   1944 "A basis for scaling qualitative data." American Sociological Review 9:139–150.
3. Guttman, L.
   1947 "The Cornell technique for scale and intensity analysis." Educational and Psychological Measurement 7: 247–279.
4. Guttman, L.
   1947 "On Festinger's evaluation of scale analysis." Psychological Bulletin 44: 451–465.
5. Congressional Directory.
   1946 79th Congress, 2nd Session, United States Government Printing Office, Washington, D.C.
6. Congressional Directory.
   1947 80th Congress, 1st Session, United States Government Printing Office, Washington, D C.
7. (Anonymous)
   1946 "Facts for November, men and issues." New Republic, September 23, 1946, 115:363–374.
8. (Anonymous)
   1947 "The 80th Congress; The sellout." New Republic, August 4, 1947, 117: 15–25.

CHAPTER **29**   Seating Aggregation as an
Index of Attitude*

DONALD T. CAMPBELL, WILLIAM H. KRUSKAL
AND WILLIAM P. WALLACE

The social sciences are at present overdependent upon voluntary verbal self-description by questionnaire or interview. This method is subject to weaknesses, such as voluntary or unconscious distortion, self-consciousness, reactive effects upon attitudes, and awkwardness of administration. More important, even though voluntary verbal self-description eventually be judged the best of all methods, every method contains systematic irrelevancies which can only be ascertained through a strategy of joint application of methods as different as possible.[1] It is in the service of

From Donald T. Campbell, William H. Kruskal and William P. Wallace, "Seating aggregation as an index of attitude." *Sociometry* 1966, *29*, 1–15. Copyright 1966 by the American Sociological Association, and reproduced by permission. Errata in the original printing have been corrected.

* The contributions of Donald T. Campbell and William P. Wallace to the preparation of this paper were supported by Project C998 Contract 3–20–001 with the Media Research Branch, Office of Education, U.S. Department of Health, Education and Welfare, under the provisions of Title VII of the National Defense Education Act. William H. Kruskal's work was carried out in the Department of Statistics, University of Chicago, under partial sponsorship of the Statistics Branch, Office of Naval Research. Reproduction in whole or part is permitted for any purpose of the United States government.

[1] Eugene J. Webb, Donald T. Campbell, Richard D. Schwartz, and Lee Sechrest, *Unobtrusive Measures: Non-*

developing such other measures that this study of seating aggregation is presented.

Where seating in a classroom is voluntary, the degree to which the Negroes and whites present sit by themselves rather than mixing randomly is a presumptive index of the degree to which acquaintance, friendship, and preference are affected by race. Such voluntary clustering by race will be termed "aggregation," as opposed to the enforced separation connoted by the term "segregation."

Just as an attitude questionnaire has its irrelevant components such as response sets, social desirability factors, social class differences in willingness to use hostile vocabulary for any purpose, etc., so such a measure as seating aggregation is distorted by factors irrelevant to the concept of interest. Observation of the high degree of racial clustering or aggregation at the typical annual banquet of a society dedicated to removing racial barriers reflects no doubt the biased opportunities for prior acquaintance rather than the racial attitudes of the persons involved. So too in a classroom, the tendency to sit with friends from one's neighborhood and previous schools provides a bias perhaps more directly

reactive Research in the Social Sciences. Chicago: Rand McNally, 1966.

reflecting acquaintance opportunity than lack of good will. None the less, if within a classroom there are marked shifts in aggregation from time to time, these might reflect shifts in interracial fear and good will superimposed on the baseline provided by prior acquaintance opportunity. Or if two schools drawing from the same community provide markedly different aggregation indices, these differences might be attributed to attitudinal factors. The illustrative data of the present study are primarily of this latter case.

The aggregation index—Among the many possible ways one might measure aggregation, we chose to base a measure on the number of Negro-white seating adjacencies, that is, the number of pairs of row-wise adjacent seats, one of which is occupied by a Negro student, the other by a white student. (Seats separated by an aisle, and seats with empty seats in between, are not considered to be adjacent.) The number of adjacencies by itself, however, is not suitable as an index. For one thing, it is clearly influenced by the total number of students and by the proportions of Negro and white students. Some kind of baseline and yardstick are necessary. In principle, a realistic stochastic model for the seating of students should be used, but not enough is known about the phenomenon to warrant work on such a model. Instead, we have used a baseline and yardstick corresponding to expected number and standard deviation of adjacencies derived from a randomness assumption, namely that the seats were randomly chosen as regards race, but that the pattern of occupied seats was fixed. Details are given in the Appendix.

The index used was

$$I = (A - EA)/\sigma_A,$$

where

A = observed number of adjacencies
EA = expected number of adjacencies under randomness
σ_A = standard deviation of number of adjacencies under randomness.

The expressions for EA and σ_A are in terms of

N = total number of students in a class
M = number of Negro students
$N - M$ = number of white students
K = number of groups of row-wise contiguous students (including isolates)
K_1 = number of students with no one next to them (isolates).

In these terms

$$EA = 2\frac{M(N-M)}{N(N-1)}(N-K)$$

$$\sigma_A^2 = 2\frac{M(N-M)}{N(N-1)}(2N - 3K + K_1) +$$
$$4\frac{M(M-1)(N-M)(N-M-1)}{N(N-1)(N-2)(N-3)}$$
$$[(N-K)(N-K-1) - 2(N - 2K + K_1)] -$$
$$4\frac{M^2(N-M)^2}{N^2(N-1)^2}(N-K)^2.$$

Figure 1 shows a typical seating chart from the study. In this case

$$N = 22, M = 6, K = 10, K_1 = 4, A = 1,$$
$$EA = 4.99 \text{ and } \sigma_A = 1.51.$$
$$I = \frac{1 - 4.99}{1.51} = -2.64.$$

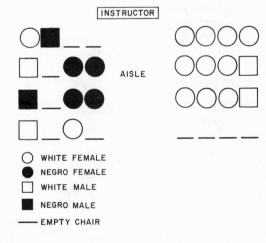

WHITE FEMALE
NEGRO FEMALE
WHITE MALE
NEGRO MALE
EMPTY CHAIR

Figure 1. Sample seating chart from Normal U., 1964.

Negative values of I indicate more aggregation than under randomness, and positive values indicate less aggregation than that under randomness.

Data sources—The data of major interest come from classrooms observed at two colleges in the Fall of 1963 and 1964. These two colleges had in a previous unpublished study provided the two extremes of most prejudiced and least prejudiced white students in a comparison of five colleges scattered over the nation, including one southern white college. Both were located in the same northern metropolis. Both consisted entirely of commuter students. Both had substantial minorities—as colleges go—of Negro students. Both had unbiased administrative policies and Negro faculty members. One, which we shall call Downtown U., was by reputation militantly liberal on the race issue. The other, which we shall call Normal U., attracted primarily students seeking teaching credentials, and apparently of predominantly traditional, nonintegrationist attitudes. Also available were seating charts for classes from Normal U. in 1951 and for 1963 from a Junior College which was located in this same northern metropolis. The basic data pool is described in Table 1. In this table the 1963–1964 data have been pooled. Inspection showed no trends within this period.

The 1963–1964 data were collected by an observer who entered the classroom as though a student and from a convenient vantage point prepared the seating chart. The 1951

observations were made by the administrator of a test while the test was being taken by the students, no record being made of the sex of the students. It must be noted that the observations on any one class were collected by a single observer. Consequently, difficulties in observer identification of Negro and white students present an unchecked source of error. Although it is presumed this problem produces a negligible error, it would be desirable to have several observers in each classroom to assess inter-observer variation, and if possible to check these against self-identification.

Any errors of identification almost certainly lead to underestimation of the number of Negroes present, given the current U.S. norms. This would make the expected number of adjacencies too low in classrooms where Negroes are in the minority. The number of observed Negro-white adjacencies would be overestimated where a Negro-Negro adjacency was recorded as an NW, and underestimated where an NW was recorded as a white-white adjacency. If aggregation occurs to the same degree among the potential passers on whom errors have been made, the net error would probably be one of overestimation of Negro-white adjacencies, which, when combined with the downward error of expected adjacencies, leads the computed indices to be underestimates of aggregation. There is no reason to believe that in the present data such errors have been distributed in any systematic manner. (The di-

TABLE 1

BASIC DATA POOL

	Number of Classes			of Negroes		of Whites		Percentage	
	Total	All of One Race	All of One Sex	Male	Female	Male	Female	Negro	Female
Downtown U. 1963–64	23	2	1	34	24	335	160	10%	33%
Normal U. 1963–64	20	0	0	49	103	164	215	29%	60%
Junior College 1963	12	1	0	59	79	106	23	52%	38%
Normal U. 1951	19	0	?	89		435		17%	?

chotomous recording made should be more accurately described as Negro and non-Negro, as there were a few oriental students who were classified as white.)

The courses sampled covered a variety of liberal arts classes. The selection of classes was haphazard but not random. During a class hour the experimenter observed as many classes as he could, selecting the classes to be observed systematically on the basis of their location, e.g., the second class sampled in a given hour would be one located near the first class sampled. This selection method was judged to be sufficiently unrelated to observed characteristics that statistical procedures based on randomness might be tentatively used. Approximately three class hours were needed for the collection of the data from each school. This gives rise to the possibility that some students may have been observed in more than one classroom. The possibility of some dependence between classrooms thus cannot be ruled out, but is judged to be of minor importance. Observations at both schools were made within a week of each other in both 1963 and 1964, with no incidents of racial relevance occurring during the period of observation.

RESULTS

The generality of aggregation by race—Table 2 shows the basic results for the class indices. (Classes not having members of both races have been omitted.) All schools have a negative mean index, indicating fewer Negro-white seating adjacencies than would be expected by chance. Using the t test all of these means are statistically significantly different from zero at the $p < .01$ level. Most individual classes show negative indices, although there are a few that do not.

School differences in aggregation—The distributions of the aggregation-index values for each school appear in Figure 2. In Figure 2, D.U. refers to the Downtown U., 1963–1964 samples, N.U. refers to the Normal U., 1963–1964 samples, J.C. refers to the Junior College, and N.U. '51 refers to the Normal U., 1951 sample. The two schools of major interest show a statistically significant difference in aggregation indices in the expected direction. The Downtown U. mean of −.81 was significantly less negative than the Normal U. mean of −1.50 with a t of 2.46, 39 degrees of freedom, $p < .02$ (a two-sided test of significance). The difference was in the same direction and to about the same degree in the 1963 and 1964 data taken separately. The utility of the index as a measure of attitude thus receives some confirmation.

The degrees of differentiation that the index provides is, however, by no means as sharp as that provided by the earlier unpublished questionnaire data. In 1951, anonymous questionnaire data on attitudes toward Negroes were collected from six classes at Downtown U. and nine at Normal U. When

TABLE 2

RACIAL AGGREGATION INDICES

	Downtown U. 1963–1964	Normal U. 1963–1964	Junior College 1963	Normal U. 1951
Mean index	−.81	−1.50	−1.41	−1.05
Standard deviation	.81	.98	1.46	1.53
t from zero index	4.50	6.82	3.20	3.00
Number of classes	21	20	11	19
Number of classes with positive indices	3	1	2	6

Note: Differences in numbers of classes from Table 1 reflect discarding of classes with M or N-M equal to zero.

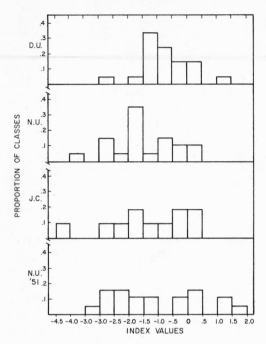

Figure 2.   Distribution of index values for D.U., N.U., J.C., and N.U. '51.

means are computed for the white students in each class, the two schools show no overlap on either a direct attitude scale or a multiple choice information test scored for anti- and pro-Negro bias in the alternatives selected.[2] The *t* ratios for the difference between the two schools, computed for an *n* of classes, were 5.74 for "direct" scores and 8.62 for "indirect" scores, these values being much larger than the *t* of 2.46 for the aggregation index even though fewer classes were involved. Different years, different classes, and different constructs are involved. It is, of course, presumptive to assume that had anonymous questionnaire data been collected in 1963–1964 the differences would have remained as

---

[2] This test was an improved version of tests reported in brief in Donald T. Campbell, "The Indirect Assessment of Social Attitudes," *Psychological Bulletin,* 47 (January, 1950) p. 21, and in Robert E. Rankin and Donald T. Campbell, "Galvanic Skin Response to Negro and White Experimenters," *Journal of Abnormal and Social Psychology,* 51 (July, 1955), p. 32 [Chapter 31 in this volume].

large as they were in 1951, but this is the only comparison available. Since no measures of anti-white attitudes were taken from the 1951 Negro students, only the white data have been examined. The aggregation index is presumably a joint product of the dislikes and fears of both Negroes and whites. (In more refined data collection, the total sequence of seat-taking might be examined in such a way as to isolate actions symptomatic of white attitudes from those symptomatic of Negro attitudes.) The lesser degree of prejudice-differential for the aggregation index might be regarded as another illustration of a recurrent observation in northern settings that overt actions are less prejudiced than anonymous questionnaire responses.

Aggregation changes over time—For Normal U. the difference between the 1951 data and that for 1964 was not statistically significant. Corresponding attitude test data from the school for the time trend are not available, although general public opinion surveys show a decrease in prejudice for this decade.[3] The direction of shift for the index is counter to this national trend. While the proportion of Negroes attending Normal U. increased between 1951 and 1964, this proportion seems, as shown below, to be unrelated to bias.

Aggregation by sex—As is commonly noted, classroom seating shows aggregation by sex. The computation of indices for sex aggregation was thought to be of value both as a check on the index and to provide a comparison for the racial aggregation indices. Table 3 shows the basic values for the indices of aggregation by sex. (Sex was not recorded in the 1951 data from Normal U., and classes have been omitted which did not have members of both sexes.) The general finding is one of significant sex aggregation in all schools.

Within the classrooms there is significant aggregation by sex and there is significant aggregation by race. However, the difference between sex and race aggregation is not sta-

---

[3] Herbert H. Hyman and Paul B. Sheatsly, "Attitudes on Desegregation," *Scientific American,* 211 (July, 1964) pp. 16–23.

TABLE 3

AGGREGATION INDICES FOR SEX

	Downtown U. 1963–1964	Normal U. 1963–1964	Junior College 1963
Mean index	−.90	−1.36	−.77
Standard deviation	1.36	.98	1.18
t from zero index	3.10	6.18	2.26
Number of classes	22	20	12
Number of classes with positive indices	4	2	4

tistically significant when computed by a paired-sample t test on the 51 classes for which both indices were available (Race mean = −1.20, Sex mean = −.99, t = 1.24, df = 49, p < .25). Since pooling across schools may be inappropriate, the analyses were repeated considering each school separately. None of the resultant t's approached statistical significance.

Joint effect of sex and race—The following analysis asks whether or not the number of adjacencies is particularly low when the adjacency crosses both race and sex. That is, do adjacencies between Negro men and white women or between Negro women and white men occur still less frequently than do adjacencies between persons differing on race alone, or on sex alone. No adequate approach to this problem was found. What has been explored are fragmented indices, paying attention only to the two subgroups involved, and treating all other persons as though they were empty seats. This analysis has been limited to those classes providing persons in

all four race-sex subgroups. (Downtown U. contributed three classes, Normal U., 1963–1964 contributed eleven classes, and the Junior College contributed three classes to this analysis.) Table 4 shows the results of this analysis. While the two indices crossing both race and sex average lower (more negative) than either of the other pairs, they both fall within the range of indices provided by the other subgroups. Using class-by-class paired-sample t's for the averages of these pairs, no significant differences were found (cross Sex and Race *vs.* cross Race t = 1.85; cross Sex and Race *vs.* cross Sex, t = 1.53; cross Sex *vs.* cross Race, t = .20, df = 16 in each case). Thus while a slight trend toward a joint effect was present, it did not approach usual standards for statistical significance. This approach has inadequacies on logical grounds, and a better approach is being sought.

Control analyses—It is very difficult to achieve descriptive indices of degree of effect which are comparable with assurance across

TABLE 4

AGGREGATION INDICES WITH FRAGMENTED CLASSES

	Cross Race and Sex		Cross Race		Cross Sex	
	MN-FW	MW-FN	MN-MW	FN-FW	MN-FN	MW-FW
Mean index	−1.20	−1.26	−.66	−1.21	−.60	−1.34
Average subclass size	15.00	17.59	14.82	17.76	9.47	23.12
Number of classes	17	17	17	17	17	17
Number of classes with positive index	1	4	6	3	5	2

heterogeneous conditions of size and proportion. For this reason, certain control analyses have been done. It is possible that the index might not be comparable between two classes varying widely in the proportion of Negroes present. Computing the correlation between this proportion and the resulting index for each of the four samples the following correlation coefficients were obtained: Downtown U., 1963–1964, $r = -.21$; Normal U., 1963–1964, $r = +.37$; Junior College, $r = -.13$; Normal U., 1951, $r = +.13$. None of these coefficients reached a usual level of statistical significance.

Class size is somewhat more problematic. The correlation between the aggregation index and class size for the four samples was as follows: $r = -.18$ for Downtown U., 1963–1964; $r = -.17$ for Normal U., 1963–1964; $r = -.75$ for the Junior College; and $r = -.14$ for Normal U., 1951. Of the above correlations, only that in the Junior College reached statistical significance ($p < .01$, df $= 10$). All of the correlations were negative, which suggests that larger classes show more racial aggregation. Larger classes probably come from freshman and sophomore courses, and the correlation may thus indicate improved race relations as a function of maturity, familiarity, etc. Unfortunately, course levels were not recorded. The class size correlations with aggregation by sex did not approach statistical significance ($r = +.01$ for Downtown U., 1963–1964; $r = -.11$ for Normal U., 1963–1964; $r = -.18$ for the Junior College). These latter results do not support an interpretation that the aggregation index is artificially influenced by class size. In any event, the class size correlation does not affect the interpretation of the Downtown U.–Normal U. aggregation differences, as the 1963–1964 mean sizes for these two are 26.33 and 26.55 respectively, and the class-size correlations within these schools did not reach an acceptable level of statistical significance.

In some respects the index neglects features that might artificially affect the number of Negro-white adjacencies. Thus no use is made of the number of vacant seats nor their possible location so as to buffer Negro-white adjacency. Undoubtedly in many instances a shortage of seats increases Negro-white adjacencies in a manner not reflecting the preferences of the persons involved. As a partial check on this, the proportion of empty seats was correlated with the race aggregation index. The resulting correlations were $+.12$ for Downtown U., $+.24$ for Normal U., 1963–1964, and $+.55$ for the Junior College. The correlations are not statistically significant and are in the opposite direction from that expected, showing the larger the proportion of empty seats the less aggregation. For sex aggregation, these correlations were $-.04$, $+.18$, and $-.49$ for Downtown U., Normal U., 1963–1964, and the Junior College respectively. None of these correlations reached statistical significance. Thus neglect of empty chairs does not in these data appear to have produced misleading effects. Another feature which an ideal index might attend to is the number or proportion of row-ends where no adjacency is possible. Thus an arrangement of the same number of chairs into a pattern of many short rows reduces the opportunities for adjacency in comparison with an arrangement of fewer longer rows. This attribute varied so little in the present study that no control correlation has been computed. Even though empty seats and row ends probably do not distort the present data, the development of a more complex index which would take these into account seems desirable.

DISCUSSION

While there is no indication that the index is of high precision or purity, the results do encourage further exploration. The index might be used, for example, as a before-and-after measure in studies of class presentations designed to improve race relations. One of the most needed studies is the examination of shifts in the degree of mutual trust. A cooperating group of instructors could easily produce a daily series of seating charts in classes in which written classroom work takes place.

The index can also be applied in any other situation in which unidimensional adjacency can be noted. One recurrent class of situations of this type is in the waiting lines for cafeterias, theater tickets, time-clock punching, etc. For waiting lines, the formula is simpler, as K becomes 1, and the number of adjacencies become one less than the number of runs, a much studied topic.[4]

The adjacency index is but one of a larger class of potential aggregation indices. Consider a school playground in which many of the pupils can be identified as participating in activity groups, be they baseball games, hop-scotch, penny-pitching, etc. Utilizing children so classified, one could examine racial composition in terms of a contingency table in which columns were Negro and white, and in which each play group constituted a row. In a similar way, ethnic bias in isolates versus group-involved could be computed. A time-series of such indices from multiracial schoolyards might provide an index of changing tensions.

Another way of conceptualizing aggregation is in terms of the steepness of the interracial boundary—and note that the schoolroom and school yard indices must come from essentially boundary conditions; they are not available for either all white or all Negro schools. If one considers, for example, the residences, sidewalks, stores and public services on a street which crosses the Negro-white boundary at right angles, the more aggregation there is, the "steeper" the racial boundary, i.e., the narrower the transition area in which there is mixed racial presence, the more nearly the shift is from 100 per cent Negro to 100 per cent white, without blocks, stores, sidewalk segments, etc., which have both Negroes and whites present. For presences for which daily decisions and changes are possible, such as shopping for groceries, an increase in the steepness of the boundary might indicate an increase in ten-

sion, as Negroes feel reluctance to shop in predominantly white stores and as whites feel reluctance to shop in predominantly Negro ones. Such considerations move us close to the sociological literature on city indices of segregation computed from census data.[5]

APPENDIX—COMBINATORIAL DERIVATION[6]

Suppose that there are K unbroken sequences of row-wise contiguous occupied seats, containing $n_1, n_2, \ldots, n_k$ seats respectively. Each end of a sequence is bound by either an empty seat or a row end. Let $N = \sum_{i=1}^{K} n_i$ be the total number of occupied seats.

Consider random arrangements of two kinds of units, M of one and $N - M$ of the other, over the occupied seats. In our case, there are M Negro students and $N - M$ white students. Let a random variable corresponding to each seat take the value 0 or 1 as the seat is occupied by a Negro or white student. Then the random variables of interest, arranged in the K sequences, are

$$X_1, X_2, \ldots, X_{n_1};$$
$$X_{n_1+1}, X_{n_1+2}, \ldots, X_{n_1+n_2};$$
$$\vdots$$
$$X_{N-n_K+1}, X_{N-n_K+2}, \ldots, X_N.$$

Note that the sum of all N Xs is $N - M$. It is assumed that all $\binom{N}{M}$ ways of assigning

[4] K. A. Brownlee, *Stati.tical Theory and Methodology in Science and Engineering,* Second Edition, Wiley, New York, 1965, pp. 224–232, and Samuel S. Wilks, *Mathematical Statistics,* Wiley, New York, 1962, pp. 144–150.

[5] Otis Dudley Duncan and Beverly Duncan, "A Methodological Analysis of Segregation Indexes," *American Sociological Review,* 20 (April, 1955); Otis Dudley Duncan, Ray P. Cuzzort, and Beverly Duncan, *Statistical Geography,* Glencoe, Illinois: The Free Press, 1961; Linton C. Freeman and John Pilger, "Segregation: a Micro-Measure Based upon Compactness," Residential Segregation Study, Maxwell School of Citizenship and Public Affairs, Syracuse, New York, October 19, 1964; Linton C. Freeman and John Pilger, "Segregation: A Micro-Measure Based upon Well-Mixedness," Residential Segregation Study, Maxwell School of Citizenship and Public Affairs, Syracuse University, February 12, 1965.

[6] The development of the aggregation index as presented in the appendix is by William H. Kruskal.

M 0s and $N - M$ 1s to the N Xs are equally likely. That is, the model is one of complete randomness conditionally on the given pattern of occupied seats.

The statistic of major interest is the number of adjacencies, A, which may be written

$$A = |X_1 - X_2| + \ldots + |X_{n_1 - 1} - X_{n_1}|$$
$$+ |X_{n_1 + 1} - X_{n_1 + 2}| + \ldots +$$
$$|X_{n_1 + n_2 - 1} - X_{n_1 + n_2}|$$
$$\vdots$$
$$+ |X_{N - n_K + 1} - X_{N - n_K + 2}| + \ldots +$$
$$|X_{N-1} - X_N|,$$

with the convention that if any sequence contains a single member ($n_i = 1$), no corresponding absolute difference appears in the sum. For convenience set $U_i = |X_i - X_{i+1}|$, so that

$$A = \{U_1 + \ldots + U_{n_1 - 1}\} +$$
$$\{U_{n_1 + 1} + \ldots + U_{n_1 + n_2 - 1}\} + \ldots +$$
$$\{U_{N - n_K + 1} + \ldots + U_{N - 1}\}.$$

Each U_j takes the values 0 and 1; 1 means an adjacency, and 0 a nonadjacency.

The next step is to compute some first and second moments in order to obtain the expectation and variance of A, EA and $\sigma_A{}^2$. These results may be regarded as a specialization of work by P. A. P. Moran or as a generalization of standard manipulations in the study of runs.[7]

Clearly $EU_j = $ Prob $\{X_j \neq X_{j+1}\} = 2 \frac{M \ (N - M)}{N \ (N - 1)}$, since

Prob $\{X_j = 1$ and $X_{j+1} = 0\} = $ Prob $\{X_j = 0$ and $X_{j+1} = 1\} = \frac{M}{N} \frac{N - M}{N - 1}.$

Hence $EA = 2 \frac{M \ (N - M)}{N \ (N - 1)} (N - K).$

Since $U_j = U_j{}^2$, $E(U_j{}^2)$ is also $2 \frac{M \ (N - M)}{N \ (N - 1)}.$

Next turn to $E(U_j U_{j+1})$. A convenient way of finding this is to notice that $(U_j - U_{j+1})^2$ takes the values 0 and 1, the latter if

[7] P. A. P. Moran, "The Interpretation of Statistical Maps," *Journal of the Royal Statistical Society,* Ser. B, 10 (1948), pp. 243–251.

and only if $X_j \neq X_{j+2}$. This event has the same probability as $X_j \neq X_{j+1}$. Hence

$$E(U_j - U_{j+1})^2 = 2EU_j{}^2 - 2E(U_j U_{j+1}) = EU_j{}^2,$$

so that

$$E(U_j U_{j+1}) = \tfrac{1}{2} EU_j = \frac{M(N - M)}{N(N - 1)}.$$

Finally, we need $E(U_j U_k)$ with $|j - k| > 1$. A conditional argument provides this readily, for $E(U_j U_k) = $ Prob $\{ U_j = U_k = 1\}$. Given $U_j = 1$, one Negro student and one white student are already sitting in seats j and $j + 1$. Hence the *conditional* expectation of $U_j U_k$ (remember that $|j - k| > 1$) is just EU_k but with M diminished by one and N by 2, i.e.,

$$2 \frac{M - 1}{N - 2} \frac{N - M - 1}{N - 3}.$$

But Prob $\{U_j = U_k = 1\} = $ Prob $\{U_k = 1| U_j = 1\}$ Prob $\{U_j = 1\}$. Hence the desired expectation is

$$\left[2 \frac{M - 1}{N - 2} \frac{N - M - 1}{N - 3} \right] \left[2 \frac{M}{N} \frac{N - M}{N - 1} \right] =$$
$$4 \frac{M(M - 1)}{N(N - 1)} \frac{(N - M)(N - M - 1)}{(N - 2)(N - 3)}.$$

Since $E(U_j U_k)$ does not depend on j,k when $|j - k| > 1$, we may as well write it $E(U_j U_{j+2})$ for simplicity of notation.

Turn now to $E(A^2)$. From the expression for A in terms of sums of Us, we see that

$$
\begin{aligned}
E(A^2) = & \text{ (number of } U_j\text{'s in sum)} \times E(U_j{}^2) \\
& + \text{ (number of } U_j U_{j+1} \text{ products possible)} \times E(U_j U_{j+1}) \\
& + \text{ (number of } U_j U_k, |j - k| > 1, \\
& \quad \text{products possible)} \times E(U_j U_{j+2}).
\end{aligned}
$$

There are clearly $N - K$ U_j's in the sum. Ask next how many $U_j U_{j+1}$ products are possible, and to this end set

$K_1 = $ number of X sequences with just one member,

$K_2 = $ number of X sequences with just two members,

$K_* = $ number of X sequences with more than two members, so that $K = K_1 + K_2 + K_*$. K_1 is the number of isolates and K_2 the number of isolated pairs.

Only the K_* sequences (those with more than two X's) give rise to $U_j U_{j+1}$ products, and the ith of these sequences gives rise to $2(n_i - 2)$ such products. (The factor 2 is there because, for example, both $U_1 U_2$ and $U_2 U_1$ must be counted.) Summing $2(n_i - 2)$ over the K_* sequences, we get

$$2[(N - K_1 - 2K_2) - 2K_*] = 2[N - 2K - K_1].$$

Now how many products of form $U_j U_{j+2}$ are there? Each of the K_2 sequences contributes $N - K - 1$ such products, so from that source we obtain a total of $K_2(N - K - 1)$. The ith K_* sequence contributes $2(N - K - 2) + (n_i - 3)(N - K - 3)$ $U_j U_{j+2}$ products, to give a total from this source of

$$2K_*(N - K - 2) + (N - K_1 - 2K_2 - 3K_*)(N - K - 3),$$

which may be expressed as

$$(N - K - 1)(N - K - K_2) - 2(N - 2K + K_1).$$

Adding the prior $K_2 (N - K - 1)$ gives the final number of $U_j U_{j+2}$ products

$$(N - K)(N - K - 1) - 2(N - 2K + K_1).$$

(As a check, note that the total number of all three kinds of products is, correctly, $(N - K)^2$.)

Putting these results together, we have

$$\sigma_A^2 = 2 \frac{M(N - M)}{N(N - 1)} (N - K) +$$

$$2(N - 2K + K_1) \frac{M(N - M)}{N(N - 1)} +$$

$$4[(N - K)(N - K - 1) - 2(N - 2K + K_1)]$$
$$\frac{M(M - 1)(N - M)(N - M - 1)}{N(N - 1)(N - 2)(N - 3)} -$$
$$4 \frac{M^2(N - M)^2}{N^2(N - 1)^2}(N - K)^2$$

$$= 2 \frac{M(N - M)}{N(N - 1)}(2N - 3K + K_1) +$$
$$4 \frac{M(M - 1)(N - M)(N - M - 1)}{N(N - 1)(N - 2)(N - 3)}$$
$$[(N - K)(N - K - 1) - 2(N - 2K + K_1)] -$$
$$4 \frac{M^2(N - M)^2}{N^2(N - 1)^2}(N - K)^2.$$

Various partial checks may be made. For example, the formulas are symmetric in M and $N - M$. Again, if $N = K = K_1$, i.e., if all the units are isolates, A must be zero; EA and σ_A^2 do indeed properly turn out to be also zero. Again, if $K = 1$ and $K_1 = 0$, A is just one less than the number of runs in a sequence of N objects of two kinds, so that the above results may be compared with well-known formulas[8]

$$EA = \frac{2M(N - M)}{N}$$

$$\sigma_A^2 = \frac{2M(N - M)[2M(N - M) - N]}{N^2(N - 1)}.$$

After algebraic simplification, this specialization does provide a consistency check. Finally, our results may be derived as special cases of those given by Moran.[9]

Depending on the relative magnitudes of $M, N, N - M, K,$ and K_1, approximations to the rather lengthy variance formula may be worked out. One may also consider asymptotic normality of A.

---

[8] For example, see p. 570 of W. Allen Wallis and Harry V. Roberts, *Statistics, a New Approach*, Glencoe, Illinois: Free Press, 1956.

[9] P. A. P. Moran, *op. cit.*, p. 245.

CHAPTER 30 Attitude Measurement and Prediction of Behavior: an Evaluation of Conditions and Measurement Techniques*

CHARLES R. TITTLE AND RICHARD J. HILL

The degree of relationship between measured attitude and other behavior continues to be investigated and debated.[1] Some social scientists now conclude that accurate prediction of behavior from attitude measures is not possible with the techniques generally employed. Green, for instance, states that "many

From Charles R. Tittle and Richard J. Hill, "Attitude measurement and prediction of behavior: an evaluation of conditions and measurement techniques." *Sociometry*, 1967, *30*, 199–213. Copyright 1967 by the American Sociological Association, and reproduced by permission of the authors and publisher.

* We wish to acknowledge the helpful criticisms and suggestions we have received from Alexander L. Clark and Gary I. Schulman.

[1] Two more recent and noteworthy studies are: Pamela K. Poppleton and G. W. Pilkington, "A Comparison of Four Methods of Scoring an Attitude Scale in Relation to Its Reliability and Validity," *British Journal of Social and Clinical Psychology*, 3 (February, 1964), pp. 36–39; and Lawrence S. Linn, "Verbal Attitudes and Overt Behavior: A Study of Racial Discrimination," *Social Forces*, 43 (March, 1965), pp. 353–364 [Chapter 27 in this book]. For general discussions of the issue see: Donald T. Campbell, "Social Attitudes and Other Acquired Behavioral Dispositions," in Sigmund Koch, editor, *Psychology: A Study of a Science*, Vol. 6, New York: McGraw-Hill, 1963; and Melvin L. DeFleur and Frank R. Westie, "Attitude as a Scientific Concept," *Social Forces*, 42 (October, 1963), pp. 17–31.

investigations have found that specific acts or action attitudes often cannot be predicted very accurately from elicited verbal attitudes."[2] Deutscher recently reintroduced the issue in most general terms when he again questioned the assumption that verbal responses reflect behavioral tendencies.[3] However, if the issue is examined on the basis of available evidence, no conclusion can be reached with a satisfactory degree of confidence.

In addition to conventional standards of research, adequate investigation of the problem appears to require that several methodological conditions be fulfilled. First, it would seem obvious that a particular attitude should be measured using a multi-item instrument constructed according to a replicable set of procedures and resulting in at least the objective ordering of respondents. The general superiority of multi-item instruments over single-item measures and introspective order-

[2] Bert F. Green, "Attitude Measurement," in Gardner Lindzey, editor, *Handbook of Social Psychology*, Cambridge: Addison-Wesley, 1954, p. 340.

[3] Irwin Deutscher, "Words and Deeds: Social Science and Social Policy," *Social Problems*, 13 (Winter, 1966), pp. 235–254.

ings of data has been discussed at length. The argument will not be reviewed here.[4]

Second, derivation of an appropriate criterion of non-attitudinal behavior would appear to necessitate consideration of action taking place under typical social circumstances. Preferably, a behavioral measure or index should refer to sets of acts indicative of consistent or patterned action. The concept of attitude usually implies some form of cognitive and affective organization in terms of which an individual responds to an aspect of the world.[5] Further, if attitudes are cognitive and affective organizations which result from normal socialization processes, it seems reasonable to assume that the correspondence between attitude and other behavior will be highest in those situations which the individual has come to define as normal and common. The individual encountering a situation which is characterized by unfamiliar contingencies is not likely to have a well-structured attitudinal organization relevant to behavior in that situation. Attitudinally influenced response is not seen as the equivalent of a deterministic reflex. Many situational contingencies enter into any particular action situation in ways which influence response. Given these considerations, attitude measures should be least predictive of behaviors occurring in situations which (1) are alien to the subject's customary behavioral context or (2) call for aberrant behavior in a familiar action context.[6] Attitude measures should be most predictive of behavior in situations which occur repetitively within the common behavioral context of the individual. With respect to the general relationship, then, the criteria

of most relevance should reflect those behaviors which are repetitious and which take place under usual social circumstances.

When studies designed specifically to evaluate the relationship between measured attitude and other behavior are examined with these considerations in mind, the degree of discrepancy is found to be partially a function of the methodological strategies employed. Table 1 summarizes the results of a review of previous research.[7] Studies were classified by the measurement instrument employed, the kind of behavioral criterion which was used, and the type of situation under which the behavior occurred. For purposes of this classification, several behaviors occurring over time, or the same behavior repetitively engaged in, were considered to constitute a configuration of patterned behavior. With respect to the behavioral circumstances, the studies were categorized into two groups—

---

[4] Cf. Clyde H. Coombs, "Theory and Methods of Social Measurement," in Leon Festinger and Daniel Katz, *Research Methods in the Behavioral Sciences*, Chicago: Holt, Rinehart and Winston, 1953; and Lee J. Cronbach, *Essentials of Psychological Testing* (2nd edition), New York: Harper and Row, Publishers, 1960, pp. 130–131.

[5] Daniel Katz and Ezra Stotland, "A Preliminary Statement to a Theory of Attitude Structure and Change," in Sigmund Koch, editor, *Psychology: A Study of a Science*, Vol. 3, New York: McGraw-Hill, 1959.

[6] Campbell, *op. cit.*

[7] These studies include: Richard T. LaPiere, "Attitudes vs. Actions," *Social Forces*, 13 (December, 1934), pp. 230–237; Bernard Kutner, Carol Wilkins, and Penny Rechtman Yarrow, "Verbal Attitudes and Overt Behavior Involving Racial Prejudice," *Journal of Abnormal and Social Psychology*, 47 (July, 1952), pp. 649–652 [Chapter 30 in this book]; Richard T. LaPiere, "Type-Rationalizations of Group Antipathy," *Social Forces*, 15 (December, 1936), pp. 232–237; Douglas W. Bray, "The Prediction of Behavior from Two Attitude Scales," *Journal of Abnormal and Social Psychology*, 45 (January, 1950), pp. 64–84; Stephen M. Corey, "Professed Attitudes and Actual Behavior," *Journal of Educational Psychology*, 38 (April, 1937), pp. 271–280; Michael Zunich; "A Study of the Relationship Between Child Rearing Attitudes and Maternal Behavior," *Journal of Experimental Education*, 30 (December, 1961), pp. 231–241; Melvin L. DeFleur and Frank R. Westie, "Verbal Attitudes and Overt Acts: An Experiment on the Salience of Attitudes," *American Sociological Review*, 23 (December, 1958), *op. cit.*; Linn, *op. cit.*; C. Robert Pace, "Opinion and Action: A Study in Validity of Attitude Measurement," *American Psychologist*, 4 (July, 1949), p. 242; Herbert W. Rogers, "Some Attitudes of Students in the R. O. T. C.," *Journal of Educational Psychology*, 26 (April, 1935), pp. 291–306; Gardner Murphy, Lois Barclay Murphy, and Theodore M. Newcomb, *Experimental Social Psychology*, New York: Harper and Brothers, 1937, pp. 894–912 (three studies are reviewed); Gwynne Nettler and Elizabeth Havely Golding, "The Measurement of Attitudes Toward the Japanese in America," *American Journal of Sociology*, 52 (July, 1946), pp. 31–39; and Poppleton and Pilkington, *op. cit.*

those that utilized a behavioral criterion representing normal action alternatives and those that employed unusual options. In some cases the research report indicated that the subjects probably defined the situation as atypical. For example, in the Kutner study, it was graphically illustrated that the subjects were dealing with an undefined situation. In instances where no detailed information was provided, we used our own judgment following the general prescription that laboratory situations represented unusual behavior contexts or options.

In addition, the studies were classified as to whether a low, moderate, or high relationship between attitude and the behavioral criterion was observed. In cases where no actual measures of association were provided, the reported conclusions were taken as the basis of classification. Where measures of association were available, association below .35 were classified as showing little relationship, associations between .35 and .59 were considered to represent moderate associations, and associations of .60 or above were classified in the high category.

Obviously, the results reported in Table 1 do not include all investigations concerned with the relationship between attitudes and other behaviors. For example, several consistency tests using "known groups" have been undertaken but are not reported here because the nature of the known groups was such that it was impossible to make inferences about individual behaviors as corresponding to individual attitudes.[8] In addition many other investigations have used certain kinds of attitude measures as predictors within specific substantive contexts. Such studies permit little direct inference about the general relationship of concern here. The research selected for inclusion deals specifically with attitudes and corresponding individual behavior. These studies are those most frequently cited in connection with the argument and to our knowledge are considered to be the crucial investigations of the problem.

It is apparent from Table 1 that the degree of correspondence between measured attitude and other behaviors varies not only with the measure of attitude used, but also with the criterion which is taken as an indicator of behavior. Of the four studies that most nearly fulfill the methodological requirements set forth above, three show attitude measures to be highly associated with behavioral patterns. Considering all 15 studies with no regard for their limitations, six report little relationship, three report moderate (or low-to-moderate) relationship, and six report high relationship. In view of these results, Campbell's conclusion is apparently inescapable: "The degree of correspondence is, for the most part, yet to be discovered."[9] The above reconsideration suggests that the degree of correspondence observed is at least a function of (1) the measurement techniques employed, (2) the degree to which the criterion behavior constitutes action within the individuals' common range of experience, and (3) the degree to which the criterion behavior represents a repetitive behavioral configuration.

The investigation reported below had two purposes. The first concern was to determine the degree of correspondence between measured attitude and other behavior which would be observed when (1) the technique employed to measure attitude consisted of a multi-item instrument constructed according to replicable procedures which result at least in the objective ordering of respondents, (2) the criterion behaviors occurred within the common behavioral context of the individual, and (3) the behavioral situation occurred repetitively in the life experience of the individual.

The second purpose was the evaluation of the relative predictive efficiency of four frequently used measurement techniques in terms of the degree to which these techniques result in the ability to predict behavioral configurations.

---

[8] See Corey, *op. cit.* for a review of some of these studies.

[9] Campbell, *op. cit.*, p. 162.

TABLE 1

SUMMARY OF STUDIES OF CORRESPONDENCE BETWEEN MEASURED ATTITUDE AND BEHAVIORAL PATTERNS

Study	Attitude Measure	Criterion	Circumstances	Correspondence
LaPiere	Hypothetical single question	Single act	Unusual	Low
Kutner	Single question	Single act	Unusual	Low
LaPiere	Stereotypical single question	Patterned behavior	Normal	Low
Bray	Summated rating scale	Single set of acts	Unusual	Low
Corey	Thurstone-Likert scale	Patterned behavior	Normal	Low
Zunich	Summated rating scale	Single set of acts	Unusual	Low
DeFleur	Summated differences scale	Single act	Unusual	Moderate
Linn	Intuitive scale	Single act	Unusual	Moderate
Pace	No indication	Patterned behavior	Normal	Low to Moderate
Rogers	Battery of single questions	Patterned behavior	Normal	High
Murphy (1)	Thurstone scale	Patterned behavior	Normal	High
Murphy (2)	No indication	Patterned behavior	Normal	High
Murphy (3)	No indication	Patterned behavior	Normal	High
Nettler	Thurstone scale	Patterned behavior	Normal	High
Poppleton	Thurstone, scored 4 ways	Patterned behavior	Normal	High

DEVELOPMENT OF ATTITUDE MEASURES

It was suggested above that adequate investigation of the first problem required utilization of multi-item instruments. But since several measuring techniques are in vogue, it seemed desirable to employ more than one of them. The techniques evaluated were: (1) Thurstone successive-interval technique, (2) a semantic differential procedure, (3) a summated-rating (Likert) technique, and (4) a Guttman type scale. In addition, a simple self rating of attitude was examined. The efficiency of each of the five measures was assessed in terms of its correspondence with five criteria of behavior. The assessment was made under the conditions discussed above. These conditions were expected to maximize the relationship between measured attitudes and criterion behaviors.

Others have argued that if one wishes to predict a particular set of behaviors he should attempt to measure an attitude that is specific for a given individual as he relates to that class of behavior.[10] Given this argument, maximizing the credibility of the present study required an attempt to measure a specific rather than a general attitude. One would not expect to predict an individual's personal behavior with respect to his own marriage from a measure of his attitude toward marriage as a social institution. In the present instance, attitude toward personal participation in student political activity was taken as an appropriate measurement objective.

One hundred forty-five statements thought to reflect such an attitude were placed on a successive interval continuum by 213 student judges. The statements were formulated by the authors and several graduate students, using the literature on political participation in the larger society for suggestive outlines. These items were oriented around eight possible channels of individual political activity: (1) voting in student elections, (2) belonging to student political groups, (3) taking part in student political party activities, (4) taking part in student campaign activities, (5) keeping informed about student politics, (6) contact with student government officials, (7) interpersonal discussion of student politics, and (8) personal office holding or seeking.

The panel of judges consisted of entire classes of students, selected to give a broad representation of the student population. The statements were printed in eight-page booklets with the pages arranged randomly, and were submitted for judging with the customary instructions.[11] Following the procedures discussed by Edwards, successive-interval scale and Q values for the statements were calculated.[12] Fifteen statements were selected so that the scale values were approximately evenly spaced on the continuum and Q values were minimal.[13] For the test sample, the median scoring technique was used.[14]

The summated rating scale was built from the same basic 145 statements. Four editors independently classified the statements as to their favorable or unfavorable content. Those statements about which all four agreed were submitted to a separate sample of 213 students. The subjects were asked to respond to each statement on a five-point scale: strongly agree, agree, undecided, disagree, strongly disagree. Responses were weighted in the standard Likert fashion from zero to four. The fifteen items that discriminated best between the top fifty and the bottom fifty subjects were selected for this scale.

A semantic differential employing nine ad-

---

[10] Linn, op. cit. and DeFleur and Westie, "Attitude as a Scientific Concept," op. cit., p. 30.

[11] The Seashore and Hevner method of rating items was used. See Robert H. Seashore and Kate Hevner, "A Time-Saving Device for the Construction of Attitude Scales," Journal of Social Psychology, 4 (August, 1933), pp. 366–372.

[12] Allen L. Edwards, Techniques of Attitude Scale Construction New York: Appleton-Century-Crofts, 1957, pp. 123–138. An internal consistency test yielded an Absolute Average Deviation of .034, a value slightly higher than usually reported when the method of successive intervals is used to scale stimuli.

[13] This was not entirely possible, since only a few statements were found to have scale values near the middle of the continuum.

[14] Edwards, op. cit., p. 145.

jectival pairs was constructed for five concepts: (1) voting in student elections, (2) discussing student political issues, (3) holding student political office, (4) helping in a student political campaign, and (5) keeping informed about student politics. The nine adjectival pairs utilized were: good-bad, valuable-worthless, clean-dirty, pleasant-unpleasant, wise-foolish, fair-unfair, complex-simple, active-passive, and deep-shallow. The first six pairs represent the evaluative or attitude dimension. They were interspersed with the remaining three to obscure the purpose of the measurement (a procedure recommended by the originators of the semantic differential).[15] Pairs were selected using the criteria suggested by Osgood and his associates. Scores on all five concepts were summed and a mean taken as an ordinal measure of attitude toward personal participation in student political activity.

A set of items constituting a Guttman scale was derived using the same responses as those utilized for constructing the summated rating scale. A random sample of 95 questionnaires was selected from the 213 respondents. The statements were examined for scalability using the Cornell technique. Ten items, six dichotomous and four trichotomous, were found to form a scale with a coefficient of reproducibility of .928 and a minimal reproducibility of .635. All error appeared to be random.

These Guttman attitude items were retested for scalability after being administered to the test sample ($N = 301$). The items met the criteria of scalability for this sample but only when used in dichotomous form. Accordingly the four trichotomous items were collapsed into dichotomies. The final scale had a coefficient of reproducibility of .930 and a minimal marginal reproducibility of .751.

Menzel's coefficient of scalability for these data was .717,[16] and Schuessler's Test I resulted in a probability of less than .001.[17]

Once the instruments were constructed they were incorporated into a questionnaire including items about the student's background, participation in student political activity, and his group affiliations on the campus. In addition, the questionnaire included an item eliciting a self-rating of attitude toward student politics on a continuum from zero to eight. This questionnaire was administered to two large sections of a course in marriage and the family, which was composed of a widely variant student population. Freshmen were eliminated from consideration as were students who failed to provide complete data. The final set of subjects was composed of 301 upper-class students.

DEVELOPMENT OF CRITERION MEASURES

The criterion behavior was indexed in several ways. First, the voting behavior of each subject was determined by inspecting student-voting records in an election held one week prior to the administration of the questionnaire. Second, the respondent's report of his voting behavior for the previous four elections was taken as a behavioral indicator. Third, an index of behavioral patterns was constructed by combining responses to questions about frequency of engagement in various types of student political activity. Eight activities were found to form a Guttman scale for the 301 subjects. These activities included frequency of participation in meetings of a student assembly, frequency with which the individual had written to or talked with a student representative concerning an issue, frequency of voting over the past four elec-

---

[15] Charles E. Osgood, George S. Suci, and Percy H. Tannenbaum, *The Measurement of Meaning,* Urbana: The University of Illinois Press, 1957. The same six evaluative pairs were used by Osgood and his associates in comparing the semantic differential with other measures of attitude. See pp. 192–195 [contained in Chapter 13 of this volume].

[16] Menzel suggests the level of acceptance for scales at somewhere between .60 and .65. Cf. Herbert Menzel, "A New Coefficient for Scalogram Analysis," *Public Opinion Quarterly,* 17 (Summer, 1953), pp. 268–280.

[17] Karl F. Schuessler, "A Note on the Statistical Significance of the Scalogram," *Sociometry,* 24 (September, 1961), pp. 312–318.

tions, frequency of engagement in campaign activities on behalf of a particular candidate, frequency of reading the platforms of candidates for student political office, and frequency of discussion of student political issues in talking with friends. When the items were dichotomized, the scale was characterized by a coefficient of reproducibility of .907 and a minimal marginal reproducibility of .698. Again error appeared to be random. Menzel's coefficient of scalability was .675 and Schuessler's Test I yielded a probability of less than .001.

The fourth index of student political participation was devised by summing, in Likert fashion, the categories of response concerning frequency of engagement in ten types of student political activity. These activities included the eight previously mentioned as well as the frequency of personal office seeking and response to an item indicating whether the respondent had ever written a letter of protest to the student newspaper. A fifth measure of participation was an adaptation of the standard Woodward-Roper index of political participation involving a modified scoring of five of the activities already listed.[18]

The five criterion indexes were designed to represent alternate methods of measuring the same behavioral patterns. The degree of association between the criterion measures is reported in Table 2. In general the magnitude of association is relatively high. All measures

of association are in the expected direction and are significantly non-zero at a probability level less than .001. These results suggest that the various indexes measured approximately the same aspects of the students' political involvement.

The degree of interrelationship of the several attitude measures varied considerably (see Table 3). This points up the fact that various methods of measuring the same characteristic may result in the ordering of individuals quite differently. Presumably the variation is accounted for by error factors intrinsic to the measurement techniques. An assessment of the extent to which such factors affect the predictive power of the several instruments in this specific instance is presented below. Moreover, the present research design permitted certain inferences to be made about the nature of the error factors involved.

The behavioral indexes included one "objective" indicator and several "reported" indicators of activity. This raises questions with respect to the adequacy of such a design for making the assessment here proposed. Specifically, it is known that reported behavior does not always correspond to actual behavior; and that the extent of error varies with kinds of information being reported.[19] In the present instance, it was possible to compare one report of a behavior with an independent record of that behavior. The subjects were asked if they had voted in the last student

---

[18] See Julian L. Woodward and Elmo Roper, "Political Activity of American Citizens," *American Political Science Review*, 44 (December, 1950), pp. 872–885.

[19] Hugh J. Parry and Helen M. Crossley, "Validity of Responses to Survey Questions," *Public Opinion Quarterly*, 14 (Spring, 1950), pp. 61–80.

TABLE 2

INTERRELATIONSHIP AMONG CRITERION MEASURES

	Vote over time	Guttman index	Likert index	Woodward-Roper index
Vote in last election	.778	.559	.636	.632
Vote over time	———	.577	.757	.789
Guttman index of political participation	———	———	.850	.721
Likert index of political participation	———	———	———	.869

TABLE 3

INTERRELATIONSHIP AMONG ATTITUDE MEASURES

	Guttman	Thurstone	Sem. Diff.	Self-Rating
Likert	.796	.588	.619	.511
Guttman	——	.445	.523	.476
Thurstone	——	——	.432	.337
Sem. Diff.	——	——	——	.387

election. This report was compared with the voting records. In 11 per cent of the cases, the report and the record did not coincide. In 28 of the 33 instances of non-correspondence, subjects reported that they had voted when in fact they had not. In the remaining five cases, the subject's name was not included in the voting records. In these latter instances, it was not possible to determine whether the error resulted from inadequacies of the student government's record-keeping procedures or whether the subjects had falsified their names. The degree of error observed corresponds closely to that reported in the analysis of the political behavior of other populations.[20] Thus, the self-reported data in this instance appear to provide a fairly close approximation to the actual behavior of the subjects. This conclusion is reinforced by the findings reported in Table 2 which indicate relatively high association between recorded vote and four reported indexes of related behavior.

The present research design, then, permitted the assessment of the relative efficiency of scaling techniques by determining the correspondence of five measures of attitude to five measures of other behavior, including a single act and four indexes of reported configurations of behavior. All the criterion indexes were composed of, or referred to, behaviors occurring under normal social circumstances, and they represented referents for specific non-hypothetical attitude components.

[20] See Charles R. Tittle and Richard J. Hill, "A Note on the Accuracy of Self-Reported Data and Prediction of Political Activity," *Public Opinion Quarterly* (1968) Volume 31, pp. 103–106.

FURTHER PROCEDURES

The attitude measures and criterion indexes used in this study were treated as ordinal data. A frequency distribution for each attitude scale was obtained, and the categories were then collapsed into six ordered classes, following the convention of equalization of marginals. The Guttman and Woodward-Roper indexes of participation also were collapsed into six categories. The seven categories of the summated index of participation were maintained to prevent a serious maldistribution of category frequencies. The association between each scale and each index was measured by the Goodman-Kruskal gamma. Since gamma is somewhat sensitive to marginal distributions, and perhaps, the number of cells in a contingency table, care was taken to make comparisons across rows where tables with approximately equal cell numbers and marginal distributions were involved.

RESULTS

The results reported in Table 4 indicate that only a moderate degree of correspondence between measured attitude and other behavior can be observed when (1) scaling techniques are employed to measure attitude and (2) the behavioral criterion is based upon a consideration of a series of acts occurring under normal circumstances. On the other hand, the data do show that the degree of correspondence observed is at least in part a function of the methodological conditions which maintain.

TABLE 4

ASSOCIATIONS[1] BETWEEN ATTITUDE MEASURES AND BEHAVIORAL INDEXES

Behavior Index	Attitude Measure					
	15-item Likert	10-item Likert	Guttman	Self	Sem. Diff.	Thurstone
Record vote	.504	.459	.391	.285	.350	.318
Vote over time	.493	.423	.329	.365	.309	.213
Guttman index	.553	.559	.421	.410	.335	.248
Likert index	.619	.612	.535	.495	.364	.257
W-R index	.548	.535	.419	.425	.335	.238
Mean association	.543	.518	.419	.396	.339	.255

[1]Gamma.

The data support the argument that greater correspondence between measured attitude and other behavior can be found when the behavioral criterion incorporates a wide range of activity with respect to the attitude object under consideration. Although the findings are not decisive, they do reveal that in five of six instances greatest association was found between the attitude measures and the Likert-type index which was derived from ten distinct kinds of behavior. The data also show that, in general, lower association was found for the voting indexes than for the Guttman and Woodward-Roper indexes based respectively on eight and five kinds of activity. Such results support the contention that the appropriate criterion measure to use in evaluating the predictive efficacy of attitude measure is one that includes sets of acts indicative of consistent or patterned behavior.

With respect to the assessment of the alternative measurement strategies, the results indicate that there is wide variation in the predictive power of the various instruments. In this instance, the Likert scale was clearly the best predictor of behavior. It was most highly associated with every one of the five behavioral indexes. The Thurstone scale showed the poorest correspondence—in only one case did it produce better prediction than any of the other measures. In fact, in four of five instances a simple self rating of attitude provided better results than the elaborate Thurstone procedure.

DISCUSSION

On the basis of a reconsideration of the relevant literature, it was maintained that multi-item attitude instruments would have considerable utility as predictors of behavior when such behavior represents a normal configuration of repetitive actions. The findings provide only modest support for this contention.

It could be argued that these findings strengthen the indictment against attitude measures as predictive tools. It is clear that attitude measurement alone, as examined herein, is not totally adequate as a predictor of behavior. However, when it is possible to obtain an average association of .543 using a Likert scale in its crude form, it seems entirely possible that technical refinements and additional methodological considerations could increase predictive efficiency. Investigation of the performance of the various measuring instruments suggests certain refinements and considerations meriting further exploration.

Analysis of the present data indicates that the differential predictive power of the various measurement approaches may be at least partially attributable to differences in reliability. Split-half reliability coefficients based upon the Spearman-Brown correction formula[21] were as follows: the Likert scale—.95; the semantic differential measure—.87; the Guttman scale—.80; and the Thurstone scale—.67. While the order in terms of reliability does not correspond perfectly with the predictive ordering, it does place the Likert and Thurstone measures in the same relative positions. The Likert scale was found to be the best predictor and to exhibit the greatest reliability, while the Thurstone scale is the poorest predictor and the least reliable. The findings with respect to the range of reliability are similar to those reported in other studies using Likert and Thurstone procedures. In addition, the available evidence suggests that in cases where the two types of scales are of equal length, one can expect the Likert scale to exhibit higher reliability.[22]

Differential reliability, however, does not seem to be a complete explanation for the findings. The Guttman scale exhibits lower observed reliability than the semantic differential, yet it performs considerably better as a predictor. In like manner the single-item self-rating of attitude would reasonably be expected to be less reliable than the multiple-item semantic differential and Thurstone scales, yet it is found to be a better predictor than either of these two scales.

It might also be argued that the superiority of the Likert over the Guttman technique can be accounted for by the fact that the original Likert scale was composed of 15 items while the Guttman scale contained only ten items. Since in general the greater the length of a test, the higher is its reliability,[23] it seemed desirable to rescore the Likert scale using the ten "best" items rather than the 15

"best" items. The data in Table 4 shows that this procedure had little effect on the results. The ten-item Likert scale was still superior to the ten-item Guttman scale as well as to each of the other attitude measures.

A second factor appears to be the differential extent to which the various scaling procedures result in the derivation of scales incorporating a specificity dimension. Although each scale was designed to measure the same specific attitude relating to personal participation in student political activity, the various scales do differ substantially with respect to the content specificity of the actual items incorporated. This observation is based on the assumption that response to an item is likely to be more specific for an individual if the item contains some self-reference. Thus, the larger the number of self-referent items included in a scale, the more specific is response likely to be. Comparison of the Likert, Guttman, and Thurstone scales in terms of the proportion of self-referent items derived for the final measuring instrument revealed a ranking corresponding exactly to the predictive ranking. For this comparison, items containing the personal pronouns "I" or "me," were considered to be self-referent in content. The Likert scale is found to rank first with 87 per cent of the items self-referent, the Guttman scale is second with 60 per cent and the Thurstone scale is ordered last with only 20 per cent of the items including a reference to self.

There are other technical differences between the different measuring procedures which may have some bearing on the findings. In addition to the advantage of greater reliability and specificity, the Likert technique also seems to have the particular advantage of providing for the operation of an intensity factor. Because scoring is influenced by the degree as well as direction of response to each item, intense judgments weight the final score assigned to an individual. Hence, an ordering of subjects by the summated rating procedure is not only a ranking on a favorable-unfavorable dimension, but a ranking influenced by how strongly the subject

---

[21] To this point, the data have been treated as ordinal. The use of the Spearman-Brown procedure makes interval assumptions. However, to the authors' knowledge there exists no ordinally-based procedure which provides a reasonable alternative to the Spearman-Brown approach.

[22] Edwards, *op. cit.*, pp. 159–169.

[23] Harold Gulliksen, *Theory of Mental Tests,* New York: John Wiley and Sons, 1950, pp. 74–86.

feels. A respondent who holds a favorable attitude but who does not feel intensely about it will consequently be ranked lower than one who holds a favorable attitude and supports that attitude with intense feelings.

Development of efficient means for handling such components as intensity and specificity may offer recognizable advantages for improving the predictive efficiency of attitude scales. The Guttman procedure for intensity analysis represents one technique for handling an additional dimension. But as ordinarily practiced, it lacks the advantage of permitting individual scores to be "corrected" for intensity (other than in a gross dichotomous sense). There is nothing, however, to prevent some combination of content score and intensity score to derive a "total" score. Certainly such possibilities deserve more exploration.

The semantic differential as a measure of attitude appears to suffer a serious disadvantage. Subjects tend to respond in a set. They observe that "desirable" things appear on one side of a continuum and "undesirable" things appear on the other. The discriminal process then apparently becomes a matter of self-evaluating overall attitude and marking the scale accordingly, with little distinction between the various adjectival pairs. Interspersing reversed continua probably only serves to make the respondent's task more difficult without fundamentally altering the problem. In this instance, the tendency for subjects to adopt a response set probably accounts for the fact that the semantic differential procedure resulted in a measure having high reliability but low predictive validity.

The findings in regard to the Thurstone technique are somewhat contrary to general methodological thinking with respect to attitude measurement. The Thurstone scale has been considered by some as the standard against which other attitude measures are to be compared. In addition to the factors of reliability and item-specificity, the poor showing of the Thurstone scale might also be influenced by the existence of a hiatus between the scaling of items and the process of measuring attitudes once the items are scaled. The judging procedure itself introduces a number of perceptual variables, the total effect of which has not been fully explored. Moreover, the nature of the typical response to Thurstone scales raises questions about the general adequacy of the Thurstone procedure. It is a common observation that respondents do not always endorse contiguous items. Indeed, subjects often endorse a wide range of items.[24] This does not make sense in light of the rationale of the procedure, and it may be largely responsible for some degree of unreliability and unpredictability.

The data presented here and the results of previous research with attitude measures strongly suggest that the error factors accounting for the differential predictability are to some extent intrinsic to the several measurement procedures. This conclusion, of course, cannot be advanced as compelling since any particular instance of the application of a given measuring technique or instrument represents only one of many possible applications. As such it is subject to various random errors. The crucial questions concerning these measurement procedures can only be answered convincingly when the results of numerous applications are available.

---

[24] George J. Dudycha, "A Critical Examination of the Measurement of Attitude Toward War," *Journal of Social Psychology,* 18 (November, 1943), pp. 383–392; Selltiz, C., M. Jahoda, M. Deutsch and S. W. Cook, *Research Methods in Social Research.* New York: Holt, Rinehart and Winston, 1959, pp. 359–365; and Otis Monroe Walter, Jr., "The Improvement of Attitude Research," *Journal of Social Psychology,* 33 (February, 1951), pp. 143–146.

SECTION **VI** **Physiological Reaction Techniques**

Overview

Self-report techniques of attitude measurement require at least two assumptions: 1) that the respondent is aware of his attitude with respect to an object (or can determine his attitude through introspection), and 2) that the respondent is both willing and able to report his attitude without distortion (either intentionally or unintentionally). That these assumptions are sometimes violated, in unknown degrees and with undetermined consequences, is unequivocal.

Another possible behavioral specimen for attitude inference is autonomic response. There are two primary reasons for optimism. First, the respondent is unable to inhibit or alter the response voluntarily. Second, there presumably is a close relationship between such physiological responses and the emotional (or affective) states of the respondent. Thus, there is hope that autonomic responses to stimuli containing the attitude object may provide a direct and measurable reference to the emotional component of attitude.

The early hope that specific autonomic responses could be paired with each emotion has been abandoned. In its place is a more empirically valid belief that physiological measures can be employed to indicate emotional arousal. The selections which follow serve to illustrate the use of autonomic responses as a basis for inferring attitudes.

One of the most frequently used autonomic responses is the electrical conductance of the skin. It has long been known that the epidermis (skin) will serve as an electrical conductor and that its resistance to the flow of electrical currents varies with the emotional state of the organism. The Galvanic Skin Response is the current notation for this autonomic response. Measurement is accomplished by attaching two electrodes to the skin, introducing a weak electrical charge and calculating the amount of resistance to conduction, usually expressed in ohms.

The selection by Rankin and Campbell (Chapter 31) reports one of the earliest successful uses of the GSR as a measure of attitude: i.e., the GSR measure showed a general trend of correlation with other attitude measures. Their study was replicated, with some procedural modifications by Porier and Lott (Chapter 32) who report no correlation between GSR responses to race of experimenter and other measures of attitude toward Negroes. The failure to replicate the earlier findings is attributed to the experimental procedure.

Results similar to those of Rankin and Campbell were obtained by Westie and DeFleur (Chapter 33) under quite different experimental conditions. Two differences are noteworthy. Westie and DeFleur used visual representations of Negroes (slides) whereas the Rankin and Campbell study and the Porier and Lott replication used a

Negro experimenter as a way of presenting the attitude object. Also, the non-physiological attitude measures were different. In addition, Westie and DeFleur found finger pulse to be related to their paper-and-pencil measure of attitude, but the pattern of relation was not parallel to the GSR findings. There is evidence in their data that physiological measures are influenced by factors other than attitudes, the sex of the respondent in particular.

A second selection reporting findings on the relation of GSR to visual representations of the Negro is provided by Vidulich and Krevanick in Chapter 34. Their results are consistent with those of Rankin and Campbell and of Westie and DeFleur (although they make no reference to the latter work). It should be noted also that sex influences the level of GSR in the Vidulich and Krevanick study.

These selections present a reasonably accurate account of the use of GSR as a basis for attitude inference. There does appear to be some convergence of findings when GSR is used with other behavior specimens, whether the GSR is a response to the attitude object or to its visual representation. However in research such as is reported by Porier and Lott GSR should be used with caution.

It was noted earlier that autonomic responses are indicators of emotional arousal. There is considerable evidence that extreme affective states, both positive and negative, give rise to similar autonomic responses. The findings reported by Vidulich and Krevanick indicate this. The GSR levels of *both* high- and low-prejudiced groups were greatest in response to the critical stimuli. It is, therefore, possible that autonomic responses may serve as valid indicators of strong attitudes but be insensitive to their direction. Obviously, this would be a serious limitation on their utility.

Recent work with pupillary constriction and dilation offers some hope for a physiological measure capable of indicating both degree and direction of autonomic arousal. Professor Woodmansee, whose work has been central to the use of pupillography in attitude research, prepared Chapter 35 especially for this volume as a summary and critical analysis of pupil response as a measure of attitudes. His conclusion does not encourage the initial optimism that pupillary constriction and dilation might serve as a bidirectional measure of autonomic arousal.

The final selection by Mueller (Chapter 36) provides a comprehensive review of the rationale for the use of physiological measures of autonomic responses, of early efforts to relate emotional states to autonomic responses, and of the development of GSR and pupillography, concluding with Professor Mueller's critical evaluation of physiological techniques of attitude measurement.

CHAPTER **31** Galvanic Skin Response to Negro and White Experimenters[1]

ROBERT E. RANKIN AND DONALD T. CAMPBELL

This study reports an experiment demonstrating a differential galvanic skin response (GSR) on the part of white college men to incidental contacts by a Negro and a white experimenter. The study was undertaken because of its methodological implications and for the light it might throw on the adequacy of current conceptions of social attitude phenomena.

There are a number of characteristics of the GSR which recommended it as a potential measure of attitudes. For one thing, the GSR is highly sensitive, although this sensitivity also becomes a source of difficulty in providing experimental control. A second advantage is the general inability of the subject to inhibit the response voluntarily. Third, the GSR has repeatedly shown itself related to affect or to favorable and unfavorable evalu-

From Robert E. Rankin and Donald T. Campbell, "Galvanic skin response to Negro and white experimenters," *Journal of Abnormal and Social Psychology*, 1955, *51*, 30–33. Copyright 1955 by the American Psychological Association, and reproduced by permission.

[1] This report is based upon the first author's master's thesis (8) done under the direction of the second author and Dr. Delos D. Wickens. The present authors are indebted to Dr. Wickens for his help and for the use of his GSR equipment, and to the Psychology Department through Dr. H. E. Burtt for providing funds for the payment of the research assistant who played the role of the Negro experimenter.

ations of stimuli, although its correlation with decision processes complicates its interpretation in some experiments (1, 5). Previous unsuccessful efforts to use the GSR in the diagnosis of social attitudes differ from the present study in various ways, especially in that they utilized verbal statements about the object of the attitude (1, 4, 5, 9).

The outline of the present experiment can be stated briefly as follows: The subjects were called in to participate in a word-association test involving emotion-provoking terms such as "love," "flunk," "mother," and "petting." During the experimental period, a Negro and a white experimenter alternated in readjusting a dummy GSR apparatus attached to the left hand. The recording GSR apparatus remained in contact on the right hand. In addition, for some of the subjects, verbal attitude measures of a direct and an indirect type were obtained in separate classroom sessions.

METHOD

The subjects (*Ss*) were seated in a sound-proofed room entered from the outer hall through a control room which contained the recording apparatus. The *S* sat in a chair which provided both a left and a right arm rest. On *S*'s right hand were clamped the electrodes, with the positive electrode resting on the palm of the hand, the negative on the back. Good contact was assured by using electrode jelly under the zinc plates. On S's left wrist was placed the dummy apparatus consisting of electrodes, two simulated electrical poles, with wires attached, the whole apparatus being held in place by a leather band. The GSR recording apparatus employed was essentially the same as that described by Haggard and Gerbrands (7). This included the use of an external current of 2.25 microamps, and RCA volt ohmyst with a General Electric photoelectric recording microammeter combined to form a DC vacuum tube voltmeter with which the voltage across the S's electrodes could be graphically recorded and evaluated in terms of resistance. Further details on this apparatus may be obtained from the full report (8). By pressing a switch when entering and leaving the experimental chamber, the experimenter (E) could record his presence and absence in the experimental chamber.

The Es alternately took one of two roles. We will call these *Experimenter* (E) and *Assistant* (A) in the following presentation. The E took S through the control room, where A could be seen, and into the experimental room. Then E read these instructions:

This is an experiment to test your reactions to certain words. During the experiment your right arm will be strapped to that board with this clamp fastened across your hand. On your left wrist we will place another apparatus. Please try not to move your right hand during the experiment. You are free to move your left hand. Wait for one of the experimenters to adjust and remove the apparatus. When the experiment begins, I shall sit in the other room and read to you slowly a list of words. Following each word you are to call out the first word you associate with the one I read. Are there any questions?

During this period A established S's base level and made the necessary settings on the recording apparatus. When the instructions had been read and the apparatus attached, E left the room. The S was left alone in the experimental room for a 2- or 3-minute period,

to make sure that an adequate base level for the GSR had been established. Then A entered the chamber and made the first adjustment of the dummy left-hand apparatus. He left promptly, and after another period of silence lasting some 30 seconds, E entered, made a second adjustment on the dummy apparatus, and left, thus providing the second experimental contact. After a further 30-second period of silence for the S, E began reading the words to the S from the control room. After ten words had been read and responded to by S (taking about two minutes) E again entered the chamber and made the third adjustment of the dummy apparatus. After another pause of 30 seconds, the four remaining words were read, at which time A entered and made the fourth and final adjustment of the dummy apparatus. After another half minute of silence, the S was released. Each experimental contact-period lasted about 20 seconds.

The experiment was run in two counterbalanced forms. In Form A E was white, a graduate student in psychology, aged 23, 5'9" in height, 155 pounds in weight. A was a Negro graduate student in education, aged 32, about 5'11½" in height, weight 192 pounds. In Form B the roles were reversed with the Negro playing the role of E and the White playing the role of A. The two experimental forms taken together provide a counterbalanced design in which the effects of (a) the person making the contact, (b) the four different contacts, and (c) the form of the experiment could be analyzed. The design is shown more compactly in Table 1. Forty male Ss, aged 19–36, were selected at random from the files of beginning psychology classes during the summer quarter 1950 at The Ohio State University. Since all students were required to spend some time as experimental subjects, it was possible to secure the cooperation of the total group originally selected. The individual experimental sessions were spread out over a two-week period, with Form A and Form B sessions being alternated. As far as could be told from the comments and questions of the Ss to the Es and to

TABLE 1

EXPERIMENTER MAKING CONTACT

Contact	Negro	White	Totals by Contact
1	49.74	34.50	84.24
	A	B	
2	42.41	44.35	86.76
	B	A	
3	34.16	28.56	62.72
	B	A	
4	42.11	29.21	71.32
	A	B	
Totals by Experimenter	168.42	136.62	

Totals by Form: A = 164.76; B = 140.28

Note.—Letters in cells indicate the form of the experiment (A or B) from which the data were taken.

their classroom instructors, all accepted the experiment as a word-association study, and were unaware that the adjustment of the left hand apparatus by Negro or white Es represented the relevant dimension of the study.

RESULTS

The quantification of GSR records is a complicated problem which has generated a considerable methodological literature. In the present study the response was defined as the difference in GSR level between the time when E entered the chamber and the highest point achieved before he left the chamber. The GSR is thus a response not only to the tactual contacts necessitated in the readjustment of the left hand apparatus, but also of the visual stimuli of entering the room and approaching the subject. While arbitrary, this definition of the response avoided subjective interpretations from the GSR trend line, where clear-cut single deflections are often lacking. The response thus defined was quantified in terms of log change in conductance, as suggested by Haggard (6). These values, multiplied by 10^8, are summed in Table 1.

Table 1 shows the cell and marginal totals

and gives the plan of the experimental design. There are three potential experimental dimensions or classification criteria confounded into a two dimensional counterbalanced arrangement. These are (a) the experimenter making contact, Negro or white; (b) the contact, first, second, third, or fourth; and (c) the form of the experiment, A or B.

In Table 2 is shown the analysis of variance of these data.[2] There are several difficulties encountered when repeated measurements are made from the same individual and when at the same time each individual is not rep-

TABLE 2

ANALYSIS OF VARIANCE

Source	SS	df	Var	F	p
Experimenter	6.32	1	6.32	15.41	.001
Contact	9.97	3	3.32	8.26	.001
Row × Col	4.08	3			
Form	3.91	1	3.91	9.54	.01
Res Int	.17	2	.08		
Within Cells	62.43	152	.41		

resented in all cells. Insofar as our major effects of experimenter and contact are concerned, all of the marginal totals are equated with regard to subjects. As in latin square designs, this equation is based upon the assumption that there is no significant interaction between the specific form of the experiment and the recruitment of subjects. As a check, significant effects have been confirmed by t tests between pairs of cells.

From Table 2 it is apparent that there is a highly significant differential response to the two Es, with the greater response being made to the Negro. In further support of this finding, the t value between the initial contact in Form A and the initial contact in Form B is 4.4, $p < .001$. In terms of the intention of the experiment, this highly significant differential response to Es would be interpreted as a differential response to race. While this

---
[2] The writers are indebted to Dr. David Bakan of the University of Missouri for advice in the design of the analysis.

interpretation is undoubtedly the most likely, it is nevertheless arbitrarily made. The two *E*s differed in size, etc., in addition to skin color. To be definitive for an interpretation in terms of race, the experiment would have to be run with a sampling of a number of different white and Negro *E*s. In this sense, this experiment must be interpreted as highly preliminary and makes its most definitive contribution in showing, for the first time as far as is known, that the GSR will differentiate between persons as stimuli. However, considering that the *E*s were both strangers to the subjects, it seems most likely to the present writers that this differential response is primarily attributable to race.[3]

The analysis of variance in Table 2 also indicates a highly significant difference between the four contacts. While the marginal totals as shown in Table 1 do not reveal an orderly progression, there is some general indication of an adaptation process, in that the later contacts produce less effect than the earlier contacts. This is particularly clear in comparison of the cell totals for contacts two and three, in which, for both forms, the same experimenter made two contacts in a row. In both instances, a marked reduction of degree of response on the second contact can be noted. These two comparisons both provide significant *t* tests, at the .001 level for Form A, the .05 level for Form B.

It can also be noted from Table 2 that the classification criterion "Form of Experiment" also produces significant differences. This might reflect chance sampling differences in the two populations, which become apparently significant when an *N* of contacts rather than an *N* of persons is used. This interpretation would be consistent with the role of counterbalancing the two forms as a control. A second interpretation would assume that the two experimental forms would, if replicated, continue to show differential responsiveness, in that the Form B

subjects had had more opportunity to adapt to the Negro *E* in the preliminary phases of the experiment, prior to the first experimental contact.

CORRELATION WITH ATTITUDE TEST SCORES

If the differential response to the two experimenters is to be interpreted as reflecting a common social attitude, individual differences in response differential become relevant attitude measures. For this purpose each individual was given a single GSR score, by subtracting the sum of his responses on the two contacts by the white *E* from the sum of the responses on the two contacts by the Negro *E*. Thirty-six of the 40 subjects obtained positive scores, a split which has a probability of less than .0000001 where a 50–50 split represents chance expectancy.

As a classroom exercise appropriate for the portion of the elementary course dealing with social psychology, the regular instructors administered an information test and a direct attitude test about the American Negro. The information test provided alternative answers which could be rated in their degree of favorableness or unfavorableness. Examples are as follows: "In the records of the state of Illinois, 17 births out of 1000 on the average are illegitimate for the White population. For Negro births the rate is: (*a*) 17; (*b*) 30; (*c*) 55; (*d*) 72; and (*e*) 151." "In intelligence tests made in New York City schools comparing Negro and White children, it has been found that the average IQ of white children is 100, and the average IQ of Negro children is: (*a*) 85; (*b*) 89; (*c*) 95; (*d*) 100; and (*e*) 106." The rationale for utilizing information tests in the indirect diagnosis of attitudes has been presented elsewhere (2). The direct attitude test asked the person to describe his own feelings about Negroes in terms of 25 prepared statements to be endorsed with five levels of agreement and disagreement (3). These two tests were stapled together and the answers from both placed upon a single IBM answer sheet, upon

---

[3] While the differential response is highly significant, it should perhaps be noted that for two-thirds of the subjects the GSR deflections were greater to the association words than to contacts by either *E*.

which the students also recorded the date and state of birth, but not their names.

A number of complications prevent this portion of the study from having the degree of control and sampling adequacy which characterize the first part. In a number of instances birth dates were omitted and matching of test with GSR was impossible, and attendance on the classroom testing day was low. In the end it was possible to match only 26 of the 40 subjects, and the matched subjects do not seem to be representative. Whereas the range in GSR scores for the whole group of 40 was from -1.7 to $+3.7$, the matched cases show a range of only from $-.1$ to $+1.9$.

There was one further complication. The instructors found it appropriate to administer the classroom tests at about the middle of the period during which the individual experimental sessions were being made. Thus some subjects received their attitude tests prior to the experiment and others received the experiment first. Those subjects who took the direct attitude test after the GSR session were significantly more hostile than those who took the attitude test prior to the GSR, $p < .001$. Whatever interpretation be given to this finding, it certainly indicates an undesirable interaction between the experimental procedure and the attitude testing process, either through modification of attitude expressions or through a recruitment differential made possible by the incomplete matching.

The correlations among the three scores are shown in Table 3, separately for four subgroups, divided in terms of form of experiment and priority of test vs. experiment. In view of the small number of cases involved, the results shown in Table 3 cannot be interpreted as demonstrating conclusively any correlation between the GSR measure and either the direct or the indirect test. However, the general trend of the results seems encouraging enough to justify further exploration. Insofar as the meager data can be trusted, the anonymous direct test seems to come off distinctly better than the anonymous indirect test in terms of predicting the GSR response.

TABLE 3

RANK-ORDER CORRELATIONS BETWEEN
GSR AND VERBAL ATTITUDE
MEASURES

Score	Form A		Form B	
	Test First ($N = 4$)	Exper. First ($N = 9$)	Test First ($N = 6$)	Exper. First ($N = 5$)
GSR × Direct	.40	—.08	.43	.90
GSR × Indirect	.20	—.09	.10	.40
Direct × Indirect	.70	.21	.71	.70

SUMMARY

Forty white male subjects participated in what was nominally a word association test with GSR being recorded. Two Es, one Negro and one white, alternated in making simulated readjustments of a dummy apparatus attached to the S's left wrist, while a right-arm apparatus remained in operation. A highly significant difference in GSR response to the two Es was found. A significant adaptation process was manifested in lessening degrees of response during the successive contacts. An attempt to correlate the degree of differential response to the Negro and white E with direct and indirect attitude tests was weakened by difficulties in matching and timing. The limited results are in general positive, and favor the direct test over the indirect, but are not of clear statistical significance.

REFERENCES

1. Abel, T. M.
    1930 "Attitudes and the GSR." Journal of Experimental Psychology 13:47–60.
2. Campbell, D. T.
    1950 "The indirect assessment of social attitudes." Psychological Bulletin 47:15–38.

3. Campbell, D. T., and B. R. McCandless.
   1951   "Ethnocentrism, xenophobia, and personality." Human Relations 4: 185–192.
4. Cattell, R. B., E. F. Maxwell, B. H. Light, and M. P. Unger.
   1949   "The objective measurement of attitudes." British Journal of Psychology 40:81–90.
5. Chant, S. N., and M. D. Salter.
   1935   "The measurement of attitude toward war and the galvanic skin response." Journal of Educational Psychology 28:281–289.
6. Haggard, E. A.
   1949   "On the application of analysis of variance to GSR data: I. The selection of an appropriate measure." Journal of Experimental Psychology 39:378–392.
7. Haggard, E. A., and R. Gerbrands.
   1947   "An apparatus for the measurement of continuous changes in palmar skin resistance." Journal of Experimental Psychology 37:92–98.
8. Rankin, R. E.
   1951   "The galvanic skin response as a physiological measure of social attitudes." Unpublished master's thesis, The Ohio State University.
9. Raven, B. H.
   1949   "The use of the galvanic skin response to investigate semantic generalization of politically toned stimulus words as affected by political attitudes." Unpublished master's thesis, The Ohio State University.

CHAPTER 32

Galvanic Skin Responses and Prejudice[1]

GARY W. PORIER AND ALBERT J. LOTT

While some support can be found in the literature for consistency among the components of attitudes (e.g., Campbell, 1947; DeFleur and Westie, 1958; Harding, Kutner, Proshansky, and Chein, 1954), Secord and Backman (1964) state that

... sufficient empirical evidence is not yet available in support of consistency among affective, cognitive, and behavioral components of prejudice. Moreover, forces toward consistency may in many instances be counteracted by strong emotional anchorage of the affective component. Because prejudice involves strong emotions it should be tied to those physiological functions associated with the emotions [pp. 427-428].

Investigations of such physiological functions have tended to focus on galvanic skin responses (GSR) resulting from *indirect* exposure to the object of prejudice. For example, in a series of studies by Cooper and his associates (Cooper, 1959; Cooper and Pollock, 1959; Cooper and Siegel, 1956; Cooper

From Gary W. Porier and Albert J. Lott, "Galvanic skin responses and prejudice." *Journal of Personality and Social Psychology*, 1967, 5, 253-259. Copyright 1967 by the American Psychological Association and reproduced by permission of the authors and publisher.
[1] This paper is based upon the first author's thesis for the MA degree at the University of Kentucky.

and Singer, 1956), GSRs were recorded for subjects when a complimentary statement was read about a group against whom they were strongly prejudiced. GSRs to these statements were greater than to similar statements about groups toward whom subjects felt less antipathy. Similarly, when GSRs of white subjects viewing colored slides of Negroes in various social contexts were recorded in a study by Westie and DeFleur (1959), prejudiced subjects were found to give larger GSRs than nonprejudiced subjects.

While the above studies have provided physiological evidence for the emotional involvement in prejudice, they did not use a face-to-face situation between a prejudiced subject and the object of his prejudice. An investigation by Rankin and Campbell (1955) did just this and found a significantly greater level of GSR to a Negro than to a white experimenter on the part of white male subjects. In their experimental situation (ostensibly a study of word associations and anxiety) the Negro and white experimenters made incidental hand contacts with a subject while his GSR was recorded. Verbal attitudes toward Negroes were measured by paper-and-pencil tests in separate classroom sessions, but the correlation between attitude test scores and the GSR measure yielded inconclusive results. Since the Rankin and Campbell investigation represents a kind of ideal approach to studying the emotional component of prejudice, it was the intent of the present study to replicate it, while making use of an improved design. The methodological problems associated with the Rankin and Campbell study and the steps taken in the present study to reduce or eliminate them are listed below:

1. Rankin and Campbell used only one Negro and one white experimenter to provide the stimulus contacts for the subjects. The present replication utilized a sample of Negro and white experimental assistants. The need for sampling stimulus populations, especially characteristics of experimenter stimuli, was early recognized by Brunswik (1947), and more recently by Hammond (1954) and McGuigan (1963). Regarding the Rankin and Campbell study specifically, Masling (1960) has noted that ". . . since he [Negro experimenter] was 9 years older, $2\frac{1}{2}$ inches taller and 27 pounds heavier than the white E, there was no conclusive proof that the difference, [in the subject's GSR] was a function of skin color [p. 75]."

2. In the Rankin and Campbell study the white experimenter had responsibility for all preliminary instructions and operations (attaching the electrodes), perhaps allowing time for adaptation to occur. The simple novelty or surprise of the appearance of another person, Negro or white, could, perhaps, have counfounded their results. In the present experiment all preliminary manipulations were handled by an experimenter who took no part in the later experimental contacts.

3. Some subjects took their verbal attitude tests prior to the experiment and some afterwards in the Rankin and Campbell study. It was found that those subjects who took them after the GSR session were significantly more hostile than those who took them before. By having all subjects take the attitude test from one to several weeks prior to the experiment

proper, this interaction was avoided in the present study, while at the same time separating the two situations by a relatively long time interval.

4. Of the direct and indirect verbal attitude tests used by Rankin and Campbell, only the former had any relationship to the GSR. Only direct attitude measures were utilized in this study.

5. The word lists used in the present study were composed of words with known emotionality based on previous GSR studies (Smith, 1922), whereas this information was not available for the words used by Rankin and Campbell.

With the above points in mind, an altered replication was carried out using the GSR as the measure of emotion, the California E Scale (Adorno, Frenkel-Brunswik, Levinson, and Sanford, 1950; Chapman and Campbell, 1959), and Rokeach's (1960) Opinionation Scale as the verbal measures of attitude, and two different word lists, one made up of emotion-provoking words and the other of neutral words.

The present study also tested the following prediction: a positive relationship will be found between GSR differences to physical contact by Negro and white experimental assistants and scores on both the E Scale and Opinionation Scale, and this relationship will be greater for the E Scale than for the Opinionation Scale since the former measures attitudes toward Negroes (and other ethnic minorities or outgroups) directly while the latter purports to measure a more "general intolerance" based primarily on belief systems.

METHOD

Subjects

A sample of 60 white males, drawn from approximately 237 male members of the introductory psychology laboratory sections and three other lower division psychology classes at the University of Kentucky, served as subjects. All were volunteers fulfilling a course requirement for participation in some experiment during the semester.

Apparatus

The GSR apparatus consisted of a dermohmmeter and an attached calibrated strip chart recorder. (A detailed description of the dermohmmeter and chart recorder can be found in Porier, 1963.)

The wires from the dermohmmeter to the subject were attached to a set of C-shaped plastic clamps which assured firm contact and a constant pressure through the use of electrode jelly. A dummy set of wires was attached to the subject's left hand in every case. The wires led from the hands, under the door, and to their respective attachments (the dermohmmeter and the table leg for the dummy wire) in the control room. The only other object in the experimental room besides the subject, chair, desk, and wired electrodes leading to the control room was a tape recorder on which a recording of the stimulus words used in the word-association test was played. The tape recording of the two lists of words was made to insure standardization of inflection and emphasis.

Procedure

A week or more before the GSR session, the E Scale and Opinionation Scale, in a combined form of 58 items, was administered to all the classes from which the subjects were later obtained.

The 18-item E Scale and half the items stated in a positive direction and the other half in a negative direction to control for an acquiescence response set (Chapman and Campbell, 1959). These items were alternated with 40 positively and negatively stated items of the Opinionation Scale, American Version—Form C (Rokeach, 1960). To avoid any possible biasing effects in the GSR situation, the subjects' attitude scales were not scored until the experiment was completed.

In the experimental situation, each subject was met individually and asked to participate in a word-association test in which his emotional reactions to a list of words would be measured. The experimenter responsible for monitoring the equipment escorted the subject from a waiting room, through the control room, into the experimental room. After the electrodes were attached to subject's hands, the experimenter informed him that there would be a 10-minute waiting period and left the experimental room.

The GSR apparatus was turned on at this point to establish the subject's basal level of resistance. After an initial period of fluctuation, the resistance level generally became a slowly but steadily increasing positive function on the recording chart. When sufficient time for this level to be reached had elapsed (approximately 10 minutes), the same experimenter again entered the experimental room and read the following instructions:

"This is an experiment to test your reactions to certain words. During the experiment these electrodes will remain attached to your hands. Please try to remain as still as possible, and especially try not to move your hands. Wait for one of the assistants to adjust and remove the apparatus. When the experiment begins, I shall turn on this recorded list of words and leave the room. Following each word you are to call out the first word you associate with the one you hear from the recorder. Are there any questions?

"Please remain as still as possible until the experiment begins."

The experimenter turned on the tape recording of either the emotional or neutral word list, according to the condition being run at the time, and left the room. A clock-timer switch was thrown simultaneously to enable the experimenter to time the entrance of an experimental assistant so as to coincide with a blank space on the tape. The chart recorder switch was also turned on at this point to begin taking the record of the subject's GSR. The tape recordings of the word lists were divided into the following segments:

1. A 3-minute blank space to further allow the subject's base line of response to become well established after the experimenter's exit from the experimental room.

2. *First experimental contact.* A 1-minute blank period in which a white or Negro assistant entered the experimental room from the control room, made an "adjustment" on the dummy electrodes on the left hand (which was in closest proximity to the door from the control room), and left, being in the room approximately 20 seconds, as instructed.

3. *Second experimental contact.* Another 1-minute blank period in which a Negro or white

assistant went through the same procedure as the previous assistant.

4. The first 10 words from the word list, spaced at 20-second intervals to allow for the latency and return to prior level of the GSR.

5. *Third experimental contact.* Another 1-minute period of blank tape, during which the Negro or white assistant entered again and made another "adjustment" for 20 seconds.

6. The completion of the word list, during which the final four words were spaced at 20-second intervals as above.

7. *Fourth experimental contact.* The fourth and final experimental contact made by the white or Negro assistant following the same procedure as above.

8. A final 1-minute period of blank tape to allow the GSR level to return to the level prior to stimulation.

The recording chart was marked at the time an assistant entered the room and at the time he returned. For purposes of this experiment, and in line with the method employed by Rankin and Campbell, the dependent measure was the difference in GSR level between the time when an assistant entered the experimental room and the lowest point indicating the greatest reaction achieved before he left the room.

At the end of the experimental session the true purpose of the experiment was explained to each subject. Subsequent questions of a general nature about the experiment were answered, the importance of secrecy concerning the purpose of the experiment was stressed, and the subject was dismissed.

An attempt to control for age and size differences in the assistants was made by matching the Negro and white assistants for a particular experimental session as nearly as possible on these dimensions. A further attempt to minimize any differences in clothing and incidental appearance was made by having both assistants wear knee-length white lab coats during the experiment. Twelve Negro undergraduate, graduate, and medical students, and 21 white graduate students served as experimental assistants.

The experiment was run in two counterbalanced sequences. In Sequence A, the white assistant made the first and fourth contacts, and the Negro assistant the second and third (W-N-N-W). In Sequence B, the Negro assistant made the first and last contact, and the white

assistant the second and third (N-W-W-N). The two sequences and the two word lists provide four possible combinations of conditions, as follows, with 15 subjects in each: (*a*) A-E (Sequence W-N-N-W, emotional word list),[2] (*b*) A-N (Sequence W-N-N-W, neutral word list),[3] (*c*) B-E (Sequence N-W-W-N, emotional word list), and (*d*) B-N (Sequence N-W-W-N), neutral word list.

RESULTS

The suggestions made by Haggard (1947) for statistical treatment of GSR data were followed in this study. Each of the four dependent measure scores (as previously described) obtained on each subject was converted into a log change in conductance. This conversion of the GSR data is also similar to the procedure used by Rankin and Campbell (1955).

In order to reduce the GSR data to a single score for each subject (i.e., to obtain a measure of the difference in reaction to the Negro and white assistants), the sum of the two converted GSR scores to the white assistant was subtracted from the sum of the two converted GSR scores to the Negro assistant. This procedure produced a single GSR *bias* score for each subject.

Whether contacts by the Negro and white assistants were different with the emotional and neutral word lists was first tested by t test. The 30 GSR *bias* scores obtained under the emotional word list (Conditions A-E and B-E) were found not to differ significantly ($t = .07$) from those obtained under the neutral word list (Conditions A-N and B-N). Since varying the emotionality and neutrality of the word lists had no effect on the results, the data from these lists were combined in subsequent analyses.

Product moment correlations between the GSR *bias* scores and scores on the two verbal measures of prejudice were obtained. The predicted relationship between GSR and E

---

[2] Some examples of emotional words are love, flunk, divorce, and mother.

[3] Some examples of neutral words are pencil, give, table, and pond.

Scale scores was confirmed at the .01 level of significance ($r = .38$, $N = 60$), while the relationship between GSR and the Opinionation Scale failed to reach significance ($r = .13$, $N = 60$).

Present Results Compared with Those of Rankin and Campbell

A first attempt to determine whether a differential GSR reaction was made to the Negro and white assistants was carried out by a t test between the 60 combined GSRs to the two white contacts and 60 combined GSRs to the two Negro contacts. The analysis indicated no significant difference between the two ($t = 1.31$, $p > .05$), and thus represents a failure to replicate the Rankin and Campbell (1955) finding.

The single GSR *bias* score of each subject in the present study is shown in Figure 1. These scores ranged from −1.60 to 1.55. Keeping in mind that a positive score means a greater overall reaction to the Negro as opposed to the white assistant, and noting the similarity to a normal distribution, the breakdown of positive and negative scores (32 plus, 28 minus) leads one to reject the possibility of a general differential reaction to Negroes on the part of the white subjects in this experiment. In the Rankin and

Campbell study, however, 36 of 40 subjects had positive GSR *bias* scores; such a split has a probability of less than .0000001, while a 50–50 split represents chance expectancy.

To further compare the results of the present study with those of Rankin and Campbell, the mean GSR scores made to white assistants and those made to Negro assistants on each of the four contact occasions were plotted by sequence of contact (Sequence A, W-N-N-W; Sequence B, N-W-W-N) for both studies. This comparison is shown in Figure 2. (Some of the raw data for this figure came from Rankin, 1951.)

Rankin and Campbell found that the sequence of contact had a significant effect at less than the .01 level of significance. However, most of this effect was present in the initial contact with some adaptation present for Contacts 2 and 3 and the effect again being present on Contact 4. A t test for Contact 1 between the means of Sequence A (W-N-N-W) and the means of Sequence B (N-W-W-N) of the present study was nonsignificant ($t = .475$), and the remaining three between-condition mean comparisons show the means to be even closer together than those for Contact 1.

Comparing the curves representing the two sequences which were obtained from both studies, it can be seen that a comparatively

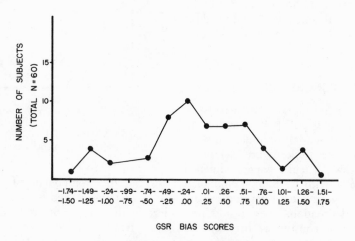

Figure 1.   Distribution of GSR bias scores (total sample).

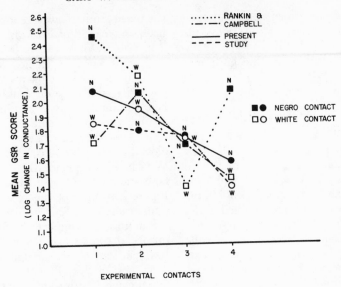

Figure 2. Comparison of Rankin and Campbell's mean GSR scores (plotted by sequence) with the mean GSR scores of the present study.

steadily decreasing curve was found for both sequences in the present study, suggesting that no matter what sequence was used, a more definite continuous adaptation to the stimuli (Negro or white assistants) was taking place than that suggested by the Rankin (1951) and Rankin and Campbell (1955) data. The steadily decreasing function which results when the conditions are combined further suggests this adaptation effect. This function, using the total mean of each contact, is shown in Figure 3.

DISCUSSION

The low but significant correlation between the GSR *bias* scores and E Scale scores indicates that differential prejudice toward Negroes (and other minority groups), as inferred from this particular paper-and-pencil test, is associated with differential emotional reactions to Negroes and whites in a face-to-face behavioral situation. These results provide evidence for consistency between the cognitive and emotional components of negative attitudes. In the present study, affective

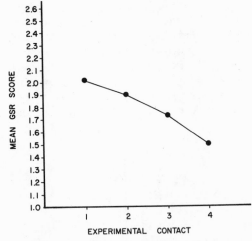

Figure 3. Combined trial means illustrating the adaptation effect in the present study.

and cognitive components of prejudice were measured and related by providing the subjects with actual contacts (a physical touch of the hand) by a sample of Negro and white experimental assistants. What the subjects said they would do or feel when responding in a paper-and-pencil situation was compared with their involuntary emotional reactions in an interpersonal situation. The correlation between E Scale and GSR is in agreement with data from Westie and De Fleur (1959), in which prejudiced subjects tended to give greater levels of autonomic response to color slides of Negroes than did an unprejudiced group.

The nonsignificant relationship obtained between responses to the Opinionation Scale and GSR *bias* scores warrants some comment.[4] Rokeach (1960) has suggested that the Opinionation Scale is a measure of general prejudice under which racial prejudice, as a special case, may be subsumed. Under the conditions of the present investigation, the subjects had no differential information concerning the Negro and white assistants except that they differed in skin color. According to recent findings of Stein, Hardyck, and Smith (1965),

When subjects are forced to evaluate stimulus individuals in terms of their beliefs, then belief-congruence is more important than race. But when the belief component is not provided, spelled out in considerable detail, subjects will react in racial terms on the basis of assumptions concerning the belief systems of others, and of emotional or institutional factors [p. 289].

Since a nonsignificant correlation between Opinionation Scale scores and GSRs emerged in this study, where belief similarity or dissimilarity was not made experimentally salient, it appears that the authors' subjects did not assume major belief differences between the Negro and white assistants, and we are therefore led to the conclusion that the subject sample was relatively low in racial prejudice. Support for this interpretation comes from three sources: (*a*) No significant differential GSR reaction was found to the Negro assistants as compared with the white assistants; (*b*) as a group, the subjects had

relatively low mean scores on the E Scale;[5] (*c*) the results of a study by Byrne and Wong (1962) showed that "highly prejudiced subjects were found to assume greater attitude dissimilarity between themselves and a Negro stranger than between themselves and a white stranger; for subjects low in prejudice the assumed dissimilarity scores for whites and Negroes did not differ [p. 253]." If the authors' subjects are regarded as low in prejudice, there is now no reason to expect them to have assumed greater belief dissimilarity between themselves and the Negroes than between themselves and the whites.

The discrepancy of the present results with those of Rankin and Campbell, in that no differential GSR was found to the Negro assistants as compared with the white assistants when all subjects were combined, may best be explained, in the view of the present authors, by procedural differences in present person stimuli (Negro and white assistants) to the subjects (as well as the other controls mentioned earlier). Rankin and Campbell used only one Negro and one white stimulus person, whereas the present study utilized a group of each. When many individual difference characteristics are canceled out through a grouping procedure, it appears that the color of the assistant's skin was not significant enough to produce differential galvanic skin reactions in the type of subjects used in this experiment.

REFERENCES

Adorno, T. W., E. Frenkel-Brunswik, D. J. Levinson, and R. N. Sanford.
1950   The Authoritarian Personality. New York: Harper.
Brunswik, E.

---

[4] In addition to the total opinionation score, right and left opinionation were correlated separately with GSR *bias* scores. Neither was significantly related to the GSR score (right $r = -.033$, left $r = .198$).

[5] For the 60 experimental subjects the following scores were obtained: mean E Scale score = 63.22 out of a possible 126.00; mean score of anti-Negro items = 18.47 out of a possible 42.00, using a 7-point scoring system ranging from a low item score of 1 to a high item score of 7. The total pool of 237 means from which the subjects were drawn showed the following scores: mean E Scale score = 66.94 out of a possible 126.00; mean anti-Negro score = 20.09 out of a possible 42.00.

1947   Systematic and Representative Design of Psychological Experiments. Berkeley: University of California Press.

Byrne, D., and T. J. Wong.
1962   "Racial prejudice, interpersonal attraction, and assumed dissimilarity of attitudes." Journal of Abnormal and Social Psychology 65:246–253.

Campbell, D. T.
1947   "The generality of a social attitude." Unpublished doctoral dissertation, University of California, Berkeley.

Chapman, L. J., and D. T. Campbell.
1959   "The effect of acquiescence response-set upon relationships among the F scale, ethnocentrism, and intelligence." Sociometry 22:153–161.

Cooper, J. B.
1959   "Emotion in prejudice." Science 130: 314–318.

Cooper, J. B., and D. A. Pollock.
1959   "Identification of prejudicial attitudes by the GSR." Journal of Social Psychology 50:241–245.

Cooper, J. B., and H. E. Siegel.
1956   "The GSR as a measure of emotion in prejudice." Journal of Psychology 42: 149–155.

Cooper, J. B., and D. N. Singer.
1956   "The role of emotion in prejudice." Journal of Social Psychology 44:241–247.

DeFleur, M. L., and F. R. Westie.
1958   "Verbal attitudes and overt acts: an experiment on the salience of attitudes." American Sociological Review 23:667–673.

Haggard, E. A.
1947   "On the application of analysis of variance to GSR data: I. the selection of an appropriate measure." Journal of Experimental Psychology 51:180–189.

Hammond, K. R.
1954   "Representative versus systematic design in clinical psychology." Psychological Bulletin 51:180–189.

Harding, J., B. Kutner, H. Proshansky, and I. Chein.
1954   "Prejudice and ethnic relations." Pp. 1021–1061 in G. Lindzey (ed.), Handbook of Social Psychology. Reading, Massachusetts: Addison-Wesley.

Masling, J.
1960   "The influence of situational and interpersonal variables in projective testing." Psychological Bulletin 57:65–85.

McGuigan, F. J.
1963   "The experimenter: a neglected stimulus object." Psychological Bulletin 60:421–428.

Porier, G. W.
1963   "The relationship between the galvanic skin response and prejudicial attitudes." Unpublished master's thesis, University of Kentucky.

Rankin, R. E.
1951   "The galvanic skin response as a physiological measure of social attitudes." Unpublished master's thesis, Ohio State University.

Rankin, R. E., and D. T. Campbell.
1955   "Galvanic skin responses to Negro and white experimenters." Journal of Abnormal and Social Psychology 51: 30–33.

Rokeach, M.
1960   The Open and Closed Mind. New York: Basic Books.

Secord, P. F., and C. W. Backman.
1964   Social Psychology. New York: McGraw-Hill.

Smith, W.
1922   The Measurement of Emotion. New York: Harcourt, Brace.

Stein, D. D., J. A. Hardyck, and M. B. Smith.
1965   "Race *and* belief: an open and shut case." Journal of Personality and Social Psychology 1:281–289.

Westie, F. R., and M. L. DeFleur.
1959   "Autonomic responses and their relationship to race attitudes." Journal of Abnormal and Social Psychology 58: 340–347.

CHAPTER **33** Autonomic Responses and Their
Relationship to Race Attitudes[1]

FRANK R. WESTIE AND MELVIN L. DEFLEUR

This is an experimental study of autonomic responses of prejudiced and unprejudiced persons viewing interracial situations. Changes in galvanic skin resistance, finger pulse, duration and amplitude of heart beat, and duration of heart cycle were recorded. The relationship of these measures to race attitudes as indicated both by scales and by open-ended interviews suggests that attitude-response syndromes include emotional tensions and affective feeling tones not under the individual's direct voluntary control or subject to his conscious examination. Experimental exploration of this more subtle dimension of attitude behavior may lead to a clearer understanding of the concept "attitude."

Most direct approaches to the assessment of

From Frank R. Westie and Melvin L. DeFleur, "Autonomic responses and their relationship to race attitudes." *Journal of Abnormal and Social Psychology,* 1959, *58,* 340–347. Copyright 1959 by the American Psychological Association and reproduced by permission of the authors and publisher.

[1] We wish to acknowledge our indebtedness to the Social Science Research Council for financial assistance and to Rolland C. Davis of the Indiana University Psychology Department who gave generously of both his time and equipment in connection with the physiological measurements. The recording of physiological responses was partially supported by funds under contract No. nr 908 (03) between the Office of Naval Research and the Indiana University Foundation.

attitudes rest upon at least two tacit assumptions: (*a*) that people can introspectively assess what their attitudes are (or "would be" under some hypothetical circumstance) toward the attitude object in question, and (*b*) assuming that people *do* know what their attitudes are, that they are both willing and able to communicate these faithfully to the investigator. This foundation of assumptions, upon which modern structured attitude scaling rests, stands in need of critical examination. We question whether all attitudinal phenomena exist for subjects on such a verbalized level of awareness as to permit them to look into themselves, and then say, in effect, "this is how unfavorable I am." If this aspect of a person's image of himself is unclear, there is scant possibility that it can be effectively communicated to the investigator, regardless of his ingenuity in constructing orderly scales. Furthermore, if attitudes include deep-seated emotional orientations, respondents may be incapable altogether of either perceiving or communicating such information. Measurement of such emotional orientations is not possible with traditional paper-and-pencil techniques.

This is not to say that structured scales and paper-and-pencil techniques are useless. On the contrary, we have used them extensively in the present research. The point is rather that they do not yield the whole picture of attitudinal behavior, but provide an image of only one dimension, the verbal.

We find it useful to conceive of attitudinal phenomena as a multidimensional complex, without any assumption of a one-to-one correspondence between the dimensions. One dimension is the emotional orientation we seek to examine; another is the verbalized behavior; still a third dimension includes overt approach-avoidance acts which to many seem to be the "real" behavior that attitude scales should predict. All of these are actual behaviors and constitute important aspects of the attitude complex. Such phenomena exist as recurrent behaviors, and the task of attitude research, as conceived here, is a search for consistency of response within these dimensions.[2]

Although existence of such dimly perceived feeling states is not difficult to demonstrate, their measurement proves to be a somewhat more exacting task. For example, many persons who have had experience in interviewing white people about their attitudes toward Negroes have felt a shortcoming in standard paper-and-pencil techniques. Individuals are frequently encountered who are determined to be "big" about the "Negro question," not only to the interviewer but to themselves. The strictly verbal picture that emerges from such interviews is that of a person who is generally favorable in his attitudes toward Negroes. But more subtle responses speak eloquently of another picture—a certain uneasiness, the

clenched fist, the restless stirring, the new atmosphere of forced friendliness—all of this following closely upon a pleasant, relaxed, easygoing atmosphere built around a discussion of an affectively neutral topic. We have observed that this change occurs when the first question about Negroes is asked. Although the interviewer may be quite aware of these subtle cues, he ordinarily lacks techniques with which to control, quantify, or record such responses.

Considerations of this sort led the writers to embark upon a study of emotional tensions in situations of race relations, as indicated by autonomic responses. The relationship of such responses to measures of race attitudes obtained by more structured methods may allow meaningful exploration of this neglected dimension of attitudes.

The problem may be stated as follows:

1. Are there consistencies in autonomic response associated with exposure to objects toward which persons have (scale-measured) attitudes?

2. If there are measurable associations between autonomic responses and attitudinal involvement, what is the direction of the (scale-measured) attitudinal involvement? Do those persons most unfavorable in their verbal response to the attitude-object manifest more pronounced autonomic responses than those more favorable in their verbal responses? Or is the reverse true?

METHOD

The investigating involved three phases: the attitude testing program, the measurement of autonomic responses to attitude stimuli, and the postexperimental interview.

The Attitude-Testing Program

Subjects (Ss) were selected on the basis of scores on the Summated Differences scales.[3]

---

[2] The reviews of the literature of the past thirty years by Allport (1935), Campbell (1950), and Green (1954) all stress that one characteristic is almost uniformly mentioned in attitude definitions: consistency of behavior, either in action toward the attitude object or in verbalizing about it. This usage, in effect, equates the term attitude to a probability (of recurrent behavior). Campbell's definition, as paraphrased by Green, expresses this focus: "An individual's social attitude is an enduring syndrome of response consistency with regard to a set of social objects. Many theorists more specifically include in their definitions some statement concerning "emotional overtones," "affective feeling states," or some similar phrase.

[3] For a detailed description of the manner in which these scales were constructed, their reliability coefficients, etc., see Westie (1953).

These scales require the S to indicate the degree to which he is willing to associate (in a variety of social settings) with Negroes of a variety of socioeconomic levels as compared to whites of comparable socioeconomic levels. The total score, based on the summated differences between responses to whites and Negroes of the same socioeconomic level, provides an index of positive or negative verbal attitudes toward Negroes. This battery of scales, made up of some 500 items, was administered to 250 freshmen students at a large university. From this population, a control group of 23 Ss was matched in over-all frequency distribution with an experimental group of the same size in terms of age, sex, social class, residential history, and previous contact with Negroes. The experimental ("prejudiced") group was selected from students who scored in the upper 25 per cent of the Summated Differences scale, while the control ("unprejudiced") group was drawn from those scoring in the lower 25 per cent of the distribution. Half of each group were males, the other half females.

The Laboratory Study

In the laboratory study, the Ss of each group were exposed individually to a series of colored photographic slides depicting whites and Negroes in various situations. During these presentations the S was connected to apparatus designed to measure GSR (galvanic skin response), FP or finger pulse volume (measured by plethysmograph), amplitude and duration of heartbeat (measured by electrocardiograph), duration of heart cycle (time required for the heart to pass from one state to the same state again, as measured by cardiotachometer). The physiological measures required about an hour per S. The data were gathered during a 12-week period.

The colored slides were posed and photographed specifically for this study. They were projected through a port into a small air-conditioned room where the S sat relaxed in a chair. Each slide portrayed two "good-looking" young adults sitting side-by-side looking at each other with a pleasant, friendly expression. One slide was included for each possible combination of males and females, whites and Negroes. In additon to these pair slides, a set of four single-person slides was included, portraying a single member of each race and sex. The age of the person photographed approximated that of the Ss. The models were dressed in dignified apparel; the background behind the seated persons included a small table with a lamp and a partial view of a window with a drapery. The white and Negro models appearing in the slides were not known to the Ss. The slides were thus designed to avoid the arousal of strong autonomic reactions for reasons extraneous to the problem at hand.

A suitable rest and standardization period was allowed for each S after being attached to the apparatus. Each S was then shown the 12 stimulus slides. The four single-person slides were shown as a first set, followed by eight pair slides. For both the first set and the second set, an independently drawn random order of presentation was used for each S so as to control for serial effects. Each slide was shown for 30 seconds with a 30-second rest between each presentation.

Although five separate autonomic physiological responses to these slides were recorded, the present paper considers only two of these: the GSR, recorded through electrodes placed on the palm, and finger pulse volume (FP), registered by an electrode at the end of the index finger. An index of change in GSR patterns was devised which states changes in skin resistance as a percentage of the resistance at the beginning of each stimulus presentation. Since the GSR activity was permanently recorded by a stylus on a recording drum, it was possible to synchronize such changes with the exact time of stimulus presentation. A similar system was used for recording FP changes. Amplified FP activity was permanently recorded on a separate drum paper, and synchronization of this record with the presentation of the stimuli was also possible.[4]

The Post-experimental Interview

Each S was interviewed immediately following the measurement of his physiological responses. During this hour-long session, which took place in an office far removed from the laboratory, the S responded to a variety of structured and open-ended questions intended to help in giving meaning to the physiological responses. Projective interpretations were elicited to slides comparable to those he viewed in the laboratory, and topics such as the S's previous experiences with Negroes, his personal and social background, his reference groups, and his degree of willingness to be photographed with Negroes were explored.

RESULTS

Quantified variations in these physiological responses were arranged in a factorial analysis of variance design. The statistical analysis was complicated by the fact that each set of slides (single person slides vs. paired slides), and each physiological measure yielded separate data.

In addition, for the GSR, the continuous kymograph records provided several ways of obtaining measures of the results. Thus, GSR responses to the single-person slides were analyzed on the basis of measures made during the *first third* of the 30-second period during which each S viewed each slide. Similarly, the *last two thirds* of each stimulus presentation provided the basis of another complete analysis. Still another analysis was made of changes in autonomic activity during each 30-second stimulus period taken as a unit. From these various combinations, six analyses were completed.

In the present paper only the analysis of the last two thirds of the stimulus period is presented. Although the results of the different analyses are quite similar, our data seem to indicate that fullest response occurred during this last 20-second period of the stimulus presentation.[5]

Table 1 shows the general statistical design and gives the mean level of finger pulse (FP) response to the single-person slides by various categories of Ss to the different types of slides. In addition, the usual summary table for the analysis of variance, based on the FP responses to the single-person slides, appears in Table 2. A verbal summary of the significant sources of variance in all unreported analyses is given in Table 5.

Examination of Table 1 indicates that FP activity was generally less for females than for males, but Table 2 reveals that the difference is not significant. Similarly, the data in Table 1 show that prejudiced Ss had generally lower levels of FP response to the Negro slides than the unprejudiced Ss, but, again, the difference is not significant. The reaction patterns of these two S groups to the white slides were very similar. However, statistically significant results are evident when both S sex and S attitude are taken into account jointly. This finding can be

---

[4] Space does not permit discussion of details concerning the apparatus, the recording devices, the nature of the laboratory, methods of translating response records into quantitative indices, etc. The apparatus is described in detail in Davis, Siddons, and Stout (1954). The procedure employed in the quantification of the kymograph records was relatively simple. For the finger pulse records, the greatest amplitude of finger pulse volume for a 5-sec. period (2.5 to 7.5 sec. after onset of stimulus) was divided by the greatest amplitude of FP volume for a 5-sec. interval preceding the onset of stimulus.

The GSR measures were obtained by taking the maximum peak during a response period as a proportion of the response amplitude before the onset of the stimulus. Simple millimeter measures of the records were used in both cases.

[5] The remaining analyses, including four variance summaries and four tables of means, have been deposited with the American Documentation Institute. . . .

The analysis followed that suggested by Edwards (1950) for the situation where repeated observations are made on several groups of Ss. The interaction between individual Ss and the stimulus conditions within a given group was taken as the error term for comparison between sets of columns. Mean squares based on row comparisons are divided by a combined "between subjects" term to obtain the appropriate F value.

TABLE 1

MEAN LEVELS OF FINGER PULSE (FP) RESPONSE TO THE SINGLE-PERSON SLIDES

| Subject Variables | Stimulus Variables | | | | | |
| | White Slides | | | Negro Slides | | |
	White Female	White Male	Mean for White Slides	Negro Female	Negro Male	Mean for Negro Slides
Male: Prejudiced	.755	.953	.854	.953	.978	.966
Unprejudiced	.924	1.690	1.307	1.135	.970	1.052
Female: Prejudiced	1.224	1.376	1.300	1.744	1.252	1.498
Unprejudiced	.990	1.018	1.004	.873	.928	.900
Mean for males	.840	1.322	1.081	1.044	.974	1.009
Mean for females	1.107	1.197	1.152	1.309	1.090	1.200
Mean for prejudiced	.989	1.164	1.077	1.348	1.115	1.232
Mean for unprejudiced	.957	1.354	1.115	1.004	.949	.976

Note.—Lower numerical values indicate greater physiological response (see footnote 6). Relative response ranges can be interpreted as follows: Response levels before each stimulus presentation equal 1.000. A value such as 1.744 (prejudiced females responding to Negro female slides) indicates a 74 per cent response change in the direction of decreased FP activity.

more clearly understood by comparing the "mean for white slides" with the "mean for Negro slides" for each of the four S types (Table 1). Prejudiced males and prejudiced females both gave smaller FP reactions to the Negro slides than to the white slides.[6] On the other hand, unprejudiced males and unprejudiced females showed no such decrease in level of FP response toward Negro slides, ac-

[6] Unusually high numerical values found in such cases as prejudiced females viewing Negro female slides (Table 1) need careful interpretation. The 1.744 numerical value represents a 74% decrease in FP activity over the preceding 30-sec. rest period. This seems difficult to account for in terms of relaxation of the arterioles of the finger. Rather, it would seem that the stroke volume of the heart had increased to a point where it more than cancelled the constriction response. If this is the case, the suggested inverse relationship between verbal attitude and FP activity may prove with further research to be a more complicated product of heart action and arterial constriction; a product whose components are each related to the verbal attitude variable in a different way. Independent measures of heart stroke were attempted in the present research but proved unusable. Further research on this problem should give careful consideration of this possible alternative interpretation of the suggested inverse relationship between FP activity and attitudinal predisposition.

tually showing a higher level of FP activity. This comparison suggests an *inverse* relationship between degree of prejudice and autonomic response as measured by FP activity. This relationship is complicated, however, by the fact that the two sexes reacted generally with somewhat different levels of activity. That is, while the direction of response was similar for prejudiced persons of both sexes, the greatest degree of FP activity was shown by prejudiced males while viewing white female slides, and the smallest response was by prejudiced female Ss viewing Negro female slides.

The analysis of the GSR means (Table 3) for the single-person slides reveals that the prejudiced group tended to give greater levels of autonomic response to the Negro slides than did the unprejudiced group, suggesting a *direct* relationship between prejudice and GSR. In each of the three parallel analyses previously mentioned, a similar pattern of significant results appeared.

Table 3 also reveals that GSR responses by all S types were consistently greater to slides portraying males than to those showing fe-

TABLE 2

ANALYSIS OF VARIANCE FOR FINGER PULSE RECORDS, SINGLE-PERSON SLIDES

Source of Variation	df	Mean Square	F
Between subjects	33		
a. Between subject types	3		
1. Between sexes	1	.83	.929
2. Between attitude types	1	.46	.515
3. Sex × attitude interaction	1	4.26	4.770*
b. Between subjects of same type	30		
1. Prejudiced males	7		
2. Unprejudiced males	7		
3. Prejudiced females	9		
4. Unprejudiced females	7		
Within subjects	102		
a. Between stimulus conditions	3		
1. White vs. Negro slides	1	.00	.000
2. Male vs. female slides	1	.11	.222
3. Race × sex interaction	1	1.67	3.370
b. Interactions, subjects, and stimulus conditions	99		
1. Interaction between subject, *types* and stimulus conditions	9	.36	
2. Pooled interaction between individual subjects and stimulus conditions	90	.495	
Total	136		

* Indicates significance at or beyond .05 level.

males. The same situation prevails in all three analyses of the single-person slides.

In summary of the FP and the GSR analyses of the single-person slides, prejudiced Ss manifested different levels of autonomic activity than unprejudiced Ss while viewing Negro slides as compared to white slides. Prejudice and FP activity tended to be inversely related, while prejudice and GSR activity tended to be directly related. In addition, the sex of the S influenced the level and direction of response.

We turn now to a summary of the analyses of the pair slides, restricting our discussion to the GSR data.

Table 4 shows the mean levels of response toward the various types of slides. A significant F value (see Table 5) was obtained for GSR reactions to slides portraying persons of the "same sex" versus those presenting "mixed sex" pairs. The means of the lower part of Table 4 show that Ss gave greater responses to slides portraying persons of the same sex.

It should be kept in mind, however, that by the time the pair slides were presented to the Ss, they had already reacted to the set of single-person slides. The Ss tended generally to respond with lesser magnitude, indicating a "jading" effect had set in by the time that the pair slides were presented.

The statistically significant findings of the experiment can be listed briefly as follows:

Finger Pulse Analysis

1. The degree of autonomic response accompanying exposure to the slides was related to the sex and attitudes of the Ss taken in combination. The response of greatest magnitude was by prejudiced males viewing white female slides. The response of smallest magni-

TABLE 3

MEAN LEVELS OF GSR RESPONSE, SINGLE-PERSON SLIDES, LAST TWO-THIRDS OF STIMULUS

Subject Categories	Stimulus Conditions					
	White Slides			Negro Slides		
	White Female	White Male	Mean for White Slides	Negro Female	Negro Male	Mean for Negro Slides
Males: Prejudiced	.948	.981	.965	.932	.957	.940
Unprejudiced	.920	.934	.927	.840	.901	.870
Females: Prejudiced	.901	1.058	.980	.886	.953	.920
Unprejudiced	.928	1.111	1.020	.892	.879	.886
Mean for males	.934	.958	.946	.886	.929	.905
Mean for females	.915	1.085	1.000	.889	.916	.903
Mean for prejudiced	.925	1.020	.973	.909	.955	.930
Mean for unprejudiced	.924	1.022	.973	.866	.890	.878

tude was by prejudiced females viewing Negro female slides (Tables 1 and 2).

2. Prejudiced Ss of both sexes showed lesser levels of FP activity while viewing Negro slides as compared to white slides, while un-prejudiced Ss of both sexes showed greater reactions to Negro slides as compared to white slides, suggesting an inverse relationship between FP activity and prejudice (Tables 1 and 2).

TABLE 4

MEAN LEVELS OF GSR RESPONSE, PAIR SLIDES LAST TWO-THIRDS OF STIMULUS

Subject Variables	Stimulus Variables					
	Same-Race Slides			Mixed-Race Slides		
	Same Sex	Mixed Sex	Mean for Same Race	Same Sex	Mixed Sex	Mean for Same Sex
Males: Prejudiced	1.030	1.037	1.033	1.256	.935	1.096
Unprejudiced	1.046	.979	1.013	1.015	.949	.982
Females: Prejudiced	1.004	1.017	1.001	.962	.993	.976
Unprejudiced	.953	.946	.950	1.173	.932	1.053
Mean for males	1.038	1.008	1.023	1.136	.942	1.039
Mean for females	.979	.982	.981	1.068	.963	1.015
Mean for prejudiced	1.016	1.027	1.022	1.109	.964	1.036
Mean for unprejudiced	1.000	.963	.982	1.094	.941	1.018

	Same-Sex Slides	Mixed-Sex Slides
Mean for prejudiced	1.062	.991
Mean for unprejudiced	1.042	.952
Mean for males	1.037	.925
Mean for females	1.023	.972

TABLE 5

SUMMARY OF SOURCES OF VARIANCE FOR ALL ANALYSES

Physiological Variable	Slide Stimuli	Stimulus Period	Significant* Source of Variance	Direction of Relationship
FP	Single-person slides	First ⅓ of period		(See Tables 1 and 2)
GSR	Single-person slides	First ⅓ of period	White vs. Negro slides	Average S's response greater to white slides with prejudiced S's response greater to Negro slides
			Male vs. Female slides	Response greater to male slides for all S types
GSR	Single-person slides	Last ⅔ of period	White vs. Negro slides	Average S's response greater to white slides with prejudiced S's response greater to Negro slides
			Male vs. Female slides	Response greater to male slides for all S types
GSR	Single-person slides	Entire period	White vs. Negro slides	Average S's response greater to white slides with prejudiced S's response greater to Negro slides
			Male vs. Female slides	Response greater to male slides for all S types
GSR	Pair slides	First ⅓ of period	none	
GSR	Pair slides	Last ⅔ of period	Same-sex vs. mixed-sex slides	Response greater to same-sex slides for all S types
GSR	Pair slides	Entire period	none	

* Significant at the .05 level.

Galvanic Skin Response Analysis

1. Prejudiced Ss, in the single-person slide analysis, showed greater responses toward Negro slides than did unprejudiced Ss (Table 3).

2. The Ss as a whole, regardless of sex or attitude, gave consistently greater responses to slides portraying males than to slides portraying females (Table 3).

3. In the analysis of the pair slides, the Ss as a whole showed higher levels of autonomic response toward slides portraying persons of the same sex as compared to mixed sex pairs (Table 4).

DISCUSSION

How do these findings bear on the problem as stated originally? The most simple and general answer that can be given to this question is that responses to attitude objects include nonrandom autonomic physiological patterns that are related to characteristics of the S, characteristics of the object, and combinations of these characteristics. There is evidence that the attitudinal predispositions of our Ss, as measured by our attitude scales, were related to some extent to their autonomic response patterns. There is also ample evidence that the response patterns were complicated by the influence of other variables. The sex category of the S operated in various ways to determine partially the direction and magnitude of response. In addition, a person's autonomic responses were influenced by the racial and sexual categories of the attitude object, and the ways in which attitude objects were paired together.

What do these data mean in terms of traditional categories of affective orientation? It cannot be assumed that conspicuous physiological changes manifested by an S upon being exposed to a stimulus object indicate simple favorability or unfavorability toward the attitude object, regardless of his scale-measured attitudes toward that object. It is easy to fall into thinking, especially when the stimuli are "race objects," that high response indicates a negative attitude. Actually, such responses could be due to a number of conditions. Conflicting feelings, indecision, or even positive involvement might result in large autonomic responses. There are probably many other interpretative possibilities besides these. The present research makes no attempt to assign simple meaning to the responses. Our aim was to determine if measurable patterns of autonomic physiological response exist and, if so, are they related to scale measured attitudes?

Finally, in attempting to evaluate the experimental data, two aspects of our method should be kept in mind. First, it would have been easy to design the slide stimuli so that larger autonomic responses were evoked. It will be recalled that our slide stimuli were deliberately made "conservative." That is, suggestive poses, body contact, unusual clothing, or facial expressions were deliberately avoided, so that if autonomic responses occurred it came in spite of the avoidance of these secondary cues. Further explorations of this problem could well include more open portrayal of emotion-arousing interracial scenes. There is every reason to presume that response consistencies under such circumstances would be more clear-cut. Another variable that might well be introduced is the

influence of well-defined social roles. For example, the Negro man and white girl portrayed together might evoke entirely different response patterns depending upon whether they were shown lying on a beach together clad in bathing suits, or talking together in a church with the Negro in a clergyman's robes. Such social roles were not included in the present research, but they may importantly influence attitudinal responses.

The second aspect of method which may have placed limitations on the magnitude of response is the order in which the slides were presented. Every S viewed the four single-person slides before being presented the pair slide stimuli. It is clear that there was a tendency for GSR activity to become dampened with rapidly presented stimuli. Since the data for the pair slides were collected during the last half of the laboratory session, differences between reactions might tend to be obscured. Further experimentation should use a reduced number of stimuli. One or two preliminaries at the start, followed by not more than four or five should be a maximum.

In terms of their implications for the attitude concept, the over-all results indicate that attitudinal responses include autonomic physiological activity that is related to the attitudinal characteristics of the individual as measured by more standard means.[7] They are also related to the sex of the responding individual and to features of the object of response. Clearly, there is little point in attempting to interpret these physiological responses as the "true attitude." Rather, it seems more useful to regard these responses as another dimension of attitudinal behavior to be considered along with the verbal and overt action dimensions.

-----

[7] A recent article by Rankin and Campbell (1955) analyzes GSR responses of male students to a Negro by the ingenious device of having a Negro experimenter touch the Ss while "adjusting" the apparatus. This problem of attributing the response to the racial aspects of the situation vs. a reaction to a particular person is discussed [Chapter 31 in this volume].

Although one need not assume that this dimension must correspond with other dimensions in a one-to-one fashion, it would seem theoretically useful and empirically possible to establish the nature of the relationship between the various dimensions for particular populations under given circumstances. Our findings, however modest, indicate that further research along these lines may prove useful not only for clarifying the construct "attitude," but also for increasing our knowledge of the empirical referents of the construct.

SUMMARY

The problem was to determine if autonomic response was associated with exposure to objects toward which individuals have (scale-measured) attitudes. That is, do persons who are unfavorable in their verbal response to Negroes also manifest different autonomic responses to slides portraying Negroes than do those more favorable in their verbal response? The 46 subjects, half of whom were males and half females, were divided into a prejudice and unprejudiced group on the basis of a verbal attitude test. They were then exposed to photographic slides portraying Negroes and whites in various combinations of race and sex. The finger pulse and GSR activity of each subject was recorded during these presentations.

The data indicate that greater GSR responses (but smaller FP responses) were given to Negro slides by prejudiced subjects, but the autonomic activity was influenced by the sex of the subject as well as the race and sex characteristics of the stimulus slides. Such autonomic activity may be considered as another dimension of attitudinal behavior to be considered along with the verbal and overt action dimensions. Additional research is needed before simple meaning can be assigned to the involvement of autonomic activity in attitudinal behavior.

REFERENCES

Allport, G. W.
1935 "Attitudes." In C. Murchison (ed.), Handbook of Social Psychology. Worcester, Massachusetts: Clark University Press.

Campbell, D. T.
1950 "The indirect assessment of social attitudes." Psychological Bulletin 47:15–38.

Davis, R. C., G. F. Siddons, and G. L. Stout.
1954 "Apparatus for recording autonomic states and changes." American Journal of Psychology 67:343–352.

Edwards, A. L.
1950 Experimental Design in Psychological Research. New York: Rinehart.

Green, B. F.
1954 "Attitude measurement." In G. Lindzey (ed.), Handbook of Social Psychology. Cambridge, Massachusetts: Addison-Wesley.

Rankin, R. E., and D. T. Campbell.
1955 "Galvanic skin response to Negro and white experimenters." Journal of Abnormal and Social Psychology 51:30–33.

Westie, F. R.
1953 "A technique for the measurement of race attitudes." American Sociological Review 18:73–78.

CHAPTER 34

Racial Attitudes and Emotional
Response to Visual Representations
of the Negro

ROBERT N. VIDULICH AND FRANK W. KREVANICK

INTRODUCTION

That strong attitudes are accompanied by
great emotional support has been advanced
by numerous authors (4, 9, 13). With respect to racial attitudes, the few available
studies suggest a positive relationship between racial attitudes and emotional response. Emotionality is defined in these
studies by a physiological reaction, the galvanic skin response (GSR). Although GSR
is not specific to emotion, it appears in any
number of states which are generally presumed to be emotional, such as startle, amusement, fear, anger, sexual excitation, and
euphoria.

Rankin and Campbell (11), in a study
using both Negro and white experimenters,
found significant differences in GSR between
high-prejudiced and low-prejudiced Ss when
the two experimenters alternated in adjusting a dummy apparatus attached to each S's
wrists. Cooper and Siegel (2) had Ss rate 20

From Robert N. Vidulich and Frank W. Krevanick,
"Racial attitudes and emotional response to visual representations of the Negro," *Journal of Social Psychology*,
1966, *68*, 85–93. Copyright 1966 by the Journal Press,
and reproduced with permission of the authors and
publisher.

ethnic groups while undergoing simultaneous GSR recording. Twenty of 23 Ss who
displayed strong nationality antipathies on a
previously administered scale gave greater
GSRs to stimulus words (e.g., Jew and Russian) toward which they had already indicated strong negative attitudes. Cooper and
Singer (3) found that all strong attitudes,
both favorable and unfavorable, are accompanied by heightened emotionality, but that
the GSR is greater for objects of strong negative attitudes than for objects of strong positive attitudes.

In the present study an attempt was made
to determine further the relationship between
racial attitudes and physiological emotionality, as measured by the GSR. Specifically, we
were concerned with the emotional responsiveness of individuals high or low in anti-
Negro feelings to visual stimuli with or without Negro content. Two hypotheses were
proposed: (*a*) high-prejudiced Ss evidence
greater GSRs to photographs of Negroes
and Negro-white interactions than do low-
prejudiced Ss and (*b*) photographs of Negroes and Negro-white interactions elicit
greater GSRs than do photographs of whites
or photographs of nonhuman content for
all Ss.

METHOD

Attitude Scale

A 40-item scale of attitudes toward Negroes was designed specifically for this study. Items were taken from several sources, including the California E and F Scales (1), a scale reported by Garrison (5), and a pool of items devised by the authors. Appropriate paraphrasing of previously used items was exercised when necessary in order that all items read in a negative direction. Items were scaled on a modified Likert technique, with a seven-point range allowing no neutral response. This scale was given to introductory psychology students by an associate of E, two weeks prior to the beginning of the experiment.[1]

A Spearman-Brown corrected split-half (odd-even) reliability coefficient of .95 was obtained from a random sample of 100 of the total pool of 214 completed scales. The total distribution of scores approximated a normal distribution but was platykurtic. The possible scoring limits ranged from 40 to 260, with a hypothetical mean of 160. The actual distribution ranged from 41 to 259, with a median of 167, a mean of 164, and a standard deviation of 37.62.

Subjects

From a total pool of 214 students enrolled in elementary-psychology courses during the fall semester of 1961 and who completed the attitude scale, 20 high scorers and 20 low scorers were selected as Ss for the present study. One-half of the Ss were males and one-half were females, each half representing the extreme scorers for the respective sexes on the obtained continuum of scores.

Apparatus and Materials

The GSR unit of a Keeler Polygraph, Model 302C, was used as the physiological measuring instrument. Automatic recording of galvanometric deflections was provided by the kymographic unit. A standard drum speed of six inches per minute was used throughout the experiment.

Owing to dampening or adaptation effects that are known to occur to prolonged stimulation in the GSR technique (11, 12), the total number of stimulus figures was held to a minimum. Stimuli consisted of 18 photographs mounted on eight-by-ten-inch cards. The selection and the categorization of the photographs were made through the agreement of three judges. Eight photographs consisted of landscapes and architectural structures, but three of these were used to calibrate the GSR unit for each S during the preexperimental period instead of as experimental stimuli. Five photographs were of Negroes or Negro-white interactions, and the remaining five were of whites approximating the actions in the Negro-Negro-white photographs. These three photograph groupings were designated as the (a) neutral-treatment, (b) critical-treatment, and (c) control-treatment conditions respectively.

To obviate any possible serial-positioning effects and to insure randomization, the stimulus photographs were shuffled prior to presentation to each S.

An isolated, quiet room was used for the experiment; and a stand containing the stimulus cards was mounted on a table three feet above the floor. The subject was seated in a chair equipped with an armrest approximately two-and-one-half feet from, and directly facing, the stand. The recording apparatus, behind a baffle that prevented S from viewing the polygraph recording, was located at right angles to S.

Procedure

Enroute to the experimental room, E said to S:

Your name has been selected randomly from a list of volunteers who are available for this research. Be assured that we are not concerned

---

[1] Copies of this scale and of the photographic stimuli used in this study are available upon request from the senior author.

with your reactions *per se*, but only in how your group does collectively.

E then ushered S into the room and requested that he be seated; then E continued:

I am going to attach this device to your hand; you will not be shocked nor will you feel anything. All I want you to do is tell me whether you like, dislike, or are indifferent to a series of pictures that I'm going to show you. Look at the pictures for several seconds before you answer.

E then attached the electrode to S's right hand and said:

It will take me a few minutes to adjust the apparatus; so please try to relax. Try to refrain from making any muscular movements or talking[2] during the experiment except to answer whether you like, dislike, or are indifferent to the pictures. Do you understand? When I say "ready," I will present the first picture.

After obtaining a basal response for S on the three neutral-calibration photographs (which took approximately three to five minutes) E uncovered the first test pictures. When the recording pen returned to the basal level,[3] E uncovered the second picture. This procedure was followed throughout the experiment, with E making appropriate record of the order of presentation and noting the S's verbalization of like, dislike, or neutral remarks on the kymogram.

Response Measures

Galvanometric deflections were analyzed according to the area contained within the tracing formed by the recording pen on the recording chart. Specifically, E counted on

[2] Greenwald (6) has shown that talking has little effect on the GSR; however, the authors felt that owing to the possible effects on tension or relaxation in S, the precaution mentioned should be taken.

[3] Hunt and Hunt (8) have shown that basal resistance is unimportant if successive measurements of GSR are made from the same level. This condition was fully met in the present study.

the chart the number of blocks (and fractions) encompassed by the tracing between the rise of the recording pen from, and its subsequent return to, the basal level.

Although the sensitivity of the galvanometer was held constant for a given S throughout the series of trials, considerable intersubject variability of course would be expected due to the different initial skin-resistance levels; consequently, it was necessary to standardize the data such that intersubject differences due to basal-resistance levels would be negated. This was accomplished by converting raw scores to T scores according to the procedure described by Guilford (7).

RESULTS

The standardized scores were subjected to a $2 \times 2 \times 3$ analysis of variance, the variables being sex (male and female), prejudice (high and low), and treatments (critical, control, and neutral). From Table 1, it is apparent that differences occurred among the various treatment conditions. Highly significant F ratios were obtained for treatments ($F = 43.88$, $p < .01$), the treatment-by-sex interaction ($F = 7.38$, $p < .01$), and the treatment-by-prejudice interaction ($F = 4.84$, $p < .01$). It should be emphasized that there were no significant differences in physiological response attributable to sex or prejudice per se, indicating that whatever differences occurred were due to the imposition of the various treatment conditions.

The mean GSRs of all experimental groups are presented in Table 2. Critical differences between the means were computed according to the procedure outlined by Lindquist (10, pp. 90–95). These differences are also contained in Table 2.

Table 2 indicates that for all Ss the critical photographs produced significantly greater mean galvanometric deflections than did the corresponding control or neutral photographs. The average GSR produced by the control photographs was, in turn, significantly greater than that elicited by the neutral photographs.

TABLE 1

ANALYSIS OF VARIANCE FOR ALL EXPERIMENTAL CONDITIONS

Source	Sum of squares	df	Mean square	F	p
Between subjects	34.339	39	.881		
Sex (S)	.093	1	.093	.10	NS
Prejudice (P)	.870	1	.870	.98	NS
S × P	1.447	1	1.447	1.63	NS
Error	31.928	36	.887		
Within subjects	3293.638	80	41.171		
Treatments (T)	1558.094	2	779.047	43.88	< .01
T × S	262.069	2	131.035	7.38	< .01
T × P	171.865	2	85.933	4.84	< .01
T × P × S	23.413	2	11.707	.66	NS
Error	1278.197	72	17.753		

The most important findings of this study, in terms of the hypotheses proposed, concern the physiological responsiveness of the high-prejudice and low-prejudice groups in the three treatment conditions. The mean GSR for the high-prejudice group was found to be significantly greater than the low-prejudice mean GSR for the critical-treatment condition, but not for the control-treatment or neutral-treatment conditions. In the latter two comparisons, the mean GSR for the low-prejudice group was greater than for the high-prejudice group, but these differences were not significant at the .05 level. Both the high-prejudice group and the low-prejudice group gave significantly greater mean GSRs to the critical photographs than to either the control or the neutral photographs.

Males gave a significantly greater mean GSR than the females to the critical photographs [compared] to the control or the neutral photographs. In fact, in the control-treatment and the neutral-treatment conditions, the females responded more than the males; but not significantly so. The male group also produced a greater mean GSR to the critical photographs than they gave to the control photographs. This difference was not found for the female group.

Even though the triple interaction of treatments by prejudice by sex was found to be nonsignificant in the analysis of variance, the differences between the means of the treatment groups for all relevant comparisons were computed to provide a more detailed understanding of the interrelationships among the three variables. These data are also presented in Table 2.

A significantly greater mean GSR to the critical photographs was obtained for the high-prejudice males than for the low-prejudice males. High-prejudice and low-prejudice females did not differ significantly for the critical photographs. No significant differences in mean GSR were found for either high-prejudice and low-prejudice males or females on the control and neutral conditions.

On the critical photographs, for the high-prejudice males, a significantly greater mean GSR was obtained than for the high-prejudice females; also, the low-prejudice males were more physiologically responsive to the critical photographs than were the low-prejudice females. These findings were not obtained for either the control-treatment or the neutral-treatment conditions.

On the comparison between physiological response to the critical, control, and neutral photographic stimuli, the following findings were obtained: high-prejudice males gave a significantly greater mean GSR to the critical

TABLE 2

Treatment Means

Subjects	N	Photographic stimuli			p value		
		Critical (a)*	Control (b)**	Neutral (c)***	(a) vs. (b)	(a) vs. (c)	(b) vs. (c)
1. All subjects	40	54.54	48.95	45.83	.01	.01	.01
2. High-prejudice Ss	20	56.32	48.14	45.13	.01	.01	.05
3. Low-prejudice Ss	20	52.77	49.76	46.54	.05	.01	.01
4. Male Ss	20	56.65	47.74	45.02	.01	.01	.05
5. Female Ss	20	52.44	50.16	46.65	n.s.	.01	.01
6. High-prejudice male Ss	10	58.69	46.43	44.87	.01	.01	n.s.
7. Low-prejudice male Ss	10	54.41	49.04	45.17	.01	.01	.05
8. High-prejudice female Ss	10	53.95	49.84	45.38	.05	.01	.05
9. Low-prejudice female Ss	10	50.93	59.48	47.91	n.s.	n.s.	n.s.

* p: 2 vs. 3 = .01; 4 vs. 5 = .01; 6 vs. 7 = .05; 8 vs. 9, n.s.; 6 vs. 8 = .05; 7 vs. 9 = .05.
** p: 2 vs. 3, 4 vs. 5, 6 vs. 7, 8 vs. 9, 6 vs. 8, 7 vs. 9, all n.s.
*** p: 2 vs. 3, 4 vs. 5, 6 vs. 7, 8 vs. 9, 6 vs. 8, 7 vs. 9, all n.s.

photographs than to the control or the neutral photographs. The same differences were found for the high-prejudice females and for the low-prejudice males on differential GSR responsiveness to the critical, the control, and the neutral photographs. The low-prejudice females did not respond significantly differently to the three treatment conditions.

A chi-square analysis of the verbalized preferences to the various photographs (between high-prejudice and low-prejudice males, between high-prejudice and low-prejudice females, and between all high-prejudice and all low-prejudice Ss) show only the critical photographs to yield any significant chi-square ratios. All of the nine possible comparisons within the critical-treatment condition, except that between the high prejudice and low-prejudice females for the neutral-response category, were significant at the .05 level of confidence. These data indicate that the high-prejudice group verbally rejected the Negro stimuli and the Negro-white stimuli, while the low-prejudice Ss expressed relatively greater preferences for these pictures.

DISCUSSION

Prior studies have demonstrated that heightened GSR is obtained by exposing persons with strong anti-Negro attitudes to Negroes in person, to statements about Negroes, and to the verbal stimulus "Negro." The present investigation extends this line of evidence to include physiological emotional reactivity to pictorial representations of Negroes.

The obtained differences in GSR between high-prejudice and low-prejudice Ss to Negro stimuli supports the widely held belief of social psychologists that prejudicial attitudes are "emotional." This view is correct insofar as the attitudes are accompanied by physiological activity; however, no evidence is available to argue against the possibility that *all* extreme attitudes or beliefs have physiological concomitants. Needed are studies that examine the differential physiological responsiveness of extreme believers on a variety of belief systems other than beliefs about ethnic groups.

The obtained sex differences in this study, indicating a greater GSR for males than for females to the critical Negro and Negro-white photographs, was unexpected because earlier investigators had not used sex as an independent variable and because we had no intuitive reason to expect males and females to react differently. A detailed examination of the mean GSRs for the four treatment groups to each critical photograph indicates the locus for the overall sex difference. The mean GSRs of the high-prejudice and low-prejudice males and females to two of the critical pictures—that of a Negro male kissing a white female and that of an integrated eating scene—were not significantly different from each other. Both high-prejudice males and low-prejudice males reacted more strongly than the combined females to the remaining three pictures of a seated Negro male, an integrated family scene, and a Negro male and a white female dancing. For the first two pictures, the mean GSRs of the high-prejudice males were significantly higher than those for the low-prejudice males; thus, while the obtained sex difference is to some extent a function of the generally heightened physiological reactivity of the high-prejudice males to the critical photographs, the fact that the low-prejudice males also produced higher than expected GSRs raised the question about the meaning of measured racial attitudes in this group. This question demands further examination.

Experimental purists can ask whether the GSRs in this study were a function *only* of the stimulus photographs or were they contaminated or mediated by the verbalized preferences elicited upon stimulus presentation? We have no data in the present study to answer this question, but plan to examine it in a future replication.

Finally, one may note that our data say nothing about what occurs physiologically to prolonged exposure to Negro stimuli for the anti-Negro S. Does the physiological response of the prejudiced person to stimuli representative of his rejected group continue unabated at the high level noted in this experiment? Does adaptation take place with subsequent lowering of the GSR? Or does continued perception of the object of negative beliefs possibly elevate autonomic reactions to an even higher level? Studies which may answer these questions are currently underway.

SUMMARY

This study investigated the degree of "emotional support" of strong racial attitudes. Specifically, the hypothesis was tested that persons with high anti-Negro prejudice exhibit greater GSRs than do low-prejudice individuals to photographic stimuli with Negro content than to non-Negro stimuli.

Forty Ss (20 male, and 20 female) who were extreme scorers among 214 introductory-level university students were asked to respond to a new 40-item, highly reliable, Likert-type Negro attitude scale. Four experimental groups of 10 Ss each were established: high-prejudice males, high-prejudice females, low-prejudice males, and low-prejudice females.

While undergoing GSR recording, each S simultaneously stated whether he "liked," "disliked," or was "indifferent to" 15 randomly presented mounted photographs matched for size and quality. Five photographs were of Negroes or Negro-white interactions (critical), five were of whites approximating the content of the critical photographs (control), and five were photographs of pastoral or architectural scenes without human content (neutral). Three additional neutral photographs were used for polygraph calibration for each S.

The response measure used was the total area of galvanometric deflection for each picture above each S's own basal level. All data were converted to standard scores to equate intersubject differences in basal skin-resistance level.

The results support the hypothesized relationship between prejudice level and stimulus treatment. Specifically, (*a*) critical stimuli elicited significantly greater GSRs for all *S*s than did control or neutral photographs; (*b*) high-prejudice *S*s gave significantly greater mean GSRs to critical photographs than did low-prejudice *S*s, but these groups did not differ on control or neutral stimuli; (*c*) similar findings held for male *S*s and female *S*s, with males producing significantly greater GSRs than females to critical photographs, but not to control or neutral photographs; (*d*) on the critical photographs, high-prejudice males were most responsive, followed by low-prejudice males, then high-prejudice and low-prejudice females; (*e*) all *S*s showed a high degree of consistency between attitude-scale response, physiological responsiveness, and verbalized preferences for the photographs.

REFERENCES

1. Adorno, T. W., E. Frenkel-Brunswik, D. J. Levinson, and R. N. Sanford.
   1950   The Authoritarian Personality. New York: Harper.
2. Cooper, J. B., and H. E. Siegel.
   1956   "The galvanic skin response as a measure of emotion in prejudice." Journal of Psychology 42:149–155.
3. Cooper, J. B., and D. N. Singer.
   1956   "The role of emotion in prejudice." Journal of Social Psychology 44: 241–247.
4. Dewey, R., and W. J. Humber.
   1951   The Development of Human Behavior. New York: Macmillan.
5. Garrison, K. C.
   1933   "A study of racial attitudes of college students." Journal of Social Psychology 4:230–235.
6. Greenwald, D. U.
   1936   "Individual differences in electrodermal response to continuum affective stimulation." Psychological Monographs 48:632–646.
7. Guilford, J. P.
   1955   Elementary Statistics in Psychology and Education. New York: McGraw-Hill.
8. Hunt, W. A., and E. B. Hunt.
   1935   "A comparison of five methods of scoring the GSR." Journal of Experimental Psychology 18:383–387.
9. Krech, D., and R. S. Crutchfield.
   1948   Theory and Problems of Social Psychology. New York: McGraw-Hill.
10. Lindquist, E. F.
    1963   Design and Analysis of Experiments in Psychology and Education. Boston: Houghton-Mifflin.
11. Rankin, R. E., and D. T. Campbell.
    1955   "Galvanic skin response to Negro and white experimenters." Journal of Abnormal and Social Psychology 51:30–33.
12. Ruckmick, G. A.
    1933   "Affective responses to the motion picture situation by means of the galvanic technique." Psychological Bulletin 30:712.
13. Young, P. T.
    1943   Emotion in Man and Animals: The Nature and Relation to Attitude and Mating. New York: Wiley.

CHAPTER 35 The Pupil Response as a Measure of Social Attitudes*

JOHN J. WOODMANSEE

A number of investigators have explored the possibility that physiological reactions might serve as indicators of social attitudes. For example, Rankin and Campbell (1955) compared the galvanic skin response (GSR) obtained from white subjects when the experimenter was a Negro with that obtained when the experimenter was white; Westie and DeFleur (1959) recorded GSR, vascular constriction, and amplitude and duration of heart cycle while the subjects viewed pictures of whites and Negroes in social situations. As Cook and Selltiz (1964) observed, work in this area has been based on the assumption that the magnitude of the physiological reaction is directly related to intensity of feeling or affect; thus, the greater the physiological response, the stronger or more

extreme the attitude is presumed to be. There are problems, however, in inferring the nature or direction of the attitude from the physiological response. Most measures of physiological reaction give direct indication only of the extent of autonomic arousal; they do not reveal whether the corresponding emotion is pleasurable or unpleasurable. Clearly, if a bidirectional indicator of autonomic neural activity were available, it would provide a much firmer basis for inferences about the direction of attitude. Recent work with pupillary constriction and dilation offers some hope of developing such an indicator.

HISTORICAL PERSPECTIVE

The fact that the pupil of the eye is an extraordinarily mobile structure which becomes larger when some psychological or sensory (except for light) stimulus intrudes upon the system has been known for some time. In her historical review of pupillary research Loewenfeld (1958) noted that Fontana studied pupillary dilation as early as 1765. Fontana demonstrated that the pupils which are contracted during sleep, dilate widely when a subject is suddenly awakened. He found that this reaction occurred even in the presence of bright light. He also found that

* This work was supported in part by grants from the Air Force Office of Scientific Research (AF-AFOSR 436–63), the National Science Foundation (GS–303) and the Wake Forest Graduate Council. I thank Dr. Stuart Cook, University of Colorado; Dr. Gad Hakerem, New York State Department of Mental Health; Dr. Eckhard Hess and James Polt, University of Chicago; and Dr. Irene Loewenfeld, Columbia University for their advice and encouragement in the formative stages of the research on which this report is based. Appreciation is also extended to Deborah Newsome and Michael Kirby for their assistance as co-experimenters.

This chapter was prepared especially for this volume.

when a cat's eye was exposed to a beam of bright light and the animal was hurt or frightened at the same time, the pupils dilated and remained large until the cat calmed down. This effect has been termed pupillary reflex dilation and is defined as that increase in pupil size elicited by sensory or emotional stimuli, or by spontaneous thoughts or emotions.

Many investigators have noted the reflex dilation effect but the most systematic work on the phenomenon has been done by Otto Lowenstein and Irene Loewenfeld at Columbia University. A half century ago Lowenstein (1920) wrote an experimental analysis of the influence of positive and negative affect-arousing stimuli and of sensory stimuli upon the pupil. He began his paper as follows:

It is today an almost universally accepted fact that every psychic process is accompanied, in normal man, by changes in pupil diameter. When a subject is asked, for example, to count the ticks of a metronome, and when the pupils are observed simultaneously with appropriate means, it is seen that pupillary movements, that is, dilations, run parallel with the beat of the metronome. Dilation of the pupil can be observed also as accompaniment of other processes: with every increase in attention, by intellectual processes of every kind, with the beginning of volitional impulses, or with the course of emotions (p. 194).

An excellent comprehensive review and analysis of pupil research conducted by physiologists, ophthalmologists, and other vision specialists is provided by Loewenfeld (1958).

Until recently most pupil research by psychologists was in the area of classical conditioning. A considerable controversy developed over the question of whether or not the pupillary constriction that occurs with an increase in light stimulation can be conditioned to a nonadequate stimulus such as a buzzer or bell. Reviews of this controversy were done by Hilgard, Dutton, and Helmick (1949) and Young (1954; 1958). It now appears that whereas pupillary dilation is conditionable, constriction is not. Recently, Young (1965) summarized the evidence on this issue and also provided an enlightening discussion of its physiological implications.

Although interest in the area of pupillary classical conditioning research has waned, research on the pupil as an index of mental and emotional states has increased. The impetus for this renewed interest was the work of Eckhard Hess and his colleagues at the University of Chicago. Several studies from Hess' laboratory suggest that the pupil response might be used as an index of social attitudes. The first of these studies involved the presentation of five pictures to male and female subjects (Hess and Polt, 1960). The males' pupils dilated more than the females' to a picture of a female nude. The females' pupils dilated more to pictures of a partially clothed "muscle man," a woman with a baby, and a baby alone. The reaction of both sexes to a landscape scene was minimal; in fact there was a slight constriction by the males. The results were interpreted as showing that pupil dilation and interest value of the stimulus are related. In a study by Hess, Seltzer and Shlien (1965) the pupils of male homosexuals were found to dilate more to pictures of males than did the pupils of heterosexual males. The heterosexual males reacted more positively to pictures of females. The investigators judged that, as in the previous study, interest value of the stimulus was the crucial factor governing dilation. These two studies appear to confirm the reflex dilation effect which Lowenstein had described. In each case the dilation response was mediated by autonomic nervous system activity, the intensity of which depended on the sexual arousal value or interest value of the pictorial stimuli.

In another report Hess (1965) described results which apparently cannot be interpreted in terms of the pupillary reflex dilation phenomenon. Hess reported that certain visual stimuli, when shown repeatedly to subjects, elicit a constriction response. Examples of these stimuli are a picture of a boy with crossed eyes, an underwater scene of a shark swimming, and the remains of several emaciated victims of a Nazi concentration camp. Subjects who disliked these pictures dilated on the first few exposures until the shock value was diminished. Continued viewing (after three to five exposures) of the pictures resulted in constrictions. Hess reasoned that the constriction to these pictures was mediated by an aversion to them.

If Hess is correct in assuming that interest and liking result in pupillary dilation while an unpleasant feeling results in pupillary constriction, the pupil should have potential as an involuntary, bidirectional index of liking and disliking in regard to attitudinal objects.

He summarized one attitude study which appears to confirm the bidirectional quality of the pupil reaction. Pictures of presidents and presidential candidates were used as the stimuli. Hess photographed the pupil reaction of three groups of people to five different photographs of then President Johnson and five of Senator Goldwater along with a single photograph of former Presidents Kennedy and Eisenhower. One group then read anti-Johnson material, another read anti-Goldwater material, and the third read excerpts from a psychology journal that had no political content. Then each group was retested. The people who read anti-Johnson material showed a slightly smaller response than previously to Johnson and a slightly larger response than previously to Goldwater. Extremely anti-Goldwater material had a different kind of effect. While it caused the expected decrease in response to Goldwater, it also caused a large drop in response to Johnson and even Eisenhower. The only person unaffected was Kennedy. Hess concluded that this may indicate that bitter campaign propaganda can shift a person's attitude toward politicians in general. He believed that Kennedy was spared for obvious reasons.

The purpose of this paper is to evaluate the potential of the pupil as an index of social attitudes. To do so, I have used Hess' work as a starting point and model since only he has claimed that the pupil has a bidirectional responsiveness mediated by different affective states.

METHODOLOGICAL CONSIDERATIONS

Hess' technique—The pupillographic apparatus which Hess used in most of his studies was quite simple. His subjects peered through an opening in one end of a closed box. Stimulus slides were rear-projected on a translucent screen at the end of the box. While the subject viewed the pictures, his left eye was photographed with a motion picture camera (see illustration in Hess, 1965, p. 48).

The stimulus pictures were of two types and were presented in pairs. Preceding each emotion-arousing or test picture was an emotionally-neutral control picture. This picture was matched in overall brightness to the test slide which followed it. After ten seconds the control picture was switched off, and the test picture was presented. A sequence of as many as ten to twelve of these control-test pairs comprised the stimuli for each study. Usually the subject's pupillary reaction to the first control-test pair was disregarded since initial reactions are predictably dilations while the experimental situation is still novel. To score the response to a particular test picture Hess compared the average diameter of the pupil as photographed during the presentation of the control picture with its average size during the test picture period. This change in pupil size was expressed as a percentage of control period size so that a positive percentage indicated a larger pupil size when the subject was viewing the test picture than when he viewed the control picture. A negative percentage meant a smaller average pupil size during the test period.

Methodological problems in pupillographic experiments—Unfortunately, many important details of Hess' method have never been reported in the literature. His summary reports (Hess, 1965; 1968) give only the briefest description of his technique. Other reports (Hess and Polt; 1960; 1964; 1966; and

Hess, Seltzer and Shlien, 1956) do provide some clues as to apparatus, stimulus preparation, etc. used in the attitude studies, but they are incomplete for the researcher who wishes to replicate Hess' work.

In the studies described later in this paper an effort has been made to provide the reader with some of the missing methodological details as they were gleaned from a personal visit to Hess' laboratory. This is one reason for describing Study A in such great detail; another reason is that the results of Hess' work and mine are interpretable only in light of a large number of methodological considerations which must be presented in any critical appraisal of pupillary research findings.

It should be made clear at this point that my studies have not, except for one pilot project, been exact replications of Hess' method. It was the pilot study plus several other attempts to gather reliable data which suggested that Hess' method was, in several aspects, inadequate. A number of methodological problems were encountered which account for the changes in Study A and thereafter (Woodmansee, 1966). These problems will be discussed now before proceeding with the empirical studies that test the usefulness of the pupil in attitude measurement.

High variability of the pupillary diameter —Possibly the greatest problem in these studies stems from the fact that in diffuse light the pupil is in a constant state of unrest or oscillatory movement. This seemingly random activity has sometimes been termed "hippus." Two kinds of activity have been identified (Lowenstein and Loewenfeld, 1962). One type is a small and fairly regular oscillation of about 1 to 2 per cent of pupil diameter. The frequency of these oscillations is maximally about two per second. Efforts to determine their mechanism have been unsuccessful (e.g., Stark, 1959).

The second type of pupillary unrest involves rather massive (commonly 20 to 30 per cent of pupil diameter) and irregular waves of contraction and dilation which are correlated with changes in sympathetic nervous system activity. As Lowenstein and

Loewenfeld (1952) have shown, the pupils of a fully alert subject are fairly steady in size. However, with waning interest or fatigue the pupils begin to oscillate widely. In ever-deepening waves of sudden, spontaneous, sympathetic arousal varied with gradual boredom or drowsiness, the pupils dilate rapidly, then recontract gradually in an unsteady, wavering decline. The less aroused the subject is, and the less he tries to suppress his drowsiness, the shorter the time of initial contraction, and the more extensive and frequent the pupillary oscillations. At the moment preceding the final closing of the eyelids in sleep, the pupils are very small.

One seldom finds a steady pupil except under conditions of total darkness or bright light. In Hess' studies both of these extremes of light intensity would have a restrictive effect on pupillary reactions. Unfortunately, the dim light condition which is required if the pupil is to have a full range of movement is the very condition under which pupillary unrest is greatest (Lowenstein and Loewenfeld, 1962).

Whatever the source of variability, the high level of "noise" found in the pupil reaction obviously makes reliable measurement very difficult. One solution is to use a repeated trials design wherein the pupillary response is calculated by averaging reactions to many exposures of the same stimulus. With this method random oscillations will cancel each other out leaving the basic response to a test stimulus intact. Hakerem (1962), for example, has used this technique successfully. While increasing reliability, this solution, however, seems inappropriate in studies where the psychosensory response may change during the course of the experiment. Other approaches that come closer to retaining temporal sequence changes while reducing the effect of variability are (*a*) averaging the responses of several subjects to the same stimuli or (*b*) averaging the responses of individual subjects to a set of similar stimuli.

Extraneous stimuli dilate the pupil—Except for light, any stimulus to which the subject is not adapted will dilate the pupil. Unexpected noise, the subject's talking or being spoken to, sudden bodily movements, etc., have been found to contaminate the pupil response to the experimental stimulus. Running the experiment in a soundproof room, masking out spurious sounds with white noise, instructing the subject not to talk or move about are examples of precautions that need to be included in research designs.

A related problem is found in research designs which require that the subject make some motor response while an experimental stimulus is being presented. Simpson and Paivio (1968) have shown that even relatively effortless responses, such as pressing a key or making a verbal reply to signal some event, will enhance pupil dilation.

Control period variability—In Hess' experiments the test stimuli typically were preceded by emotionally-neutral control stimuli. One might suppose that during the control periods pupil size would recover to a fairly constant and steady level, which could then be taken as a basal size for judging the influence of the emotion-arousing test stimuli. Hopefully, the control period means would be about equal across all controls, while only the test period means would vary. This is not the case. The control period means may be expected to vary as much or *more* than the test period means. Data from an exploratory study showed that the size of the pupil during control periods was clearly affected by (*a*) the reaction to the previous test stimulus and (*b*) the general trend of autonomic arousal. Interference by the previous stimulus either enhanced or covered up control-test differences depending on the particular interaction involved. For example, if a test stimulus elicited a strong dilation response, pupil size during the control period following it was artificially enlarged. If, however, the preceding test stimulus was boring, pupil size during the next control period would be relatively smaller because of decreasing arousal.

In lengthy experiments pupil size will gradually decrease regardless of the stimuli. In one study in which the pupil was monitored continuously for more than five minutes, pupil size of most subjects increased somewhat during the first 90 seconds of the experiment, then the pupil size fell off quite rapidly. This regression effect after the first minute and a half can easily account for a 2 to 3 per cent mean pupil size decrease from one 10 second period to the next. This amounts to a built-in constriction effect using Hess' method of computing pupil size change.

Preliminary testing revealed other contaminants of the control period data. Some subjects reported that they could not keep their attention on the control picture and would think of the previous slide, anticipate what might be shown next, or give their attention to other things such as the small hot spot made on the rear projection screen by the projector lamp. It seems that subjects will improvise ways to retain their interest in a boring experiment.

Several attempts were made to provide more similar control period means and less variable intracontrol period data. Working on a hunch that some continuous mental activity might serve to steady the pupil, a variety of tasks were added while the subject viewed the control pictures. The following were tried: repeating the alphabet backwards, either orally or silently, and talking about the previous slide. None of these procedures served to make the control period data less variable.

A solution to these problems is to vary the order of control-test stimulus pairs. This serves to randomize the effects of anticipation, arousal level and inter-stimulus interaction. Even with the stimuli randomly presented, however, a subject may try to figure out which stimuli have not been seen in a given trial. The anticipation problem may be more completely controlled by having each trial presented both in random order and with a random number of control-test stimulus pairs.

Individual differences in visual acuity—Typically, approximately one out of two adults needs corrective lenses for distant vision. With Hess' apparatus this poses no difficulty in obtaining a good film record. It is nevertheless possible that some subjects cannot see the stimuli clearly and thus may have different responses than those with adequate vision. An investigator should include at least a simple visual acuity test in his procedure to screen out those with inadequate vision.

Constriction responses and the near vision reflex—I have found, as has Hess, some subjects whose pupils constrict, rather than dilate, when a test stimulus is presented. These constrictions were not the result of increased stimulus illuminance. Nor were the constrictions related to a feeling of dislike for the stimulus as Hess (1965) proposed. The effect appeared to be the result of near vision reflex.

When the eye, focused at a distant point, is refocused on a close point, a constriction occurs. The distance at which the near focusing must occur before the constriction effect begins to operate varies greatly in individual cases. In general, however, the older the person, the more pronounced the effect at a given distance. The effect is closely related to the condition called *presbyopia*, the decrement in range of focusing ability with age. Typically, most persons notice near vision difficulty by 45 years of age. For this reason subjects used in most optical experiments are under 40. However, even some young adults may show presbyoptic-like difficulty in near vision.

The extent of this problem was noted in the responses of a 50-year-old male subject to stimuli presented on the rear-projection pupillographic apparatus (see illustration in Hess, 1965, p. 48). The subject was shown several pairs of control-test pictures. His pupil response to the test stimuli early in the series was the typical dilation as he retained a focus on both control and test pictures. After several pairs he apparently focused only on the test pictures (each of which was different) and allowed his vision to blur on the repetitive controls (i.e., he focused behind the plane of projection). This shift in focus from near to a more distant plane resulted in clear-cut constriction responses of 10 to 30 per cent.

In the pupillograph built to Hess' specifications, many subjects did complain that repetitive control pictures were boring and difficult to focus on. The author himself tried to focus on the number 5 in the center of Hess' standard control picture and found great difficulty in keeping focused for more than five seconds at a time. Retaining a focus for an extended period is considerably easier if the projection screen is several meters from the eyes.

A simple solution, then, is to project all of the pictures on a more distant surface (e.g., three to four meters) than the rear of the pupillograph. This has the effect of putting the stimuli at a distance more like optical infinity for all subjects, and the probability of contamination of responses by distant-to-near focusing is lessened. This latter technique also has the advantage of eliminating the annoying hot spot on the rear-projection screen caused by the projector lamp. With forward projection no hot spot is seen, and the subject has one less potential distraction that may arouse his interest and dilate his pupils.

Fatigue effects—In a study mentioned earlier there was a general decrement in average pupil size after about 90 seconds of stimulus presentation, indicating that sympathetic arousal was declining. If arousal level drops too low, the pupil response becomes sluggish or is lost altogether. Thus, the subject must be kept alert and responsive to the stimuli throughout the experiment. A single trial should probably be no longer than 100 seconds. Frequent rest pauses help to reestablish an active level of pupil size.

Pupillary change attributable to differences in light flux—Careful control of the light reflexive effect is an obvious problem in studies using visual stimuli. Even slight increases in light energy striking the retina will result in pupillary constriction. In Hess' studies control of the light reflex was as follows: (*a*) the control and test stimulus pairs were matched for average overall brightness, (*b*) by a special photographic technique, the brightness contrasts in the test pictures were reduced to a minimal level without the loss of important details. In this way the constriction effect of looking from a dark to a relatively brighter area in a test picture was minimized, but, as Loewenfeld (1966) has suggested, the effect is still a significant influence. In preliminary testing with a set of picture stimuli that had been prepared in Hess' laboratory, an average constriction of 2 per cent resulted when a subject's gaze was shifted from a dark to a relatively brighter area of a test picture. The potential influence of the light reflex is sizable considering that pupillary changes to emotion-arousing stimuli generally average less than 5 per cent of pupil diameter (e.g., Hess and Polt, 1960; Hess, 1965; Hess, Seltzer and Shlien, 1965).

The problem is alleviated if it can be assumed that (a) individual differences in the extent of the light reflex (which are great) are randomly distributed in test groups, and (b) a subject's light sensory experience is not systematically related to his psychological reaction to the stimuli. In the latter case, for example, a subject might constrict to a test picture he did not like simply because he consistently looked at an area of the picture that was brighter than the control stimulus.

An obvious solution is not to use visual stimuli, but, if necessary, a short visual effects test is suggested. This test is described in Study A which follows.

STUDY A: THE PUPIL AS A MEASURE OF ATTITUDE TOWARD NEGROES[1]

The purpose of this study was to evaluate the pupil response as a measure of racial attitude. The strategy was to find two groups of subjects whose attitude toward Negroes was widely divergent and have them view racially toned pictures while their pupillary reactions were recorded.

Method

Subjects—The subjects were 22 Caucasian

female undergraduates at the University of Colorado. Eleven subjects had, in previous testing, expressed strong anti-Negro sentiment on the Multifactor Racial Attitude Inventory (MRAI) developed by Woodmansee and Cook (1967). The scores for these anti-Negro subjects fell in the most prejudiced quartile among students at that school. The other 11 subjects were persons who had been identified with equalitarian activities (e.g., membership in CORE, participation in civil rights protests, volunteer work in biracial projects, or marriage to a Negro). None of the subjects reported being overly tired or currently taking any medication. The order of testing subjects in the two groups was random.

Apparatus[2]—The basic recording device was a photo-pupillograph much like that used by Hess (1965, p. 48). The instrument was a light-tight box 55 cm. high, 45 cm. wide, and 80 cm. long. A subject faced into a rubber-lined opening on one end and peered through a 40 × 40 cm. opening at the opposite end toward a screen 3.6 meters from the eyes. A front surface mirror was mounted directly forward of and 12 degrees below the subject's left eye. It reflected the image of the eye to a 16 mm. Bolex reflex motion picture camera which was mounted on the outside of the box at a 90 degree angle to the subject's line of sight. The eye-to-film distance was 45 cm. The camera recorded two frames per second at an exposure speed of 0.18 seconds. The lens was a 100 mm. Macro-Yvar set at f/8. The source of illumination was a 25 watt red light bulb (G.E. 25 A/R) in a reflector positioned 20 cm. in front of and below the eye. By using this low level of illumination and high speed infrared film (Kodak HIR 430), very clear, full-frame pictures of the eye were possible with only mini-

---

[1] A more detailed account of this study and several exploratory studies which preceded it may be found in Woodmansee (1965).

[2] This pupillograph was quite simple and inexpensive but had the disadvantage of requiring tedious hand-scoring of the pupil images from a film record. More sophisticated equipment is available from commercial sources: Smith, Kline and French (see Lowenstein and Loewenfeld, 1958), Bausch and Lomb, and the Itek Corporation. See also reports by Hakerem (1962) and Green and Maaseidvaag (1967) for computerized devices.

mal constriction of the pupil by the light reflex.

A 35 mm. Bell and Howell 935 slide projector was positioned on the top and to the rear of the pupillograph. It projected in the direction of the subject's line of sight to a white mat screen. The projector was modified by placing an opaque plastic washer with a 13 mm. hole in front of the magnifying lens. This modification considerably reduced the overall intensity of the projected image. Projected in a dark room, the illuminance of a blank slide (maximum light) was 22 lumens/meter^2.

The experiment was run in a soundproof room. A small floodlamp provided a low level of diffuse background illumination on the screen (17 lumens/meter^2).

As suggested earlier an adequate research design requires some modifications in Hess' apparatus. One change made was the projection of the pictorial stimuli on a screen set at several times the distance that Hess used. This was done to reduce the effect of the near vision reflex.

A second modification in Hess' apparatus design involved repositioning the small mirror in the camera-to-eye optical system. In the pupillograph which Hess was using at the time of his 1965 article, the mirror was placed at an angle of about 15 degrees to the left and below the subject's line of sight when gazing straight ahead (left eye). With this arrangement, unless the subject looked directly into the mirror, the pupil image on film was distorted elliptically in both lateral and vertical planes. The amount of distortion varied depending on where the subject was looking in the stimulus field. In pilot testing it was found that the pupillary diameter, as measured, decreased about 5 per cent when a subject shifted his gaze from the left to the right of the blank screen (an arc of 30 degrees). Positioning the mirror so that it was still below, but directly in front of the subject's left eye, reduced the error from side-to-side eye movement. There was still the vertical distortion problem, but it was attenuated by having the scorer measure laterally across the filmed pupil image, rather than vertically

wherein the image was still subject to maximal elongation. The problem was further minimized by projecting the pictorial stimuli so that they subtended no more than ten degrees of the subject's visual field (laterally or vertically).

Materials—The test stimuli were five black and white pictures presented from 35 mm. slides. Four pictures portrayed Negroes in various situations. One showed Nat "King" Cole and a biracial group of other well-known entertainers rehearsing for a show. Cole is standing at center stage with the others seated behind him. All are laughing. Another picture showed a Negro man seated in a train with a white woman standing behind him. She has her arms around him as they look at some papers. The third picture was of two grade school boys tussling with each other across their desks at school. Both are laughing; one is a Negro. The fourth picture was of a young Negro man standing and smoking a cigarette. He is slovenly in his dress and his face bears a rather dull expression. These particular scenes were selected for two reasons. First, they were pictures which, in pretesting, were liked more by equalitarian judges than by anti-Negro judges. Second, when considered individually, the pictures differed among themselves as to their affective quality. Regardless of the rater's attitude, the scenes of the intimate couple and the slovenly man were liked less than the scenes of the boys playing and the entertainer. If Hess (1965) was correct in his assumption that states of positive and negative affect are associated with pupillary dilation and constriction, respectively, then there should be less dilation (or perhaps even constriction) to all of these pictures by the anti-Negro subjects than by the equalitarian subjects. In addition, we should find that the more unpleasant a particular scene is, the less will be the dilation (or more the constriction) response.

The fifth test stimulus was a picture of a filthy toilet and surroundings. In pretesting, this scene was strongly disliked by the raters regardless of their attitude toward Negroes. It was included not to differentiate the attitude groups, but to test Hess' notion that the pupil constricts with unpleasant stimuli. It was predicted that all the subjects, regardless of attitude, would constrict when exposed to this scene.

In addition to the life-content test pictures there were five neutral-content control pictures like those used by Hess (1965, p. 50). The control pictures had the numbers "1" through "4" in the corners and "5" in the center of a plain gray-white background. By preceding each of the test stimuli with one of these emotionally neutral pictures, a basal level of pupil size was established to which test stimuli reactions could be compared.

The stimuli were made with special care to insure that pupillary changes reflected the emotional reactions of the subject rather than differences in brightness between control and test slides, or differences due to the subject's looking from a dark to a lighter area (or vice versa) of a given picture. Hess' technique and tolerances were followed. The control and test pictures were first made nearly equal in overall brightness. Then each slide was projected on the screen exactly as the subject would see it. Using a Honeywell Pentax 3 degree spot photometer positioned in the apparatus where the subject's left eye would be, darkest-to-lightest light contrast measurements were taken on the picture. Acceptable test pictures yielded illuminance readings within a range of 18 to 24 lumens/meter^2. The white background of the control pictures measured 22 lumens/meter^2. Under these conditions the test pictures were low in brightness contrast but clear enough for the subject to see all details.

As discussed earlier, this careful preparation of the stimuli will not in itself sufficiently control for light reflexive changes in pupil size. Substantial pupillary changes which are attributable to the light reflex still occur when the gaze is shifted from a dark to a brighter area of a picture. Furthermore, individual differences in light reflexive reactions may be sizable and difficult to control. If, in this study, the anti-Negro subjects looked more often at brighter areas of the test stimuli than did the equalitarian subjects, the relatively

smaller pupils of the anti-Negro group would appear to confirm Hess' hypothesis. To evaluate this factor a special optical effects test was devised using a checkerboard-like stimulus picture. Each of the gray and white squares of this picture was about as large in area as the size of the largest dark and bright areas in any of the test pictures. In addition, the squares were as dark or bright as the darkest (18 lumens/meter^2) and brightest (24 lumens/meter^2) areas, respectively, of the test pictures.

The subjects made judgments of their liking for and interest value of the various stimuli on two rating scales. The range of the affect scale was from 0 (strong dislike, disgusting, repulsive) to 140 (like very much, makes me very happy to see this). The midpoint was 70 (neither like nor dislike). The range of the interest scale was from 0 (completely boring) to 136 (so interesting that it would never lose its attention-getting power). The midpoint on the interest scale was 68 (holds attention for quite awhile, then boring). Preliminary testing with these scales showed that their test-retest reliability (1–3 days) was: affect scale, 0.89; interest scale, 0.81.

Procedure—The subject was positioned comfortably in the apparatus. During the several minutes required for camera settings and instructions, the projection screen was illuminated and the red light in the pupillograph was on to allow for visual adaptation.

The subject was briefed on what would be happening and why. The following ideas were presented:

You are a subject because of what I know about your position on the matter of Negro-white relations. You will see four pictures with Negroes in them, and one without a Negro in it. There will also be some control pictures (showing the neutral control slide on the screen). These are used to set a light reflexive level of pupil size for comparison to the pupillary reaction during the presentation of the life content pictures. One of these control pictures will precede each of the test pictures. When a control slide is shown, you should look in each corner of the picture for the numbers "1" through "4" . . . then look at the "5" in the middle until the picture changes. There will be ten groups of pictures with a different order in each group. Not all the pictures will be seen in each group. You will be allowed to rest between groups. Do not talk or move while the pictures are being shown.

Before beginning the experimental portion of the procedure two special tests were performed.

A brief acuity test was performed to evaluate the subject's ability to see the stimuli. A modified Snellen test showed that all subjects had adequate distant vision to see the stimuli clearly. Those who required corrective lenses wore them during the experiment.

Each subject was then shown the gray and white checkerboard-like picture for eight 5-second trials, while her pupil reaction was photographed. At the beginning of each trial the subject was given an oral instruction to look at a specific "black" or "white" square in the picture. The order of areas viewed was counterbalanced. Pupil size was averaged separately across the four trials when the subject looked at a white square and across the four trials when she looked at a gray square. For all 22 subjects the average constriction to looking from gray squares to white squares was 2.10 per cent of pupil diameter. There was no difference between attitude group means on this test ($p > .05$).

Following these tests the subject was shown each of the control and test pictures for ten seconds each. The five control-test pairs were arranged in ten sets ordered at random and of varying length (two, three, or five pairs per set). The order in which the ten sets were presented was also random across subjects, but for each subject in the anti-Negro group who saw the ten sets in a particular order, there was an equalitarian subject who was shown the sets in the same order.

In the ten sets of pictures each of the five control-test pairs appeared a total of eight times. In the subsequent discussion the term presentations has been used to refer to these eight exposures of the stimuli. Upon completion of each continuous set of pictures the

subject was asked to remove her head from the apparatus and rest for at least one minute. This step was taken to reduce fatigue and to help the subject stay alert.

At the beginning of each of the ten stimulus sets a dummy control slide was presented for 30 seconds to readapt the subject's eyes to the level of light stimulation. After 30 seconds the next stimulus set was begun with the presentation of the first control-test pair. The camera and slide timer were turned on at this point. At the end of each set the red light trained on the subject's eyes went off momentarily, while the camera ran for a few seconds longer before being stopped. This procedure marked the beginning and end of each set by providing several blank frames on the film record.

After all five of the life-content pictures had been seen at least once (i.e., between the first and second presentations), the subject made liking and interest ratings on each picture including the control scene. In preparation for this task the investigator discussed a sample picture from a magazine in order to clarify what was required in the ratings.

When the ratings were completed the subject returned to the pupillograph for the remaining presentations. Upon completion, the stimuli were rated a second time for affect and interest value. The first and second set of ratings were combined for subsequent analyses.

To check on the possibility that the subjects in either group had, on the average, larger or smaller pupils simply because they looked at dark or bright areas in the test pictures, they were asked to identify what they looked at during the course of the experiment. Later, with the pictures projected as the subjects had viewed them, spot photometer illuminance readings were taken from the areas mentioned. The test groups were then compared on these data to determine whether they differed in their average light sensory experience throughout the experiment. It was found that the attitude groups did not differ on this test ($p > .05$).

Scoring the pupillographic record—A roll of developed film was scored in a special apparatus designed to magnify and project the pupil image about 25 times its life size. A high intensity movie projector presented the pupil image on the underside of a translucent screen mounted in a table top. The scorer gauged the pupil diameter laterally, measuring each frame of film with a millimeter ruler. The scorer was a nonstudent employee who was naive as to the purpose and procedure of the study. Any frame showing a blink and the succeeding frame were scored as missing data. This was done to eliminate the non-random effect of the lid closure reflex. For some persons the lid-closure reflex (Lowenstein and Loewenfeld, 1962) results in a slight constriction following a blink. This response appears on the film record frame immediately following the frame or frames of blink response. The effect generally lasts no more than one-half second.

Analysis of the data—As in Hess' studies the basic unit of analysis was the pupil response (PR) representing the change in pupillary diameter from the presentation of the control picture to the presentation of the following life-content picture, which is expressed as a percentage of pupil diameter during the control period. The first two and last two of the 20 frames of film for each ten second stimulus period were disregarded, leaving 16 frames for computation of the stimulus period mean pupil size. Hess (1965) also followed this procedure.

The PR scores for the attitude groups were compared by each stimulus and by various combinations of the Negro-content stimuli, depending on the results of the affect ratings by the two groups. It was predicted that the group having the greater liking for a given stimulus would have the more positive PR to it (positive meaning in the direction of greater dilation or less constriction). By combining the PR scores on those stimuli for which the two attitude groups differed in affect ratings, an average PR score for affect-differentiated stimuli was derived, providing another way of comparing the groups. This latter approach is Hess' technique for analyzing the data in his studies.

Results

Ratings of the stimuli—As expected, the attitude groups differed in their rated liking of the racial stimuli. The groups differed most on the intimate couple scene followed in order by the slovenly man and boys playing ($p < .05$). They did not differ significantly on the entertainers scene, however.

The groups had strong, and equal dislike for the dirty bathroom scene. The control picture was rated at about the midpoint of the liking-disliking scale by both groups.

The interest value ratings showed that the two groups saw all the test stimuli as approximately equal in their attention-getting quality. The control stimulus was considered equally boring by both groups.

Pupillary reactions—The pupillary responses to the racial stimuli are plotted in Figure 1. On presentations 1 and 2 the equalitarian subjects had more positive responses than the anti-Negro subjects. By presentation 3, and thereafter, the group differences were smaller and mixed in terms of which group had the more positive responses.

Using students' t to test the differences between attitude group means on each presentation, it was found that only on presentation 1 was there a significant effect beyond the

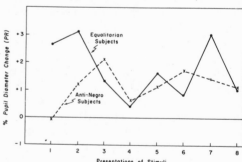

Figure 1. Per cent of pupil diameter change for equalitarian and anti-Negro subjects on each of eight presentations of four racial content stimuli.

.05 level of confidence. For presentation 1 the average PR to the four racial pictures was —0.10 per cent (s.d. = 2.14) for the anti-

Negro subjects and +2.65 per cent (s.d. = 2.06) for the equalitarian group ($p < .01$). If the entertainers scene data are not used in computing the stimulus combination averages, the group means differ even more: 3.37 per cent (s.d. = 2.37) for the equalitarian subjects, 0.37 per cent (s.d. = 1.57) for the anti-Negro subjects ($p < .01$).

In terms of individual stimuli on presentation 1, the intimate couple scene showed the greatest discrimination between group PRs ($p < .05$), followed by the slovenly man ($p < .05$), boys playing ($p < .10$), and the entertainers ($p < .10$). Note that this order is identical to the ranking of attitude group differences on the liking ratings.

The groups did not differ in their PR to the scene of the filthy bathroom on any of the eight presentations. Averaging across all 22 subjects the presentation-by-presentation PRs were all dilations to this scene: percentages were 1.84, 0.01, 0.88, 1.59, 0.14, 1.71, 0.89, and 1.77 on presentations 1 through 8, respectively.

Discussion

The results were puzzling in terms of the predictions made from Hess' findings. It was predicted that both attitude groups would have similar positive (dilation) reactions to the first few presentations of stimuli, then the anti-Negro subjects would dilate less than the equalitarian group and eventually would show constriction responses to the disliked racial pictures. Instead, the groups differed on only the first exposure of stimuli and not on subsequent presentations. Furthermore, the PRs for both groups were either positive or essentially zero on all eight presentations. There was no evidence of constriction to either the racial pictures or to the unpleasant bathroom scene.

The difference in attitude group reactions on presentation 1 deserves some attention. This finding was unexpected and had to be accepted cautiously since the probability of one such difference in eight comparisons occurring by chance was fairly substantial.

However, an analysis of the presentation 1 data suggested that this result might be reliable. When reactions to individual racial stimuli were analyzed, PR differences between attitude groups ranked identically with differences found in the subjects' verbal ratings. Perhaps an attitude-related PR did occur early in the series of repeated measures and then diminished. This possibility was supported by the results obtained when the subjects' PRs to each picture were correlated, trial-by-trial, with their ratings of liking for the pictures. Significant correlations ($p < .05$) were obtained on presentations 1 (+0.43), 2 (+0.28), and 8 (+0.20).

In Figure 2, actual pupillary diameters

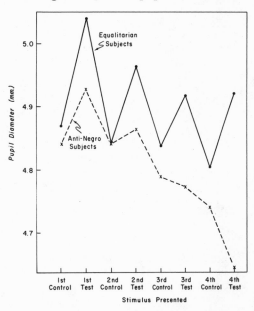

Figure 2. Actual pupil size during the sequence of control and racial test stimuli for presentation 1 only.

were plotted for each group's reactions to the individual control and test stimuli viewed in presentation 1. Note the reflex dilations to the test stimuli, and the fairly regular trend of reactions to the identical control pictures.

Since the control stimuli are essentially neutral in their arousal value, the pupil size during these periods can be considered an index of ambient or general arousal level. During control periods the equalitarian subjects' pupils were generally larger and dedilated more slowly as the sequence of pictures was shown than did the pupils of the anti-Negro subjects. It appears that the equalitarian subjects were more aroused by the stimuli than were the anti-Negro subjects.

If the difference found on presentation 1 is an arousal effect, why did it not persist? An explanation is suggested by examining the changes in actual pupil size during just the control periods for all eight presentations. Figure 3 shows that the pattern of general

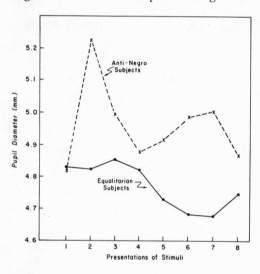

Figure 3. Actual pupil size during the course of the experiment as calculated on the basis of control period data only.

arousal changed radically by presentation 2. Whereas the equalitarian subjects' arousal level was fairly constant during the early presentations and declined slowly thereafter, the anti-Negro subjects became more strongly aroused by the second presentation and maintained a higher arousal level than the equalitarian group for the remaining presentations.

It will be recalled that the subjects made written evaluations of the stimuli between presentations 1 and 2. This step may have clarified and emphasized the fact that the experiment focused on one's feelings about Negroes. In this era of racial awareness with an increased emphasis on self-appraisal of attitudes, it could be reasoned that the subjects felt varying degrees of apprehension or uneasiness about the imminent disclosure of their true attitudes. If so, the anti-Negro group should have had the stronger emotional reactions because their declared dislike of Negroes puts them in a less socially sanctioned position than does the more socially acceptable evaluations of the equalitarian subjects. The increased emotionality of the anti-Negro subjects would result in stronger dilations to test pictures, thus bringing their PRs into line with those of the equalitarian group.

One last point needs discussion. As Figure 2 shows there was a gradual decrease in pupil size as the sequence of stimuli was presented. It should be noted that the calculation of the PR does not account for this dedilation effect. Consequently, the resulting PRs are underestimates of the dilations which occurred to the test stimuli. A more realistic method of computing the PR value is to average the control periods both before *and after* a given test stimulus period to establish a basal pupil size. When this was done on the presentation 1 data, for example, the resulting PR values were more positive than those shown in Figure 1. The means increased to $+0.36$ per cent for the anti-Negro subjects and $+2.79$ per cent for the equalitarian subjects. These are minor changes, to be sure, and the alternate method of computing the PR probably would not change the outcome of most experiments. However, as discussed elsewhere (Woodmansee, 1966) this methodological error may help explain why Hess (1965) finds pupillary constriction in his studies. Note that the pupils of my anti-Negro group also constricted -0.10 per cent or, alternately, dilated $+0.36$ per cent on presentation 1 depending on how the PR was computed.

STUDY B: AN EXTENSION OF STUDY A

Considering the results of Study A, the pupillary reaction seemed of questionable value in attitude measurement. The findings raised several questions, however. First, how reliable is the attitude-related difference in PR found on the initial presentation of stimuli in Study A? If found to be reliable, would the difference persist beyond the first presentation providing that the stimuli were not rated until the end of the study? A third question concerns the number of presentations of stimuli. Hess (1965) reported that constrictions may be expected in three to five exposures, regardless of the interval between exposures. Although eight presentations were given in Study A, perhaps more are needed to elicit the attitude-related PR. To answer these questions, Study A was repeated, with some modifications, by one of my students, Jeanne Blanchard.

Method

Subjects—The subjects were ten male and ten female Wake Forest University undergraduates. Five of the males and five of the females were selected from the upper quintile of the local distribution of Wake Forest students on the Multifactor Racial Attitude Inventory; they were clearly anti-Negro.

Stimuli—Pictures similar to those in Study A were used. There were four attitude-related pictures. One was an intimate scene of an interracial couple: a Negro man and a white woman, cheek-to-cheek and smiling. A second picture was of two disheveled Negroes: one man and one woman, both apparently drunk. A third was of a young Negro boy and a young white boy lying peacefully together on the floor. The fourth picture was of a well-dressed Negro man sitting quietly at a table on which there was a bottle of liquor.

Two other pictures were included to provide a contrast with the Negro-content pictures. These pictures were selected to be pleasant, but relatively unexciting. One was of a seascape with gulls flying over the seashore. Another pictured a cat and a dog sitting together. The numbered control picture described in Study A was also included and was paired with each test picture. The pictures were made according to brightness and contrast standards described in Study A.

Apparatus and procedure—The apparatus and procedure were the same as that used in Study A except for the following details.

The four racial pictures and the two nonracial pictures with their matched controls were arranged in 20 separate sets for viewing by the subjects. Each set also included one additional control picture placed after the last control-test stimulus pair. This additional control period was needed for the computation of the basal pupil size as explained in the next section. The 20 sets varied in number, serial position and composition of stimuli so that each test stimulus was presented a total of only 15 times. The pupil was recorded only during presentations 1, 2, 5, 10, 14 and 15. The sounds of the camera being operated were masked out by a white noise source.

After the 15 presentations were concluded, the subjects rated all pictures for the amount of affect they had experienced when shown the picture. Compared to the equalitarian group the anti-Negro subjects clearly gave stronger ratings of dislike to three of the Negro-content pictures. On the fourth racial picture (the two slovenly Negroes) and the two nonracial pictures (seascape and animals) the group ratings of liking did not differ at the .05 level of confidence.

Results

Computation of the PR to each test stimulus was done two ways: (1) as in the previous study basing the PR on pupil size during the test period as contrasted with the reaction to the preceding control period, and (2) using an average of *both* preceding and succeeding control periods as a basal level of pupil size. These computational alternatives were found to yield only minor differences, but there was a tendency for the latter method to result in more positive (as if dilating) results than the former.

Data were analyzed separately for each of the six presentations which were photographed. PRs for the four racial pictures were first combined for analysis. Both attitude groups showed only dilation responses to the racial pictures. The order of magnitude was 6 per cent to 7 per cent on the average for the early presentations and 3 to 6 per cent for the later presentations. Dilation responses were still occurring for both anti-Negro and equalitarian subjects on the fourteenth and fifteenth presentations. No difference between groups was found on any presentation. Nor were there any observable trends in this direction.

When the racial pictures were considered individually, the results were similar to those obtained when the stimuli were combined. In contrast to Study A there were no differences in PRs to the various racial stimuli on the first presentation or any subsequent one.

Reactions to the two nonracial pictures (seascape, animals) were also analyzed. The results were similar to those above. The only difference in reactions to the nonracial pictures was that the degree of dilation seemed somewhat, although not markedly, less.

Implications from Studies A and B

Judging from the results of Studies A and B the pupil response appears to hold no promise as an index of attitude toward Negroes. The difference in attitude group responses on presentation 1 in Study A was not found in Study B. In addition, the two major changes in procedure (increasing stimulus presentations from 8 to 15, and eliminating the rating task between stimulus presentations 1 and 2) appeared not to have had any effect on attitude group responses. The subjects, regardless of attitude, dilated regularly to both Negro content and nonracial pictures.

In neither Study A nor B was there the constriction-with-aversion effect which Hess (1965) obtained when he used pictorial stimuli. Since our studies used stimuli to which the subjects reacted with varying degrees of unpleasantness, we too should have found constrictions. What would account for this discrepancy in our findings? Considering the multitude of methodological problems found in this type of research, it is possible that

Hess' results are artifacts of his experimental design. As outlined earlier in this paper and elsewhere (Woodmansee, 1966), there are several special sources of error which can confound pupillographic studies. Hence, a major part of this paper has been devoted to describing these methodological problems because it is felt that careful experimental control is an absolute prerequisite if we are to understand the pupil reaction.

Reviewing briefly, there are three major effects which could account for Hess' constriction finding with unpleasant pictures. First, there is the light reflexive effect of viewing contrastingly dark and bright areas within photographs. It has been found that the light reflex is operative even with low contrast stimuli, and it must be shown that subjects who constrict were not simply looking at bright areas of a test picture relative to where they looked during a basal period.

Hess (1965) did claim, on the basis of a special experiment, that the role of the light reflex must be minimal compared to the psychological effects of exposure to the stimuli. In his demonstration a basal level was set by having the subject look at a blank screen with the slide projector turned off. Then a picture was presented on the screen with the projector; thus the stimulus was at all points brighter than the control level of the blank screen. On the basis of the light reflex alone, the pupil size change should be a constriction. However, some subjects constricted while others dilated. Hess claimed that those who constricted found the stimulus distasteful. Unfortunately, this is a circular argument and does not show that a constriction response could not have resulted from an increase of light flux.

The near vision reflex is a second source of constriction in cases in which a subject fails to maintain a constant focus on both control and test pictures. In one of Hess' studies (Hess and Polt, 1964) an accommodation effects test was described which appears to be a check on the near vision reflex problem in that particular experiment. It is not known whether the near vision reflex was evaluated in subsequent studies. As mentioned earlier it has been shown that subjects have difficulty retaining their focus on uninteresting pictures (e.g., the numbered control slide) in the Hess pupillograph. Possibly his subjects who constricted to an unpleasant picture were doing so because they focused sharply on the picture after merely staring "through" the previous control picture. This certainly is no less critical a problem in pupillographic research than is the light reflex.

The third major source of constriction is what I term the arousal decrement effect. Pupil size decreases when sympathetic arousal falls off with loss of interest, deepening fatigue, or simply adaptation to a new stimulus situation. Basing the PR on change in pupil size from one period to the next yields PRs with a built-in constriction bias because pupil size typically decreases during the course of an experiment. Again, Hess (1965) did not discuss this problem nor did he provide data which could be checked for the extent of this effect.

Besides these major problems, other difficulties (e.g., the distortion in filmed pupil images because of the way the eye-to-camera optical system is arranged, high pupillary variability, order and anticipation effects) could also result in misleading evidence.

STUDY C: AN ATTEMPT TO ELICIT CONSTRICTION WITH NEGATIVE AFFECT

Turning away from methodological considerations alone, there is the possibility that Hess' stimuli aroused a different kind or different intensity of negative affect than stimuli used in Studies A and B. Hess used quite repugnant photographs (e.g., the bodies of concentration camp victims) to arouse affect. Even the filthy bathroom scene in Study A was probably not nearly as aversive as many of Hess' pictures.

As it turns out, it is difficult to find a laboratory-contrived visual stimulus which can be guaranteed to arouse strong negative affect. The average college sophomore is re-

markably flexible and adaptive in the grimmest of experimental situations. For example, I once used a gruesome photograph of the amputated remains of a leg and foot. A panel of judges voiced universal disgust when shown this picture, but also thought that it was a fascinating scene which would hold a subject's interest for a long time! This interest in the stimulus certainly was not negative affect, but positive affect instead. To be useful a picture should arouse a genuine repulsion reaction without much else.

At the University of Colorado in the summer of 1966 a coed was brutally murdered in a music practice room of one of the much-used buildings. A newspaper photograph taken shortly after the incident showed the murder scene with blood on the floor and the outline of the girl's body where it lay. Since the local newspapers had carried full details of the affair for a considerable period of time there was every reason to think that the picture could reinstate, particularly in female subjects, a genuinely uncomfortable affect. Some preliminary exploration substantiated the fact that the picture served to bring back the strong negative feelings which had occurred at the time of the murder. It was felt that this stimulus had the affect-arousing qualities needed to give Hess' constriction-aversion hypothesis a fair test.

Method and Results

Within two weeks of this frightening crime, and with the murderer still at large, I tested 14 coeds who were thoroughly familiar with all the public details of the crime.

The murder scene picture was shown in three blocks of three 10-second exposures each. To obtain a basal level of pupil size another photo of a similar room, furnished in a commonplace and uninteresting manner, was used preceding and following each test slide. The test and control slides were low in brightness contrast and carefully matched to reduce light reflexive effects as in the previous studies. In the two test intervals between the three blocks of trials the subject was allowed to examine freely the test and control pictures. She was left alone for two minutes in the research room during these periods. This procedure was intended to facilitate the transition described by Hess, from a state of arousal (producing dilation) to a state of aversion (producing constriction).

The subjects were assigned to two groups on the basis of their self-reported affective reactions to the testing situation. If, in the postexperimental interview, a subject *clearly* felt repelled, disgusted, or sickened she was included in the aversive reaction group ($N = 8$). Subjects with other reactions (neutral, or in the case of one subject, positive affect) were assumed to approximate a control group for purposes of comparison ($N = 6$). Figure 4 shows the results. These findings

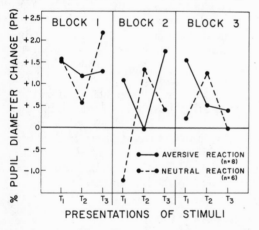

Figure 4.   Per cent of pupil diameter change to the murder scene stimulus for subjects who felt negative affect and those who did not.

were essentially reflex dilations. The one instance of apparent constriction—the initial trial of the non-affected subjects in Block 2 —was not different from zero at the .05 level. Furthermore, the two groups did not differ on any of the nine trials.

Discussion

The results do not support the hypothesis that unpleasant affect is accompanied by

pupillary constriction; in fact, the opposite seems true: affect, whether negative or positive, is accompanied by reflex dilation. Other studies testing Hess' hypothesis have found the same pattern. Nunnally, Knott, Duchnowski and Parker (1967) used a series of affectively neutral, positive and negative pictures in a pupil study. The negative stimuli were quite comparable to Hess' (e.g., a woman with a cancerous growth on her neck and upper chest), but there was no evidence of pupillary constriction to these pictures. Collins, Ellsworth and Helmreich (1967) used stimuli comparable to those of Studies A and B(e.g., soldiers drilling, a Negro man and white woman holding hands) and found a zero correlation between pupil change and the evaluative dimension of the semantic differential. In a study by Koff and Hawkes (1968) children were shown photographs of self-selected friends and nonfriends. Pupil changes were equal dilations to both kinds of stimuli. Although each of these three studies was designed to test the aversion-constriction hypothesis, none involved more than a single exposure of the stimuli. A fair test of Hess' finding must employ a repeated exposure design such as that used in Studies A, B, and C.

At this point it should be recalled that Hess (1965) reported his aversion-constriction effect only with visual materials. For this reason Studies A, B, and C used pictorial stimuli exclusively. It is possible, and indeed logical, to reason that any affective stimulus, regardless of which sense modality is involved, should evoke a characteristic pupil response.[3] There are several recent studies which tested Hess' hypothesis by using nonvisual stimuli. One group of studies used affectively-toned words or groups of words presented orally (Bergum and Lehr, 1966; Collins *et al.,* 1967; and Egan, 1968). Bergum and Lehr also presented their verbal materials visually in the form of pictures. This mode of presentation

---

[3] Of interest in this regard is the statement by Shakhnovich (1965) that, as part of orienting reflexive behavior, the pupil dilates, except in the case of orienting to visual material, where the pupil typically constricts.

was used in other studies (Paivio and Simpson, 1966; Nunnally, Knott and Duchnowski, 1967; and Peavler and McLaughlin, 1967). Of these several studies apparently only Egan's (1968) used a repeated exposure design: six repetitions of pleasant (e.g., moonlit beach), neutral (e.g., plastic cup), and negative (e.g., rotting corpse) phrases. The general finding in all these studies is that the pupil does not constrict, but conversely dilates, when unpleasant verbal material is heard or seen.

In a study of taste preference Hess and Polt (1966) reported that they were able to differentiate between dilations to various liquids. They noted, however, that their unpleasant drinks (quinine solution and concentrated lemon juice) also elicited dilations.

In one study reported by Pitts and Ernhart (1967) electrical shock was used to condition an aversive response to the number 3. On extinction trials the orally presented 3 elicited only dilation responses. In a second study using unpleasant (rotten garlic), pleasant (allspice), and neutral (water) odors, dilations again resulted.

In another odor study (Woodmansee, 1967) hydrogen sulfide gas was used as an aversive stimulus. Dilations were again the typical response throughout the 20 separate presentations of the odor stimulus. Although the magnitude of the dilations decreased with repeated odor presentations, there was no tendency for constrictions eventually to occur.

In contrast to all the studies with negative results, there is one study which appears to support Hess. Bernick and Oberlander (1968) instructed their subjects to think about various topics in an attempt to determine the effects of internal vs. external reference, verbalization vs. non-verbalization, degree of pleasantness on pupil size. They found that the subject's pupils were smaller during periods of concentration on personal problems than during more pleasant moments.

Taken as a group, the studies done outside of Hess' laboratory do not encourage the notion that the pupil is a bidirectional index of affect. The studies which provided for repeated exposure to the unpleasant stimulus had essentially the same findings as those studies which used a single exposure design. With one exception the results in these studies were consistent in showing that the pupil dilates when something serves to arouse the subject. Pleasant and unpleasant words, pictures, odors, and tastes all elicited dilations.

SUMMARY AND CONCLUSIONS

The purpose of this paper has been to judge the potential of the pupil reaction as a measure of social attitudes. In this effort the work of Eckhard Hess and his colleagues served as a point of departure, since it was Hess who encouraged the use of the pupil in attitude measurement. Three studies were described in which the aim was to test directly the validity of Hess' proposal.

In Study A subjects who were known to differ greatly in their attitude toward Negroes were shown a group of pictorial stimuli while pupillary changes were recorded. The stimuli were known to arouse differing feelings among the subjects, and those affective reactions were predictable from the subjects' racial attitude. According to Hess, both groups should have reacted similarly to the first few presentations, but after viewing the pictures several times the anti-Negro subjects should have had less positive (i.e., constriction or less dilation) pupil reactions to the racial stimuli than would the equalitarian subjects. The predicted attitude group difference occurred, but only on the first of eight exposures of the pictures rather than the later exposures. Study B showed that the unexpected findings of Study A were not reliable. What Studies A and B did find was that subjects may be expected to dilate consistently on viewing racially-toned pictures, regardless of their own attitude toward Negroes.

In describing Studies A and B much attention was given to the wide variety of methodological problems which could confound the interpretation of pupillographic studies. Our inability to confirm Hess' notion that the pupil reaction is a bidirectional index of affect or attitudes was discussed in the context of methodological errors which may serve to explain his results.

Study C was done on the hunch that in Studies A and B we had not really produced in our subjects the same kind or intensity of affect that Hess had when he found that certain pictures were accompanied by pupillary constriction. Again, there were no findings which could encourage the use of the pupil as a bidirectional index of pleasant and unpleasant emotional states. As in the first two studies the subjects dilated whether they felt neutral or uncomfortable about the stimulus.

Taken as a whole, Studies A, B and C and all other studies which are relevant to the issue suggest that the pupil does not measure attitude or qualitatively different affective states. There is ample evidence, however, that the pupil, in its reflex dilation reaction, may be used to indicate arousal, attentiveness, interest, and perceptual orienting.

REFERENCES

Bergum, B., and D. Lehr.
1966   Prediction of Stimulus Approach: Core Measures Experiment 11. Rochester, New York: Xerox Corp. (Research Report R66–36).

Bernick, N., and M. Oberlander.
1968   "Effect of verbalization and two different modes of experiencing on pupil size." Perception and Psychophysics 3: 327–330.

Collins, B. E., Phoebe C. Ellsworth, and R. L. Helmreich.
1967   "Correlations between pupil size and the semantic differential: an experimental paradigm and pilot study." Psychonomic Science 9:627–628.

Cook, S. W., and Claire Selltiz.
1964   "A multiple indicator approach to attitude measurement." Psychological Bulletin 62:36–55.

Egan, T.
1968   "Pupillary response to verbal phrases differing in affect." Unpublished manuscript, Attitude Research Laboratory, Institute of Behavioral Science, University of Colorado.

Green, D. G., and F. Maaseidvaag.
1967   "Closed-circuit television pupillometer." Journal of the Optical Society of America 57:830–833.

Hakerem, G.
1962   "Instrumentation for research in pupillography." Psychopharmacology Service Center Bulletin 2:11–14.

Hess, E. H.
1965   "Attitude and pupil size." Scientific American 212:46–54.
1968   "Pupillometric assessment." Pp. 573–583 in J. M. Shlien (ed.), Research in Psychotherapy. Washington, D.C.: American Psychological Association.

Hess, E. H., and J. M. Polt.
1960   "Pupil size as related to interest value of visual stimuli." Science 132:349–350.
1964   "Pupil size in relation to mental activity during simple problem-solving." Science 143:1190–1192.
1966   "Changes in pupil size as a measure of taste difference." Perceptual and Motor Skills 23:451–455.

Hess, E. H., A. L. Seltzer, and J. M. Shlien.
1965   "Pupil response of hetero- and homosexual males to pictures of men and women: a pilot study." Journal of Abnormal Psychology 70:165–168.

Hilgard, E. R., C. E. Dutton, and J. S. Helmick.
1949   "Attempted pupillary conditioning at four stimulus intervals." Journal of Experimental Psychology 39:683–689.

Koff, R. H., and T. H. Hawkes.
1968   "Sociometric choice: a study in pupillary response." Paper presented at American Educational Research Association. Chicago: (February).

Loewenfeld, Irene E.
1958   "Mechanisms of reflex dilation of the pupil. Historical review and experimental analysis." Documents Ophthalmologica 12:185–448.
1966   "Pupil size." Survey of Ophthalmology 11:291–294.

Lowenstein, O.
1920   "Experimentelle Beiträge zur lehre von den katatonischen pupillenveränderungen. Monatschrift fur Psychiatrie und Neurologie 47:194–215.

Lowenstein, O., and Irene E. Loewenfeld.
1952 "Disintegration of central autonomic regulation during fatigue and its reintegration by psychosensory controlling mechanisms." Journal of Nervous and Mental Diseases 115:1–21 and 121–145.
1958 "Electronic pupillograph." AMA Archives of Ophthalmology 59:352–363.
1962 "The pupil." Pp. 231–267 in H. Davson (ed.), The Eye. Volume 3, New York: Academic Press.
1964 "The sleep-waking cycle and pupillary activity." Annals of the New York Academy of Sciences 117:142–156.

Nunnally, J. C., P. D. Knott, and A. J. Duchnowski.
1967 "Association of neutral objects with rewards; Effects of different numbers of conditioning trials and of anticipated reward versus actual reward." Journal of Experimental Child Psychology 5:249–262.

Nunnally, J. C., P. D. Knott, A. Duchnowski, and R. Parker.
1967 "Pupillary response as a general measure of activation." Perception and Psychophysics 2:149–155.

Paivio, A., and H. M. Simpson.
1966 "The effect of word abstractness and pleasantness on pupil size during an imagery task." Psychonomic Science 5:55–56.

Peavler, W. S., and J. P. McLaughlin.
1967 "The question of stimulus content and pupil size." Psychonomic Science 8: 505–506.

Pitts, C., and Claire B. Ernhart.
1967 "Pupillometrics." Unpublished manuscript, Central Midwestern Region Educational Laboratory. St. Ann, Missouri.

Rankin, R. E., and D. T. Campbell.
1955 "Galvanic skin response to Negro and white experimenters." Journal of Abnormal and Social Psychology 51:30–33.

Shakhnovich, A. R.
1965 "On the pupillary component of the orienting reflex during action of stimuli specific for vision and non-specific (extraneous) stimuli." Pp. 249–258 in L. G. Voronin, A. N. Leontiev, A. R.

Luria, E. N. Sokolov, and O. A. Vinogradova (eds.), Orienting Reflex and Exploratory Behavior. Volume 3 Washington, D.C.: American Institute of Biological Sciences.

Simpson, H. M., and A. Paivio.
1968 "Effects on pupil size of manual and verbal indicators of cognitive task fulfillment." Perception and Psychophysics 3:185–190.

Stark, L.
1959 "Stability, oscillations, and noise in the human pupil servomechanism." Proceedings of I(nstitute) of R(adio) E(ngineers) 47:1925–1939.

Westie, F. R., and M. L. DeFleur.
1959 "Autonomic responses and their relationship to race attitudes." Journal of Abnormal and Social Psychology 58: 340–347.

Woodmansee, J. J.
1965 "An evaluation of the pupil response as a measure of attitude toward Negroes." Unpublished doctoral dissertation, University of Colorado.
1966 "Methodological problems in pupillographic experiments." Proceedings of the 74th annual convention of the American Psychological Association. Washington, D.C.: APA 133–134.
1967 "The pupil reaction as an index of positive and negative affect." Paper presented at the meeting of the American Psychological Association. Washington, D.C.: (September).

Woodmansee, J. J., and S. W. Cook.
1967 "Dimensions of verbal racial attitudes: their identification and measurement." Journal of Personality and Social Psychology 7:240–250.

Young, F. A.
1954 "An attempt to obtain pupillary conditioning with infrared photography." Journal of Experimental Psychology 48:62–68.
1958 "Studies of pupillary conditioning." Journal of Experimental Psychology 55:97–110.
1965 "Classical conditioning of autonomic functions." Pp. 358–377 in W. F. Prokasy (ed.), Classical Conditioning. New York: Appleton-Century-Crofts.

CHAPTER 36 Physiological Techniques of Attitude Measurement

DANIEL J. MUELLER

In psychological measurement a distinction is commonly made between highly structured and straightforward techniques, and the less direct, unstructured, or even disguised measurement methods. The advantage of the latter is that they tend to be unobtrusive. If the subject does not know what is being measured, or even that he is being subjected to psychological testing, he will not be on guard; he will be less likely to bias his responses. The more disguised the measurement process, therefore, the more the subject is likely to respond as he truly feels or believes rather than as he thinks he should.

Such techniques are especially useful in the measurement of socially undesirable, "shameful," or otherwise disvalued beliefs, traits, feelings, emotions, and attitudes. Extending this idea, one could argue that if disguised behavioral and verbal measures produce no awareness of measurement by the subject, then physiological indices should be all the more effective. In addition to being easily disguised, they are much more difficult to regulate consciously than are verbal and behavioral responses.

This chapter was prepared especially for this volume. The author wishes to acknowledge the invaluable criticisms and editing of Dr. Gene F. Summers and Dr. Martin Fishbein in the preparation of this paper.

Physiological indices are the bodily processes that are regulated by the autonomic (as opposed to the somatic) nervous system. The functioning of all of the visceral organs as well as the heart and the glands is included in this category. Within these boundaries, the psychologist interested in relating psychological states to "extra-normal" bodily changes has a lot of room for measurement. The bodily processes falling under this heading include all circulatory, respiratory, and digestive functions as well as body chemistry, body temperature, water balance, skin electrical conductance, pupillary dilation, and others. In this chapter we are especially interested in the use and usability of changes in these physiological processes as a basis for the measurement of attitudes.

Before considering the physiological measures of attitudes, however, let us examine the literature dealing with the general relationships between physical and mental states. A majority of the research on these relationships has been done in conjunction with the study of emotion, which serves as the background for physiological attitude measurement. Since the research into the nature of emotion wrestled with a good many of the problems involved in physical-psychological relationships long before the concept of attitude arrived at its present state,[1] we need to examine briefly the emotion-physiological research in order to gain a fuller understanding of the relationship between attitudes and physiology.

EMOTION AND AUTONOMIC CHANGES

Some 75 years ago, working independently, two psychologists—William James and C. G. Lange—championed the theory that bodily changes are directly related to emotional states (Cannon, 1927). Since that time, literally hundreds of researchers (equipped with cardiotachometers, sphygmometers, gasometers, plethysmographs, ballistocardiographs, pneumographs, electromyographs, electroencephalographs, galvanometers, polygraphs, and a host of other ingenious and sometimes ominous measuring devices) have set out to determine the exact nature of the relationship postulated by James and Lange. The object of these studies has been to provide science with a detailed listing of the autonomic changes that accompany each emotion, by which the various emotional states could be empirically distinguished from one another. With few exceptions, these undertakings have been virtual failures.

This is not to say that various mental states do not effect physiological changes or vice versa. Bodily changes are commonly observed during emotional arousal, but, if there are physiological distinctions among the various emotional states, these "differences are at best rather subtle and the variety of emotional states are by no means matched by an equal variety of visceral patterns" (Schachter and Singer, 1962, p. 380).

There are a few exceptions. Mittlemann

and Wolff (1939, 1943) reported different emotional correlates for the rise than for the fall in finger temperature. A rise in temperature, which they claim is caused by vasodilation, seems to result from feelings of emotional security; a fall in temperature seems to occur during times of anxiety, anger, fear, guilt, embarrassment, and humiliation.

In two separate studies, researchers have reported finding different physiological conditions for fear and anger. Wolf and Wolff (1943) observed the lining of the stomach of a subject who had a gastric fistula. Whenever there was worry or fear, the mucosa became pale; both stomach motility and digestive secretion were inhibited. Hostility, resentment, or anxiety produced a red lining and an increase in stomach motility and acid secretion. Ax (1953) noted that anger-producing and fear-producing stimulus conditions "were accompanied by ... physiological reaction patterns which ... were clearly different for the two stimuli" (p. 441). He measured pulse, heartstroke volume, respiration, face and finger temperature, skin conductance, and muscle potential, as well as diastolic and systolic blood pressure.

In a 1945 review of the literature, Arnold concluded that there are "three different physiological states corresponding to three different emotions: fear, with predominantly sympathetic excitation; anger, with strong parasympathetic excitation; and excitement or elation, with moderate parasympathetic activity" (Arnold, 1945, p. 45).

Almost all the remaining research in this area can be summed up by saying that all emotions are accompanied by a widespread increase in the level of activation or of energy mobilization. In itself this is an important and useful finding—physiological measures can be employed to verify experimentally induced emotional arousal. But it is now quite clear that emotion differentiation through the measurement of changes in bodily functions is out of the question.

This turn of events has been a puzzle to a good many psychologists. However, Stanley Schachter (1962) developed a plausible and

---

[1] In contemporary social psychology, attitude is commonly defined as a set or a readiness to respond to a stimulus object in a manner consistent with one's beliefs, feelings, and action tendencies towards that object. There is a general consensus that affect (evaluation) is the major dimension of attitude. Some social psychologists—notably Osgood and Tannenbaum (1955) and Fishbein (1965)—prefer a unidimensional definition in which affect alone constitutes attitude.

intriguing explanation for how a single body state can generate a whole series of widely different emotions (or vice versa). Following up experiments by Marañon (1924), Cantril and Hunt (1932), and Landis and Hunt (1932), Schachter and Singer administered sympathomimetic drugs (adrenalin and ephedrine) to subjects in order to produce a pattern of sympathetic discharge common to strong emotional states. However, they did not inform some of their subjects of the reactions that they would experience from the drugs. They found that in this state of sympathetic activation (for which no immediately appropriate explanation was available), subjects could be readily manipulated into states of euphoria, anger, and amusement simply by varying their cognitive setting. In his original experiment, Marañon found that subjects in this state of activation (but without cognitive reason for a true emotional response) reported feeling as if they were afraid or as if awaiting a great happiness. Cognition, it seems, plays a vital part in the determination of emotional states.

Two studies (which were, in effect, the inverse of the above) varied the level of activation while controlling for cognition. Using drugs, Schachter and Wheeler (1962) induced varying levels of sympathetic activity in subjects viewing a humorous movie. They found that the degree of overt amusement was directly related to the degree of manipulated sympathetic activity. In an ingenious study with paraplegics, Hohmann (1962) found that subjects with lesions in the spinal cord experienced much less excitation of their emotions than they had experienced prior to the time of their injury. Furthermore, the higher the lesion on the spinal cord (and consequently the less the visceral sensation), the greater the decrease in excitation. Schachter and Singer have summarized these findings as follows:

An emotional state may be considered a function of physiological arousal and of a cognition appropriate to this state of arousal. . . . Cognitions arising from the immediate situation as interpreted by past experience provide the framework within which one understands and labels his feelings (p. 381).

If we accept Schachter and Singer's conclusions, emotion is composed of some combination of physiological activation and cognition. In order to measure emotion, it thus becomes necessary to measure both of these factors. Attitude, like emotion, is based upon cognition, but unlike emotion it may or may not be accompanied by a state of bodily activation.

If it is impossible for a system of cognitions that relates to a stimulus object to exist without the development of an attitude about the object, it seems reasonable to conclude that attitude plays a significant role in the development of emotional states. Since strongly held attitudes are often accompanied by activation (as we shall see later), the theoretical distinction between strong attitude and emotion becomes, it seems, somewhat meaningless. What, for instance, is the difference between a very strong liking and love? And where is the dividing line between an extremely negative attitude and hate? Realizing this interrelationship among attitude, emotion, cognition, and activation (i.e., that cognition is a necessary component of both attitude and emotion and that activation is necessary only to emotion), it is apparent that activation-based measurement techniques alone are not good measures of emotion, and are of even less value in the assessment of attitude.

GALVANIC SKIN RESPONSE, EMOTION, AND ATTITUDE

Without a doubt, the most widely used index of activation level in psychological research is the electrical conductance of the skin.[2] As

---

[2] While there is substantial agreement that the GSR is a functional measure of activation and while it is widely used for that purpose, there are dissenters. Lacey and Lacey (1958) claim that a single autonomic index (including the GSR) is not enough for an accurate evaluation of activation. These authors feel that several measures should be used for an accurate assessment of phys-

with the physiological changes already mentioned, the level of skin conductance is an autonomic response. Its discovery is usually accredited to Féré (1888). Although a good deal of preliminary work had already been done, it was Féré who first popularized the skin response measure with psychologists. Connecting two electrodes to the skin to form a complete circuit, and then introducing weak electrical charges, he noted that the electrical conductance of the body changed as various stimuli were presented. Féré's explanation was that the varying conduction level was due to vasodilation.

Two years later, Tarchanoff (1890) discovered that no outside current was necessary because of the slight electrical charge in the human body. This current flow is measurable and is conducted in different amounts as the person is exposed to various stimuli. Tarchanoff's theory was that these variations in conductance level result from the secretory activity of the sweat glands.

In 1902, Sommer propounded a muscular theory of skin conductance. In succeeding years, little evidence was developed to support this theory. It is an established fact that muscular activity does relate to skin conductance level, but this relationship can be explained on the basis of either sweat gland activity or vasodilation. The muscular theory was thus short lived.

Densham and Wells (1927) reported that no skin conductance reading can be obtained when the epidermis is removed. Shortly thereafter, Richter (1929) noted that there was a striking fall in resistance level when even a small needle prick was made in the skin under the electrode. These findings seemed to establish the presence of the undamaged skin as necessary for electrical conductance changes, and thus pretty well

iological arousal. Malmo, who himself has for years used the GSR and other autonomic indices to measure activation, now believes he has evidence that these physiological measures may actually not be measuring activation, but motivation (1965). The gradients in these measures (including the GSR) during mental activity, he finds, are not indicative of the patterns of activation level.

precluded the vascular theory. But the secretory proponents were still divided into two camps: (1) those who attributed conductance level to the presence of sweat in and on the skin and (2) those who felt that it was dependent on a change in the sweat glands preceding actual secretion.

Darrow (1932) demonstrated quite convincingly that the electrical changes in the skin consistently preceded (by about one second) the increase of moisture on the surface of the skin. Thus, sweat volume could not be a vital factor in the level of skin conductance. In a comprehensive review of research into the nature of the skin response, McCleary (1950) concluded that "it seems likely that the GSR [skin conductance level] is dependent on sweat gland activity. . . . [It is] the result of some pre-secretory change in the sweat glands" (p. 109). There is, to date, no absolute consensus about the nature of the skin response, but this issue need not concern us here.

The earliest name given to skin conductance level was psychogalvanic reflex (PGR). But since the response is neither psychic nor a reflex, this name has fallen into disrepute. Galvanic skin response (GSR) is by far the most popular name today, but even the galvanic usage is technically not correct. Probably, the most precise name for this phenomenon is electrodermal response (EDR). In deference to current usage, however, we will refer to this measure as the GSR. Up to this point we have been referring to the skin response as a measure of electrical conductance. While conductance is measurable as such, it is more common to measure the opposite—resistance to conduction. In the GSR this resistance is generally measured in ohms.

As noted earlier, the GSR can be measured with or without the introduction of an outside current. The endosomatic GSR (no current applied) is more convenient—all that is needed is a galvanometer and a pair of electrodes. But the exosomatic method (external current applied) has some advantages. "It yields a measure of the absolute level of conductance as well as of the changes, and seems a little more dependable" (Woodworth and Schlosberg, 1964, p. 138). The great majority of recent experiments have used the latter method.

With both methods, a number of different measurements are possible. Hunt and Hunt (1935) compared five methods of scoring the exosomatic GSR: (a) the frequency of response, relative to the total number of applications of the stimulus; (b) the change in the number of ohms of resistance with each deflection; (c) the change in the number of ohms of resistance, relative to total bodily resistance; (d) the change in the number of ohms of resistance per stimulus, as a percentage of the individual's total range of deflection for all stimuli at a particular session; and (e) the differences in conductance, as opposed to those in resistance. After a statistical comparison of these five scoring methods, the authors concluded that "the absolute number of ohms of deflection offers a simple and adequate method of scoring the galvanic skin response" (p. 387). Furthermore they suggest that another measure, such as the percentage of frequency of occurrence, would be beneficial as a supplemental measure.

Yet another GSR measurement possibility is the absolute level of conductance (basic conductance) at a given time, as opposed to measures of the rapid variations that result from stimulation. Woodworth and Schlosberg feel that this measure "has received less attention than it deserves" (p. 137).

Most of the studies relating GSR to attitude have dealt with strong, negative attitudes. Typically, a comparison has been made between attitudes, as measured by paper-and-pencil techniques, and the GSR in response to the stimulus object. Rankin and Campbell (1955) [Chapter 31 in this volume] found highly significant differences in GSRs for white male subjects when Negro and white experimenters adjusted an apparatus on each subject's wrist. A subsequent significance test between GSR responses and prejudice scores on a paper-and-pencil attitude test yielded inconclusive results.

Measuring attitudes toward ethnic groups, Cooper and Siegel (1956) observed greater GSRs in response to the names of negatively valued groups than to those of neutrally valued groups. In a related study Cooper and Singer (1956) measured GSRs when complimentary statements were made about disvalued ethnic and national groups and when derogatory statements were made about groups that were favorably viewed. These investigators found greater GSRs in response to objects of strong negative attitudes than for objects of strong positive attitudes. From these studies, they felt that they had clearly demonstrated that "prejudices are emotionally fortified" or that "prejudices are emotional attitudes" (p. 246).

By this they simply mean that prejudices (strongly held negative attitudes) are accompanied by physiological activation. Or, as stated previously, strongly held attitudes (i.e., those strong enough to be accompanied by sympathetic or parasympathetic arousal) are, in fact, emotions and can be measured as such.

Westie and DeFleur (1959) [Chapter 33 in this volume] reported that white subjects who scored in the upper 25 per cent on an attitude scale measuring prejudice toward Negroes registered significantly higher GSR readings when they were exposed to colored slides of Negroes than did those subjects who scored in the lower 25 per cent on the attitude scale.

In a more recent study, Vidulich and Krevanick (1966) [Chapter 34 in this volume] compared the GSRs of high- and low-prejudiced white males and females (as measured by an attitude scale) in response to pictures of whites interacting, whites and Negroes interacting, Negroes interacting, and landscapes. All subjects (male and female, high- and low-prejudiced) manifested significantly greater mean GSRs for the Negro and the Negro-white interaction pictures than for the white interaction and landscape pictures. High-prejudiced subjects manifested significantly greater mean GSRs for pictures of Negro and Negro-white interaction than did low-prejudiced subjects. The responses of these groups to pictures of whites interacting and of landscapes were not significantly different.

With one exception, all of the above experiments employing GSR in the assessment of prejudice level have used indirect exposure (verbal and visual images) to the object of prejudice. The one exception is the study by Rankin and Campbell, where Negro and white experimenters actually touched the subjects. The Rankin and Campbell study was replicated, with some refinements, by Porier and Lott (1967) [Chapter 32 in this volume]. In this study, the California E Scale and Rokeach's Opinionation Scale were used as self-report measures of prejudice. The authors report that: (a) E Scale scores, but not Opinionation scores, were found to correlate significantly with GSR responses to Negro and white experimenters and (b) the Rankin and Campbell findings of differential GSR responses (for all subjects) to Negro and white experimenters was not reproduced. Porier and Lott speculated that failure of the E Scale scores to correlate significantly with GSR responses may be due to the generally low level of prejudice in all sample members. (The smaller the variance on any given measure, the less the likelihood for a correlation to be significant. Low prejudice and, thus, relatively little variance in prejudice scores is a common problem in using college students in experiments such as those reported here.)

These studies indicate that broad ranges of attitudinal differences can be distinguished by means of GSR measurement. Subjects with strong negative attitudes (perhaps also with strong positive attitudes) toward Negroes and other ethnic and national groups can indeed be differentiated from subjects with weak or neutral attitudes.

A further study by Cooper and Pollock (1959) indicates that not only nominal, but also ordinal-level attitude measurement is possible with this technique. These researchers recorded GSRs in response to the names of ethnic and national groups, pre-

dicted attitudes from this GSR data, and verified their predictions with a paper-and-pencil, paired-comparison test (a design almost exactly the reverse of the Cooper and Singer study). The ranking of the GSR magnitudes correlated highly (a Spearman rank-order coefficient of .82) with rank order on the paired-comparisons test.

These findings suggest that for strong attitudes, the GSR may be able to supply better interval-level data than attitude scales (where an interval level of measurement is attained only through a process of arbitrary weightings). Based upon this evidence, it seems justified to conclude that the GSR is a legitimate and useful measurement technique for attitudes having a magnitude above the level of emotional arousal. The important question remaining is how are GSRs affected by weaker attitudes—those below the level of physiological activation?

Ruckmick (1933) and Greenwald (1936) have reported on the use of a galvanometer to measure affect below the level of emotional activation. GSR measurements were taken continuously as subjects viewed motion pictures. These were movies that would not cause emotional arousal. Greenwald reports a close relation between the GSR and the conscious affective life, as indicated by a verbal report. He concludes that "our data justify the use of GSR as a physiological indicator of the majority of affective changes, including many which are less intense than emotions" (p. 26).

However, Greenwald defines affect as "humor, amusement, and mild laughter"—a definition that is considerably different from the like–dislike continuum which generally constitutes the definition of affect for attitude theorists. A close inspection of Greenwald's data reveals that the GSR-affect relationship is not nearly as clear cut as he would have us believe. He reports several instances in which a large GSR deflection occurred, but where no affect was reported by the subject (bodily movements and speech were apparently among the causes for this) and where affect was reported without a significant GSR deflection being observed. Furthermore, he had a great deal of difficulty in categorizing verbal reports as affect or not affect. Beyond that, who is to say that his subjects were not experiencing emotional arousals? All things considered, we can hardly consider this work as evidence that GSR can effectively measure attitudes below the level of emotion.

A discussion evaluating the GSR as a measure of mental activity would not be complete without the mention of an article by Landis (1930). His evaluation is overwhelmingly negative; a more scathing critique is hardly imaginable:

I find in going through the literature that the psychogalvanic reflex has been elicited by the following varieties of stimuli . . . sensations and perceptions of any sense modality (sight, sounds, taste, etc.), associations (words, thoughts, etc.), mental work or effort, attentive movements or attitudes, imagination and ideas, tickling, painful or nocive stimuli, variations in respiratory movements or rate, suggestion and hypnosis, emotional behavior (fighting, crying, etc.), relating dreams, college examinations, and so forth. . . . Forty investigators hold that it is specific to, or a measure of, emotion or the affective qualities; ten others state that it is not necessarily of an emotional or affective nature; twelve men hold that it is somehow to be identified with conation, volition, or attention, while five hold very definitely that it is nonvoluntary; twenty-one authorities state that it goes with one or another of the mental processes; eight state that it is the concomitant of all sensation or perception; five have called it an indicator of conflict and suppression; while four others have used it as an index of character, personality, or temperament (p. 391).

Landis equates the GSR with basal metabolism and blood pressure as a measure of the psychological states of the body. In the end, he blames a large part of the difficulty on the psychological concepts that are supposed to be measured:

There is something seriously wrong with our psychological notions. The psychological categories [emotion, attitude, volition, ideation, etc.]

need either a thorough overhauling or to be scrapped (p. 397).

As for the fascination the GSR holds for psychologists, Landis attributes this to the belief that they have finally discovered a method for detecting and measuring emotion, and to the fact that the exactness and precision of the instruments "fosters the delusion that emotion is a precisely defined psychological process."

Clearly, GSR measurement does present a number of substantial problems, both theoretical and methodological. As Landis has pointed out, almost any stimulus, external or internal, may cause a change in resistance level. In something of an understatement, Morgan and Steller (1950) admit that "it may be too sensitive . . . it may signal too many different events. . . . It comes out whenever a stimulus or idea sets a person in readiness or expectancy of something happening" (p. 557).

The GSR may be affected by the sound of a door closing, by an incidental thought about a test, lover, movie, mother, etc., by body temperature, skin thickness, speech, the movement of a limb, a feeling of expectation or relief, and so on, ad infinitum. In addition, neither the basic conductance level nor the amount of change in resistance, in response to a given stimulus, is constant from subject to subject or for that matter in a single individual from one time to another. Even the nature and placement of the measuring equipment is critical. A strong current causes itching; a very weak one reduces efficiency of measurement. Exosomatic GSR varies inversely with electrode size; endosomatic GSR is relatively independent of electrode size. Alternating current produces different effects than does direct current. The palms of the hands are the best body areas for resistance measurement; the soles of the feet are almost as good; the brow is not bad, but the wrists and the backs of the hands give poor measurements. Yet another factor that must be taken into account is the dampening or routine effect. Unless there are very long intervals between successive stimulations, the GSR falls off rapidly as the series progresses.[3]

Since the time of Landis' studies, a number of the faults of GSR measurement have been reduced or overcome. Equipment has become more or less standardized; the interrelation of the several possible measurements (frequency of response, basic conductance level, absolute degree of change in resistance level, relative change, etc.) is better understood; the plethora of contaminating variables is more fully realized and usually better controlled; and, perhaps most important of all, psychological conceptions of emotion and attitude have been overhauled and at least tentatively clarified.

Nonetheless, it now appears clear that the GSR is not the ultimate technique for the measurement of emotion or attitude. If all stimuli other than the experimental variable could be entirely controlled (which in itself is literally impossible), the GSR would be an excellent measure of physiological activation, and indeed of emotional level and the strength of very strong attitudes. But it can never be expected to differentiate among emotional states, nor can it be expected to measure the strength of attitudes below the level of physiological arousal nor the direction of affect (positive or negative), simply because it cannot measure or assess cognition.

PUPILLARY DILATION AND ATTITUDE MEASUREMENT

In many respects the most promising physiological attitude assessment technique to be discussed herein is the measurement of constriction and dilation of the pupil of the eye, or pupillography. For centuries, physiologists,

neurologists, ophthalmologists, and psychologists have been aware of a relationship between various mental states and pupil size.

Gump (1962) reported that Chinese jade dealers used pupil dilation as a measure of their customers' interest in particular stones. But only in recent years has the nature of this relationship begun to be clarified. Early in the century, German scientists noted a correlation between the degree of mental activity (or central nervous system activity) and pupil size (Bumke, 1911). In studying the nervous system further, Kuntz (1929) found that emotions of pleasure as well as fear are often accompanied by pupillary dilation.

More recently, Rubin (1960) found that the speed of pupillary constriction is related to the level of cholinesterase in the cerebral cortex (which in turn relates to conditioning). Holmes (1967) found that the speed of pupillary constriction and dilation are significantly related to performance in verbal conditioning, as well as to introversion. Lowenstein and Loewenfeld (1962) discuss the physiological mechanics of pupillary reflex dilation, which they define as "dilatation elicited by sensory or emotional stimuli, or by spontaneous thoughts or emotions" (p. 236). After testing the sensitivity of pupillary response to visual, auditory, and physiological stimuli (and anticipation of the same), Nunnally and his associates (Nunnally, Knott, Duchnowski, and Parker, 1967; Nunnally and Rileigh, 1967) reported that all the evidence seems to indicate that pupil size is a valid index of many types of activation.

Parkman[4] used pupil dilation measurements to validate sex role identity. She measured the pupil dilation of high school juniors in response to pictures of a muscular young male and of a young girl. The pupils of female subjects dilated significantly when exposed to the picture of the young male, and pupils of male subjects dilated significantly when exposed to the picture of the young female.

To date, the most exhaustive research re-

[3] For further insight into the problems of GSR standardization and for more detailed accounts of the sources of error variance in GSR measurement, see Elliot (1964), Edelberg (1966), Edelberg and Burch (1962), Harter, Eason, and White (1964), Martin (1960, 1963), Martin and Venables (1966), Venables (1955, 1956, 1963), Venables and Sayer (1963), Venables and Martin (1967), Wenger (1940), Wenger, Clemens, and Cullen (1962), Wenger and Irwin (1935, 1936), and Darrow (1933).

[4] Personal communication with Dr. Margaret Parkman of Cornell University.

lating pupil dilation to attitude has been carried out by Hess in his laboratory at the University of Chicago. Hess describes his technique as follows:

The subject peers into a box, looking at a screen on which we project the stimulus pictures. A mirror reflects the image of his eye into a motion picture camera. First we show a control slide that is carefully matched in overall brightness to the stimulus slide. . . . Meanwhile the camera, operating at the rate of two frames per second, records the size of his pupil. After 10 seconds the control slide is switched off and the stimulus slide is projected 10 seconds. . . . To score the response to a stimulus, we compare the average size of the pupil as photographed during the showing of the control slide with its average size during the stimulus period. . . (1965, p. 2).

In his early experiments, Hess talked about the "interest value," "emotionality," and "pleasure value" of visual stimuli (Hess and Polt, 1960). More recently, he has come to equate pupil dilation with positive response and constriction with negative response—very clearly inferring an affective dimension. For example, dilation is regularly produced when heterosexual male subjects view female pinup pictures and when female subjects and homosexual male subjects view pictures of nude or seminude males (Hess, Seltzer, and Shlien, 1965). Females experienced greater pupil dilation than did males when pictures of a baby and of a mother and baby were flashed on the screen (Hess and Polt, 1960).

One substantial advantage of the pupil-size change measurement technique over other physiological measurement methods is that levels of attitude strength below the level of general physiological arousal can be differentiated: "There is a continuum of responses that ranges from extreme dilation for interesting or pleasing stimuli to extreme constriction for material that is unpleasant or distasteful. . . . In the presence of uninteresting or boring stimuli we find only a slight random variation in pupil size" (Hess, 1965, p. 6). Another advantage is that very slight differences in the degree of attitude strength

can be measured. Male subjects, for instance, record greater dilation when viewing pinups than when viewing landscapes; subjects who are hungry make a more extreme response to pictures of food than do those who are not. Better-tasting orange flavored beverages elicit a greater dilation than those whose flavor is of a poorer quality.

Seemingly, even very minute affective differences can be differentiated by this technique. In fact, Hess presents some evidence that pupil response, in some cases, can reveal preferences in which the actual taste differences are so slight that subjects cannot consciously articulate them.

According to Hess, stimuli other than visual sensory ones can evoke similar pupillary responses. Pleasant-tasting liquids, pleasant odors, and music cause pupil dilations in most subjects. Admittedly, these findings are less clear cut, however, than are those using visual stimuli. For instance, Hess has not been able to explain why unpleasant-tasting liquids often cause dilation (the usual positive response) or why all kinds of music apparently cause the pupils to increase in size for all subjects.

Hess has not worked extensively with attitude formation and change, but his measurement method seemingly can be a useful tool for research in this area. On one occasion, he measured subjects' pupil size in response to a picture of an anonymous person. He then read to the subjects a passage which indicated that the man whose picture they had seen was a former commandant of the Nazi concentration camp at Auschwitz. A subsequent exposure to the picture, and a concomitant pupillary measurement, revealed that a more negative attitude had clearly been developed.

The most controversial finding reported by Hess is that pupil constriction accompanies exposure to unpleasant and unappealing stimuli: "Constriction is as characteristic in the case of certain aversive stimuli as dilation is in the case of interesting or pleasant pictures" (Hess, 1965, p. 49). This reaction was reportedly observed when subjects were shown pictures of a cross-eyed or crippled child and of dead soldiers on the battlefield. According to Hess, male subjects experienced pupil constriction when exposed to pictures of fully-clothed male figures; females had the same reaction while viewing pictures of sharks or of seminude female pinups.

If true, this finding indicates the existence of a bidirectional (negative as well as positive) physiological index of affect. Unfortunately, the validity of the negative-affect pupil-constriction relation has not been unequivocally demonstrated. When extremely repugnant pictures are shown (e.g., dead soldiers on the battlefield or piles of corpses in a concentration camp), a large initial increase in pupil size is observed before the expected constriction occurs. Hess attributes this dilation to a shock factor. But Hess himself was unable to confirm the occurrence of constriction for other than visual stimuli. He noted that certain unpleasant olfactory, taste, and auditory stimuli did not produce the expected constriction (1965). Hess' findings and his interpretations of them are not accepted everywhere without question. In some circles, they are viewed with a great deal of disbelief and pessimism.

Woodmansee (1965) has objected to Hess' single-trial design on the grounds that the stability of the pupil response is very low. Using both a single- and multiple-trial design, he has replicated some of Hess' experiments. In one study, he exposed anti-Negro female subjects, and "equalitarian" female subjects to racial content pictures. On the first trial, Hess' findings were substantiated. The anti-Negro subjects experienced a slight decrement in pupil dilation. On subsequent trials (eight in all), the constriction response did not occur. Woodmansee suggests that the constriction response found in the first trial may be only an apparent constriction. The anticipation of an unpleasant stimulus may cause dilation during the control measurement. Thus, the actual presence of the disliked stimulus serves as a relief from the anticipatory excitation, which causes an apparent constriction. The same experiment

(this time with fifteen trials) was conducted by one of Woodmansee's students (Woodmansee, 1967). "Again, there was no evidence of constriction for those subjects who were assumed to dislike the stimuli" (p. 3).

On the chance that the aversive stimuli in these experiments were not unpleasant enough to register a substantial negative effect, Woodmansee (1967) in another experiment, used as a stimulus a photograph of a murdered college girl; the subjects were other college students from the same school. The experiment took place less than two weeks after the murder while the killer was still at large. Fourteen female subjects were placed into either an aversive reaction group or a non-affected group on the basis of their self-reported reactions to the photo. Of the nine exposures for each group, eight of the mean reactions for the aversive group were dilations. Furthermore, the groups did not differ significantly on any of the nine trials. On the basis of these studies, Woodmansee concludes that the pupil constriction reported by Hess was the result of some systematic methodological error (as suggested above).

In a fourth study by Woodmansee (1967), twelve male subjects were told that they would be exposed to several whiffs of hydrogen sulfide gas (aversive stimuli). Six of the twelve were, in fact, exposed to the gas (experimental group) and six were not (control group). "The experimental group showed the typical dilation responses across all twenty odor trials. . . . For the control group we found apparent constriction responses on nine out of the first ten trials" (p. 5). Woodmansee's explanation is that the pupils were dilated in the process of anticipating the H_2S; then "dedilated" when the odor failed to be sensed, causing what appeared to be pupil constriction.

Experiments by Nunnally and his associates substantiate Woodmansee's notion of anticipatory dilation. In one study (Nunnally, Knott, Duchnowski, and Parker, 1967), 30 male college students were led to believe that on a given signal a gun would be fired in the experimental room. Nunnally, *et al.* report a very regular increase in pupil size during the anticipatory phase and a very regular decrease during the relief phase. (Subjects had been assured during the latter phase that the gun would not be fired.) Similar results were reported for anticipated muscle strain (Nunnally and Rileigh, 1967).

Otto Lowenstein (who coined the term "pupillography" some 40 years ago) and his colleague Irene Loewenfeld have spent many years in the study of pupillary dilation. Loewenfeld has severely criticized Hess' work. In an unpublished letter to the *Scientific American* (the journal in which Hess' most comprehensive article on pupillary attitude measurement had been published) she states that: (a) Hess' review of the literature on pupillary dilation studies indicates "disregard of many hundreds of superior previous efforts" and (b) "the content of an emotion or an idea does not affect the direction of the pupillary response.... All sensory, emotional, or intellectual stimuli (with the exception of light) dilate the pupil and none of them constrict it."[5] Commenting on an article in the *New York Times* that discussed Hess' work, Loewenfeld (1966) wrote that (*a*) visual images (as used by Hess) were an unfortunate choice of stimuli because of the complications in controlling "brightness, color, area, and retinal distribution of the various images;" and (*b*) "the assumption that pleasant emotions dilate the pupil whereas unpleasant ones constrict it is not merely unsupported, but is contrary to fact" (p. 294). In conclusion, Loewenfeld wrote: "This critique has been written in order to dissociate our methods and our goals unmistakably from 'research' of this kind" (p. 294).

In a recent piece of research, Hess and Polt (1966) have reported additional findings from their research on pupillary dilation. A record was kept of the changes in pupil size while a series of five orange drinks, interspersed with drinks of water, were presented to sixteen subjects. These authors report "a significant difference in pupillary responses

to the orange stimuli and ... [no] significant difference in pupillary responses to water" (p. 454). One orange drink in particular consistently produced a much greater pupillary response than did the other orange drinks or the water. It is suggested that "the pupil of the eye may reflect ongoing stimulation to all cortical centers" (p. 451). In a critique of this study, Dooley and Lehr (1967) have pointed out serious weaknesses in experimental design, controls, and data analysis.

A major reason for the lag in the research on psychological-pupillographic relationships is the necessity for advanced technological methodology and hardware for accurate pupil size and rate-of-change measurement. Direct observation and photographic methods have now largely given way to cinematography (Machemer, 1933; Lowenstein and Friedman, 1942; Petersen, 1956; and Dureman, Scholander and Salde, 1961) and highly sophisticated photo-electronic scanning devices (Matthes, Matthes, Brunn, and Falk, 1941; Cüppers, 1951 and 1954; Ataev, 1953; Glezer, 1953; and Lowenstein and Loewenfeld, 1958).

A brief synopsis of the major methodological problems in pupillographic experiments is found in a paper presented by Woodmansee at the 1966 American Psychological Association convention. He describes four complications in the accurate measurement of pupil size change and suggests possible solutions. The problems are: light reflexive effect, arousal decrement effect, effect of the near-vision reflex, and high pupillary variability.

Light reflexive effect refers to the problem of controlling the light level of visual stimuli, or being able, in some manner, to distinguish the effect of varying light levels from the psychological effect of the stimulus object on pupillary dilation. In one study Woodmansee (1965) found pupil constrictions ranging from 1 to 5 per cent of basal pupil width when the subjects' gaze shifted from a dark to a bright area of a single photographic stimulus—a change equal to or greater than that typically noted for emotion-arousing stimuli.

[5] Personal communication with Dr. Irene Loewenfeld of Columbia University.

As Loewenfeld (1966) has pointed out, controlling for the light reflex is wellnigh impossible; stimuli other than visual ones should be employed. Hess corrected for this effect by equating test and control pictures for overall brightness, and reducing brightness contrasts in test pictures as much as possible without the loss of important detail (1965).Woodmansee (1965) went one step further. He not only equated overall brightness, but constructed checkerboard-like control slides with white and gray squares equal in size and illumination to the white and gray areas of the experimental slides. His 1966 experiments suggested that the light reflex can be controlled by running multiple trials—on the assumption that these effects will occur in a random fashion, thus balancing out one another. He spells out a short visual effects test whereby this assumption can be checked.

No matter what the stimuli (pleasant, aversive, control), an initial arousal followed by a rapid decrease in such arousal occurs during a series of stimulus presentations. (In alert subjects, this decrease in arousal occurs after about 100 seconds; sooner in tired subjects.) With the arousal, the pupil dilates; with the decrement, it constricts (actually dedilates). Thus, the assumption that the basal level, as measured in response to initial control images (e.g., checkerboard-like slides), will remain constant throughout a series of stimulus presentations is subject to error. Woodmansee (1966) suggests that (a) the order of presentation of stimuli should be varied, (b) lengthy trials should be avoided, and (c) control measurements should be taken after each stimulus presentation.

The third problem is that everyone, upon close viewing of an object, experiences convergence of the eyes and accommodation of the lenses. Individuals vary with regard to the exact distance at which this near-focusing is called for—older persons tending to near-focus at greater distances than young ones. This accommodation requires muscle strain and causes a slight pupillary constriction. Woodmansee (1966) has noted that subjects who must near-focus on the experimental stimuli will sometimes relax their eyes on control slides. This eye-muscle relaxation is accompanied by dilation; if not partialed out, this factor will lead to an error variance greater than the true variance. Woodmansee suggests using young (under 30) subjects and presenting stimuli at a distance farther than that requiring accommodation or near-focusing.

The complication of high pupillary variability, even under constant light conditions [as much as 10 to 20 per cent over several seconds, as reported by Woodmansee (1966)], causes test-retest reliability to hover at an undesirably low level (about .30 in single-trial designs). This reliability coefficient can be raised slightly by averaging pupil response across repeated trials. [Woodmansee (1965) reported a split-half reliability coefficient of .43 in an eight-trial design.]

For a more technical discussion of the physiological mechanics of pupillary light-reflex, reactions to near-vision (accommodation), reflex dilation (psychological), and pupillary unrest, see Lowenstein and Loewenfeld (1962), Davson (1963), and Loewenfeld (1958). For a detailed historical review of pupillographic development, see Loewenfeld (1958).

Doubtless, the reader has noticed that almost the entire emphasis of this discussion has been on GSR and pupillary dilation. The reason for this emphasis is that there has been relatively little attitude research using other physiological indices, largely because the research reported has been singularly fruitless.

Westie and DeFleur, in the study cited earlier, also measured (in addition to GSR) finger-pulse volume, the amplitude and duration of heartbeat, and the duration of the heart cycle. They reported that finger-pulse volume tends to relate to prejudice (not statistically significant); they do not report the results from the other three autonomic variables. Lawson (1954) reported that there is a tendency (not significant) for attitude shift to relate to palmar sweat fluctuations.

In a study with positive results, Volkova (1953) found that Russian children who were conditioned to salivate in response to the word good were also found to salivate in response to positively valued (good) statements. Statements such as, "The Young Pioneer helps his comrade," reportedly elicited a much greater salivation than did statements such as, "The Fascists destroyed many cities." It would be interesting to see a replication of this study and additional research using salivation as a measure of attitude. Relatedly, Eysenck and Eysenck have recently (1967a, 1967b) reported that salivation level caused by orally administered lemon juice is a valid index of introversion.

In a short discussion of physiological measures of attitude, Cook and Selltiz (1964) concluded: "Most measures of physiological reaction give direct indications only of the extent of arousal; they do not reveal whether the corresponding emotion is pleasurable or unpleasurable" (p. 38 in this volume).

SUMMARY AND CONCLUSION

A review has been made of the literature linking physiological conditions to attitudinal states in an attempt to evaluate the usefulness of physiological measures in the assessment of attitude. Our analysis has led us to a broader discussion of the relationships between particular physiological states and psychological states in general, with particular emphasis on physiological-emotional relationships. A large part of the problem in establishing such relationships has been that the psychological constructs (attitude and emotion) are so broadly defined; perhaps variously defined or ill-defined would be a more accurate appraisal. (This observation is now more true of the construct of emotion; recent years have seen a good deal of convergence in the definitions of attitude.)

Emotion, from its inception, has been considered a weak psychological construct. In 1933, Meyer predicted that the term emotion would eventually disappear from psychology.

Duffy (1941) suggested that emotion was a term of convenience that would be used in lieu of specific explanations of certain human behaviors, but that in the interest of more precise investigation the use of the word should be abandoned.

Some writers have contended that emotion should be located on an evaluative or positive-negative dimension. For instance, Arnold (1960, 1967) defined emotion as a "felt tendency away from something appraised as harmful, unsuitable, or burdensome, or toward something appraised as pleasurable, beneficial, or useful" and furthermore, "evaluation [liking or disliking] arouses this action tendency" (1967, p. 125). This definition of emotion is difficult to distinguish from the conative component of many contemporary definitions of attitude.

Plutchik (1962) points out that many emotions exist that simply cannot be located on an approach-avoidance continuum. Floyd Allport (1924) related pleasurable emotions to the parasympathetic nervous system and unpleasurable emotions to the sympathetic nervous system. Gellhorn and Loofbourrow (1963) report that for emotions of moderate intensity, Allport's generalization is accurate, but "as the degree of emotional excitation increases, the hypothalamic downward discharge does not remain restricted to one division of the autonomic system" (pp. 368-369). Consequently, there is no autonomic distinction even between positive and negative emotions at high levels of arousal.

While most social psychologists would agree that activation is a necessary component of any emotional expression, a precise definition of emotion is made even more difficult by recent charges that activation theory, too, is in need of serious revision. Specifically, it has been suggested that there is no single state of physiological arousal, but rather that there are several arousals. While these are positively correlated, they are not coterminous (Lacey, 1967). More detailed discussions of contemporary theories of emotion are presented in Lindsley (1951), Plutchik (1962), and Gellhorn and Loofbourrow (1963).

Attitude is an inclination or response set toward a stimulus object. It is the result of the combined beliefs (and feelings) that a person holds with regard to that object. The major dimension of attitude is affect (i.e., evaluation).

In some characteristics attitude and emotion are identical: both have a cognitive basis, both can be placed along an evaluative or affective dimension, and both include an action tendency toward the stimulus object. The major distinctions between these constructs are that (i) affect is the major (if not the only) dimension of all attitudes, whereas emotions may fall along other dimensions as well as being positive or negative, and (ii) emotions always include a physiological arousal, whereas only very strong attitudes are accompanied by activation. This means that very strong attitudes are, in fact, a special case of emotion; or in other words, attitudes strong enough to elicit physiological arousal are no different from affective emotions.

A number of physiological conditions are affected by activation. Some are more directly related than others, and therefore are better indicators of activation. GSR is probably the best single measure (if testing conditions are highly controlled and extraneous interference is kept at a minimum). GSR can be used to measure the strength of emotions and of strong attitudes (i.e., those accompanied by physiological arousal). It cannot, however, be used to measure the degree or direction of affect, nor can it differentiate among cognitions. The usability of GSR in attitude measurement is limited to cases where the existence of affect and its direction have already been established, and where the attitude is strong enough to elicit activation.

The only physiological measure that holds any promise in the measurement of affect (evaluation) is pupil-size change. The evidence is quite convincing that positive attitude is accompanied by pupillary dilation. Whether negative attitude causes constriction—thus making pupil-size change a bidirectional physiological index of attitude—is a matter for further research.

The major advantage of physiological attitude measurement techniques over the more common self-report, pencil-and-paper attitude scales is that physiological indices are much less subject to conscious control by the subject. Furthermore, these measures can easily be disguised. Pupillary attitude testing can be carried out under the guise of ophthalmological research, for example. Furthermore, it is believed that pupillographic methods can be used to measure attitudes of which the subject is not cognizant, ones that he could not express on a conscious level. Because of these advantages, pupillographic attitude measurement holds some promise as a practical means of measuring attitudes in commercial as well as social-psychological research. (For a discussion of the use of pupillometrics in advertising research, see Van Bortel, 1968).

The limitations of pupillographic attitude measurement are, however, still monumental. A negative-attitude, pupil-constriction relationship has not been unequivocally demonstrated to date; the reliability of pupillary attitude measurement is discouragingly low; the complicated hardware necessary for pupillary measurement is expensive; and its bulkiness and sensitivity make field research almost impossible. [Hess (1968) reports the development of a portable pupil response apparatus, but Hess' instrumentation is rather unsophisticated compared to the elaborate photo-electric scanning equipment now available.]

For the present, these limitations all but preclude the practical use of pupillography for attitude measurement. If reliability can be improved, pupillography will surely become a valuable tool in attitude research, including special cases of applied attitude measurement where attitudes are not consciously established or where subjects are reticent to disclose socially undesirable attitudes. Its use together with more conven-

548 DANIEL J. MUELLER

tional methods (to overcome the problems of low reliability and lack of knowledge of affective direction) probably constitutes the most rational application of pupillography in attitude measurement at this time.

REFERENCES

Allport, F. H.
1924 Social Psychology. New York: Houghton Mifflin.

Arnold, Magda B.
1945 "Physiological differentiation of emotional states." Psychological Review 52:35–48.
1960 Emotions and Personality. New York: Columbia University Press (2 volumes).
1967 "Stress and emotion." Pp. 123–140 in M. H. Appley and R. Trumbull (eds.), Psychological Stress. New York: Appleton-Century-Crofts.

Ataev, M. M.
1953 "A method for simultaneous recording of pupillary reactions and EEG during conditioning in man." (in Russian) Sechenov Journal of Physiology 39:622–626.

Ax, A. F.
1953 "The physiological differentiation between fear and anger in humans." Psychosomatic Medicine 15:433–442.

Bumke, O.
1911 Die Pupillen Storungen, Die Geistes, und Nervenkrankheiten. Jena:Fischer.

Cannon, W. B.
1927 "The James-Lange theory of emotions." American Journal of Psychology 39:106–124.
1929 Bodily Changes in Pain, Hunger, Fear, and Rage. New York: Appleton.

Cantril, H., and W. A. Hunt.
1932 "Emotional effects produced by the injection of adrenalin." American Journal of Psychology 44:300–307.

Cook, S. W., and Claire Selltiz.
1964 "A multiple-indicator approach to attitude measurement." Psychological Bulletin 62:36–55.

Cooper, J. B., and D. Pollock.
1959 "The identification of prejudicial attitudes by the GSR." Journal of Social Psychology 50:241–245.

Cooper, J. B., and H. E. Seigel.
1956 "The galvanic skin response as a measure of emotion in prejudice." Journal of Psychology 42:149–155.

Cooper, J. B., and D. N. Singer.
1956 "The role of emotion in prejudice." Journal of Social Psychology 44:241–247.

Cüppers, C.
1951 "Eine neue methode zur stetigen registrierung der konsensuellen pupillenreaktion." Klin. Mbl. Augenheilk 119:411.
1954 "Die fortlaufende registrierung der direkten und der konsensuellen pupillenreaktion." V. Graefes Arch. Augenheilk 155:588.

Darrow, C. W.
1932 "The relation of the galvanic skin reflex curve to reactivity, resistance level and perspiration." Journal of General Psychology 7:261–273.
1933 "Considerations for evaluating the galvanic skin reflex." American Journal of Psychiatry 13:285–298.

Davson, H.
1963 The Physiology of the Eye. Boston: Little, Brown.

Densham, H. B., and H. M. Wells.
1927 "The mechanism by which the electrical resistance of the skin is altered." Quarterly Journal of Experimental Physiology 18:175–184.

Dooley, P., and D. J. Lehr.
1967 "Critique of a pupillary response experiment." Perceptual and Motor Skills 25:603–604.

Duffy, Elizabeth.
1941 "Emotion: an example of the need for reorientation in psychology." Psychological Review 41:184–198.

Dureman, I., T. Scholander, and H. Salde.
1961 "An apparatus for pupillography with intermittent infrared light." Journal of Psychosomatic Research 5:224–226.

Edelberg, R.
1966 "Response of cutaneous water barrier to ideational stimulation: a GSR component." Journal of Comparative and Physiological Psychology 61:28–33.

Edelberg, R., and N. R. Burch.
1962 "Skin resistance and galvanic skin re-

sponse." Archives of General Psychiatry 7:163–169.

Elliot, R.
1964 "Physiological activity and performance: a comparison of kindergarten children with young adults." Psychological Monographs 78 (whole 587): 1–33.

Eysenck, Sybil B. G., and H. J. Eysenck.
1967a "Physiological reactivity to sensory stimulation as a measure of personality." Psychological Reports 20:45–46.
1967b "Salivary response to lemon juice as a measure of introversion." Perceptual and Motor Skills 24:1047–1053.

Féré, C.
1888 "Note sur les modifications de la resistance electrique sous l'influence des excitations sensorielles et des emotions." Compt. Rend. Soc. de Biol. 5: 217–219.

Fishbein, M.
1965 "A consideration of beliefs, attitudes, and their relationships." Pp. 107–120 in I. Steiner and M. Fishbein (eds.), Current Studies in Social Psychology. New York: Holt, Rinehart, and Winston.

Gellhorn, E., and G. N. Loofbourrow.
1963 Emotions and Emotional Disorders. New York: Hoeber.

Glezer, V. D.
1953 "Constriction of the pupil by conditional reflex." (in Russian) Sechenov Journal of Physiology 39:571–579.

Greenwald, D. U.
1936 "Some individual differences in electrodermal response to continuous affective stimulation." Psychological Monographs 48: (whole 214).

Gump, R.
1962 Jade: Stone of Heaven. New York: Doubleday.

Harter, M. R., R. G. Eason, and Carroll T. White.
1964 "Effects of intermittent visual input disruption, flicker-rate, and work time on tracking performance and activation level." Perceptual and Motor Skills 19:831–848.

Hess, E. H.
1965 "Attitude and pupil size." Scientific American 212:46–54.
1968 "Pupillometrics." In F. M. Bass, C. W.

King, and E. A. Pessemier (eds.), Applications of the Sciences in Marketing Management. New York: Wiley.

Hess, E. H., and J. M. Polt.
1960 "Pupil size as related to interest value of visual stimuli." Science 132:349–350.
1966 "Changes in pupil size as a measure of taste differences." Perceptual and Motor Skills 23:451–455.

Hess, E. H., A. L. Seltzer, and J. M. Shlien.
1965 "Pupil response of hetero- and homosexual males to pictures of men and women." Journal of Abnormal Psychology 70:165–168.

Hohmann, G. W.
1962 "The effect of dysfunction of the autonomic nervous system of experienced feelings and emotions." New York: Paper read at the Conference on Emotions and Feeling at New School for Social Research.

Holmes, D.
1967 "Pupillary response, conditioning, and personality." Journal of Personality and Social Psychology 5:98–103.

Hunt, W. A., and Edna B. Hunt.
1935 "A comparison of five methods of scoring the galvanic skin response." Journal of Experimental Psychology 18:383–387.

James, W.
1884 "What is emotion?" Mind 19:188–205.

Kuntz, A.
1929 The Autonomic Nervous System. Philadelphia: Lea and Febiger.

Lacey, J. I.
1967 "Somatic response patterning and stress: some revisions of activation theory." Pp. 14–37 in M. H. Appley and R. Trumbull (eds.), Psychological Stress. New York: Appleton-Century-Crofts.

Lacey, J. I., and Beatrice C. Lacey.
1958 "Verification and extension of the principle of autonomic response-stereotype." American Journal of Psychology 71:50–73.

Landis, C.
1930 "Psychology and the psychogalvanic reflex." Psychological Review 37:381–398.

Landis, C., and W. A. Hunt.
1932 "Adrenalin and emotion." Psychological Review 39:467–485.

Lawson, E. D.
1954 "Attitude shift as related to palmar sweating in group discussion." Unpublished doctoral dissertation: University of Illinois.

Lindsley, D. B.
1951 "Emotion." Pp. 473–516 in S. S. Stevens (ed.), Handbook of Experimental Psychology. New York: Wiley.

Loewenfeld, Irene E.
1958 "Mechanisms of reflex dilation of the pupil. Historical review and experimental analysis." Documenta Ophthalmologica 12:185–448.
1966 "Comment on Hess' findings." Survey of Ophthalmology 11:293–294.

Lowenstein, O., and E. D. Friedman.
1942 "Pupillographic studies. I. Present state of pupillography; its method and diagnostic significance." Archives of Ophthalmology 27:969–993.

Lowenstein, O., and Irene E. Loewenfeld.
1958 "Electronic pupillography." Archives of Ophthalmology 59:352–363.
1962 "The pupil." Pp. 231–267 in H. Davson (ed.), The Eye. Volume 3, London: Academic Press.

McCleary, R. A.
1950 "The nature of the GSR." Psychological Bulletin 47:97–113.

Machemer, H.
1933 "Eina kinematigraphische methode zur pupillen-messung und registrierung der irisbewegung." Klin. Mbl. Augenheilk 91:302–316.

Malmo, R. B.
1965 "Physiological gradients and behavior." Psychological Bulletin 64:225–234.

Marañon, G.
1924 "Contribution a l'étude de l'action emotive de l'adrenaline." Review of French Endocrinology 2:301–325.

Martin, Irene.
1960 "Variations in skin resistance and their relationship to GSR conditioning." Journal of Mental Science 106:281–287.
1963 "Delayed GSR conditioning and the effect of electrode placement on measurements of skin resistance." Journal of Psychosomatic Research 7:15–22.

Martin, Irene, and P. H. Venables.
1966 "Mechanisms of palmar skin resistance and skin potential." Psychological Bulletin 65:347–357.

Matthes, H., K. Matthes, W. Brunn, and R. Falk.
1941 "Untersuchungen uber die pupillenreflexe beim menschen." Pflugers Arch. Ges. Physiol. 244:644.

Meyer, M. F.
1933 "That whale among the fishes—the theory of emotions." Psychological Review 40:292–300.

Mittlemann, B., and H. G. Wolff.
1939 "Affective states and skin temperature: experimental study of subjects with 'cold hands' and Raynaud's syndrome." Psychosomatic Medicine 1:271–292.
1943 "Emotions and skin temperature: observations on patients during psychotherapeutic (psychoanalytic) interviews." Psychosomatic Medicine 5:211–231.

Morgan, C. T., and E. Steller
1950 Physiological Psychology. New York: McGraw-Hill.

Nunnally, J. C., and W. J. Rileigh.
1967 "Pupillary response in relation to anticipation of emotion-provoking events." Washington, D.C.: Paper presented at American Psychological Association convention (September).

Nunnally, J. C., P. D. Knott, A. Duchnowski, and R. Parker.
1967 "Pupillary response as a general measure of activation." Perception and Psychophysics 2:149–155.

Osgood, C. E., and P. H. Tannenbaum.
1955 "The principle of congruity in the prediction of attitude change." Psychological Review 62:42–55.

Petersen, P.
1956 "Die pupillographie und das pupillogramm, eine methodologische studie." Acta. Physiol. Scand., 37(supplement 125):1–141.

Plutchik, R.
1962 The Emotions. New York: Random House.

Porier, G. W., and A. J. Lott.
1967 "Galvanic skin responses and prejudice." Journal of Personality and Social Psychology 5:253–259.

Rankin, R. E., and D. T. Campbell.
1955 "Galvanic skin response to Negro and white experimenters." Journal of Abnormal and Social Psychology 51:30–33.

Richter, C. P.
1929 "Physiological factors involved in the electrical resistance of the skin." American Journal of Physiology 88:596–615.

Rubin, L.
1960 "Pupillary reactivity as a measure of adrenergic-cholinergic mechanisms in the study of psychotic behavior." Journal of Nervous and Mental Disease 130:386–400.

Ruckmick, G. A.
1933 "Affective responses to the motion picture situation by means of the galvanic technique." Psychological Bulletin 30:712–713.

Schachter, S.
1964 "The interaction of cognitive and physiological determinants of emotional state." In L. Berkowitz (ed.), Advances in Experimental Social Psychology. Volume 1. New York: Academic Press.

Schachter, S., and J. Singer.
1962 "Cognitive, social and physiological determinants of emotional state." Psychological Review 69:379–399.

Schachter, S., and L. Wheeler.
1962 "Epinephrine, chlorpromazine, and amusement." Journal of Abnormal and Social Psychology 65:121–128.

Sommer, R.
1902 "Zur messung der motorischen begleiterscheinungen psychischer zustande." Beitrage zur Psychiatr. Klinik 1 Wein: 143–164.

Tarchanoff, J.
1890 "Uber die galvanischen erscheinungen an der haut des menschen bei reizung der sinnesorgane und bei verschiedenen formen der psychischen tatigkeit." Pflug. Arch. Ges. Physiol. 46:46–55.

Van Bortel, F. J.
1968 "Commercial applications of pupillometrics." In F. M. Bass, C. W. King, and E. A. Pessemier (eds.), Applications of the Sciences in Marketing Management. New York: Wiley.

Venables, P. H.
1955 "The relationships between PGR scores and temperature and humidity." Quarterly Journal of Experimental Psychology 7:12–18.
1956 "Some findings on the relationship between GSR and motor task variables." Journal of General Psychology 55:199–202.
1963 "Amplitude of the electrocardiogram and level of skin potential." Perceptual and Motor Skills 17:54.

Venables, P. H., and Irene Martin.
1967 "The relation of palmar sweat gland activity to level of skin potential and conductance." Psychophysiology 3:302–311.

Venables, P. H., and E. Sayer.
1963 "On the measurement of the level of skin potential." British Journal of Psychology 54:251–260.

Vidulich, R. N., and F. W. Krevanick.
1966 "Racial attitudes and emotional response to visual representations of the Negro." Journal of Social Psychology 68:85–93.

Volkova, B. D.
1953 "Some characteristics of conditioned reflex formation to verbal stimuli in children." Sechenov Journal of Physiology 39:540–548.

Wenger, M. A.
1940 "A study of individual differences in electrical resistance." Psychological Bulletin 37:576.

Wenger, M. A., T. L. Clemens, and T. D. Cullen.
1962 "Autonomic functions in patients with gastrointestinal and dermatological disorders." Psychosomatic Medicine 24:267–273.

Wenger, M. A., and O. C. Irwin.
1935 "Variations in electrical resistance of the skin in newborn infants." Proceedings of the Iowa Academy of Science 42:167–168.
1936 "Fluctuations in skin resistance of infants and adults and their relation to muscular processes." University of Iowa Studies in Child Welfare 12(1):141–179.

Westie, F. R., and M. L. DeFleur.
1959 "Autonomic responses and their relationship to race attitudes." Journal of Abnormal and Social Psychology 58:340–347.

Wolf, S., and H. G. Wolff.
  1943 Human Gastric Function. New York: Oxford University Press.
Woodmansee, J. J.
  1965 "An evaluation of the pupil response as a measure of attitude toward Negroes." Unpublished doctoral dissertation: University of Colorado.
  1966 "Methodological problems in pupillographic experiments." Proceedings of the 74th Annual Convention of the American Psychological Association. 133–134.
  1967 "The pupil reaction as an index of positive and negative affect." Paper presented at the American Psychological convention, Washington, D.C. (September).
Woodworth, R. S., and H. Schlosberg.
  1964 Experimental Psychology. New York: Holt, Rinehart and Winston.

Indexes

Author Index

Subject Index

18-303

Date Due

OCT 2 0 '78			
MAR 1 0 '77			
SEP 20 '79			
JUL 1 6 1981			
SEP 1 3 1984			

Demco 293-5